MOON

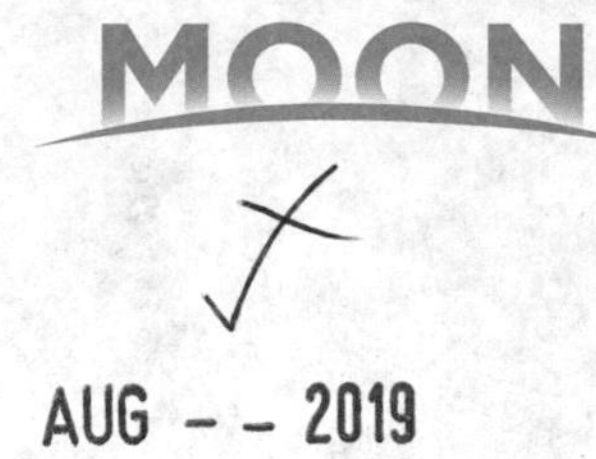

AMALFI COAST

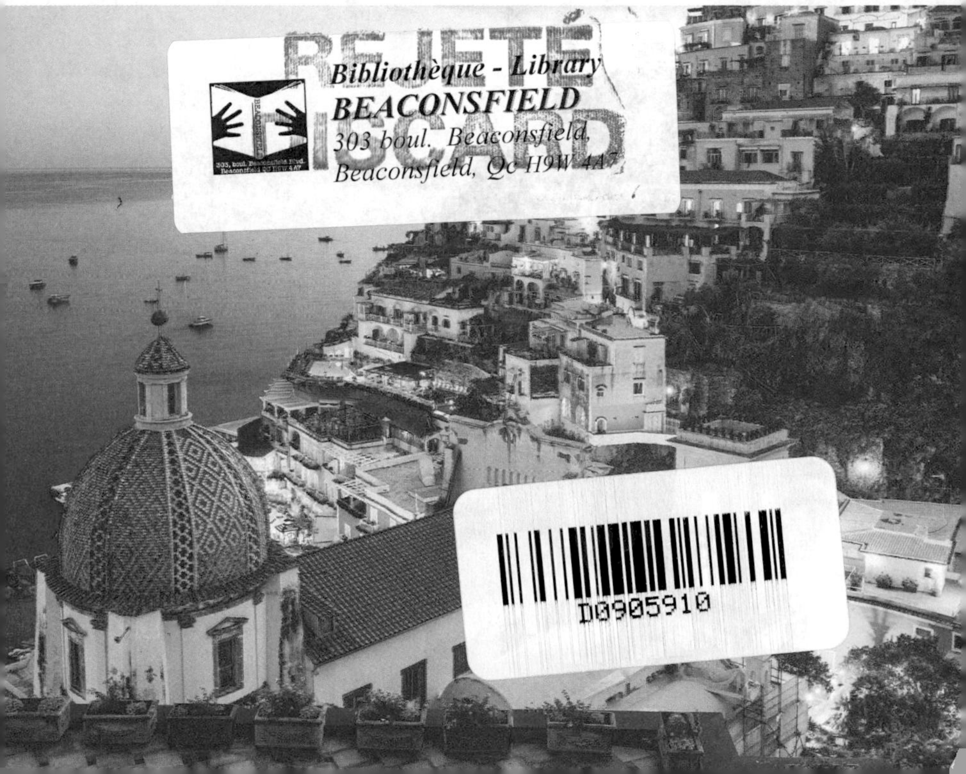

LAURA THAYER

Contents

Discover Amalfi Coast **6**
15 Top Experiences 10
Planning Your Time 22
• If You Want... 25
• If You Have... 27
• Best Festivals 28
Best of the Amalfi Coast 30
• Best Food and Drink Experiences . 33
Best Beaches 34
Sorrento and Island-Hopping 36
• Fun for Families 38
Outdoor Recreation and Seaside Relaxation 39

Amalfi Coast **41**
Itinerary Ideas 51
Positano 56
Praiano 77
Furore 84
Conca dei Marini 88
Amalfi 93
Atrani 116
Ravello 120
Scala 137
Tramonti 142
Minori 144
Maiori 149
Cetara 154
Vietri sul Mare 161
Salerno 168

Sorrento and the Sorrentine Peninsula **182**
Itinerary Ideas 186
Sorrento 191
Sorrentine Peninsula 210

Capri **224**
Itinerary Idea 228
Sights 229
Beaches 240
Sports and Recreation 242
Entertainment and Events 246
Shopping 248
Food 251
Accommodations 255
Information and Services 258
Transportation 258

Ischia and Procida **261**
Itinerary Ideas 268
Ischia Town 272
Casamicciola Terme 283
Lacco Ameno 289
Forio 296
Serrara Fontana, Sant'Angelo, and Barano d'Ischia 303
Procida 310

Naples **320**
- Itinerary Ideas 326
- Sights 331
- Sports and Recreation 353
- Nightlife 354
- Entertainment and Events 355
- Shopping 358
- Food 361
- Accommodations 368
- Information and Services 373
- Getting There 373
- Getting Around 375
- Around Naples 379

Pompeii, Herculaneum, and Vesuvius **392**
- Itinerary Ideas 396
- Pompeii 397
- Herculaneum 408
- Vesuvius 413

Background **417**
- The Landscape 417
- Plants and Animals 419
- History 421
- Government and Economy 431
- People and Culture 434

Essentials **441**
- Transportation 441
- Visas and Officialdom 447
- Recreation 448
- Food 449
- Shopping 453
- Accommodations 454
- Health and Safety 456
- Conduct and Customs 457
- Practical Details 460
- Traveler Advice 465

Resources **469**
- Glossary 469
- Italian Phrasebook 470
- Suggested Reading 473
- Suggested Films 475
- Internet and Digital Resources 476

Index **478**

List of Maps **490**

AMALFI COAST
Caivano
Acerra
Cardito
Giugliano in Campania
A1
Qualiano
Melito di Napoli
Casandrino
Casalnuovo di Napoli
A16
Marano di Napoli
Casavatore
NAPLES INTERNATIONAL AIRPORT
Sant' Anastasia
A1
Cercola
Pollena Trocchia
Gauro Park
A56
Naples
A3
San Giorgio a Cremano
A3
Pozzuoli
Portici
Ercolano
Monte di Procida
Bay of Pozzuoli
HERCULANEUM
Bacoli
Torre del Greco
Canale di Procida
Procida
Procida
Gulf of Naples
Forio
Ischia
Ischia
Canale d'Ischia
Barano d'Ischia
Vico Equens
SS163
Sorrento
Massa Lubrense
SORRENTINE PENINS
Marina del Cantone
Punta Campanella
Capri
Capri
Tyrrhenian Sea
SWITZERLAND
AUSTRIA
HUNGARY
SLOVENIA
MALPENSA
Como
VENICE MARCO POLO
Milan
Venice
CROATIA
Genoa
Ravenna
BOSNIA AND HERZ.
Pisa
Florence
Livorno
Ancona
Siena
Adriatic Sea
ITALY
Pescara
ROME LEONARDO DA VINCI
ROME
NAPLES
Sassari
Olbia
Bari
Naples
Salerno
Sardinia
Tyrrhenian Sea
Lecce
Cagliari
Crotone
Catanzaro
Palermo
Messina
Sicily
Catania
© MOON.COM

A16
Nola
San Paolo Bel Sito
Mercogliano
Atripalda
Avellino
Monteforte
Irpino
Palma Campania
San Gennaro
Vesuviano
Ottaviano
Forino
Serino
Montella
San Giuseppe
Vesuviano
A30
Solofra
Sarno
Poggiomarino
San Valentino
Torio
Castel
San Giorgio
Mercato
San Severino
San Marzano
sul Sarno
Fisciano
Scafati
Pagani
Nocera
Inferiore
Nocera Superiore
Baronissi
Angri
A3
Acerno
Corbara
Sant'Antonio
Abate
Cava de' Tirreni
Gragnano
Montecorvino
Rovella
Tramonti
di Stabia
Vietri sul Mare
Salerno
SS163
MONTE LATTARI
Minori
Maiori
Ravello
Cetara
Pontecagnano
Positano
Amalfi
Furore
Eboli
Bellizzi
Battipaglia
Praiano
Conca dei
Marini
Amalfi Coast
Gulf of Salerno
Paestum
Agropoli
0
5 mi
5 km

DISCOVER

Amalfi Coast

With its pastel-hued homes clinging to the cliffs between mountain and sea, tempting beaches lined with colorful umbrellas, and postcard-worthy views in every direction, the Amalfi Coast is one of Italy's most popular travel destinations—and for good reason. This remarkable coastline is rich in natural beauty, culture, and history. Mix in a splash of warm southern Italian hospitality and that's the charm of the Amalfi Coast.

Though its popularity means you certainly won't be discovering the Amalfi Coast on your own, you'll also find opportunities to wander off the beaten path. There are quiet piazzas where the scent of Sunday *ragù* (meat sauce) fills the air, little restaurants where you can eat impossibly fresh fish just steps from the sea, and hiking trails through terraced lemon groves that climb up the mountains.

Plan to spend time exploring the area, for just a short distance away you'll find sunny Sorrento, Paestum with its incredibly well-preserved Greek temples, and the ancient cities of Pompeii and Herculaneum frozen in time. Or go island-hopping from chic Capri to Ischia's thermal spas or to tiny Procida, where the sea laps at brightly colored fishing boats in the island's picturesque Marina Corricella harbor.

Clockwise from top left: traditional Amalfi ceramics; a street on Capri; Marina Corricella on the island of Procida; Pompeii; mussels; evening on the Amalfi Coast.

When you're ready for a burst of energy, head to Naples, where, to the soundtrack of buzzing scooters and Neapolitan songs, there lies an exciting and rewarding city. Often described as gritty, loud, and chaotic, Naples is all that—and yet so much more. It is a city that has been defying easy definition for centuries. It is, quite simply, a city to be experienced.

Few places in the world have as many layers as Naples, and only by experiencing it can you begin to unravel its fascinating tangle of culture, history, and, of course, food. Go underground in Napoli Sotterranea to see ancient ruins, climb the walls of medieval castles, and get lost in the twists and turns of the city's busy streets, filled with baroque architecture. When it's time to take a break, taste pizza in its birthplace. Around the next corner, you might just find that Naples has a way of making you fall in love with its vibrant charms just when you least expect it.

From secluded villages on the Amalfi Coast to hidden treasures in Naples, soothing spa experiences in Ischia, and unforgettable views in Capri, get ready to encounter a part of Italy that will capture your heart and leave you longing for more. One thing is for sure: You'll make travel memories to last a lifetime.

Clockwise from top left: the Path of the Gods route from Agerola to Nocelle; the Marina Piccola beach with Faraglioni rocks in the distance on Capri; Villa Cimbrone in Ravello; beachside restaurant in Positano.

15 TOP EXPERIENCES

1 Gazing up at Positano's colorful cascade of buildings from the town's **Spiaggia Grande** beach (page 62).

2 Hiking deep into **Valle delle Ferriere,** the mountain valley above Amalfi, to see waterfalls and ruins of old paper mills (page 100).

3 Climbing the grand staircase of the **Duomo di Amalfi** to visit the town's cathedral, peaceful Cloister of Paradise, and fine small museum (page 96).

4 Soaking up the Mediterranean sun on the beach in the picture-perfect **Marina Piccola** in Capri (page 241).

5 Dining at the edge of the sea in Sorrento's charming **Marina Grande** harbor (page 199).

6 Riding the chairlift up to the top of **Monte Solaro,** the highest point on Capri with breathtaking views over the entire island (page 237).

7 Standing right on the edge of the Terrace of Infinity at **Villa Cimbrone** in Ravello, taking in the sweeping panoramic view of the Amalfi coastline (page 124).

8 Admiring the incredible detail of the inlaid woodwork treasures on display at Sorrento's **Museobottega della Tarsialignea** (page 195).

9 **Kayaking** the rugged coastline of the Amalfi Coast from the seaside village of **Nerano,** near the tip of the Sorrentine Peninsula (page 220).

10 Discovering the incredible antiquities at the **Museo Archeologico Nazionale** in Naples, home to one of the world's finest collections of archaeological treasures (page 331).

11 Climbing atop the **Castello Aragonese** and exploring the medieval castle, churches, and ruins on a tiny islet off Ischia (page 272).

12 Savoring traditional **Neapolitan pizza** in Naples, famous as the birthplace of pizza (page 367).

13 Walking down the streets of **Pompeii,** an ancient Roman town frozen in time by the eruption of Mount Vesuvius in AD 79 (page 397).

14 Relaxing in one of **Ischia's many spas,** absorbing the healing properties of the thermal waters (page 286).

15 Strolling along **Marina Corricella** in Procida, where brightly colored fishing boats bob in a harbor lined with buildings that were once the homes of fishermen (page 310).

Planning Your Time

Where to Go

The Amalfi Coast

The first sight of the Amalfi Coast is a travel experience not easily forgotten. Whether you're sailing into Amalfi's harbor or inhaling the sweet scent of wisteria mixed with salty sea air in Positano, you'll be captivated by the **rugged coastline,** rocky **secluded beaches,** and **famous views** that have been luring travelers for centuries.

With a cascade of pastel-colored buildings seemingly stacked up, one on top of another, **Positano** is one of the most visited spots on the coastline. **Amalfi,** the namesake town of this region, has a scenic port and a fascinating history dating back to the Middle Ages, when it was a maritime republic. Set high in the mountains, the town of **Ravello** is a big draw for its lovely gardens and panoramic views. While many visitors only see Positano, Amalfi, and Ravello, there are **10 more towns and tiny villages** to discover on the UNESCO World Heritage-protected Amalfi Coast. Plus, just east of the coast lies the city of **Salerno,** with its attractive *lungomare* (waterfront), maze of medieval streets in the historic center, and remarkable cathedral. More tranquil than Naples, Salerno is a good home base in this area for travelers who like a bigger city vibe.

Sorrento and the Sorrentine Peninsula

With its convenient setting between Naples and the Amalfi Coast, **Sorrento** is a popular spot for travelers looking to explore all the top destinations in the area. With **panoramic views** across the Gulf of Naples, a **historic center**

Faraglioni rocks off Capri

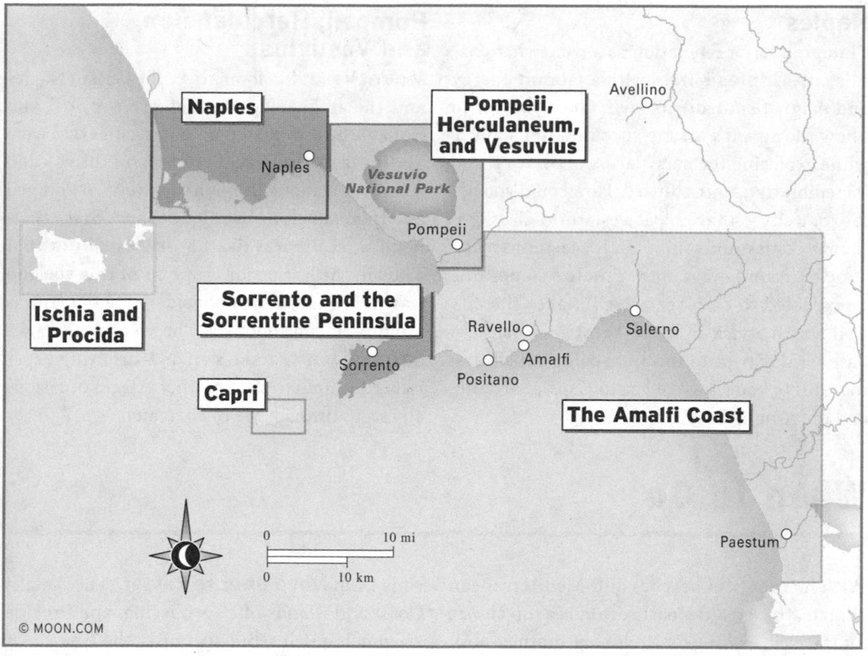

full of shops and restaurants, and picturesque **Marina Grande harbor,** this vacation setting combines beauty, charm, and convenience. Ferry service from Sorrento's harbor offers connections to Naples, Capri, Ischia, and the Amalfi Coast. Along the **Sorrentine coastline,** there are **quaint towns** and **beautiful coves** for swimming that are a bit farther off the beaten path than you'll find on the nearby Amalfi Coast.

Capri

This **small island** set in the Mediterranean, just off the tip of the Sorrentine Peninsula, is justifiably famous for its stunning views. Of course, this means it does draw crowds, especially during the high season, but that doesn't mean you should miss out on its exceptional beauty. Stop in the bustling **Piazzetta,** the heart of Capri town, pick up a souvenir of your visit (or just browse) along the **chic shopping streets,** and don't miss iconic views of the **Faraglioni rocks.** There's also a quieter side of the island to discover as you **hike** to incredible overlooks, ride a chairlift to **Monte Solaro,** the island's highest point, and get lost exploring narrow pathways past **bougainvillea-draped villas.** Whether you're planning a day trip from the Amalfi Coast, Sorrento, or Naples, or staying longer, there are plenty of ways to enjoy Capri's beauty without being overwhelmed by the crowds.

Ischia and Procida

These two islands in the Gulf of Naples boast natural beauty to spare and an abundance of local charm, yet they don't draw the day-tripping crowds like Capri. Known as the Green Island, **Ischia** is a lush retreat with little towns, beautiful beaches, and **thermal spas.** The spas have been an attraction on Ischia since ancient Roman times. Spend a day dedicated to wellness and relaxation in a thermal spa, or discover natural hot springs and steaming sand beaches around the island. Located nearby is the tiny island of **Procida,** famous for its **colorful architecture** and **scenic beaches.**

Naples

Though it has a reputation as a somewhat chaotic city, **Naples** buzzes with a vibrant energy and magnetism truly its own. Once you get to know the city, it's easy to succumb to its allure while exploring the many layers of **history** and incredibly **dynamic culture.** How could you not fall for a city with royal palaces, world-class museums, castles, and some of Italy's tastiest **street food**? Around every corner there's something unexpected to discover, which makes the city well worth a visit in itself. Yet it's also a great base for day trips to the archaeological sites in the Gulf of Naples as well as to Capri, Sorrento, and the Amalfi Coast.

Pompeii, Herculaneum, and Vesuvius

Mount Vesuvius looms over the Gulf of Naples and the archaeological sites of **Pompeii** and **Herculaneum,** thriving Roman cities that were destroyed by the violent eruption of the volcano in AD 79. Walking through the streets of Pompeii and Herculaneum is a unique chance to see firsthand what life was like for **ancient Romans.** Though the last major eruption of this volcano was in 1944, it is still considered active and is monitored continuously. The volcano is now a **national park,** and it's an awe-inspiring experience to climb to the top where steam occasionally seeps through the rocky crater.

When to Go

With its beautiful beaches and Mediterranean climate, the Amalfi Coast region is a top choice for travelers looking for a relaxing summer holiday. **High season** in this area runs from **Easter through October,** and **July and August** are the busiest months. During this peak period, everything is open and in full activity, and you can expect higher prices for accommodations and even rentals for sun beds and umbrellas at some beach clubs (*stabilimenti balneari*). For leisurely beach days, your best bet is to visit between June and August, and often September as well. August is peak season, so expect beaches to be full and public transportation to be at max capacity.

The spring shoulder season is a gorgeous time to visit the Amalfi Coast, especially as the wisteria blooms and the temperatures warm up. **April and May** are two of the best months to visit the coastline to enjoy all it has to offer before things get too warm and busy in the summer. The weather usually stays very nice through **October and November,** offering a great autumn shoulder season, when you can hike on the Amalfi Coast and catch a glimpse of autumnal hues across the mountainsides. **Low season** runs from **November to Easter.** The Amalfi Coast and islands of Capri, Ischia, and Procida are much quieter, but still offer the fine views and far smaller crowds. During low season, many accommodations and restaurants will close for a period, especially on the Amalfi Coast and islands.

The question of whether to visit the Amalfi Coast and islands off-season depends on the type of travel experience you want. If you're dreaming of a beach holiday, you'll need to visit during the summer. If you'd prefer cooler temperatures for sightseeing and hiking, a shoulder season may be preferable. Though the area can be a bit rainy off-season, it usually doesn't last for long and there are many clear, crisp days when the beauty of the Amalfi Coast is a splendor to discover.

Note that the impact of high and low season will be more noticeable in beach destinations on the Amalfi Coast and islands, such as Capri, than in larger cities like Salerno and Naples. On the Amalfi Coast, many hotels and restaurants and some shops close, and ferry service stops during low season. However, you'll find fewer seasonal closings in the Sorrento area as well as on the islands of Ischia and Procida, but check

If You Want...

vineyards among the hills along the Amalfi Coast, at Ravello

PURE RELAXATION

- **Ischia:** Nothing says tranquility like thermal spas where you can soak up the healing properties of the water in serene natural settings.
- **Conca dei Marini** or **Nerano:** These little towns on the Amalfi Coast and Sorrentine Peninsula, respectively, are secluded, quiet spots full of seaside charm.

HISTORY

- **Naples:** Go underground to see the ancient urban plan of the city, and don't miss the stunning baroque churches, royal palaces, and world-class museums.
- **Pompeii** and **Herculaneum:** History enthusiasts shouldn't miss a visit to these ancient cities, which were frozen in time by the eruption of Mount Vesuvius in AD 79.
- **Paestum:** This ancient city features well-preserved Greek temples that date from the 5th and 6th centuries BC.

FOOD AND WINE

The Campania region is incredibly rich when it comes to delicious food and locally produced wines.

- **Tramonti, Furore,** and **Ravello:** The vineyards in and around these towns, a few of which offer tours and tastings, produce the Costa d'Amalfi DOC (Denomination of Controlled Origin) wines.
- **Cetara** and **Capri:** Seafood is a gastronomic highlight of the entire region, with standout offerings like the anchovies in Cetara and sea urchin in Capri.
- **Naples:** This gateway to the Amalfi Coast region is the birthplace of pizza.

HIKING AND OUTDOOR ADVENTURE

Once only connected by footpaths and trails, the towns of the Amalfi Coast are a dream for hikers.

- **Sentiero degli Dei, Positano:** With endless coastal views, this trail (the name of which translates to Pathway of the Gods) above Positano is one of the most popular hikes in the area.
- **Valle delle Ferriere, Amalfi:** This trail above Amalfi passes by the ruins of the town's once busy paper mills.

in advance as many places do still close for the winter period, including the thermal parks. Accommodations and restaurants in Naples and Salerno are usually open all year, with the Christmas holiday time being very popular for both cities.

Before You Go

Passports and Visas

For travelers visiting Italy from the United States, Canada, Australia, and New Zealand, there are currently no visa requirements for visits of fewer than 90 days. You'll only need a passport that is valid at least three months after your planned departure date from the European Union. For stays longer than 90 days, you will need to apply for a visa at the Italian embassy in your home country before you travel.

For EU citizens, or citizens of the non-EU member states of the EEA or Switzerland, there are no visa requirements for traveling to Italy. You can enter Italy with your passport or National Identity Card.

Travelers from South Africa will need to procure a Schengen Visa to enter Italy. This currently costs €60 for adults (€35 for children aged 6-12, and free for children younger than 6).

You can check for the latest information on visa requirements and other restrictions at Italy's Farnesina website (http://vistoperitalia.esteri.it).

Transportation

BY AIR

The Aeroporto Internazionale di Napoli, also referred to as Capodichino, is well connected with flights from across Italy as well as international flights from more than 80 cities. Direct flights from the United States, however, are limited and are only available from May to October. The airport is very near Naples, only about 3.7 miles

the unforgettable view arriving by ferry to Capri

If You Have...

- **Three Days:** Enjoy the highlights of the Amalfi Coast, spending one day each in **Amalfi, Positano,** and **Ravello.**
- **Five Days:** With two extra days, you can add on a day trip to the island of **Capri** and a day in **Cetara,** a lovely seaside village known for its seafood, especially *alici* (anchovies).
- **One Week:** If you have a full week, add a couple of days in **Sorrento,** and make it your base to explore its charming historic center and the ruins of one of the ancient towns near Mount Vesuvius, like **Pompeii,** which is an easy day trip from Sorrento by train.
- **Two Weeks:** With an additional week, you can make it to **Naples** and base yourself there for 2-3 days, visiting the city's incredible museums and churches and, of course, eating plenty of pizza. From Naples, take a day trip to see the **Reggia di Caserta,** the lavish 18th-century royal palace and gardens that are among the largest in Europe. End your holiday relaxing on the island of **Ischia,** famous for its thermal spas, with the option of hopping over to the neighboring island of **Procida.**

(6 km) northeast of the city center, and is the main airport for the entire region.

BY TRAIN

Naples and Salerno are major stops for trains operated by the Italian national railway company **Trenitalia** (www.trenitalia.com), with Regional, InterCity, and high-speed trains connecting the region to destinations across Italy. The private company **Italotreno** (www.italotreno.it) also offers high-speed trains to both Naples and Salerno from Torino, Milan, Venice, Bologna, Florence, Rome, and many other smaller cities. The **Circumvesuviana** train line (www.eavsrl.it) connects Naples with Pompeii, Herculaneum, and Sorrento. The closest train stations to reach the Amalfi Coast are in Salerno and Sorrento.

BY FERRY

Ferries offer an excellent way to move around the Amalfi Coast and Sorrentine Peninsula, and are necessary to reach Capri, Ischia, and Procida. The **Porto di Napoli** (Port of Naples) is one of the largest in Italy, offering ferry service to Capri, Ischia, Procida, and destinations on the Sorrentine Peninsula. Ferry service from Salerno and along the Amalfi Coast runs seasonally from Easter through October.

BY BUS

Bus companies like **Flixbus** (www.flixbus.com) offer service to Naples and Salerno from cities across Italy. Local buses provide an inexpensive option to get around the Amalfi Coast, islands, and larger cities like Naples and Salerno. Since ferry service along the Amalfi Coast is seasonal, buses are the best way to get around during the off season (November-Easter).

BY CAR

Given the famously chaotic traffic of Naples, the narrow and curvy Amalfi Coast Road, and congested island roads, driving is not recommended in this area. With train, bus, and ferry options available, it is best to stick to public transportation, especially if you're traveling during high season.

What to Pack

Amalfi Coast style is relaxed, so when you're packing, think casual yet elegant resort wear. Formal clothes may be required for fine dining and opera in Naples, but even fine dining in the coastal areas and islands is often a more casual affair. For women, a scarf can come in handy for layering, and to tuck into your bag as a shoulder wrap to use when you visit churches. Though

Best Festivals

From moving religious processions to gastronomic events, festivals offer a unique chance for visitors to experience local life and traditions in Italy. There are many festivals throughout the year in this region. Here are a few highlights in the Amalfi Coast and Naples area to mark on your calendar.

AMALFI COAST

Positano

- **Ferragosto:** While Ferragosto is a national holiday, it is also a religious festival celebrating the Assumption of the Virgin Mary in the main church of Positano. Watch the traditional processions and spectacular fireworks displays over the sea. **Maiori** hosts a similar celebration. *August 15.*

- **Festa del Pesce:** Seafood enthusiasts will love the annual Fish Festival held in Positano on the Spiaggia di Fornillo (Fornillo Beach). *Last Saturday in September.*

Amalfi

- **Festival of Sant'Andrea:** The biggest festivals of the year in Amalfi are dedicated to Sant' Andrea, the town's patron saint and protector. Don't miss seeing the incredible running of the statue of the saint up the steps of the Duomo di Amalfi at the end of the procession. *June 27 and November 30.*

- **New Year's Eve:** Amalfi rings in the new year with a massive fireworks display over the harbor and music in Piazza Duomo that lasts well into the early hours of the morning. *December 31.*

Ravello

- **Ravello Festival:** Called the City of Music, Ravello hosts an important music and performing arts festival every year with concerts, exhibitions, and events. *June-August.*

Cetara

- **Notte delle Lampare (Night of the Fishing Lights):** The town famous for anchovies hosts a food festival on the beach and recreates the traditional fishing method of using light to attract fish after dark. *July.*

A procession carrying the statue of Sant'Andrea descends the steps of the Duomo.

SORRENTO

- **Settimana Santa (Easter week):** Easter is a major holiday in Italy, and in Sorrento you can see two impressive processions through town. *Good Friday.*

ISCHIA

- **Festa a Mare agli scogli di Sant'Anna (St. Anne Sea Festival):** A fun blend of tradition, folklore, and religious celebrations, this festival includes a boat procession and fireworks over the Castello Aragonese in Ischia. *July 26.*

NAPLES

- **Festival of San Gennaro:** The patron saint of Naples is celebrated three times a year with important religious festivals complete with processions and miracles. *Saturday before the first Sunday in May, September 19, and December 16.*

- **Napoli Pizza Village, Naples:** The traditional Neapolitan pizza is celebrated in this fun food festival that takes over the waterfront in Naples. *June.*

wisteria in the Villa Rufolo garden in Ravello

dress codes are not always strictly enforced, modest dress is recommended at religious sites where tank tops and short skirts or shorts are not considered appropriate attire.

Beachwear and swimsuits are a must if you're traveling during the summer. Cover-ups are a good idea, too, as it's not permitted to walk around most towns (even beachside towns) only wearing swimwear. Pack sun protection and a hat for beach days.

Whether you're climbing the steps of Positano, visiting the museums of Naples, or walking along the dusty streets of ancient Pompeii, comfortable shoes are a must. If you plan to hike on the Amalfi Coast or islands, bring good footwear with plenty of support. For the rocky beaches, a pair of flip-flops or water shoes will save your feet.

Pack a European plug adapter and converter for your electronic devices. You'll also want to bring plenty of memory cards or film for photos, as the endless fine views and landscape will inspire you to snap more photos than you expect.

Best of the Amalfi Coast

The Amalfi Coast's alluring vistas are what draw many travelers to this rugged coastline, but there is so much to see and experience in the area that it's well worth spending a week to see the highlights. This seven-day itinerary includes the top spots on the Amalfi Coast along with time to enjoy the charms of Sorrento, discover historic Naples, walk among the ruins of ancient Pompeii, and take in the natural beauty of Capri. This itinerary works best in season (Easter-October), when the ferries are running and everything is open.

Day 1: Amalfi

With its central location on the Amalfi Coast, the town of **Amalfi** is a convenient home base for sightseeing. Start your first day in the town's central Piazza Duomo at the historic **Pasticceria Pansa** with coffee and a freshly baked *sfogliatella*. Join the Amalfi Lemon Experience tour in the morning to visit a sixth-generation family-run lemon grove in Amalfi. Nearby, stop to see the **Museo della Carta** to learn more about Amalfi's fascinating history of paper making. Enjoy shopping along the town's main street and stop in at **Trattoria Da Maria** for home-cooked specialties. Back in Piazza Duomo, climb the steps to visit the **Duomo di Amalfi,** with its peaceful Cloister of Paradise, excellent small museum, and crypt dedicated to the town's patron Sant'Andrea. Take an evening stroll along the harbor and watch the sunset with an *aperitivo* at **Gran Caffè** before enjoying a relaxed dinner overlooking the sea at **Ristorante Marina Grande.**

Day 2: Positano

Start your second day on the Amalfi Coast by catching a ferry in the morning to **Positano,** which is only a short yet very scenic 25-minute cruise along the coastline. You'll arrive right on the **Spiaggia Grande** beach with the Chiesa di Santa Maria Assunta in the middle. Climb the

a captivating view of Amalfi from the sea

Ravello's Piazza Duomo

steps to visit the church and see its much-loved Byzantine icon. From the Spiaggia Grande, follow the cliff-hugging Via Positanesi d'America walkway over to **Spiaggia di Fornillo,** a very scenic and quieter spot for swim. Rent a sun bed from **Da Ferdinando** and enjoy a fresh lunch at their beach restaurant. Later in the afternoon head back to Positano's town center to explore the maze of streets lined with tempting boutiques. Catch the last evening ferry back to Amalfi and for dinner grab a table under the lemon trees at **Pizzeria Donna Stella** in the heart of Amalfi.

Day 3: Ravello

Head into the mountains of the Amalfi Coast by hopping on the City Sightseeing open-top bus to **Ravello.** Visit the town's elegant central piazza and stop in the **Duomo.** Enjoy a hearty home-cooked lunch at **Trattoria da Cumpà Cosima.** Take a leisurely walk through the quiet streets of Ravello to reach the **Villa Cimbrone.** Stroll along the wisteria-covered pathway to the Terrace of Infinity, where the blue sea and sky blend into one breathtaking vista. Enjoy shopping for ceramics in Ravello's town center before heading to the chic **Palazzo Avino** hotel for evening cocktails on their romantic terrace overlooking the coastline. It's such an enchanting setting that you'll be tempted to stay on for dinner at the hotel's Michelin-starred **Rossellinis** restaurant. Catch a late bus or taxi back down to Amalfi.

Day 4: Sorrento

From the Amalfi Coast, move your home base over to the north side of the Sorrentine Peninsula to the city of **Sorrento.** After dropping off your bags at your accommodation, head out to explore the ***centro storico,*** the historic center, of Sorrento, which is largely pedestrian-only and lined with shops and restaurants. Enjoy beautiful views over the Gulf of Naples from the **Villa Comunale** gardens and stop for a light lunch at **D'Anton Design & Bistrot** in the pretty **Piazza Sant'Antonino.** Head to the **Museobottega della Tarsialignea** to admire the collection of inlaid woodwork, a traditional craft in Sorrento. In the evening, stroll down to the **Marina**

Grande harbor. With its old-world fishing village atmosphere, it's a charming spot for dinner by the sea.

Day 5: Capri

Spend a day on the enchanting island of **Capri.** Take the ferry from Marina Piccola in Sorrento, and after only about 30 minutes you'll be on the famously beautiful island. From the Marina Grande port, take a boat tour around the island with the option to see the **Grotta Azzurra,** the Blue Grotto with its shimmering electric blue water. Back in Marina Grande, take the **funicular train** up to Capri town. Meander through the shop-lined streets and stop for a **traditional Caprese lunch** at Ristorante Michel'angelo. Walk off a delicious lunch by strolling down to the **Giardini di Augusto,** where you'll find a perfect view of the Faraglioni rocks. On the way back, stop at Carthusia for beautiful Capri-made perfumes, soaps, and home scents. Enjoy an *aperitivo* in the bustling Piazzetta, Capri's place to see and be seen, before hopping on the funicular train back down Marina Grande to catch the ferry back to Sorrento for a divine dinner at **Il Buco.**

Day 6: Day Trip to Pompeii

Set off today for a day trip to the ruins of **Pompeii,** which you can easily reach by taking the Circumvesuviana train from Sorrento. After about a 30-minute ride, get off at the "Pompeii Scavi – Villa dei Misteri" stop and cross the street to the Porta Marina entrance. Plan on about three hours to explore the archaeological site to see the highlights, stop for a light lunch at the café inside the site, and really experience what life was like in an ancient Roman town. Take the train back to Sorrento and then transfer to Naples by ferry or Circumvesuviana train. The more scenic option is the ferry from Sorrento's Marina Piccola port to Naples, where you'll arrive at the Molo Beverello after about 45 minutes. After settling in to your accommodation, head out to explore your neighborhood and enjoy some Neapolitan street food like the classic fried pizza.

Day 7: Naples

End your trip with a day in the historic center of **Naples.** Start in the morning at the **Museo Archeologico Nazionale,** where you can explore one of the world's most important archaeological collections. Then head over to the **Piazza del Gesù Nuovo** and enjoy a walk down **Spaccanapoli,** a straight street that is named for the way it cuts right through the historic center. Take a left on Via San Gregorio Armeno and enjoy perusing the workshops where you can see artisans creating traditional nativity scenes. Not far away, stop in the **Duomo di Napoli** to see the city's most important church and lavishly decorated chapel dedicated to San Gennaro. Next head over to **Piazza del Plebiscito** to admire the elegant Palazzo Reale and Basilica di San Francesco da Paola with its curved colonnade. Stop for true **Neapolitan espresso** at the Gran Caffè Gambrinus at the edge of the piazza. Cross the Piazza Trieste e Trento and go inside the **Galleria Umberto I** shopping center to admire the soaring glass dome. Watch the sunset from the **Castel dell'Ovo** with fine views of the Gulf of Naples. For dinner, have a traditional **Neapolitan-style pizza** just steps from the sea at Sorbillo's Lievito Madre al Mare pizzeria.

Best Food and Drink Experiences

When it comes to delicious gastronomic experiences, the Amalfi Coast is just as rich as it is with fine views. Walk among lemon groves, see *limoncello* being made, and learn how to re-create traditional lemon-infused recipes at home. Go in search of the best pizza in Naples or simply relax by the sea with a glass of locally made Costa d'Amalfi DOC white wine, which is the perfect refreshing touch on a hot summer day.

limoncello

LEMONS AND LEMON PRODUCTS

The Amalfi Coast's distinctive lemons grow on terraced groves along the coastline. In Amalfi, the **Amalfi Lemon Experience** tour gives you the chance to visit the lemon gardens of the Aceto family, who have been cultivating lemons for six generations. See how they make *limoncello*, the traditional lemon-infused liqueur, and bring some home with you from their shop, **La Valle dei Mulini,** near the town's main square. Between Minori and Maiori on the Amalfi Coast are some of the largest lemon groves, and you can enjoy a scenic walk called the **Sentiero dei Limoni** connecting the two towns. On Capri, spend a fun day learning traditional Caprese pasta, dessert, and *limoncello* recipes at the **Lemon Twist** cooking class taught by local chef Gianluca D'Esposito at Ristorante Michel'angelo.

PIZZA

Nowhere will you taste pizza quite like Neapolitan-style pizza, which was invented in Naples in 1889. Of course, to find your favorite means stopping in a few of the most iconic pizzerias like **L'Antica Pizzeria da Michele** or **Sorbillo** as well as some of the newer yet top-ranked spots in the city such as **Pizzaria La Notizia** or **50 Kalò.** Outside of Naples you'll also find excellent pizza, like the unique long pizza made to share at **Pizza a Metro da Gigino** in Vico Equense. In Salerno, head to **Pizzaria Criscemunno,** next to the Cattedrale di Salerno, for excellent pizza cooked in the traditional wood-fired oven.

SEAFOOD

Seafood is the main gastronomic specialty in the entire area and one you'll find highlighted in nearly every restaurant. **Trattoria Da Lorenzo** in Scala on the Amalfi Coast is an excellent spot for seafood, as is **Porta Marina** in Sorrento, where the seafood is caught by local fisherman just steps from the seaside restaurant. Some of the most traditional dishes are pasta with *vongole* (clams) or *cozze* (mussels), but also freshly caught fish, tuna, squid, and octopus. A very localized seafood specialty can be found in Cetara on the Amalfi Coast, which is noted for its *alici*, or anchovies, that are served fresh and preserved with oil. You can also find *colatura di alici*, which is a strong fish oil made from anchovies in Cetara that is thought to have origins dating back to the ancient Roman *garum* fish oil. **Ristorante San Pietro** in Cetara is a great spot to try anchovies and *colatura di alici*.

WINE

Wine enthusiasts will want to plan some time exploring the vineyards of the Amalfi Coast, where grapes are grown in steep terraces on the mountainside at **Cantine Marisa Cuomo** in Furore, tucked away in a mountain valley at the **Tenuta San Francesco** and **Cantine Giuseppe Apicella,** and overlooking the coastline at **Le Vigne di Raito** in Vietri sul Mare. On the slopes of Monte Epomeo in Ischia, **Casa d'Ambra** is one of the island's leading wine producers and has been growing grapes since 1888.

Best Beaches

Looking for places to spend the best beach days where you can swim in the turquoise sea, soak up the sun, and enjoy a good dose of local character while you're at it? Here's a list of the finest beaches on the Amalfi Coast, Sorrentine Peninsula, and islands.

Amalfi Coast

BEST BEACHES FOR SWIMMING AND WATER SPORTS

- **Marina di Praia, Praiano:** This is a beautiful small beach for swimming, where you can also find windsurfing lessons and equipment available for rent.
- **Duoglio, Amalfi:** Set on a rocky beach west of Amalfi, this is a popular local spot for windsurfing and kayaking, with both rentals and lessons available.
- **Minori:** The beach here is a lovely spot for swimming; you can also rent a clear kayak and paddle over to a natural waterfall west of town.

BEST BEACHES TO SEE AND BE SEEN

- **Spiaggia Grande, Positano:** Here you'll find a large beach with colorful umbrellas and the iconic view of Positano in the background.
- **Laurito, Positano:** This beach is home to the Treville Beach Club, one of the most chic beach clubs on the Amalfi Coast.

BEST BEACHES FOR FAMILIES

- **Spiaggia di Fornillo, Positano:** This is a quieter beach in Positano, away from the hustle and bustle of the Spiaggia Grande.
- **Atrani Beach:** This beach has a fine, dark sand that is more comfortable for families with young kids compared to the pebbly and rocky beaches of the coastline.
- **Maiori Beach:** The longest beach on the Amalfi Coast is made of small pebbles and sandy areas. The waterfront area is also perfect for seaside walks and for kids to run and play.

Maiori Beach

Set below a historic watchtower, Cetara's beach is one of the loveliest on the Amalfi Coast.

HIDDEN GEMS

- **Arienzo, Positano:** Set in a small cove east of Positano, this beautiful little beach can be reached by a long flight of steps or boat service from Positano.
- **Santa Croce, Amalfi:** One of the prettiest and most secluded rocky beaches on the Amalfi Coast, this spot is only accessible by boat.
- **Cetara:** One of the most picturesque beaches on the coastline, Cetara's beach is surrounded by a fishing village and a 14th-century watchtower.

Sorrento and the Sorrentine Peninsula

- **Marina Grande, Sorrento:** For a characteristic beach experience in Sorrento, head to the Marina Grande fishing village, where a small beach and bathing platforms are set in the harbor lined with colorful fishing boats.
- **Marina del Cantone, Nerano:** Set right near the tip of the Sorrentine Peninsula, this is a gorgeous natural setting for swimming in the clear sea or exploring the untouched coastlines nearby by kayak.

Capri

- **Marina Piccola:** The picturesque small harbor on Capri's southern side is one of the island's most beautiful spots for a swim, with a host of options for seaside dining and *stabilimenti balneari* offering beach services.
- **Punta Carena:** At the southernwesternmost tip of the island, this rocky beach is set below Capri's pink and white lighthouse at Punta Carena.

Ischia

- **Baia di San Montano, Lacco Ameno:** Set in a horseshoe-shaped bay, this beach is surrounded by the lush tranquility that makes Ischia such an ideal holiday escape. Plus, it's also home to the Negombo thermal water park, one of the finest on the island.

- **Spiaggia dei Maronti, Barano d'Ischia:** The longest beach on Ischia is also a great spot for swimming with the clear water, sandy beach, and view down the coastline to the seaside village of Sant'Angelo.

Procida

- **Spiaggia della Chiaia:** Located near the charming Marina Corricella with its pastel-hued buildings, this is the ideal spot for a relaxing beach day on Procida.

Sorrento and Island-Hopping

If you've seen and done the Amalfi Coast and are looking to explore Sorrento and the beautiful islands of the Gulf of Naples, this itinerary has you covered. Spend a couple of nights based in Sorrento before hopping over to Ischia to discover an oasis of relaxation and beauty.

Day 1: Sorrento

Start off your day in Sorrento's central **Piazza Tasso** watching the busy square come to life while sipping a cappuccino at Fauno Bar. Spend the morning exploring the historic center, visiting the **Cattedrale di Sorrento,** and admiring the view of the Gulf of Naples from the Villa Comunale gardens. Meander down to the Marina Grande seaside village for lunch by the sea. In the afternoon, discover Sorrento's tradition of inlaid woodwork and marvel at the pieces on display at the **Museobottega della Tarsialignea.** End a fine day of sightseeing and walking with a delicious meal at **L'Antica Trattoria** in the historic center.

Day 2: Day Trip to Capri

Catch the ferry from Sorrento's Marina Piccola port for the quick 30-minute ride over to Capri. After landing in the Marina Grande port, catch a bus or taxi up to **Anacapri.** Stroll down **Via Axel Munthe** to find a lovely view overlooking Marina Grande. Hop on the chairlift up to the top of **Monte Solaro,** the highest point on the island, for panoramic views of the island and on a clear day across the Gulf of Naples to Ischia and Procida. Take a bus or taxi down to Capri town and stroll through the bustling Piazzetta and head to **Ristorante Il Geranio** for a relaxed lunch with beautiful views over the island. Enjoy a picture-perfect glimpse of the Faraglioni rocks from the **Giardini di Augusto** before heading back to the Piazzetta to catch the funicular train down to Marina Grande and the ferry back to Sorrento.

Days 3-4: Ischia

Take the first morning ferry from Sorrento across the gulf to **Ischia,** only a 60-minute ferry ride. You'll arrive at the port in Ischia town, which is a convenient home base for exploring the island. Drop your bags at the hotel and set off via taxi or bus to the town of **Lacco Ameno** on the northwest side of the island. Stop here to stroll along the waterfront and enjoy a light and fresh lunch at **Terra Madre.** Hop in a taxi for a quick ride up to the **La Mortella** gardens and soak up the luscious natural setting while walking through the terraced gardens. Catch another taxi outside the garden over to the **Chiesa del Soccorso** in Forio, a small church with brilliant white façade set atop a panoramic overlook. Walk down through the historic center of Forio before catching a bus or taxi back to Ischia Porto for an evening stroll along the lively **Vittoria Colonna.** Enjoy dinner steps from the sea at **Cap' e' Fierr** right on the Spiaggia di San Pietro in Ischia town.

Spend your second day on Ischia exploring a castle and relaxing at the island's oldest thermal spa. Start off the day in Ischia Ponte, a great area for shopping near the **Castello Aragonese.** Walk out to the islet where the Castello Aragonese sits via the pedestrian causeway and take the elevator up to the top. Spend the morning exploring the fascinating walled castle with churches, ruins, and fine views. Next take a taxi from Ischia Ponte up to the **Fonte delle Ninfe Nitrodi** thermal

Riding the chairlift to Monte Solaro on Capri is fun and offers stunning views.

spa, where you can enjoy a one-of-a-kind experience soaking up the healing properties of the thermal water, relaxing in the sun, and savoring lunch at their lovely nature-inspired restaurant. Explore the southern side of the island by heading down to the pedestrian-only seaside village of Sant'Angelo for tranquil dinner by the sea at **Deus Neptunus.**

Day 5: Day Trip to Procida

From the port at Ischia town, catch a morning ferry over to nearby **Procida,** just about a 20-minute boat ride away. Stop to try the traditional *la lingua* pastry at **Bar dal Cavaliere** in the port before meandering through the charming streets of the island up to **Terra Murata,** the medieval fortified town on the island's highest point. Visit the impressive **Abbazia di San Michele Arcangelo** church before walking down to **Marina Corricella,** a charming seaside village with buildings awash in pastel colors. Walk along the harbor lined with fishing boats and dine by the sea at **Il Pescatore.** Make your way back to the port and catch a ferry returning to Ischia. Splurge for special island farewell dinner at **La Lampara** restaurant atop the Miramare e Castello hotel for a fine dining experience with equally fine views.

Fun for Families

While the Amalfi Coast is famous as a honeymoon and romantic destination, it's also a fun and memorable area to visit for families. From exploring the beautiful coastline on a clear-bottomed kayak to climbing castles and eating pizza in its birthplace, here are some of the best experiences for families.

AMALFI COAST

- Spend a day swimming and collecting sea glass and pebbles at the beautiful **Spiaggia di Fornillo** in Positano, where the clear water and calmer beach is a great option for families.
- Learn firsthand how paper was traditionally made and even try to make it yourself on a tour at Amalfi's **Museo della Carta.** Kids won't look at paper the same way again after seeing how much work used to go into its creation.

SORRENTO AND THE SORRENTINE PENINSULA

- Take a close-up look at the remarkable inlaid woodwork at the **Museobottega della Tarsialignea** and have fun picking out scenes from daily life, animals, and Mount Vesuvius among the elaborate designs.
- **Rent a clear kayak** from Chasing Syrens at the Marina del Cantone beach in Nerano and set off on a family adventure exploring the coastline from the sea.

ISLANDS

- Thrill the kids with a ride up the chairlift to the top of Capri's **Monte Solaro** for incredible views overlooking the island.
- Enjoy a **boat tour** around the island of Capri for the best views of the famous grottoes and caves. Watch the excitement as the boat cruises right through the hole in the middle of the Faraglioni rocks.
- Explore the **Castello Aragonese** on Ischia: Complete with macabre crypts, abandoned prisons, and interesting ruins, there are a lot of real-life tales to uncover here.

Spiaggia di Fornillo

NAPLES

- Climb to the top of **Castel Sant'Elmo** for a view dominating Naples and see who can point out first the other two castles of Naples, the Castel Nuovo and the Castel dell'Ovo, along the waterfront far below.
- Older kids will find a **Napoli Sotterranea** tour fascinating and spooky as it leads deep into the underground of the city to reveal intriguing layers of the past.

HERCULANEUM AND VESUVIUS

- Get a look at ancient Roman life at **Herculaneum,** which is much smaller and easier to explore for kids than Pompeii.
- For the adventurous young travelers, a climb to the top of **Mount Vesuvius** is a thrilling travel experience. Maybe you'll even see a glimpse of steam seeping from the crater!

Outdoor Recreation and Seaside Relaxation

From soaring mountains to tiny beach coves, the Amalfi Coast offers such a varied natural landscape to explore and enjoy. This itinerary is based in Amalfi, taking advantage of its central location, and highlights the best outdoor experiences, including a good deal of hiking balanced with time spent discovering the beauty of the coastline and recovering with relaxing beach time.

Day 1

Set off in the morning to explore the beautiful green valley above Amalfi. Follow Amalfi's main street up from Piazza Duomo and continue following signs to the **Valle delle Ferriere.** The hike leads past ruins of old mills and along a peaceful stream with waterfalls and deep into the valley where you'll discover an almost tropical setting. Stop for lunch on the way down at **Agricola Fore Porta,** a rustic restaurant setting serving fresh homegrown fare. Continue back down the mountain and to the center of Amalfi and stop for a refreshing gelato at **Cioccolato Andrea Pansa** in Piazza Duomo. Head to the **Marina Grande** beach in Amalfi for a swim to relax. For dinner, stroll over to the neighboring village of Atrani and enjoy dinner by the sea at **Le Arcate.**

Day 2

Start the day with a good breakfast at your accommodation before lacing up comfortable walking shoes, packing some water, and catching the bus from Amalfi up to Agerola. Get off in Bomerano to begin the **Sentiero degli Dei,** or the Pathway of the Gods, one of the most impressive and scenic walks on the Amalfi Coast. The walk takes about 3-4 hours and ends in **Nocelle,** a *frazione* (hamlet) above Positano. Continue along the road

hiking around the top of the Valle delle Ferriere

to **Montepertuso,** another *frazione*, for a hearty lunch at **La Tagliata.** Catch a local bus down to the center of Positano and head all the way down to the beach to give your legs a rest or go for a swim at the **Spiaggia Grande,** with the town's vertical stack of colorful buildings the perfect backdrop. Catch the last ferry back to Amalfi. Stop in at **Trattoria Da Maria** in Piazza Duomo for a delicious wood-fire cooked pizza and glass of local Costa d'Amalfi wine.

Day 3

Give your legs a rest from hiking by renting a scooter in Amalfi and heading east down the coastline on the **Amalfi Coast Road** (SS163) through Minori, Maiori, and along the curvy road all the way to Cetara. Park your scooter down by the port and enjoy a walk along the pretty harbor. Stop for lunch at **Ristorante Pizzeria Al Convento** to savor some of the local seafood specialties—don't miss trying the *alici* (anchovies)! Afterward, head back in the direction of Amalfi and keep an eye out just west of Cetara for the road that leads down to **Erchie.** This secluded seaside village is the perfect spot for a peaceful afternoon swim. Hop back on your scooter and enjoy the evening ride back to Amalfi. For dinner, catch the boat service from Amalfi to the **La Tonnarella** restaurant on the beach in Conca dei Marini for a laid-back seaside dinner.

Day 4

Take the bus up into the mountains to the town of **Ravello.** Stop for a coffee at **Caffe Calce** in the Piazza Duomo and watch the town come to life. Visit **Villa Rufolo,** where you can climb to the top of the 13th-century Torre Museo watchtower to get a bird's-eye view over town and down the coastline. Continue soaking up the good views while enjoying lunch at **Ristorante Garden.** Work off lunch by walking down the **ancient stone steps** connecting Ravello to the seaside town of Minori. The walk takes about an hour and leads through sleepy villages and terraced olive groves. Reward yourself with a leisurely *aperitivo* and dinner along the *lungomare* (waterfront) followed by a much-deserved dessert from **Sal de Riso** before catching the bus back to Amalfi.

Day 5

For a final day of pure relaxation, catch the boat service to **Santa Croce beach** just west of Amalfi. Spend the day relaxing in the sun and for lunch enjoy dining steps from the beach at **Da Teresa.** As the sun begins to fade behind the mountains, head back to Amalfi by boat and enjoy a *limoncello* spritz and people-watching at one of the outdoor cafés in Piazza Duomo. Enjoy a farewell dinner overlooking the sea at **Lido Azzurro** in Amalfi.

Amalfi Coast

With a beauty that has been captivating travelers for ages, the Amalfi Coast's dramatic scenery, charming villages, rocky beaches, and famous views have made this area one of Italy's most popular travel destinations. **Positano,** known as the Vertical City, is one of the biggest draws, with its pastel-hued buildings scattered down the mountainside to the beach. **Amalfi** is the namesake town of the coastline and was the seat of a powerful maritime republic in the Middle Ages. High above Amalfi in the mountains, **Ravello** stretches out across a promontory with sweeping views of the coast.

While Positano, Amalfi, and Ravello are the most visited towns, the region comprises 10 other towns and tiny villages, each one offering a unique glimpse of local living and the intense natural beauty of the Amalfi Coast. While a visit to this UNESCO World Heritage protected

Itinerary Ideas 51
Positano 56
Praiano 77
Furore 84
Conca dei Marini 88
Amalfi 93
Atrani 116
Ravello 120
Scala 137
Tramonti 142
Minori 144
Maiori 149
Cetara 154
Vietri sul Mare 161
Salerno 168

Highlights

Look for ★ to find recommended sights, activities, dining, and lodging.

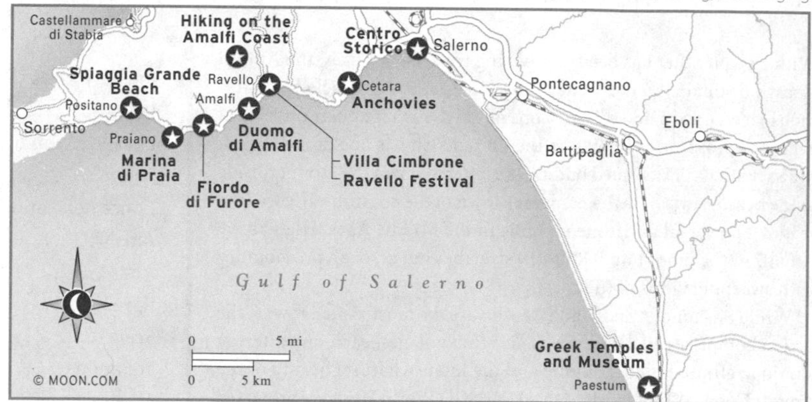

★ **Spiaggia Grande Beach, Positano:** The heart of Positano is the town's main beach, lined with colorful umbrellas. This is the beach to see and be seen, so settle onto a sun bed, soak up the sun, and enjoy the view (page 62).

★ **Marina di Praia, Praiano:** Wooden fishing boats and sunbathers vie for space on this pretty beach hidden away in a small cove. Stroll along a pathway carved out of the cliffside for a scenic walk (page 80).

★ **Fiordo di Furore:** This tiny fjord with famous views cuts a sliver into the rugged Amalfi coastline. Hike down to the minuscule beach for the best view (page 85).

★ **Duomo di Amalfi:** Step back in time to the splendor of Amalfi's medieval past at this impressive cathedral sitting atop a grand staircase in the town's main square (page 96).

★ **Villa Cimbrone, Ravello:** Gaze into endless beauty from the Terrace of Infinity in these beautifully landscaped gardens, where the sky and sea blend into one tantalizing view (page 124).

★ **Ravello Festival:** With the lights of the Amalfi Coast twinkling in the distance, the City of Music hosts outdoor concerts in the Villa Rufolo gardens during this annual summer music and performing arts festival from June to August (page 128).

★ **Hiking on the Amalfi Coast:** From the Pathway of the Gods to waterfalls and ruins above Amalfi, there are plenty of walks or hikes on the Amalfi Coast to take in extraordinary views far away from the crowds (page 134).

★ **Cetara's anchovies:** With a fishing history dating back to Roman times, Cetara is known for its seafood. Anchovies are a specialty in local dishes, and they're celebrated with a festival every summer in July in this small town off the main tourist path (page 158).

★ **Centro Storico, Salerno:** Meander through the maze of narrow streets in Salerno's medieval historic center, with its lively atmosphere, excellent shopping options, and important historic landmarks (page 168).

★ **Paestum Greek Temples and Museum:** Marvel at the well-preserved Greek temples, and admire the archaeological treasures uncovered at the museum (page 179).

coastline isn't complete without seeing the top three towns, it's well worth the time to wander a bit off the beaten path. Linger awhile in **Praiano** to enjoy the best vantage point for sunsets, eat freshly caught seafood in a hidden cove in **Conca dei Marini,** and wash it down with wine grown in improbably steep vineyards in **Furore.** Hike to medieval watchtowers and crumbling church ruins in **Scala,** walk among the lemon groves high above Minori, and try the local anchovies in **Cetara.** There's so much to discover along the Amalfi Coast.

Just beyond **Vietri sul Mare,** a town famous for its ceramic production, the Amalfi Coast flows right into the large port city of **Salerno.** Though it's off the radar for many travelers, Salerno is a fascinating city with a wealth of history and a more tranquil setting than nearby Naples. Explore the medieval city center, stroll along the *lungomare* (waterfront), climb to the castle high above the city, and visit the impressive cathedral. With excellent train and ferry service, it's a good home base for travelers who enjoy a city vibe.

Beyond the tempting beaches and sparkling blue Mediterranean Sea, the not-to-be-missed archaeological site of **Paestum** is only a short jaunt from Salerno. Its remarkable temples stand as testimony to the historical richness of this area. From these Greek temples to the Roman ruins in **Minori** and the medieval splendor of Amalfi, the history of the Amalfi Coast is a tapestry set against one of the most splendid backdrops in Italy.

So pack a pair of comfortable shoes and set off to explore the Amalfi Coast with all its magnificent twists and turns, history, and exquisite Mediterranean beauty.

GETTING TO THE AMALFI COAST

Salerno is the closest major train station to the Amalfi Coast. **Trenitalia** (www.trenitalia.com) operates frequent train service between Naples and Salerno daily with travel times ranging from 40 minutes to 1 hour 25 minutes, depending on the type of train. From the station you can catch SITA SUD buses to the Amalfi Coast or walk a short distance to the port nearby, where ferries depart for the Amalfi Coast towns and to Capri seasonally April-October.

There is also a train station in **Sorrento.** The **Circumvesuviana train** line operated by EAV (www.eavsrl.it) connects Naples with the archaeological sites of Pompeii and Herculaneum as well as Sorrento. The full journey from Naples to Sorrento takes about 60 minutes. This regional commuter train runs frequently throughout the day and is an inexpensive way to travel between Naples and Sorrento. To reach the Amalfi Coast from Sorrento, you can catch a SITA SUD bus right outside the Sorrento train station, or if you are headed to Positano, Amalfi, Minori, Maiori, or Cetara in season, you may also be able to take a ferry.

GETTING AROUND THE AMALFI COAST

The landscape of the Amalfi Coast is a rugged one, with its famously twisty road weaving up and down and connecting the coastline towns situated both at sea level and dotted across the mountainsides. While it's certainly not the most straightforward area to explore, with a little preparation you'll be navigating the Amalfi Coast like a pro in no time.

By Car and Scooter

The **Amalfi Coast Road** (Strada Statale 163, also abbreviated as **SS163**) winds its way along the Amalfi Coast from Vietri sul Mare west to Positano. As the only road along the coastline, and a very narrow and curvy one at that, it can become quite packed, especially during the peak seasons around Easter and from July to August. Driving this unique and congested road is not for the faint of heart.

Previous: Positano; lemons growing around Amalfi; the ruins of the Basilica di Sant'Eustachio, Scala

Amalfi Coast and Paestum

A30

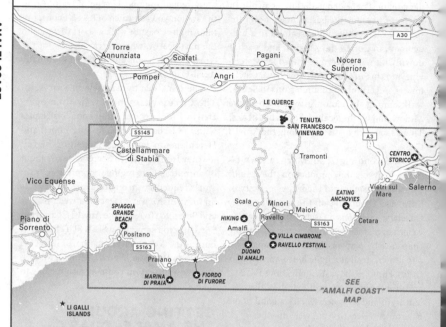

Torre Annunziata

Scafati

Pagani

Nocera Superiore

Pompei

Angri

LE QUERCE

TENUTA SAN FRANCESCO VINEYARD

SS145

A3

Castellammare di Stabia

Tramonti

CENTRO STORICO

Vico Equense

Salerno

Vietri sul Mare

EATING ANCHOVIES

Scala

Minori

Maiori

SPIAGGIA GRANDE BEACH

HIKING

Ravello

Cetara

Piano di Sorrento

Amalfi

SS163

Positano

VILLA CIMBRONE

RAVELLO FESTIVAL

SS163

DUOMO DI AMALFI

Praiano

MARINA DI PRAIA

FIORDO DI FURORE

SEE "AMALFI COAST" MAP

LI GALLI ISLANDS

Gulf of Salerno

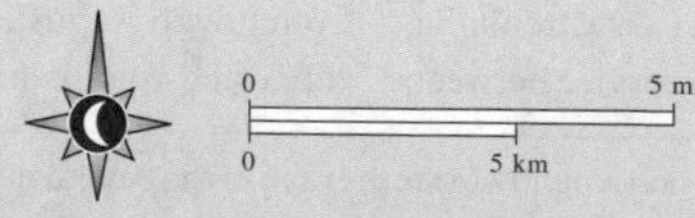

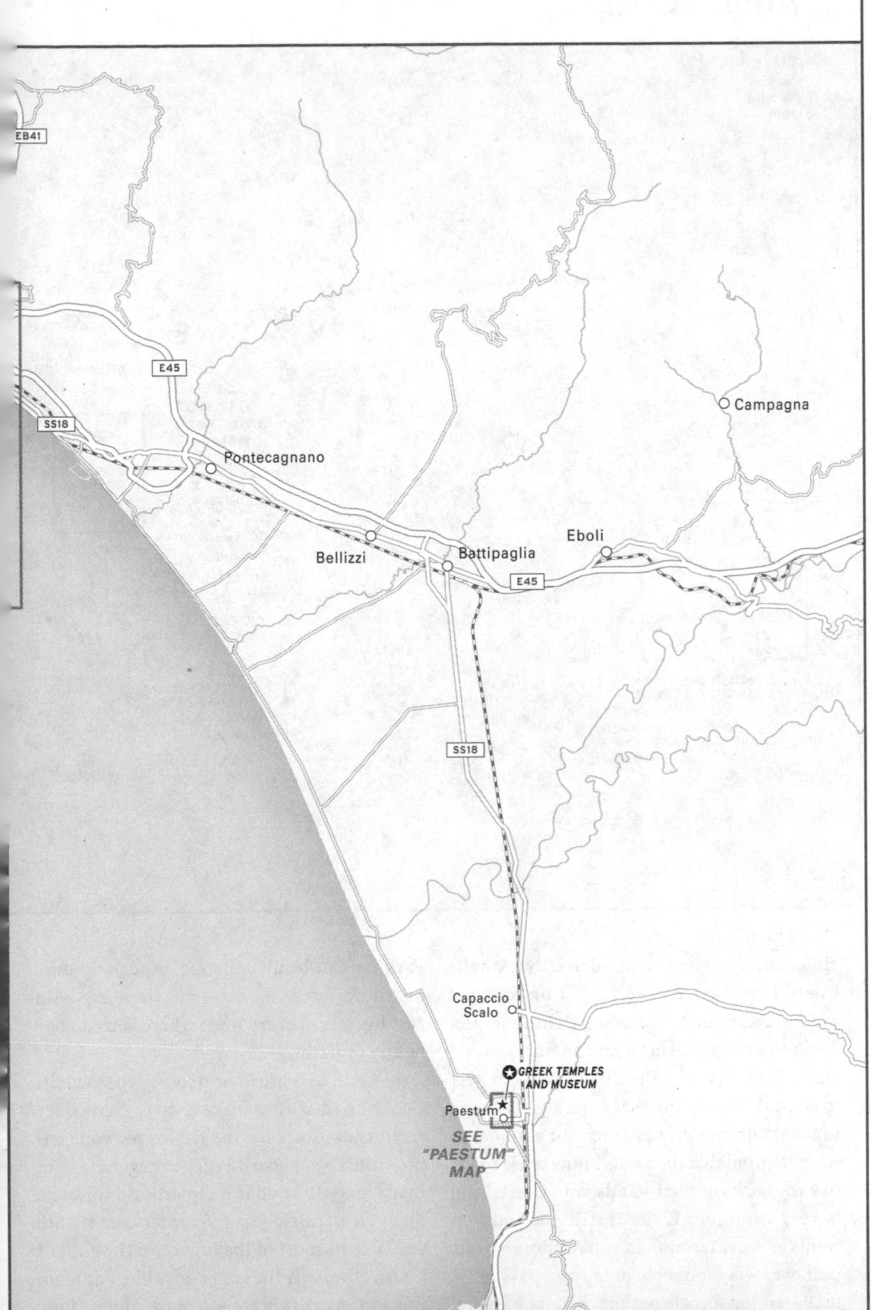
EB41
E45
SS18
Campagna
Pontecagnano
Bellizzi
Battipaglia
Eboli
E45
SS18
Capaccio
Scalo
GREEK TEMPLES
AND MUSEUM
Paestum
SEE
"PAESTUM"
MAP

Amalfi Coast

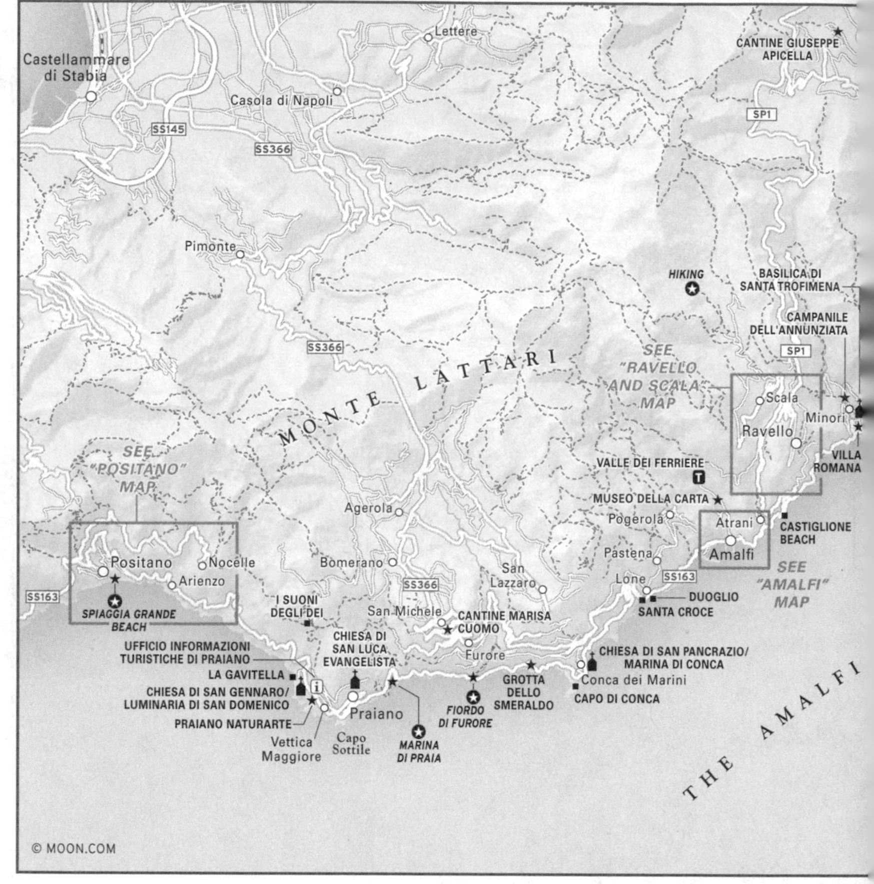

However, if you're keen to drive the Amalfi Coast Road, be prepared for the unexpected around every curve, including tight squeezes, backing up if necessary, and the occasional traffic jam. If you're the driver, don't expect to enjoy those famous views, because it's hard to take your eyes off road even for a moment. Keep in mind that the locals know these roads like the backs of their hands, and overtaking is very common. If the traffic behind you wants to move faster than you're comfortable, pull over when possible to let cars pass or be prepared for sometimes precarious passing.

Parking can be a challenge, especially during the summer months, but there are paid parking lots in every town where you can pay hourly or daily.

For the adventure of driving the Amalfi Coast Road with a bit less stress, consider renting a scooter for the day or for your entire visit. They make it easier to negotiate tight roads and allow you to zip around (or even through!) traffic jams. Scooter rentals are available in most of the towns on the Amalfi Coast, especially the larger ones like Positano, Praiano, Amalfi, Ravello, and Maiori. Many

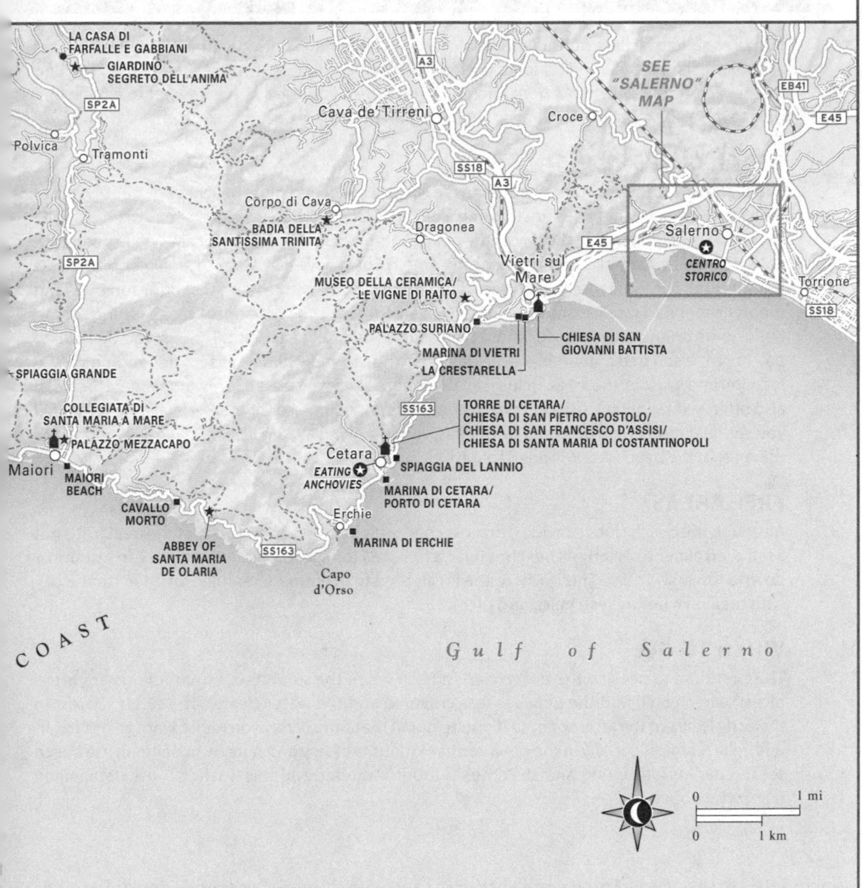

companies will even deliver a scooter right to your hotel or accommodation on the Amalfi Coast for a small fee. Bring an ID if you plan to rent a scooter. While parking can be a bit easier with a scooter, it can still be a challenge in the height of summer from July to August. Paid parking areas for scooters are available in every town along the coastline.

By Bus

PUBLIC BUSES

The Amalfi Coast towns are well connected with buses operated by **SITA SUD** (tel. 089/386-6701; www.sitasudtrasporti.it; starting at €1.30 per person) that run along the Amalfi Coast Road and to towns located higher in the mountains along the coastline. Amalfi is a central bus hub along the Amalfi Coast Road, with the main bus lines running from Salerno to Amalfi and from Amalfi to Sorrento. Buses for Ravello and Scala depart from Amalfi. Positano has internal bus lines operated by **Mobility Amalfi Coast** (tel. 089/813-077; info@mobilityamalficoast.com; €1.70-1.80) that circle the internal road though town and

Tips for a Day at the Beach

With a rugged coastline dotted with picturesque swimming spots, the Amalfi Coast's beaches are among its most alluring features during the summer months. If you're dreaming of soaking up the Mediterranean atmosphere and diving into the turquoise sea, here's what to expect and how to make the most of your time at the beach on the Amalfi Coast.

BEACH CLUBS

The first thing to know is that the coast here is quite rocky and most beaches are pebbly rather than sandy. You'll want to be sure to bring a pair of beach flip-flops or water shoes to enjoy walking on the beach. Spending the day at the beach lounging on the rocks is not always very comfortable. However, nearly all beaches along the Amalfi Coast have at least one *stabilimente balneare* (beach club). These are often wooden structures built right on the beach that offer sun beds and umbrella rentals, as well as showers (often just an outdoor shower to rinse off), changing rooms, bathrooms, and usually a bar for snacks and drinks, or a full restaurant. Though you do have to pay to rent a sun bed and umbrella (usually starting around €10 per person, depending on the location and season), the rates include all the other services available. A few *stabilimenti balneari* also offer kayaks for rent, but don't expect to find snorkeling gear or the like available for rent. If you see neat rows of sun beds and umbrellas, you're looking at a *stabilimente balneare*, and to use that part of the beach you will need to pay.

FREE AREAS

Although the beach clubs provide the most comfortable way to spend a day at the beach, it's not a required expense. Nearly all beaches have a free area (*spiaggia libera*), where you can just throw down a towel and relax. This is where the locals tend to be, sometimes fully outfitted for the day with their own umbrellas, chairs, and picnics.

WHEN TO GO

The best time to head to the beach depends on when the sun hits it, but mornings are often nicest, when you'll find the beaches less crowded and the water clearer. The sun is hottest in the early hours of the afternoon, so if you're going that time of day you might want to opt for an umbrella rental, especially in the peak summer months of July and August. In general, the beach season begins late spring and stretches through October, and this is when most *stabilimenti balneari* are open.

circulate to the areas in the mountains above town.

To ride the SITA SUD buses, tickets need to be purchased in advance in local *tabacchi* (tobacco) stores or some bars. Tickets follow the Unico Campania (www.unicocampania.it) pricing system, where you can pay for individual journeys or daily passes. Ticket prices depend on the length of the journey and start at €1.30. Or opt for a **COSTIERASITA ticket** for €10 (€12 for one that also includes the internal bus lines for Positano) that covers all bus rides for 24 hours to and from Agerola, Amalfi, Atrani, Cetara, Conca dei Marini, Furore, Maiori, Massa Lubrense, Meta di Sorrento, Minori, Positano, Piano di Sorrento, Praiano, Ravello, Salerno, Sant'Agnello, Scala, Sorrento, Tramonti, and Vietri sul Mare. Validate your ticket only on the first bus you take and be sure to write your name and birth date on the ticket where indicated. Don't forget to validate your tickets when boarding at the small machine located behind the driver. Ticket inspectors do circulate on the routes and will fine you if you haven't properly validated your ticket.

CITY SIGHTSEEING

City Sightseeing (www.city-sightseeing.it; Apr.-Oct.; from €5 per person) has three bus lines on the Amalfi Coast, including one from Sorrento to Positano and Amalfi, one that connects Amalfi and Ravello, and another route connecting Amalfi with Minori and Maiori. Buses are bright red and easy to spot, with the Amalfi-Ravello line often having open-top buses that offer a great view. These are a little more expensive than the public buses, but they are far more comfortable. Tickets are purchased onboard, and these buses only allow as many passengers as they have seats, so you won't have to worry about standing-room-only situations. Ticket prices also include audio guides in English.

TIPS

Buses are an inexpensive way to get around the Amalfi Coast and avoid the stress of driving on the Amalfi Coast Road. The road, however, remains busy and tricky, which means that bus schedules are very challenging to run precisely on time. If you're planning to travel by bus, be prepared to wait and to deal with crowds during the summer season. The public SITA SUD buses are popular with locals and travelers alike and can be absolutely jam-packed during the peak of the summer season. Lines for getting the bus are rarely orderly, and buses can also be so full that they are unable to stop to pick up passengers. This frustrating experience is most likely to occur during July and August.

Be aware that the SITA SUD buses on the Amalfi Coast are not the easiest to navigate for first-time visitors. You will need to push a button on the bus to request your stop as buses don't stop unless requested or there are passengers to pick up. Stops are not numbered and are not announced in advance in any way, so finding your stop can be a bit of a challenge. Some drivers will announce the biggest stops, for instance in Positano, but it is best not to rely on it. If you have an international data plan for your smartphone, Google Maps can be helpful for tracking your location and helping you know when to get off. Bus stops are marked by a small blue sign saying SITA.

If you are traveling with luggage, you will need to take the SITA SUD bus, not the City Sightseeing bus, and it will need to be stored below the bus before boarding. Be sure to let the driver know you must retrieve luggage before getting off the bus.

By Ferry

Traveling around the Amalfi Coast by ferry is the most comfortable and least stressful way to navigate the coastline. It's also a scenic way

a ferry departing from Amalfi

to get around because you'll enjoy fine views of the Amalfi Coast from the sea. Ferry service connects many towns on the Amalfi Coast, including Positano, Amalfi, Minori, Maiori, Cetara, and Salerno. Amalfi and Positano are the main ferry terminals along the coastline, with the option to transfer to smaller boats to reach Minori, Maiori, and Cetara. Ferry service to Vietri sul Mare is set to begin in summer 2019. Boat service to Salerno, Capri, and Sorrento is also available seasonally from the towns of Positano, Amalfi, Minori, Maiori, and Cetara.

Travelmar (tel. 089/872-950; www.travelmar.it; €3-12 per person) and **Alicost** (tel. 089/871-483 weekdays, 089/948-3671 weekends; www.alicost.it; €8-26.90 per person) are the main ferry companies connecting Salerno, the Amalfi Coast, Capri, and Sorrento. Tickets can be purchased online in advance or at ticket booths near the ferry terminals. From Positano, **Positano Jet** (tel. 089/811-164; www.lucibello.it; €18.50-21 per person) offers ferry service connecting Positano, Amalfi, and Capri.

Keep in mind that ferry service is seasonal and only runs from about **Easter** through the beginning of **November.** Naturally, the service is also dependent on the weather and sea conditions. Even though rough seas rarely prohibit service in the summer, during the shoulder seasons of April to May and October, it's a good idea to have a backup plan for other transportation options in mind.

By Taxi

Taxis provide a comfortable way to get around the Amalfi Coast, but this is also the most expensive option. Taxis that transport visitors between towns operate differently from city taxis insofar as the fares aren't usually based on time or distance but on the journey. A ride from one town to the next can cost €40 or more, even if it's a short drive, and this can add up quickly, so be sure to negotiate and agree with the driver on a price before departing.

One time you may want to splurge on a taxi transfer is when you arrive or depart from the Amalfi Coast. Public transportation is not particularly easy to negotiate with luggage, so booking a private transfer to or from the airport or other point of arrival can help alleviate some stress.

PLANNING YOUR TIME

Many travelers see the Amalfi Coast on a day excursion from a cruise ship, or from nearby Naples or Sorrento. Though spending a day is better than not visiting at all, a single day only gives you a brief look at the view and a small taste of what the towns along the coast have to offer. To explore the area more deeply, plan to spend at least three days to allow time to visit the three main towns on the coast—Amalfi, Positano, and Ravello—along with a bit of time to relax on the beach: the area's hottest commodity. With a week, there is plenty of time for hiking, visiting smaller towns, enjoying water sports or boating along the coastline, and adding day trips to nearby destinations, such as Capri or Sorrento, and archaeological sites like Pompeii and Paestum.

Expect bigger crowds—especially during the peak summer months from June through August—in Positano, Amalfi, and Ravello, as they're the most visited towns on the coast. Visit during the shoulder seasons or consider staying in smaller towns like Atrani, Minori, Scala, or Cetara to avoid the crowds.

For shorter visits, Amalfi makes an excellent home base, thanks to its central location and transportation connections. Although Positano is well connected to other towns by ferries, the public buses that pass by at the top of town are often very crowded.

Itinerary Ideas

ESSENTIAL AMALFI COAST

Make the most of a shorter stay on the Amalfi Coast by hitting the three most popular towns. Amalfi is a great starting point for delving deeper into the history of the Amalfi Coast, and a visit isn't complete without seeing Positano. Then head up into the mountains to explore Ravello, famous for its fine views of the coastline and peaceful gardens.

Day 1: Amalfi

- Start in the center of town in the **Piazza Duomo,** where you'll find a striking view of the Duomo di Amalfi. Visit the historic bakery and coffee shop **Pasticceria Pansa** for the best espresso and cappuccino in Amalfi as well as one of their tempting *sfogliatella* (shell-shaped pastry).
- Climb the long staircase to visit the **Duomo di Amalfi,** taking time to savor the peacefulness of the Cloister of Paradise, admire the treasures in the museum, and see the crypt of Sant'Andrea, the town's patron saint.
- Just steps from Piazza Duomo, stop at **Trattoria Da Maria** for excellent wood-fire oven pizza and a glass of locally produced wine.
- Walk off lunch with a stroll along the harbor, passing by rocky beaches and multihued fishing boats all the way to the end of the **Molo Foraneo** pier for a panoramic view looking back to Amalfi.
- Find out more about Amalfi's important role in the history of papermaking at the **Museo della Carta**. You can even try your hand at making paper!
- To take home a souvenir of traditional handmade paper, which is still produced at an antique mill in the valley above Amalfi, stop in **La Scuderia del Duca** near the Arsenale for a lovely selection of stationery, journals, and gifts.
- Watch the sunset accompanied by the sound of the sea with drinks at **Gran Caffè,** which overlooks Marina Grande beach, and make a toast to all of Amalfi's charms.
- Enjoy a relaxed dinner overlooking the beach at **Ristorante Marina Grande.**

Day 2: Positano

- If you're not based in Positano, the best way to arrive is by ferry to enjoy the spectacular view of the town from the sea. The ferry docks right at the Spiaggia Grande beach; walk along the beach and climb the steps to visit the **Chiesa di Santa Maria Assunta.** Step inside to see the town's prized Byzantine icon hanging above the altar.
- Stroll along **Via Positanesi d'America** over to the Spiaggia di Fornillo beach and pick out a sun bed from **Da Ferdinando** for some relaxation in the sun. When it's time for lunch, enjoy a fresh meal just steps from the beach at their restaurant.
- Spend the afternoon exploring all the little pathways lined with boutiques. Stroll along **Viale Pasitea** to find an excellent selection of some of Positano's popular fashion and homeware shops.
- Stop for a fresh juice from **Casa e Bottega.**

Itinerary Ideas

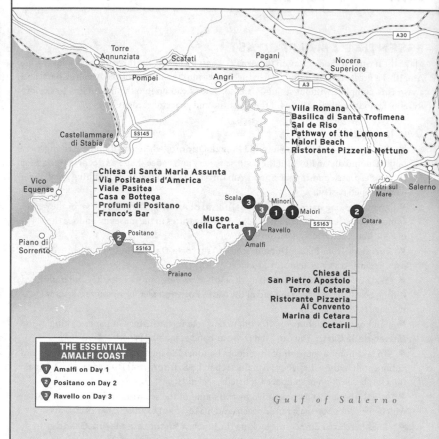

A30
Torre Annunziata
Scafati
Pagani
Nocera Superiore
Pompei
Angri
A3
Castellammare di Stabia
SS145
Villa Romana
Basilica di Santa Trofimena
Sal de Riso
Pathway of the Lemons
Maiori Beach
Ristorante Pizzeria Nettuno
Chiesa di Santa Maria Assunta
Via Positanesi d'America
Viale Pasitea
Casa e Bottega
Profumi di Positano
Franco's Bar
Vico Equense
Salerno
Vietri sul Mare
Scala
Minori
Maiori
Cetara
Museo della Carta
Ravello
SS163
Amalfi
Positano
Piano di Sorrento
SS163
Praiano
Chiesa di San Pietro Apostolo
Torre di Cetara
Ristorante Pizzeria Al Convento
Marina di Cetara
Cetarii

THE ESSENTIAL AMALFI COAST

1 Amalfi on Day 1
2 Positano on Day 2
3 Ravello on Day 3

Gulf of Salerno

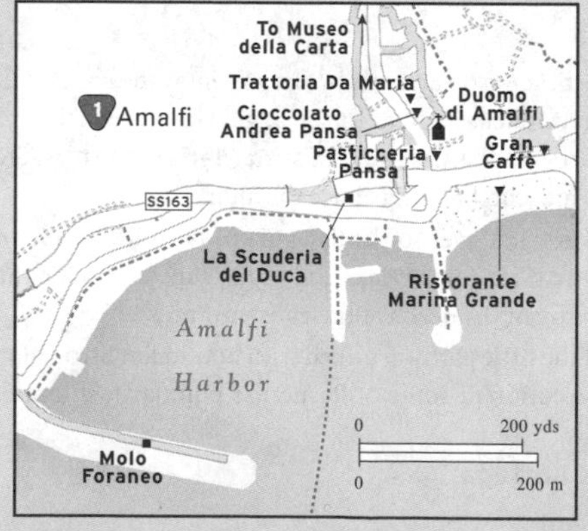

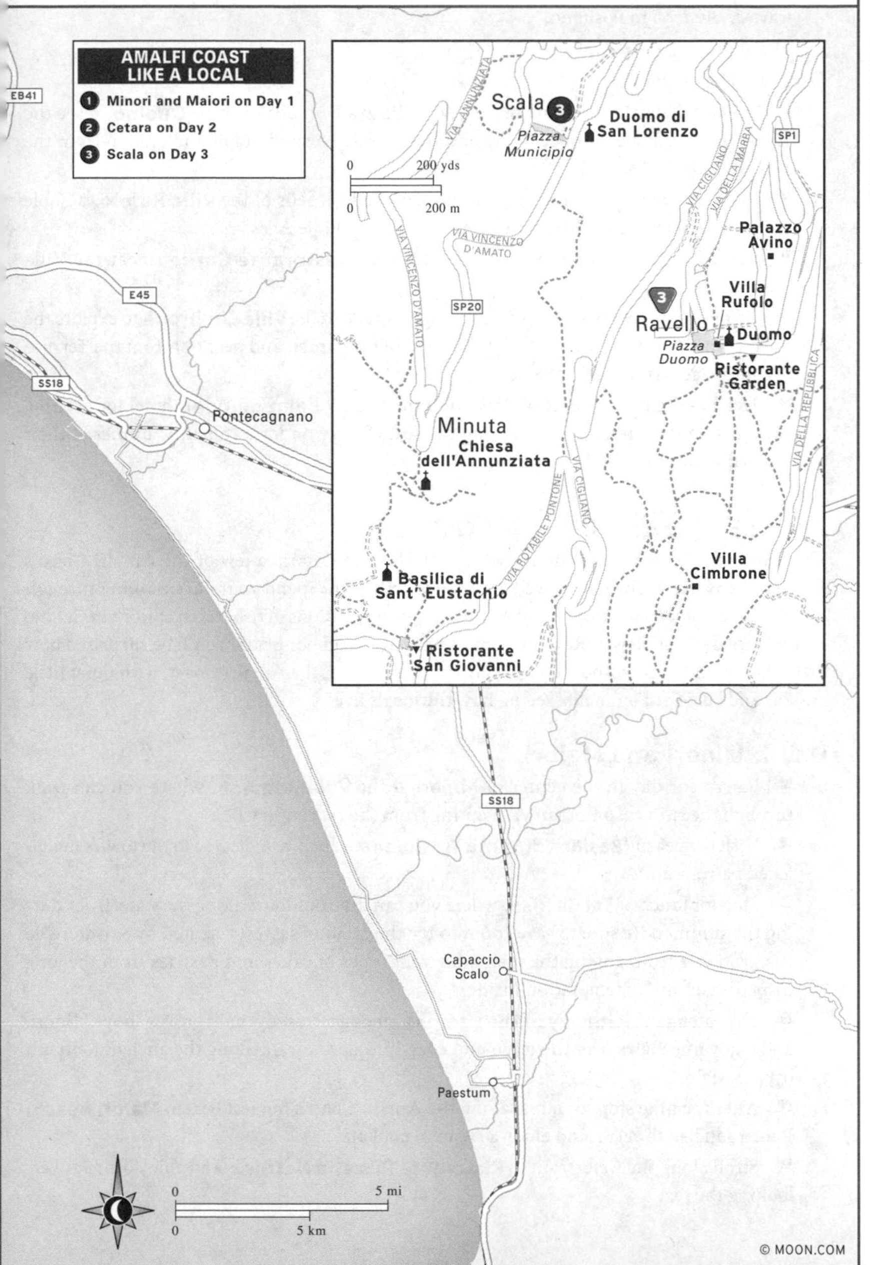
AMALFI COAST LIKE A LOCAL
1 Minori and Maiori on Day 1
2 Cetara on Day 2
3 Scala on Day 3
EB41
E45
SS18
Pontecagnano
Capaccio Scalo
Paestum
0
5 mi
0
5 km
Scala
3
Piazza Municipio
Duomo di San Lorenzo
0
200 yds
0
200 m
VIA ANNUNZIATA
VIA VINCENZO D'AMATO
SP20
SP1
VIA CIGLIANO
VIA DELLA MARRA
Palazzo Avino
Villa Rufolo
Ravello
Duomo
Piazza Duomo
Ristorante Garden
VIA DELLA REPUBBLICA
Minuta
Chiesa dell'Annunziata
VIA ROTABILE PONTONE
Villa Cimbrone
Basilica di Sant' Eustachio
Ristorante San Giovanni
© MOON.COM

- Shop for perfume at **Profumi di Positano** to take a little of the sweet scent of Positano home with you.
- As the sun begins to set, enjoy a *spritz* at **Franco's Bar** before hopping on the ferry to wave *arrivederci* to Positano.

Day 3: Ravello

- Spend the day in the heart of Ravello in Piazza Duomo. Visit the **Duomo** to see the 12th-century paneled bronze doors and the mosaic-covered pulpit and ambon from the 12th-13th centuries.
- Just off of Piazza Duomo, explore the terraced gardens of the **Villa Rufolo,** a noble estate created by the wealthy Rufolo family in the Middle Ages.
- Savor lunch with a panoramic view from the **Ristorante Garden** near the Villa Rufolo.
- Enjoy a leisurely walk after lunch through Ravello to the **Villa Cimbrone** to explore the town's other famous garden. Walk to the end of the garden and peer out from the Terrace of Infinity across the Gulf of Salerno.
- Head to the highest part of Ravello to the elegant **Palazzo Avino** hotel for evening cocktails on their terrace overlooking the sea. Or stay on for a romantic dinner at their Michelin-starred Rossellinis restaurant.

AMALFI COAST LIKE A LOCAL

This three-day itinerary highlights Minori, Scala, and Cetara, a few of the Amalfi Coast's smaller towns that aren't on the well-trodden tourist path. Spend your days walking through the ruins of a Roman summer villa in Minori, watch generations of fishermen at work in Cetara, and admire the best view of Ravello from its peaceful neighbor Scala. You'll be surprised how little distance it takes to find a completely different side of the Amalfi Coast, with quiet little piazzas and beautiful moments seeing how the locals live.

Day 1: Minori and Maiori

- Start your day in the center of Minori at the **Villa Romana,** where you can walk through the ruins of a Roman villa dating from the 1st century BC.
- Visit the nearby **Basilica di Santa Trofimena,** which is dedicated to the town's much-loved patron saint.
- Stop for lunch at **Sal de Riso,** where you can dine outdoors along the waterfront during the summer. Be sure to save room to try the famous desserts created by Salvatore de Riso. Choose from among the many different types of cakes and pastries from the long display cases full of temptation inside.
- Hike along the **Pathway of the Lemons** among terraced lemon groves above Minori, and enjoy fine views over the town and coastline as you walk along the ancient footpath over to Maiori.
- After the hike stop for a rest along the Amalfi Coast's longest beach, **Maiori beach.** Rent a sun bed to relax, and enjoy a swim to cool off.
- Stroll along the waterfront to **Ristorante Pizzeria Nettuno** and enjoy dinner overlooking the sea.

Day 2: Cetara

■ Give your legs a day of rest after the walk with a day visiting the picturesque seaside town of **Cetara.** Arriving by ferry is the most beautiful option from Easter through October, but you can also easily reach Cetara by SITA SUD bus year-round.

■ Follow the main street, Corso Garibaldi, to the short staircase on the right leading up to the **Chiesa di San Pietro Apostolo,** where you can admire the modern bronze doors depicting the Saints Peter and Andrew.

■ Next to the church, follow the staircase up to the road and continue right until you reach the **Torre di Cetara.** Visit the tower's museum and stop outside on the balcony of the tower for a beautiful view over Cetara.

■ Return to the main street and stop for lunch at the **Ristorante Pizzeria Al Convento** overlooking a pretty piazza. Find a table in the tree-lined outdoor area and enjoy sampling Cetara's famous *alici* (anchovies) in a variety of ways. The restaurant also makes a delicious pizza if anchovies don't tempt you.

■ Find a spot along the **Marina di Cetara** and soak up the Mediterranean sun and views alongside locals as their kids splash in the sea.

■ Enjoy a leisurely walk back toward the ferry along the beach and stop in **Cetarii** to take home a taste of Cetara, such as their jarred *alici*, tuna, and other locally made products.

Day 3: Scala

■ Take the bus up into the mountains above Amalfi to the center of **Scala** at Piazza Municipio.

■ Visit the **Duomo di San Lorenzo** dedicated to the town's patron saint.

■ To the right of the church, walk down the short flight of steps to a large terrace in the **Piazza Municipio,** where you'll enjoy an excellent view of Ravello across the valley.

■ Walk along Via Torricella for about 10 minutes to **Minuta,** where you'll find the **Chiesa dell'Annunziata** and a fine overlook with Amalfi far below.

■ Hike from Minuta down the valley toward Amalfi. The first stop is in the *frazione* (hamlet) of Pontone, where you'll follow signs to see the ruins of the 12th-century **Basilica di Sant'Eustachio.**

■ Stop for a rest mid-hike for lunch at **Ristorante San Giovanni** in Pontone. The outdoor dining area boasts a fine view across the valley to Ravello.

■ Continue the hike down the mountain to Amalfi. If you haven't already visited, you can stop to visit the **Museo della Carta** in Amalfi to learn more about Amalfi's papermaking history.

■ Continue down Amalfi's main street to the Piazza Duomo and stop in **Cioccolato Andrea Pansa** for a well-deserved gelato or chocolate treat: all locally made right in Amalfi.

Which Amalfi Coast Town Is Best for You?

With 13 different towns to choose from and each one more beautiful than the last, it can be hard to decide where to stay during your holiday on the Amalfi Coast. Each town is appealing in its own way, but not every town is the right home base for every type of traveler. If you're planning a quick visit to the Amalfi Coast of 1-3 days, Amalfi is the most convenient base with its easy bus and ferry connections to help you see the highlights of Amalfi, Positano, and Ravello. If you're staying for longer or just enjoy being a bit off the beaten path, this section will help you find the right spot. Whether you're looking for the best beaches, easiest access to hikes, a relaxing holiday with a cultural twist, or a family-friendly spot, here's a look at the top towns recommended for different vacationing styles.

BEST FOR BEACHES

- **Positano:** For a beach-themed holiday, Positano offers a host of different options, from the colorful Spiaggia Grande to the more secluded Spiaggia di Fornillo and tiny beaches reached by boat service from the center of town.
- **Conca dei Marini:** The seaside Marina di Conca retains an old-world feel from when it was just a sleepy fishing village. There's also a very scenic beach at the Capo di Conca promontory.
- **Amalfi:** The namesake town of the Amalfi Coast is another convenient option for beach lovers. You'll find many beaches right in town as well as the beautiful Santa Croce beach only a short boat ride away.

BEST FOR FOODIES

- **Minori:** From the lemon groves above town to a long tradition of pasta making and the tempting sweets created by one of Italy's most noted pastry makers, Minori is connected to its past and present by food. Every August these traditions are celebrated during the Gusta Minori (A Taste of Minori) food and cultural festival.

Positano

With its romantic mosaic of pastel-hued buildings clinging to the cliffside, Positano has a seemingly impossible beauty that captures the hearts of travelers. Set in a steep ravine, the town climbs from the beach to the mountains above. The Amalfi Coast Road winds its way through the top of Positano, leaving much of the town accessible only by a meandering smaller road or the town's famous steps. Whether you arrive by boat at sea level or by car or bus higher up, steps are everywhere in Positano. What did you expect in a town nicknamed the Vertical City? Fortunately, there are plenty of captivating views to stop and enjoy along the way.

Spiaggia Grande is the heart of town, and many of the main sights are within a short stroll—or climb—from the beach. With a relaxed yet chic atmosphere, Positano is the place for shopping, soaking up the sun, and perfecting the art of *la dolce vita*, Amalfi Coast style.

ORIENTATION

One glimpse of Positano, either from the sea or from the Amalfi Coast Road above the city, and it's easy to see why it's called the Vertical City. More than any other town along the Amalfi Coast, Positano is set into the steep mountainside, with buildings that seem to be

- **Cetara:** Famous for its fishing fleet, and fresh anchovies and tuna, Cetara is home to many fine restaurants where you can enjoy seafood specialties like the coveted *colatura di alici*, an oil made from anchovies that is similar to the ancient Roman *garum*.

BEST FOR HIKING

- **Scala:** Hike to a 15th-century watchtower, explore the valley above Amalfi with its paper mill ruins, and wander through sleepy villages that are among the most charming on the Amalfi Coast.
- **Nocelle (Positano):** Sitting right by the starting point of the famous Sentiero degli Dei (Pathway of the Gods), Nocelle is a tiny village with immense views. Besides the Sentiero degli Dei, there are hikes up into the mountains around Positano in nearby Montepertuso.
- **Ravello:** With its scenic setting on a promontory, Ravello is well situated for hikes to the neighboring towns in the surrounding valleys like Minori and Atrani.

BEST FOR ART LOVERS

- **Amalfi:** As the heart of the Republic of Amalfi in the Middle Ages, Amalfi boasted wealth that brought the town many artistic treasures, which can be seen in the Duomo di Amalfi, the Museo della Carta, and the Museo della Bussola e del Ducato Marinaro di Amalfi (Museum of the Compass and Duchy of Amalfi).
- **Vietri sul Mare:** The Amalfi Coast's homegrown art form is hand-painted ceramics, and the center of ceramic production in the area is the town of Vietri sul Mare. Visit the scores of ceramic shops and don't miss the town's ceramics museum, Museo della Ceramica.
- **Salerno:** While the Amalfi Coast isn't particularly known for its museums, neighboring Salerno has a selection of excellent small museums, including the archaeological treasures at the Museo Archeologico Provinciale and an excellent collection of religious art at the Museo Diocesano.

stacked, one on top of the other. The center of town is near the Spiaggia Grande beach where Via Marina Grande runs along the beach, lined with restaurants and shops. Overlooking the beach, the **Chiesa di Santa Maria Assunta** sits right in the heart of Positano with the town rising behind it. Ferries arrive and depart from the large cement pier at the westernmost edge of Spiaggia Grande. From near the pier, the Via Positanesi d'America hugs the cliffside and leads to the **Spiaggia di Fornillo.** Along the way, you can see the Li Galli islands, an archipelago of three small islands located off the coast of Positano.

From the Chiesa di Santa Maria Assunta, Via dei Mulini is a bougainvillea-covered pedestrian-only walkway that leads up to **Piazza dei Mulini.** This is where you'll meet the Viale Pasitea, or the internal road that runs through Positano from two points along the Amalfi Coast Road (SS163), from the Chiesa Nuova area near the *Comune* (town hall) and the Bar Internazionale on the western side of the town to the Sponda intersection on the eastern side of town. This road is one way from the west side to the east and is lined with shops and restaurants. Public SITA SUD buses running along the Amalfi Coast Road stop at the Sponda intersection and near the Bar Internazionale at Chiesa Nuova. Local Positano buses also circulate around Viale Pasitea through Positano. By car or bus, the Piazza dei Mulini is the closest spot that you can reach to the Spiaggia Grande, and from there you will need to walk. Positano is a town best explored on foot, but do expect a lot of steps and steep walkways.

High above Positano in the mountains

Positano

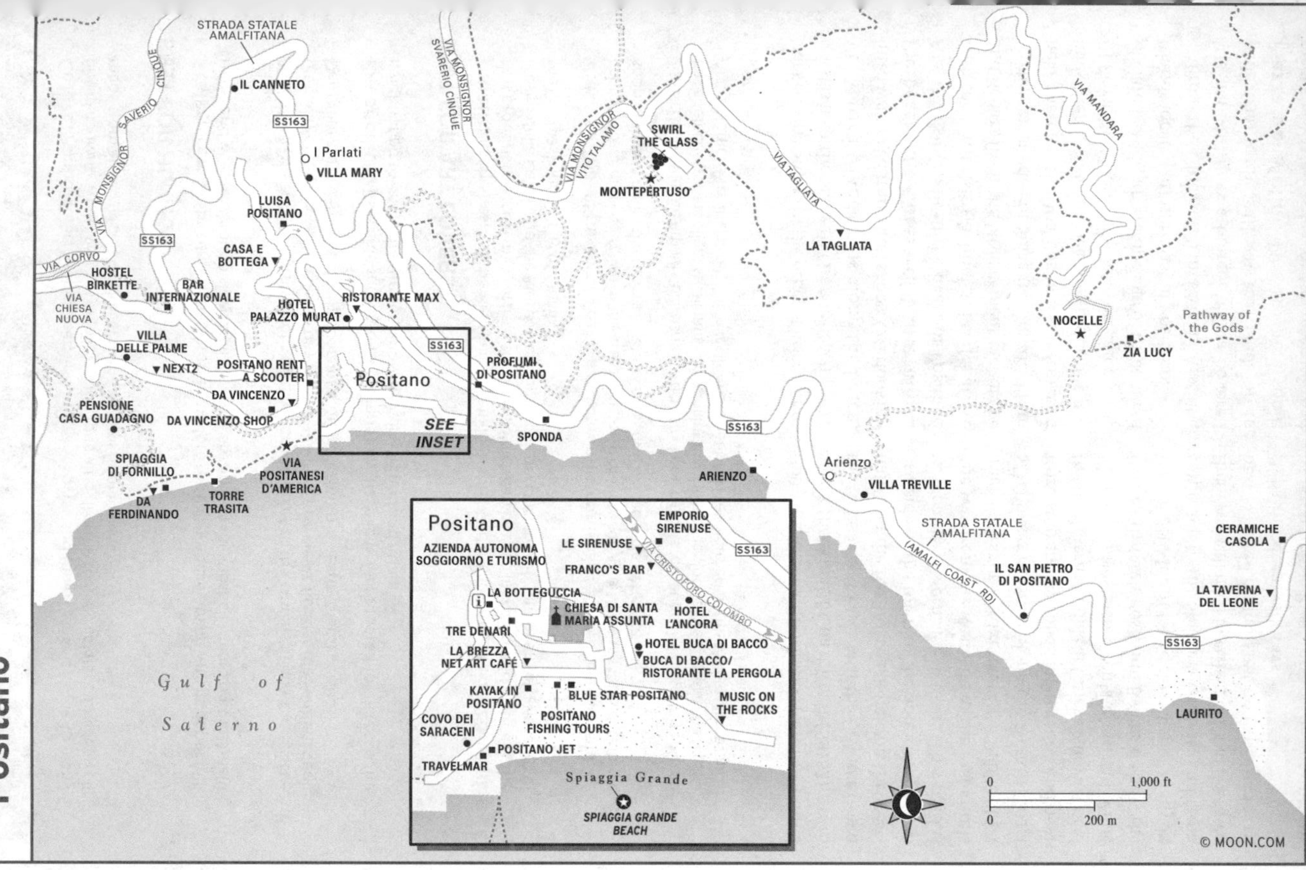
STRADA STATALE AMALFITANA
IL CANETO
SS163
VIA MONSIGNOR SAVERIO CINQUE
VIA MONSIGNOR SVARERIO CINQUE
I Parlati
VILLA MARY
LUISA POSITANO
CASA E BOTTEGA
VIA CORVO
HOSTEL BIRKETTE
VIA CHIESA NUOVA
BAR INTERNAZIONALE
HOTEL PALAZZO MURAT
RISTORANTE MAX
VILLA DELLE PALME
NEXT2
POSITANO RENT A SCOOTER
DA VINCENZO
PENSIONE CASA GUADAGNO
DA VINCENZO SHOP
Positano
SEE INSET
PROFUMI DI POSITANO
SPONDA
SPIAGGIA DI FORNILLO
DA FERDINANDO
TORRE TRASITA
VIA POSITANESI D'AMERICA
VIA MONSIGNOR VITO TALAMO
SWIRL THE GLASS
MONTEPERTUSO
VIA TAGLIATA
LA TAGLIATA
VIA MANDARA
NOCELLE
Pathway of the Gods
ZIA LUCY
ARIENZO
Arienzo
VILLA TREVILLE
STRADA STATALE AMALFITANA
(AMALFI COAST RD)
IL SAN PIETRO DI POSITANO
CERAMICHE CASOLA
LA TAVERNA DEL LEONE
LAURITO
Gulf of Salerno
Positano
AZIENDA AUTONOMA SOGGIORNO E TURISMO
LA BOTTEGUCCIA
CHIESA DI SANTA MARIA ASSUNTA
TRE DENARI
LA BREZZA NET ART CAFÉ
KAYAK IN POSITANO
COVO DEI SARACENI
POSITANO JET
TRAVELMAR
POSITANO FISHING TOURS
BLUE STAR POSITANO
LE SIRENUSE
EMPORIO SIRENUSE
FRANCO'S BAR
VIA CRISTOFORO COLOMBO
HOTEL L'ANCORA
HOTEL BUCA DI BACCO
BUCA DI BACCO/ RISTORANTE LA PERGOLA
MUSIC ON THE ROCKS
Spiaggia Grande
SPIAGGIA GRANDE BEACH
0
1,000 ft
0
200 m
© MOON.COM

are two *frazioni*, or small villages, called **Montepertuso** and **Nocelle.** These are peaceful areas noted for their breathtaking views and convenient location for hiking around Positano. To the east of Positano along the coastline are several smaller beaches, the largest and easiest to reach being the **Arienzo beach** and **Laurito beach.** Set into rocky coves, these beaches are accessible by long staircases from the Amalfi Coast Road or by boat service from Positano's Spiaggia Grande.

SIGHTS

Chiesa di Santa Maria Assunta

Via Marina Grande; tel. 089/875-480; www.chiesapositano.it; 8am-noon and 4pm-8pm daily; free

Situated near the Spiagga Grande beach right in the heart of the town, Positano's most important church is surrounded by colorful buildings climbing up the mountainside. The church is topped with a ceramic-tiled dome in a striking geometric pattern of yellow, green, blue, and white. This local style appears on several churches along the Amalfi Coast, including those in Praiano, Cetara, and Vietri sul Mare.

Built over the ruins of a Roman villa, the church likely dates back to the second half of the 10th century, but what can be seen today was built much later. An open square in front of the church is decorated with artwork by the noted Italian artist Mimmo Paladino. Along one side, a four-level bell tower from 1707 stands separate from the church. Mounted to the bell tower is an ancient marble plaque depicting a *pistrice*, a mythological creature that's part dragon, part winged horse, and part sea monster.

Step inside the church to find a bright white neoclassical interior with gold decorative elements. Above the altar hangs the church's most treasured possession, a Byzantine icon of the Madonna from the 13th century. How the icon ended up in Positano is the stuff of legends. It is said that that the icon was aboard a ship sailing along the coastline, but when it reached Positano, the wind stopped and the boat was stranded. After trying everything, the sailors heard a voice calling out, "*Posa, posa!*" ("Put me down, put me down!") The captain took the icon ashore and suddenly the wind began blowing. This is also, according to local legend, how Positano came by its name. Walk up to the altar and take a closer look at Positano's rare icon, which depicts a regal Madonna with crown, blue scarf, and flowing gold robes.

Below the church lie the ruins of an ancient Roman villa, as well as later medieval crypt areas of the church. The **Museo Archeological Romano Santa Maria Assunta** (Piazza Flavio Gioia 7; tel. 331/208-5821; 9am-9pm daily Apr.-Oct., 10am-4pm Nov.-Mar.; €15, credit card only) offers guided visits of the Roman villa and archaeological area. Groups are limited to a maximum of 10 people and the visit lasts about 30 minutes. To preserve the site, it is kept at a cool temperature, so a jacket or layers are recommended. Tickets can be booked in advance or purchased at the ticket booth next to the bell tower.

Via Positanesi d'America

Via Positanesi d'America from Via Marina Grande to Via Fornillo

This pathway, carved into the mountainside, connects Positano's two main beaches, Spiaggia Grande and Fornillo. Surrounded by the warm scent of pine trees in the sun and looking over at the stunning turquoise sea below, it's a lovely walk to escape the crowds on Spiaggia Grande.

The pathway begins with a small staircase near the cement ferry pier at the western end of Spiaggia Grande and follows the curve of the mountains past the **Torre Trasita** watchtower. Continue along the pathway and you'll spot a tiny beach called Marinella di Positano, tucked away in a tiny cove below. In the distance, you'll see the **Spiaggia di Fornillo** with its distinctive Torre di Clavel watchtower. The walk over to Fornillo takes about 15 minutes and is mostly an inclined walkway that is a bit steep in parts, with only a few steps along the way.

Li Galli Islands

Sirenuse Islands, Positano

Just off the coast of Positano lie three small islands that have captivated travelers since ancient times. According to the ancient Greek historian and geographer Strabo, these islands were home to mythical siren creatures with human heads and bird-like bodies. Li Galli (The Roosters) refers to this half-bird characteristic. According to myth, the sirens were not exactly hospitable: They lured sailors to their death with their beautiful music and songs. You may recall the story in Homer's *The Odyssey:* Odysseus filled his sailors' ears with wax and had them bind him to the mast of his ship as they sailed past the sirens, so he could hear their intoxicating song and live to tell the tale. When they failed to capitvate Odysseus, the sirens, named Ligea, Leucosia, and Parthenope, died from humiliation, it is said, and were transformed into the three islands we see today.

In more recent times—the 14th century—a watchtower that is still standing was built on the ruins of an earlier Roman tower. Eventually, the islands were sold to private owners. In 1924, Russian choreographer and dancer Léonide Massine transformed the islands into a luxurious private villa with help from the French architect Le Corbusier. Rudolf Nureyev, another famous Russian dancer, later added lavish decorative touches to the island's villa. Though the property is still privately owned today, it's possible to boat around and through the archipelago. You can swim in the beautiful waters around the islands if you rent a boat or go on a private or group boat tour from Positano. Onshore, you'll have a fine view of the islands from Spiaggia Grande or from the walk along Via Positanesi d'America to Spiaggia di Fornillo.

Montepertuso

Montepertuso, Positano

Located improbably high in the mountains above Positano, Montepertuso is a quiet little part of town that seems worlds away from the busy beach scene below. Its quiet and spectacular setting overlooking Positano makes Montepertuso a fine spot for hiking or enjoying a relaxed lunch or dinner to savor the fine views. Situated at about 1,150 feet (350 m), this area is best known for the distinctive hole in **Monte Gambera,** which can be seen from far below. This *pertuso* (the Neapolitan word for hole) gives the village its name. Local legend says that the hole was created during an epic battle between the Madonna and the devil, and as she called on divine strength to defeat evil, a hole was driven straight through the mountain. This dramatic story is reenacted every summer during the town's local festival on July 2 with fireworks set off from the hole and a firelight procession that begins near the hole and travels to the church of Montepertuso, dedicated to Santa Maria delle Grazie. Hiking through the hole above Montepertuso offers remarkable views over Positano. To reach the hole, follow the steps that start near the restaurant Il Ritrovo in the center of Montepertuso. The village can be reached by local bus from Positano or by hiking about 1,500 steps from the center of Positano. The steps to Montepertuso start from the Amalfi Coast Road in the upper part of town and lead toward the town's cemetery. When the steps split, follow the direction leading up and continue to Montepertuso.

Nocelle

Nocelle, Positano

For centuries, Nocelle was reachable only by rugged pathways through the mountains to Montepertuso nearby and Positano below. This area, which sits at about 1,475 feet (450 m) was likely settled in the 10th century by people fleeing for safety after Saracen pirate attacks. Given the remote setting, it's no surprise that a rural lifestyle still reigns here. Terraced gardens dot the mountainside around the quiet village center. Nocelle is mostly a stopover point for hikers finishing or starting the Sentiero degli Dei (Pathway

1: the Via Positanesi d'America with the Li Galli islands visible on the horizon **2:** The Chiesa di Santa Maria Assunta sits at the heart of Positano.

1

2

of the Gods), which passes through the village, or one of many other mountain hikes in the area. Thanks to a narrow road built from Montepertuso, this sleepy little village is now accessible by bus or car. However, hiking is certainly the nicest way to visit. The steps connecting Nocelle to Positano begin from the Amalfi Coast Road near Arienzo Beach, but it is much easier to start in Nocelle and go down instead of starting in Positano and going up.

BEACHES

Life in Positano is intimately connected to the beach, just as it has always been for the town's lucky residents. From the Spiaggia Grande in the heart of Positano to tiny beaches set in coves a short boat ride away, the town has plenty of beaches to choose from during your stay. Three of the most popular beaches are also designated Blue Flag beaches, a special ranking that the Foundation for Environment Education gives to beaches with the finest water quality. Whether you like being in the center of activity or are looking for seclusion and romance, there's a beach for you in Positano.

TOP EXPERIENCE

★ SPIAGGIA GRANDE

Via Marina Grande

With its perfectly aligned rows of beach umbrellas and chairs, Positano's main beach is a sight to see. This picture postcard of a town wouldn't seem complete without the unique burst of color and buzz of activity found here. Surrounded as it is by the cascade of buildings spilling down the mountainside right to the edge of the beach, it is an absolutely stunning setting.

Standing on the beach, you get one of the best views of the vibrant Vertical City. Right at the center of town just steps from the beach is the Chiesa di Santa Maria Assunta with its multicolored dome. Above that rises the center of Positano, and even farther above, the villages of Nocelle and Montepertuso are tucked away on the mountainside. There's always been something unreal and artistic about Positano, and it's on display at its very best when you walk along the Spiaggia Grande.

More than 1,000 feet (300 m) long, this Blue Flag designated beach is lined with a series of beach clubs. Located in the middle of the beach, **L'Incanto** (Marina Grande 4; tel. 089/811-177; www.lincantopositano.com; daily May-Oct.; starting at €20 for one bed and umbrella) is a good choice with sun beds, umbrellas, beach services, and drinks and snacks available at the Blue Bar right on the beachfront. However, there is also a free section of the beach, where you can simply throw down a towel in any open space you might be able to find. Expect crowds on the Spiaggia Grande, especially during the summer months, but that's an essential part of the scene. The beach can be quite busy, and it's a popular swimming spot. However, with a lot of boat traffic in the summer, a safe swimming area is marked off by lines of buoys and is somewhat limited.

SPIAGGIA DI FORNILLO

Via Fornillo

Positano's second-largest beach is a wonderful option for a relaxing day by the sea with a little less hustle and bustle than Spiaggia Grande. Sitting below the Fornillo neighborhood, this beach is reached on foot by following the scenic Via Positanesi d'America. Pass the Torre Trasita watchtower and continue until the pathway leads through a tunnel and down to the beach level.

There are several beach clubs here to choose from, such as **Da Ferdinando** (Via Fornillo 24; tel. 089/875-365; daferdinando1953@gmail.com; 8am-8pm mid-May-mid-Oct.; €10-13 for sun bed and umbrella). If you walk all the way to the end of the beach, near where it ends at the large rocks, there is a free beach where it's lovely to swim near the **Torre di Clavel.** The water at this Blue Flag beach

1: Arienzo beach east of Positano offers boat service from Positano. **2:** Positano's Spiaggia Grande with colorful rows of beach umbrellas

LIDO "BAGNI D'ARIENZO"
ARIENZO
1
2

is clear and refreshing, particularly in the morning.

During the beach season (Apr.-Oct.), the *stabilimenti balneari* at Fornillo also offer boat service from near the corner of Positano's cement pier. The boat service is complimentary for clients, so keep in mind that when you hop off you'll be expected to rent a sun bed or dine at the beachside restaurant.

ARIENZO

Via Arienzo

Set in a ravine east of Positano's Spiaggia Grande, this scenic beach is accessible by 269 steps from the Amalfi Coast Road. It is a picturesque little Blue Flag beach, and one of the few rocky beaches near Positano that is reasonably accessible from the road, albeit after a pretty good hike down those steps, and back up at the end of the day. However, the **Bagni d'Arienzo** beach club (Via Arienzo 16; tel. 089/812-002; www.bagnidarienzo.com; 10am-6:30pm mid-May-mid-Oct.; €15 per person) offers free boat service from Positano's main pier for clients. With sun beds, umbrellas, showers, changing rooms, and an excellent restaurant and bar, it's a lovely escape from the busy beaches in Positano. Sun bed and restaurant reservations in advance are highly recommended. With a southwesterly setting, the beach days are longer here than at Positano's other beaches, and it's a fine spot for swimming with very clear water.

LAURITO

Via Laurito

Halfway between Positano and Praiano, this rocky beach is set in a cove far below the Amalfi Coast Road. Named after the *lauro* (laurel) plants growing in the area, the beach is accessible by a long staircase of about 500 steps through thick Mediterranean vegetation. The most comfortable way to arrive is by boat service from Positano's main cement pier. Look for the small boats from **Ristorante Da Adolfo** (Via Laurito 40; tel. 089/875-5022; www.daadolfo.com; reservations only by phone) or the **Treville Beach Club** (Laurito Beach; tel. 089/811-580; www.trevillebeachclub.it; 10am-7pm May-Sept.; €30 per person). As space is limited at this secluded beach, booking in advance is highly recommended at both establishments to reserve a sun bed or restaurant table. Athough it's a small beach, the water is beautiful and it's an excellent spot for swimming and exploring the rocky coastline surrounding the beach.

SPORTS AND RECREATION

With a naturally dramatic landscape stretching from pebbly beaches to soaring mountains, Positano is an ideal location to spend time outdoors exploring the area's natural beauty. Get out on the water on a kayak tour or boat excursion to discover the hidden coves and tiny beaches nearby. The mountain pathways above Positano are excellent for hiking, or climbing for the more adventurous. No matter what activity you choose, you'll be rewarded with incredible views along the way.

Hiking

PATHWAY OF THE GODS (Sentiero degli Dei)

Piazza Paolo Capasso, Bomerano

In a rugged landscape famous for beautiful views and hiking, there's one particular trail that is often considered the most breathtaking. The Pathway of the Gods (Sentiero degli Dei), is a 3.7-mile (6-km) rugged mountain trail stretching from Bomerano in Agerola to Nocelle above Positano. Passing along the mountains high above the sea, the trail is dotted with Mediterranean vegetation and offers panoramic views overlooking Praiano, Positano, and Capri in the distance.

The pathway can be hiked in both directions, but most people choose to start in Bomerano's Piazza Paolo Capasso and enjoy the hike toward Positano. To reach Bomerano by public transportation, you'll need to take the SITA SUD bus on the line from Sorrento to Amalfi, which you can catch at either the Chiesa Nuova stop or the Sponda stop in Positano, and then transfer to the bus from

Amalfi to Agerola. Mention to the driver when boarding that you're hiking the Sentiero degli Dei and they'll usually announce the stop in Bomerano. Look for the signs for the Sentiero degli Dei from the Piazza Paolo Capasso and follow the walkway out of town. Eventually, the road ends and a trail begins, passing by some lonely abandoned houses with sweeping views between mountains and the sea. The landscape and views are spectacular, and you'll want to allow for plenty of time to stop and take photos.

While the hike isn't exceptionally hard, it is quite remote along the route. Part of the pathway is a mountain trail, so good walking shoes are recommended. The hike from Bomerano to Nocelle takes about three hours, depending on the number of rests and photo breaks you take. Once you're in Nocelle, you can take a local bus or follow the steps down to Positano.

The pathway is more popular during the summer months from June to August, but is also at its hottest then, because much of the hike is not shaded. If you're hiking in the summer, get an early morning start and take plenty of water, which can be refilled at public fountains in Bomerano and Nocelle. Spring and autumn are excellent times to hike the Pathway of the Gods.

A local guide can also really add to your enjoyment of this hike. A knowledgable guide will help you notice the best spots, and learn about the history of the area and local vegetation along the way. Since hiking paths can involve numerous steps, guides can also recommend the best hikes tailored your abilities and time available. For a private guided excursion, local guide **Anna Naclerio** (tel. 335/731-5259; annanaclerioguida@gmail.com; 5-6 hour private hiking tour €200) loves sharing her passion for the landscape and nature. **Zia Lucy** (Via Pizzillo 14; tel. 339/272-0971; www.en.zialucy.com; Mar.-Dec.; small group tours €55-60 per person) also offers private and small-group guided hiking excursions.

Rock Climbing

DIREZIONE VERTICALE

Montepertuso, Positano; tel. 338/727-9878; www.direzioneverticale.it; climbing excursions available year round; starting at €100

With rugged Mediterranean landscape and incredible views, the Lattari Mountains are a dream setting for mountain climbers. For more than 17 years, Cristiano Bacci from the Associazione La Selva (tel. 347/166-9308; www.associazionelaselva.it) has worked on curating excellent climbing areas in the

hiking Sentiero degli Dei in Nocelle

Positano area around Montepertuso, Nocelle, and the Pathway of the Gods. Direzione Verticale, founded by expert climber Francesco Galasso, who has worked closely with Bacci, offers sport climbing excursions with equipment and guide in the Positano area as well as all of the climbing areas of the Amalfi Coast. They also organize deep-water soloing combined with kayak or boat tours. To stay close to the climbing area above Positano, the Associazione La Selva also offers yoga retreats, natural cosmetic products, and room rentals in a gorgeous rustic setting that is dedicated to natural living.

Water Sports

KAYAK IN POSITANO

Spiaggia Grande; tel. 333/614-5247; www.kayakinpositano.it; 8am-8pm daily Apr.-mid-Nov.; €30 for 4 hours

With a convenient location right on Spiaggia Grande, Kayak in Positano offers kayak rentals as well as tours along the Amalfi Coast. Start with as little as €10 for one hour to enjoy a simple paddle around Positano. Half-day and full-day rentals are available for longer excursions. Want some expert guidance on finding hidden grottoes, caves, and the best beaches? A variety of excursions from Positano to Praiano and along the coastline are available from €40-95 per person.

POSITANO FISHING TOURS

Spiaggia Grande cement pier; tel. 334/980-674; www.positanofishingtours.com; Apr.-Nov.; from €400 per group

Founded by Alberto Russo and his father, two passionate fishermen, this family-run company offers a unique way to experience the Mediterranean sea. Join these expert fishermen for a fun time fishing along the Amalfi Coast. Choose from a half day, full day, sunset and night, or even giant squid fishing options. It's not often you can learn traditional fishing techniques to catch giant squid from the depths of the Mediterranean. All fishing excursions are private and customized to your interests and schedule.

Boat Tours

BLUE STAR POSITANO

Via Del Brigantino 1; tel. 334/235-4122; www.bluestarpositano.it; Easter-early Nov.; small group tours from €65 per person, private from €400 per group

Seeing the Amalfi Coast from the sea is a must, and Blue Star offers small group or private boat excursions along the Amalfi Coast or to Capri. With a team dedicated to customer service, and offering excellent assistance in English and many other languges, Blue Star is a popular choice with travelers. Join a small group tour with a maximum of 12 people for a day trip excursion along the Amalfi Coast, with free time ashore in Amalfi. You can also book a private boat for a fully customized tour experience. Book in advance online or simply pass by their booth right on the Spiaggia Grande to join group excursions or book a private excursion.

Wine Tours

SWIRL THE GLASS

Via Pestella 70; tel. 366/123-1358; www.swirltheglass.com; flexible schedule available daily Apr.-Oct.; tastings from €70 per person, tours from €180 per person

Discover the wines of Campania and the Amalfi Coast with the guidance of professional sommelier Cristian Fusco, who was born and raised in Positano. Let Cristian guide you on a wine tour where you'll have a wonderfully authentic experience visiting a local vineyard to learn more about the unique Amalfi Coast winemaking process, from the vine to the bottle. Half-day and full-day wine tours include transporation, a vineyard and winery tour, lunch, and wine tasting. Wine tastings in Positano are also available.

ENTERTAINMENT AND EVENTS

Positano as the sun sets is a magical place to be. Though the town isn't known for its lively nightlife, it is one of the finest spots to enjoy a sunset on the Amalfi Coast. Grab a table at a bar or beachside restaurant and enjoy cocktails as the sun sinks behind the mountains. Compared to the hustle and bustle of Positano during the day, when ferries bring in crowds of day-trippers, the evening delivers a much more relaxed atmosphere.

For a memorable evening, consider dinner with a sea view followed by drinks or dancing at the town's one notable nightclub. Or enjoy a moonlit stroll along the sea and after-dinner drinks by the water's edge. If you enjoy local experiences and cultural events, time your visit for one of Positano's annual festivals.

Nightlife

MUSIC ON THE ROCKS

Via del Brigantino 19; tel. 089/875-874; www.musicontherocks.it; 10:30pm-4am daily Apr.-Oct.

The one vibrant exception to Positano's otherwise sedate nightlife scene is Music on the Rocks. This nightclub is literally on the rocks, as it's set in a cave carved out of the mountainside just steps from the sea. For more than 40 years, this has been a hot spot for music and dancing on the Amalfi Coast, and it still attracts national and international DJs and musicians. There is a cover charge, but it varies depending on the events taking place.

FRANCO'S BAR

Via Cristoforo Colombo 30; tel. 089/875-066; www.francosbar.com; 5pm-12:30am daily May-Oct.; €6-18

Next door to the stylish Le Sirenuse hotel and named after one of its founders, Franco's Bar is one of the most chic spots in Positano. As the sun sets and Positano turns all rosy-hued, a *spritz* never looked so good. The warm ambiance lingers on well into the night, making this a great choice for after-dinner drinks.

Festivals and Events

FERRAGOSTO

Spiaggia Grande and various locations; Aug. 14-15

Although Ferragosto is a public holiday celebrated in August throughout Italy, it takes on special meaning in Positano. Roman emperor Augustus declared Ferragosto a holiday in 18 BC to celebrate the summer harvests. The holiday also falls on the Catholic day honoring the Assumption of the Virgin Mary. Because Positano's main church is dedicated to the Santa Maria Assunta, or the Assumption of the Virgin, Ferragosto marks the town's largest religious celebration of the year. Festivities start on August 14 with a re-creation of the arrival of the icon of the Virgin Mary and continue through August 15, capped off by an incredible fireworks display over the sea. With a wonderful blend of religious meaning and tradition, and a few pirates thrown in, Ferragosto in Positano is a festive summer experience. Check with the tourist office for the schedule of events.

POSITANO PREMIA LA DANZA LÉONIDE MASSINE

Spiaggia Grande and various locations; tel. 089/812-3535; www.positanopremialadanza.it; early Sept.

Positano celebrates its long tradition with the world of dance during this annual festival in early September, named in honor of the great Russian ballet dancer and choreographer Léonide Massine, who was enamored of Positano and once owned the Li Galli islands. Each year, usually in early September, this festival brings dancers from around the world for events, workshops, and performances on a special stage constructed on Spiaggia Grande.

FESTA DEL PESCE

Spiaggia di Fornillo; www.festadelpesce.net; last Sat. in Sept.

With Positano's deep connection to the sea and fishing tradition, it's no surprise that this town puts on a festival dedicated to seafood. The Festa del Pesce (Fish Festival) takes over the Spiaggia di Fornillo beach on the last Saturday in September for an extravagant evening of fresh seafood, music, and fun. People from throughout Positano work together to create a variety of seafood offerings and the event always ends up feeling just as much a celebration of Positano's community pride as its wonderful cuisine.

SHOPPING

Shopping in Positano is all about fashion, as it has been since the 1960s when the seaside town became a favorite of stylish vacationers, and there are still shops that create their designs right in Positano. The perfect complement to that new summer wardrobe is a pair of custom-made leather sandals, another local tradition still going strong in Positano.

The main shopping area centers around the Chiesa di Santa Maria Assunta and follows Via dei Mulini up to where it meets the internal road Viale Pasitea that winds through Positano at Piazza dei Mulini. Follow Viale Pasitea west to find some of Positano's most traditional fashion and houseware shops. In the other direction, follow Via Cristoforo Colombo east uphill toward Sponda, at the intersection with the Amalfi Coast Road, to enjoy a gorgeous view overlooking Positano and a treasure trove of shops to browse along the way.

Clothing and Shoes

★ LUISA POSITANO

Via Pasitea 78; tel. 089/875-549; www.luisapositano.it; 9am-9pm daily

Full of beautifully patterned fabrics, classic linen, and summery styles, this boutique was founded by Luigia Pollio, known as Luisa, who was a model during the glamorous '60s in Positano. Her children have continued the family enterprise and all of their traditionally Positano designs are handmade in the workshop located right below the boutique. Come here to add a touch of Positano's color and style to your wardrobe.

EMPORIO SIRENUSE

Via Cristoforo Colombo 107; tel. 089/812-2026; www.emporiosirenuse.com; 9am-7pm Apr.-Oct.

Just across the street from the elegant Le Sirenuse hotel, this equally chic boutique features the ready-to-wear resort fashion line and home decor collection custom-designed by Carla Sersale, the wife of Le Sirenuse's owner, Antonio Sersale. Featuring collaborations with top artists and designers from around the world, Positano's artistic tradition beautifully endures at this one-of-a-kind boutique.

★ TRE DENARI

Via del Saracino 8-9; 089/875-062; mcpositano@yahoo.it; 8:30am-9pm, closed Jan.-Feb.

Find beautiful sandals and a large selection of both men's and women's shoes at this friendly shop at the base of the steps of the Chiesa di Santa Maria Assunta. Comfortable handmade leather loafers come in every color under the sun to match vibrant Positano fabrics.

LA BOTTEGUCCIA

Via Regina Giovanna 19; tel. 089/811-824; www.labottegucciapositano.it; 9am-10pm Mar.-Oct.

This tiny shop has been a Positano fixture since it was founded in the early 1960s. Inside, you'll find Dino, son of the shop's founder, pounding away at work, creating handmade sandals. Stop by and have your measurements taken, and he'll create a custom pair while you wait.

Ceramics and Home Goods

CERAMICHE CASOLA

Via Vito Savino 1 and Via Del Saracino 30 (Positano center), and Via Laurito 49 (Positano showroom and factory); tel. 089/811-382; www.ceramicacasola.it; 9am-8pm, closed Dec. 1-Mar. 14

Just try to pass the colorful ceramics on display here and resist going inside for a closer look. With a variety of patterns and styles, from traditional Amalfi Coast patterns to more contemporary geometric designs, this shop has an excellent selection and several locations around town. They can also ship larger orders to your home.

DA VINCENZO SHOP

Via Pasitea 200; tel. 089/875-128; shop@davincenzo.it; 9:30am-9:30pm, closes 10:30pm in summer

A tempting and well curated selection of ceramics, custom linen designs, tableware, and locally sourced products are on display in this inviting shop. A highlight is the La Selva natural soap and skincare line, all handmade in the mountains above Positano.

La Moda Positano

Positano fashion

There's one thing you can't miss while shopping in Positano, and that's all the boutiques with colorful displays of clothing spilling out into the narrow streets of the town. Positano is known for fashion, and it has its own unique style called *La Moda Positano* (Positano Fashion). Perfect for a seaside town, the local style includes flowing linen in Mediterranean hues, lace, and relaxed chic beachwear: perfect for a day of lounging in the sun in Positano.

Also worked into many of today's fashion designs in Positano is a delicate bobbin or pillow lace, called *merletto a tombolo*, which is an intricate lace textile made by weaving and braiding thread. Nuns at one of Positano's convents were experts at this handiwork and passed it down for generations, thanks to a school they created at the end of the 19th century to teach locals the craft.

During a visit in 1847, English writer John Ruskin noticed the unique and colorful style of the locals, which was also appreciated by the many artists and writers who sought refuge and creative freedom in secluded Positano. Yet it wasn't until the 1950s and 1960s, when the jet-set travelers arrived in Positano and began wearing the local styles, that the rest of the world became aware of the colors and refreshing style of Positano. There's always been an element of avant-garde to the local style, and it's said that Fornillo beach is one of the first spots the bikini appeared on the beaches of Italy.

Today you'll be spoiled for choice as you stroll along the streets and climb the famous staircases of Positano. Whether you're looking for a crisp linen shirt, a beach cover-up, or a bikini to remember the beaches of Positano, you'll find a rainbow of pastel hues and relaxed designs to choose from. For the finishing touch, pick up a pair of handmade leather loafers or have a pair of sandals custom made to fit your feet.

Perfume

PROFUMI DI POSITANO

Via Cristoforo Colombo 175; tel. 089/875-057; www.profumidipositano.it; 10am-10pm

Since the 1920s, the Barba family have produced soaps and perfumes right in Positano. Take home the sweet scents of Positano with their locally made products featuring classic Mediterranean scents that are natural to the area, such as lemon, jasmine, wisteria, citrus, and almond blossoms.

FOOD

Positano's diverse landscape, stretching from the sea deep into the mountain forests high above town, is reflected in the local cuisine, which you'll find ranges from freshly caught seafood to heartier staples like grilled meat and locally grown vegetables. There's a wide range of very high-quality restaurants, whether you're just visiting for the day or making Positano your home base. Reservations are a good idea for much of the season.

Seafood

★ DA VINCENZO

Via Pasitea 172; tel. 089/875-128; www.davincenzo.it; noon-2:45pm and 6:15pm-10:45pm daily Mar.-mid-Nov.; €25-50

An excellent spot for traditional Positano cooking in a friendly setting. The indoor dining area spills out onto the sidewalk during nice weather. While you'll find a varied menu, seafood is a specialty here and is nicely prepared. The pasta is handmade, and when it's paired with fresh seafood like mussels or prawns, it is a sure win. Reservations are a must, especially for dinner.

RISTORANTE MAX

Piazza dei Mulini 22; tel. 089/875-056; www.ristorantemax.it; 9am-11pm daily Apr.-Oct.; €35-80

This eatery is located just off Positano's busy pedestrian-only Via dei Mulini. Follow a narrow staircase down to find a peaceful restaurant opening to a pretty garden patio. With walls lined with wine and an impressive art collection, the setting is one of a kind. The menu is predominently seafood-based, and the *zuppa di pesce* (fish soup) is a definite highlight. Cooking classes are offered in the mornings on the terrace (€150 per person, reservation required).

LA TAVERNA DEL LEONE

Via Laurito 43; tel. 089/811-302; www.latavernadelleone.com; 1pm-3pm and 7pm-11pm Wed.-Mon., Aug. open daily, closed early Jan.-mid-Feb.; €12-20

Since 1965 this restaurant has been a popular choice with locals and travelers alike. Located between Positano and Praiano, above Laurito beach, La Taverna del Leone is excellent for seafood. Try the *tortelli* (stuffed pasta) filled with lobster and a delicate and creamy lemon-infused buffalo milk cheese, or the pasta with fresh caught local fish like *scorfano* (red scorpionfish), as famous for its frightening appearance as it is for its delicate flavor.

BUCA DI BACCO

Via Rampa Teglia 4; tel. 089/875-699; www.bucadibacco.it; noon-3pm and 7pm-10:30pm Apr.-Oct.; €14-25

Overlooking a lush green pergola with the Spiaggia Grande beach just beyond, this restaurant has been a Positano tradition since the 1950s. Seafood is a natural choice, and there are excellent appetizers as well as classic pasta dishes with clams, lobster, or *baccalà* (cod). For the main course, try their grilled octopus, fried mixed seafood platter, or grilled fresh fish. There are plenty of non-seafood options on the menu, too, and the Black Angus sirloin is especially good.

Regional Cuisine

LA TAGLIATA

Via Tagliata 32B, Montepertuso; tel. 089/875-872; www.latagliata.com; noon-3:30pm and 7pm-10:30pm mid-Mar.-early Nov.; €30-40

Head high into the mountains to Montepertuso for an entirely different take on local dining in Positano. Here, far from the sea, the menu is based on organic vegetables grown on terraces around the restaurant, handmade pasta, and, above all, grilled meat. The portions are generous and the setting has a rustic charm. The views overlooking Positano and the coastline are as popular as the excellent food. The restaurant is sometimes open off-season between November and March, usually on Sunday for lunch, but call in advance to confirm.

DA FERDINANDO

Via Fornillo 24; tel. 089/875-365; daferdinando1953@gmail.com; 8am-8pm mid-May-mid-Oct.; €7-15

Whether you're looking for a relaxing day at the beach or a refreshing seaside meal, this *stabilimente balneare* (beach club) and restaurant is a great choice right on Spiaggia di Fornillo. Sun beds and umbrellas are available (€10-13), and when you're ready to eat just head up to the restaurant area overlooking the beach. The *caprese* (salad with tomatoes and buffalo mozzarella) tastes even better by the sea, as does *parmigiana di melanzane* (eggplant parmesan) and their unique *caponata*, a refreshing take on a *panzanella* bread and tomato salad, which they prepare with tomatoes, mozzarella, tuna, olives, and bread. Catch their boat service from Positano's main cement pier.

NEXT2

Viale Pasitea 242; tel. 089/812-3516; www.next2.it; 6:30pm-11pm Apr.-Oct.; €20-38

Founded by Tanina Vanacore, the mastermind behind the popular Casa e Bottega nearby, and now run by her daughter Carmela, this is an elegant choice for dinner with tastefully designed seating both indoors and outdoors on the terrace surrounded by jasmine. Seafood and meat options share equal billing on the menu, with the *conchiglioni* (large shell-shaped pasta) stuffed with ragù sauce and *stracciatella di burrata* (a deliciously creamy cheese) being top choices. You can't go wrong with the mixed grilled seafood or the meatballs served with roasted polenta. Reservations are recommended.

★ CASA E BOTTEGA

Viale Pasitea 100; tel. 089/875-225; casaebottegapositano@gmail.com; open 8:30am-4:30pm Apr.-Oct.; €12-18

When you're ready for a break from pizza and pasta, this is your place. The menu highlights delicious organic fare and features plenty of healthy options like salads, smoothie bowls, and juices. Try the zucchini spaghetti with pesto and *mozzarella di bufala*; the chicken, avocado, and tomato salad; or the lovely orzo with grilled zucchini, avocado, and orange-infused shrimp. A buffet displaying freshly made sweets is tempting for dessert. The restaurant includes a shop with a well-curated selection of ceramics, linens, and housewares that might just find their way home with you.

RISTORANTE LA PERGOLA

Via del Brigantino 35; tel. 089/811-461; www.bucadibaccolapergola.com; 8:30am-11pm Mar.-mid-Nov.; €20-50

This restaurant is just steps from the Spiaggia Grande beach. Set under a broad pergola, it is a lovely choice for breakfast or morning coffee, lunch, an *aperitivo* at sunset, or a romantic dinner. The menu features a little of everything, with excellent *scialatielli ai frutti di mare* (handmade local pasta with seafood), grilled fish, a variety of hearty salads, and pizza. The house pizza with cherry tomatoes, fresh arugula, *mozzarella di bufala*, and parmesan is a wonderful choice.

Cafés

LA BREZZA NET ART CAFÉ

Via del Brigantino 1; tel. 089/875-811; www.labrezzapositano.it; 8:30am-midnight Easter-Nov.; €3-12

With a scenic setting right at the corner of

Fresh salads, juices, and light meals are made with organic ingredients at Casa e Bottega.

Positano's Spiagga Grande, this will quickly become your go-to bar for any time of the day, thanks to its convenient location and great options throughout the day. La Brezza Net Art Café is open for breakfast, with both sweet and savory choices, and offers drinks and snacks or light meals throughout the day. Free Wi-Fi is available. Just below the café, check out Bio Brezza for fresh fruit, juice, and smoothies to go.

ACCOMMODATIONS

If you're thinking of splurging on accommodations for your Amalfi Coast stay, Positano is a great place to consider stretching the budget. With some of the finest hotels that are regularly voted among the best in all of Italy by travelers, Positano knows how to do luxury and service without losing the laid-back style and local, family-run feel of the Amalfi Coast. However, there are affordable options as well, that are still centrally located and provide the same views for which Positano is so famous.

Whatever your budget, one key to enjoying your stay in Positano is booking well in advance. Positano is one of the most popular destinations on the Amalfi Coast, and accommodations of all sizes fill up very early, despite the vast number of options in town. If you have your heart set on a particular hotel or budget range, book as early as possible.

Given the vertical nature of Positano, it's best to plan in advance as well when it comes to your arrival and departure. Check with your accommodation to see if they offer assistance with luggage. Sometimes this is available for an extra charge, but in Positano this is well worth it, especially if you're staying near the beach or lower part of Positano and arriving by car or bus. Nothing puts a damper on a holiday faster than hauling a suitcase through the cobblestone walkways and up or down the steps of Positano!

Under €100

HOSTEL BRIKETTE

Via G. Marconi 358; tel. 089/875-857; www.hostel-positano.com; closed Nov.-Easter; €45 shared room

The Amalfi Coast doesn't boast many hostels, but this one makes up for the shortage by offering those gorgeous Amalfi Coast views at a very good rate. The super-clean rooms are decorated with a cheery design, and all feature air-conditioning: a nice plus during the summer months. Room configurations vary, and you can choose from shared dorm rooms that sleep 4-10 people. Some premium shared rooms offer en suite bathrooms, sea views, and terraces. A private room with double bed and en suite bathroom is also available. There are plenty of breakfast options, and the staff are friendly and ready to help with local information and tips. The hostel is located at the top of Positano just west of the Chiesa Nuova bus stop.

€100-200

VILLA DELLE PALME

Viale Pasitea 252; tel. 089/875-162; www.inpositano.com; closed mid-Nov.-Feb.; €180 d

Family-run since 1959, this charming small hotel near the top of Positano really has a knack for making guests feel at home. The family is always on hand to help with recommendations, getting around, and anything needed for a pleasant stay. With panoramic views over town and decor in classic Amalfi Coast shades of turquoise and blue, all nine rooms include a private terrace or balcony. Breakfast is served on the shared terrace or on your own private terrace, which is a lovely way to start your day in Positano.

IL CANNETO

Via G. Marconi 87; tel. 089/875-881; www.ilcannetopositano.it; closed Nov. 15-Mar. 25; €120 d

Set in a lush valley surrounded by the natural landscape of Positano, this small eight-room hotel offers simple yet very clean rooms. Each one features a terrace with sea view. It is located a 15-minute walk above the center of town, but with access to local buses nearby. Note that the hotel rooms are only reachable by stairs (about 80 steps), but there is a lift for luggage. Free parking is available for small vehicles.

€200-300

PENSIONE CASA GUADAGNO

Via Fornillo 34/36; tel. 089/875-042; www.pensionecasaguadagno.it; closed Nov. 10-mid-Mar.; $220 d

Situated above Fornillo beach, this small pensione with seven rooms offers a comfortable stay in a quieter area of Positano. The sea-view rooms are worth the extra splurge and feature private terraces. Fornillo beach is accessible via steps, or walk along Viale Pasitea, or hop on an internal bus nearby to reach the center of Positano quickly. Rates are much more affordable outside of high season.

VILLA MARY

Via Liparlati 53; tel. 089/857-216; www.villamary.it; closed Jan.-Feb.; €255 d

This charming B&B is one of Positano's most popular, and for very good reason. Situated in a historic house from the late 1700s, five beautiful suites all offer private terraces with sea views, and an abundant breakfast is served every morning. You'll appreciate the attentive service and friendliness of Tiziana and her husband Antonio, who welcome guests and truly make them feel at home. They are also on hand to help arrange transporation and activities in the area. A newly added solarium with small pool and panoramic views is an added bonus.

HOTEL BUCA DI BACCO

Via Rampa Teglia 4; tel. 089/875-699; www.bucadibacco.it; open Apr.-Oct.; €280 d

Tucked away behind the Chiesa di Santa Maria Assunta and just steps from the beach, this hotel could hardly be more centrally located. There are 46 rooms ranging from standard rooms, with or without sea views, to superior rooms with balconies or terraces with sea views. The hotel's excellent restaurant overlooking the beach is open for all meals and is a great feature. Because the hotel is near the beach and a bit of a hike to the nearest road, baggage transport and parking are available (at an extra cost).

Over €300

★ HOTEL L'ANCORA

Via Cristoforo Colombo 36; tel. 089/875-318; www.hotelancorapositano.com; closed Nov.-Easter; €320-370 d

Run by the same management as the Covo dei Saraceni hotel down by the beach, this hotel in the upper part of Positano offers spectacular views over town. The 18 rooms are large and full of light thanks to the private balconies and terrraces. There are two lovely suites with outdoor hot tubs on private terraces. Breakfast is served in the hotel's restaurant with excellent views of Positano.

COVO DEI SARACENI

Via Regina Giovanna 5; tel. 089/875-400; www.covodeisaraceni.it; closed Nov.-Easter; €490 d

With an enviable position overlooking Spiaggia Grande, this hotel has one of the most convenient locations for enjoying Positano. The beach is just steps from the front entrance, as is the pier to catch a ferry along the coast or to Capri. The hotel's 66 rooms vary from classic rooms to a variety of gorgeous suites. The pool terrace offers stunning views of Positano where you can soak up the sun away from the crowds just below.

IL SAN PIETRO DI POSITANO

Via Laurito 2; tel. 089/812-080; www.ilsanpietro.it; open Apr.-Oct.; €750 d

This marvelous five-star hotel is a hidden oasis on the Amalfi Coast, located a little more than a mile (2 km) east of Positano. Its gorgeous garden terraces and 57 rooms decorated with beautiful ceramics in the traditional style offer a peaceful respite. Dining is a pleasure at the hotel's Michelin-starred restaurant, Zass, or in the seaside Carlino restaurant for al fresco meals. Committed to highlighting local produce, including products from the hotel's own gardens, the thoroughly modern kitchen was completely remodeled in 2016 to be eco-sustainable. The hotel's private beach with convenient elevator access and complimentary boat excursions are nice perks during the summer months.

HOTEL PALAZZO MURAT

Via dei Mulini 23; tel. 089/875-177; www.palazzomurat.it; closed early Nov.-Mar.; €1,300 d

Situated right in the heart of Positano, just next to the Chiesa di Santa Maria Assunta, this historic home from the 1800s was once the preferred summer residence of Gioacchino Murat, the King of Naples and brother-in-law of Napoleon. There's a timeless feel to the hotel's 32 rooms with their elegant historical details, antique decor, and unforgettable views of Positano. The courtyard garden is dotted with lemon trees, roses, and flowers that add a sweet scent around the restaurant and pool area. This is the place to seek out a peaceful stay in the center of Positano.

★ LE SIRENUSE

Via Cristoforo Colombo 30; tel. 089/875-066; www.sirenuse.it; open late Mar.-Oct.; €2,200 d

Since 1951, the Sersale family have specialized in personalized luxury and unforgettable stays in a setting that exudes modern elegance while still retaining the air of a family home. Le Sirenuse's 58 rooms and suites embody classic Positano style with traditional ceramic floors, a medley of antique and modern design, and private balconies or terraces with sea views in most rooms. You'll feel like a movie star as you lounge by the outdoor heated pool or enjoy dining at one of the many restaurant options, from the Michelin-starred La Sponda Restaurant to the Poolside Bar and Restaurant, Champagne and Oyster Bar, or chic Franco's Bar.

VILLA TREVILLE

Via Arienzo 30; tel. 089/812-2411; www.villatreville.it; closed Nov.-Mar.; €2,218 d

The most delicious slice of Amalfi Coast luxury has a name: Villa Treville. Overlooking Arienzo beach with Positano in the distance, this was once the home of the great Italian film and opera director Franco Zeffirelli. This remarkable five-star luxury boutique villa has 16 rooms and suites surrounded by lush garden terraces that perfectly frame the dreamy view down the coastline toward Positano. With exquisite service, plenty of chic spots to relax outdoors, a plunge pool, seaside sun loungers, on-site restaurant and lounge bar, and private boat service to and from Positano, it's truly a dream holiday destination on the Amalfi Coast.

INFORMATION AND SERVICES

Tourist Information

AZIENDA AUTONOMA SOGGIORNO E TURISMO

Via Regina Giovanna 13; tel. 089/875-067; www.aziendaturismopositano.it; 8:30am-7pm daily, closes 4:30pm Nov.-Mar.

Positano's tourist office is located not far from Spiaggia Grande and is open throughout the year. To find it, walk straight ahead from the cement ferry pier and you'll find it on the left as you pass under an archway. English-speaking staff are on hand to answer your questions about Positano and any special events that might be on during your visit, and offer a selection of maps and local information.

Postal Services

To mail letters and packages, Positano's post office (Poste Italiane; Via Guglielmo Marconi 318; tel. 089/875-142; www.poste.it; 8:20am-1:45pm Mon.-Fri.) is located in the upper part of town near the *Comune* (town hall).

GETTING THERE

By Car and Scooter

Positano is situated toward the western end

of the Amalfi Coast and is 11 miles (18 km) west of Amalfi and 27 miles (43.5 km) west of Salerno on the Amalfi Coast Road (SS163). From Ravello, which is 15.5 miles (25 km) east of Positano, take the SS373 road down the mountain to connect with the Amalfi Coast Road (SS163) and continue west on the road to Positano. Sorrento is 9 miles (15 km) away on the northern side of the Sorrentine Peninsula. You will need to follow SS145 south over the mountains of the Sorrentine Peninsula until it merges with the Amalfi Coast Road (SS163) and head east to reach Positano. Naples is 37 miles (60 km) away from Positano, and the drive is along the A3 autostrada south until Castellammare di Stabia, where the (SS145) road begins. Follow that west along the coastline to Sorrento and then continue on to reach the Amalfi Coast Road (SS163) for Positano. Though the distances don't seem far, keep in mind that the roads along the Sorrentine Peninsula are very twisty and narrow. Drive time to Positano is usually 50 minutes from Amalfi, a little over an hour from Ravello, and about 45 minutes from Sorrento. From Salerno, the drive is about 2 hours, while from Naples plan for about 2 hours, and that's without traffic. During the tourist season from Easter through October, expect longer drive times.

Parking in Positano can come with a hefty price tag, from €3-5 per hour or €20-30 per day, depending on the season and location. You'll find parking lot options as you drive along Viale Pasitea, especially in the Piazza dei Mulini area. This is a convenient parking area as the Spiaggia Grande and heart of Positano are just a short walk down Via dei Mulini. If you're staying in Positano, check with your accommodation in advance for the best parking options.

By Ferry

Ferry service on the Amalfi Coast runs seasonally, from around Easter through the beginning of November. Ferries arrive at, and depart from, the large cement pier on the western end of the Spiaggia Grande beach. Tickets can be purchased at the ticket booths in colorful wooden stands along the pier. Because there is no port and the pier is open to the sea, ferry service to Positano is dependent on good weather and sea conditions. Sometimes even if ferries are running, stops in Positano can be limited or canceled if the sea is rough. Though this rarely happens during the summer months, it is a stronger possibility in the shoulder seasons of early spring or October. So if you're traveling by ferry, it's good to have alternative transportation options in mind, just in case.

Ferry service to Positano from Amalfi, Minori, Maiori, Cetara, and Salerno is operated by **Travelmar** (tel. 089/872-950; www.travelmar.it; €8-12 per person). There are ferries throughout the day every 1-2 hours from about 9:30am to 6pm. For some routes, you may need to transfer boats in Amalfi to reach Positano. Travel time to Positano by ferry from Salerno is about 70 minutes, from Cetara about 35 minutes, 40 minutes from Maiori (with change in Amalfi), 35 from Minori (with change in Amalfi), and 25 minutes from Amalfi. It's a good idea to purchase your tickets in advance online or via the Travelmar app, especially during the peak season from June through September.

Alicost (tel. 089/811-986; www.alicost.it; €15-21.30 per person) is the main ferry service connecting Capri and Sorrento to Positano, with service from Amalfi and Salerno as well. They offer one daily trip from Capri (more available June-Sept.) and two daily trips from Sorrento. The ferry ride from Capri to Positano takes about 45 minutes, while from Sorrento it's about 50 minutes. Tickets can be purchased online in advance. Another option to Positano from Capri is **Positano Jet** (tel. 089/811-164; www.lucibello.it; €9-21 per person). Operated by the Lucibello boat company, this ferry service runs three trips each day, and the journey is about 40 minutes. They also operate two to three ferries a day from Amalfi to Positano, and the journey is about 25 minutes.

By Bus

The public bus line connecting Positano to Sorrento and the rest of the towns on the Amalfi Coast, as far as Salerno is operated by **SITA SUD** (tel. 089/386-6701; www.sitasudtrasporti.it; from €1.30). Buses stop in Positano at two stops: Chiesa Nuova and Sponda. If you're staying in the upper part of Positano, the Chiesa Nuova stop is likely the most convenient option, while if you're staying in the center of Positano near the beach, the Sponda bus stop is the best choice. To reach Positano from Ravello or towns east of Amalfi to Salerno, you will first need to take the bus to Amalfi and then transfer to the Amalfi-Sorrento line to reach Positano. The bus ride from Sorrento to Positano takes about an hour, and from Amalfi the journey is a little less.

City Sightseeing (www.city-sightseeing.it; Apr.-Oct.; from €10 per person) offers a more comfortable way to travel to Positano from Sorrento and Amalfi. They stop in Positano at the Sponda stop. Tickets are purchased onboard, and audio guides for the journey are included in the price. This is not a hop-on hop-off bus service; instead you buy a tickets for each ride. However, after the first ticket subsequent tickets on the same day are €6 instead of €10. Note that if you are traveling with luggage you will need to take the SITA SUD bus.

By Taxi

To get to Positano by taxi, it is best to book in advance. **Positano Drivers** (tel. 338/888-6572 and 339/886-9182; www.positanodrivers.com; starting at €100) offers transfers from Naples, Sorrento, and other destinations along the Amalfi Coast.

GETTING AROUND

By Car and Scooter

There's a one-way internal road through Positano that starts on the western edge of town near the Chiesa Nuova. To access the lower part of Positano, follow Viale Pasitea, which winds through Positano down to Piazza dei Mulini and then changes name to Via Cristoforo Colombo as it climbs out of town to rejoin the Amalfi Coast Road at Sponda, the intersection with the Amalfi Coast Road. To reach Montepertuso and Nocelle, follow the Amalfi Coast Road west from the center of Positano and soon you'll find a large turn-off with a sign pointing toward Montepertuso and Nocelle. This is Via Corvo and it becomes Via Monsignor Saverio Cinque, which leads first to Montepertuso and continues along to Nocelle. The drive to Montepertuso takes about 10 minutes, and it's about 15 minutes to Nocelle.

With the narrow roads of the Amalfi Coast, a small rental car is a good idea. Even better, **Positano Car Service** (Via Cristoforo Colombo 2 ; tel. 089/875-867;www.positanocarservice.com; starting at €110 per day) offers pint-sized Smart cars for you to zip around the Amalfi Coast. If you want to rent a scooter, **Positano Rent a Scooter** (Via Pasitea 99; tel. 089/812-2077; www.positanorentascooter.it; from €70 per day) offers a variety of options, including the classic Italian brand Vespa.

By Bus

Mobility Amalfi Coast (tel. 089/813-077; info@mobilityamalficoast.com; €1.70-1.80) provides bus service along Positano's internal road and to Nocelle, Montepertuso, and Praiano. Buses pass about every half hour for the internal route 9am-midnight. The service to Nocelle, Montepertuso, and Praiano is much more limited and runs more or less hourly. Tickets can be purchased in *tabacchi* or onboard.

By Taxi

Taxis in Positano are independently owned and charge flat fees based on the destination, rather than calculating according to distance covered or drive time. As a result, prices are higher than you might expect, compared to taxis in most cities, but you can also expect to find very high-quality vehicles. You can generally find a taxi at Piazza dei Mulini during the season from April to October, but do budget for more than €20 just to move around Positano, and a ride from Positano to Nocelle and Montepertuso can cost €30-40. Before departing, tell the driver where you need to go and agree on a price.

On Foot

Positano isn't called the Vertical City for nothing. Getting around town means navigating a lot of steps or inclined walkways. From Piazza dei Mulini down to the beach, you'll walk on a cobblestone path mixed with steps, making it a bit of an expedition if you have a lot of luggage. If you're staying near the beach, it is worth asking in advance if your accommodation offers a luggage service; there may be an additional fee, but it will be well worth it. Comfortable shoes and sandals are a good idea for getting around Positano. This is the place to forgo those elegant heels and opt for a nice pair of flats for evenings out.

Praiano

Between Positano and Furore, the Amalfi coastline juts out into the sea and Praiano spills down two sides of a mountain ridge that ends in a gently curved cape named **Capo Sottile.** The eastern side is called **Praiano** while **Vettica Maggiore** is the name of the western side of town facing Positano. One thing is guaranteed: The views are gorgeous on both sides. As the Amalfi Coast Road weaves through the town, you might just drive right on through. Without a large central piazza or particularly easy parking, many travelers miss the chance to stop and explore this lovely little town.

Despite its mountainside setting, Praiano has always had a strong connection with the sea. Its ancient name, Antica Plagianum, likely derives from the Latin for "open sea" because the town sits on a cape along the Amalfi Coast. The town has long been known for fishing, including the production of nets, and later coral fishing. Evidence of the fishing tradition can be seen at the **Marina di Praia beach,** which is often covered with small wooden boats and heaps of fishing cages and nets.

The Amalfi Coast Road runs right through Vettica Maggiore and Praiano, allowing you only a glimpse of the town unless you stop and explore. In Vettica Maggiore on the western side of Capo Sottile, you'll find the beautiful **Chiesa di San Gennaro** with a large terrace in front, offering spectacular views of Positano. At sea level far below is the rocky **La Gavitella beach.** Just east of the Chiesa di San Gennaro, a narrow road leads up into higher parts of Praiano and meanders through the town until meeting back down at the Amalfi Coast Road on the eastern side of Capo Sottile. Continue on the Amalfi Coast Road east to find the charming Marina di Praia beach set in a tiny cove.

For some time, Praiano has been a hidden oasis for travelers who enjoy staying somewhere off the beaten path. And with its dreamy setting, suspended between the mountains and sea, Praiano offers a quiet charm that is closely connected to nature. Though this town is certainly no longer off the radar, it is by no means as busy as its next-door neighbor Positano. It's an excellent choice for a home base if you're looking for a quieter and more local experience than you'd find in larger towns along the coast.

SIGHTS

Chiesa di San Gennaro

Piazza San Gennaro; Vettica Maggiore; tel. 089/874-799; piobozza@virgilio.it; 9am-noon and 4pm-8pm, open until 10pm in summer

Driving through Vettica Maggiore on the Amalfi Coast Road, you'll see the colorful ceramic-tiled dome and bell tower of the Chiesa di San Gennaro sitting just below the road. This large church dates back to 1589 and was constructed on the site of an older church, which was also dedicated to San Gennaro (St. Januarius), an important bishop, martyr, and patron saint of Naples. The baroque interior is richly decorated with an equally ornate ceramic floor. The large piazza in front of the church is a lovely spot to admire the view of Positano in the distance and gaze all the way down the coastline to the island of Capri. Here is where the dramatic Luminaria di San Domenico celebrations take place at the beginning of August. If you're in Praiano on September 19, December 16, or the first Sunday in May, you'll likely catch the local celebrations with special Masses and processions honoring San Gennaro.

Chiesa di San Luca Evangelista

Piazza San Luca; tel. 089/874-247; www.sanluca.org; 3pm-7pm Mon.-Fri., 8:30am-noon and 3pm-7pm Sat.-Sun., open until 10pm daily in summer

Although not as striking as the Chiesa di San Gennaro with its majolica dome, the Chiesa di San Luca Evangelista holds a special place in Praiano, as it is dedicated to the town's patron saint. The pretty piazza in front of the church is reason enough to visit here, and inside this 16th-century church are lovely baroque ornaments, including a hand-painted majolica floor from 1789, depicting San Luca surrounded by a decorative pattern of flowers and birds. Praiano celebrates its patron saint with a festival, including special Masses and processions on October 18, the first Sunday of July, and Easter Monday.

Praiano NaturArte

Various locations; free

Walking is the best way to discover the charms of the Amalfi Coast's towns. Praiano offers extra incentive with a unique artistic experience: The town has created more than 150 permanent art installations around town and strung them together into eight suggested walks, each one leading to a collection of ceramic or stone artworks created by eight different artists. The works blend harmoniously with the landscape to create an outdoor museum experience, and pieces by local artists showcase the town's traditions, myths, and history. Walks vary from short routes without too many steps to longer, more challenging walks. An excellent choice is itinerary No. 5, with artwork created by Lucio Liguori, a ceramic artist from Vietri sul Mare. Inspired by the sea, the pathway is dotted with brightly colored ceramic likenesses of sea creatures native to the area, like anchovies, squid, and tuna, as well as ceramic panels showing scenes from the traditional fishing life in Praiano. To enjoy this walk, follow Via Breve down from the Amalfi Coast Road to Via Massa, which leads to the Chiesa di San Gennaro and continues on as Via Rezzola. Plan for about 40 minutes for this walk. Visit the **Ufficio Informazioni Turistiche di Praiano** for a map of the NaturArte walks.

BEACHES

Given the town's setting above the sea, Praiano is a little more limited when it comes to beach access than some of the other towns on the Amalfi Coast. However, what it lacks in quantity is absolutely made up in quality.

LA GAVITELLA

Cala della Gavitella, Vettica Maggiore

Situated below Vettica Maggiore, this small and very rocky beach is a bit of a hike from the center of Praiano. Yet, it's lovely with great views down the coast toward Positano. However, be prepared for the climb back up, which is just over 400 steps. The beach is served by a *stabilimente balneare* (beach club), but there is also space where you can sunbathe and swim for free. Head to the rockier end of the beach if you're looking for a more secluded spot; the water is lovely here

1: The colorful dome of the Chiesa di San Gennaro stands out in Praiano. **2:** Marina di Praia is a popular spot for swimming but also for the local fishermen.

1

2

for swimming, even though it's rocky and access to the sea is via a ladder down to the water.

★ MARINA DI PRAIA

Via Marina di Praia

A fishing village and an important access point to the sea since ancient times, Marina di Praia is one of the most captivating beaches along the entire coastline. Set in a deep ravine with little houses and a tiny whitewashed church, this beach still has the atmosphere of a fishing village. Sunbathers vie for space with brightly painted wooden fishing boats pulled up on the beach. You'll also probably spot fishing nets and cages, signs that tradition is still going strong here. Besides the incredibly clear and clean water, one of the most appealing features of Marina di Praia is the **walkway** cut into the cliffside that leads from the beach about 400 meters along the rugged coastline. Follow the scenic pathway past the medieval **Torre a Mare** watchtower all the way to the entrance of the iconic Africana Famous Club.

One of the best aspects of Marina di Praia is its easy access. A small road leads from the Amalfi Coast Road to a gentle slope of steps down to the beach. Like much of the coastline, the beach is pebbly. Sun beds are available for rental or find a spot in the crowded free area among the fishing boats. There are also some cement platforms along the walkway where locals sunbathe and where rock jumping is popular.

Given the steep cliffs on both sides, the sun hits Marina di Praia only during the middle hours of the day. Yet, the location is just as enchanting in the evening or after dark, thanks to the beautiful walk along the sea and excellent restaurants.

SPORTS AND RECREATION

Praiano's rocky stretch of coastline is ideal for water sports. Just head down to Marina di Praia where you'll find options for kayaking, boat trips, and even diving excursions.

WINDSURF & KAYAK PRAIANO

Marina di Praia; tel. 339/483-5115; www.windsurfpraiano.it; 9:30am-7pm May-Oct.; kayak rental from €10 per hour

Set off from the beach and explore the coastline while kayaking or stand-up paddleboarding around Praiano. It's the best way to enjoy the area's natural beauty while getting a bit of exercise in as well. In addition to kayak and paddleboard rentals, Windsurf & Kayak Praiano offers windsurfing lessons for all skill levels (starting at €100), as well as kayak excursions (€40-95 per person) along the coastline.

LA BOA CHARTER & DIVING

Marina di Praia; tel. 089/813-3034; www.laboa.com; 8am-9pm daily May-Oct.; from €90 per person

Discover the underwater beauty of the Amalfi Coast on a diving excursion from Praiano. La Boa Charter & Diving has two diving centers on the Sorrentine Peninsula, where the company offers immersions and boat excursions. The one in Marina di Praia is the starting point for dives along the Amalfi Coast. All immersions include an instructor and equipment. There are many types of dives possible, ranging in experience level from easy immersions below Vettica Maggiore to challenging dives around the Li Galli islands for very advanced divers.

ENTERTAINMENT AND EVENTS

Praiano is a tranquil town known mostly for its moving religious and cultural celebrations throughout the year. Rather surprisingly, it's also home to the most notable nightclub on the Amalfi Coast.

Nightlife

With a stunning view down the coastline toward Positano, the Vettica Maggiore side of Praiano is an ideal place to enjoy a beautiful sunset. After dark, dinner by the sea in Marina di Praia is a captivating experience. For after-dinner drinks and dancing, follow the cliffside walk from Marina di Praia to the Amalfi Coast's most striking nightclub.

AFRICANA FAMOUS CLUB

Via Terramare 2; tel. 089/874-858; www.africanafamousclub.com; 9pm-4am Sat. in May, daily June-Sept.; cover charge varies

Since the 1960s, this unique nightclub has been a hot spot for music and entertainment on the Amalfi Coast. The entire club is located in a cave carved out of the moutainside, just 32 feet (10 m) above the sea level. This unique space features a large dance floor, DJ station, VIP area with private tables, and terrace overlooking the sea. Music genres include lounge and disco, and there are often themed nights during the summer. There's a dress code, so avoid casual clothing or beachwear, and instead opt for evening club attire. It's a good idea to call in advance to verify opening hours and dates because the club is also a popular spot for private events and can be closed to the public on certain dates. You can arrive on foot by following the pathway from Marina di Praia, or come via the nightclub's boat service from Positano, Amalfi, and Maiori. There's also shuttle bus service available for the entire Amalfi Coast if you reserve in advance.

Classical Music

I SUONI DEGLI DEI

(The Sounds of the Gods)

Sentiero degli Dei; tel. 089/874-557; www.isuonideglidei.com; every Wed. in May, Sept., and Oct.; free

There are few more impressive settings for an open-air concert than the Sentiero degli Dei pathway high above Praiano. This incredible concert series of classical and contemporary music is not only set against the backdrop of the Amalfi Coast, but also immersed in nature in various settings, including among the ruins of the Santa Maria a Castro church that sit at at 1,194 feet (364 m) above the sea. Accessing the concerts means hiking the **Pathway of the Gods;** the hike is strenuous but extremely rewarding, but do dress accordingly with hiking or good walking shoes. For more details on reaching the concert locations, contact the organization for tips or to arrange a guide.

Festivals and Events

LUMINARIA DI SAN DOMENICO

Piazza San Gennaro, Piazza San Luca, and various locations; www.luminariadisandomenico.it; Aug. 1-4; free

Every summer, the Luminaria di San Domenico—a visually stunning festival that is imbued with cultural and religious significance—takes over Praiano. Celebrated for more than 400 years, this event starts from the Convento di Santa Maria a Castro above Praiano, where there was once a strong devotion to San Domenico. The festival re-creates the legend of San Domenico's mother, who had a dream before he was born of a dog with a torch in his mouth setting the world on fire; this was believed to signify that the newborn would carry the word of God to the world. Today the journey of the fire is represented with thousands of candles around town and religious celebrations. The events culminate with about 3,000 candles decorating the Piazza San Gennaro, where performing fire dancers re-create the story of San Domenico.

FOOD

TRATTORIA DA ARMANDINO

Via Praia 1; tel. 089/874-087; www.trattoriadaarmandino.com; 1pm-3:30pm and 7pm-11pm daily, mid-Mar.-Oct.; €35

Right at the edge of the sea in picturesque Marina di Praia, this restaurant has a way of making you feel right at home. Owners Armando and Carmela have been running this restaurant since 1986, and it's a popular spot with locals. Seafood is the specialty here, with a home-cooked touch. Try the pasta with *totani* (squid), the delicious risotto with lemon and shrimp, or fried fresh seafood. The restaurant is also open as a bar for coffee and drinks 9am-11pm.

LA MORESSA ITALIAN BISTRO & LOUNGE BAR

Piazza Moressa 1; tel. 089/935-5017; www.lamoressa.it; 8am-midnight daily Mar.-Nov.; €30

Open throughout the day, this restaurant offers a little of everything along with a panoramic terrace to enjoy the view. Whether you're stopping in for breakfast, a pizza for lunch, or looking for a romantic spot for dinner and drinks, this is a good choice in Praiano. There are some excellent non-seafood specialties like the pizzas, pork with an apple sauce, and pasta with *provolone del Monaco* cheese and walnuts from Sorrento.

IL PIRATA

Via Terramare; tel. 089/874-377; www.ristoranteilpirata.net; 12:30pm-10:30pm Easter-Oct.; €20

From the beach in Marina di Praia, follow the Via Terramare walkway carved into the mountain and before long you'll happen across this restaurant with outdoor seating on terraces overlooking the sea. Naturally, this is the place to enjoy seafood, including excellent *crudo di pesce* (raw fish), *totani e patate* (squid and potatoes), or pasta with freshly caught fish, yellow tomatoes, and basil. Il Pirata is also open 9am-6pm as a solarium for visitors to enjoy the sun, and the bar carved into the mountain is usually open late.

ACCOMMODATIONS

€100-200

LOCANDA COSTA DIVA

Via Roma 12; tel. 089/813-076; www.hotelspraiano.com; closed Nov. 3-Feb. 28, €180 d

Enjoy lovely views of the coastline dotted with watchtowers from this hotel nestled in between terraces of lemon and olive trees and lush gardens. All of the rooms and suites feature special touches like vaulted ceilings and frescoed walls, ceramics from Vietri sul Mare, and colorful decor. The hotel's restaurant with an outdoor dining terrace surrounded by lemon trees is a dreamy dining spot.

€200-300

HOTEL MARGHERITA

Via Umberto I 70; tel. 089/874-628; www.hotelmargherita.info; open mid-Mar.-Oct.; €218 d

With a bright and classic Amalfi Coast decor, and extremely friendly service, this hotel offers a peaceful escape thanks to its lovely pool overlooking the sea, excellent on-site restaurant, cooking class experiences (from €60 per person), and handy services like a shuttle van to the beach and to Positano. If you want a sea-view room (and you do), make sure to request one of the 24 rooms (out of 28) that include private terraces.

HOTEL TRAMONTO D'ORO

Via Gennaro Capriglione 119, Vettica Maggiore; tel. 089/874-955; www.tramontodoro.it; open Apr.-Oct., €279 d

Praiano is one of the best spots on the coast to enjoy sunsets, and there's no better spot than this hotel, whose name means "golden sunset." Facing toward Positano, with views down the coastline all the way to the Faraglioni Rocks off of Capri, the hotel also includes a nice pool, spa and wellness center, and restaurant. For a sea view, ask for a superior room or one of the even more upscale types; the Mediterranea rooms are especially fine.

Over €300

CASA ANGELINA

Via Gennaro Capriglione 147, Vettica Maggiore; tel. 089/813-1333; www.casangelina.com; open Apr.-Oct.; €780

Perhaps no place frames views of the Amalfi Coast quite as beautifully as this boutique hotel with its unique take on contemporary luxury. Here a white-on-white color scheme—with 15 unique shades—creates a simple yet refreshing setting to enjoy the 180-degree sea views of Positano, Capri, and the Amalfi Coast. The hotel's 40 exquisite rooms offer a variety of themes and configurations, including two stunning suites. Looking for something secluded? Check out the four Eaudesea Experience Rooms, old fishermen's houses converted into luxury accommodations. Soak up the sun and fine views from the swimming pool, which is surrounded by sun beds and umbrellas. Guests also have a reserved area at La Gavitella beach, accessible via a modern glass elevator and about 200 steps. The spa's custom treatments are perfectly relaxing, and the modern gym is so tempting you won't even mind working out while on holiday. At the restaurant **Un Piano Nel Cielo,** chef Leopoldo Elefante creates a refined menu to be savored in a spectacular setting overlooking the coastline.

INFORMATION AND SERVICES

UFFICIO INFORMAZIONI TURISTICHE DI PRAIANO

Via Gennaro Capriglione 116b, Vettica Maggiore; tel. 089/874-557; www.praiano.org; Mon.-Sat. 9am-1pm and 5pm-9pm June-Sept., and 9am-1pm and 4:30pm-8:30pm Oct.-May

Praiano's tourist office is located just across the street from the easy-to-spot Chiesa di San Gennaro with its multicolored dome. Stop in here for friendly help in English and you'll find all the information you need to explore the town during your stay.

GETTING THERE AND AROUND

Located only about 3.7 miles (6 km) east of Positano, Praiano is a popular base on the Amalfi Coast for travelers looking to stay a little distance outside of busier locations like Positano and Amalfi. This is a good plan as long as you keep in mind that transportation will require a bit more work. There is no port in Praiano, so unless you are driving, the only connections between Praiano and other towns are via taxi or bus.

By Car and Scooter

The Amalfi Coast Road (SS163) runs right through Praiano, making it easy to reach from nearby Positano, which is only about a 20-minute drive. The next nearest town to the east on the Amalfi Coast Road is Conca dei Marini, which is also about a 20-minute drive. The main sights in Praiano are located along or very near the Amalfi Coast Road, as it winds through the center of Praiano. However, there is a road that passes through the upper area of Praiano above the Amalfi Coast Road. This internal road intersects the Amalfi Coast Road east of Chiesa di San Gennaro where the road is called Via Giuglielmo Marconi. Eventually, it splits into Via Costantinopoli to the left, a scenic drive through the upper part of town, and Via Umberto I, which meanders through a pretty area of town with restaurants and hotels, and eventually meets up with the Amalfi Coast Road on the eastern side of Capo Sottile in Praiano.

Driving east from Praiano right on the edge of town, look for the sharp turnoff to the right with a narrow road Via Marina di Praia that leads down to the beach cove. Parking is available in Praiano and Marina di Praia in paid areas along the side of the road, or in paid parking lots that usually charge €2.50-3 per hour.

Located right beside the Chiesa di San Gennaro, **Mr Rent a Scooter** (Via Gennaro Capriglione 99, Vettica Maggiore; tel. 089/813-071; www.mrentascooter.it; 9am-7pm daily May-Oct. and otherwise by reservation, from €54 per day) has a selection of scooters you can rent daily or for longer periods. This is a fun experience and often less stressful way to get around the Amalfi Coast compared to driving a car.

By Taxi

Taxis can usually be found at the beginning of Via Giuglielmo Marconi, just off the Amalfi Coast Road east of the Chiesa di San Gennaro in Vettica Maggiore, and at the crossroads of the Amalfi Coast Road and Via Umberto I in Praiano. Look for the orange Taxi sign for more information. Taxis are independently owned, but the town of Praiano has set taxi fares to most locations on the Amalfi Coast. Fixed fares are available for 1-4 people and 5-8 people, starting from €15 to move around within Praiano town limits. The fare is €40 to Positano, €45 to Amalfi, €85 to Ravello, €80 to Sorrento, and €120 to Salerno. Be sure to notify the driver if you want a fixed rate before departure. Outside of the fixed fares, all other journeys are metered and start at €6. The tourist office in Praiano can offer the latest rates and help with any questions about taxis in Praiano.

For 24-hour taxi service as well as transfers to Praiano from the Naples airport, Sorrento, and other locations in the Amalfi Coast area, contact Praiano Taxi Service (www.praianotaxiservice.it; tel. 347/335-6845). It is a good idea to book a taxi in advance, especially for arrival and departure, or if you need to be somewhere at a specific time as buses can be delayed.

By Bus

Public buses operated by **SITA SUD** (tel. 089/386-6701; www.sitasudtrasporti.it; from €1.30) pass right through town on the Amalfi Coast Road, but they can be very crowded, so it's best to pack a dose of patience if you plan to head to Praiano by bus, and especially if you're trying to catch the bus in Praiano because buses can be so full before arriving in Praiano that they are unable to stop to pick up passengers. Stops are located throughout Praiano and Vettica Maggiore, including near the Chiesa di San Gennaro, intersections with Praiano's internal road, and above Marina di Praia.

To reach Praiano by bus from Positano, catch the bus heading to Amalfi from one of the two stops in Positano (Chiesa Nuova or Sponda), and the journey is about 25 minutes. From Amalfi, take the bus heading to Sorrento and the journey is about 25 minutes as well. To travel to Praiano from Ravello and Salerno you must first take a bus to Amalfi and then transfer to the bus to Sorrento.

You can also get to Praiano from Positano and get around Praiano by a local bus service, **Mobility Amalfi Coast** (tel. 089/813-077; info@mobilityamalficoast.com; €1.30-1.70). These smaller buses stop in Praiano at several locations, from the Chiesa di San Gennaro to Marina di Praia, roughly every hour. Tickets are available in local *tabacchi* and some other shops, or onboard for a slightly higher price.

Furore

Following the Amalfi Coast Road along the coastline, it's easy to understand why Furore has the nickname *Il paese che non c'è* (The Town that Doesn't Exist). As the Amalfi Coast Road winds its way along the coastline, it passes right below the town of Furore, which clings to the cliffside high above. The only part you'll see briefly from the road is the impressive **Fiordo di Furore,** a dramatic fjord with a tiny beach, as you pass by. To visit the rest of the town, you'll have to meander off the Amalfi Coast Road and head up into the mountains to find this village, which does actually exist, on the way to Agerola. You'll find Furore spread out along the mountainside with houses set between terraced gardens. As you follow the hairpin curves that zigzag up the mountain, you'll discover why Furore calls itself *Il Paese Dipinto* (The Painted City), which is a much more fitting title. The town is full of beautiful murals, sculptures, and artistic embellishments.

Though Furore doesn't have a cohesive town center, its evocative location, peaceful atmosphere, and stunning views make it a fine town to explore or to serve as a home base on the Amalfi Coast if you want to spend time surrounded by nature and don't mind if you're not close to the beach. With excellent hiking options nearby, Furore is an ideal base for mountain lovers.

The Vineyards of the Amalfi Coast

The idea of Italian vineyards usually conjures up images of gently rolling hills in Tuscany lined with evenly spaced rows of vines. To see the vineyards of the Amalfi Coast is quite a different experience, and one that often starts with looking up. The steep slopes and rocky terrain of the Amalfi Coast certainly doesn't seem like the place to grow grapes, but here, with a hefty dose of hard work, some incredible wines are produced in the coastline's vertical vineyards.

Grapes have been grown here for generations on terraces carved out of the mountainside and using a clever system of pergolas. In this incredibly challenging landscape, the wines that are produced are infused with the salty scent of sea breeze and the unique Mediterranean microclimate. The wines of the region are of the Costa d'Amalfi DOC or *denominazione di origine controllata*, the Italian system to indicate quality and geographically protected wine-production areas. The slopes of Ravello and higher into the Lattari Mountains in Tramonti are two other areas that are noted for their wine production. In Tramonti you can sample wines created with grapes handpicked from vines that are more than a century old. This is rare because in the mid-19th century, an aphid species from the United States destroyed many of the vines in France and Italy; however, Tramonti's remote location allowed it to largely escape the blight.

WINE TASTING

- **Furore:** Visit the **Cantine Marisa Cuomo** to try the Costa d'Amalfi DOC wines made from the grapes grown along the slopes of Furore and the Amalfi Coast.
- **Tramonti:** Along with Tramonti's rare vines, you'll find the classic local red varietals like aglianico, piedirosso, and tintore. If you prefer white wines, you'll find lovely blends with falanghina, ginestra, pepella, and biancolella grapes. Local producers like **Tenuta San Francesco** and **Cantine Giuseppe Apicella** offer vineyard tours and tastings, and you'll see their wines at many local restaurants.
- **Vietri sul Mare:** Travel down the coast to Raito, a small village above Vietri sul Mare, to visit **Le Vigne di Raito,** a newer vineyard that is continuing the local traditions of winemaking on the Amalfi Coast.

SIGHTS

★ Fiordo di Furore

Strada Statale 163 (Amalfi Coast Road) at Fiordo di Furore

The sliver of Furore's fjord with its tiny beach and old fishing village is one of the Amalfi Coast's most iconic images. However, you can only catch a glimpse of it while driving along the Amalfi Coast Road. The best way to enjoy the view and visit the beach is to arrive by bus because there is no parking nearby. Ask the driver to stop at the Fiordo di Furore stop, and after gazing down at the view, take the staircase starting at the western side of the bridge that clings to the cliff, and follow it down to reach the beach. The little cluster of houses carved into the mountainside and some wooden boats are all that's left of a fishing village that has always been Furore's only access point to the sea. It was here in this romantic spot that Italian film director Roberto Rossellini and actress Anna Magnani had a passionate affair during the filming of his 1948 movie *L'Amore*.

This nearly hidden beach still has a mesmerizing atmosphere of bygone days. During the summer season, especially around midday when the sun arrives on the beach, you'll find beachgoers along with boats arriving below the bridge to show travelers the scenic beach, and kayakers pulling up for a rest on the shore. The small beach doesn't offer a lot as far as amenities, but it makes up for it with fine views.

Every July the **Marmeeting Mediterranean Cup** (www.marmeeting.

1

2

com), a deep sea high-diving competition, comes to Furore, where divers make the jump from about 92 feet (28 m) off the bridge over the fjord into the deep water below. Though it's best to leave that to the professionals, the rocks along the walk down to the beach are popular for cliff jumping in the summer.

Cantine Marisa Cuomo

Via Giambattista Lama 16/18; tel. 089/830-348; www.marisacuomo.com; wine tasting and tours Mar.-Oct., tours only Nov.-Feb., reservations required; €75 per person for tour and tasting

Set in an improbable location along the steep slopes of Furore, this is one of Campania's most celebrated vineyards. A labor of love of husband-and-wife team Andrea Ferraioli and Marisa Cuomo, the Cantine Marisa Cuomo produces highly esteemed wines from grapes grown on nearly 25 acres of steeply sloped and terraced vineyards. The winery is noted for both its white and red wines, making this an excellent vineyard to try some of the Amalfi Coast's unique grape varietals. The falanghina and biancolella grapes create the lovely Furore Bianco wine, with delicate fruit and Mediterranean scents, while aglianico and per 'e palummo are used to make the classic Furore Rosso, a ruby red colored wine with a hint of cherry and spices. These combined with award winning *vini estremi* (extreme wines) are among the different types that connoisseurs will enjoy sampling while in the area. After grapes are harvested, the wine is produced in the winemakers' cantine, situated in a cave carved out of the mountain. Wine tastings and vineyard tours include a tour of the cantine and vineyard, and lunch or dinner accompanied by a selection of wines. Menus can vary, with gluten-free and vegetarian options also available. Tours are also offered during the winter months. Booking in advance is required.

1: terraces of vineyards on the steep slopes of Furore **2:** Fiordo di Furore beach

FOOD AND ACCOMMODATIONS

HOSTARIA DI BACCO

Via Giambattista Lama 9; tel. 089/830-360; www.baccofurore.it; restaurant open 12:30pm-3:30pm and 7:30pm-10pm daily June-Aug., closed Tues. Sept.-May, €15-28; hotel closed Jan. 8-Feb. 28; €114 d

With a long tradition of welcoming guests since their hostaria opened in 1930, this friendly restaurant and hotel will make you feel right at home. Restaurant specialties blend seafood and traditional mountain dishes, in just the way Furore sits between land and sea. Try the pasta with beans and mussels or the squid stuffed with seafood and locally grown vegetables. "Slow Food" and vegan tasting menus are available. The hotel offers 19 bright and lovely rooms with balconies or terraces and views of the sea, grapevines, or lemon groves.

AGRITURISMO SANT'ALFONSO

Via San Alfonso 6; tel. 089/830-515; www.agriturismosantalfonso.it; closed mid-Jan.-mid-Mar.; €110 d

This 17th-century farmhouse nestled along the slopes of Furore offers a comfortable spot to get away from it all while surrounded by beautiful views in a rustic setting. The nine rooms are cozy and the *agriturismo* offers a generous breakfast with freshly baked sweets included in the price. For lunch or dinner you can also dine out on the terrace overlooking the sea during good weather. There's a small chapel on-site dedicated to Sant'Alfonso Maria de' Liguori that was once part of a monastery (now the farmhouse). An air of tranquility reigns in this splendidly natural spot.

GETTING THERE

Furore is located between Praiano and Conca dei Marini, with the center of the town set in the mountainside above the Amalfi Coast Road (SS163). To reach Furore, you'll need to drive up the SS366 road, which intersects the Amalfi Coast Road (SS163) about 1.2 miles (2 km) west of Amalfi. Look for a well marked intersection with signs indicating Furore. Continue on the SS366 road as it climbs into the mountains and passes through the upper part of Conca dei Marini. Stay on the SS366, and after about 3.7 miles (6 km) more you'll arrive in Furore. The drive to Furore is about 40 minutes from Praiano, 25 minutes from Amalfi, 15 minutes from Conca dei Marini, and 40 minutes from Ravello.

The **SITA SUD** (tel. 089/386-6701; www.sitasudtrasporti.it; from €1.30) bus line connecting Amalfi to Agerola is the only one along the coastline providing access to the upper part of the town. The Fiordo di Furore is located on the Amalfi Coast Road and is accessible via the SITA SUD bus line connecting Amalfi and Sorrento. To reach the center of Furore from Amalfi by bus takes about 25 minutes. For the Fiordo di Furore, it's a 20-minute bus ride from Amalfi and a 50-minute bus ride from Positano. From Ravello and Salerno, you will need first to arrive by SITA SUD bus in Amalfi (about 25 minutes from Ravello to Amalfi, and 1 hour 15 minutes from Salerno to Amalfi) and then transfer to the Amalfi to Agerola bus line. To reach the town by ferry, the closest port is Amalfi, where you can then transfer to the SITA SUD bus to reach Furore.

Conca dei Marini

Conca dei Marini climbs vertically from the sea straight up the mountainside more than 1,300 feet (400 m). Given the vertical nature of the setting, like many of the towns between Positano and Amalfi, Conca dei Marini is very spread out with access to the lower part of town via the Amalfi Coast Road and the upper part of town via the SS366 road leading up into the mountains toward Furore and Agerola. In Conca dei Marini, you can go from swimming in the sea to sweeping views of the coastline at the top of town and back down to the distinctive **Capo di Conca** promontory with its 16th-century stone watchtower. In the small bay by the watchtower is the entrance to the **Grotta dello Smeraldo** (Emerald Grotto) with its mesmerizing green waters.

However, the town is most noted for the picturesque harbor of **Marina di Conca,** where a small cluster of houses built around the beach were once home to the town's fishermen. Here you'll find one of the Amalfi Coast's most charming beaches and gorgeous water. This sleepy fishing village was put on the map in the 1960s when the jet set, including Jacqueline Kennedy, favored the quiet setting of Conca dei Marini for summer holidays. The town still has a secluded charm that makes it a popular spot for travelers looking for a relaxed escape on the Amalfi Coast.

SIGHTS

Grotta dello Smeraldo (Emerald Grotto)

Via Smeraldo; tel. 089/831-535; info@amalfitouristoffice.it (site managed by Azienda Autonoma di Soggiorno e Turismo in Amalfi); 9am-4pm daily Apr.-Oct. (closes at 3pm Nov.-Mar.); €5

While Capri has its famous Blue Grotto, the Amalfi Coast has a cave of its own that is just as notable for its beautiful colors. The Grotta dello Smeraldo (Emerald Grotto) is named after the intense green water inside. Situated in the pretty bay at Capo di Conca, the large grotto was discovered in 1932 by a local fisherman. Unlike the Blue Grotto, however, the Emerald Grotto has an easily accessible entrance. After walking into the grotto, you climb aboard small boats to be rowed around to see the underwater sights, including the impressive stalactites and stalagmites, and, of course, the emerald water. The boat tour lasts about 15 minutes. Access to the grotto is from the Amalfi Coast Road via elevator (steps not in service) or by boat from Amalfi, offered by the **Gruppo Battellieri Costa d'Amalfi** (Via Largo Duchi Piccolomini 4, Amalfi; tel. 089/873-446; www.gruppobattellieriamalfi.com; Mar.-Nov.; €10 boat plus €5 entrance) with about seven departures daily from 9:20am to 3:20pm.

Chiesa di San Pancrazio

Via Don Gaetano Amodio 22; parrocchieconcadeimarini@yahoo.it

Follow the narrow road that leads from the Amalfi Coast Road up into the heart of Conca dei Marini, and after a few steep twists and turns you'll find this church surrounded by olive trees. There's a beautiful open space in the front lined with trees and oleander. Inside you'll find a baroque altar with marble inlays, above which is a 16th-century triptych showing the Madonna and Child with San Pancrazio and San Leonardo. Across from the church, follow the walkway leading out to the Punta Vreca overlook, which is marked by a large cross. Here, the view stretches down the coastline all the way to the Faraglioni rocks off of Capri.

BEACHES

MARINA DI CONCA

Via Marina di Conca

Unless you know where to stop to peek down over the edge you could easily drive right by one of Conca dei Marini's most appealing spots. Set far below the Amalfi Coast Road, the town's tiny beach and seaside village is often called the Borgo Marinaro, because it is where fishermen once lived. Though their homes near the beach have been transformed into restaurants, the local connection to the sea is still strong, and dining on fresh fish by the sea is a must. The incredibly clear turquoise water and charming atmosphere make this one of the best beaches along the Amalfi Coast. It's well worth the walk down the 300 steps from the Amalfi Coast Road. You'll enjoy panoramic views looking toward Amalfi in the distance. The beach has small pebbles and an easy slope into the sea, where the water is clear and the swimming terrific.

Just before reaching the beach, you'll pass the **Cappella della Madonna delle Neve,** a small chapel with important religious ties for the community. On August 5 a celebration, including a boat procession on the sea, takes place at the chapel.

It was here in the '50s and '60s that the jet set brought fame to this sleepy little fishing village. With visitors like Jacqueline Kennedy and Princess Margaret of Windsor, a touch of glamour arrived on Conca dei Marini's beach and still lingers. Here or on the nearby **Marinella di Conca** and **La Vite** beaches, you still run the chance of spotting a movie star or two.

CAPO DI CONCA

Via Capo di Conca; tel. 089/831-512; www.capodiconca.it; mid-May-Sept.; from €18

Along the Capo di Conca promontory just below the 16th-century watchtower, this is less a beach and more a rocky outcropping and series of terraces that is home to one *stabilimento balneare* that offers the chance to swim in this scenic spot. With a restaurant, bar, sun beds, and umbrellas, you will find everything needed to enjoy a day by the sea, and perhaps stretch that day into the evening with dinner by the water's edge. Climb the steep staircase near the tower for a stunning view in both directions along the coastline.

SPORTS AND RECREATION

Boat Tours

EXCLUSIVE CRUISES

Via Smeraldo 14; tel. 331/441-4506; www.exclusivecruisescapri.com; Mar.-Dec.; from €250 for self-drive and €590 for excursions with captain

Experience the natural beauty of the Amalfi Coast up close on a relaxing private boat excursion with an expert local captain at the helm. Discover hidden grottoes and the best swimming spots, and admire the coastline from the sea, away from traffic and crowds. Exclusive Cruises offers a variety of boat options, from classic Sorrentine-style wooden boats to Itama luxury speedboats and larger

1
2
3
4

yachts that are ideal for groups of family or friends. Smaller boats are also available for self-drive rentals without the need for a license. Boat excursions and transfers are available not only from Conca dei Marini, but also from all of the towns along the Amalfi Coast, Sorrento, Capri, Salerno, and Naples.

FOOD

LA TONNARELLA

Via Marina di Conca 5; tel. 089/831-939; www.ristorantelatonnarella.com; 12:30-4pm and 6:30-10pm, closed Sun.-Mon. for dinner and mid-Oct.-mid-Apr.; €40

With a great beachy vibe and very friendly service, this restaurant is an excellent choice, just steps from the sea in the Marina di Conca. Listen to the waves and dine on fresh seafood and a glass of local wine. Here on the beach where Jacqueline Kennedy once enjoyed swimming, the local specialty is named in her honor: The Spaghetti alla Jacqueline is made with zucchini, pancetta, and a generous grating of parmesan cheese. Boat service is available from Amalfi. Reservations are recommended.

LE BONTÀ DEL CAPO

Via I Maggio 14; tel. 089/831-515; www.lebontadelcapo.it; 9am-11pm Apr.-Oct.; €6-16

Located in the upper part of Conca dei Marini with a view overlooking the Capo di Conca and its watchtower far below, this restaurant is open all day with lunch served 12:30pm-2:30pm, and dinner 6:30pm-11pm. It's also perfect if you're looking for a relaxing spot for drinks or a sweet place to try out local desserts. Specialties include seafood as well as other delightful options like the ravioli with ricotta and lemon. The chef also offers limoncello and **cooking classes** (from €50 per person).

1: the charming Marina di Conca fishing village
2: a private boat excursion with Exclusive Cruises
3: traditional octopus and potato antipasto
4: Capo di Conca with its 16th-century watchtower and beach

ACCOMMODATIONS

HOTEL LE TERRAZZE

Via Smeraldo 11; tel. 089/831-290; www.hotelleterrazze.it; open mid-Apr.-end of Sept.; €229 d

Bright, colorful, and beautiful views characterize this lovely little hotel situated above the Marina di Conca beach. Of the 27 rooms, 23 offer sea views and 4 overlook gardens. All rooms feature balconies, classic Mediterranean colors, and modern design. Relax on the terraces or follow the steps (a little more than 200) down to the charming Borgo Marinaro to enjoy swimming or dining at the local seaside restaurants. No children under 16.

MONASTERO SANTA ROSA

Via Roma 2; tel. 089/832-1199; www.monasterosantarosa.com; open mid-Apr.-end of Oct.; €650 d

Set right at the edge of a cliff in a picturesque spot with impossibly beautiful views, the Monastero Santa Rosa is one of the finest hotel experiences on the coastline. Located in a convent that dates back to the 17th century, this hotel has an air of complete tranquility and lovely rooms that have preserved the essense of the unique architectural heritage of this space. All 20 rooms, ranging from superior rooms to breathtaking suites, have been individually decorated and boast spectacular sea views. The lush gardens dotted with lounge chairs and beautiful landscaping spread out over four terraces and lead down to the heated infinity pool with views you simply have to see to believe. The on-site spa offers luxurious treatments, and the hotel's restaurant, **Il Refettorio,** recently received its first Michelin star. This hotel is ideal for a secluded escape surrounded by the beauty of the Amalfi Coast.

GETTING THERE AND AROUND

By Car

Conca dei Marini is situated between the Amalfi Coast Road (SS163) and the SS366 that makes its way up into the mountains

Divine Sweets: The Sfogliatella Santa Rosa

Sfogliatella Santa Rosa pastries at the Monastero Santa Rosa

Look up in the mountains of Conca dei Marini and you'll spot the austere-looking **Monastero Santa Rosa,** perched dramatically on the edge of the cliff. Founded as a convent dedicated to Santa Rosa da Lima in the second half of the 17th century, today it is one of the Amalfi Coast's most exclusive five-star hotels.

It was in this isolated setting infused with the scents of the convent's gardens and the sea breeze, that one of the Amalfi Coast's most disctintive desserts was born. The cloistered nuns lived a tranquil life, and little did they know that one of their recipes would still be so much appreciated today. The Sfogliatella Santa Rosa dates back to the 1700s when one of the nuns created a pastry using leftover ingredients that she had on hand. Over time, the dessert developed into the Sfogliatella Santa Rosa as we know it today, a crisp layered pastry filled with citrus-infused ricotta, a rich pastry cream, and the classic touch of amarena cherries on top.

The dessert was such a success that it became a traditional treat during the festival day for Santa Rosa, which at that time took place on August 30. For more than a century, the recipe was a closely guarded secret until the early 1800s when Neapolitan pastry maker Pasquale Pintauro (who founded the Pintauro bakery you can still visit today in Naples) managed to discover the recipe, perhaps through an aunt who was a nun at the monastery. He transformed the recipe slightly into the traditional *sfogliatella* that is perhaps the most iconic dessert in the region of Campania.

Today, Sfogliatella Santa Rosa can be enjoyed at bakeries all over the Amalfi Coast and Naples area, including **Pasticceria Pansa** in Amalfi. To find it in the bakery case, look for its slightly larger size and the dollop of cream and cherries. Every summer on August 2, Conca dei Marini celebrates this famous pastry during the Santarosa Conca Festival (www.santarosaconcafestival.com).

through the upper part of town before continuing on to Furore and Agerola. There's a narrow and steep road that winds through the town, connecting the two roads with each other and with the center of the town. From the Amalfi Coast Road, look for a very large ceramic sign for Conca dei Marini; the road begins there as Via Don Gaetano Amodio and leads very steeply up. The name changes to Via Miramare as the road continues up and then again changes to Via Roma before meeting the SS366 road immediately next to the Monastero Santa Rosa hotel.

From Amalfi, the drive to Conca dei Marini takes about 15 minutes. To reach the Marina di Conca, Grotta dello Smeraldo, and the lower part of town, take the Amalfi Coast Road (SS163) west. For the upper part of Conca dei Marini, take the Amalfi Coast Road (SS163) west about 1.2 miles (2 km), and at the well-marked intersection with SS366, bear right and continue for about 2.5 miles (4 km). From Ravello, take the SS373 road down the mountain to connect with the Amalfi Coast Road (SS163) and continue west following the directions as from Amalfi. The drive from Ravello to Conca dei Marini takes about 30 minutes, following SS373 down to the Amalfi Coast Road (SS163) and then continuing west. From Furore, follow SS366 down the mountain about 10 minutes to reach the upper part of Conca dei Marini.

By Bus

For the lower part of town, the Marina di Conca, and Grotta dello Smeraldo take the **SITA SUD** (tel. 089/386-6701; www.sitasudtrasporti.it; from €1.30) bus line from Amalfi to Sorrento; it runs roughly every hour 6:30am-7pm. The journey to Conca dei Marini is about 15 minutes from Amalfi and about 35 minutes from Positano. To reach the upper part of town, take the Amalfi to Agerola line, which runs every 1-2 hours 7:10am-9pm and takes about 15 minutes. To reach Conca dei Marini by bus from Ravello, you will first need to arrive in Amalfi by bus (about 25 minutes from Ravello to Amalfi) and then transfer to one of the two lines mentioned above.

Amalfi

Once you catch a glimpse of Amalfi, it's no surprise that the Amalfi Coast's namesake town is one of the most popular spots along the coastline. The town is nestled in a valley with pastel-hued buildings climbing up both sides of the mountain and interspersed with terraces of lemon groves. The bell tower of the town's impressive cathedral marks the center of Amalfi, the beautiful **Piazza Duomo.** A powerful sea republic back in the Middle Ages, Amalfi has a fascinating history populated by dukes and duchesses, wars and wealth, innovation and undaunted curiosity for exploration that can still be seen in the town today.

With a seeming maze of streets and staircases, Amalfi is a town best explored on foot. While Piazza Duomo and the main street are home to most of the town's activity, shops, and restaurants, do spend some time wandering and exploring the quieter side streets, where you'll find arched passageways, hidden gardens overflowing with lemons, and tiny piazzas. Amalfi is about the buzz just as much as it is about these quiet spots, too, so don't miss the chance to see both sides.

Amalfi has one of the most picturesque harbors along the coastline, and a scenic *passeggiata* (stroll) leads from the Marina Grande beach along the sea all the way to the end of the Molo Foraneo, the largest pier in Amalfi, with its red port marker. From the walkway along the top of the Molo Foraneo, enjoy a stunning view looking across the harbor and back toward Amalfi. The view is captivating during the day, but especially after dark with the lights of Amalfi stretching out across the water and the salty sea breeze filling the air.

ORIENTATION

Amalfi's harbor is defined by three piers, the largest being the **Molo Foraneo** on the western side of the town. The central pier is referred to locally as the **Molo Pennello** and serves as the ferry terminal for town.

Amalfi

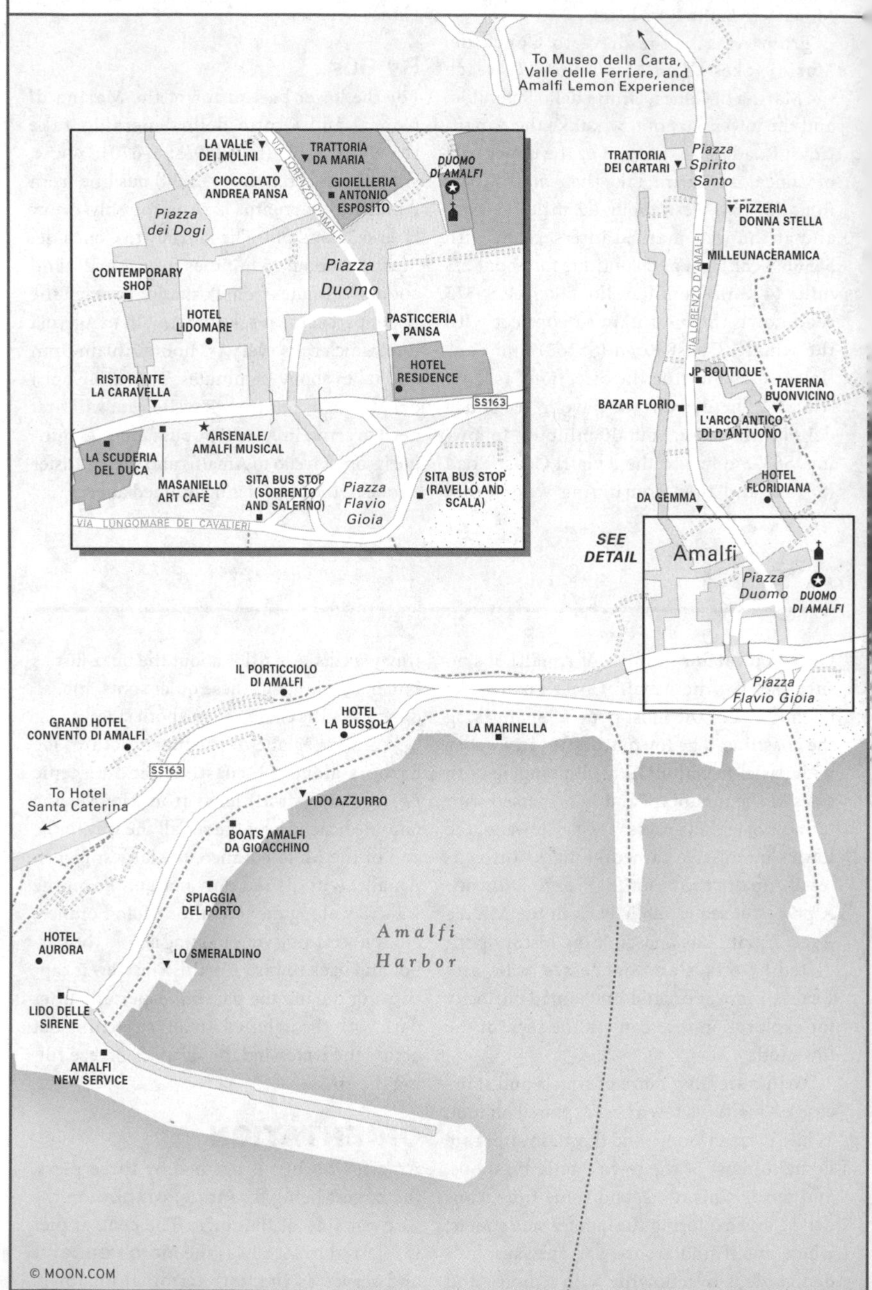
To Museo della Carta, Valle delle Ferriere, and Amalfi Lemon Experience
LA VALLE DEI MULINI
TRATTORIA DA MARIA
DUOMO DI AMALFI
CIOCCOLATO ANDREA PANSA
GIOIELLERIA ANTONIO ESPOSITO
VIA LORENZO D'AMALFI
Piazza dei Dogi
Piazza Duomo
CONTEMPORARY SHOP
HOTEL LIDOMARE
PASTICCERIA PANSA
HOTEL RESIDENCE
RISTORANTE LA CARAVELLA
SS163
LA SCUDERIA DEL DUCA
ARSENALE/ AMALFI MUSICAL
MASANIELLO ART CAFÈ
SITA BUS STOP (SORRENTO AND SALERNO)
Piazza Flavio Gioia
SITA BUS STOP (RAVELLO AND SCALA)
VIA LUNGOMARE DEI CAVALIERI
TRATTORIA DEI CARTARI
Piazza Spirito Santo
PIZZERIA DONNA STELLA
MILLEUNACERAMICA
JP BOUTIQUE
TAVERNA BUONVICINO
BAZAR FLORIO
L'ARCO ANTICO DI D'ANTUONO
HOTEL FLORIDIANA
DA GEMMA
SEE DETAIL
Amalfi
Piazza Duomo
DUOMO DI AMALFI
IL PORTICCIOLO DI AMALFI
HOTEL LA BUSSOLA
LA MARINELLA
Piazza Flavio Gioia
GRAND HOTEL CONVENTO DI AMALFI
SS163
To Hotel Santa Caterina
LIDO AZZURRO
BOATS AMALFI DA GIOACCHINO
SPIAGGIA DEL PORTO
Amalfi Harbor
HOTEL AURORA
LO SMERALDINO
LIDO DELLE SIRENE
AMALFI NEW SERVICE
© MOON.COM

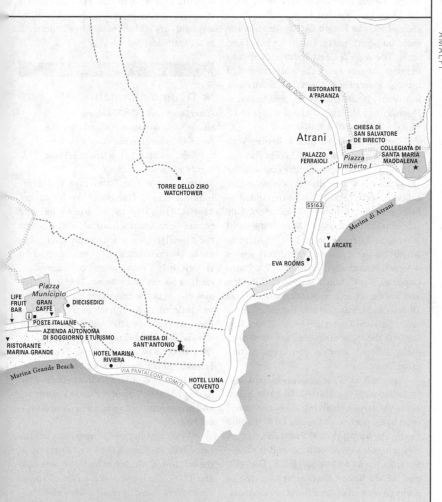

VIA DEI DOGI
RISTORANTE A'PARANZA
Atrani
CHIESA DI SAN SALVATORE DE BIRECTO
PALAZZO FERRAIOLI
Piazza Umberto I
COLLEGIATA DI SANTA MARIA MADDALENA
TORRE DELLO ZIRO WATCHTOWER
SS163
Marina di Atrani
LE ARCATE
EVA ROOMS
Piazza Municipio
LIFE FRUIT BAR
GRAN CAFFÈ
DIECISEDICI
POSTE ITALIANE
AZIENDA AUTONOMA DI SOGGIORNO E TURISMO
RISTORANTE MARINA GRANDE
CHIESA DI SANT'ANTONIO
HOTEL MARINA RIVIERA
Marina Grande Beach
VIA PANTALEONE COMITE
HOTEL LUNA COVENTO
Gulf of Salerno

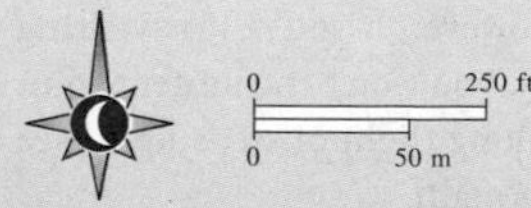

The pier to the east nearest Marina Grande beach is called the **Molo Darsena.** Near the Molo Darsena is a large traffic circle around **Piazza Flavio Gioia,** which is the main transport hub in Amalfi for buses and taxis. The Amalfi Coast Road (SS163) runs through Amalfi along the waterfront and through Piazza Flavio Gioia. Two small roads lead from Piazza Flavio Gioia into the Piazza Duomo, the very heart of Amalfi where you'll find the **Duomo di Amalfi.**

There are three main piazzas in town with the largest being the central Piazza Duomo. Follow the covered passageway opposite the Duomo to find a small, traffic-free square called **Piazza dei Dogi.** It's surrounded by cafés, restaurants, and shops. On the opposite side of town is the quiet **Piazza Municipio** where the *Comune* (town hall) is located. Amalfi has one main street called Via Lorenzo d'Amalfi (and changing names to Via Pietro Capuano, Via Cardinal Marino del Giudice, and Via delle Cartiere) starting from Piazza Duomo and leading far into the valley above town. This main street and Piazza Duomo are the best shopping areas, and are lined with many different kinds of boutiques, restaurants, and cafés.

Many of Amalfi's beaches are located right in town, with the **Marina Grande** beach being the largest. Walking along the waterfront by the port, you'll find the **La Marinella** beach, the **Spiaggia del Porto,** and at the westernmost side of town beyond the Molo Foraneo, the **Le Sirene** beach. The **Duoglio** and **Santa Croce** beaches are located in rocky coves west of Amalfi and are most easily reached by boat.

The waterfront, Piazza Duomo, and main street of Amalfi leading into the valley are all relatively flat by Amalfi Coast standards. If you plan to explore the side streets, which are much quieter, you can expect to find plenty of steps. However, if you're just visiting the main sights, you won't encounter too many, except the long flight of steps up to see the Duomo di Amalfi.

SIGHTS

Amalfi's highly photogenic Piazza Duomo is the place to start exploring town. The other top sights are all located within a short walk of the cathedral.

TOP EXPERIENCE

★ Duomo di Amalfi

Piazza Duomo; tel. 089/871-324; www.museodiocesanoamalfi.it; 9:30am-5:15pm Mar., 9am-6:45pm Apr.-June and Oct., 9am-7:45pm July-Sept., and 10am-3:15pm Nov.-Dec., closed Dec. 25 and Jan. 7-Feb. 28; €3

Sitting atop a grand staircase and overlooking Piazza Duomo, Amalfi's cathedral is dedicated to the town's beloved patron Sant'Andrea Apostolo (St. Andrew the Apostle). Most often simply referred to as the Duomo, meaning the most important church, it is a monumental complex of incredible beauty and interest. This is the religious heart of the city, where the connection to Sant'Andrea dates back to the arrival of the saint's relics in 1208. Before climbing the steps of the church, take a moment to admire the **Fontana di Sant'Andrea** in the Piazza Duomo. This fountain has a central marble statue from 1760 of Sant'Andrea in front of the X-shaped cross (one of the saint's symbols), and surrounded by angels, a siren, and mythical creatures.

While climbing the 57 steps to visit the cathedral, stop along the way to gaze up at the bell tower, which was built between 1180 and 1276. It is topped with a central round tower surrounded by small towers, all featuring interlacing arches and geometric patterns created with yellow and green ceramic tiles. Looking up to the facade of the church, you'll see the black and white striped details, mosaics glimmering in the sun, and prominent arches with white tracery opening to the entrance portico. While the exterior is full of medieval architectural elements, the facade

1: Cloister of Paradise **2:** Duomo di Amalfi

1

2

was not completed until 1891, based on a design by Neapolitan architects Errico Alvino and Guglielmo Raimondi after the earlier baroque facade collapsed during an earthquake in 1861. The current design, which was inspired by details of the 13th-century original, was implemented in a distinctly colorful 19th-century revival fashion.

At the top of the steps in the entry portico, you'll find a set of large bronze doors that date from 1065. In the center are four bronze panels depicting Sant'Andrea, San Pietro, the Virgin Mary, and Christ. On the left side of the portico is the entrance to the **Complesso Monumentale di Sant'Andrea,** which includes the **Cloister of Paradise, Museo Diocesano, Crypt of Sant'Andrea,** and the **Duomo.** The aptly named Cloister of Paradise is a peaceful garden cloister surrounded by 120 columns and intertwined arches. Built between 1266 and 1268, it was once the cemetery for Amalfi's nobility. Around the cloister, you'll find mosaic-inlaid architectural fragments, carved ancient sarcophagi, and frescos dating to the mid-14th century in the style of Giotto.

From the cloister, you'll enter the **Basilica of the Crucifix,** the oldest part of the cathedral complex that dates back to the 6th century. It now houses the **Museo Diocesano,** which displays the most impressive treasures of the Duomo di Amalfi, including reliquaries, chalices, religious paintings and sculptures, and a precious 13th-century miter made of gold, silver, and gems, and covered in tiny pearls. Follow the steps down to the **Crypt** where the relics of Sant'Andrea are held below the altar, topped with a large bronze statue of the saint. The sumptuously decorated crypt includes marble polychrome on the columns and walls, as well as ceiling and wall frescoes. The final stop on the visit to the complex is the grand **nave** of the cathedral, decorated in a baroque style dating from the early 18th century. The elegant gold-paneled ceiling has four large paintings inset into it depicting scenes of the life of Sant'Andrea. The columns are covered with richly detailed marble polychrome work and lead to an altar that features an 18th-century painting of the Sant'Andrea's crucifixion.

If you visit when the Complesso Monumentale di Sant'Andrea is closed in January and February, you can still enter the Duomo, as it is open and free to the public 7:30am-11:30am and 4pm-6:30pm.

Museo della Carta

Via delle Cartiere 23; tel. 089/830-4561; www.museodellacarta.it; 10am-6:30pm daily Mar.-Oct., 10am-4pm Tues.-Sun. Nov.-Jan., closed Feb.; €4

Discover Amalfi's long tradition of papermaking in the town's paper museum, which is located in a 13th-century mill near the top of town. The working mill offers a rare look at how paper was made in Amalfi before industrialization. Even older papermaking equipment is on display inside the mill, and during the guided tour included in the price, you'll learn about ancient and more modern methods of papermaking and get a chance to try your hand at making traditional Amalfi paper. It's fascinating to go inside one of the town's historic mills and learn how Amalfi's famous paper was made for centuries.

Arsenale

Largo Cesareo Console 3; museoarsenaliamalfi@gmail.com; 10am-2pm and 4pm-5:30pm daily; €4

Dating from the 11th century, the Arsenale, where Amalfi's naval fleet and trading ships were constructed, is the only medieval shipyard to have remained nearly intact in all of Italy. Just off Piazza Flavio Gioia, all that is left are two long naves with cross vaults and pointed arches. Today the Arsenale is home to the **Museo della Bussola e del Ducato Marinaro di Amalfi** (Museum of the Compass and Duchy of Amalfi). The museum's collection of historic prints, costumes, compasses, and photos tells the story of Amalfi's naval heritage, and its important role in the development of the compass and early maritime codes.

Chiesa di Sant'Antonio

Via Pantaleone Comite; tel. 089/871-485; curiaamalfi@pddinformatica.it; open during Mass

Just below the Hotel Luna Convento and before Amalfi's watchtower, a long zigzag staircase leads from the Amalfi Coast Road and seems to disappear. At the top of the staircase, you'll find the entrance to the Chiesa di Sant'Antonio, one of Amalfi's larger churches after the Duomo. Once dedicated to San Francesco, it's next to the cloister of San Francesco that is now part of the Hotel Luna Convento. The church was founded in 1220 on the site of an even older church. The original Gothic structure was later covered in the baroque style you see today. Just behind the altar are beautiful baroque wooden chorus stalls dating from 1593. Below in the crypt is an altar with a series of paintings depicting scenes from the life of San Francesco. The church is usually only open during Mass, and the tourist office can provide more details on the schedule.

BEACHES

Amalfi's harbor has several beaches, ranging from the popular Marina Grande beach with its rows of candy-colored umbrellas to beaches tucked away in nearly hidden spots. There are even more options for a more secluded beach day if you head west down the coastline to the small beaches located in rocky coves a short boat ride away.

MARINA GRANDE BEACH

Via Marina Grande

Historic photos show fishing boats lined up along Amalfi's largest beach, which is located just east of Piazza Flavio Gioia and the Molo Darsena. Today the scene is a little different, with the beach's buzz of energy, and colorful umbrellas and sun beds. Much of the beach is lined with restaurants that also offer sun bed and umbrella rental, along with shower and changing room facilities. For a small fee, you can pick out a sun bed and an umbrella in your favorite color and enjoy a comfortable day at the beach. **Tonino O' Beach** (Via Marina Grande; tel. 089/873-364; www.toninobeach.com; Apr.-Oct.; from €10 for sun bed and umbrella) is located on the eastern side of the beach in the best swimming area, and offers sun bed and umbrella rentals, changing rooms, showers, bathrooms, and boat rentals. However, the beach also has two free areas, located at either end of the beach. The most popular with locals is the eastern end of the beach; look for the arches supporting the Amalfi Coast Road as it winds its way out of town and head that way. Though the free beach is quite busy during the summer (that's just part of the scene), the water is gorgeous on this rocky side, especially if you swim out a bit. The water is nicest in the morning, so if you're an early riser head straight to this beach.

LA MARINELLA

Via Lungomare dei Cavalieri

Stroll along the harbor and just beyond Molo Pennello, you'll spot this minuscule beach with transparent water. Part of the **La Marinella** restaurant, this beach is only accessible via the *stabilimente balneare* (tel. 089/871-043; www.lamarinella.net; Apr.-Oct.; €10 per person). Though the beach area is limited, a platform for sunbathing is constructed during the summer months. There are steps down from the platform to the sea, and it's a good spot for families with young children because the beach has small pebbles and easy access to calm water.

SPIAGGIA DEL PORTO

Via Lungomare dei Cavalieri

Often just called the *porto* (port), this beach is along the waterfront of the harbor, with floating docks and boats moored nearby. Because there aren't any beach club services here (although there is a shower to rinse off), it's truly a local beach. The view of the harbor with boats puttering to and fro is a relaxing sight while sunbathing. The swimming area is somewhat limited, but it's refreshing for a dip in the sea.

LE SIRENE

Piazzale dei Protontini 4

Located on the western edge of Amalfi just outside the port, this is a beautiful, rocky beach with clear water for swimming and nice light well into the afternoon. The beach is private and accessible only via the **Lido delle Sirene** restaurant and beach club (tel. 089/871-756; daily Apr.-Oct.; €25 for beach entrance, two sun beds, and umbrella) where you can rent sun beds and umbrellas, and use the shower and changing room facilities. Given its setting only a short stroll from the busy center of Amalfi, this is a good option for a quieter day at the beach.

DUOGLIO

Spiaggia Duoglio

Along the rocky coastline west of Amalfi you'll find this small beach with restaurants and *stabilimenti balneari* that are built during the summer season, leaving two small areas on either end of the beach as free swimming areas. The beach is accessible via steps down from the Amalfi Coast Road, but note that the road climbs high along the coastline west of Amalfi, so to walk there you'll need to go down 400 steps to reach the beach, starting from a small stone gate just east of the intersection for SS363. (The gate is usually open 8am-7pm during the summer season, but not always.) However, the best way to reach the beach is by boat service.

For a small fee you can take the Duoglio beach service boat run by the **Gruppo Battellieri Costa d'Amalfi** (www.gruppobattellieriamalfi.com; June-Sept.; about every 30 minutes 9am-5:30pm; €4 round-trip per person) from the Molo Pennello in Amalfi. Or, if you're planning to visit one of the restaurants that offers sun bed and umbrella rental, which is the best option at this rocky beach, then you can take a free boat shuttle service from Molo Darsena. **Lido degli Artisti** (tel. 331/996-5635; www.lidodegliartisti.it; daily May-Oct.; €15) is a great choice with a boat every 30 minutes from 9am until sunset. A reservation for the boat service and beach is recommended. Round-trip boat service plus umbrella and sun bed is €15 per person.

SANTA CROCE

Spiaggia di Santa Croce

Not far west of Duoglio is one of the Amalfi Coast's most beautiful beaches. Set beneath a sheer cliff and surrounded by large rocks, this beach has stunning water and lots of beautiful natural spots to explore. Because a storm damaged the steps leading to the beach in 2011, the only way to access this beach is by boat. There are two restaurants that offer *stabilimente balneare* services and free boat service from Amalfi for clients from the Molo Darsena. Look for the small boats marked **Da Teresa** (www.ristorantedateresa.com; late Apr.-Oct.; sun bed and umbrella rental €25 per person) or **Santa Croce** (www.ristorantesantacroce.it; Apr.-Oct.). The secluded atmosphere and rocky setting make it the ideal choice for a relaxing day by the sea. If you're a good swimmer, you can swim along the coastline a short distance to the *arco naturale,* a natural arch that is also called the Lover's Arch.

SPORTS AND RECREATION

Hiking

TOP EXPERIENCE

VALLE DELLE FERRIERE

Via Paradiso (follow to top of valley)

To immerse yourself in the natural beauty of the Amalfi Coast, hike into the valley above Amalfi, where you'll find ruins of old mills, a cool mountain stream, and a surprisingly tropical landscape with waterfalls, wild orchids and cyclamen, and even a rare prehistoric fern called *Woodwardia radicans.* This area is sometimes called the Valle delle Ferriere and sometimes the Valle dei Mulini; both names refer to the ironwork factories

1: Le Sirene at the Lido delle Sirene **2:** Marina Grande Beach

1

2

and paper mills that once lined the valley and were powered by the Canneto stream. At the top of Amalfi beyond the Museo della Carta, look for the signs indicating Valle delle Ferriere and continue along Via Paradiso past terraces of lemons until it turns into a dirt pathway. The walk follows the Canneto and passes by the town's former industrial area, where you'll see ruins of old paper mills, some nearly covered in natural growth. Near the top you'll find an impressive area with waterfalls. Stop and dip your toes in the water, which is cold even in the peak of summer. The walk is a little more than 3 miles (5 km) and takes about 2.5 hours round-trip.

There are nice areas to stop for a picnic alongside the mountain stream. Or take a break at **Agricola Fore Porta** (Via Paradiso 22; tel. 339/243-6450; www.agriturismoamalfi.it; open 10am-6pm Wed.-Mon. from Easter-Dec., often closed Tuesdays), an *agriturismo* nestled into the valley along the hiking pathway about 25 minutes from Amalfi. Set in a rustic farm building, they offer a menu of only freshly made drinks and traditional dishes made with organic ingredients from their gardens.

Water Sports

LIDO DEGLI ARTISTI BEACH CLUB

Spiaggia Duoglio; tel. 331/996-5635; www.lidodegliartisti.it; May-Oct.; windsurfing rentals €18 per hour, €45 per day

Head to the tiny and very rocky Duoglio beach west of Amalfi to find the Lido degli Artisti Beach Club, which offers a windsurf school, stand-up paddleboard rentals, water skiing, and more. Windsurfing lessons are available for all ages, with a 4-day course (1 hour 30 minutes each day) starting at €180 per person. Contact to book lessons in advance. The *stabilimento balneare* also offers sun bed rentals and a restaurant for a comfortable full day at the beach.

Boat and Kayak Tours

AMALFI KAYAK

Spiaggia Duoglio, Via Mauro Comite 41; tel. 338/362-9520; www.amalfikayak.com; Apr.- Oct.; from €49 per person

For active travelers, a kayak tour is one of the best ways to experience the natural beauty of the Amalfi Coast. Amalfi Kayak offers multiple half-day and full-day excursions, where expert local guides show you the best spots along the coast. The most popular is the half-day tour from Amalfi to the Fiordo di Furore, where you'll see the beautiful coastline including the Lover's Arch near Santa Croce beach, glide by the villa where Sophia Loren once lived, and view the Fiordo di Furore up close.

During the summer months from June to September, excursions depart from the Spiaggia Duoglio beach, and during the shoulder season from April to May and October, excursions depart from the Le Sirene beach in Amalfi. Only guided tours are available, and all equipment is included in the price.

BOATS AMALFI DA GIOACCHINO

Via Lungomare dei Cavalieri 286; tel. 338/264-0895; www.boatsamalfi.it; Apr.-Oct.; from €150

Started by Amalfi local Giacchino Esposito, who left his career as a chef to be closer to the sea, this friendly family-run operation offers boat rentals and excursions with and without a captain. For independent travelers, rent a traditional wooden boat or small motor boat without the need for a nautical license and spend a day exploring the coastline. Larger boats and yachts with captain are also available for private tours along the Amalfi Coast or to Capri. Though the main season is from April to October, Gioacchino usually has boats in the water year-round. You never know when a beautiful winter day might call you out for a day on the sea.

Local Tours

AMALFI LEMON EXPERIENCE

Via delle Cartiere; tel. 089/873-211; www.amalfilemonexperience.it; 10am Mon.-Sat. Mar.-Oct.; from €25 per person

The lemon and Amalfi have been inextricably connected for centuries. There's no better way to experience this firsthand than to walk among Amalfi's historic lemon groves as you learn about the cultivation of this very special product. Since 1825, six generations of the Aceto family have been growing lemons on the steep slopes of the Amalfi Coast for six generations. The family is passionate about maintaining traditional techniques, from the dry stone wall construction that creates the garden terraces to the details of running an organic farm. A daily group tour offers the chance to meander through the Aceto family's lemon gardens, enjoy a taste of their lemon products, and visit the family's **Museum of Rural Life Arts and Crafts,** a fascinating collection of historic pieces from Amalfi's past. The final touch is a visit to the production lab, where the Acetos transform their lemons into *limoncello* and other traditional products. Book your spot for the lemon tour in advance, or private tours and experiences can also be arranged, such as a sweet Honey Lemon Experience and Tour that showcases the honey made in the lemon grove, as well as wine tastings, and cooking classes that, of course, highlight the lemon!

ENTERTAINMENT AND EVENTS

Amalfi's scenic setting and the beautiful Piazza Duomo make for a stellar backdrop for concerts, fashion shows, and seasonal events. Concerts and events take place throughout the year, but are often not promoted very extensively or far in advance, so stop in the tourist office in Amalfi to find out about upcoming programs.

However, you can count on Amalfi coming to life during several annual religious festivals, when the town becomes the setting for elaborate processions and spectacular fireworks displays from the sea. Each year is capped off by the biggest fireworks show of the year for Capodanno (New Year's Eve), which makes Amalfi the most popular location on the coast to celebrate. Whenever you visit, be sure to check the calendar for festivals, as they will give you an extraordinary experience.

Nightlife

AMALFI MUSICAL

Largo Cesareo Console 3; tel. 334/9177814; www.amalfimusical.it; 8pm Wed. and Sat. May-Oct.; €15-30

The historic arsenal of Amalfi is the evocative setting for the Amalfi Musical, a moving and entertaining performance inspired by the history of Amalfi. It brings together key moments of the town's fascinating history with stories of passion and war, and it is a unique way to see Amalfi's past brought to life. Subtitles are provided in English as well as French, German, Spanish, and Japanese. The show is 80 minutes long without intermisison.

MASANIELLO ART CAFÈ

Largo Cesareo Console 7; tel. 089/871-929; info@masanielloartcafe.it; 9am-3am, closed Mon. for lunch Feb.-Mar.; €8-12

If you're looking for the nightlife scene in Amalfi, this is the place. Although it's a popular spot during the day for drinks and for the best hamburger (yes you read that right) in Amalfi, the Masaniello Art Café really comes to life after dark. The cocktails are on point, and if you're a gin fan, don't miss trying their house-made version. Locally produced beers are also on the menu. Live music and events are scheduled throughout the year. This is the go-to spot for the younger crowd in Amalfi, and in a town that can feel somewhat touristy, it offers a refreshingly local experience.

Festivals and Events

EASTER IN AMALFI

Piazza Duomo and various locations; Holy Week and Easter Sunday

Easter is one of the biggest holidays in Italy,

with events taking place throughout the week leading up to Easter Sunday. Many towns along the coastline have Good Friday and Via Crucis (Stations of the Cross) processions through town, and Amalfi is one of the most impressive locations on the coast to experience the Easter holiday. The Via Crucis often takes place on Holy Thursday and meanders through the streets of the town, retelling the story of the crucifixion of Christ. The procession on Good Friday, representing the funeral and burial of Christ, is one of the most moving on the Amalfi Coast. After dark, the lights are turned off in Piazza Duomo, and a candlelit procession starts from the Duomo and moves down the steps and through the town. The procession is accompanied by haunting choral music and masked figures carrying the statue of Christ after being taken down from the cross, followed by a statue of the Madonna Addolorata (Virgin Mary in mourning).

Easter Sunday is a joyous day in Amalfi and is followed by Pasquetta (little Easter), which is a day traditionally spent outdoors and with family and friends. The Easter holiday is the unofficial start of the tourist season on the Amalfi Coast, and it's often very busy with traffic and visitors.

FESTIVAL OF SANT'ANTONIO

Chiesa di Sant'Antonio and various locations; June 13

The summer season gets off to a festive start thanks to the procession and celebrations in honor of Sant'Antonio (St. Anthony) on June 13. Both Amalfi and Atrani honor this saint because the Chiesa di Sant'Antonio is located not far from the tunnel that leads to Atrani. The procession is one of the most unique on the Amalfi Coast and takes places on both land and sea. It starts from the Chiesa di Sant'Antonio and follows the Amalfi Coast Road to Atrani, where it descends through town to the beach. From the beach, the statue of Sant'Antonio is carefully loaded onto a small boat. Then every member of the procession—marching band included—boards small boats that continue in a water procession to Amalfi, where they all disembark and continue on land to the Duomo di Amalfi. There's a festive atmosphere to the celebrations, including a fireworks display over the harbor after dark.

★ FESTIVAL OF SANT'ANDREA

Piazza Duomo and various locations; June 27 and Nov. 30

Twice a year Amalfi honors its patron Sant'Andrea (St. Andrew) with a grand religious festival that is one of the biggest and most popular of the year on the Amalfi Coast. Celebrations take place June 27 to remember the time Sant'Andrea is said to have heeded the prayers of the town's faithful in 1544, and protected Amalfi from a pirate attack by bringing on a sea storm so intense that it destroyed the invading ships. The November 30 celebration marks the traditional festival day honoring Sant'Andrea.

On both days, after a special Mass, a large 18th-century silver-and-gold statue of Sant'Andrea is taken down the long staircase of the Duomo and carried throughout Amalfi. The statue is even carried down to the beach where boats gather in the harbor for a blessing. The grand finale has to be seen to be believed: The large group of men carrying the statue pause at the bottom of the Duomo's 57 steps before running the statue back to the top. Once they reach the top, the piazza packed full of people bursts into applause as Sant'Andrea returns safely home.

The festive atmosphere continues with music in Piazza Duomo and a spectacular fireworks display over the harbor after dark. The two events honoring St. Andrew are similar to each other, though the summer festival usually comes with excellent weather and summertime vibes. In June, the procession begins after evening Mass, and in November it starts after a mid-morning Mass. This centuries-old festival offers a wonderful glimspe into the religious traditions of Amalfi.

1: A procession carrying the statue of Sant'Andrea descends the steps of the Duomo. **2:** lemons growing around Amalfi **3:** hiking down to Amalfi **4:** Consider renting a scooter for the day.

1
2
3
4

Historical Regatta of the Ancient Maritime Republics

Amalfi celebrates its rich heritage and the medieval splendor of the Duchy of Amalfi each year at the Regatta of the Ancient Maritime Republics (Regata delle Antiche Repubbliche Marinare). This festival brings together the four powerful maritime republics of Italy from the Middle Ages—Amalfi, Pisa, Genoa, and Venice—in a rowing contest and historical parade. Conceived in the 1940s, the first event was held in 1955, and since then has been held annually. Each city takes turns holding the regatta, which rotates each year and arrives in Amalfi every four years, usually taking place on the first Sunday in June. If your visit happens to coincide with the regatta in Amalfi (the next chance is in 2020), you are in for a very special experience.

PARADE

The Regatta of the Ancient Maritime Republics begins with a historical parade that starts from Atrani and follows the Amalfi Coast Road into Amalfi. The procession arrives in Piazza Duomo and then climbs the steps to the Duomo, which is a grand sight to see. Each of the four cities is represented in the parade with figures representing an important moment in history. For Amalfi, the period highlighted is the apex of the Duchy of Amalfi around the 10th century with rich costumes made of silk, brocade, damask, and linen. Locals from Amalfi dress as all types of historical figures for the parade, from sailors and rowers to knights, magistrates, judges, and the Duke of Amalfi. The theme for Amalfi's parade is the celebration of the marriage of the Duke's son to a noblewoman. Each town is accompanied by a band and some include flag throwers.

REGATTA

After the parade, all eyes turn to the sea for the regatta. Each city has a team of eight rowers and a helmsman who compete in wooden galleys styled after 12th-century boat designs. It's easy to spot Amalfi's team with its boat painted the traditional blue color of the Republic of Amalfi. Pisa's boat is red, Genoa's is white, and Venice's is green. The course of the regatta is 1.2 miles (2,000 m) long and begins near Cape Vettica west of Amalfi with the finish in front of the Marina Grande beach in the center of town. Amalfi has had spectacular come-from-behind wins the last two times it has hosted the regatta in 2012 and 2016. While a hometown win adds even more to the festivities, the Regatta of the Ancient Maritime Republics is always a fun celebration in Amalfi.

BYZANTINE NEW YEAR

Piazza Duomo and various locations Aug. 31-Sept 1

During the Middle Ages, the first of September was the start of the legal and fiscal new year, according to the calendar of the Byzantine Empire. Given Amalfi's strong ties to that part of the world, that date was used to appoint their elected officials with an elaborate ceremony. This cultural event is celebrated today with a historical procession including more than 100 people dressed in costumes of the former Republic of Amalfi. The event includes selecting a local Amalfitan to represent the Magister di Civiltà Amalfitana in a ceremony at the Chiesa di San Salvatore de Birecto in Atrani, followed by a procession to the Duomo in Amalfi. It is a fascinating event that is even more elaborate than the historical parade during the Regatta of the Ancient Maritime Republics that takes place in Amalfi every four years.

SHOPPING

Amalfi has a wonderful array of shops, mostly centered around Piazza Duomo and the main street leading from the piazza up into the valley and through the center of town. Here you'll find plenty of opportunities to discover the Amalfi Coast's traditional crafts and products, such as handmade paper, *limoncello* and lemon-themed items, ceramics, and clothing. Shops in Amalfi rarely close for lunch between Easter and October. During the winter months, and especially from January to February, some shops close midday for a break, on select days during the week, or for an extended holiday. The majority of the shops featured below are open year-round, with exceptions noted.

Gifts and Clothing

JP BOUTIQUE

Via Pietro Capuano 12; tel. 329/371-8648; wind592@hotmail.com; 10:30am-8pm daily

This friendly shop has a unique and refreshing selection of clothing, canvas and jute bags, and gifts. Many items are decorated with the hand-drawn designs by the young owner Gianpiero (JP for short) that include fun sayings in Italian, Amalfi-inspired patterns with anchors, and a simple yet classic pattern with fish.

CONTEMPORARY SHOP

Piazza dei Dogi 35; tel. 335/121-9319; hi@officinezephiro.com; 10am-9:30pm daily Apr.-early Nov., open until 10:30pm Aug.-Sept.

A surprisingly large and tempting selection of clothing, jewelry, accessories, and ceramics are on display in this tiny shop tucked away on a corner of Piazza dei Dogi. There's also a nice selection of books on the area, as well as detailed maps for the hiking paths along the Amalfi Coast.

Accessories

GIOIELLERIA ANTONIO ESPOSITO

Via Lorenzo d'Amalfi 12; tel. 089/871-088; avvesp@tiscali.it; 9am-10pm daily Apr.-Oct., and 9am-1pm and 3pm-8pm (closed Sun. evening and Fri.) Nov.-Mar.

Just steps from Piazza Duomo you'll find this beautiful jewelry store that has been family-run for four generations. They have a large selection of silver and gold jewelry along with traditional coral and cameo pieces, charms, crosses, and men's jewelry. The pieces inspired by the Tarì, the currency of Republic of Amalfi during the Middle Ages, make unique souvenirs or gifts. Necklaces, bracelets, and charms are available with the Tari design in gold and silver.

BAZAR FLORIO

Via Pietro Capuano 5-7; tel. 089/871-980; www.amalfibazar.com; 8:30am-10pm daily

This is the place to find a large selection of beautiful Italian leather bags and accessories of all shapes, sizes, and colors. The owners stock their own production line of bags as well as notable brands from around Italy. Need a purse to match those sandals you had custom-made in Positano or Capri? Stop in here and you'll find something tempting to bring home.

Paper

★ LA SCUDERIA DEL DUCA

Largo Cesareo Console 8; tel. 089/872-976; www.carta-amalfi.com; 10am-7pm daily Apr.-Oct., 10am-6pm closed Sunday Nov.-Mar.

Situated near the ancient arsenals where Amalfi's ships were built in the Middle Ages, this treasure trove of a shop offers an incredible selection of paper products, stationery, and prints, all created with paper handmade in Amalfi. They also have an intriguing selection of artwork, ceramics, and antiques. The store specializes in bookbinding as well, and has a great choice of journals and notebooks made with Amalfi's handmade paper.

L'ARCO ANTICO DI D'ANTUONO

Via Pietro Capuano 4; tel. 089/873-6354; www.cartadamalfi.it; 9:30am-9:30pm daily, until 11pm in Aug., closed Feb.

Follow Amalfi's main street from Piazza Duomo up into the valley, and along the way you'll find this small yet well-stocked store selling paper products handmade in Amalfi. Stationery sets, cards, and handbound journals are great choices here. They also have a good selection of books, pens, and gifts.

Ceramics

★ MILLEUNACERAMICA

Via Pietro Capuano 36; tel. 089/872-670; www.milleunaceramica.com; 9am-9pm daily Apr.-May, until 11pm June-Sept., until 8pm in Oct., winter months open with limited hours

A love for the Amalfi Coast's ceramic traditions shines through in the handpicked collections on display in this colorful ceramic shop. Owner and ceramics enthusiast Maria Anastasio works only with local artists in the Amalfi Coast area, and many pieces are custom-made for Milleunaceramica. This is a unique opportunity to support artists, mostly quite young, who are keeping alive the important ceramic-making tradition on the Amalfi Coast.

Specialty Foods

CIOCCOLATO ANDREA PANSA

Via Lorenzo d'Amalfi 9; tel. 089/873-282; www.andreapansa.it; 7:30am-11pm daily, until 1am June-Sept., closed Jan. 7-Feb. 3

If you love chocolate or have chocolate enthusiasts on your shopping list, this is the place for you. All of the products are handmade in the Pansa chocolate workshop in Piazza Municipio, using local or high-quality sourced ingredients. Try the chocolate with lemon, or the candied lemon and orange rinds dipped in chocolate. The citrus is grown on the Pansa family property called Villa Paradiso, located in the valley above Amalfi.

LA VALLE DEI MULINI

Via Lorenzo d'Amalfi 11; tel. 089/872-603; www.amalfilemon.it; 9:30am-8:30pm daily, until 11pm spring-summer, closed January 10-31

Stepping into this shop feels like you've arrived in lemon heaven. All of the *limoncello* and liqueurs are made in Amalfi in the family's laboratory at the top of the town in the Valle dei Mulini. The lemons are grown on the family's organic farm, so it doesn't get more local than this. They also have a lovely selection of local products, candies, and food specialties.

FOOD

Dining along the waterfront in Amalfi, with its beautiful harbor setting, is a memorable experience. However, don't miss the chance to explore the side streets and little piazzas in the heart of town for other unique dining choices. You'll find plenty of eateries around Piazza Duomo for a quick break or *aperitivo* with a view. Reservations are recommended, especially at the seaside restaurants to ensure you get a great table with a view.

Seafood

DA GEMMA

Via Fra Gerardo Sasso 11; tel. 089/871-345; www.trattoriadagemma.com; noon-3pm and 7pm-11pm, closed Wed. mid-Nov.-mid-Mar.; €16-28

Dating back to 1872, this is one of Amalfi's historic restaurants and it's a popular choice. The dining area also includes a terrace with views overlooking the Piazza Duomo nearby. Seafood is served brilliantly here, and the risotto with red prawns and the *zuppa di pesce* (fish soup) are excellent choices. Tasting menus are also available. Reservations are recommended.

LIDO AZZURRO

Via Lungomare dei Cavalieri 5; tel. 089/871-384; www.ristorantelidoazzurro.it; 12:30pm-3pm and 7pm-10:30pm, closed Jan. 10-end of Feb.; €15-28

With a beautiful little terrace right on the harbor of Amalfi, this restaurant is a picturesque spot for lunch or dinner. The menu is focused on local ingredients, and given the setting, seafood is naturally a specialty. Yet there's something for all tastes, with especially tempting risotto and pasta dishes. Reservations are recommended, especially for one of the coveted tables right around the edge of the terrace by the sea.

Regional Cuisine

TRATTORIA DA MARIA

Via Lorenzo D'Amalfi 14; tel. 089/871-880; www.amalfitrattoriadamaria.com; noon-3:30pm and 5:30pm-11pm daily; €12-22

For authentic home cooking and excellent wood-fire oven pizzas, head to this friendly trattoria and pizzeria just off Piazza Duomo. You truly can't go wrong here, whether you choose pizza or the seasonal pasta options like spaghetti with zucchini or fresh clams and mussels in the summer. The fried *alici* (anchovies) are a local specialty that should be experienced in Amalfi. Ask for whatever *verdure* is in season to experience the local ways of cooking fresh veggies. The comfortable air-conditioned dining room is great for hot summer days.

★ RISTORANTE MARINA GRANDE

Viale della Regione 4; 089/871-129; www.ristorantemarinagrande.com; noon-3pm and 6:30-10pm Wed.-Mon. mid-Apr.-mid-Nov.; €14-26

Enjoy the view overlooking Amalfi's main beach while dining at Marina Grande. The seasonal menu highlights regional specialties served with a creative flair, and is well balanced with seafood and meat choices. Try the *baccalà fritto* (fried salted cod) or smoked provola cheese grilled on lemon leaves to start. The spaghetti with three types of locally grown tomatoes and basil pesto is simplicity at its best, thanks to the locally sourced ingredients, such as Gentile pasta produced in the hills above Sorrento. This casually elegant restaurant also offers beach service with comfortable lounge chairs just steps from the sea.

TRATTORIA DEI CARTARI

Piazza dello Spirito Santo 5; tel. 089/872-131; societto.amalfi@alice.it; noon-3pm and 7pm-10pm; €15-25

Follow Amalfi's main street up to the Piazza dello Spirito Santo, and opposite the fountain you'll spot this small trattoria with an umbrella-covered outdoor dining terrace and small yet inviting indoor seating area. The Amalfi-style seasonal pasta dishes here are top-notch and very traditional. Try the *genovese,* a rich and tasty sauce made with meat and onions. Despite the name, this dish is local to the Naples and Amalfi Coast area.

LO SMERALDINO

Piazzale dei Protontini 1; tel. 089/871-070; www.ristorantelosmeraldino.it; 11:45am-3pm and 6:45pm-11:15pm daily July-Aug., closed Wed. other months, closed Jan.-Feb.; €13-27

A classic option right on the waterfront in Amalfi, this restaurant and pizzeria has a large indoor dining area and terrace with a gorgeous view of Amalfi's harbor. The pizza cooked in a wood-fire oven is outstanding, and the *pappardelle all' astice* (wide tagliatelle pasta with lobster) and grilled fresh fish are equally tempting. For diners who don't care for seafood, the steak and lamb are also excellent.

TAVERNA BUONVICINO

Largo Santa Maria Maggiore 1; tel. 089/873-6385; www.tavernabuonvicino.it; 12:30pm-2:30pm and 6:30pm-10:30pm daily Apr.-Oct., 12:30pm-2:30pm and 6:30pm-10:30pm Tues.-Sat. and 12:30pm-2:30pm Sun. Nov.-Mar.; €12-23

Set on a tiny piazza under the bell tower of the Santa Maria Maggiore church, this taverna is a great restaurant choice for excellent home cooking in a tranquil setting. Try the *pappardelle con crostacei e sfusato Amalfitano* (thick pasta noodles with shellfish and local Amalfi lemon), a house specialty that highlights the fresh flavors of Amalfi. Save room for the house-made artisan desserts. Afterward, stroll through the side streets and catch a glimpse of the quieter side of Amalfi.

RISTORANTE LA CARAVELLA

Via Matteo Camera 12; tel. 089/871-029; www.ristorantelacaravella.it; noon-2:30pm and 7pm-11pm, closed Tuesdays mid-Nov.-Christmas and Jan. 10-Feb. 10; lunch tasting menu €50 per person (minimum two people), dinner tasting menu €90-135 per person

This gem of a restaurant is not only Amalfi's only Michelin-starred restauarant, but also it's the first southern Italian restaurant to have held that honor. Amalfi born and raised, chef Antonio Dipino is a proud custodian of tradition in many beautiful forms. The restaurant itself is situated in a building that dates to the 1100s and once belonged to the Piccolomini Family, early Dukes of Amalfi. Inside the restaurant and a nearby art gallery is housed the finest collection of local ceramics on the Amalfi Coast. Foodwise, the tasting menus change seasonally, but the *Tubettoni di Gragnano con ragù di pesce* (Pasta from Gragnano with a ragout of fish) is an exceptional first course followed by locally caught *pezzogna* fish stewed with Greco di Tufo wine, fennel, sun dried tomatoes, and fresh mint.

Il Sole nel Piatto (The Sun in the Dish), the restaurant's lemon soufflè, deserves a special mention. For wine enthusiasts, the Enoteca offers a remarkable selection. Reservations are highly recommended.

Pizzeria

PIZZERIA DONNA STELLA

Via Salita d'Ancora 4; tel. 338-358-8483; donna.stella@alice.it; noon-3:30pm and 7pm-10:30pm Wed.-Mon. Apr.-Oct., dinner only Nov.-Mar.; €7-14

If eating pizza fresh from the wood-fire oven under a lemon tree pergola sounds just right, then you'll enjoy this pizzeria. A small indoor dining area is available during inclement weather. There are plenty of options for different pizzas, with lots of fresh toppings to try. The specialty is Pizza Annabella, prepared with mozzarella and *ricotta di bufala*, black olives, and arugula. Appetizers, seasonable vegetables, and a selection of pasta and main course dishes are also available.

Bakeries and Cafés

★ PASTICCERIA PANSA

Piazza Duomo 40; tel. 089/871-065; www.pasticceriapansa.it; 7:30am-11pm, until 1am June-Sept., closed Jan. 7-Feb. 3; pastries from €2-3.50

Since 1830, this bakery has been a fixture in Amalfi right on Piazza Duomo. The fifth generation of the Pansa family proudly runs the family bakery and they have made it one of the most popular in the area for pastries, traditional Christmas and Easter desserts, and chocolates. The candied lemon and citrus peels start in the family's property above Amalfi and are transformed into delicious sweets. Try the *sfogliatelle* (shell-shaped pastry), *delizia al limone* (lemon cake), or any of the sweets on display. You truly can't go wrong!

GRAN CAFFÈ

Corso delle Repubbliche Marinare 37/38; tel. 089/871-047; www.bargrancaffeamalfi.it; 7:30am-1am Tues.-Sun. Oct.-Jan., Mar.-July, daily Aug.-Sept.; €5-10

Open all day with an outdoor dining area overlooking Marina Grande beach, this is a popular spot with locals and travelers for everything from a morning espresso or cappuccino to a light lunch or an *aperitivo* as the sun sets. During the summer months the lively atmosphere continues until late. The *bruschette* and salads are particularly good and fresh, but they also offer pizzas and daily specials for those who want something more substantial. There's an extensive drink menu, but you can't go wrong with a classic *spritz* or their unique version with *limoncello.*

LIFE FRUIT BAR

Largo Scario 6; tel. 089/871-611; lifeamalfi@outlook.it; 7am-2am daily, closes at 10pm in winter; €2-8

Set in a charming little piazza across the Amalfi Coast Road from the Marina Grande beach, this is a great spot for a fresh and healthy break. Excellent for espresso or cappuccino, the bar also serves fruit, yogurt, smoothies, and fresh-pressed juice.

ACCOMMODATIONS

Amalfi offers a large range of accomodations, from small B&Bs to extraordinary five-star hotels with that family-run touch that is a inviting characteristic of luxury on the Amalfi Coast. If you're looking for a unique experience, consider a stay in one of Amalfi's two former monasteries that have been transformed into lovely hotels with incredible views overlooking the harbor.

€100-200

HOTEL LIDOMARE

Largo Piccolomini 9; tel. 089/871-332; www.lidomare.it; €145 d

This family-run hotel is situated in a historic palazzo dating back to the 1400s that was once the home of the wealthy Piccolomini family. Situated on a quiet piazza near Piazza Duomo, the palazzo offers 18 rooms, 9 of which include balconies with sea views, and are large

---

1: Soak up the Amalfi atmosphere at the outdoor seating of the Gran Caffè. **2:** swimming pool by the sea at the Hotel Santa Caterina

1

2

and decorated with colorful ceramic tiles and antique touches. Also interesting is the well preserved kitchen with its antique wood-burning stove and ceramic tiles from Vietri sul Mare. The hotel is open year-round, so it's a great option for off-season stays, too.

HOTEL FLORIDIANA

Salita Brancia 1; tel. 089/873-6373; www.hotelfloridiana.it; open Apr.-Oct.; €150 d

Situated right in the center of Amalfi, this hotel is wonderful choice for easy access and beautiful rooms. The 12th-century palazzo includes beautiful features like a salon from the 1700s with lavish decor and a sumptuously frescoed ceiling. The 13 rooms vary in style from standard rooms to junior suites with Jacuzzi tubs. Parking is available at no extra charge.

IL PORTICCIOLO DI AMALFI

Via Annuziatella 38; tel. 089/873-096; www.amalfiporticciolo.it; open mid-Mar.-mid-Nov.; €190 d

Set in the upper part of town with a sweeping view over the harbor, this welcoming B&B offers an authentic Amalfi stay in its five simply decorated, comfortable rooms. Breakfast can be served on the large terrace with panoramic views or delivered to your room. The terrace can be enjoyed any time of the day and is a lovely spot for evening cocktails. Note that the B&B is only accessible via a long and steep staircase from the center of Amalfi or from an easier, yet still inclined, 10-minute walk along the road followed by steps. However, once at the B&B you are rewarded with a peaceful setting.

€200-300

HOTEL AURORA

Piazzale dei Protontini 7; tel. 089/871-209; www.aurora-hotel.it; open Apr.-Oct.; €219 d

Well situated in a quiet spot overlooking a rocky beach and Amalfi's harbor, this family-run hotel has 28 spacious rooms with sea views, some with large terraces that are perfect for sunbathing. You can also take advantage of the hotel's private beach access nearby. Service is very friendly, and breakfast is served on a bougainvillea-covered terrace with fine views. Three fully equipped apartment rentals are also available in the center of Amalfi and start at €180 per day (3-night minimum).

HOTEL LA BUSSOLA

Via Lungomare dei Cavalieri 16; tel. 089/871-533; www.labussolahotel.it; open mid-Mar.-mid-Nov. and for New Year's Eve; €250 d

With a great central location overlooking the harbor, this hotel offers a welcoming stay. Located in what was once a pasta factory (how Italian!), the 50 rooms vary from mountain-view rooms to those with partial or side sea views to full sea-view rooms with lovely balconies. The large terrace and solarium is a great spot to soak up the sun. Hotel staff are dedicated to making guests feel welcome and sharing ideas for the best things to see and do in the area.

HOTEL RESIDENCE

Via delle Repubbliche Marinare 9; tel. 089/871-183; www.residencehotel-amalfi.it; open from Apr.-Dec.; €285 d

It doesn't get more central than this hotel located right on Piazza Flavio Gioia, opposite Marina Grande beach. Set in a noble palace from the 18th century, the 27 rooms are well appointed and decorated with a designer's eye for color and detail. Rooms feature balconies or terraces with sea or Piazza Duomo views. The indoor dining area and small outdoor dining terrace are equally lovely.

DIECISEDICI

Piazza Municipio 13; tel. 089/872-737; www.diecisedici.com; open early Mar.-early Nov. and for New Year's Eve; €290 d

You'll find this B&B on a quiet piazza behind the Duomo. It has easy access to the Marina Grande beach and six rooms, four of which feature beautiful sleeping loft areas and two that are situated on an upper level with a glimpse of the sea. The ceramic floors are striking, and the decor is modern. Minimum stay requirements vary, depending on the season. There's no elevator, but the accommodations are located on the 2nd or 3rd floors and well worth the climb.

Over €300

HOTEL LUNA CONVENTO

Via Pantaleone Comite 33; tel. 089/871-002; www.lunahotel.it; open Mar.-Dec.; €320 d

One of Amalfi's most romantic spots, the Hotel Luna Convento is situated in a former monastery that dates back to 1200s and is located near the seaside watchtower at the eastern edge of town. Inside, there's a peaceful cloister that transports you back in time. All of the rooms feature sea views, and each one has its own unique style thanks to the historic nature of the building. The hotel also owns the **Torre Saracena** restaurant across the street, offering the chance to dine with incredible views. Below the watchtower, down a meandering staircase of about 80 steps, you'll find a saltwater pool and sunbathing terrace with access to the sea and splendid views of Atrani.

HOTEL MARINA RIVIERA

Via Pantaleone Comite 19; tel. 089/871-104; www.marinariviera.it; open two weeks before Easter-early Nov.; €465 d

Offering a beautiful view overlooking Amalfi's Marina Grande beach, this boutique hotel offers 35 rooms with sea views. Accommodations vary from standard to deluxe rooms and suites with balconies. The hotel's rooms are all unique and well appointed, and the corridor connecting the rooms was excavated from the mountainside. The solarium and pool are perfect for enjoying the sunshine and views, away from the crowds.

GRAND HOTEL CONVENTO DI AMALFI

Via Annunziatella 46; tel. 089/873-6711; www.ghconventodiamalfi.com; open Apr.-early Jan.; €700 d

This remarkable hotel is situated in a 13th-century Cappuchin monastery that has been completely transformed into a five-star hotel, while retaining the peaceful atmosphere and incredible architectural details of the original building, including the stunning cloister and church of San Francesco. Set more than 260 feet (80 m) above the sea, with an elevator from the Amalfi Coast Road for easy access, this property offers spectacular views that are beautifully framed by the terraced lemon gardens and the Monks' Walk with bougainvillea-covered columns. The hotel's 53 rooms and suites have sea views and a refined style that complements the hotel's reflective nature and modern comfort. The infinity pool overlooks Amalfi below and is the place to be in the summer.

HOTEL SANTA CATERINA

S.S. Amalfitana 9; 089/871-012; www.hotelsantacaterina.it; open Apr.-Oct.; €1,038 d

Located just west of Amalfi's town center, the Hotel Santa Caterina blends modern elegance with a comfortable atmosphere, thanks to the Gambardella family, who have run the hotel for more than 100 years. Enjoy picture-perfect views of Amalfi from your own private balcony, the dining terrace, or lush gardens surrounding the sprawling 19th-century villa. Take the elevator or follow a meandering path down to the rocky private beach with a saltwater pool carved into the cliff. Decorated with Mediterranean colors and hand-painted majolica, 36 rooms offer partial to full sea views, while suites feature direct sea views. Stunning garden suites offer the perfect romantic getaway. Additional deluxe accomodations are available in the nearby Villa Il Rosso.

INFORMATION AND SERVICES

Tourist Information

AZIENDA AUTONOMA DI SOGGIORNO E TURISMO

Corso delle Repubbliche Marinare 11; tel. 089/871-107; www.amalfitouristoffice.it; 9am-1pm and 2:30pm-6pm May-Oct., morning only Nov.-Apr.

Amalfi's tourist office can offer maps and helpful information in English on local sights, getting around, and more. You'll find it located opposite Marina Grande beach in a courtyard. The courtyard entrance is just to the left of the post office (Poste Italiane), which is easier to spot.

Medical and Emergency Services

OSPEDALE COSTA D'AMALFI

Via Civita 12; tel. 089/873-150; www.aslsalerno.it

The only hospital along the Amalfi Coast is in Castiglione, a *frazione* of Ravello, a little more than a mile (1.7 km) east of Amalfi. Follow the Amalfi Coast Road east to the crossroads of SS373 road to Ravello. After a tight hairpin curve, the hospital is located on the left. There is a 24-hour *pronto soccorso* (emergency room). For **emergency services,** dial 118 for ambulance and urgent care.

Postal Services

POSTE ITALIANE

Corso delle Repubbliche Marinare 31; tel. 089/830-4831; www.poste.it; 8:20am-7:05pm Mon.-Fri.

Amalfi's post office is located opposite the Marina Grande beach and is the only spot in town that offers shipping services for mailing letters and packages.

GETTING THERE

With its larger harbor and convenient central location, Amalfi is a transportation hub along the coastline for buses and ferries. This makes it a popular base for exploring the area by public transportation.

By Car and Scooter

Amalfi is centrally located along the Amalfi Coast, about 15.5 miles (25 km) west of Salerno and 10 miles (16 km) east of Positano. The Amalfi Coast Road (SS163) runs right through Amalfi at sea level. The drive from Salerno to Amalfi takes about an hour, while the drive from Positano to Amalfi is about 45 minutes to an hour or more, depending on the time of year. From Ravello, follow the SS373 down to where it intersects the Amalfi Coast Road at Castiglione and take a right to continue to Amalfi. The drive from Ravello takes about 20 minutes. From Naples, there are multiple options for driving to Amalfi: There are two passes over the mountains, the Valico di Chiunzi above Tramonti and the pass through Agerola. Since the tract of road between Tramonti and Ravello is technically closed (although traffic does pass through), many travelers choose to take the pass via Agerola. Follow the A3 highway south out of Naples and exit at Castellammare di Stabia and follow the SS145 to the intersection with the SS366 that leads up the mountains, through Agerola, and down to the Amalfi Coast on the other side. It ends at the Amalfi Coast Road (SS163), where you'll bear left and shortly arrive in Amalfi. This drive from Naples to Amalfi takes about 1 hour 30 minutes. You can also stay on the A3 highway until Vietri sul Mare and then take the Amalfi Coast Road west to Amalfi to see more of the coastline. This option takes about 1 hour 45 minutes.

Amalfi has several paid parking lots, including limited parking right along the waterfront near Piazza Flavio Gioia, behind the Molo Foraneo, and the **Luna Rossa** parking garage (www.amalfimobilita.com) carved entirely out of the mountain. Prices vary from €1 to €5 per hour, depending on the time of year, with the highest rates being charged from April through September. However, during the peak periods it is not unusual for all parking to be full. If you're arriving by car, contact your accommodation in advance to try to reserve a spot, as many offer parking at an additional cost.

By Ferry

Right in the center of Amalfi's harbor is the Molo Pennello pier where the ferries arrive and depart. Along the western side of the pier, you'll find the smaller boats that travel to and from the beaches nearby and the Emerald Grotto in Conca dei Marini. The end of the pier is where the larger ferries from Salerno, Positano, Capri, and Sorrento dock. Tickets can be purchased at the booths at the beginning of the pier, and they can also be purchased in advance from many operators, which is a good idea during the busiest time of year from June through September.

The most frequent ferry service to Amalfi is operated by **Travelmar** (tel. 089/872-950; www.travelmar.it; €8-12 per person). During the ferry season from April to early November, there are regular arrivals—6-11, depending on departure point—throughout the day from Positano, Minori, Maiori, Cetara, and Salerno. From Positano the ferry ride is about 25 minutes, from Minori about 10 minutes, from Maiori 15 minutes, from Cetara 40 minutes, and from Salerno about 35 minutes. Tickets can be purchased online in advance, or via the Travelmar app.

Alicost (tel. 089/811-986; www.alicost.it; €19.80-21.30 per person) offers daily ferry service to Amalfi from Capri, Sorrento, Positano, Minori, and Salerno. There are usually 1-4 departures from Capri to Amalfi (more during the peak summer period from June-September). Exact times can vary seasonally, so check the schedule in advance. The ferry from Capri to Amalfi takes about 1 hour 20 minutes. To reach Amalfi from Sorrento, there are 1-2 ferries daily and the journey time is about an hour. Many of the ferries from Capri and Sorrento also stop in Positano.

By Bus

Amalfi is the central hub along the coastline for the public **SITA SUD** buses (tel. 089/386-6701; www.sitasudtrasporti.it; from €1.30) with service from all of the most popular spots in the area. Two main bus lines run along the Amalfi Coast Road and arrive in Amalfi. From Salerno, buses pass through Vietri sul Mare, Cetara, Maiori, Minori, and Atrani before arriving in Amalfi. The other main line departs from Sorrento and passes through Positano, Praiano, and Conca dei Marini before arriving in Amalfi. From Salerno, the bus ride to Amalfi is about 1 hour 15 minutes. From Sorrento, expect the ride to be about 1 hour 40 minutes. From Positano, the bus journey takes about 50 minutes. There is also a bus line that circulates between Ravello and Scala to Amalfi, with a travel time of about 25 minutes to Amalfi from either Ravello or Scala.

Buses for Salerno and Sorrento arrive and depart from Via Lungomare dei Cavalieri at the western edge of Piazza Flavio Gioia. The signage for each route is not very clear, but the final destination is listed on the top front of each bus. Buses to Ravello and Scala arrive and depart from the eastern side of Piazza Flavio Gioia near the beach (there's a sun-protective awning that is marked for Ravello and Scala).

The red **City Sightseeing** buses (www.city-sightseeing.it; Apr.-Oct., from €5 per person) provide a more comfortable journey. There are multiple lines to Amalfi, including ones from Sorrento (with a stop in Positano), from Ravello, and from Minori and Maiori. From Sorrento the bus ride takes about 1 hour 25 minutes, from Positano about 50 minutes, and from Amalfi and Minori about 30 minutes. The buses from Ravello are open-top, which is enjoyable on a sunny day. Because they only allow as many passengers as they have seats, these buses aren't overcrowded like the public buses can be. The stop in Amalfi is at the Ravello/Scala SITA stop on the eastern side of Piazza Flavio Gioia. Audio guides for the journey are included in the price, and tickets can be purchased onboard or from the assistant before boarding.

Pintour (tel. 081/879-2645; www.pintourbus.com; €20 adults, €10 children up to 12 years) offers a convenient and affordable bus service to Amalfi from the Naples airport (Aeroporto Internazionale di Napoli at Capodichino). The service is available seasonally from April to early November. Buses depart from the bus terminal located outside the arrivals hall at the airport. The bus stops at Pompeii and every town along the Amalfi Coast from Vietri sul Mare to Amalfi, where it stops right in Piazza Flavio Gioia. Tickets can be booked in advance online, which is a good idea. There are usually about five departures from the airport for Amalfi daily, but check exact times in advance, as they can change from season to season. The journey takes about 1 hour 55 minutes.

By Taxi

To reach Amalfi by taxi transfer service, Amalfi Turcoop (tel. 081/873-1522; www.amalfiturcoop.it; transfers starting at €110) offers private transfers from any point of arrival in the area to Amalfi. Booking a transfer in advance is the most convenient and easy way to arrive in Amalfi.

GETTING AROUND

By Bus

Amalfi does have a small mini bus service, **Amalfi Mobilita** (tel. 089/873-518; www.amalfimobilita.com; €0.50) that runs from the western end of the port near the Piazzale dei Protontini to near the top of the town at the Valle dei Mulini stop, passing through Piazza Flavio Gioia and Piazza Duomo along the way. Service runs about every half hour from 8am until 8pm. Tickets cost €0.50 and can be purchased onboard. However, Amalfi is very walkable from end to end.

By Car and Scooter

Looking to explore the coastline by car or zip around like a local on a scooter? **Amalfi New Service** (Piazzale dei Protontini; tel. 089/871-087; www.amalfinewservice.it; 8:30am-8pm) offers scooters and a variety of car rentals, including new and vintage options. Car rental rates start at €70 per day, while scooters are €60 for the first day and €40 for each additional day. Scooters are available to rent from March through November, and car rentals are available all year.

By Taxi

Taxis are easy to find in Amalfi. The taxi stand is located on the western side of Piazza Flavio Gioia, and taxis are available year-round. The city of Amalfi has set taxi fares, which are clearly marked on the sign near the taxi stand or on the Comune di Amalfi website (www.amalfi.gov.it/taxi). The set fares depend on the number of passengers and the distance covered. To ride around Amalfi to hotels in the area (convenient if you have luggage), the cost begins at €10-€25 for 1-4 people and €15-30 for 5-8 people. There are also set fares from Amalfi to Ravello of €40-50, from Amalfi to Positano (€70-80), and most of the towns on the Amalfi Coast. All other journeys are based on the taxi meter rate that starts at a minimum of €6. If you would like the fixed rate, you must let the driver know before you depart.

Atrani

If you haven't heard of Atrani that might be because it is the smallest town in all of Italy by surface size, with a footprint of only 0.05 square miles (0.12 square km). Located just east of Amalfi, this pint-sized town packs quite a punch when it comes to charm. The town is settled into the Valle del Dragone, with its pastel-hued buildings seemingly stacked one on top of the other. The Amalfi Coast Road curves around the **Collegiata di Santa Maria Maddalena,** with its colorful dome, and cuts right across the front of town with an arched bridge.

Atrani's beautiful jumble of buildings and maze of streets have inspired many artists and writers over the centuries, perhaps most notably M.C. Escher, who was captivated by the labyrinthine setting. Travelers feel like they've stumbled across a hidden gem when they discover little Atrani, which has all the conveniences of Amalfi just a short walk away. If you're looking for a central stay with an out-of-the-way feel, consider making Atrani your home base on the Amalfi Coast.

SIGHTS

Piazza Umberto I

This is one of the Amalfi Coast's most charming squares: when you step into Piazza Umberto I, it's like you've taken a big step back in time. Surrounded as it is by buildings with arches, balconies, and the staircase leading up to the **Chiesa di San Salvatore de Birecto,** it feels like time has stood still in this little piazza. In fact, it's a popular location for films and commercials looking for an old-world feel. Find a seat at a café, order an *aperitivo,* and take some time to soak up the peaceful atmosphere.

Collegiata di Santa Maria Maddalena

Largo Maddalena; usually open in the evening at 5pm for mass

In a dramatic location, jutting out above the beach of Atrani, the Collegiata di Santa Maria Maddalena was built in 1274 in honor of Saint Mary Maddalena, to whom the town is strongly devoted. Built and remodeled over the centuries, the church has a fascinating patchwork of architectural styles and designs, from its striking yellow and green majolica-tiled domes to the stark white and stone 16th-century bell tower to its gleaming white facade: the only example of rococo architecture on the Amalfi Coast. Inside, the church's baroque decor is well preserved, including 17th- and 18th-century paintings and a 16th-century portrait of Santa Maria Maddalena with Sant'Andrea and San Sebastiano above the altar by Giovanni Angelo d'Amato, a painter from Maiori active on the Amalfi Coast and in Naples from the late 16th century to early 17th century.

Chiesa di San Salvatore de Birecto

Piazza Umberto I; assatrium@libero.it; 10:30am-1pm and 4pm-6pm, afternoons only during summer; €2

This small church is among the most interesting on the Amalfi Coast, and thanks to a local association it is open for a small fee. Climb the staircase from Piazza Umberto I, and beyond the iron gate is the entrance to the church, which was founded in the 10th century. The interior has been restored to reveal different layers of history that are well worth uncovering. It was here that the dukes of the Republic of Amalfi were crowned in the Middle Ages, and the church has always had a strong religious and cultural tie to Amalfi. In addition to the beautiful interlaced arches inside, there are bronze doors from 1087, architectural elements uncovered during the restoration, as well as marble sculptures, including a unique piece with peacocks, and religious sculptures and paintings.

BEACHES

MARINA DI ATRANI

With a quaint town setting and the Collegiata di Santa Maria Maddalena rising above, Atrani's beach is one of the most often photographed on the Amalfi Coast. During the summer months, this popular beach is lined with umbrellas and sun beds. Yet even on the busiest days it tends to be less crowded than the Marina Grande beach in Amalfi nearby. The water is extremely clear and the beach even has some dark sandy areas that are a welcome relief from the pebbles and large stones of most of the beaches along the coast. Several *stabilimenti balneari* (beach clubs) offer everything needed for a relaxing day by the sea.

CASTIGLIONE BEACH

SS163 Amalfi Coast Road at Castiglione

Although it's located just around the corner from Atrani, this beach technically belongs to the city of Ravello and is named after the Castiglione area of Ravello that is just above the beach. It is only accessible by a long staircase of a little more than 180 steps from the Amalfi Coast Road, just east of Atrani, or by swimming over from the Marina di Atrani, which is only about 460 feet (140 m) away. During the beach season, there's a *stabilimente balneare* (beach club) that offers sun bed and umbrella rentals, as well as snacks and food. With its beautiful water and small soccer field, this beach is very popular with teenagers from Ravello and surrounding towns during the summer.

FESTIVALS AND EVENTS

FESTIVAL OF LA MADDALENA

Collegiata di Santa Maria Maddalena, Piazza Umberto I, and various locations; July 22

Atrani celebrates its patron Santa Maria Maddalena, or La Maddalena, with a grand summer festival every year on July 22. Colorful lights appear all over town and a stage is erected in Piazza Umberto I for concerts. The procession begins at the Collegiata di Santa Maria Maddalena and follows the road down to the beach and through the village, with several stops for blessings along the way. After dark, a fabulous fireworks show is set off from barges in the sea, just off the coastline. It's a spectacular show, offering a unique glimpse into Atrani's deep devotion to La Maddalena and a fun way to spend a warm summer evening on the Amalfi Coast.

LA NOTTE DI MASANIELLO

Piazza Umberto I and various locations; www.stelledivine.it; first Sat. in Sept.

Dedicated to Atrani's revolutionary son Masaniello, this event transforms the entire town into an open-air theater with a blend of historic renactments, concerts, and Atrani's culinary traditions, especially seafood. Performances take place throughout the streets of Atrani, and different food stalls serve a menu of specialties from local restaurants, winemakers, and producers.

FOOD

LE ARCATE

Largo Orlando Buonocore; tel. 089/871-367; www.learcate.net; noon-3:30pm and 7pm-11pm, closed Mon. and mid-Nov.-early Mar.; €8-26

It doesn't get much more romantic than this restaurant with its outdoor dining area situated below a series of arches (*arcate*) that give this place its name. There's an indoor dining area carved into the mountain like a little sea cave, but when the weather is warm, a table right by the sea with a view of Atrani is the place to be. Seafood here is excellent, starting with the classic Antipasto Le Arcate, a mix of seafood served up in different styles. Next try the *scialatielli della costiera,* a traditional handmade pasta with clams, mussels, and fresh tomatoes, followed by the *cuoppo* (paper cone) of fried frish. There are plenty of non-seafood options as well, like zucchini blossoms stuffed with ricotta, pasta with smoked *provola* cheese and eggplant, or *provola* grilled on lemon leaves. The pizza cooked in a wood-fire oven is also excellent.

RISTORANTE A'PARANZA

Via Comunale Traversa Dragone 1; tel. 089/871-840; www.ristoranteparanza.com; 12:30pm-3pm and 7pm-11pm, closed Tues. (except in Aug.) and Jan. 6-31; €12-30

Follow Atrani's main street from the Piazza Umberto I, and after a short distance you'll find this restaurant tucked away on the right. You'll feel as if you've stumbled across a hidden gem. The setting is elegant and the menu is dedicated to maintaining local traditions. Seafood is the specialty here, such as the *paccehro di gragnano* (large pasta tubes made on the Sorrento Peninsula) or the *zuppa di pesce* (fish soup) made with the fresh fish of the day. Save room for dessert and try their *pasticciotto,* a local favorite with a rich cream and black cherries. Reservations are recommended, especially on the weekend.

ACCOMMODATIONS

EVA ROOMS

Via Gabriele di Benedetto 3; tel. 089/872-875; www.evarooms.it; Apr.-Oct.; €140

This small and welcoming B&B has two bright, spacious rooms with a dreamy view overlooking Atrani and the coastline toward Salerno. Each room has a balcony with table

---

1: the rococo facade of the Collegiata di Santa Maria Maddalena **2:** steps lead up to the Chiesa di San Salvatore de Birecto **3:** Atrani's beach is one of the most charming on the Amalfi Coast.

1
2
3

and chairs for enjoying breakfast and savoring the view after dark, as Atrani is lit up beautifully and the lights dance across the sea.

PALAZZO FERRAIOLI

Via Campo 16; tel. 089/872-652; www.palazzoferraioli.it; open mid-Apr.-Oct. 31; €200

It is a little tricky to find the entrance to this hotel, but wandering through the charming streets of Atrani is one of the best things to do in this picturesque town. Once you climb the steps to this 19th-century aristocratic family residence that has been turned into a boutique hotel, you'll see that the view over Atrani with the sea beyond is worth every step. Inside you'll enjoy a stay surrounded by modern design, with an elegant dining room, spa, and roof terrace offering sun beds and a fabulous view. The 25 rooms vary in style and size, but all have a clean modern design with select rooms inspired by iconic actresses.

GETTING THERE AND AROUND

Getting to and around Atrani is quite easy. The Amalfi Coast Road (SS163) winds its way right around the tiny town and over the beach and main piazza on a bridge supported by arches. There's a bus stop in the middle of the bridge for the **SITA SUD** buses (tel. 089/386-6701; www.sitasudtrasporti.it; from €1.30) from Amalfi, Salerno, Scala, and Ravello. The bus journey from Salerno to Atrani is about 1 hour 15 minutes, while from Ravello and Scala it is about 25 minutes. To reach Atrani from Positano, take the bus first to Amalfi and continue on foot or transfer to the bus line to Salerno and get off at Atrani (this is likely only worthwhile if you're traveling with luggage from Positano to Atrani). Amalfi is just a 10-minute stroll away along the Amalfi Coast Road, or once you're through the tunnel along the Amalfi Coast Road on the west side of Atrani, look on the right for a well-marked pedestrian tunnel entrance for a more direct and traffic-free (but less scenic) walk direct to Piazza Municipio in Amalfi. Parking for cars and scooters is available for hourly rates in a small lot near the beach or at the **Luna Rossa** parking garage (www.amalfimobilita.com) between Atrani and Amalfi.

The **Pintour** (tel. 081/879-2645; www.pintourbus.com; €20 adults, €10 children up to 12 years) bus service connecting the Naples airport to the Amalfi Coast stops at Atrani. Service is available seasonally from April to early November and costs €15 per person. Catch the bus at the bus terminal located outside the arrivals hall at the airport. The bus stops at Pompeii and along the Amalfi Coast, including a stop in Atrani at the bus stop along the Amalfi Coast Road in the center of town. It's a good idea to book tickets in advance via the Pintour website. The bus ride from Naples airport to Atrani takes about 1 hour 45 minutes.

Ravello

Along with Positano and Amalfi, Ravello is one of the most visited towns on the Amalfi Coast and for very good reason. The city sits at 1,200 feet (365 meters) above sea level and stretches across a long, flat promontory that juts out of the mountains between two deep valleys. An eye-catching sight from every angle, Ravello offers a completely different experience from the seaside towns, as well as a unique vantage point and sweeping views down the coastline in both directions.

Ravello's history is tied closely to Amalfi, as Ravello was a part of the Republic of Amalfi in the Middle Ages. Its grand villas and palazzos, many now home to luxury hotels, were once the residences of wealthy merchants who built the remarkable churches that dot the town. Today the grounds of two of the largest estates, **Villa Rufolo** and **Villa Cimbrone**, offer visitors the chance to explore their beautifully landscaped gardens and take in their famous views.

A place of inspired beauty, Ravello has been a haven for artists for centuries. Known as the City of Music, the town produces a rich and varied calendar of performances throughout the year, including the annual summer **Ravello Festival.**

While Ravello is a popular spot for travelers, the town remains tranquil even during the busiest summer months. Its charming pedestrian-only areas, including Piazza Duomo, give it a feeling of being far away from traffic. Summer evenings are especially enchanting when the day-trippers have moved on and music is in the air during the Ravello Festival. If you can't get enough of the famous Amalfi Coast views, be sure to plan time to explore Ravello's beautiful gardens and enjoy one of the most relaxing towns on the coast.

ORIENTATION

The center of Ravello sits high above sea level and the Amalfi Coast Road (SS163), which does pass through Castiglione, a *frazione* (hamlet) of Ravello. From the Amalfi Coast Road in Castiglione, the SS373 road leads up into the mountains to the town center. This road is even narrower than the Amalfi Coast Road (yes that is possible!), and a traffic light controls the flow of cars, alternating directions in the high season (roughly Easter through October) as well as during winter holidays. Along the drive from Castiglione up to Ravello, you will pass through Civita, another *frazione* of Ravello, as well as two crossroads, the first leading to Pontone and the second, Scala. Keep following the road straight past the well-marked turn-off on the left to Pontone, and at the Scala crossroad bear right to reach Ravello's town center.

Approaching Ravello from the SS373 leads to one of the town's two tunnels. Before the tunnel to the right, Via della Marra leads to the Chiesa di Santa Maria a Gradillo and beyond to Ravello's largest paid parking area. Continuing through the tunnel from SS373 leads to the other side of Ravello. After exiting the tunnel, take a right and follow Via Giovanni Boccaccio; it ends at a small piazza in front of the town's second tunnel, which leads directly into the Piazza Duomo. Traffic is restricted through this tunnel to the rest of Ravello.

The heart of Ravello is **Piazza Duomo,** right in the center of town, where you'll find the town's largest church, great shopping and dining options, and the entrance to Villa Rufolo, one of the two famous gardens in town. The Villa Cimbrone is located at the tip of the promontory and is well worth the 15-minute walk to reach it, not only to see the splendid views and gardens but also to pass through a quietly beautiful part of town. To reach Villa Cimbrone, head down Via dei Rufolo from Piazza Duomo and follow signs that lead up a series of staircases and meandering pedestrian-only walkways to the entrance of the gardens.

SIGHTS

Duomo

Piazza Duomo; tel. 089/858-311; www.chiesaravello.it; 9am-12pm and 5:30pm-7:30pm daily; free

Ravello's most important church reflects the sun with its white facade. Founded in the 11th century, it has gone through many renovations over its long history. However, the latest refurbishments served to restore many of the medieval features and to preserve later baroque additions. At the top of a small flight of steps, the entrance to the church is marked by a pair of bronze doors that were created in 1179 by Barisano da Trani, whose bronze work can also be seen on the Monreale Cathedral in Sicily and the Trani Cathedral in Puglia. Ravello's intricately designed church doors feature 80 panels of bas-relief designs depicting religious figures and scenes.

The nave of the church seems stark in comparison to the richly decorated raised transept with its baroque design. The columns

Ravello and Scala

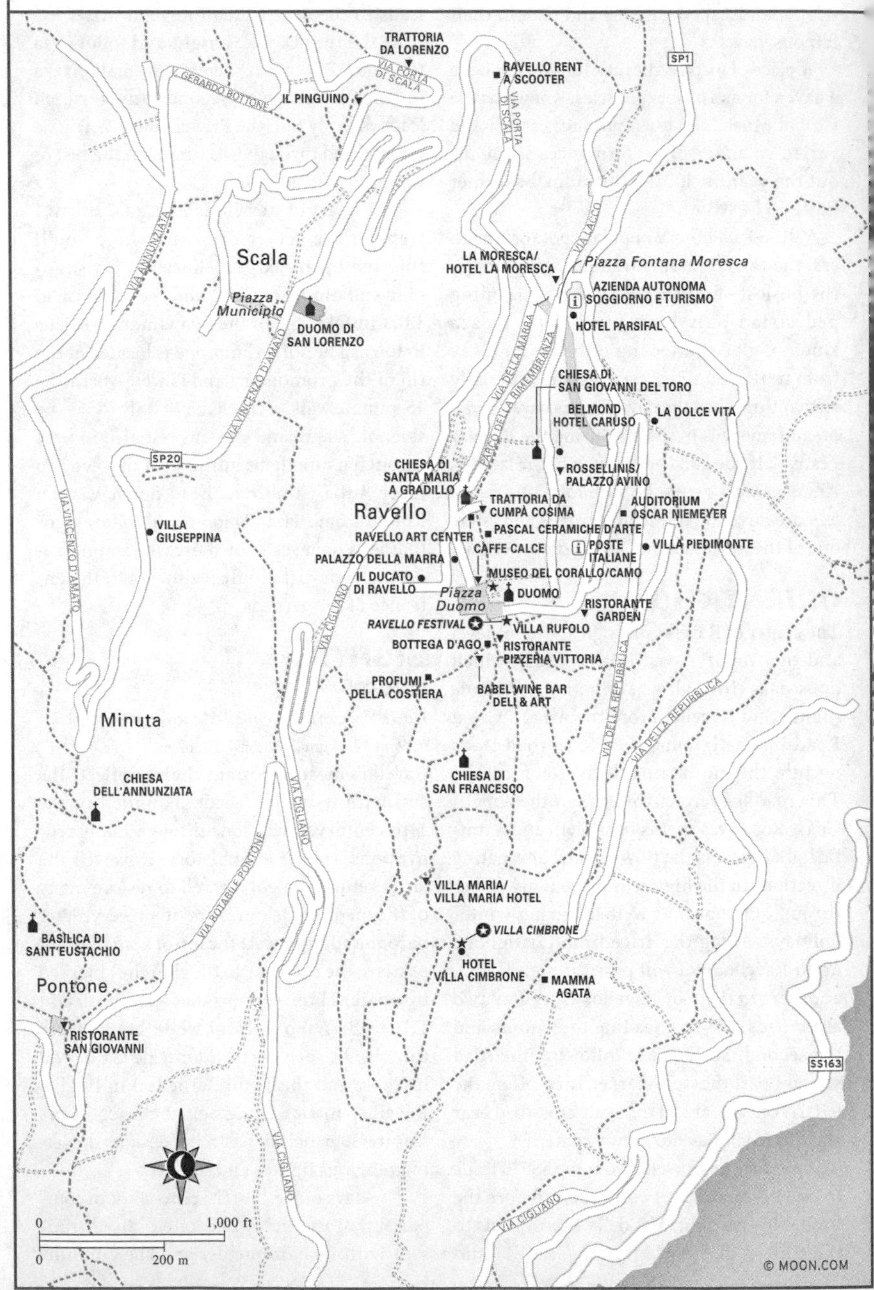

that line the nave are topped with antique capitals, taken from ancient sites in the area. Along the nave are two remarkable works of religious art. On the left side is a 12th-century ambon with mosaics depicting the story of Jonah and the whale. The winged monster devouring Jonah is a *pistrice*, a mythical sea creature with a long snake-like tail and wings. Just opposite, a pulpit from the 13th century fills a large section of the aisle. Covered with intricate mosaics, the pulpit features six spiral columns supported by lions. It was created for Nicola and Sigilgaida, two members of the wealthy Rufolo family who were the founders of this church. Take time to look at all the beautiful details, from the expressive faces of the lions to the mosaic designs and the eagle statue sitting at the top.

To the left of the altar is an ornate chapel that is dedicated to San Pantaleone (St. Pantaleon), the town's patron saint. Behind the 17th-century chapel altar is a reliquary containing the blood of the saint. It is said that every year on July 27, the saint's festival day, the blood liquefies in the reliquary: a religious miracle that just can't be explained!

Museo dell'Opera del Duomo

Piazza Duomo 7; tel. 089/858-311; www.museoduomoravello.com; 9am-7pm daily; €3

More historical treasures are on display in the crypt of the church, which houses the Museo dell'Opera del Duomo. Among the pieces on display are reliquaries, paintings, and architectural pieces like the remains of an impressive tabernacle from 1279 that was donated by Matteo Rufolo and was above the main altar until the 18th century. When the church doors are closed, you can still visit the church by paying a small fee to visit the museum.

Villa Rufolo

Piazza Duomo; 089/857-621; www.villarufolo.com; daily year-round 9am-5pm, last entrance 4:30pm; €7

Take a walk back in time while exploring the gardens of the Villa Rufolo. This sprawling estate belonged to the wealthy Rufolo family during the Middle Ages. The property was largely saved from ruin thanks to Scottish industrialist Francis Nevile Reid in the 19th century. Climb to the top of **Torre Museo,** a 13th-century tower that has been transformed into a museum, to learn the fascinating history of the villa through historic photos, videos, and archaeological finds on display. As a bonus, you get an incredible bird's-eye view over Ravello from the top. While exploring the villa, you'll spot traces of the unique architectural style of the Amalfi Coast, blending Arabic, Sicilian, and Norman influences. Don't miss the cloister with its delicate twin columns supporting intricate interlocking foliate arches.

The terraced gardens are dotted with wisteria-covered pergolas that frame the incredible view, fountains, and romantic nooks. Floral beds are planted seasonally with colorful flowers to complement the beautiful bougainvillea vines, hydrangeas, roses, and cypress and pine trees, along with Mediterranean herbs and plants. There's an air of enchantment in the gardens, which inspired Richard Wagner's opera *Parsifal* after a memorable visit he made in 1880. Today the musical tradition continues as the Villa Rufolo hosts the celebrated Ravello Festival every year from June to August. While the gardens are at their best from early spring through the fall, the views and Torre Museo make a visit to Villa Rufolo worthwhile throughout the year.

Museo del Corallo

Piazza Duomo 9; tel. 089/857-461; www.museodelcorallo.com; 10am-noon Mon.-Thurs.; free with appointment

Just to the left of the stairs leading up to the Duomo, look for the entrance to this lovely shop owned by master coral carver Giorgio Filocamo. Though the shop looks small from the outside, waiting within is a treasure trove of coral masterpieces. Enter the small museum area at the back of the shop, where Giorgio has curated an impressive personal collection that represents his family's heritage and long tradition in coral carving. There's everything from beautiful jewelry and decorative pieces to religious art. To visit the museum, it's best to make an appointment in advance. After visiting the collection, stop in for a look at Giorgio's fine jewelry and carved pieces for sale in the shop **CAMO.**

Chiesa di San Giovanni del Toro

Via San Giovanni del Toro 3; tel. 089/857-977; www.ravellotime.com; request opening hours at tourist office

Located atop the highest spot of Ravello, this church sits in what was once the walled-off, noble quarter of town. With architectural elements reflecting Byzantine and Sicilian-Arab influences, the church reveals the wide influences the town's merchants brought back with them during the Middle Ages. The church was founded in 975 and the original portico has been lost to time, although a small flight of stairs remains to reach the church. Major restorations over the course of the 20th century have preserved many of the original elements of the church's medieval design. Along the nave is a splendid mosaic-covered pulpit that most likely dates to the 13th and 14th centuries. There are still traces of the frescoes that once covered the walls along the apse as well as some 14th-century frescoes in the crypt.

Chiesa di Santa Maria a Gradillo

Via Gradillo; tel. 089/858-311; www.chiesaravello.it; contact the Duomo for opening hours

Founded around the 11th century, this church has three apses and architectural elements (like its interlacing arches) that bear a resemblance to the nearby **Chiesa di San Giovanni del Toro.** It was here that the nobles of Ravello met to discuss city and public affairs. An intense restoration from 1958-63 removed the baroque elements that were added in the 18th century, and restored many of the original medieval features, which reveal Ravello's unique blend of Byzantine and Sicilian-Arab architectural influences. Small glass panels in the floor reveal the original mosaic floor below. Unlike other churches in Ravello, this one is often open throughout the day.

Piazza Fontana Moresca

This pretty piazza has an 18th-century fountain with statues of a lion and an ox that are replicas of the originals from the medieval tabernacle that once stood in the Duomo (the originals were stolen in 1975). Near the fountain, what remains of the **Chiesa di Sant'Agostino** was transformed into a memorial in 1968 with a plaque on the right of the portico listing the names of Ravello citizens who perished in World War I and World War II. Just beyond the fountain to the right is a terrace where you can enjoy a nice view of the coastline.

Chiesa di San Francesco

Via San Francesco 13; tel. 089/857-146; www.ravellofrancescana.it; free

The Chiesa di San Francesco is located through a large portico along the walkway to Villa Cimbrone. The church dates from the 13th century, and is said to have been founded when St. Francis of Assisi passed through Ravello in 1222 on the way to Amalfi. The original Gothic-style interior was later covered during a late baroque renovation. Below the altar is a memorial for the beatified Bonaventura da Potenza, a Franciscan monk who died in Ravello in 1711. To the right of the church entrance is a doorway leading to the cloister of San Francesco, which is often used to display artwork. It's a peaceful spot to stop and rest on the way to Villa Cimbrone.

TOP EXPERIENCE

★ Villa Cimbrone

Via Santa Chiara 26; tel. 089/857-459; www.hotelvillacimbrone.com/gardens; 9am-sunset daily; €7

At the tip of the promontory where Ravello sits is the lush green estate called Villa Cimbrone, which is now a five-star hotel with beautiful gardens that are open to the public. Although it's a 15-minute walk with

1: Ravello's Piazza Duomo **2:** the gardens of Villa Cimbrone **3:** a view of the hamlet of Torello on the hike from Ravello to Minori **4:** Villa Rufolo

some hills and steps to navigate from the center of Ravello, the peaceful gardens and stunning views make this one of the top highlights of the entire Amalfi Coast. The estate has been in this coveted location in Ravello since ancient Roman times, when it was called Cimbronium. Villa Cimbrone was home to noble Ravello families during the Middle Ages, but by the end of the 19th century, it was largely abandoned. It was rediscovered by Ernest William Beckett, Lord Grimthorpe, an English banker and politician, who fell in love with the estate and purchased it in 1904. He revived the gardens with the help of local gardeners as well as notable English garden designers and architects like Gertrude Jekyll, Vita Sackville-West, and Edwin Lutyens. The resulting gardens blended original Renaissance features like a long central avenue with traditional English elements, such as the temples, grottoes, tearoom, and lovely rose garden.

As you enter the gardens, visit the serene **Gothic cloister** with its pointed arches and spiral columns, blending Arab, Sicilian, and Norman architectural details. Then continue down the aptly named **Avenue of Immensity** that is the main artery through the garden, leading from the entrance to the **Terrace of Infinity.** The avenue is covered with wisteria vines, and if you visit during spring when the wisteria is blooming, it is heavenly. From the Avenue of Immensity, wander off and explore the beautifully landscaped gardens. You'll see the **Rose Terrace,** with its geometric flower beds planted with roses that bloom from May to October. Nearby is the open pavilion tearoom, decorated with columns in the style of the cloister at **Villa Rufolo** and panels of green and yellow ceramic tiles. It was here that Lord Grimthorpe often gathered with members of the Bloomsbury Group, an association of English writers, philosophers, and artists, including author Virginia Woolf. There's still an artistic air, as if you might just happen across an artist at an easel or a writer scribbling away in a notebook.

At the end of the Avenue of Immensity, the pathway leads through a pavilion with a statue of Ceres before opening to the Terrace of Infinity. Here, at the very tip of Ravello, the sweeping view blends sky and sea into a panorama that seemingly never ends. Looking down the sheer cliff is not for the faint of heart. The terrace is rimmed with 18th-century marble busts that add to the romance of the setting. Follow the pathway back to the entrance that leads through terraced gardens dotted with sculptures, grottoes, and little overlooks with beautiful views of the valley below. Don't miss the pathway leading under oak, alder, and chestnut trees to Eve's Grotto, where you'll find a marble statue of Eve by Bolognese artist Adamo Tadolini (1788-1868). You can also walk around a temple dedicated to Bacchus; this is where Lord Grimthorpe's ashes were interred, so he could eternally rest in the gardens he loved.

SPORTS AND RECREATION

Ravello is a tranquil spot that is ideal for a relaxing holiday. Visitors are surrounded by nature and the incredible views that make the town a popular destination. Although Ravello doesn't have beaches near the center of town like other vacation spots in this region, there are interesting hikes to nearby villages. Or spend the day delving into local culinary traditions at a cooking class, complete with a picture-perfect view.

Hiking

With its setting on a promontory between two mountain valleys, Ravello is a great starting point for hiking in the area. Plan to take your time, because there are a lot of steps and panoramic views along the way. The local hiking maps produced by **Cart&guide** (www.carteguide.com; English and Italian versions available; €5 each) are very detailed and make excellent companions for exploring on foot. Maps are also available at Bric a' Brac (Piazza Duomo 4; tel. 089/858-6228), a shop located right in Piazza Duomo.

RAVELLO TO MINORI

Set in the valley below Ravello, the town of **Minori** is your destination on a beautiful hike down an ancient stone pathway that was the only connection between the two towns before roads were built in the 19th century. There are several different pathways leading down the mountain from Ravello to Minori, but the most enjoyable starts at the center of Ravello and passes through the tiny village of **Torello** before meandering through terraces of lemon trees and olive groves down to Minori. The walk descends from about 1,200 feet (365 m) down to the sea level in Minori, so be prepared for a lot of steps. There aren't places to stop for refreshments along the way, so bring water for the hike.

Start in Piazza Duomo in Ravello and follow the pathway just to the left of the entrance tower to Villa Rufolo. Ceramic signs point the way to Minori as the steps lead past several tiny churches. Stop in Torello to admire the **Chiesa di San Michele Arcangelo.** While usually only open during Mass, this small church has a charming piazza and portico. After Torello the steps are steeper but the views are spectacular as you zigzag down with the sea seemingly just beyond. Follow the steps down all the way to the *lungomare* (waterfront) in Minori, which has some nice benches: a welcome sight after all those steps down the mountain. If you walk at a leisurely pace, the hike takes about an hour. To return to Ravello from Minori, you will first need to get to Amalfi since there are no direct buses from Minori to Ravello. Catch the ferry from the pier in Minori to Amalfi and then take the SITA SUD bus back up to Ravello. Or on Via Roma along the waterfront in Minori, you can also catch the SITA SUD bus to Amalfi and then transfer to the bus to Ravello.

RAVELLO TO ATRANI

Hiking down the valley on the western side of Ravello will take you to **Atrani,** and Amalfi is located just a short stroll beyond on the Amalfi Coast Road. Just like the hike to Minori, there are various routes. One option is to follow the steps near Santa Maria a Gradillo down the valley and follow the signs to Atrani. You'll walk along a pathway with stone steps that follows the river valley down to the top of Atrani and then passes through the tiny village to the sea.

Another scenic option is to follow Via della Repubblica past the Auditorium Oscar Niemeyer down to the **Chiesa di San Cosma.** Follow Via San Cosma, a foothpath that alternates between flat walkways and steps, and leads beyond the church and hugs the mountainside below Villa Cimbrone. Very steep steps lead down toward the sea through the Civita area of Ravello, just above Castiglione. Look for Via San Nicola near Civita, a gorgeous walk high above the Castiglione beach, that takes you directly down into Atrani.

This is a hike where it's good to have a map because some options can lead to long stretches of walking along the SS373, the narrow road connecting Ravello and Scala with the Amalfi Coast Road. Avoid these options because the SS373 is very narrow and congested, making it an unpleasant walk compared to the other options described here. Hiking from Ravello to Atrani will take an hour or a little longer, depending on the route you choose. The landscape is quite secluded and you won't find many options for refreshments during the walk, so carry your own water. From Atrani along the bridge over the center of town or from Piazza Flavio Gioia in Amalfi, you can catch the SITA SUD bus back up to Ravello.

Cooking Class

MAMMA AGATA

Piazza San Cosma 9; tel. 089/857-845; www.mammaagata.com; classes offered Mon., Tues., Thurs., Fri. mid-Mar.-Oct., closed Aug. 11-28; starting at €180 pp

Located in a tranquil spot in Ravello, Mamma Agata is a little culinary haven where cooking is a family passion and truly a family affair. Mamma Agata, who began cooking on the Amalfi Coast at a very early age, was the inspiration for this cooking school created by her daughter Chiara Lima. In cooking classes, Mamma Agata and Chiara's husband, Gennaro—also a talented chef and sommelier—share their traditional family recipes, home-cooking style, locally produced and organic products, and a wealth of local cooking secrets. After the demonstration cooking class, an exquisite lunch is served on the terrace with panoramic views over their gardens and the Amalfi Coast.

ENTERTAINMENT AND EVENTS

Ravello is a remarkable setting after dark with its sweeping views of the coastline and twinkling lights in the distance. Known as the City of Music, it offers no shortage of concerts and musical events throughout the year. Though the town is rather quiet at night when it comes to nightclubs, you'll find an assortment of bars with outdoor seating surrounding the Piazza Duomo. During the Ravello Festival, these are lively places for pre- or post-concert drinks.

Nightlife

CAFFE CALCE

Viale Richard Wagner 3; tel. 333/173-7568; www.caffecalce.com; 8am-midnight daily May-Sept., 8am-9pm Tues.-Sun. and closed Mon. Oct.-Apr.; €2-7

On a corner of Piazza Duomo, to the left of the church, this popular local coffee shop, bar, and *pasticceria* (pastry shop) has covered outdoor seating as well as a small indoor seating area. The outdoor area is a great spot to enjoy drinks after dark and soak up the atmosphere. The pastries made on-site are a special treat if you're looking for something sweet to go with your cappuccino in the morning or for dessert after dinner. They also offer light meals, snacks, and gelato.

Concerts

RAVELLO CONCERT SOCIETY

Annunziata Historic Building, Via della Annunziata; tel. 089/842-4082; www.ravelloarts.org; concerts usually held Mon., Wed., and Fri.-Sat. at 8:30pm Mar.-Dec.; €27.50

The Ravello Concert Society has been presenting concerts since 1933 in beautiful historic locations throughout Ravello. Because the season runs most of the year, it's a wonderful opportunity to enjoy a concert in the City of Music, no matter when you visit. Classical and contemporary concerts take place in the **Annunziata Historic Building** (a beautiful setting in a former 13th-century church), as well as in the **Ravello Art Center,** which is located near the Chiesa di Santa Maria a Gradillo. Note that the entrance to the Annunziata Historic Building is at the top of about 90 steps, so concertgoers with mobility issues should select a concert at the Ravello Art Center. Concerts do often sell out, so it's a good idea to purchase in advance.

AUDITORIUM OSCAR NIEMEYER

Via della Repubblica 12; tel. 089/857-977; www.ravellotime.com; contact tourist office for visiting information

Since 1997, the Amalfi Coast has been a UNESCO World Heritage Site, which tells you there has been very little new construction in the area. One distinctive exception is the Auditorium Oscar Niemeyer, which takes its name from its designer, Brazilian architect Oscar Niemeyer. With Ravello's music and art tradition, a state-of-the-art concert hall for year-round performances was needed, and this venue was inaugurated in 2010. The sweeping curved roofline of the bright white building is a striking addition to Ravello's cityscape. A variety of shows are staged here throughout the year, from concerts during the Ravello Festival to movies during the winter months. The large terrace in front of the auditorium is often used for art installations during the Ravello Festival.

Festivals and Events

★ RAVELLO FESTIVAL

Villa Rufolo and various locations; tel. 089/858-422; www.ravellofestival.com; June-Aug.; €25-70

Inspired by Ravello's visitor in 1880, Richard Wagner, the Ravello Festival began in the

1: the swooping modern lines of the Auditorium Oscar Niemeyer in Ravello **2:** Ravello Festival stage and performance in the Villa Rufolo

1
2

1930s and became a yearly event in the 1950s. While exploring the Villa Rufulo gardens, Wagner was so captivated by their enchanting beauty that they served as the inspiration for the magical garden of Klingsor in his opera *Parsifal*. The town transformed that musical moment into a tradition of performances and events. At first, the festival was dedicated primarily to Wagner's music, but over time it has transformed into an excellent, varied festival, featuring classical, opera, jazz, and contemporary performances, as well as ballet, dance, theater, and cultural events and exhibitions. The majority of the performances take place on a specially constructed stage in the Villa Rufolo gardens, the scene of Wagner's inspiration, with the Amalfi Coast serving as a one-of-a-kind backdrop. Other events are held in the Auditorium Oscar Niemeyer and at various locations in Ravello. Concerts take place throughout the week during the festival, and the schedule is usually announced around May each year with tickets available online shortly thereafter. Tickets frequently sell out for concerts, so book as soon as tickets go on sale to avoid disappointment.

FESTIVAL OF SAN PANTALEONE

Duomo di Ravello and various locations; July 27; contact tourist office for program of events

Ravello celebrates its patron San Pantaleone (St. Pantaleon) with a religious festival that starts in the Duomo and takes over the entire town. The festivities take place on July 27, the date San Pantaleone was martyred in AD 305, and the date that it's said the blood of the saint miraculously liquifies. After a special Mass, a procession following a statue of the saint meanders through the narrow streets, accompanied by the town's faithful. Concerts take place in the piazza, and after dark a huge fireworks display is set off above Ravello. The sight is just as magificent overhead as it is from across the valley in Scala, where you can enjoy a full view overlooking Ravello.

SHOPPING

With a fine selection of boutiques, ceramic stores, and local products, Ravello is a nice spot for shopping on the Amalfi Coast. You'll find most of the shops around Piazza Duomo and the two streets that branch off from the square: **Via San Francesco** heading toward Villa Cimbrone, and **Via Roma** in the opposite direction.

RICORDI DI RAVELLO

Piazza Duomo 12; tel. 089/858-403; ricordidiravello@hotmail.com; 9:30am-9pm daily Mar.-Nov.

Located right on the edge of Ravello's main square, this shop has a lovely collection of linen clothing, scarves and shawls, cashmere sweaters, and accessories. The styling is crisp, and the colors and patterns are perfectly in tune with the Amalfi Coast.

BOTTEGA D'AGO

Via Trinità 7; tel. 328/653-6291; www.bottegadago.it; 10am-1:30pm and 2:30-8:30pm

This small family-run boutique is an intimate affair where custom-designed women's clothing and accessories are handmade onsite. Every piece is created by designer Laura D'Agostino, and the boutique is a collaboration with her husband Anthony Cantarella. There's always a tempting selection to admire, from handprinted fabrics to stylish crocheted bags and elegant pieces you'll want to add to your wardrobe.

PASCAL CERAMICHE D'ARTE

Via Roma 22; tel. 089/858-576; www.ceramichedarte.com; 8am-10pm daily Mar.-Oct. (open Nov.-Feb. but contact for daily opening hours)

A fine selection of ceramics is on display at this large shop in the center of Ravello. The pieces on display are curated by Pasquale Sorrentino, who is passionate about handpicking and creating beautiful designs. You'll also find more garden furniture, tables, and vases at a satellite shop with a natural outdoor setting in Ravello at Via della Marra 14, not far from Piazza Duomo.

PROFUMI DELLA COSTIERA

Via Trinità 37; tel. 089/858-167; www.profumidellacostiera.it; 8:30am-7pm daily May-Oct., 8:30am-5pm Nov.-Apr.

Stop in here to find a large selection of locally made liqueurs, including the iconic *limoncello* (lemon liqueur) made with Amalfi Coast lemons. For something a little different, don't miss the liqueur with *finocchietto selvatico* (wild fennel) or other popular varieties made with melon, strawberries, or liquorice.

FOOD

With a setting suspended between land and sea, Ravello offers traditional cuisine that reflects both the mountains and the ocean. Expect to find options ranging from freshly caught seafood to hearty meat dishes or *crespolini*, a local dish of rich and creamy stuffed crepes that are baked in the oven. If you're just visiting for the day, you'll want to pick a restaurant where you can enjoy the view. Longer stays will present you with the chance to try some of the excellent local pizzerias and trattorias, too.

Regional Cuisine

RISTORANTE GARDEN

Via Boccaccio 4; tel. 089/857-226; http://lnx.gardenravello.com; noon-3pm and 7:30pm-10pm daily, closed mid-Nov.-Jan. and Tues. Nov. to Easter; €16-25

With a large terrace and sweeping views, this is a great choice for dining with those iconic Ravello views as the backdrop. The menu is varied and offers excellent choices, even if you aren't into seafood. However, if you are, it is very delicately prepared here, including *spaghetti con le vongole* (with clams) that is top-notch.

ROSSELLINIS

Via San Giovanni del Toro 28; tel. 089/818-181; www.palazzoavino.com/en/Dining/Rossellinis, 7:30pm-midnight daily, closed Nov.-Mar.; €35-45

For a special dining experience, this Michelin-starred restaurant at Ravello's luxurious Palazzo Avino hotel delivers on fine dining, atmosphere, and excellent views. Carefully curated tasting menus (starting at €130 per person) are available, or you can choose to order a la carte. The menu changes seasonally, but if it's available, try the *mezzi paccheri con scampi, burrata e ricci di mare* (pasta with prawns, burrata cheese, and sea urchins); it is exceptional. Reservations are highly recommended.

TRATTORIA DA CUMPÀ COSIMA

Via Roma 44; tel. 089/857-156; noon-4pm and 6pm-11pm daily Mar.-Dec., noon-4pm and 6pm-11pm Tues.-Sun. and closed Mon. Jan.-Feb.; €15-40

Tucked away on a small street near the Chiesa di Santa Maria a Gradillo, this trattoria is the real deal when it comes to home cooking. Netta Bottone, with her apron neatly tied around her waist, serves up local specialties with an emphasis on hearty fare. Can't choose just one pasta from the menu? Try the sample platter that combines some of the restaurant's daily choices, or go for the *crespolini:* Netta's take on this local dish of baked stuffed crepes is out of this world. The meat is also a great choice; it's especially fresh because the family runs the butcher shop next door.

LA MORESCA

Piazza Fontana Moresca 8; www.lamorescaravello.com/it/cucina; 12:30pm-3:30pm and 7:30pm-11pm daily, closed Nov.-Easter; €12-18

In a quiet location on Piazza Fontana Moresca, this traditional trattoria offers both indoor seating as well as a nice outdoor dining terrace. It's a peaceful spot to savor Ravello's relaxed atmosphere and local specialties. Quality of ingredients and traditional flavors are highlighted in dishes like spaghetti with *colatura di alici* (anchovy oil), walnuts, pine nuts, and cherry tomatoes. The wine list is well curated and features mainly Amalfi Coast and Campania wines, as well as other fine wines from across Italy.

VILLA MARIA

Via Santa Chiara 2; tel. 089/857-255; www.villamaria.it/en/restaurant; noon-5pm and 7pm-10pm daily Palm Sunday through Oct.; €25

You'll find this charming restaurant on the way to Villa Cimbrone. Step into a garden courtyard of the Hotel Villa Maria. Under a wisteria-covered pergola, there's a peaceful dining area where you can relax and enjoy excellent local cooking with a view across the lush green valley to Scala. Vegetarian and gluten-free menus are available.

Pizzeria

RISTORANTE PIZZERIA VITTORIA

Via dei Rufolo 3; tel. 089/857-947; www.ristorantepizzeriavittoria.it; noon-3pm and 7pm-11pm daily Apr.-Oct.; €5-20

Just a few steps from Piazza Duomo, this bustling restaurant has a large menu based on local specialties. There are meat and seafood-based options, as well as pizza, which makes this spot a great choice for families.

Wine Bar

BABEL WINE BAR DELI & ART

Via Santissima Trinità 13; tel. 089/858-6215; www.babelravello.com; 11:30am-3:30pm and 7pm-10pm daily, €6-15

For a light lunch, dinner, or drinks, head to this wine bar, just a short jaunt from Piazza Duomo. Try one of the excellent salads for a refreshingly healthy option with a local twist, like the fabulous buffalo *bresaola* (air-dried salted meat) and fig salad with white truffle honey. There are also creative *bruschette* topped with lovely combinations like goat cheese and caramelized onion, or creamy *burrata* cheese with pesto and tomato confit. Choose from local beer and wines in an artistic setting.

ACCOMMODATIONS

Ravello is noted for its five-star hotels, but there are plenty of options available, from cute B&Bs set in historic buildings to seaside villas. While there are a great deal of accommodations in Ravello, it's still a very good idea to book well in advance, especially because it's a popular location for destination weddings.

If relaxing by the sea or pool is key for your holiday, keep in mind that there aren't any beaches in Ravello near the center of the town. You can compensate by picking a hotel with a lovely pool and those fine Ravello views, or choose one with direct sea access or a private beach club.

Under €100

PALAZZO DELLA MARRA

Via della Marra 3; tel. 089/858-302; www.palazzodellamarra.it; closed Jan.; €80 d

Just a few steps from Piazza Duomo, this B&B is set in a historic palazzo once belonging to the Della Marra family, who were important nobles in 13th-century Ravello. The four rooms have views over the Piazza Duomo or across the valley to Scala. The family also offers an apartment rental right in the center of Ravello. This B&B offers a central location and excellent service.

€100-200

IL DUCATO DI RAVELLO

Piazza Duomo (Rampe B. Gambardella); tel. 089/857-837; www.ilducatodiravello.com; €140 d

Situated just below Piazza Duomo, this B&B offers large, well-furnished rooms and a comfortable stay right in the center of Ravello. With views across the green valley to Scala, it feels immersed in nature. The outdoor terrace where breakfast is served has the same fine views.

LA DOLCE VITA

Via Crocelle 23/25; tel. 089/858-320; www.dolcevitaravello.com; open all year; €150 d

La Dolce Vita (The Sweet Life) B&B truly does offer a sweet stay with its large rooms and sweeping views of the coastline. Choose from one of two studios or one-bedroom apartments, each one with large windows, patio or terrace, and a cheery design. Located next to the Auditorium Oscar Niemeyer, it's only a short stroll to the center of Ravello.

HOTEL PARSIFAL

Viale Gioacchino d'Anna 5; tel. 089/857-144; www.hotelparsifal.it; €165 d

Taking its name from Wagner's opera inspired by Ravello, this hotel certainly has an enchanting setting. Sitting high atop Ravello, it was founded as a convent in 1288 and was converted into a hotel in 1948. There's a tranquil atmosphere in the hotel's lovely terraces, central cloister, and 17 rooms. This charming hotel has a family feel and offers the kind of gorgeous Amalfi Coast views that you'd find at the five-star hotels nearby, yet at a much more affordable price point.

€200-300

VILLA MARIA HOTEL

Via Santa Chiara; tel. 089/857-255; www.villamaria.it; €220 d

Follow the walk leading to Villa Cimbrone, and near the entrance to the gardens you'll find this hotel through a small garden courtyard. The villa is beautifully decorated and still maintains the air of a noble residence. The spacious rooms are full of light from the large windows, and there are terraces with excellent views of the tranquil valley and the sea in the distance. With handpainted majolica tiled floors and antique furnishings, the rooms boast historic elements as well as all the modern comforts. The hotel restaurant is set below a wisteria-covered pergola in the courtyard and is a top choice in Ravello. The hotel is open year-round, but the restaurant is open seasonally from Palm Sunday until early November.

HOTEL VILLA SAN MICHELE

Via Carusiello 2, Castiglione; tel. 089/872-237; www.hotel-villasanmichele.it; mid-Mar.-early Nov., €230 d

This beautiful white villa is set on a series of terraces cascading down to the sea and offers a peaceful escape on the Amalfi Coast. The 12 rooms are decorated in shades of blue and white to blend perfectly with the incredible views. Explore the lush garden terraces and follow the steps that meander all the way down to the sea. Prices include lunch or dinner. While the setting is spectacular, note that this hotel's location in Castiglione means that it's not as convenient to restaurants or shopping as many of the other accommodations listed. However, bus stops are located above the hotel, and walking along the Amalfi Coast Road takes you to Atrani in about 10 minutes and Amalfi in about 20 minutes.

the infinity pool at the Belmond Hotel Caruso

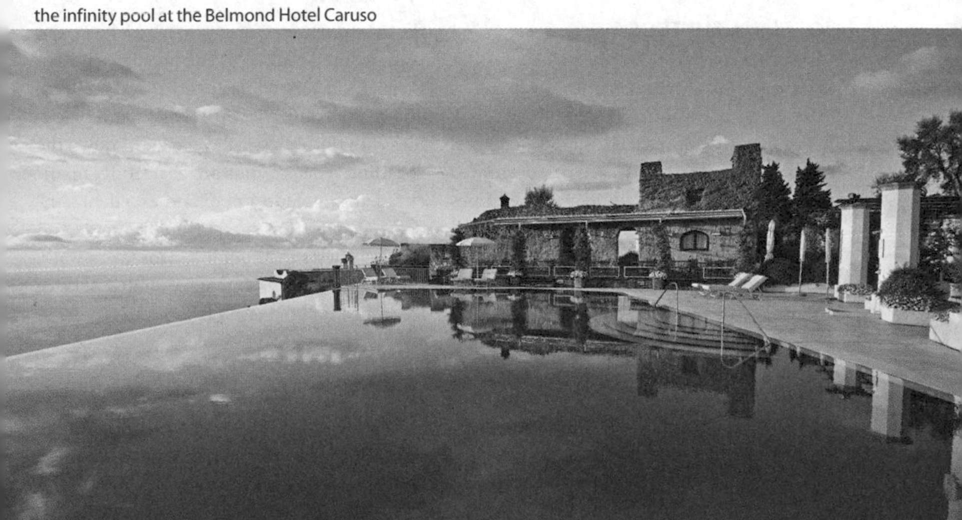

Hiking on the Amalfi Coast

With spectacular views and rich natural beauty, the mountainous landscape of the Amalfi Coast is truly ideal for hiking. The towns and tiny villages dotted along the coastline are interconnected by pathways that were the only way to get around before the Amalfi Coast Road was built during the 19th century. Most of the original footpaths have been preserved and are relatively well maintained. What this means for hikers today is that getting from town to town on foot is actually quite easy, as long as you plan for a lot of steps!

TIPS

Though there is some intense hiking in the higher points of the Lattari Mountains along the coastline, the hikes or walks that most travelers enjoy follow the ancient stone pathways connecting the towns in this area. Here are a few tips and suggestions to enjoy walks and hikes on the Amalfi Coast.

- **Footwear:** Unless you need added support, you'll be fine with a pair of comfortable sneakers or walking shoes.
- **Maps:** Popular hikes and pathways connecting the towns along the Amalfi Coast are fairly well marked. However, **Cart&guide** (www.carteguide.com; English versions available; €5 each) makes detailed maps that can be purchased in bookstores and shops in the area.
- **Steps:** Expect a lot of steps wherever you are hiking on the Amalfi Coast. The ancient stone steps and pathways can be very irregular and steep, and going down a large number of steps can be very hard on the knees. If this is an issue, consider walking from the lowest starting point to the highest, and plan a more relaxed activity for the day after a long hike like the Sentiero degli Dei in Positano.
- **Essentials:** Bring plenty of water as well as sun protection and a hat in the summer months. Fountains that you find along the way all have potable water so you can refill bottles.

HOTEL LA MORESCA

Piazza Fontana Moresca 8; tel. 089/857-912; www.lamorescaravello.com; open Easter-Oct.; €250 d

Situated in a tranquil area of Ravello on Piazza Fontana Moresca, this boutique hotel has nine gorgeous rooms, each one decorated in a unique style with striking local ceramics and views overlooking Ravello, the sea, and the valley over to Scala. This is a great choice for travelers who like small hotels and unique design. The excellent on-site restaurant is an added bonus.

VILLA PIEDIMONTE

Via della Repubblica 1; tel. 089/745-0036; www.villapiedimonte.com; Apr.-early Nov., €299 d

This sprawling 12th-century villa just below the Auditorium Oscar Niemeyer has been transformed into a great holiday spot in Ravello. The 22 rooms are crisp and modern, and many feature lovely terraces and balconies with those classic Ravello views down the coastline. The grounds are beautifully manicured and include a pool and excellent sunbathing spots. On-site parking is ample and free for guests. Although it's not far to walk, there's also a complimentary shuttle service from the hotel to Piazza Duomo.

Over €300

HOTEL VILLA CIMBRONE

Via Santa Chiara 26; tel. 089/857-459; www.hotelvillacimbrone.com; open Apr.-Oct.; €572 d

Nestled in beautiful gardens, Villa Cimbrone

HIKES

Trail	Starting Point	Hiking Time	Description
Pathway of the Gods	Bomerano (in Agerola) or Nocelle (near Positano)	3 hours	Mountain trail with panoramic views of Praiano, Positano, and Capri.
Valle delle Ferriere	Amalfi	2.5 hours	Hike in the valley above Amalfi, passing old paper mills and waterfalls.
Ravello to Minori	Ravello	1 hour	Ancient stone steps lead down through lemon and olive trees to Minori.
Ravello to Atrani	Ravello	1.5 hours	Various stone pathways go down the valley to Atrani and farther to Amalfi.
Torre dello Ziro Watchtower	Pontone (near Scala)	2 hours	Visit this 15th-century watchtower via a mountainside trail with views of Atrani from above.
Scala to Amalfi	Scala	45 min	Stairway hike through villages with a quick detour to the ruins of an old basilica. Can be combined with Valle delle Ferriere hike
Pathway of the Lemons	Minori	1 hour	Walk through lemon groves on this mountain trail that was once the only way to get between Maiori and Minori.

is a stunning property, offering the rare chance to enjoy a luxurious stay on a 12th-century estate. The hotel and its rooms are full of historic charm and remarkable details like frescoed ceilings, marble fireplaces, and handpainted ceramic floors. The pool and private garden area for guests are perfectly manicured. The hotel isn't accessible by car, but it's a pleasant 10-minute walk from Piazza Duomo.

BELMOND HOTEL CARUSO

Piazza San Giovanni del Toro 2; 089/858-801; www.belmond.com/HotelCaruso; open Apr.-Oct.; €920 d

Situated in an 11th-century palazzo, this luxury hotel offers a sumptuous stay full of historic charm. Top-notch guest services and beautiful gardens add to the luscious setting. Perched between sky and sea with a stunning view overlooking the coast, the infinity pool is the stuff that travel dreams are made of. The classically styled rooms range from double to exclusive suites, and feature balconies, terraces, or private gardens. Some overlook the town or garden instead of the sea. Check in advance if a sea view is a must.

PALAZZO AVINO

Via San Giovanni del Toro 28; tel. 089/818-181; www.palazzoavino.com; open Apr.-Oct.; €1,150 d

This impeccably designed luxury hotel is situated in a grand, private 12th-century villa and includes 33 double rooms and 10 suites, each one more spectacular than the last. Explore the terraced gardens, which include a solarium and pool. Or take the complimentary shuttle down to the Clubhouse by the Sea, where you can dine seaside, soak up the sun and swim in the small pool, or enjoy direct access to the sea. This is a unique feature for a hotel located in the center of Ravello.

INFORMATION AND SERVICES

Tourist Information

AZIENDA AUTONOMA SOGGIORNO E TURISMO

Piazza Fontana Moresca 10; tel. 089/857-096; www.ravellotime.com; 9am-6pm daily (until 3pm Nov.-Feb.)

Ravello's tourist office is located in the pretty Piazza Fontana Moresca, where you'll find a fountain and view across the valley to Scala. Stop in if you have questions or need local information, and the English-speaking staff will be happy to help.

Medical and Emergency Services

OSPEDALE COSTA D'AMALFI

Via Civita 12; tel. 089/873-150; www.aslsalerno.it

The Amalfi Coast's only hospital is located in Ravello, but not in the center of town. It is on the SS373 road that connects Ravello with the Amalfi Coast Road (SS163). The hospital is located in Castiglione, a *frazione* of Ravello, just before the intersection with the Amalfi Coast Road. It is a little more than 3 miles (5 km) and a 15-minute drive (without traffic) from the center of Ravello. The hospital has a 24-hour emergency room (*pronto soccorso*). To receive **emergency services** in Italy, dial 118 for ambulance and urgent care.

Postal Services

POSTE ITALIANE

Via Giovanni Boccaccio 21; tel. 089/858-6631; www.poste.it; 8:20am-1:35pm Mon.-Fri.

To find Ravello's post office from the central Piazza Duomo, walk through the large tunnel to the left of the Villa Rufolo entrance, take a left, and walk along Via Giovanni Boccaccio only a short distance to find the post office on the left. This is where you'll go to mail letters or packages.

GETTING THERE

By Car and Scooter

Ravello sits at 1,200 feet (365 m) above sea level along the Amalfi Coast, about 4 miles (6.7 km) from Amalfi. It is not located along the Amalfi Coast Road (SS163), but can be reached by following SS373 from the crossroads at Castiglione. The road to Ravello is among the trickiest roads on the coast, as one section is very narrow. During the tourist season from Easter through October, there is a traffic light to limit traffic to one way during the day. If you're driving this road, go slowly and be prepared to back up if needed. The drive from Amalfi to Ravello takes about 20 minutes, depending on traffic and the time of year. From Positano, the drive is about an hour along the Amalfi Coast Road east to SS373 and then up to Ravello. To reach Ravello from Salerno, this drive is about 1 hour as well along the Amalfi Coast Road west to SS373 and then up to the center of town.

By Bus

Given the tricky roads and limited parking, one of the best ways to arrive is by bus. The local public bus company **SITA SUD** (tel. 089/386-6701; www.sitasudtrasporti.it; from €1.30) has a bus line connecting Ravello with Scala and Amalfi. Buses arrive every 30-60 minutes throughout the day, depending on the time of year. There are two bus stops in Ravello. The Galleria Nuova stop is located on Via Giovanni Boccaccio near the entrance to the tunnel that leads to Piazza Duomo. The Gradillo stop is just below the Chiesa di Santa Maria a Gradillo. The bus ride from Amalfi to Ravello takes about 25 minutes. To reach Ravello by bus from Salerno, Positano, and other locations on the Amalfi Coast, you will first need first to arrive in Amalfi by bus and then transfer to the SITA SUD bus line to Ravello.

The easy-to-spot, bright red **City Sightseeing** (tel. 081/877-4707; www.city-sightseeing.it; Apr.-Oct., from €5 per person) buses are a more comfortable option for traveling from Amalfi to Ravello. These open-top buses arrive in Ravello at the Galleria Nuova area just like the SITA SUD buses. Yet, because they only admit as many passengers as they have seats, they are never as overcrowded as a SITA SUD bus might be. Tickets are purchased onboard and include an audio guide in many languages.

GETTING AROUND

Ravello is a small town and it is best explored on foot once you've arrived by bus or parked your car or scooter. A well-marked paid parking lot is located below Piazza Duomo and is accessed by following Via della Marra below the Chiesa di Santa Maria a Gradillo. A small parking lot is available below the Auditorium Oscar Niemeyer, and paid parking is also available along the side of the roads surrounding Ravello. Expect to pay about €3 per hour for parking. Scooter parking is available near the Chiesa di Santa Maria a Gradillo and on Via della Repubblica leading down to the Auditorium Oscar Niemeyer. Scooter parking costs €1.50 an hour or €8 for the day.

If you'd like to rent a scooter in Ravello, check out **Ravello Rent A Scooter** (Via Porta di Scala 1; tel. 366/951-5631; www.ravellorentascooter.com; mid-Mar.-mid-Nov.; starting at €65). This company will deliver your scooter rental to your accommodation for a small extra fee.

Scala

Considered the oldest settlement on the Amalfi Coast, Scala is believed to have been founded in the fifth century by shipwrecked Romans who fled to the rugged mountains for protection. Over time, the town's prosperity grew in connection with the Republic of Amalfi, which led to a period of great affluence and the construction of Scala's impressive churches.

Located just across the valley from Ravello in the mountains above Amalfi and Atrani, Scala is one of the Amalfi Coast's hidden gems. It stretches across the mountainside and is composed of six different *frazioni*, or villages: **Minuta, Campidoglio, Santa Caterina, San Pietro,** and **Pontone.** The center of Scala is at **Piazza Municipio,** which is where the **Duomo di San Lorenzo** is located as well as the main bus stop and shopping area in town. Via Toricella heads south out of Piazza Municipio and makes a large circuit around town, connecting Minuta, Campidoglio, Santa Caterina, and San Pietro. The peaceful village of Pontone is reached by taking Via Valle delle Ferriere from the SS373 road; Pontone lies in a more secluded area between Scala and Amalfi.

Scala's serene atmosphere feels worlds away from the pace of modern-day life and makes it the ideal home base, surrounded by nature. You'll enjoy hiking and savoring the beauty of the Amalfi Coast just a short distance from two of the coastline's major destinations.

SIGHTS

Scala's beautiful setting, stretching out across the valley, is one of its most attractive sights. While exploring the town's *frazioni*, stop to visit the churches, as they offer a glimpse into Scala's important history as a part of the Republic of Amalfi. Wealthy families built large estates in the area and founded the churches you can still visit today.

Piazza Municipio

Piazza Municipio between Via Vescovado and Via Torcella

This piazza is the heart of Scala. It is where you'll find the Duomo di San Lorenzo as well as all the town's shops and city hall.

The square is dominated by the façade of the Duomo, but just to the right you'll find a stone fountain and beyond that, a terrace with great views of Ravello across the valley. In the piazza opposite the Duomo, a plaque honors Gerardo Sasso, a monk from Scala who, during the 12th century, was the founder of the Order of the Knights of Malta (*Cavalieri dell'Ordine dell'Ospedale di San Giovanni di Gerusalemme)*. At that time, Scala was a part of the Republic of Amalfi, which is why you'll spot the familiar symbol of Amalfi, the eight-pointed Maltese cross, on the plaque.

Duomo di San Lorenzo

Piazza Municipio; 10:30am-6pm daily

Dedicated to San Lorenzo, the Duomo of Scala is an impressive church for what is now a small, peaceful town. Step inside and you'll see that the massive space with large white columns is crowned with three large paintings on the ceiling depicting scenes of the life of San Lorenzo, the town's patron saint. In the center of the aisle on the floor, there's a large majolica ceramic scene from 1853 depicting a large shield with a lion climbing a ladder, which refers to the town's name (*scala* means steps). The shield is surrounded by cherubs holding an ornate garland of flowers. Follow the steps on the right aisle down to the church's crypt, the Gothic-style Cripta del Paradiso with its delicate pink and white detailing. At the far end is the striking tomb of Marinella Rufolo, a noblewoman from Ravello in the 1300s.

Chiesa dell'Annunziata

Piazza Minuta; open only during Mass generally Sunday at 6pm

Set in the *frazione* of Minuta, one of the prettiest spots in Scala, this church is among the oldest on the Amalfi Coast. Founded in the 11th century, it features a portico with a 15th-century fresco of the Madonna above the central door. Be sure to visit the crypt to see the extraordinary frescoes, also from the 12th century, with a variety of scenes including the Miracle of San Nicola of Bari. From the piazza outside the church there's a panoramic view down the valley with the Basilica di Sant'Eustachio and just a glimpse of Amalfi in the distance.

Basilica di Sant'Eustachio

Via Sant'Eustachio; tel. 333/255-7163; www.basilicasanteustachio.business.site; 10am-noon and 2pm-6pm daily, free

Located between Minuta and Pontone, the ruins of the 12th-century Basilica di Sant'Eustachio are a romantic sight sitting atop a small promontory. This was once a lavish church built by the noble d'Afflitto family of Scala, but what remains today are just traces of its former glory. Walk through the ruins and enjoy the marvelous panoramic views across the valley from the Villa Cimbrone in Ravello to Atrani, Pontone, and Amalfi.

Pontone

Via Valle delle Ferriere, Pontone, Scala

This tranquil *frazione* of Scala sits halfway between Scala and Amalfi, and is often a peaceful respite for hikers exploring the area. Its pretty little piazza is full of trees and **Blu Bar** (Piazza San Giovanni 2; tel. 089/872-639; 8am-midnight daily from Mar.-Oct., 8am-1pm and 5pm-8pm Mon.-Sat. Nov.-Feb.) is a great spot to relax. Also on the piazza you'll find the bell tower and **Chiesa di San Giovanni Battista**, which was founded in the 12th century. If the church is open, step inside to find a somewhat surprising pastel-colored baroque interior.

Pontone is reachable by steps from Minuta or Amalfi, and more easily by a small road that branches off of the SS373 between Castiglione on the Amalfi Coast Road and Ravello. There's a handful of public SITA buses on the Amalfi, Scala, and Ravello line that also stop in Pontone.

1: detail on the Duomo di San Lorenzo **2:** Stop to take in the view of Amalfi while walking down the steps from Scala. **3:** Sit and enjoy the quiet atmosphere in Pontone's little piazza.

1
2
3

HIKING

TORRE DELLO ZIRO WATCHTOWER

Sitting atop the mountain between Amalfi and Atrani is the 15th-century Torre dello Ziro watchtower, which was built on top of an earlier defensive tower from the 12th century. Though it is much more visible from Amalfi and Atrani, the only way to reach the watchtower is by hiking from Scala. Start in Pontone where Via Pisacane branches off of the Via Valle delle Ferriere and follow the signs to the Torre dello Ziro. The rugged pathway hugs the mountainside as it climbs toward the tower. Along the way there's a spectacular view looking down on Atrani. You can explore the area around the tower and walls before climbing to a higher viewpoint for a bird's-eye view of Amalfi. Plan for it to take about two hours round-trip to hike to the tower and back.

SCALA TO AMALFI

This gorgeous hike leads from Scala down through the mountain valley to Amalfi and passes through the villages of Minuta and Pontone along the way. Start by following the steps from Via Torricella down to Minuta to the Chiesa dell'Annunziata. From the piazza in front of the church, take the staircase behind the fountain down and follow signs to Amalfi. When you reach the top of Pontone, the pathway divides with two options for passing through Pontone. Take the pathway on the right to visit the ruins of the **Basilica di Sant'Eustachio** before descending a steep staircase into Pontone. Stop for a rest in the piazza before continuing down the steps toward Amalfi.

The stairacase zigzags through terraces of lemon groves and hugs the mountainside before it reaches the first houses at the top of Amalfi. The pathway leads down to Amalfi's main street and eventually the Piazza Duomo.

Another option once you arrive in Pontone is to hike into the Valle delle Ferriere to explore the waterfalls and ruins of ancient mills before descending back into Amalfi. From Piazza San Giovanni in Pontone, follow signs for the Valle delle Ferriere leading deep into the valley. From the Valle delle Ferriere, follow signs pointing back down to Amalfi. The hike from Scala to Amalfi takes 45 minutes, but plan to spend at least twice as long if you're going to explore the **Valle delle Ferriere.**

ENTERTAINMENT AND EVENTS

While Scala's peacefulness is one of its best features, the town also knows how to put on a good festival. Whether it's feting the town's patron saint or putting on one of the best food festivals along the Amalfi Coast, Scala's annual events are worth marking your calendar.

FESTIVAL OF SAN LORENZO

Piazza Municipio; Aug. 10

Scala's patron saint is celebrated with a big summer festival on August 10, the traditional day the saint is honored. Events center around the Duomo di Scala—which is dedicated to San Lorenzo—and include a religious procession with a statue of the saint, music in the piazza, stalls selling food, and a big fireworks display over the town after dark.

FESTA DELLA CASTAGNA (Chestnut Festival)

Piazza Municipio; www.discoverscala.com; October (dates vary)

Chestnut trees fill the valley around Scala, and in autumn the annual harvest is celebrated with a big food festival (*sagra*) completely dedicated to chestnuts. The entire center of town is transformed into a rustic setting with various stalls selling local specialties like *gnocchi* and pasta made with chestnuts or chestnut flour and a variety of tempting chestnut cream-filled desserts as well as roasted chestnuts. Traditional games take place in Piazza Municipio, including tug of war and a donkey race with each of the *frazioni* of Scala vying to win. A stage is set up in the piazza for concerts by local bands. The festival usually takes place over two weekends in October, with the dates varying depending on the harvest.

FOOD AND ACCOMMODATIONS

TRATTORIA DA LORENZO

Via Frà Gerardo Sasso 10; tel. 089/858-290; www.trattoriadalorenzo.com; 12:30pm-3pm and 7:30pm-10:30pm Apr.-mid-Oct., closed Mon.; €50

The entrance to this gem of a restaurant is through a pretty garden with olive trees leading to a small inside seating area and a beautiful terrace with a glimpse of Ravello in the distance. You'll want to try their array of antipasti, which includes a selection of fish and local vegetable dishes. Seafood is the highlight here, and the pasta and fresh local fish like *scorfano* (red scorpionfish) or *rana pescatrice* (angler) are exceptionally good. Save room for the creative desserts if you can!

IL PINGUINO

Via Frà Gerardo Sasso 7; tel. 089/857-304; www.pinguinobb.it; 12:30pm-3pm and 7:30-11pm Wed.-Mon., closed Tues. (open daily in Aug.), closed Jan.-Feb.; €10-22

This family-run restaurant and B&B is a local favorite with its excellent home cooking, wood-fire oven pizza, and warm hospitality. The eggplant parmesan is a great place to start, followed by spaghetti with beans and mussels, a regional specialty you won't find on many menus. The pizza is also top-notch. The rooms (€150 d) are clean and bright, and the breakfast options are delicious.

RISTORANTE SAN GIOVANNI

Via Santa Maria, Pontone; tel. 089/872-582; www.ristorantesangiovanni.com; 10am-4pm and 7pm-midnight daily from Mar.-Nov.; €9-20

Located next to the Chiesa di San Giovanni Battista in Pontone, this is a great spot to stop for lunch while hiking in the Scala area. There's both an indoor dining area and a lovely outdoor covered terrace with views across the valley to Ravello. You'll enjoy excellent pizza, hearty pasta dishes, and an especially good grilled meat platter.

VILLA GIUSEPPINA

Via Torricella; tel. 089/857-106; www.villagiuseppinacostadamalfi.it; closed Nov. 15-Mar. 15; €120

With a quiet setting and gorgeous views across the valley to Ravello, this small hotel offers a very welcoming stay with friendly service. Of the 20 rooms available, about half include large private terraces with panoramic views. Breakfast is served on the vine-covered terrace, and if you can time your visit to when the wisteria blooms, it is especially magical. The hotel also boasts a pool with the same fabulous views of Ravello.

GETTING THERE AND AROUND

Scala is located across the Valle del Dragone from Ravello and is easily reached by car or bus. From Ravello, you can even walk to Scala in about 30 minutes. To reach Scala from the Amalfi Coast Road, follow the SS373 road at Castiglione up toward Ravello. Before reaching Ravello, look for the large ceramic sign for Scala and turn left. From there the road leads to the center of town and if you continue to follow it, it makes a large loop around the different parts of town. The drive to Scala is about 5 minutes from Ravello, 20 minutes from Amalfi, and a little over an hour from either Positano or Salerno.

The local bus company **SITA SUD** (tel. 089/386-6701; www.sitasudtrasporti.it; from €1.30 per person) has a bus line that connects Scala to Ravello and Amalfi, with service every 30-60 minutes throughout the day, with more frequent service from April-October. All buses to Scala stop in the Piazza Municipio in the center of town, while only a handful each day stop in the *frazioni* of Scala, including Pontone and Minuta. The bus ride from Ravello to Scala is about five minutes, while from Amalfi it's about 25 minutes. To reach Scala by bus from Positano or Salerno, first take the bus to Amalfi where you can transfer to the bus line serving Scala and Ravello.

Tramonti

Deep in the Lattari Mountains above Ravello and Maiori, Tramonti is the green heart of the Amalfi Coast. The town once played an important role in defending the Republic of Amalfi along the pass through the mountains, while the river Reginna, which runs down the valley to Maiori, was used to power the local ironworks and paper mills.

The town's name means "among the mountains," which perfectly describes its setting nestled in a lush valley and spread out into 13 different areas that are connected by a narrow road that winds through sleepy villages, terraced gardens, and pergolas of grapevines so close to the road that it seems you could reach out and touch them while driving by. It's those grapevines that bring most visitors to quiet Tramonti, because wine from this region is a real treasure of the Amalfi Coast. Vines have been growing here for more than a thousand years. If you enjoy a rural and natural landscape, or good wine, plan to stop in Tramonti.

SIGHTS

Tramonti's sights and mountain setting are best appreciated while exploring the different villages spread out around the valley.

Giardino Segreto dell'Anima

Via Telese, Campinola; tel. 347/879-0007; www.giardinosegretodellanima.com; Apr.-Oct.; free with required reservation

This secret garden is tucked away in a spot that is easy to miss if you aren't looking for it. Yet, garden enthusiasts will be happy to explore this large garden spreading out over more than 32,000 square feet (3,000 square meters) on eight large terraces. The rose garden has more than 350 varieties, the citrus garden 25 different varieties, and the entire garden has more than 1,200 different types of plants to discover. Admission is free, but visitors must make an appointment in advance to join a tour.

Tenuta San Francesco Vineyard

Via Solficiano 18, Corsano; tel. 089/876-748; www.vinitenutasanfrancesco.com; reservation required; from €35 per person

Since 2004, Tenuta San Francesco has been a forerunner in the production of highly respected wines from the Amalfi Coast. They've brought modern production into a cantina dating back to the 1700s, and with a little more than 22 acres this is one of the largest vineyards in Tramonti. Vineyard tours and a variety of tasting options are available, but reservations are required.

Cantine Giuseppe Apicella

Via Castello S.Maria 1, Capitignano; tel. 089/856-209; www.giuseppeapicella.it; reservation required; from €25 for tour and tasting

For generations the Apicella family has produced wine in the Tramonti valley, and today the vineyard is run by Giuseppe Apicella and his wife along with their two children. The family is passionate about continuing the important wine-producing tradition and tending the vines, the oldest dating back to the early 20th century. Wine tastings and tours through the vineyards and the cantina are available.

FOOD AND ACCOMMODATIONS

Tramonti's local specialties take inspiration from the natural setting and include hearty meat dishes, locally produced cheese, chestnuts, and pizza.

TRATTORIA SAN FRANCESCO DI POLVICA

Piazza Polvica 17, Polvica; tel. 339/440-1041; s.francisco2000@libero.it; noon-3pm and 7:00pm-11:30pm Thurs.-Tues., closed Wed.; €7-15

Head to this welcoming restaurant and pizzeria to try Tramonti's unique style of pizza, which is a little different and a bit thicker than the traditional Neapolitan style. Pizza maker Francesco Maiorano and his wife Pamela Viggiano are the masterminds behind this restaurant, which is dedicated to Tramonti's traditional home cooking based on high-quality ingredients. Try the pasta with locally grown beans or sauces prepared with the variety of tomato called Re Fiascone, which is cultivated locally.

LE QUERCE

Località Chiancolelle; tel. 338/203-2931; ag.querce@hotmail.it; 12:30pm-3pm and 7:30pm-midnight, closed Mon. Nov.-Apr.; €20-40

This rustic restaurant located at the top of a steep and narrow mountain road specializes in grilled meat as well as traditional local dishes like pasta with mushrooms or wild boar. The steaks are enormous and the best you'll find on the Amalfi Coast. From the small parking area you can see to the other side of the mountains toward Naples.

LA CASA DI FARFALLE E GABBIANI

Piazza Campinola, Campinola; tel. 089/856-469; www.farfalleegabbiani.it; closed Nov. 4-Dec. 6; €78

This charming B&B is immersed in the natural setting that characterizes Tramonti. It includes a garden terrace with solarium and chairs for relaxing. The rooms are decorated in a simple yet natural way with oak-beamed ceilings. All rooms have a view of the sea in the distance: a nice reminder that it's only about 5 miles (8 km) away!

GETTING THERE AND AROUND

Given Tramonti's rural setting, with 13 different areas sprawling across the valley in the Monte Lattari, the best way to get to and explore the town is by car or scooter. Two main roads pass through Tramonti, connecting it with Ravello and Maiori on the Amalfi Coast. The SP1 (Strada Provinciale 1) begins in Ravello and runs through the western side of Tramonti while the SP2a starts in Maiori and passes along the eastern side of Tramonti. Both the SP1 and SP2a meet at the Valley of Chiunzi (Valico di Chiunzi), the pass over the Lattari mountains from the southern side of the Sorrentine Peninsula to the northern side. From there, the SP2b road continues down the northern side of the mountains where it meets the highway to Naples and Salerno. A narrow internal road connects the small rural areas of Tramonti. From the SP2a on the eastern side of Tramonti, take a left at a well marked intersection onto the SP141 and follow the road as it meanders through the terraced vineyards and tiny hamlets to the other side of Tramonti, connecting to the SP1 road on the western side of the town.

To reach Tramonti from Maiori, follow the SP2a road up into the valley and you'll reach the town after a 15-minute drive. From Amalfi and Positano, follow the Amalfi Coast Road (SS163) east to Maiori and then take SP2a to Tramonti. From Salerno, take the Amalfi Coast Road west to Maiori and continue along the SP2a. The drive to Tramonti from Amalfi takes about 35 minutes, from Positano about an hour and 15 minutes, and from Salerno a little over an hour. From Naples, follow the A3 highway south and exit at Angri Sud and follow signs for Valico di Chiunzi and continue along the SP2a road to the pass, where you can continue along either the SP1 or SP2a roads to Tramonti. From Naples, plan for about a 1-hour drive to Tramonti.

Note that the road SP1 from Ravello to Tramonti is currently closed due to a landslide. However, many drivers pass through with caution. Choosing an alternate route is recommended, especially if it is or has been raining. If you take this road, proceed at your own risk, as insurance may not cover any incidents that occur on a road that is technically closed.

Minori

Minori sits at the base of a beautiful valley surrounded by terraced gardens of lemons. Called Rheginna Minor in the Middle Ages, this town has a vibrant cultural and gastronomic heritage that is still very much alive and well. Minori's mountain stream, called Regginolo, once powered papermaking mills and pasta factories. Yet it was the town's agricultural tradition of lemon farming that left a lasting mark on Minori.

Minori is home to an archaeological treasure in the form of an expansive Roman villa dating from about the first century BC. The excavated parts of the villa are located right in the center of town. Not far away is the grand **Basilica di Santa Trofimena,** dedicated to Minori's very special patron saint. The small, well-manicured waterfront stretches along the beach and is the popular spot for locals to enjoy a *passeggiata* (stroll) throughout the day. On the eastern end of town you'll spot the **Fontana Moresca,** a fountain with two carved stone lions and, in the middle, a column that was most likely taken from an ancient site.

Though it is not far from Amalfi and Ravello, Minori has a more laid-back feel because it is just that little bit off the beaten path. It's an excellent base to enjoy a holiday surrounded by the Amalfi Coast's charms.

SIGHTS

Most of Minori's sights are located along the waterfront or right in the center of the town. Though its main sights can be visited in a half day, plan to linger because there are some great walks in the area and a picturesque beach to soak up the sun.

Basilica di Santa Trofimena

Piazza Cantilena; tel. 089/854-1503; www.santatrofimena.it; 7:30am-noon and 5pm-7:30pm

The religious heart of Minori is the beautiful Basilica di Santa Trofimena, which sits in a small piazza not far from the beach. The first church to stand on this spot dates back to the seventh century, but after the saint's relics miraculously arrived on the beach in Minori, a new church was constructed. The church played an important role on the Amalfi Coast, and from 987 to 1818 it was the seat of a bishop and therefore held the position of a cathedral.

The church you see today dates from the baroque period, though it underwent significant restorations in the 19th century. The elegant stucco architectural details in gray and white blend baroque and neoclassical elements into one unique style. Its interior has a Latin cross floor plan with a nave, two side aisles, and a dome over the crossing. The oldest part of the church is the crypt holding the relics of Santa Trofimena.

Villa Romana

Via Capo di Piazza 28; tel. 089/852-893; www.villaromanaminori.com; 9am-one hour before sunset daily, closed May 1, Dec. 25, and Jan. 1; free

Enjoying the natural landscape of Minori has been a pastime since the Romans sailed along the coast and spotted this scenic beach and lush valley setting. We know this thanks to a large Roman villa dating from about the first century BC that has been excavated right in the center of town. Of all the ruins uncovered along the Amalfi Coast, the Villa Romana is the largest. Sprawling out over 2,500 square feet (232 square meters), the villa offers a rare glimpse into the Roman lifestyle along the Amalfi Coast.

The multilevel villa includes a large dining area and nymphaeum, with beautiful mosaics, frescoes, and the remains of what was once a waterfall. Though much of the villa is closed to visitors, it's possible to envision how grand the villa once was if you walk around the portico surrounding the large courtyard. The pool was once in the center of the villa, meaning the garden area was much larger than we can see today. Near the entrance is a small museum of archaeological items uncovered in Minori and the surrounding areas.

Campanile dell'Annunziata

Via Torre Annunziata

On the eastern mountain slope above Minori, you can spot a striking bell tower, which is all that remains from the Chiesa dell'Annunziata, a church from the 12th century. While there are only ruins of the church that the bell tower was once connected to, from the outside on the steps next to the tower you can see the Byzantine-Arab architectural influences in the intricate geometric diamond and cross patterns and style of the bell tower. To reach the tower, follow the steps from the center of Minori for the Campanile dell'Annunziata. A narrow staircase leads through a residential area with little terraced gardens to the top of town and the bell tower. If you would like to continue your walk, the Sentiero dei Limoni begins nearby.

BEACHES

SPIAGGIA GRANDE

Via Roma

Minori's pretty beach stretches out in front of the town and offers a lovely view of the surrounding valley. The beach has several beach clubs (*stabilimenti balneari)* like **Chalet de Mar** (Lungomare; tel. 089/851-721; www.chaletdemaramalficoast.it; May-Oct.; starting at €15 for two sun beds and umbrella), offering sun bed and umbrella rentals as well as showers, changing rooms, and beachside snack bars or restaurants. On both ends of the beach, there are open areas where you can throw down a towel and enjoy the beach for free. The beach is popular with families, and because it faces south for sunshine most of the day and is a pleasant spot for swimming. **Boat Service** (tel. 328/302-9603; www.boatservice.org; May-Oct.; kayak rental starting at €15 per hour) offers kayak, clear kayak, and pedal boat rentals right on the beach in Minori.

HIKING

PATHWAY OF THE LEMONS (Sentiero dei Limoni)

Via Torre Annunziata

Before the Amalfi Coast Road was built in the first half of the 19th century, the only connection between Maiori and Minori on land was a rugged pathway over the mountain. This scenic walk is now called the Sentiero dei Limoni (Pathway of the Lemons) because it passes through the terraces of lemon groves above Minori and Maiori. This was once the largest area for growing the local *sfusato amalfitano* lemons, which were harvested and carried down the mountain to Minori and Maiori and then exported around the world. The lemon groves are still lovingly maintained and the walk offers beautiful views along the way.

Starting from the **Campanile dell'Annunziata** in Minori, follow Via Torre, which hugs the mountainside with terraced lemon gardens above and below. Stop at the **Belvedere Mortella**, a little overlook off the walkway that offers great views of the town, the Basilica di Santa Trofimena, and beach below. The pathway passes through a little area called Torre with a small church dedicated to San Michele Arcangelo before continuing around to Maiori. It takes about an hour to walk from Minori to Maiori.

FESTIVALS AND EVENTS

During the summer months Minori often hosts concerts and cultural events along the waterfront or in the Villa Romana, so keep an eye out for event postings around town. In addition to the festivals for the town's patron saint throughout the year, Minori also celebrates Easter with moving religious processions from the Basilica di Santa Trofimena.

FESTIVAL OF SANTA TROFIMENA

Basilica di Santa Trofimena; July 13, Nov. 5, and Nov. 26-27

The people of Minori celebrate their patron saint with three big religious festivals throughout the year, each date

NICIPIO
BASILICA S TROPHIMENAE V.M
1
2
3
4

honoring a special occasion connected to Santa Trofimena. Each festival includes special Masses in the Basilica, religious processions with a treasured statue of the saint, and fireworks displays over the sea.

GUSTA MINORI

Various locations; tel. 089/854-1609; www.gustaminori.it; August

Once an important center for pasta making and still strongly connected with the Amalfi Coast's traditional lemon cultivation, Minori is proud of its gastronomic heritage. This culinary tradition is usually feted during the last week of August with a multiday festival called Gusta Minori (A Taste of Minori), which celebrates local products and blends food, art, and cultural events into a fun summer event.

FOOD AND ACCOMMODATIONS

SAL DE RISO

Via Roma 80; tel. 089/877-941; www.salderiso.it; 7am-1am daily; €5 individual pastries and €8-16 for entrees and pizzas

Saving room for dessert is a must thanks to Minori's famous pastry chef Salvatore de Riso, who has created not only a heavenly spot for sweets but also for excellent dining in his hometown. The menu is focused on the highest-quality local ingredients and includes gourmet pizza, salads, sandwiches, and even a great hamburger. You really do want to save room for dessert though! You'll find an incredible selection of pastries, gelato, and cakes, all beautifully presented. You really can't go wrong, but the *delizia al limone*, a lemon cream infused cake, and *ricotta pera e cioccolato*, a lovely cake made with ricotta, pears, and chocolate, are both divine.

GIARDINIELLO

Corso Vittorio Emanuele 17; tel. 089/877-050; www.ristorantegiardiniello.com; 12:15pm-3pm and 6:30pm-11:30pm; €11-18

Along the main street that cuts through the center of Minori, you'll find this restaurant with a beautiful pergola-covered garden where you can dine outside when the weather is fine. The menu highlights seafood, and it's done remarkably well. However, you could also go for the local *ndunderi*, a traditional Minori pasta dish of small dumplings made with flour and ricotta served with tomato sauce and smoked mozzarella. The menu also includes plenty of excellent non-seafood options as well as pizza.

PALAZZO VINGIUS B&B

Via San Giovanni a Mare 19; tel. 089/854-1646, www.palazzovingius.it; open Mar.-Oct.; €120 d

This lovely B&B has nine welcoming and comfortable rooms with excellent sea views. The balcony rooms are worth paying extra to enjoy sitting outside and taking in the views day and night. Entrance to the B&B is from the Amalfi Coast Road as it winds out of the town to the west, or from a staircase of about 50 steps from near the beach. An elevator is in the works for the near future.

INFORMATION AND SERVICES

PRO LOCO

Via Roma 32; tel. 089/877-087; www.prolocominori.it; 9am-1pm and 4pm-9pm May-Sept., and 9am-1:30pm and 3:30pm-8:30pm Oct.-Apr.

Located right along the waterfront, Minori's tourist office is friendly and well-stocked with information about the town and surrounding area. The English-speaking staff are happy to share information and answer any questions.

GETTING THERE AND AROUND

Minori is located 2.5 miles (4 km) east of Amalfi and about 13 miles (21 km) west of Salerno on the Amalfi Coast Road (SS163). There is a small public parking lot near the

---

1: Minori's graceful Basilica di Santa Trofimena **2:** the ancient Villa Romana **3:** the procession during the Festival of Santa Trofimena **4:** Minori's beach is a relaxing spot to swim.

beach on the western edge of town where you can park hourly for a small fee. Parking is relatively limited, so arriving by bus or ferry is recommended. Minori is very small and easy to get around on foot.

By Ferry

Minori is well connected to other towns along the Amalfi Coast via the ferry service by **Travelmar** (tel. 089/872-950; www.travelmar.it; €8-12 per person). Boats arrive at Minori's small pier from Amalfi, Maiori, Cetara, Salerno, and Positano. Tickets are available online in advance, or via the Travelmar app. Ferries operate seasonally from April through early November, with boats departing hourly from 8:30am to 7pm (times vary, depending on the departure point). From Salerno the trip to Minori is about 40 minutes, from Positano about 25 minutes, and from Amalfi only about 10 minutes. **Alicost** (Salerno; tel. 089/227-979; www.alicost.it; €24.40) runs a daily ferry connecting Capri and Minori from April to October. Be sure to check the schedule in advance, as they usually only offer one daily departure in the evening from Capri to Minori and one in the morning from Minori to Capri. The trip takes about an hour and 30 minutes from Capri to Minori.

By Bus

Minori is served by the public **SITA SUD** (tel. 089/386-6701; www.sitasudtrasporti.it; from €1.30) buses on the Amalfi-Salerno line. Buses arrive about every hour throughout the day, depending on the time of year. The main stop is along the Via Roma (the waterfront) opposite the small road leading to the Basilica di Santa Trofimena. From Amalfi the journey to Minori is about 15 minutes and from Salerno about an hour. From Positano, you will need to take the bus to Amalfi and then transfer to the bus to Salerno and get off in Minori.

The bright red **City Sightseeing** (tel. 081/877-4707; www.city-sightseeing.it; Apr.-Oct.; from €5 per person) buses circulate between Amalfi, Minori, and Maiori. However, the service only offers a couple of evening departures from Amalfi to Minori (5:15pm and 5:45pm). The trip from Amalfi to Minori takes about 15 minutes. Check the exact times in advance, as it can change. An audio guide is provided and tickets are purchased onboard.

To reach Minori by bus from the Naples airport, **Pintour** (tel. 081/879-2645; www.pintourbus.com; €20 adults, €10 children up to 12 years) runs a bus service seasonally from April to early November. Catch the bus at the bus terminal located outside the arrivals hall at the airport. The bus stops at Pompeii and along the Amalfi Coast, including at Minori along the waterfront on Via Roma and at Via Gatto 59. Do book your tickets in advance via the company website. The journey from the airport to Minori takes about an hour and 35 minutes.

Maiori

Maiori sits at the base of a wide valley with a long beach that is one of the town's key attractions, especially during the summer months. With the longest beach on the coast, Maiori was the trading center of the Republic of Amalfi in the Middle Ages and was home to the largest arsenals for shipbuilding. Where its beaches were once lined with sailing ships, fishing boats, and nets, today there are lines of brightly colored beach umbrellas and sun beds. The beach itself has been the setting for significant moments in the town's history, starting with the recovery of a statue of **Santa Maria A Mare** (Madonna of the Sea) in 1204, a focal point for the town's faithful that is now on display in the Collegiata di Santa Maria a Mare.

Maiori's beach was the setting for another historical event on September 8, 1943, when it was the location for part of Operation Avalanche, or the landing of Salerno, during World War II. Allied troops landed on the beach and then followed the pass over Chiunzi on their way to Naples. On October 25, 1954, a massive storm caused a flood that destroyed much of the central part of the town. Many of Maiori's more modern buildings along the seafront and main street, **Corso Reginna,** date from the period after the flood. Yet the charming and wide waterfront (*lungomare*) walkway is a beautiful place to enjoy a *passeggiata* (stroll), which is a popular pastime with locals.

The Amalfi Coast Road (SS163) runs through Amalfi at sea level just alongside the *lungomare* walkway. In the center of town, the main street of Maiori, Corso Reginna, runs perpendicular to the *lungomare* up into the valley. This pedestrian-only street is lined with shops, cafés, and restaurants. After walking a short distance up Corso Reginna, the small Piazza Raffaele D'Amato opens on the left with a narrow yet steep staircase that leads up to the Collegiata di Santa Maria a Mare. Continuing on Corso Reginna leads to **Palazzo Mezzacapo** on the left, and more shops and dining options.

Maiori covers a large swath of the coastline east of the center of the town toward Cetara. Following the Amalfi Coast Road east out of town leads past the **Abbey of Santa Maria de Olearia** (Abbazia di Santa Maria de Olearia). To reach the seaside village of Erchie, which is technically part of Maiori, continue east on the Amalfi Coast Road until a small road splits off sharply to the right, the Via Provinciale, which meanders down to Erchie, set well below the Amalfi Coast Road.

As one of the largest towns on the Amalfi Coast, Maiori is a popular destination, thanks to its many hotels, sandy beach, and *lungomare* with beautiful views of the coastline.

SIGHTS

One of the most pleasurable things to do in Maiori is to stroll along the *lungomare* or relax on the beach. Corso Reginna is where you'll find the majority of the town's sights, restaurants, and shops.

Collegiata di Santa Maria a Mare

Piazzale Mons. Nicola Milo; tel. 089/877-090; www.santamariuamaremaiori.it; 8am-noon and 5pm-8pm

Maiori's largest church sits on the western side with a scenic position overlooking the town. Founded as a small church carved into the rocks, it was later expanded in the 13th century after an important sculpture of the Madonna was discovered in Maiori. As the story goes, in 1204 a ship sailing back from the Orient had aboard a beautiful statue of the Madonna and Child that was saved in Constantinople. However, during a terrible storm it was lost overboard, only to be found by fishermen from Maiori. The church was then dedicated to Santa Maria a Mare, and the statue still stands above the high altar of the church. The statue is carved from cedar wood from Lebanon and depicts the Madonna holding the baby Jesus, wearing gold crowns and rich robes in red, blue, and gold.

The church has a simple yet refined pale yellow baroque style facade from the 1700s, a 14th-century bell tower, and a dome covered with green and yellow ceramic tiles in a geometric diamond pattern. Inside, the church has three naves and is decorated in a baroque style with the same sense of elegance. The town celebrates its patron saint on August 15 with a grand religious festival that coincides with the national Italian holiday **Ferragosto,** which celebrates the feast of the assumption of Mary.

Palazzo Mezzacapo

Corso Reginna 71; tel. 333/890-7653; www.maioricultura.it; 10am-1pm and 4pm-8pm, closed Monday; free

Once the home of the marquis Mezzacapo, an influential noble family of Maiori, this beautiful palazzo is now home to the town's *Comune* (city hall), library, and archive; the palazzo also hosts art exhibitions and events. Elements from the 18th-century structure are still visible, such as the ornate frescoed ceilings, which can be seen in the spaces used for exhibits. The lovely garden to the left of the palazzo is planned in the shape of the Malta Cross, the eight-pointed cross that is the symbol of Amalfi; it is designed to reflect the members of the Mezzacapo family, who had ties with the Order of the Knights of Malta. The garden features fountains, roses and other seasonal flowers, and offers a fine view up to the Collegiata di Santa Maria a Mare.

Abbazia di Santa Maria de Olearia

Strada Statale Amalfitana 43; tel. 333/890-7653; www.maioricultura.it; 3:30pm-6:30pm Wed. and Sat., 10am-1pm Sunday, open late Mar.-Nov. 1; free

Set in an isolated curve along the Amalfi Coast Road about 2.5 miles (4 km) east of Maiori, this small abbey is easy to miss, but it is one of the most evocative examples of medieval religious life on the Amalfi Coast. Founded in the 11th century, the space is carved into the mountainside and divided into three chapels sitting one on top of the other. In what remains of the abbey, you can see remarkable examples of medieval frescoes, along with architectural details that give a sense of the original space. The peaceful setting and expansive view make this a naturally contemplative spot. Note that car parking is not available near the abbey, so arriving by bus or scooter is the best option. You will need to ask the driver to stop at the abbey, because it is not a frequent stop.

BEACHES

If you enjoy the buzz of a busy beach scene, head to the main beach in town. Otherwise you'll enjoy exploring some of the smaller beaches nearby or heading down the coast to Erchie, a small seaside village that is technically considered part of Maiori.

MAIORI BEACH

Amalfi Coast Road (SS163)

Stretching from the port to a historic watchtower on the eastern side, Maiori has the longest beach on the Amalfi Coast at over a half a mile (almost 1 km) long. The beach is split nearly in two where there's a divide for the river that runs down the valley. It's lined with a host of beach clubs to choose from, and many hotels have private beach areas for their guests. There are also small free areas along the beach, including the westernmost side near the port. By Amalfi Coast standards, the beach is quite sandy rather than pebbly, and the water is clear and lovely for swimming. The services available and pleasant conditions make this beach a good choice for families.

SALICERCHIE

SS163, .75 miles (1.2 km) east of Maiori

Just beyond Maiori's distinctive watchtower is a tiny beach tucked away in a semicircular bay, which gave the beach its name. The beach can be reached by following a staircase of about 160 steps leading down from the Amalfi Coast Road, which is right above the western side of the beach. There are some small grottoes near the beach for good swimmers and explorers to discover. Because parking is not available near the steps to the beach, it's best to arrive by SITA SUD bus (catch the bus direction Salerno); the closest stop is at the Torre Normanna watchtower. Continue on foot about 500 feet (150 m) east to find the steps down to the beach. From the center of Maiori, the walk is about 0.6 miles (1 km) and 20 minutes east along the Amalfi Coast Road.

CAVALLO MORTO

SS163, 1.75 miles (2.8 km) east of Maiori

This incredibly scenic beach is set in a little bay with clear turquoise water. A sheer rock cliff soars from the beach to where the Amalfi Coast Road passes high above. This pretty spot is accessible only by sea, and is a popular spot for boats to drop anchor. If you rent a boat or hire a private boat excursion along the Amalfi Coast, stop here to dive into the stunning water and explore the beach.

MARINA DI ERCHIE

Erchie

Overlooked by most travelers, the seaside village of Erchie (err-KEY-eh) has a beautiful beach with all the services needed for a relaxing day by the sea. It's a scenic setting with the 16th-century watchtower **Torre Cerniola** set on a rocky peninsula near the beach. Though it's well off the beaten path for day-trippers, Marina di Erchie is a popular beach in the summer, thanks to the gorgeous clear water, convenient parking lots not far from the beach, and the services of many beach clubs. From Maiori, the best way to reach Erchie is via the public SITA SUD bus. Catch the bus in the direction of Salerno along the *lungomare* in Maiori and ask to get off in Erchie. The stop for Erchie is along the Amalfi Coast Road, and from there you'll need to follow the narrow Via Provinciale road about .4 miles (700 m) downhill to reach the beach. The center of the beach is occupied by a handful of beach clubs (*stabilimenti balneari*), and the extreme ends of the beach offer small, free beach areas. For a comfortable day at the beach with sun beds, umbrellas, changing room, and beach services, head to **Lido Edelvina** (Via Capo Tomolo, Erchie; 8am-6:30pm daily May-Sept.; starting at €15 for two sun beds and one umbrella).

Maiori's long beach stretches out along the waterfront.

SPORTS AND RECREATION

Boat Rentals

CAPONE SERVIZI MARITTIMI

Lungomare Amendola; tel. 089/853-895; www.capone-servizi-marittimi.business.site; Apr.-Oct.; starting at €35 for group tours and €70 for a half-day (4 hours) self-drive rental

The coastline between Maiori and Erchie is one of the most beautiful, untouched stretches of the Amalfi Coast. With tiny beaches and grottoes to discover, it's ideal for exploring with a self-drive boat or on a guided boat excursion. Capone Servizi Marittimi offers small boats that can be rented without a license by the hour, as well as small group and private boat tours along the Amalfi Coast and to Capri. The Minicrociera (minicruise) is a pleasant 4 hour small group tour along the coastline with an optional stop to visit the Grotta dello Smeraldo (Emerald Grotto) in Conca dei Marini.

FESTIVALS AND EVENTS

CARNIVAL

Maiori port and lungomare; Sunday and Tuesday before Ash Wednesday

Maiori comes to life after the winter season with a massive citywide celebration for Carnival (*Carnevale*), which takes place the Sunday and Tuesday before Ash Wednesday. Groups in Maiori build massive handmade floats, with colorful designs often inspired by historic or mythical characters or contemporary figures, that are paraded down the long waterfront along with costumed bands and locals. There are also games, mini amusement park-type rides for kids, and stalls selling candy and toys along the waterfront.

FESTIVAL OF SANTA MARIA A MARE

Collegiata di Santa Maria a Mare, various other locations; August 15

The biggest event of the year in Maiori centers around the Collegiata di Santa Maria a Mare and the celebration of the town's patron saint that takes place on August 15. This is the peak of summer in Italy, as it is also Ferragosto (Feast of the Assumption of Mary), a public holiday celebrated throughout country. All of this means busy beaches, big crowds, and religious events. In Maiori you'll find special Masses around the holiday, as well a procession through town followed by a huge fireworks display set off from a barge on the sea after dark.

FOOD AND ACCOMMODATIONS

Maiori has plenty of options when it comes to dining. Along the waterfront and the main street, Corso Reginna, there are bars and bakeries to start your day with something sweet; eateries for a light lunch, pizza, or seafood; and places that buzz after dark and are ideal for an *aperitivo* or drinks.

RISTORANTE PIZZERIA NETTUNO

Via Gaetano Capone 1; tel. 089/877-594; nettunoristorante@live.it; 12:45pm-3:30pm and 7:45pm-11:30pm daily from May-Oct. and closed Wed. from Nov.-Apr.; €9-22

With a great setting right on the sea at the eastern edge of the beach, this restaurant and pizzeria is an excellent choice for local specialties and pizza. The pasta dishes are generous and the pizza—with a slightly thicker crust than is common in the area—can also be made larger than the standard personal size, which is great for families or sharing.

TORRE NORMANNA

Via D. Tajani 4; tel. 089/877-100; www.torrenormanna.net; 12:30pm-2:30pm and 7pm-10:30pm daily Apr.-Oct., closed Wed. from Nov.-Mar. (winter closure from second week of Nov. to the first week of Dec. and from the second week of Jan. to the second week of Feb.); €16-30

If you like the idea of dining in a 13th-century watchtower as the waves crash below, you'll enjoy the setting of this restaurant, with its sweeping views of the coastline toward Amalfi. Run by the four Proto brothers, Torre Normanna showcases their passion for local ingredients and love of tradition as well as experimenting with new flavors. Reservations are recommended.

HOTEL BOTANICO SAN LAZZARO

Via Lazzaro 25; tel. 089/877-750; www.hbsl.com; closed Nov.-mid-Apr.; €395 d

If you enjoy truly unique hotels, the Hotel Botanico San Lazzaro—set above Maiori and immersed in a garden setting—is the place for your Amalfi Coast stay. Set in a 19th-century home belonging to the Cimini family, who are still the owners today, this five-star boutique hotel offers a one-of-a-kind stay; it's surrounded by gardens full of everything from lemon trees to exotic plants. The 19 rooms and suites are thoroughly modern, while maintaining an old world feel, and all offer beautiful panoramic views. With a spa, pool, restaurant, and bar all on-site, this hotel has everything you need. Set above Maiori, the hotel is reached by a panoramic elevator.

INFORMATION AND SERVICES

AZIENDA AUTONOMA SOGGIORNO E TURISMO

Corso Reginna 71; tel. 089/877-452; www.aziendaturismo-maiori.it; 9am-5pm Nov.-Mar., 9am-1pm and 2pm-6pm Apr.-Oct.

Maiori's tourist office is located on the town's central shopping street, which runs perpendicular to the Amalfi Coast Road through town. From the waterfront, walk up Corso Reginna and you'll find the office in the garden area next to the Palazzo Mezzacapo. English-speaking staff are on hand to help with any questions and provide information about Maiori.

GETTING THERE

By Car

Maiori is set at the base of a wide river valley, 3.5 miles (5.7 km) east of Amalfi and about 12.4 miles (20 km) west of Salerno on the Amalfi Coast Road (SS163). To reach Maiori by car along the Amalfi Coast Road, the drive is about 40 minutes from Salerno, 20 minutes from Amalfi, and an hour from Positano. From Ravello, follow SS373 down to where it meets the Amalfi Coast Road at Castiglione and take a left to continue along the Amalfi Coast Road to Maiori. From Naples, take the A3 highway south, exit at Angri Sud, and follow signs for Valico di Chiunzi. You'll continue along the SP2a road through Tramonti and down the valley to Maiori. The drive from Naples to Maiori takes about an hour and 20 minutes.

By Ferry

Travelmar (tel. 089/872-950; www.travelmar.it; €3-11 per person) operates ferry services to Maiori from Amalfi, Minori, Cetara, Salerno, and Positano seasonally from April to early November. Times and schedules vary by departure point, but generally run from about 8:30am to 7pm, about every hour. The ferry ride from Salerno to Maiori takes 30 minutes, while from Positano it is 25 minutes, from Amalfi and Cetara it's about 15 minutes, and it's only five minutes from Minori to Maiori. Tickets are available online in advance, or via the Travelmar app.

To reach Maiori from Capri, **Alicost** (Salerno; tel. 089/227-979; www.alicost.it; €19.80-21.30 per person) is the ferry service you want. There's usually only one trip per day, so check the schedule in advance. Plan for the journey from Capri to Maiori to take about an hour and 40 minutes.

By Bus

Maiori is on the public **SITA SUD** (tel. 089/386-6701; www.sitasudtrasporti.it; from €1.30 per person) bus line from Amalfi-Salerno as well as a line that connects Maiori to Tramonti, Nocera, and Cava de' Tirreni. Buses stop in Maiori at several points along the waterfront. To reach Maiori by bus, the journey is about 20 minutes from Amalfi, 55 minutes from Salerno, and 20 to 40 minutes from Tramonti, depending on where you depart. From Ravello and Positano, you will first need to arrive in Amalfi by bus, then transfer to the Amalfi-Salerno line and get off in Maiori.

City Sightseeing (tel. 081/877-4707; www.city-sightseeing.it; Apr.-Oct.; from €5 per person) runs a line that connects Amalfi and Minori to Maiori. The service is quite limited to reach Maiori, with only a couple of arrivals in the evening (5:45pm-6:15pm). However, there are also two departures in the morning (9:15 and 9:45) to reach Minori and Amalfi. Check the times in advance, as it can change. Tickets are purchased onboard and include an audio guide available in multiple languages.

If you're traveling from the Naples airport to Maiori, **Pintour** (tel. 081/879-2645; www.pintourbus.com; €20 adults, €10 children up to 12 years) offers an affordable bus service seasonally from April to early November. Catch the bus at the terminal located outside the arrivals hall at the airport. The bus stops at Pompeii and along the Amalfi Coast, including three stops for Maiori, at Erchie, at the crossroads of the SP2a, and near the port at Via Giovanni Amendola 41. It's a good idea to book your tickets in advance on Pintour's website. The trip from the airport to Maiori takes about an hour and 30 minutes.

GETTING AROUND

Maiori is a comfortable town for walking and exploring, because it is largely flat. The Amalfi Coast Road runs through town, and between the road and the beach is a wide and tree-lined sidewalk called the *lungomare* (waterfront), which is a popular place to stroll along the sea. Midway along the waterfront, the Corso Reginna begins at the Amalfi Coast Road and runs perpendicular to the Amalfi Coast Road up through the town. Corso Reginna is Maiori's main shopping street; it is also pedestrian-only and a great place for walking. To the east of Corso Reginna is the intersection where the SP2a road to Tramonti meets the Amalfi Coast Road.

Although it's part of Maiori, the *frazione* of **Erchie** is about 5.5 miles (8.6 km) east along the Amalfi Coast Road. To get there by public transport, take the SITA SUD bus in the direction of Salerno and get off in Erchie after about 10 minutes.

You'll find a small paid public parking lot by the beach in Maiori at the intersection of Corso Reginna. There's also paid parking along the north side of the Amalfi Coast Road as it runs through Maiori.

Cetara

A town of unexpected charm and deep traditions, Cetara is a wonderful example of just how much there is to discover on the Amalfi Coast. Situated in a relatively isolated valley along the coastline between Vietri sul Mare and Maiori, the town has a beautifully preserved feel with its historic buildings along the seafront, a beach scattered with colorful fishing boats, and a maze of old streets opening onto piazzas where locals chat and children play.

Here the sea is everything and never seems far away. Cetara has the best equipped fishing fleet on the Amalfi Coast that is still active in the Mediterranean, with the specialty being tuna. The town is also known far and wide for anchovies, and even if you think you don't care for them, you've got to at least try anchovies in Cetara. It's a culinary experience not to be missed! Generations of Cetara's fishermen have brought in hauls of these tasty tiny fish since ancient Roman times.

Many travelers catch only a glimpse of this beautiful town and its brightly colored church dome from the Amalfi Coast Road (SS163) as they're driving through, which is a real shame. If your time is limited, stop for a stroll along the town's main road, **Corso Garibaldi,** which leads from the **Piazza San Francesco** down to the port and beach; it's one of the prettiest stretches along the coastline. Via Marina runs along the town's main beach over to the base of the **Torre di Cetara** watchtower. However, to visit the tower, you'll need to follow the Amalfi Coast Road to the eastern edge of town, as the only entrance is directly from the road. From Piazza San Francesco, Corso Garibaldi goes under the bridge of the Amalfi Coast Road and continues up into town and the **Piazza Martiri Ungheresi,** where more shops and accommodations are located.

For a home base on the Amalfi Coast full of charm and off the well-worn path, consider a stay in Cetara, which is also connected to the rest of the coastline by ferry service.

SIGHTS

Torre di Cetara

Corso Umberto I 4; tel. 089/262-911; www.torredicetara.it; 10:30am-1pm May- Sept.; free

Rising above the eastern edge of the beach, the town's historic watchtower dates back to the 14th century. Yet, a close look reveals multiple layers built one on top of the other over the centuries. The original cylindrical part of the watchtower is closest to the sea, with a larger square-shaped section added later. The top two levels were added at the end of the 1800s. Today, the tower houses a museum that highlights local artists and the town's history, and provides a venue for temporary exhibitions. During exhibitions the tower is sometimes open extended hours. Visitors get a rare chance to see the interior of one of the Amalfi Coast's historic watchtowers, while enjoying a fine view overlooking the town.

Chiesa di San Pietro Apostolo

Via San Giacomo; 5pm-8pm daily

Dedicated to Cetara's beloved patron, San Pietro Apostolo (St. Peter), this beautiful church boasts an eye-catching green and yellow majolica tiled dome that is reminiscent of the Chiesa di Santa Maria Assunta in Positano. Though the church dates back to 988, it has been remodeled and restored multiple times over the centuries. Today the neoclassical facade has a set of bronze doors, created in 2005 by Italian sculptor and painter Battista Marello. The doors depict Saint Peter and Saint Andrew, both fisherman, surrounded by a swirling net full of tiny fish: a nod to the longstanding fishing tradition that is part of local life. The interior, a single-nave floor plan with side chapels, boasts a late baroque design with rich décor. Tucked away on the side of the church is a bell tower dating back to the 1300s. The church is usually only open in the evenings during Mass.

Chiesa di San Francesco d'Assisi

Piazza San Francesco, open only on special occasions

Sitting on a small piazza just below the point where the Amalfi Coast Road winds through the center of town, this convent dates back to the end of the 14th century. Once a sprawling structure, a church is all that remains, while the cloister is now a lovely restaurant and other parts of the convent have become the town hall. The church itself dates from 1585, and though the facade is quite simple, inside the single-nave church features beautiful frescoes on the ceiling from the 1600s. Although located right in the center of town, this small church is open only occasionally. Stop in the Pro Loco, the town's tourist information center, just across the street below Piazza San Francesco for more details on when it might be open.

Chiesa di Santa Maria di Costantinopoli

Piazza Europa; 5pm-8pm daily

Follow the main road, Corso Garibaldi, up into the valley, and on the left you'll find this small, pastel pink church behind a gated entrance. It dates from the second half of the 19th century and was largely rebuilt after being nearly ruined in 1910 during the massive flood that destroyed much of Cetara. Though the Chiesa di Santa Maria di Costantinopoli is not as old as many local churches, it holds a special place in the hearts of many locals, especially its statue of the Madonna and Child, which is carried in a religious procession in through town during the celebration for Santa Maria di Costantinopoli that takes place June 9-10.

BEACHES

Cetara is set along a particularly scenic and sparsely inhabited stretch of the coastline that is dotted with numerous tiny beaches stretching west toward Erchie and east toward Vietri sul Mare. Though these little beaches are certainly beautiful, the majority are only accessible by sea. The following beaches are right in Cetara or are accessible on foot.

MARINA DI CETARA

Via Marina

Cetara's main beach stretches out in front of the town's characteristic houses, from the parking lot beside the port to the rocky base of the Torre di Cetara. You'll find both a beach club with sun beds you can rent for the day and, closer to the parking area, a free beach (*spiaggia libera*). With its beautiful clear water, colorful houses, and historic watchtower, Cetara's beach is one of the most picturesque of the entire coastline and is a great spot for swimming.

PORTO DI CETARA

Via Galea

This small beach is located on the western edge of Cetara, just outside of the port. Walk all the way down to the end of the parking area at the port, and outside the pier is an angular beach that was created in the mid 1980s during contruction after a massive earthquake. Over time, it has become a lovely beach that is often a little less crowded than the main beach, but it is a popular spot with locals for swimming. The small beach is split in two with half being a free area and the other a tiny beach club.

SPIAGGIA DEL LANNIO

Via Lannio

Follow the small walkway that starts in front of the Torre di Cetara down to reach this secluded beach. Although it might be a little out of the way, that doesn't mean it's not popular. The sandy beach and clear water makes this a hot spot in the summer. Find an open space on the free beach, the sandy side of the beach on the right, which gets sun longer into the afternoon, or head to the beach club for all the comforts, including sun bed rentals and dining options.

FESTIVALS AND EVENTS

FESTIVAL OF SAN PIETRO

Chiesa di San Pietro, various locations; June 29

The biggest event of the year in Cetara is the summer celebration for the town's patron San Pietro. After a special Mass, a religious procession leads up to the top of town and then back down to the beach where boats are waiting for the traditional blessing. The procession then returns to the church, where the statue of the saint is run up the flight of steps leading to the church. A unique feature of the procession is that the statue of the saint is carried through town on a platform shaped like a boat, representing San Pietro's role as patron of fishermen. As the statue is taken through town, the bearers lilt back and forth to give the impression that the saint is navigating through the sea. Afterward, the town is bustling with people—especially along the beach—waiting for the huge fireworks display from the sea.

NOTTE DELLE LAMPARE

Largo Marina, various locations; tel. 089/261-593; www.nottedellelampare.it; July; €10 for tasting menu

This food festival not only celebrates the town's famous anchovies, but also re-creates a traditional fishing technique using large lights attached to a boat. This attracts the fish to the surface and they are then caught in a massive net. It's quite a piece of choreography to pull off, and it's possible to go out on boats and watch the fishing from up close. Boats depart from Cetara at 8pm and cost €10 per person (tickets available at the **Travelmar** ferry ticket

1: Colatura di Alici made in Cetara by Cetarii **2:** Set below a historic watchtower, Cetara's beach is one of the loveliest on the Amalfi Coast.

1

2

☆ Little Fish with a Big Flavor: Cetara's Anchovies

Cetara's long fishing tradition is embedded in the town's name, which is thought to come from a host of different Latin or even ancient Greek words all having to do with fishing. Whatever the exact origin, it's clear that fishing has been an important part of the economy for most of the town's history. Cetara's fishing fleet is still very active, and you'll spot both larger fishing boats and the colorful little wooden rowboats bobbing in the port. The specialties of the area are tuna caught in the deeper waters of the Mediterranean off the coast and the popular anchovies (*alici*). Rich in omega-3, iron, and other nutrients, anchovies have long been a key part of the local diet in Cetara.

Even if you think you're not keen on anchovies, give them a chance in Cetara as you've never tasted anything quite like it. The tiny fish are filleted and prepared in a number of different ways, including marinated in vinegar or lemon, breaded and fried, used in a variety of pasta dishes, baked in the oven, and used as a pizza topping. You'll find *alici* prepared in many traditional ways on the menus in all of Cetara's restaurants.

COLATURA DI ALICI

The most prized production is *colatura di alici*, a deep amber-colored oil made from pressing anchovies. This intensely flavored oil is thought to be the descendent of an ancient Roman *Garum*, a creamy fish sauce created by salting and preserving fish, which was produced in Pompeii.

The process to create *colatura di alici* is passed down through generations of fishermen in Cetara, and many families have their own secret recipes. It starts with freshly caught anchovies that are placed in wooden barrels, called *terzigni*, and covered with salt. The fish are usually caught from March through July so that the heat of the summer can help advance the maturation process. The barrels are weighted down on the top, and the anchovies are slowly pressed inside. Months later when it's finished, a small hole is punctured in the bottom of the barrel to release the precious liquid, which has a super-concentrated fish and salt flavor.

The *colatura di alici* is traditionally ready at the beginning of December, when the Festa della Colatura di Alici takes place in town. The oil is then used to flavor the pasta and fish dishes customarily made on Christmas Eve. However, *colatura di alici* is used year-round to add extra flavor to everything from *antipasti* to pasta dishes and fresh vegetables.

PLACES TO TRY

In addition to the food shops and restaurants in Cetara, not to mention the annual festivals, there are a number of places to try the famous anchovies and anchovy oil. Here are a few that stand out:

- **Trattoria Da Maria, Amalfi:** Fried anchovies are a specialty here (page 108).
- **La Moresca, Ravello:** Come here for the traditional spaghetti with anchovy oil (page 131).
- **Il Principe e la Civetta, Vietri sul Mare:** The *spaghetti al pesto vietrese* combines anchovies with capers, sun dried tomatoes, pine nuts, and another Amalfi specialty, lemon (page 165).

booth in the port). The fishermen bring their catch to shore where it is served fresh on the beach. Buy a €10 ticket for the tasting menu and enjoy fish that's as fresh as can be. The celebrations and music continue well into the night. Dates vary depending on the lunar calender, which plays an important role in anchovy fishing.

FESTA DELLA COLATURA DI ALICI

Hotel Cetus, various locations; www.colaturadialici.it; early December

The year wouldn't be complete in Cetara without a festival dedicated to the town's celebrated *colatura di alici* (oil made from pressing anchovies). The events take place over two to three days in the first half of December, coinciding with the bottling of the season's *colatura di alici*, which is made from anchovies caught along the Amalfi Coast from the end of March to mid-July. Festival events center around celebrating local history and traditions. The most popular part involves special tasting menus themed around *colatura di alici* being made available at restaurants and pizzerias in town.

SHOPPING

CETARII

Via Largo Marina 48/50; tel. 089/261-863; www.cetarii.it; 9am-1:30pm and 3:30pm-9pm

Just steps away from the beach, follow a small ramp up to reach this shop where there's an excellent variety of local products on display. Naturally, the focus is on tuna and anchovies, and this is the spot to find jars of the *tonno rosso* (red tuna) caught in the Mediterranean, as well as anchovies preserved in oil and salt and the famous *colatura di alici*. Not sure what to buy, or just curious to try out some of the delicacies? Cetarii also offers product tastings and gourmet sandwiches accompanied by locally made Amalfi Coast wines.

FOOD

Gourmands will be glad to have Cetara on their radar. With such a strong fishing tradition, it's no surprise that the local restaurants specialize in fresh seafood, but the lemon trees and vegetables grown in the verdant valley above town play a prominent role in the town's cuisine as well. Here, the flavors of land and sea blend into unique dishes that you'll find only in Cetara.

RISTORANTE PIZZERIA AL CONVENTO

Piazza San Francesco 16; tel. 089/261-039; www.alconvento.net; noon-3:30pm and 7pm-11:30pm; €10-13

As the name suggests, this restaurant is set inside a former convent right next to the Chiesa di San Francesco. It overlooks a pretty square along the town's main street. The space has been transformed into a comfortable dining area with a rustic and welcoming feel that's further enhanced by the friendly service. There's an outdoor dining area beneath the trees, overlooking the piazza. The pizza is excellent and you can't go wrong with the seafood dishes, which highlight local tuna and anchovies. Try the *genovese di tonno*, a twist on the classic Neapolitan pasta sauce made with tuna instead of beef.

RISTORANTE SAN PIETRO

Piazza San Francesco 2; tel. 089/261-091; www.sanpietroristorante.it; 12:45pm-2:45pm and 7:45pm-11pm daily July-Aug., closed Jan., closed Tues. Feb.-June and Sept.-Dec.; €10-18

Cetara's gastronomic traditions are well-preserved in this popular local restaurant. Here you can sample the blending of locally grown products with fresh seafood in dishes like the pasta with fresh anchovies and wild fennel. The *zuppa antica pompei* is a local specialty that is made with *farro* (spelt wheat), fish, and *colatura di alici*. Vegan and vegetarian menus are available. Reservations are recommended.

ACCOMMODATIONS

CETARA ALBERGO DIFFUSO

Piazza Martiri Ungheresi 14/16; tel. 089/262-014; hotelcetaraalbergodiffuso@gmail.com; €100 d

This hotel is *diffuso*: spread out in a variety of charming locations around Cetara's main piazza. However, with a central reception and breakfast room, as well as attentive service, it offers all the conveniences of a traditional hotel. There are seven rooms and three additional accomodations with mini kitchens available.

B&B MARA

Parco degli Ulivi 3; tel. 089/261-896; www.bbmara.com; open Jan.-Oct.; €100 d

You'll feel like you're at home at this welcoming B&B with a great setting above the center of town near the Torre di Cetara. The three rooms are bright and very colorful. Enjoy a view overlooking the beach, watchtower, quaint port, and down the coastline from the rooms and terrace of the B&B.

HOTEL CETUS

Corso Umberto 1; tel. 089/261-388; www.hotelcetus.com; open year round; €260 d

Impressively built into the cliffside below the Amalfi Coast Road, this hotel offers a unique Amalfi Coast stay. Its 37 rooms all have beautiful sea views, and each includes a private balcony or terrace. Although located a short 10 minute walk from the center of Cetara, the hotel makes up for this with an on-site restaurant, bar, and access to the hotel's private beach, Tuoro Vecchio. The beach club offers sun beds, umbrellas, and an American bar.

INFORMATION AND SERVICES

PRO LOCO

Corso Garibaldi 15; tel. 089/261-593; www.prolococetara.it; 8am-8pm

Located below Piazza San Francesco on Cetara's main road leading down to the beach, the town's friendly tourist office is a great spot to stop in for local information, specific details about openings of the smaller churches, and more. Information and assistance are available in English.

GETTING THERE AND AROUND

Located about 6 miles (10 km) west of Salerno, Cetara offers a more secluded feel while still well connected via ferry and bus to Salerno and other towns along the Amalfi Coast. Cetara is very small and enjoyable to explore on foot.

By Car

The Amalfi Coast Road winds through Cetara just above the center of town, passing over the town's main street, Corso Garibaldi, with a small bridge. Just east of the bridge, a narrow road called Via Francesco Prudente (marked with a sign for the "Centro") splits off the Amalfi Coast Road and leads down to Corso Garbaldi to the left, and Corso Federici leading to Piazza Martiri Ungheresi to the right. To reach Cetara from Salerno, it's a 25-minute drive west on the Amalfi Coast Road. From Positano and Amalfi, follow the Amalfi Coast Road east to Cetara with a drive time of about an hour and 25 minutes from Positano or 40 minutes from Amalfi. From Ravello, the drive takes about 50 minutes; first follow the SS373 road down to the Amalfi Coast Road at Castiglione and then continue east to Cetara. Once you're in Cetara, hourly paid parking is available in a large lot next to the port.

By Ferry

Travelmar (tel. 089/872-950; www.travelmar.it; €5-12 per person) operates ferry services from Salerno, Maiori, Minori, Amalfi, and Positano to Cetara. Ferry service is available seasonally from April through early November, with departures roughly hourly for Cetara 9am-6pm (times vary depending on departure point). A ferry ride from Salerno or Maiori to Cetara takes about 15 minutes, from Minori about 25 minutes, from Amalfi about 40 minutes, and from Positano about 65 minutes. Tickets are available online in advance, or via the Travelmar app.

It's possible to reach Cetara from Capri by the **Alicost** (Salerno ticket office tel. 089/227-979; www.alicost.it; €24.40) ferry service, which offers one departure for Cetara in the evening and one return to Capri in the morning. The ferry ride from Capri to Cetara takes a little less than two hours.

By Bus

Cetara is located along the public **SITA SUD** (tel. 089/386-6701; www.sitasudtrasporti.it; from €1.30) bus line from Amalfi to Salerno, and buses arrive about every hour depending on the time of year. The main stop in town is right in the center where Corso Garibaldi meets the Amalfi Coast Road. The bus journey from Salerno takes about 30 minutes and from Amalfi about 45 minutes. From Positano and Ravello, you will first need to travel to Amalfi by bus and then continue on the Amalfi-Salerno line to Cetara.

To reach Cetara from the Naples airport, **Pintour** (tel. 081/879-2645; www.pintourbus.com; €20 adults, €10 children up to 12 years) runs a convenient bus service seasonally from April to early November. Catch the bus at the terminal located outside the arrivals hall at the airport. The bus stops at Pompeii and along the Amalfi Coast, including a stop right in the center of Cetara. Book your tickets in advance via Pintour's website. The trip from the airport to Cetara takes just over an hour.

Vietri sul Mare

From the pastel-hued buildings of Positano to the bright lemons and the brilliant shades of blue in the sea, the Amalfi Coast bursts with color. The most colorful spot of all just might be the town of Vietri sul Mare, which is famous for its longstanding tradition of ceramics. As the easternmost town on the coastline, Vietri sul Mare is also known as the gateway to the Amalfi Coast. With its colorful ceramics shops spilling out onto the street, artistic heritage, and lovely views down the coast, it makes a very fetching impression.

Vietri sul Mare is divided into two areas, with the center of town at the top and Marina di Vietri at sea level, where you'll find a large beach or boats to reach smaller and more secluded beaches nearby. The multihued dome of the town's main church, the **Chiesa di San Giovanni Battista,** marks the center of town and is surrounded by a maze of little streets, including the main **Corso Umberto I.** That's where you'll want to go to find one ceramic shop after another, each more tempting than the last. Spend time trying to find your favorite and then head up into the mountains to **Raito,** a *frazione* of Vietri sul Mare, to visit the town's interesting ceramic museum to learn more about the history of ceramic production in the area.

While **ceramics** are certainly the appeal for day-trippers passing through town, Vietri sul Mare has a refreshingly traditional and less touristy feel than many of the more famous towns along the Amalfi Coast. This lesser known town is an excellent place to discover a different side to the Amalfi Coast.

SIGHTS

The ceramic shops in town are among Vietri sul Mare's main attractions. The town is practically a ceramic museum itself, with all of the colorful murals and designs decorating the walls, houses, and shops.

Chiesa di San Giovanni Battista

Via San Giovanni 18; tel. 089/210-219; s.giovannidivietri@diocesiamalficava.it; 8:30am-1pm and 5:30pm-8pm daily

Vietri sul Mare's religious and artistic traditions blend beautifully at this church right in the center of town, with its bold blue, yellow, and green ceramic tiled dome. Situated on a tiny yet charming little piazza surrounded by houses, the entrance of the Chiesa di San Giovanni Battista features a round ceramic mural above the entrance showing San Giovanni Battista (St. John the Baptist) against a backdrop of Vietri sul Mare. The mural dates from 1946 and replaced a rose window that was damaged during World War II. The church was originally founded toward the end of the 10th century, but the structure we see today dates to the last major restoration in 1732 in the baroque style. The single-nave church is decorated in a pale pink with ornate white stucco work and lovely light that comes in from the large windows around the base of the dome.

A Colorful Tradition of Ceramics in Vietri sul Mare

The Salerno area has a long tradition of ceramic production dating back to the 5th century BC thanks to natural clay caves. Archaeological excavations have revealed that vessels were produced to transport wine, oil, and other products even before Romans settled in the area. But the ceramic production on a larger scale began developing at the end of the 15th century when the local ceramic factories began working in a more industrial manner.

Every angle in Vietri sul Mare features colorful ceramics.

Production ebbed and flowed over the centuries with slower periods interspersed with moments when creativity flourished and brought new life to the ceramic factories. One of the most notable peaks is known as the German Period, which started in the early 20th century with the arrival of German artists and other Europeans, who brought with them new styles and influences, such as the Expressionism movement. The peak of this design period took place from the 1920s to the start of the second world war.

Artists like Richard Dölker, Irene Kowaliska, Lisel Oppel, and Bab Thewalt Hannasch, to mention just a few, developed a distinctive style as they experimented with new colors and found inspiration in the local people and the warm Mediterranean landscape. Everyday scenes like fishermen and women carrying water urns on their heads, local architecture, and elements of daily life served as colorful artistic inspiration. Even the humble and hardworking donkey was memorialized in clay, and has ever since been one of the ceramic symbols of Vietri sul Mare. The local ceramic style in Vietri sul Mare varies by artist but often involves bright Mediterranean colors like turquoise, yellow, and blues.

Ceramic production continues today with a handful of ceramic factories, smaller shops, and individual artists who continue this creative tradition on the Amalfi Coast.

Museo della Ceramica

Villa Guariglia, Via Nuova Raito, Raioti; tel. 089/211-835; 9am-3pm Tues.-Sun.; free

If you love the ceramics on the Amalfi Coast and are curious to find out more about the history and traditions, head to Vietri sul Mare's Provincial Museum of Ceramics located in Raito. The museum is situated in the Torretta Belvedere, an old tower on the grounds of the Villa Guariglia, a large estate now owned by the Province of Salerno. Opened in 1981, the museum tells the story of ceramic production in the Vietri sul Mare area with displays of beautiful pieces of religious art and household items. There is also an excellent collection of pieces from Vietri sul Mare's German Period in the early 20th century; these are noted for their modern style and for the introduction of decorative themes inspired by the local landscape and traditions. A detailed brochure with information in English is available.

Le Vigne di Raito

Via San Vito 9, Raito; tel. 328/865-1452; www.levignediraito.com; year round; reservation required; wine tasting and tour from €55

Situated along a mountain slope in Raito, this vineyard is a labor of love for owner Patrizia Malanga. She fell in love with the area in 2001 when she began the intense work of recovering and restoring a 5-acre (2-hectare) plot of terraced land back to life. Because the area had a tradition of wine production, she set to work planting a new vineyard and creating wine that would capture the scents of the beautiful landscape of Raito. Since 2007, Malanga has been producing Ragis Rosso, a deep and rich red wine made with aglianico and piedirosso grapes. Later came Vitamenia, a dry rosato with notes of citrus. Since 2011, Le Vigne di Raito has been certified organic by I.C.E.A, the Italian organization that regulates organic products. Patrizia's hospitality makes you feel right at home during a visit to the vineyard. Stop by for a wine tasting and tour that lasts about 2.5 hours, or stay longer for lunch or dinner after the wine tasting and tour (4 hours, starting at €95 per person). You can also take a cooking class that highlights traditional local dishes like eggplant parmesan, homemade pasta, and local desserts (6-7 hours, €250 per person).

Badia Della Santissima Trinita

Via Abate Michele Morcaldi 6, Cava de' Tirreni; tel. 347/194-6957; www.badiadicava.it; guided tours available 8:30am-noon; €3

Located outside of Vietri sul Mare in the mountains above Cava de' Tirreni, this Benedictine abbey dedicated to the Holy Trinity dates back to 1011 when it was founded by St. Alferius, who retired to a small cave in the area to live as a hermit. Over the centuries it grew into a sprawling and impressive abbey that houses an incredibly rich artistic, architectural, and religious heritage. Although it is still an active abbey, it's possible to take a guided tour to see the splendid basilica, cloister, richly decorated rooms, museum, and cemetery excavated below the church. While not on the usual tourist path, the abbey is absolutely a treasure to discover and worth a visit before exploring the historic center of nearby Cava de' Tirreni.

BEACHES

MARINA DI VIETRI

Via Cristoforo Colombo

Vietri sul Mare's seaside *frazione*, called Marina di Vietri, has one of the most expansive beaches on the Amalfi Coast. While the beach was created naturally, its size is the result of a 1954 flood that washed massive amounts of mud down the valley from the mountains high above town. The beach is divided into two sections by the river Bonea, and both sides of the beach offer a large selection of beach clubs (*stabilimenti balneari*) as well as free areas. From the eastern side, you can get an especially good view of the **I Due Fratelli** rock formation with two large rocks jutting out of the sea off the coastline: one of the symbols of Vietri sul Mare. The beach is popular in summer as it's the first large beach on the coastline near Salerno. The water is great for swimming, especially in the area around I Due Fratelli.

LA CRESTARELLA

Via Cristoforo Colombo 27

Surrounded by rocky cliffs, this small beach stretches out below the 16th-century Torre Crestarella watchtower just east of I Due Fratelli. During the summer, the beach is reached via a private entrance from Via Cristoforo Colombo to the beach club **La Crestarella** (Via Cristoforo Colombo 27; tel. 327/576-6591; www.torrecrestarella.eu; 9am-6:30pm daily May-Sept.; €24 for two adults, umbrella, and two sun beds). La Crestarella offers parking, sun bed and umbrella rentals, and a restaurant.

FESTIVALS AND EVENTS

With its large beach area, Marina di Vietri is a popular spot for concerts during the summer. Most events are seasonal and dates are posted locally. Check with the tourist office for any scheduled events during your visit.

FESTIVAL OF SAN GIOVANNI BATTISTA

Chiesa di San Giovanni Battista and various locations; June 24

On June 24 the town of Vietri sul Mare honors its patron, San Giovanni Battista (St. John the Baptist), with a town-wide celebration. After Mass in the evening, the statue of the saint is carried through town on a long procession accompanied by a marching band and the town's faithful. Find a spot in the small piazza in front of the Chiesa di San Giovanni Battista for a good view of the procession as it leaves the church.

CERAMICS SHOPPING

Ceramics are naturally the focus for shopping in Vietri sul Mare, and the joy comes in the sheer abundance of choices. Though ceramic shops seem to be tucked away in every nook and cranny, you'll find the majority of shops along Corso Umberto I in the heart of town. Spend time exploring, visiting shops, and talking to the locals, and find the style that catches your eye. All of the shops can help you arrange shipping services so you don't have to overload your luggage.

CERAMICA ARTISTICA SOLIMENE

Viadotto Madonna degli Angeli 7; tel. 089/210-243; www.ceramicasolimene.it; 9am-8pm Mon.-Fri., 9am-1:30pm and 4pm-8pm Sat., 10am-1:30pm Sun.

A visit to this ceramic factory is a must for ceramic or architecture enthusiasts, as it is one of Vietri sul Mare's—and perhaps the entire Amalfi Coast's—most distinctive buildings. The factory is literally covered in small circular orange and green tiles, in a unique design that was created in the 1950s by Italian architect Paolo Soleri, who had studied with Frank Lloyd Wright in the U.S. Inside you'll find a large selection of ceramics ranging from iconic designs featuring various animals to more abstract artistic pieces. You can also catch a glimpse inside the ceramic factory where artists are at work producing the famous Solimene ceramics.

CERAMICA PINTO

Corso Umberto I 31; tel. 089/210-271; www.ceramicapinto.it; 10:30am-1:30pm and 4pm-8pm Mon.-Sat.

One of Vietri sul Mare's important ceramic-making families, the Pinto family, have produced beautiful ceramics in the factory

Stop in the Ceramica Margherita shop for traditional ceramics.

located along Corso Umberto I in the center of town since Vincenzo Pinto purchased the entire building in 1910. Today his granddaughter, Rosaura Pinto, continues the family tradition and runs the ceramic factory, which you can spot easily by the large ceramic murals decorating the walls. Stop in the showroom to see a display of their tableware, vases, lamps, tiles, and more.

ARTEMIKA

Corso Umberto I 63; tel. 340/428-7478; enzadarienzo@live.it; 9am-1:30pm and 4pm-8pm daily

This small and colorful shop is full of tempting ceramics that are all created and produced by owner Enza d'Arienzo and her family. The designs are bright and modern with a touch of whimsy, and are handpainted on everything from vases to candleholders, lamps, platters, decorative objects, and dishes. In the back of the shop, you'll likely see ceramic production in process.

CERAMICA MARGHERITA

Corso Umberto I 45; tel. 089/763-130; www.ceramicamargherita.com; 9am-1pm and 3:30pm-8pm daily

Everything colorful and ceramic under the sun can be found in this large shop along Vietri sul Mare's main street. They also produce a style of ceramics called "sabbiato" (sandblasted) for its unique textured appearance.

FOOD

IL PRINCIPE E LA CIVETTA

Via Giuseppe Mazzini 137; tel. 089/763-2201; www.ilprincipeelacivetta.it; noon-3pm and 7pm-11pm daily Apr-Oct., noon-3pm and 7pm-11pm Mon.-Tues. and Thurs.-Sat., noon-3pm Sun. Nov.-Mar.; €10-18

Located right in the center of Vietri sul Mare, this restaurant is tucked away in the former display galleries of the historic Ceramica Pinto factory. Beautiful ceramics and a spacious dining area are the setting for an excellent gastronomic experience. Choose from plenty of seafood options: The *spaghetti al pesto vietrese* is a house specialty made with fresh anchovies, capers, sun dried tomatoes, pine nuts, herbs, and a touch of lemon. You'll also find plenty of meat and vegetarian options on the menu.

RE MAURÌ

Via Benedetto Croce; tel. 089/763-3687; www.remauri.it; 12:30pm-2:30pm and 7:30pm-11pm Thurs.-Mon., Wed. dinner only, closed Tues.; €28-40

One of the Amalfi Coast's fine dining experiences can be found in Vietri sul Mare. This gourmet restaurant is guided by experienced chef Lorenzo Cuomo, who has worked at top restaurants throughout Italy. After only two years, Re Mauri was awarded its first Michelin star, and the level of creativity and service is very high. The menu varies throughout the year by season and ingredients, with the defining elements being Chef Cuomo's simple and elegant way of blending traditional flavors. Reservations are recommended.

ACCOMMODATIONS

B&B PALAZZO PINTO

Via Giuseppe Mazzini 137; tel. 340/101-2255; www.palazzopinto.it; closed mid-Jan.- Feb.; €80 d

Surround yourself with the beauty of Vietri sul Mare's ceramics at this small B&B. The four double rooms feel like you're staying in a ceramic museum, as they are designed with ceramics from the Pinto family ceramic factory, including decorative floors, fully tiled en suite bathrooms, and gorgeous tables and lamps everywhere you look. The B&B is connected to the factory and is located right in the center of Vietri sul Mare, off of Corso Umberto I.

LLOYD'S BAIA HOTEL

Via Enrico de Marinis 2; tel. 089/763-3111; www.lloydsbaiahotel.it; €129 d

Step into this hotel right off the Amalfi Coast Road. To reach your room and the hotel's beautiful terraces and restaurant you'll need to go down. That's right, this hotel is built into the cliffside, and you'll feel suspended between sky and sea while enjoying the views overlooking the coast and Salerno's port nearby. The hotel has 130 rooms of various sizes, but all feature sea views and are decorated in Mediterranean colors and, naturally, the ceramics of Vietri sul Mare. Another perk here is the private beach below the hotel that can be reached by elevator. The central area of the beach is reserved exclusively for hotel guests, and along with the beachside bar, is available for a small additional fee daily.

PALAZZO SURIANO

Via Madonna Dell'Arco 30; tel. 089/234-450; www.palazzosuriano.it; €189 d

Situated in a beautiful palazzo from the 1700s and surrounded by terraced gardens, this property is a remarkable find on the Amalfi Coast. The palazzo is situated on the western side of Vietri sul Mare in a scenic spot below the Amalfi Coast Road. The beach at Marina di Vietri is accesible on foot by following a small road and about 40 steps. The six rooms, some with balconies and sea views, are decorated in a warm style that blends beautifully with the historic details of the building, like the wood-beamed ceilings and frescoed walls. The public spaces, including a library with sea views, are all curated with antiques and well preserved historic and artistic touches.

INFORMATION AND SERVICES

PRO LOCO

Via Orazio Costabile 4; tel. 089/211-285; www.prolocovietrisulmare.it; 10:30-12:30 daily May-Sept., Fri.-Sun. only Oct.-Apr.

Vietri sul Mare's tourist info point is located just above Piazza Matteotti and can be easily reached following Via XXV Luglio up to the small triangular piazza where the Pro Loco is set in a small well-marked building. The friendly English-speaking staff can offer information on Vietri sul Mare and getting around, and help answer any Amalfi Coast travel questions.

GETTING THERE

Despite its large beach, Vietri sul Mare has not been connected by ferry service for many years. However, ferry service to and from Salerno and other towns along the Amalfi Coast is scheduled to start in summer 2019. Check with **Travelmar** (tel. 089/872-950; www.travelmar.it) for more detailed information. Otherwise, the closest port is located in nearby Salerno.

By Car

Vietri sul Mare is the eastern gateway to the Amalfi Coast. The town begins just west of the Port of Salerno and marks the beginning point for the Amalfi Coast Road (SS163). From the *lungomare* and center of Salerno, follow Via Roma (SS18) west out of the historic center. The road climbs above the port and in about 10 minutes leads directly to Vietri sul Mare. From Positano and Amalfi, follow the Amalfi Coast Road east to Vietri sul Mare. From Ravello, first drive down the SS373 to reach the Amalfi Coast Road at Castiglione before continuing east. The drive to Vietri sul Mare from Positano takes about an hour and 45 minutes; it's about 50 minutes from Amalfi, and an hour from Ravello. If you're coming from Naples, take the A3 highway south to the Vietri sul Mare exit, and expect a drive time of about 50 minutes.

By Bus

Vietri sul Mare is located along the **SITA SUD** (tel. 089/386-6701; www.sitasudtrasporti.it; from €1.30 per person) bus line connecting Amalfi to Salerno. Buses run roughly every hour from Amalfi in the direction of Salerno, 5:15am-9pm daily and 5:55am-9:30pm from Salerno toward Amalfi. The bus ride from Amalfi takes about an hour, while from Salerno it's about 15 minutes. To reach Vietri sul Mare from Positano and Ravello, first take the bus to Amalfi and transfer to the Amalfi-Salerno line. Buses stop at the western side of town at the start of the Amalfi Coast Road (SS163) across from Piazza Matteotti, and at the eastern side of town near the Ceramica Artista Solimene building.

You can also take **Busitalia Campania** (www.fsbusitaliacampania.it; from €1.10 per person) line 1 or 4 to get from Salerno to Vietri sul Mare. Bus line 1 runs every 30-60 minutes, 7am-10pm. Bus line 4 runs about every hour 6:45am-11pm. The ride to Vietri sul Mare takes about 10 minutes.

To arrive in Vietri sul Mare from the Naples airport, **Pintour** (tel. 081/879-2645; www.pintourbus.com; €20 adults, €10 children up to 12 years) offers a convenient bus service seasonally, from April to early November. Catch the bus at the terminal located outside the arrivals hall at the airport. The bus stops at Pompeii and along the Amalfi Coast including two stops in Vietri sul Mare: one near Piazza Matteotti at the start of the Amalfi Coast Road and one at the crossroads leading up to Raito and Albori. It's a good idea to book your tickets in advance via the Pintour website. The trip from the airport to Vietri sul Mare takes about 50 minutes.

By Train

Vietri sul Mare is the only town on the Amalfi Coast with a train station. The "Vietri sul Mare-Amalfi" station is situated above the center of town and is serviced by local **Trenitalia** (www.trenitalia.com) trains from Salerno and Naples. Trains from Salerno depart every 30 minutes 5am-9pm. The journey is about 8 minutes and costs €1.20. From Naples, trains depart every 30 minutes 5:40am-9:30pm. The journey takes about an hour and 15 minutes, and prices start at €4.70. It's a 10-minute downhill walk following a winding cobblestone street to the center of town from the train station.

GETTING AROUND

The center of Vietri sul Mare where all the shops are located is relatively flat and walkable. To reach the Marina di Vietri, follow Via Orazio Costabile from Piazza Matteotti down through town to sea level.

By Car

The center of Vietri sul Mare is easy to navigate on foot, so if you have a car, you may want to leave it parked while you're here. Limited paid parking is available in Piazza Matteotti or in parking areas along the beach in Marina di Vietri. The six *frazioni* of Vietri sul Mare are scattered along the mountainside west of the center of town. To reach Raito, follow the Amalfi Coast Road west, and shortly you'll see a sign marking Raito and a turnoff to the right. This road, the SP75, winds up the mountain to Raito and takes about 10 minutes to reach. Parking is available along the side of the street in Raito.

By Bus

The **Busitalia Campania** bus lines (www.fsbusitaliacampania.it, from €1.10 per person) connect Vietri sul Mare with Cava de' Tirreni, and provide a local bus service to the *frazioni* of Vietri sul Mare, and between the town center and Marina di Vietri. Look for line 68 to reach Marina di Vietri and Raito from the center of Vietri sul Mare. Buses run every hour to hour and a half 6:30am-8:30pm; the journey from the town center to Marina di Vietri takes 6-8 minutes and to Raito takes about 8 minutes. From early June to early September, the 63 bus runs between Marina di Vietri and the center of town every 30 minutes, 7am-6:30pm; it is a comfortable way to reach the beach in Vietri sul Mare without the walk. To reach Cava de' Tirreni, take the No. 4 bus and get off at the train station in Cava de' Tirreni. This line runs every hour 6:45am-11pm, and the journey is about 15 minutes.

Salerno

Just beyond Vietri sul Mare where the Lattari Mountains drop down to a flat plain, the city of Salerno stretches out along a large gulf. Set between two of the most beautiful coastlines in Italy—the Amalfi Coast to the west and the Cilento Coast to the south—Salerno is a vibrant and traditional southern Italian city. Despite its scenic setting and proximity to the Amalfi Coast, Salerno has an off-the-beaten-path atmosphere that appeals to many travelers. The Amalfi Coast flows right into Salerno, where you can explore the medieval historic center, catch a show at the elegant **Teatro Giuseppe Verdi,** stroll along the waterfront, or visit the **Castello di Arechi** for a bird's-eye view over Salerno.

Salerno has a rich heritage dating back to the early Middle Ages, when it was a flourishing Lombard principality that was noted for its culture and learning. This town was the birthplace of the **Schola Medica Salernitana,** the first medical school in the west. The history of Salerno can be seen in the city's impressive Romanesque cathedral dedicated to St. Matthew, and in the **Museo Archeologico Provinciale.** Not far from Salerno you can uncover even more of the area's ancient origins while visiting the ruins of **Paestum,** where you'll find some of the best-preserved Greek temples in the world.

For travelers who enjoy a city vibe, a stay in Salerno is a great alternative to Naples. With a train station and port right in the center of the city, you'll have easy access to day trips to the Amalfi Coast, Paestum, Capri, and also to Pompeii and Naples. There's a wealth of history to uncover, and all the top spots in the area are just a train or ferry ride away.

ORIENTATION

Though Salerno is a large city, the top sights are primarily located in the historic center or along the waterfront (*lungomare*). An important shipping center, Salerno's large port on the western side of the city serves as both a commercial and touristic port where cruise ships dock, and ferry service for the Amalfi Coast and Capri departs from the Molo Manfredi at the Stazione Marittima di Salerno. From the port, the *lungomare* is a pleasant place to stroll along the sea and stretches to Piazza Concordia where you'll find another touristic port called the Masuccio Salernitano. This port offers more frequent ferry service to the Amalfi Coast and Capri.

Salerno's train station is located about two blocks north of Piazza Concordia. Roughly parallel to the *lungomare*, the Corso Vittorio Emanuele starts at the train station and continues west through the city to the Piazza Sedile di Portanova. From there, follow Via Mercanti into the medieval ***centro storico*** (historic center) of Salerno. Then follow Via Mercanti to Via Duomo and take a right to reach the **Cattedrale di Salerno.** The city's museums, most intriguing churches, and excellent shopping are all located along Corso Vittorio Emanuele and the historic center.

At the western end of the *lungomare* is a lovely park called the Villa Comunale, and next to it is the Teatro Giuseppe Verdi. The best way to get around Salerno is on foot, because as you visit the sights you can explore the maze of streets in the medieval city center, one of the most characteristic and charming spots in the city.

SIGHTS

★ Centro Storico

Between Piazza Sedile di Portanova and Piazza Matteo Luciani, and between Via Roma and Via Torquato Tasso

The *centro storico* (historic center) of Salerno has origins dating back to Roman times, around 197 BC, when the city was founded as Salernum. A few remains of the ancient city can be seen at the Tempio di Pomona, ruins

Salerno

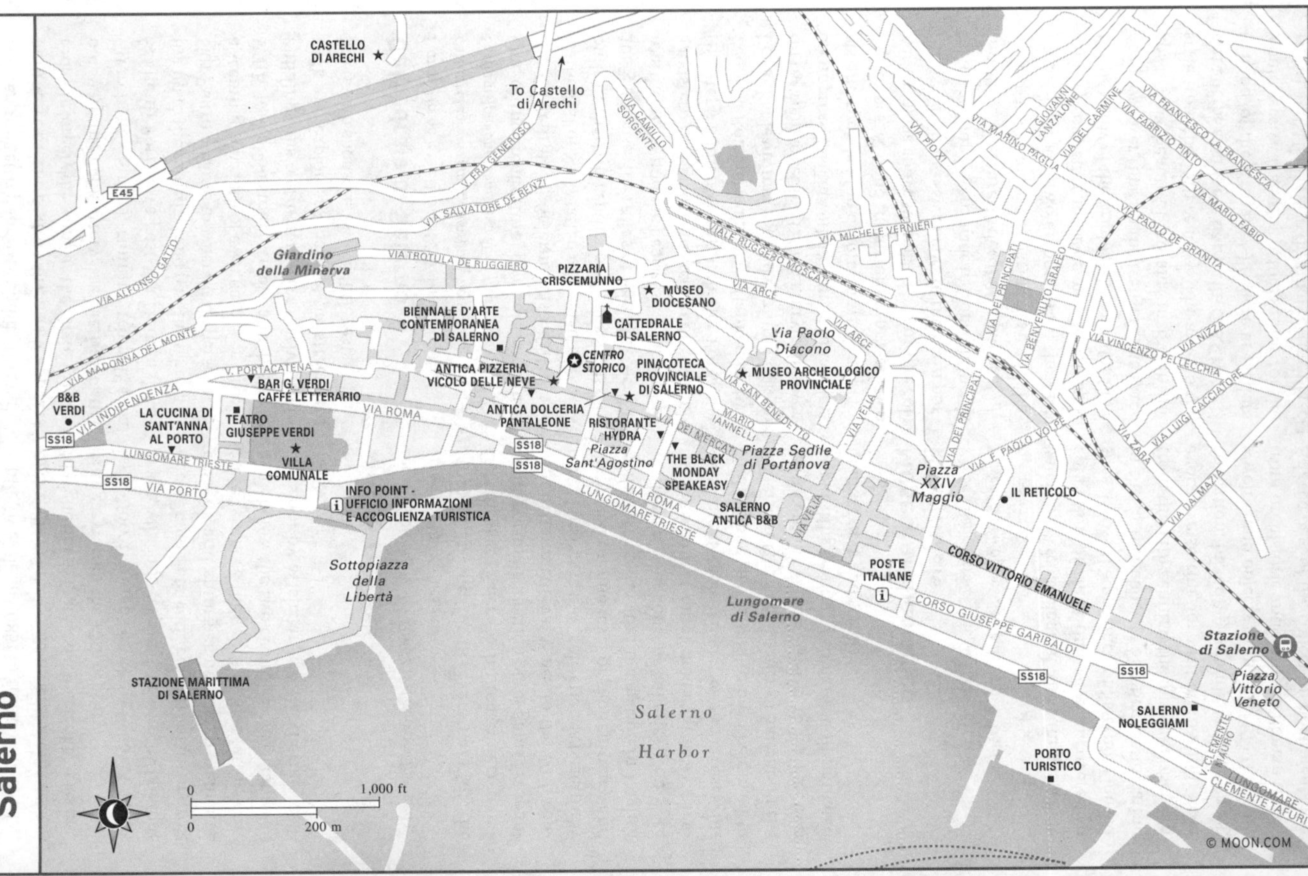
CASTELLO DI ARECHI
To Castello di Arechi
E45
V. FRA GENEROSO
VIA SALVATORE DE RENZI
VIA CAMILLO SORGENTE
VIA ALFONSO GATTO
Giardino della Minerva
VIA TROTULA DE RUGGIERO
VIA MADONNA DEL MONTE
PIZZARIA CRISCEMUNNO
MUSEO DIOCESANO
CATTEDRALE DI SALERNO
BIENNALE D'ARTE CONTEMPORANEA DI SALERNO
CENTRO STORICO
ANTICA PIZZERIA VICOLO DELLE NEVE
PINACOTECA PROVINCIALE DI SALERNO
ANTICA DOLCERIA PANTALEONE
RISTORANTE HYDRA
Piazza Sant'Agostino
THE BLACK MONDAY SPEAKEASY
SALERNO ANTICA B&B
MUSEO ARCHEOLOGICO PROVINCIALE
Via Paolo Diacono
VIA ARCE
VIALE RUGGERO MOSCATI
VIA MICHELE VERNIERI
V. PORTACATENA
BAR G. VERDI CAFFÈ LETTERARIO
B&B VERDI
VIA INDIPENDENZA
LA CUCINA DI SANT'ANNA AL PORTO
TEATRO GIUSEPPE VERDI
VILLA COMUNALE
VIA ROMA
SS18
LUNGOMARE TRIESTE
VIA PORTO
INFO POINT - UFFICIO INFORMAZIONI E ACCOGLIENZA TURISTICA
Sottopiazza della Libertà
STAZIONE MARITTIMA DI SALERNO
VIA DEI MERCANTI
MARIO IANNELLI
VIA SAN BENEDETTO
Piazza Sedile di Portanova
VIA VELIA
VIA DEI PRINCIPATI
VIA BENVENUTO GRAFEO
VIA F. PAOLO VOLPE
Piazza XXIV Maggio
IL RETICOLO
POSTE ITALIANE
CORSO VITTORIO EMANUELE
CORSO GIUSEPPE GARIBALDI
Lungomare di Salerno
Salerno Harbor
Stazione di Salerno
Piazza Vittorio Veneto
SALERNO NOLEGGIAMI
PORTO TURISTICO
V. CLEMENTE MAURO
LUNGOMARE CLEMENTE TAFURI
VIA PIO XI
VIA MARINO PAGLIA
V. GIOVANNI LANZALONE
VIA DEL CARMINE
VIA FRANCESCO LA FRANCESCA
VIA FABRIZIO PINTO
VIA MARIO FABIO
VIA PAOLO DE GRANITA
VIA NIZZA
VIA VINCENZO PELLECCHIA
VIA LUIGI CACCIATORE
VIA ZARA
VIA DALMAZIA
0 1,000 ft
0 200 m
© MOON.COM

of a Roman temple, next to the Duomo, which is often the setting for art exhibits throughout the year. The *centro storico* as it appears today is largely the same as the medieval layout, with the main artery, the **Via Mercanti** (Merchant's Street), running from Piazza Sedile di Portanova past Via Duomo, leading up to the cathedral and past the Chiesa di San Pietro a Corte to where it disperses into a seeming labyrinth of even narrower streets. With its cobblestone streets and historic buildings, the *centro storico* is a lovely area to walk and explore, as many of the streets are lined with shops, cafés, and little restaurants.

Cattedrale di Salerno

Piazza Alfano I; tel. 089/231-287; www.cattedraledisalerno.it; 8am-8pm Mon.-Sat., 8:30am-1pm and 4pm-8pm Sun.; free

One of the architectural gems of Campania, the Cattedrale di Salerno, also called the Cathedral of San Matteo or the Duomo, was built in the 11th century and consecrated in 1085; it houses the **relics of San Matteo** (St. Matthew). Behind the neoclassical facade lies a masterpiece of Norman architecture. Climb the steps and enter through the Porta dei Leone, a Romanesque portal flanked by two lions that leads into a grand atrium. Look up on the right to see the 12th-century bell tower, an impressive sight with its sturdy square levels and rounded top decorated with interlacing arches. Around the atrium runs a portico with a loggia above supported by antique columns. The impressive doors to the main portal to the church were made in Constantinople in 1099 and feature 42 decorative panels.

Step inside to find a soaring nave with baroque décor and two ambons from the 12th century covered in intricate mosaic patterns. While many of the original decorations have been lost over time, in the transept the three apses have beautiful mosaics in Byzantine style from the 13th century. The apse to the right of the altar is the **Cappella dei Crociati** (Chapel of the Crusaders), where crusaders would receive a blessing before sailing for the Holy Land. Here is also the final resting place for Pope Gregorio VII, who died in Salerno while in exile in 1085. In the apse to the left of the altar is the grand funeral monument to Margherita di Durazzo, Queen of Naples and Hungary, from the 15th century.

Follow the steps on the left down to the crypt, which is resplendent with its baroque décor, complete with polychromatic marble designs and shimmering golden elements. Here is where the relics of St. Matthew are held, below the two central bronze statues of the saint by Michelangelo Naccherino from 1622.

Museo Diocesano

Largo Plebiscito 12; tel. 089/239-126; 9am-1pm and 3pm-7pm Thurs.-Tues.; €2

Housed in the former seminary of the Cattedrale di Salerno, this museum contains an important collection of religious art spanning from medieval times to the 20th century. The impressive collection is beautifully displayed on one level of the seminary and well illustrated, with information in English available throughout the galleries. You'll see the fine collection of medieval ivory carvings, and notable reliquaries and crosses, including one that is said to have belonged to Roberto il Guiscardo, ruler of Salerno in the 11th century. There's also a rich collection of paintings, antique coins, and illuminated manuscripts and scrolls.

Museo Archeologico Provinciale

Via San Benedetto 28; tel. 089/231-135; www.museoarcheologicosalerno.it; 9am-7:30pm Tues.-Sun.; €4

Salerno's Archaeological Museum has a fine collection of finds that were uncovered in sites across the province of Salerno. Housed in the former abbey of San Benedetto dating from the 11th century, the museum offers an evocative setting for visitors to admire the collection, including ceramics, bronze vases, jewelry, and objects from daily life that date from prehistoric antiquities to Roman times. A large part of the collection documents the

Etruscan-Campano settlement of Fratte in the northern part of modern-day Salerno, where a large part of the museum's collection was uncovered. A special room is dedicated to the museum's important bronze statue of the Head of Apollo dating from the 1st century BC. A detailed map and information are available in English.

Pinacoteca Provinciale di Salerno

Via Mercanti 63; tel. 089/258-3073; museibiblioteche@provincia.salerno.it; 9am-7:45pm Tues.-Sun.; free

Set in the historic center along Via Mercanti, this museum is located in the 17th-century Palazzo Pinto. The collection is based on the original collection belonging to the Pinto family, and predominantly covers paintings and other works from the 15th through the 18th centuries that were donated or saved from churches or other locations throughout the province of Salerno. The collection comprises mainly religious works, but also includes landscapes and portraits. Important works include 17th-century paintings by Giovanni Battista Caracciolo and 18th-century works by Francesco Solimena, two important Neapolitan artists. An interesting section is dedicated to foreign artists who were inspired to visit the area by earlier travelers on the Grand Tour, and features paintings and drawings of scenes from the Amalfi Coast. The museum also hosts special exhibits throughout the year. Information is available in English throughout the museum.

Villa Comunale

Via Roma and Via Lungomare Trieste; 8am-midnight Apr.-Oct., 8am-8pm Nov.-Mar.; free

Just next to the Teatro Giuseppe Verdi along the waterfront, you'll find this public garden, which was created in 1874. It's a quiet retreat to stroll through or enjoy a rest on one of the many benches. The garden was constructed around an 18th-century fountain called the Fontana del Tullio, and statues of political and military figures are dotted throughout the garden. During the Luci d'Artista Christmas light festival from November to January, the Villa Comunale is transformed into a magical garden with light installations, tunnels, and plenty of whimsy.

Giardino della Minerva

Vicolo Ferrante Sanseverino 1; tel. 089/252-423; www.giardinodellaminerva.it; 9:30am-8pm June-Aug., closed Monday, some earlier closing times, depending on the season; €3

In the early 1300s, this garden was used as the botanical garden for the Schola Medica Salernitana medical school, which makes it one of the oldest in Europe. Tucked away in a residential area, the gardens are spread out along the slope in the upper part of Salerno below the Castello di Arechi. After an in-depth restoration in 2001, the gardens were revitalized and replanted with many of the species mentioned in medieval medical texts. The gardens now have more than 380 species of plants and are as educational as they are beautiful, offering a peaceful spot with some lovely panoramic views overlooking Salerno and the sea.

Castello di Arechi

Via Croce; tel. 089/227-237; www.ilcastellodiarechi.it; 9am-5pm Tues.-Sat., 9am-3pm Sun.; €4

Situated in the mountains about 980 feet (300m) above Salerno, this castle dating back to the eighth century is named after the Lombard duke Arechi II, who transferred his kingdom from Benevento to Salerno. The castle was part of the Lombard defensive system and was added to over the centuries, with each new invasion and change of power in Salerno. The on-site **Museo Medievale** (Medieval Museum) houses historical finds uncovered during various restoration projects on the castle, including collections of ceramics, glass vessels, iron and bronze objects from daily life, as well as weapons. Besides the fine views overlooking the city and Gulf of Salerno, the castle's rugged walls are an evocative setting to delve deeper into Salerno's history.

1
2
3
4
M2
OUTLET
STREET
CAFE
ARTE
LFATTIVA

SPORTS AND RECREATION

LUNGOMARE

Lungomare Trieste

Stretching out nearly a mile (1.5 km), the *lungomare* (waterfront) of Salerno is a pedestrian-only garden lined with trees overlooking the Gulf of Salerno and Amalfi Coast. It leads from near the Villa Comunale gardens to Piazza Concordia and is a popular spot to enjoy a *passeggiata* (stroll) with a lovely view with the ports of Salerno nearby and the beginning of the Amalfi coastline to the west.

ENTERTAINMENT AND EVENTS

Salerno has a lively entertainment scene. Even in winter when the Amalfi Coast is sleepy, Salerno's **Luci d'Artista** Christmas light festival attracts large numbers of visitors during the holiday season. Salerno's nightlife scene keeps the *centro storico* and *lungomare* buzzing well after dark. On Via Roma from Via Antica Corte to the Villa Comunale, you'll find about every type of bar and restaurant.

Nightlife

BAR G. VERDI CAFFÈ LETTERARIO

Piazza Matteo Luciani 28; tel. 320/897-2096; barverdi1910@yahoo.it; 6:30am-1am Tues.-Fri., 6:30am-11pm Mon., 6:30am-2pm and 5pm-1am Sat.-Sun., closed two weeks mid-Aug.; €3-5

Located across the street from the Teatro Giuseppe Verdi, this coffee shop has been a hub of creativity for the theater since it opened in 1910. Inside, you'll find photos of the artists who have visited, which is a tradition that continues today during the theater season. The eclectic décor and quirky style are the perfect setting for a literary café that also hosts weekly events that range from music and theater to book presentations and children's programs. There's even a small independent bookstore inside. They roast their own beans, so this is the place for coffee lovers. You'll also find organic teas, fresh juices, and homemade desserts, as well as wine and cocktails.

THE BLACK MONDAY SPEAKEASY

Via Mazza 26; tel. 348/263-7594; 8pm-3am Oct.-Apr.; €8-20

This unique speakeasy offers fine cocktails and drinks, a vintage vibe, a friendly local setting, and frequent live music performances. This cozy spot is open only from autumn through spring. It's the perfect spot to warm up with a drink after seeing the holiday Luci d'Artista lights.

Performing Arts

TEATRO GIUSEPPE VERDI

Piazza Matteo Luciani; tel. 089/662-141; www.teatroverdisalerno.it; season May-Dec.; tickets starting at €10 for concerts and €25 for operas

Inaugurated in 1872, Salerno's Teatro Giuseppe Verdi is an impressive venue to experience a concert or show. Inspired by the grand Teatro San Carlo in Naples, the architects created a smaller version that was then decorated by celebrated Neapolitan artists. The stunning interior of the theater, one of the few remaining original wooden 19th-century theaters in Italy, has been beautifully restored with its brilliant red seats, four tiers of boxes, shimmering gold details, and a ceiling mural depicting Gioachino Rossini surrounded by muses. The lyric, concert, and ballet season runs from May to December, but there are often concerts and performances throughout the year.

Festivals and Events

FESTIVAL OF SAN MATTEO

Cattedrale di Salerno and various locations; September 21

On the traditional day honoring San Matteo, September 21, Salerno celebrates its patron saint with a religious festival that is fittingly grand for an apostle and evangelist. The evening procession leads through the streets of the *centro storico* with statues of San Matteo, San Giuseppe, San Gregorio VII, and the saints Gaio, Ante, and Fortunato,

---

1: the Villa Comunale gardens **2:** Cattedrale di Salerno **3:** strolling through Salerno's medieval historic center **4:** the Castello di Arechi in the mountains above Salerno

accompanied by marching bands. As the procession makes its way through the narrow streets, balconies are packed with onlookers and the streets are lined with people leaving just enough room for the procession to squeeze through. For a moment, city activity pauses and time seems to stand still during this annual event that has taken place for centuries. After the procession a Mass is given in the crypt of the Duomo, followed by concerts in Piazza Alfano I, Piazza Cavour, and Piazza Amendola. The finishing touch is a huge fireworks display after dark.

LUCI D'ARTISTA

Villa Comunale and the historic center; lucidartista.comune.salerno.it; early Nov.-mid-Jan.

There are holiday lights and then there's the Luci d'Artista, which takes Christmas lights to a whole new level. Starting in November, the entire city is decorated with elaborate light displays that transform an evening stroll through the city into a dreamlike experience. Every little street and piazza is covered with lights, each with its own theme. A soaring Christmas tree graces Piazza Sedile di Portanova and the Villa Comunale is always decked out with an abundance of light displays, often shaped like animals and whimsical floral designs, to create an enchanted garden setting.

BIENNALE D'ARTE CONTEMPORANEA DI SALERNO

Palazzo Fruscione, Vicolo Adelberga 19; tel. 335/667-6408; www.biennaleartesalerno.com; Oct.-Nov.; free

Salerno's annual contemporary art festival presents works by artists in a variety of different media. Events include the art exhibit, concerts, book presentatations, and other cultural programs. The artwork is displayed in Palazzo Fruscione, a remarkable historic building dating back to Norman times.

SHOPPING

Salerno is a fun destination for shopping if you're looking for a variety of larger Italian brands as well as locally owned shops. While much of the *centro storico* is good for shopping, the best spots are located along two main streets and the area surrounding them. Keep in mind that Salerno keeps to traditional shop closing times, so most will close for lunch from around 1:30pm to 4:30pm and many are also closed Monday morning, especially during the winter.

Shopping Districts

CORSO VITTORIO EMANUELE

Corso Vittorio Emanuele between Piazza Vittorio Veneto and Piazza Sedile di Portanova

Corso Vittorio Emanuele is the main shopping street in Salerno and runs from the train station at **Piazza Vittorio Veneto** to **Piazza Sedile di Portanova.** Lined with shops, cafés, and restaurants, this tree-lined street has limited traffic and makes a pleasant place to stroll. Along the way, you'll find larger department stores like **OVS** as well as Italian and international brand clothing, jewelry, and shoe shops like **United Colors of Benetton** (Corso Vittorio Emanuele 70; tel. 089/254-139; 10am-9pm daily); **Alcott** (Corso Vittorio Emanuele 29; tel. 089/232-169; 10am-9pm Mon.-Sat., 10am-2pm and 5pm-10pm Sun.), **Intimissimi** (Corso Vittorio Emanuele 190; tel. 089/910-0102; 10am-1:30pm and 4:30-8pm daily), and a multilevel **Feltrinelli bookstore** (Corso Vittorio Emanuele 230; tel. 199/151-173; 9:30am-8:30pm Mon.-Fri., 9:30am-9:30pm Sat., 10am-9pm Sun.).

CENTRO STORICO

Via Mercanti starting from Piazza Sedile di Portanova and turning into Via Dogana Vecchia and Via Portacatena, plus cross streets like Via Duomo and many more

Cross Piazza Sedile di Portanova and look for the narrow entrance to Via Mercanti, the original merchant area of medieval Salerno. This is the entrance into the oldest part of the city, where you'll find smaller artisan shops mostly selling clothing and jewelry. The maze of little streets that cross Via Mercanti are also fun to explore.

La Botteguccia al Duomo (Via Duomo 43; tel. 089/222-687; vm@viamercanti.sa.it; 9:30am-1:30pm and 4pm-8:30pm Tues.-Sat., 10am-1:30pm Sun., 4pm-8:30pm Mon.) is located across from the Cattedrale di Salerno and is a lovely artisan leather workshop where you'll find handmade bags, shoes, and accessories.

Stop in **Sciglio** (Via Duomo 46; tel. 089/296-1785; www.sciglio vintage.com; 10am-1pm and 5pm-8:30pm Tues.-Sat., 5pm-8:30pm Sun.-Mon.) for a beautifully curated selection of vintage clothing as well as illustrations, ceramics, jewelry, accessories, and artwork all created by a group of young and talented local artists.

Keep following Via Mercanti west as it changes into Via Dogana Vecchia and Via Portacatena and don't miss exploring all of the little cross streets, like Via Duomo, in the historic area. At the western end of the *centro storico*, look for **DecoBirds Ceramiche** (Via Portacatena 21/23; tel. 347/480-5208; 10am-2pm and 3pm-8:30pm Mon.-Sat., 10am-2pm Sun.), where owner Donatello Ciao is often at work hand-painting the cheerful ceramics on display; many pieces feature birds, which is his unique personal touch.

FOOD

Much larger than the towns along the Amalfi Coast, Salerno has a thriving restaurant scene with an abundance of options. You'll find excellent pizza, with influences from nearby Naples, as well as trattorias to enjoy local specialties, and even a variety of international options. You don't have to walk far in the *centro storico* to find a host of restaurant options; there are also plenty of choices along the *lungomare* and near the Villa Comunale.

Regional Cuisine

RISTORANTE HYDRA

Via Antonio Mazza 30; tel. 089/ 995-8437; www.ristorantehydra.com; 7:30pm-midnight Tues.-Fri., 12:30-3pm and 7:30pm-midnight Sat.-Sun.; €15-50

Just off of Via Mercanti, this is a fine spot for lunch or dinner. With a beautiful minimalist décor, the restaurant offers the opportunity to dine inside or outside in their garden setting, right in the historic center. The menu is creative and highlights both seafood and meat; their grilled menu is a highlight, along with wood-fired pizza.

LA CUCINA DI SANT' ANNA AL PORTO

Via S. Teresa 1; tel. 320/857-4215; www.lacucinadisantannalporto.com; 7:30pm-1am Mon., Wed., Thurs., 1pm-4pm and 7:30pm-1am Fri.-Sun.; €8-16

Located near the Villa Comunale gardens and Teatro Giuseppe Verdi, this restaurant specializes in seafood, and it doesn't get fresher. The carpaccio and *tartare* (raw fish) are excellent, as is the fish of the day, grilled or baked in the oven. Pasta is served with all types of seafood, or you can opt for the *zuppa di pesce*, soup made with a variety of fish and shellfish.

Pizzeria

PIZZARIA CRISCEMUNNO

Via Romualdo II Guarna 15; tel. 089/296-6164; www.criscemunno.it; 7:30pm-11:30pm; €3.50-8.50

For an excellent Neapolitan-style pizza right in the heart of the historic center, head to this pizzeria right next to the Cattedrale di Salerno. The restaurant boasts a dining terrace overlooking the piazza and the distinctive bell tower of the cathedral. With only the finest-quality locally sourced ingredients and a perfect blend of traditional and creative cooking, the pizzas are delicious masterpieces. Try the classic Margherita with mozzarella, tomato, and a drizzle of olive oil, or go for one of their unique creations like the *Cenere* pizza topped with potatoes, smoked *provola di bufala* (buffalo provolone), and *caciocavallo* cheese.

ANTICA PIZZERIA VICOLO DELLA NEVE

Vicolo Della Neve 24; tel. 089/225-705; www.vicolodellaneve.it; 7pm-2am Mon.-Tues. and Thurs.-Sat. and 12:30pm-4pm Sun., closed Wed.; €7-15

Located down a tiny side street in the historic

center off of Via Mercanti, this small restaurant is an iconic spot for pizza and hearty home cooking, all from the traditional wood-fired pizza oven. In addition to pizza, try the *pasta e fagioli* (pasta with beans) or the *baccalà con patate* (cod with potatoes), two of their classic dishes.

Bakery

ANTICA DOLCERIA PANTALEONE

Via Dei Mercanti 75; tel. 089/227-825; www.dolceriapantaleone.it; 8:30am-2pm and 4:30pm-8:30pm Mon.-Sat., 8:30am-2pm Sun.; €2-18

Right in the historic center, this bakery was founded in 1868 and is still the spot to try classic Campania desserts as well as Salerno specialties. You'll catch the sweet scent even before you arrive at the entrance to what was once a church. For something very local, try the *scazzetta*, a brilliant red-hued cake with chantilly cream, wild strawberries, and a strawberry glaze. Or try the *dolce della strega* (dessert of the witch) flavored with Strega liqueur made in Benevento, a city inland in Campania.

ACCOMMODATIONS

Under €100

IL RETICOLO

Via Giovan Angelo Papio 14; tel. 089/995-8585; www.ilreticolobebsalerno.it; open year round; €75 d

Located in the historic center about a 10-minute walk from the train station, this B&B offers four bright rooms, each one named after a town in the area that is featured in a panoramic photo in the room. The building has an elevator and two wheelchair-accessible rooms. Private parking is also available for a daily fee.

€100-200

B&B VERDI

Via Indipendenza 5; tel. 345/341-6372; www.bbverdi.it; open year round; €100 d

This friendly B&B is located not far from the Teatro Giuseppe Verdi and the Villa Comunale. Its three rooms are comfortable, and all offer private bathrooms: two are en suite and one has its private bathroom outside the room. The breakfast is abundant, and both sweet and savory options are offered. Note that if you're arriving by train or ferry, the B&B is located on the other side of town and you'll need to catch a bus or taxi from the terminals.

SALERNO ANTICA B&B

Via Masuccio Salernitano 8; tel. 089/253-156; www.salernoantica.com; €130

With an ideal location just off of Piazza Sedile di Portanova, this lovely B&B is set in a historic palazzo dating back to the 1400s. The building has been remodeled and includes an elevator. The three large rooms are all beautifully appointed, and owner Daniele Abbondanza is on hand to help with local information and suggestions. This is a wonderful find right in the heart of the Salerno's historic center.

INFORMATION AND SERVICES

Tourist Information

INFO POINT TURISTICO COMUNE DI SALERNO

Corso Vittorio Emanuele 193; tel. 089/662-951; www.comune.salerno.it; 9am-1pm and 5pm-8pm Mon.-Fri., 9am-1pm Sat., closed Sun.

The tourist office for the city of Salerno is located in the heart of the shopping district along Corso Vittorio Emanuele. It's not that easy to spot from the street, but look for the Burger King and head inside the Galleria Capitol, a mini shopping center, and you'll find it up a short staircase on the right.

INFO POINT - UFFICIO INFORMAZIONI E ACCOGLIENZA TURISTICA

Via Lungomare Trieste 7/9; tel. 089/231-432; www.eptsalerno.it; 9am-7pm Mon.-Sat. year-round, and 9am-7pm Sun. May-Sept.

Located across the street from the southeast corner of the Villa Comunale, this tourist office is run by the Province of Salerno and covers the entire area, including the city of

Salerno and the Amalfi Coast. The English-speaking staff can help with detailed information on the area, events, and transportation.

Medical and Emergency Services

OSPEDALE SAN LEONARDO

Via San Leonardo; tel. 089/671-111; www.sangiovannieruggi.it

Salerno's hospital is located about 5 miles (8 km) southeast of the historic center in the San Leonardo area of the city. The fastest way to reach it from the center of Salerno is to take the Tangenziale di Salerno highway just east of the train station south to the exit for Ospedale-San Leonardo, and the hospital is directly at the exit. The drive is about 15 minutes, depending on traffic. It is a large hospital with a 24-hour *pronto soccorso* (emergency room). If you need **emergency services** to come to you, dial 118 for ambulance and urgent care.

Postal Services

POSTE ITALIANE

Corso Giuseppe Garibaldi 203; tel. 089/275-9749; www.poste.it; 8:20am-7:05pm Mon.-Fri.

For letter- and package-mailing services, you'll find Salerno's main post office along the Corso Giuseppe Garibaldi in the center of the city. There's also a smaller Poste Italiane office near the train station (Piazza Vittorio Veneto 7; tel. 089/229-998; 8:20am-1:35pm Mon.-Fri.).

GETTING THERE

By Car

Salerno is located east of the Amalfi Coast and is quite easy to reach from all towns along the coastline. From Positano and Amalfi, head east on the Amalfi Coast Road (SS163) and Salerno is located just beyond Vietri sul Mare. The drive from Positano takes an hour and 45 minutes, while from Amalfi it's about an hour's drive. From Ravello, first follow the SS373 road down to where it intersects the Amalfi Coast Road and take a left to continue east until you reach Salerno. The drive time from Ravello is about 1 hour 15 minutes. From Naples, follow the A3 highway south to the Salerno exit. From Naples to Salerno, plan for about a one-hour drive.

By Train

Salerno's train station, the **Stazione di Salerno** (Piazza Vittorio Veneto), is conveniently located in the center of the city and is served by Italy's national train line **Trenitalia** (www.trenitalia.com) as well as **Italo** (www.italotreno.it). There are local, regional, and high-speed trains to Salerno from cities across Italy, with trains arriving direct to Salerno or by transfering in large cities like Naples and Rome. From Naples, trains depart throughout the day, every 15-30 minutes (or even more frequently, depending on the time of day) from about 5:30am to 10:30pm. The length of the journey ranges from 40 minutes to 1 hour 25 minutes, depending on the type of train, and prices start at €4.70.

From Rome, trains also run frequently (every 10-30 minutes) from 5:30am to 11pm. The journey time varies greatly, depending on the type of train and number of transfers. The fastest and most convenient trains are the Frecciarossa high-speed trains that travel from Rome to Salerno in about 2 hours. Fares vary, depending on the train type and season, but a direct Intercity train can start around €12.90 and takes about 3 hours. The piazza in front of the station is also a bus hub, and it's a short walk to reach the Porto Turistico near Piazza Concordia for ferries.

By Bus

To reach Salerno by bus from the Amalfi Coast, **SITA SUD** (tel. 089/386-6701; www.sitasudtrasporti.it; from €1.30) runs a bus line from Amalfi to Salerno. Buses run 5:15am-9pm roughly every hour and the journey from Amalfi to Salerno takes about 1 hour, 15 minutes. The bus passes through Atrani, Castiglione (Ravello), Minori, Maiori, Cetara, and Vietri sul Mare before arriving in Salerno. To reach Salerno from points west of Amalfi, such as Positano, first take the bus to Amalfi and then transfer to the Amalfi-Salerno line.

From Ravello, take the bus to Amalfi and transfer to the Amalfi-Salerno line. Buses from the Amalfi Coast pass along the waterfront in Salerno, where you can get off at multiple stops as well as Piazza Concordia before the bus arrives at the Via Vinciprova bus hub, about 15 minutes' walk east of the train station. For the center of Salerno, you'll want to get off along the waterfront or Piazza Concordia.

From Naples, buses for Salerno depart from near the Piazza Immacolatella along the port about every 30 minutes 6am-9pm, and the journey takes about 1 hour 15 minutes. Note that the bus arrives at the bus hub at Via Vinciprova.

FlixBus (www.flixbus.it; prices starting at €4.99) offers 93 routes to Salerno from destinations all across Italy. Buses arrive at Piazza Concordia.

By Boat

Salerno's large port is divided into several areas. On the western side is the city's commerical port where large cruise ships often dock. On the eastern side not far from the train station is the Porto Turistico where ferries arrive from the Amalfi Coast. In the center is the Stazione Marittima di Salerno (Maritime Station), or Molo Manfredi, where ferries arrive from the Amalfi Coast, Capri, and the surrounding area.

PORTO TURISTICO

Piazza Concordia

Salerno's main port for ferries is the Porto Turistico, also called the Marina Masuccio Salernitano, located at Piazza Concordia. **Travelmar** (tel. 089/872-950; www.travelmar.it; €5-12) ferries arrive at the end of the pier from Cetara, Minori, Maiori, Amalfi, and Positano. Ferry service is seasonal and runs from April to early November. Departures are every 1-2 hours, 9am-7pm (depending on the departure location), and the ferry ride from Positano to Salerno takes about 70 minutes. From Amalfi, it takes about 35 minutes, from Minori about 40 minutes, from Maiori about 30 minutes, and from Cetara about 15 minutes. Tickets are available online in advance, or via the Travelmar app.

STAZIONE MARITTIMA DI SALERNO

Molo Manfredi; tel. 800/115-110; www.salernostazionemarittima.it

Salerno's maritime station at Molo Manfredi is located on the western side of the port. Architect Zaha Hadid designed the Stazione Marittima di Salerno with its sleek lines and sweeping roofline. **Alicost** (tel. 089/227-979, www.alicost.it, starting at €25.00 per person) ferries from Capri and Ischia arrive at this port, often stopping at Positano, Amalfi, Minori, Maiori, and Cetara along the way. Ferry service is available seasonally from April to October, but exact start and end dates vary each year. From Capri there are usually one or two ferry services in the evening, and the journey is a little over 2 hours. Ferries only run from Ischia to Salerno during the peak summer months, from mid-June to August or September, and the journey takes about 2 hours 55 minutes.

GETTING AROUND

Salerno's historic center is not that large, and the best way to get around is on foot. The majority of the city's main sights are very walkable. However, there are local buses that run along the town's main thoroughfares to speed up crossing the city.

By Car and Scooter

If you want to rent a car or scooter, many of the internationally known names like Hertz and Avis have offices near the Stazione di Salerno train station. Though traffic in Salerno is tame compared to nearby Naples, keep in mind that it is still a good-sized city and you should be cautious, especially when navigating traffic on a scooter. Located just across the street from the train station, **Salerno Noleggiami** (Corso Giuseppe Garibaldi 63; tel. 089/252-579; www.salernonoleggiami.it; starting at €25 per day) offers daily and longer rentals of scooters and cars.

By Bus

Salerno's local buses are run by **Busitalia Campania** (www.fsbusitaliacampania.it; from €1.10) with a large number of urban lines that crisscross the city, along with lines to nearby towns like Vietri sul Mare. Many bus lines run along the waterfront of Salerno, from west to east on Lungomare Trieste and from east to west on Corso Giuseppe Garibaldi. Main stops along the waterfront and the *centro storico* are near the Villa Comunale. There are also several stops along Lungomare Trieste and Corso Giuseppe Garibaldi, along with Piazza Concordia near the tourist port. Buses 4, 5, and 6 run frequently throughout the day, but if you're just moving around the center of Salerno to see the sights, nearly every bus that runs along the Lungomare Trieste and Corso Giuseppe Garibaldi will get you from one side of the *centro storico* to the other. Buses run frequently from about 6am to 11pm. Tickets need to be purchased before boarding and can be found in most *tabacchi* (tobacco shops), as well as some coffee shops and bars. Don't forget to validate your ticket after boarding using the machine usually located near the driver.

To reach the Amalfi Coast by bus, take the **SITA SUD** (tel. 089/386-6701; www.sitasudtrasporti.it; from €1.30) bus line from Salerno to Amalfi. From Amalfi, you can transfer to other bus lines to reach Ravello, Positano, and Sorrento. Buses depart from Via Vinciprova, with a stop in Piazza Vittorio Veneto in front of the train station as well as on Via Roma on the western edge of town, across from the Teatro Giuseppe Verdi.

★ DAY TRIP FROM SALERNO: GREEK TEMPLES AT ANCIENT PAESTUM

Not far south of Salerno is one of Italy's most remarkable archaeological treasures, the ruins of the city of Paestum with its incredibly well-preserved Greek temples. The site makes an excellent day trip from Salerno and the Amalfi Coast.

Parco Archeologico di Paestum

Via Magna Grecia 919; 082/811-023; www.museopaestum.beniculturali.it; 8:30am-7:30pm, closed Jan. 1 and Dec. 25; €9.50 for archaeological site and museum, free for children under 18

The ancient city of Paestum was founded by Greek colonists around 600 BC as Poseidonia, a defensive outpost of Magna Graecia. The city was once surrounded by an impressive wall over 23 feet (7 m) tall with towers and four entry gates, and parts of the original wall still exist, although not at the original height. Named after Poseidon, the Greek god of the sea, the colony was later conquered by the Lucanians, an Italic tribe of people on Italy's mainland, at the end of the fifth century BC. Excavations on the site have revealed how the Greek and Italic cultures blended and then later continued to transform when, in 273 BC, the city became a colony of Rome called Paestum.

While visiting the archaeological site, you'll see both Greek and Roman ruins, and it is all worth exploring in detail. A modern-day road called **Via Magna Grecia** cuts through the center of the ancient city with the archaeological area on the west side and a museum on the east side. Enter through one of the two gates along the pedestrian-only section of Via Magna Grecia and the ancient city spreads out in front of you. What captures the most attention, however, are the three incredible temples, and for very good reason as they are remarkable examples of Greek architecture.

TEMPLES

The oldest on the site is the **Temple of Hera,** also referred to as the Basilica, located near the southern side of the city. Dating from around 560 BC, it's the finest and best preserved example anywhere of early Greek temple architecture. Just to the north is the **Temple of Neptune,** the largest in Paestum that was built in the mid-fifth century BC.

Paestum

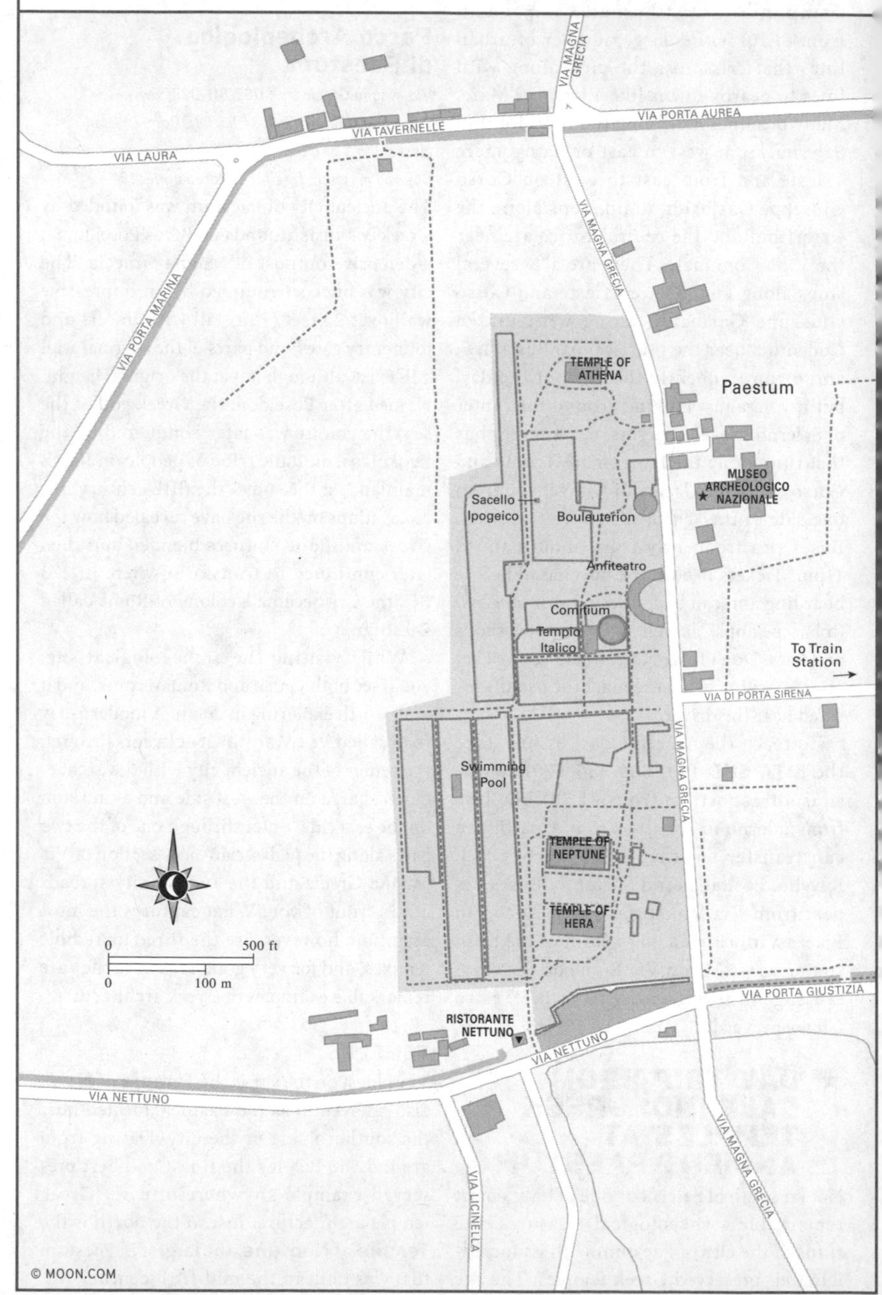
VIA MAGNA GRECIA
VIA PORTA AUREA
VIA TAVERNELLE
VIA LAURA
VIA PORTA MARINA
TEMPLE OF ATHENA
Paestum
MUSEO ARCHEOLOGICO NAZIONALE
Sacello Ipogeico
Bouleuterion
Anfiteatro
Comitium
Tempio Italico
To Train Station
VIA DI PORTA SIRENA
Swimming Pool
TEMPLE OF NEPTUNE
TEMPLE OF HERA
0
500 ft
0
100 m
VIA PORTA GIUSTIZIA
RISTORANTE NETTUNO
VIA NETTUNO
VIA LICINELLA
© MOON.COM

It's an essential example of a Doric-style temple, and although its name refers to Neptune, the later Roman name of the god of the sea, archaeological evidence has revealed it was likely dedicated to Hera or perhaps even Zeus. On the northern side of the site is the **Temple of Athena,** dating from around 500 BC; this is the only temple in Paestum where excavations have revealed with certainty that the temple was originally dedicated to Athena. Along with the temples, you can see the ruins of the agora—later transformed into the Roman forum, which was the heart of the city—as well as part of an amphitheater, thermal baths, and more.

MUSEO ARCHEOLOGICO NAZIONALE

Opposite the archaeological area across Via Magna Grecia, the Museo Archeologico Nazionale is a must during your visit to Paestum. The museum houses artifacts uncovered at Paestum, and rarely is it possible to see such a detailed portrait of an ancient city and how it changed over the centuries. Inside you'll find areas dedicated to the prehistory and protohistory of Paestum, the largest area dedicated to the Greek and Lucanian city, and a section on the Roman period.

Don't miss the extensive collection of ancient vases produced in local workshops, the room dedicated to the carved stone metopes from temples in the area, and the many incredible tombs. The most famous is the Tomb of the Diver, the only known example of a Greek burial tomb with painted figures. Captivating in their simplicity and elegance, the painted scenes date from 470 BC and show figures taking part in a symposium as well as the namesake scene showing a man diving.

Note that on the first and third Monday of the month, the museum closes at 1:40pm. During this time, the entrance price for the archaeological area is reduced to €7. The archaeological area is open until 7:30pm (last tickets at 6:50pm) year-round and is illuminated after dark. Seeing the temples lit at night is a special experience, but keep in mind that you'll need to stick to the illuminated trail only if you visit after sunset.

Food

RISTORANTE NETTUNO

Via Nettuno 2; 082/881-1028; www.ristorantenettuno.com; noon-3:30pm Tues.-Sun. Mar.-Oct., 7:45pm-11pm Tues.-Sat. June-Aug., closed Mon. all year; €10-18

Located right at the southern Porta Giustizia entrance to Paestum, this is a lovely restaurant to stop for lunch or dinner during your visit. Not only are you steps from Paestum, but there are views of the temples and archaeological site from the indoor and outdoor dining areas. The menu is broad and offers both seafood and meat-based specialties. In an area famous for buffalo mozzarella cheese, this is an excellent spot to sample locally made cheese.

GETTING THERE

From Salerno, the easiest way to reach Paestum is to catch a local train operated by Trenitalia (www.trenitalia.com; departures daily every 30 to 60 minutes 6am-9pm; journey about 30 minutes; starting at €2.90) and get off at the Paestum stop. Just across the street from the station is the Porta Sirena entrance to the archaeological area. It's a 15-minute walk through the park to reach Via Magna Grecia with the museum to the right and the archaeological area directly ahead. By car, the SP175 highway runs south from Salerno and along the coastline, and leads to the site after a 50-minute drive.

Sorrento and the Sorrentine Peninsula

Itinerary Ideas 186
Sorrento................191
Sorrentine Peninsula...210

A picturesque setting atop a rocky terrace along the rugged coastline, a well-preserved historic center, and a warm Mediterranean atmosphere are just a few of the assets that make Sorrento such a popular holiday destination. Add to that panoramic views of the Gulf of Naples and a convenient central location on the Sorrentine Peninsula, and you'll really understand Sorrento's appeal. Yet it's not until you're walking along the water's edge watching the colorful fishing boats bob in the harbor of Marina Grande, or examining the detailed inlaid woodwork on a music box that plays "Torna a Surriento" ("Return to Sorrento") that it begins to sink in. This is a city that draws you in with a its colorful streets, intoxicating *limoncello* liqueur, and those stellar views.

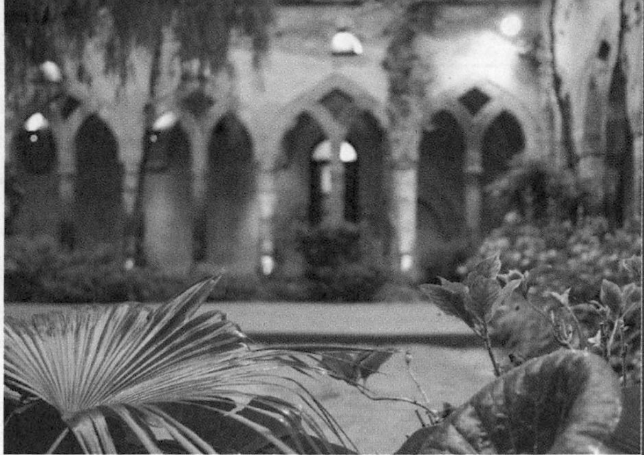

Highlights

Look for ★ to find recommended sights, activities, dining, and lodging.

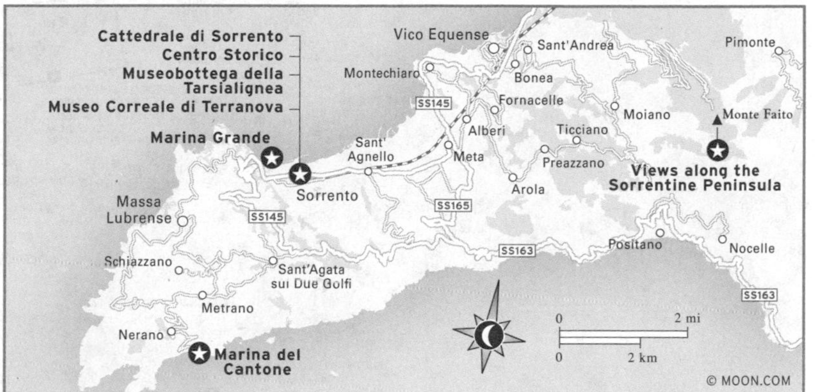

★ **Views along the Sorrentine Peninsula:** From hidden gardens in Sorrento to the height of Monte Faito, the Sorrentine Peninsula has many unforgettable vistas to discover (page 190).

★ **Cattedrale di Sorrento:** Visit Sorrento's Cathedral with its ornate baroque interior and exquisite examples of intarsia, the local tradition of inlaid woodwork (page 194).

★ **Centro Storico:** The historic center of Sorrento, with an urban footprint dating to ancient Greek and Roman settlements, is full of shops and dining spots (page 195).

★ **Museobottega della Tarsialignea:** This excellent museum is dedicated to Sorrento's long history of inlaid woodwork. You'll learn about every step of the process while exploring the extraordinarily rich collection (page 195).

★ **Museo Correale di Terranova:** This museum offers a collection of Neapolitan paintings, ceramics, and inlaid woodwork, housed in an 18th-century residence with a large garden, citrus grove, and panoramic terrace (page 198).

★ **Marina Grande:** Despite its name, the smaller of Sorrento's two ports is very charming with its traditional fishing boats lining the harbor and restaurants perfect for relaxed dining by the sea (page 199).

★ **Marina del Cantone:** Swim or sunbathe at this small and secluded beach near the tip of the Sorrentine Peninsula (page 219).

Sorrento and the Sorrentine Peninsula

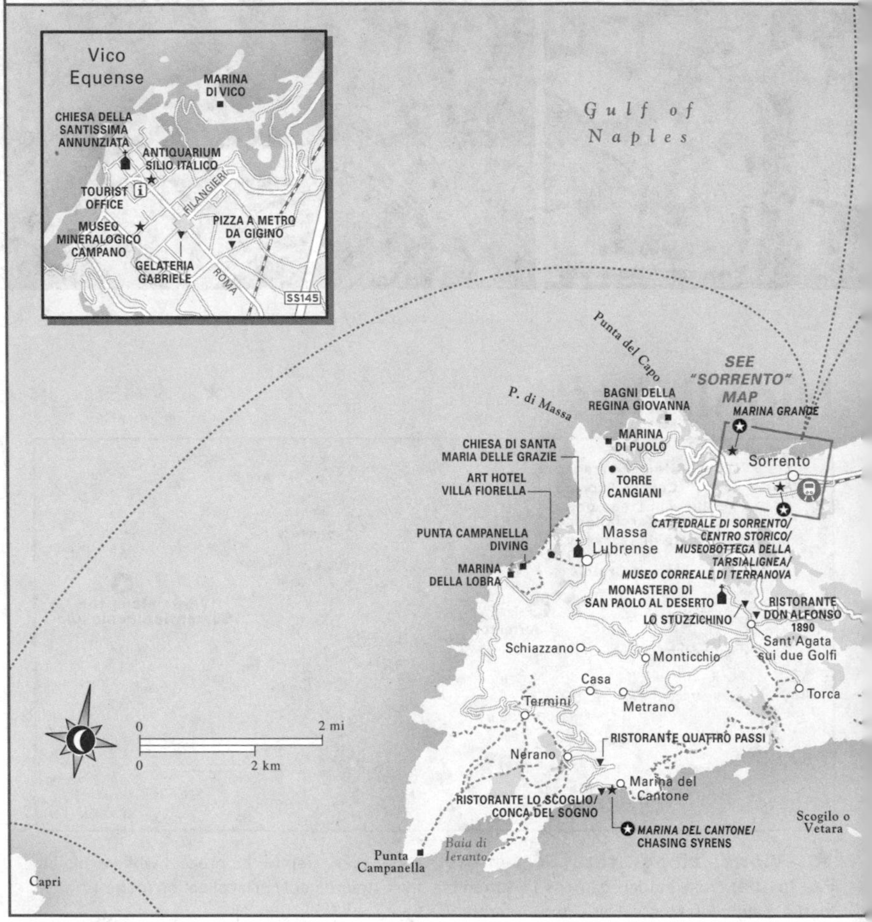

Though Sorrento is the main draw for most visitors to the area, there are many other towns to explore. Take time to visit Vico Equense, where you'll discover vineyards planted along the slopes of the mountains, famous pizza, and the majestic beauty of the Monti Lattari (Lattari Mountains) that make up the backbone of the Sorrentine Peninsula. Discover panoramic vistas and secluded seaside villages where time seems to have stood still in Massa Lubrense. Take some time to explore a bit off the beaten path, and you'll be rewarded with cable car rides to mountain peaks, kayak trips into hidden coves, hikes among olive and citrus groves that have been tended for centuries, and time to soak up the untouched natural beauty of the Sorrentine Peninsula.

Previous: The beautiful Marina del Cantone beach; lemons for sale at a market in Sorrento; Chiesa di San Francesco and Cloister

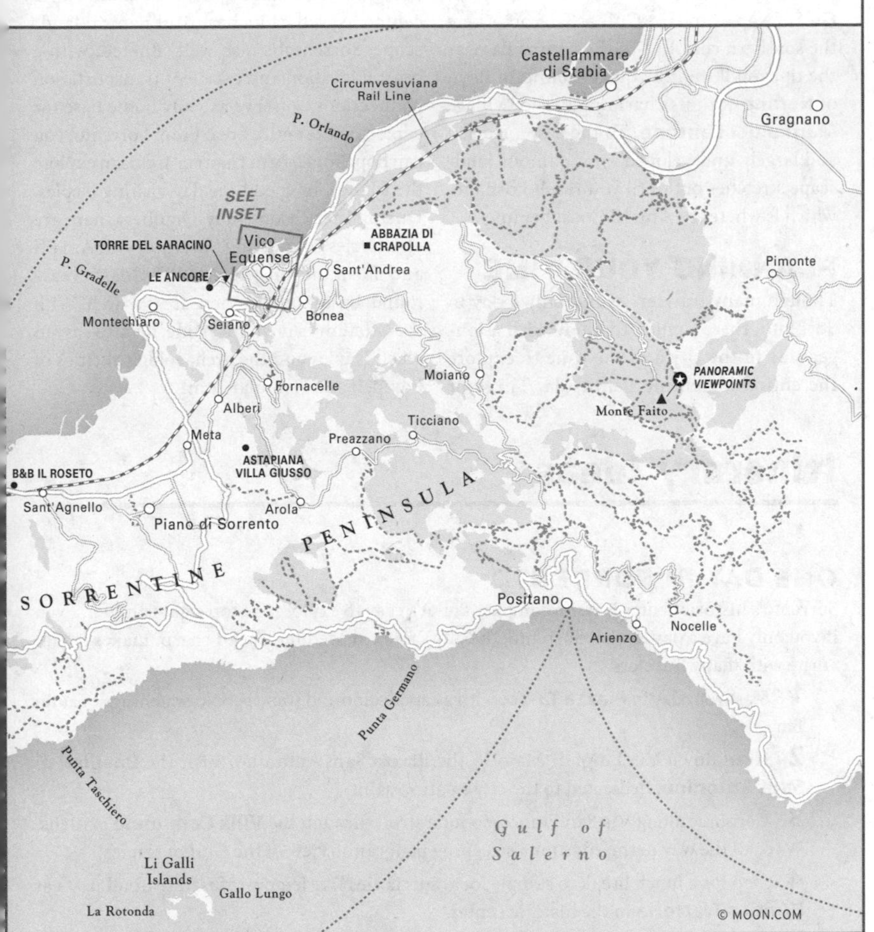

ORIENTATION

The Sorrentine Peninsula juts out from the coastline south of Naples, separating the Gulf of Naples from the Gulf of Salerno to the south. Named after **Sorrento,** its largest and most populous city, the peninsula begins west of Castellammare di Stabia and includes the towns of **Vico Equense** along the coastline, with the soaring peak of Monte Faito and the Monti Lattari (Lattari Mountains) high above. Between Vico Equense and Sorrento are the towns of **Meta, Piano di Sorrento,** and **Sant'Agnello,** all fairly well-developed areas connected seamlessly to the city of Sorrento. West of Sorrento there are small towns set among the hills and the tiny seaside villages (*frazioni*) of **Massa Lubrense** tucked into coves.

At the tip of the Sorrentine Peninsula lies **Punta Campanella,** surrounded by the Area Marina Protetta di Punta Campanella (Protected Marina Area of Punta Campanella). Sitting in a particularly scenic spot nestled in the mountains, the town of

Sant'Agata sui Due Golfi takes its name from its position, offering views of both the Gulf of Naples and the Gulf of Salerno. Along the southern coastline of the peninsula near the tip, you'll find the quiet mountain town of **Nerano** with its charming seaside village **Marina del Cantone.** To the east a rugged and largely undeveloped mountainous landscape stretches out until you reach Positano, which is where the Amalfi Coast begins.

PLANNING YOUR TIME

Though many travelers spend only a day in Sorrento, there's much to enjoy with a longer stay in the city and the time to explore the entire Sorrentine Peninsula. Three or four days will give you enough time to enjoy Sorrento's fine small museums and historic center, as well as its beautiful natural landscape. Sorrento is also well situated, with a central location and excellent transportation connections, to serve as your home base for exploring the entire area. From Sorrento, you can hop on a ferry to Capri or Ischia to explore the islands, or spend the day visiting Naples. During the season (May-October) there are also ferries connecting Sorrento with Amalfi and Positano on the Amalfi Coast; year-round, buses connect these areas as well. With the Circumvesuvian train line, it's also easy to reach Naples and the archaeological cities of Pompeii and Herculaneum.

Itinerary Ideas

ONE DAY IN SORRENTO

Sorrento's historic center is quite compact and it's easy to explore the top sights on foot. Even if you only have a day to visit Sorrento, the city's relaxed Mediterranean charm makes it a favorite with many travelers.

1 Start your day in **Piazza Tasso,** with a cappuccino and some people-watching at Fauno Bar.

2 Head down Via Luigi di Maio to the Piazza Sant'Antonino. Visit the **Basilica di Sant'Antonino,** dedicated to the city's patron saint.

3 Continue along Via San Francesco for a stroll through the **Villa Comunale** gardens. Walk all the way to the edge for a sweeping panoramic view of the Gulf of Naples.

4 Stop for a lunch break to sample local specialties like lemon-infused seafood pasta at **L'Antica Trattoria** in the historic center.

5 Follow Via Accademia to the **Museobottega della Tarsialignea** to learn more about Sorrento's long tradition of inlaid woodwork artistry.

6 Head to the **Cattedrale di Sorrento** for a look at the intricate intarsia work around the entrance.

7 Pick up some beautiful woodwork of your own as a souvenir at **Stinga Tarsia.**

8 After a long day of sightseeing and walking, unwind with a drink and a hearty meal at **Il Buco.**

One Day in Sorrento

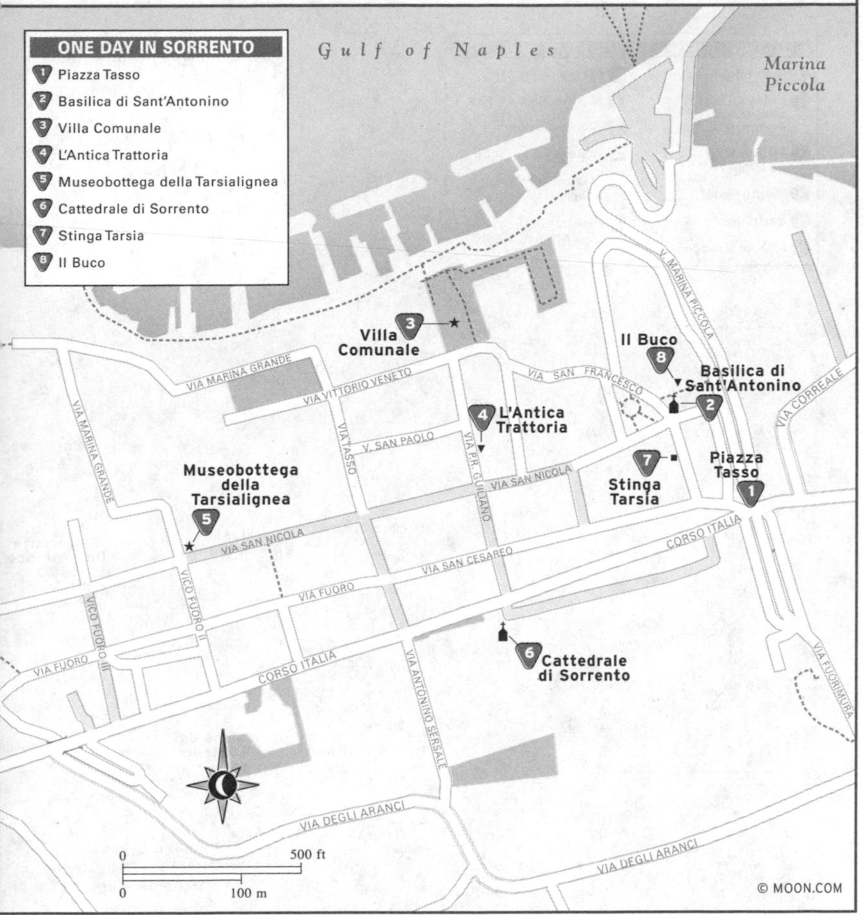

A DRIVING TOUR OF THE SORRENTINE PENINSULA

With a stunning coastline that stretches from rocky cliffs and seaside villages to farming towns and soaring mountains, the Sorrentine Peninsula is a dramatic landscape to explore by car. Though the coastal road from Sorrento toward Naples can be quite congested during the peak season, much of the rest of the peninsula allows for more relaxed driving, especially compared to the famously tortuous Amalfi Coast Road along the southern side of the peninsula. However, you should be prepared for twisty, narrow roads and, with a a sense of adventure, you'll experience everything the Sorrentine Peninsula has to offer on this two-day drive along the coastline, heading from the Naples area toward the Amalfi Coast. (You can make it a three-day itinerary by stopping to tour Sorrento in the middle.)

Driving Tour of the Sorrentine Peninsula

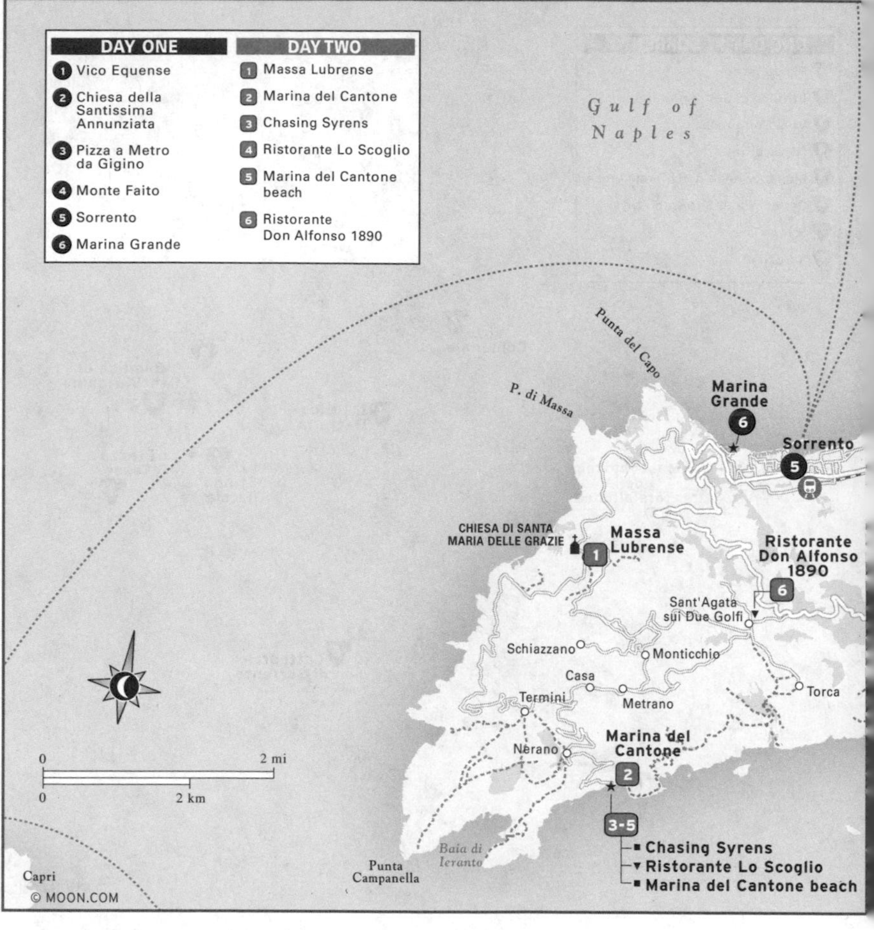

Day 1

1 Head south from Naples, and at Castellammare di Stabia follow signs for the SS145. Once you've passed through Castellammare di Stabia, the SS145 hugs the coastline on a scenic drive to reach **Vico Equense.**

2 Stop in the historic center of Vico Equense to see the panoramic views from near the **Chiesa della Santissima Annunziata.**

3 For lunch try the town's famous meter-long pizza at **Pizza a Metro da Gigino** in the center of Vico Equense.

4 After lunch, drive up to the top of **Monte Faito** for the finest views over the Sorrentine Peninsula and Gulf of Naples.

5 Continue on to **Sorrento** and check into your hotel in the evening.

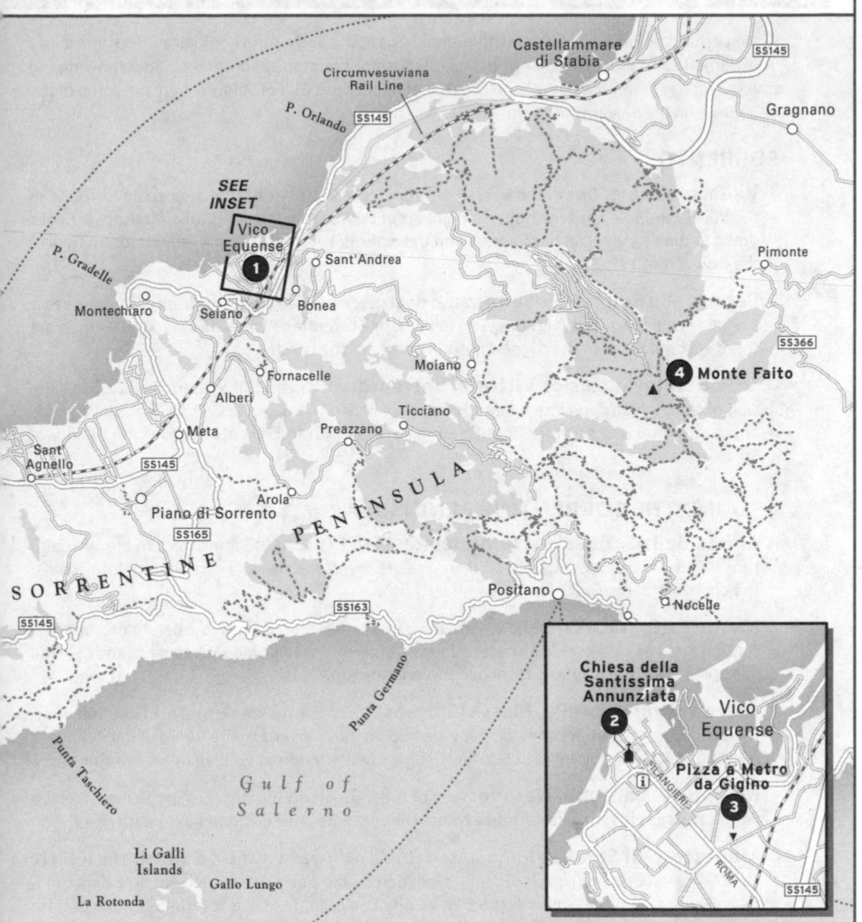

6 Stroll down to **Marina Grande** for a seafood dinner at Porta Marina, overlooking the tiny harbor of the quaint old fishing village.

Day 2

1 Set off on a leisurely morning drive west of Sorrento along the coast to **Massa Lubrense.** Stop to visit the Chiesa di Santa Maria delle Grazie and enjoy the views down the coastline from the small overlook nearby.

2 Continue along Via Nastro d'Oro through Termini and follow along the southern tip of the peninsula through Nerano down to the seaside village of **Marina del Cantone.**

3 Rent a clear kayak from **Chasing Syrens** and paddle along the coastline or join one of their excellent excursions to the most scenic spots in the area.

Best Views on the Sorrentine Peninsula

While perhaps not as well known as the Amalfi Coast, the Sorrentine Peninsula offers fine views from Sorrento and the surrounding coastline. From mountaintop panoramas to hidden swimming coves and sweeping views over both the Gulf of Naples and Gulf of Salerno, here are some of the best views on the Sorrentine Peninsula.

SORRENTO

- **Villa Comunale:** One of the best views from Sorrento is free of charge and can be found in the Villa Comunale gardens right in the heart of town. From the overlook that drops straight down to the sea, you can gaze across and get a perfect view of Mount Vesuvius looming over the Gulf of Naples.
- **Bagni della Regina Giovanna:** This tiny lagoon with an arched entrance from the sea is a divine swimming spot, and the views down the Sorrentine Peninsula along the walk to get there encompass all of the rugged natural beauty of the coastline.
- **Grand Hotel Excelsior Vittoria, Sorrento:** With beautiful gardens and views of the Gulf of Naples, you can almost hear the voice of Italian tenor Enrico Caruso, who stayed here and was famous for singing *"Torna a Surriento"* ("Return to Sorrento") about the beauty of Sorrento.

AROUND THE SORRENTINE PENINSULA

- **Chiesa della Santissima Annunziata, Vico Equense:** Dating back to the 14th century, this church is perched right on the edge of the cliff and makes a captivating sight against the backdrop of the Gulf of Naples.
- **Monte Faito, Vico Equense:** Ride the cable car up Monte Faito to a height of 3,583 feet (1,092 m) and enjoy sweeping views of the Sorrentine Peninsula, Mount Vesuvius, and the Gulf of Naples along the way, and from overlooks at the top.
- **Art Hotel Villa Fiorella, Massa Lubrense:** Located in a scenic spot in Massa Lubrense, this boutique hotel offers spectacular views down the coastline to the island of Capri. Enjoy a relaxing stay here, stop by the Cielo Sky Lounge, or enjoy dinner with an unforgettable view.
- **Marina del Cantone, Nerano:** One of the most charming beaches in the area, this is a wonderful spot to rent a kayak and explore the coastline and secluded bays nearby.
- **Monastero di San Paolo al Deserto, Sant'Agata sui Due Golfi:** The town of Sant'Agata sui Due Golfi is named for its location on the peninsula, where you'll find magnificent views of both the Gulf of Naples and Gulf of Salerno. Take in a 360-degree view of both gulfs and the island of Capri from atop this convent.

4 Refuel with freshly caught seafood at **Ristorante Lo Scoglio** overlooking the sea in Marina del Cantone.

5 Spend a leisurely afternoon relaxing on the beautiful **Marina del Cantone beach.**

6 Head back up into the mountains toward Sant'Agata Sui Due Golfi and savor an unforgettable dining experience at **Don Alfonso 1890.** Even better, book one of their lovely rooms and stay overnight so you can simply fall into bed after a delectable day.

Sorrento

Sorrento, the land long associated with the mythical sirens, has been captivating travelers for centuries. On a long, flat terrace of craggy coastline, where the cliffs drop straight to the sea, the Greeks and later Romans built a fortified town protected by its inaccessible setting and thick stone walls, parts of which are still visible around the city today. Although much of the historic center's urban plan dates back to the ancient Roman city of Surrentum, the Sorrento we see today is well cultivated as a modern holiday destination.

This friendly place, noted for its hospitality and Mediterranean charm, became a popular spot for travelers back in the 18th century during the Grand Tour. Weary after a long journey through Italy, travelers found in Sorrento a true respite where the sweet scent of citrus blossoms mingled with the salty breeze. Elegant hotels like the Grand Hotel Excelsior Vittoria are the bastions of Sorrento's old-world style and elegance with large gardens and captivating views.

Those same views are still savored by travelers from around the world today. The beautiful natural setting has long inspired artists, and a visit to the city's excellent museums reveals centuries of artwork inspired by Sorrento, including the city's important artistan craft of intarsia (inlaid woodwork). Tradition and hospitality are beautifully combined in Sorrento, where you'll enjoy discovering for yourself the city's eternal allure for travelers.

ORIENTATION

Sorrento is a small city where all of the top sights and the charming historic center are easily explored on foot. Indeed, walking is a pleasure in Sorrento compared to much of the Amalfi Coast area, because it is quite flat. However, the town sits above the sea level and its two harbors, **Marina Piccola** and **Marina Grande,** are both located below the city center. **Piazza Tasso** is the heart of Sorrento with the city's main thoroughfare, **Corso Italia,** running through it roughly east-west and parallel to the sea. Following Corso Italia east of Piazza Tasso (to the right as you're looking toward the sea) leads to the train station at Piazza Giovanni Battista de Curtis after about five minutes. From Piazza Tasso heading west (to the left if looking toward the sea), Corso Italia is pedestrian-only for a long stretch until Via degli Aranci. Lined with shops, restaurants, pubs, and cafés, Corso Italia is a lively spot for shopping and dining during the day and especially for the evening *passeggiata* (stroll).

The **historic center** of Sorrento is located north of Corso Italia up to the steep cliffside overlooking the Gulf of Naples. It's a relatively small and highly walkable area stretching from Piazza Tasso on the east to Via Sopra le Mura on the west. Following the ancient urban plan dating back to Roman times, the historic center is a grid of streets with Via San Cesareo and Via Accademia/Via San Nicola running parallel to Corso Italia and intersected perpendicularly by many small cross streets. Here you'll find excellent shopping as well as plenty of dining options while exploring the center. From Piazza Tasso, Via Luigi di Maio leads to Piazza Sant'Antonino, and from there you can follow Via San Francesco to the Villa Comunale garden.

Though the names are pretty misleading, Marina Piccola (Small Harbor) is the largest port in town, where ferries arrive and depart for destinations in the Gulf of Naples, including Naples, Capri, Ischia, and the Amalfi Coast. Marina Grande (Large Harbor) is a small port west of the historic center with a charming atmosphere that's perfect for a quiet swim or dining by the sea.

Sorrento

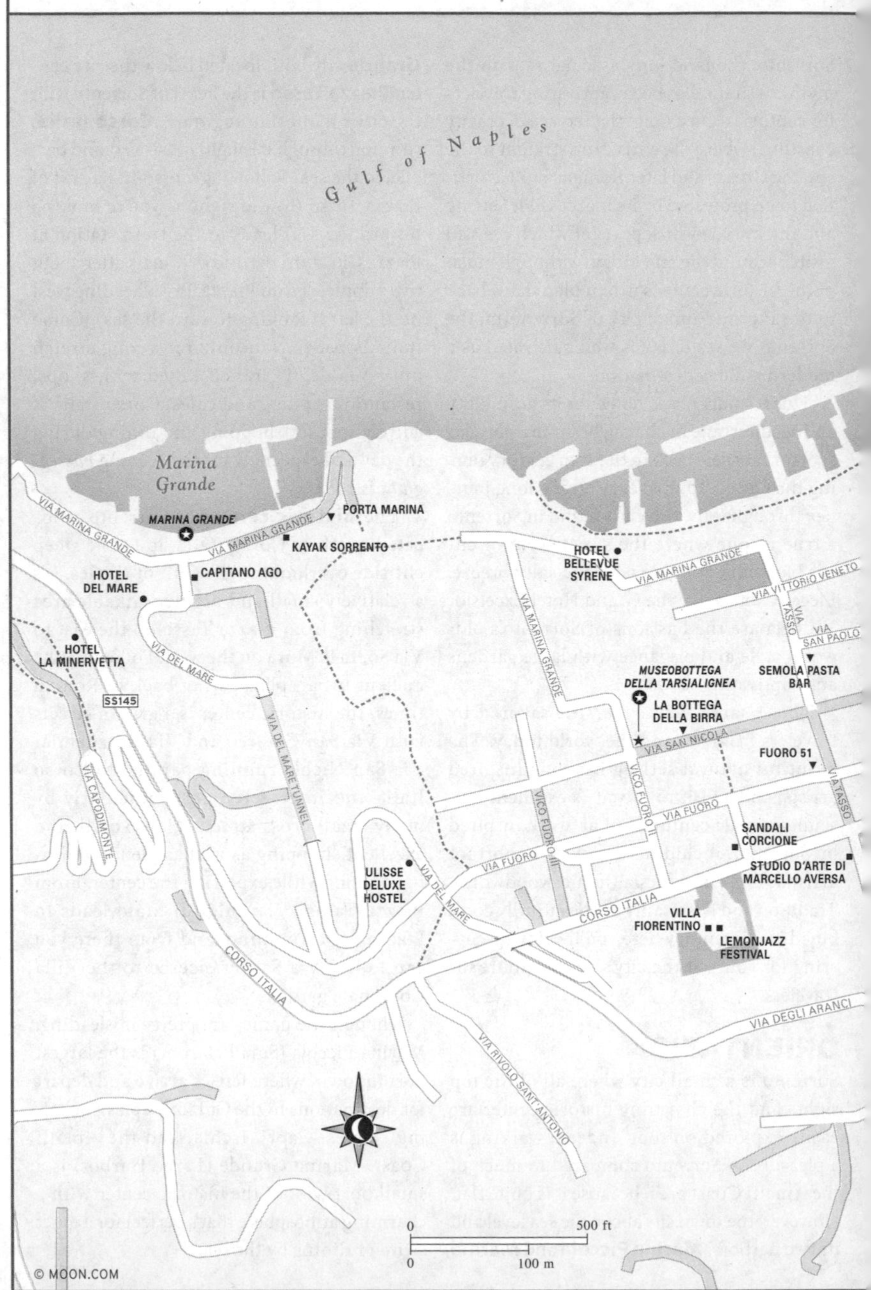
Gulf of Naples
Marina Grande
MARINA GRANDE
PORTA MARINA
KAYAK SORRENTO
CAPITANO AGO
HOTEL DEL MARE
HOTEL LA MINERVETTA
HOTEL BELLEVUE SYRENE
MUSEOBOTTEGA DELLA TARSIALIGNEA
LA BOTTEGA DELLA BIRRA
SEMOLA PASTA BAR
FUORO 51
SANDALI CORCIONE
STUDIO D'ARTE DI MARCELLO AVERSA
VILLA FIORENTINO
LEMONJAZZ FESTIVAL
ULISSE DELUXE HOSTEL
VIA MARINA GRANDE
VIA DEL MARE
VIA DEL MARE TUNNEL
SS145
VIA CAPODIMONTE
CORSO ITALIA
VIA FUORO
VICO FUORO III
VICO FUORO II
VIA SAN NICOLA
VIA TASSO
VIA VITTORIO VENETO
VIA SAN PAOLO
VIA DEGLI ARANCI
VIA RIVOLO SANT'ANTONIO
0
500 ft
0
100 m
© MOON.COM

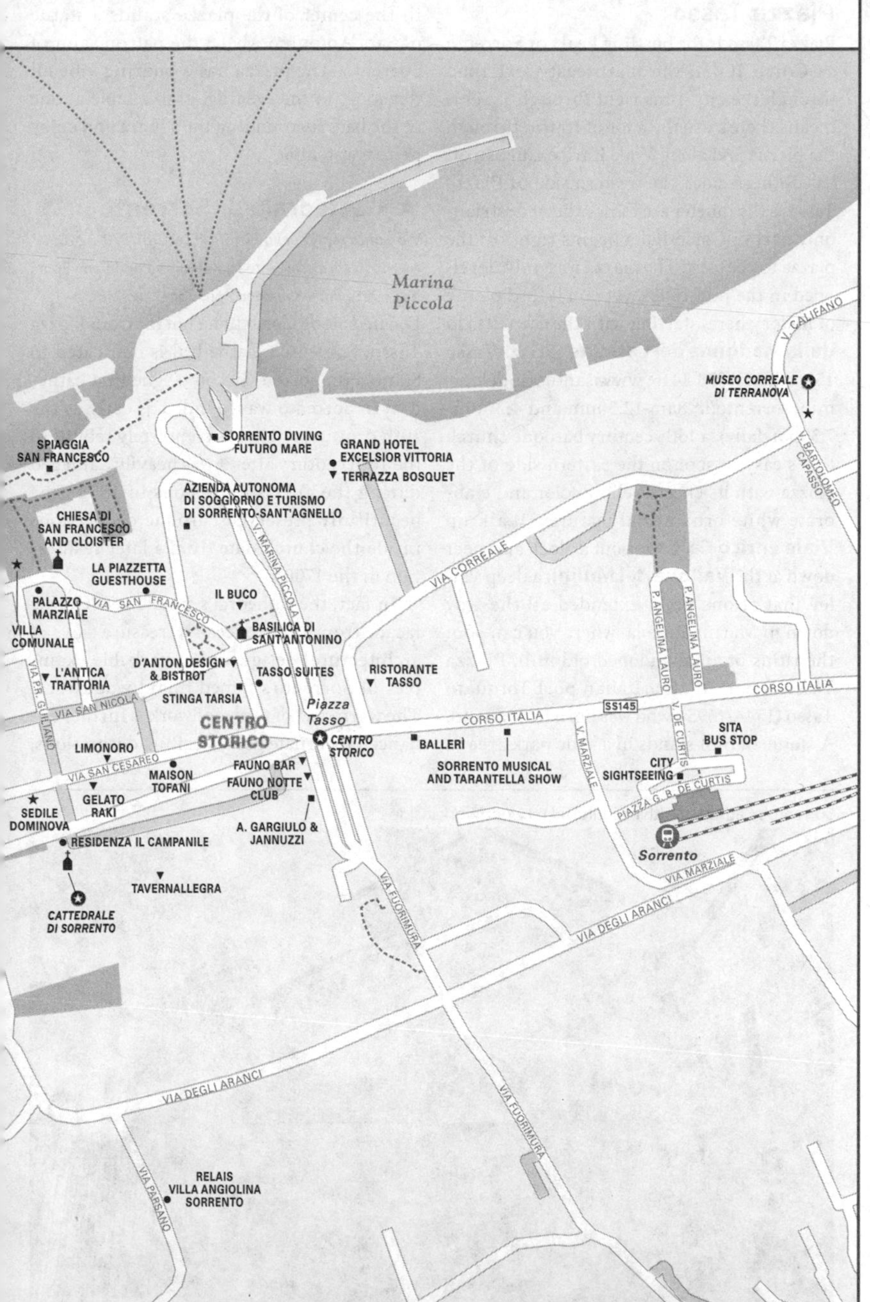
Marina Piccola
SPIAGGIA SAN FRANCESCO
SORRENTO DIVING FUTURO MARE
GRAND HOTEL EXCELSIOR VITTORIA
TERRAZZA BOSQUET
AZIENDA AUTONOMA DI SOGGIORNO E TURISMO DI SORRENTO-SANT'AGNELLO
CHIESA DI SAN FRANCESCO AND CLOISTER
LA PIAZZETTA GUESTHOUSE
PALAZZO MARZIALE
VILLA COMUNALE
IL BUCO
BASILICA DI SANT'ANTONINO
L'ANTICA TRATTORIA
D'ANTON DESIGN & BISTROT
TASSO SUITES
RISTORANTE TASSO
STINGA TARSIA
Piazza Tasso
CENTRO STORICO
CENTRO STORICO
LIMONORO
MAISON TOFANI
FAUNO BAR
FAUNO NOTTE CLUB
BALLERÌ
SORRENTO MUSICAL AND TARANTELLA SHOW
GELATO RAKI
SEDILE DOMINOVA
A. GARGIULO & JANNUZZI
RESIDENZA IL CAMPANILE
TAVERNALLEGRA
CATTEDRALE DI SORRENTO
MUSEO CORREALE DI TERRANOVA
SITA BUS STOP
CITY SIGHTSEEING
Sorrento
RELAIS VILLA ANGIOLINA SORRENTO
VIA SAN FRANCESCO
V. MARINA PICCOLA
VIA CORREALE
V. CALIFANO
V. BARTOLOMEO CAPASSO
P. ANGELINA LAURO
CORSO ITALIA
SS145
V. MARZIALE
V. DE CURTIS
PIAZZA G. B. DE CURTIS
VIA MARZIALE
VIA SAN NICOLA
VIA SAN CESAREO
VIA P.R. GIULIANO
VIA FUORIMURA
VIA DEGLI ARANCI
VIA PARSANO

SIGHTS

Piazza Tasso

Piazza Tasso is the bustling heart of Sorrento as Corso Italia, the main east-west road through the city, runs right through it. This means there's usually a lot of traffic through the piazza and along Viale Enrico Caruso off its southern side. The western side of Piazza Tasso is the quieter area since the pedestrian-only part of Corso Italia begins right off the piazza to the west. The piazza was only developed in the mid 1800s, yet you'll find plenty of history here, starting with the **Santuario della Madonna del Carmine** (Piazza Tasso 158; tel. 081/878-1416; www.santuariodelcarminesorrento.it; 8am-12:30pm and 4:30pm-7:30pm daily), a 16th-century baroque church that's easy to spot on the eastern side of the piazza with its cheery yellow color and elaborate white ornamental features. Walk up **Viale Enrico Caruso** about a block and peer down at the **Vallone dei Mulini,** a deep valley that at one point extended all the way down to Marina Piccola, where you can spot the ruins of an abandoned old mill. Piazza Tasso is named after Italian poet Torquato Tasso (1544-1595), who was born in Sorrento. A statue of him stands in a little park area at the southwestern corner of the piazza, while in the center of the piazza stands a statue of Sant'Antonino Abate, the patron saint of Sorrento. The piazza has a buzzing vibe all day long. In the evening, grab a table at one of the bars surrounding the square and enjoy people watching.

★ Cattedrale di Sorrento

Via Santa Maria della Pietà 44; tel. 081/878-2248; www.cattedralesorrento.it; 8am-noon and 5pm-8pm Apr.-Oct., 8am-noon and 4pm-7pm Nov.-Mar.

Located along Corso Italia not far from Piazza Tasso, Sorrento's Cathedral is dedicated to Saints Filippo and Giacomo. The first cathedral in Sorrento was founded as early as the 10th century, but it was completely rebuilt in the 16th century after it was heavily damaged during the Turkish invasions in 1558. The beautifully preserved baroque decorations inside the church date from a later restoration in the 1700s.

In fact, the cathedral's simple neo-Gothic façade from 1924 conceals a treasure trove of architectural design and remarkable examples of Sorrento's famed inlaid woodwork. The warm feel of the woodwork is further enhanced by ornate golden ceiling decorations,

Sorrento's Cathedral with beautiful inlaid woodwork inside

deep orange marble panels on the columns down the nave, and terra-cotta-colored detail on the arches that perfectly complement the wood accents throughout the church. Look for the detailed intarsia work inside around the wooden entrance, depicting stories from the church's history in Sorrento, as well as the stations of the cross along the two side aisles and the incredible choir stalls behind the altar that were created at the beginning of the 1900s. In the central nave near the altar stand two interesting elements: On the left is the *Cattedra*, the Bishop's throne, which dates from 1573 and incorporates columns and pieces from ancient Roman temples. Opposite is a marble pulpit, also from the 16th century, with a bas-relief sculpture depicting the baptism of Christ. Back outside, you'll spot the bell tower, constructed around the 11th century in the Romanesque style, located not far from the church. While standing on Corso Italia, there's a lovely view of the bell tower that stretches from the ancient columns at the base up through multiple levels to a clock with ceramic tiles near the top.

★ Centro Storico

Via San Cesareo north to Villa Comunale and Via Marina Grande between Via Luigi de Maio and Via Sopra le Mura

Sorrento sits on a foundation dating back to an ancient Greek settlement that later became an important urban center for the Romans, who called the town Surrentum. An ancient urban footprint is still evident today in the grid of streets that make up the *centro storico* (historic center). Until the late 1800s, when Corso Italia was built, the main street of the historic center was Via San Cesareo, which corresponds to the ancient Greek *decumano maggiore* (most important street). Walking down the cobblestoned streets today, look for grand stone entrance portals where the noble families and wealthy merchants of Sorrento built stately homes. Meander through the small historic center, which is now home to a host of shopping and dining spots, as well as churches and historic sights. Largely pedestrian-only, this area is ideal for popping in and out of shops or stopping for lunch or dinner at one of the many restaurants with outdoor seating to soak up the atmosphere of the historic setting.

Sedil Dominova

Via San Cesareo 68

While walking down the historic Via San Cesareo, you'll pass by a dark gray stone building with large arches. It's worth a stop to peer over the stone balustrade and through the wrought iron fence at the beautiful arcade of this building. Built in the 15th century with a distinct Renaissance style, the building was originally a gathering place for the town's noblemen. The ornate frescoes with their elaborate architectural details date from the 18th century. Since 1877, the Sedil Dominova has been the home of the Società Operaia di Mutuo Soccorso (Mutual Aid Society for Workers), a place for workers of Sorrento to gather and assist one another. Given the private nature of this building, it is best for travelers to admire the frescoes and architecture from outside.

TOP EXPERIENCE

★ Museobottega della Tarsialignea

Via San Nicola 28; tel. 081/877-1942; www.museomuta.it; 10am-6:30pm daily Apr.-Oct., closes at 5pm Nov.-Mar.; €8

Dedicated to Sorrento's history of intarsia (inlaid woodwork or marquetry), this museum brings to life the traditional craft and houses a large collection of pieces by master craftsmen. Set in a building from the 1700s that was once surrounded by intarsia workshops, the building itself is beautifully restored and maintains many original features, including the 18th-century hand-painted wallpaper, wooden vaults, and frescoed ceilings.

The museum's collection is displayed in three sections that span five floors. The first is dedicated to showing Sorrento in the 1800s with paintings, prints, and photographs of the town. The next section highlights intarsia in Italy from the 1400s to the 1800s, while the third area is the largest and highlights the intarsia work of Sorrento artisans in the especially rich period of the 19th century. Along with the remarkable pieces of art and furniture with inlaid designs, the museum does an excellent job demonstrating the process with displays of work tools and materials, discussions of technique, and explanations about design and innovation. Exhibits include pieces from Sorrentine artists and artists from around the world. The museum has detailed information available in English, and pullout trays below many displays contain samples of wood and additional didactics that add to an excellent visitor experience.

Basilica di Sant'Antonino

Piazza Sant'Antonino 2; tel. 081/878-1437; 9am-7pm Apr.-Oct., 9am-noon Nov.-Mar., closed during Mass at 9am Mon.-Fri. and 8am, 10am, and 11:30am Sun. and holidays.

Set on a small piazza, this church holds a special place in the hearts of Sorrento's faithful as it is dedicated to the town's patron saint, Sant'Antonino. Dating back to the 11th century, the original church design included many elements found in ancient Roman temples and villas along the coastline. In the 17th century, the church was updated in a baroque style with gilded accents while the highly decorative friezes and stucco work were added later in the 18th century. The crypt is set below the main altar area; it is accessed via two marble staircases and is supported by four marble columns from ancient temples. Even if the church is closed when you pass through Piazza Sant'Antonino, stop to peer through the gates to the right of the entrance and you'll spot a large whale bone. According to legend, this belongs to a whale that swallowed a baby who was then miraculously saved by Sant'Antonino.

Chiesa di San Francesco and Cloister

Via San Francesco 12; tel. 081/878-1269; 9am-noon and 5pm-8pm Apr.-Oct., 9am-noon and 4pm-7pm Nov.-Mar.

Founded in the eighth century as a Benedictine convent, this complex was later transformed into a Franciscan monastery, and today the church and adjacent cloister are still dedicated to San Francesco (St. Francis). While the church was redecorated many times over the centuries, the current baroque design dates from 1690-1727 and seems infused with just a touch of the Sorrento sunshine with its warm yellow tone. Be sure to visit the peaceful cloister dating back to the 13th century. It is a unique amalgam of architectural styles, with two sides of the cloister featuring pointed interlaced arches and the other two having rounded arches, along with octagonal columns and pieces from ancient sights incorporated into the design. With its romantic setting, the cloister is a popular spot for weddings, concerts, and other events.

Villa Comunale

Via San Francesco; 7:30am-8:30pm Jan.-Mar. and Nov.-Dec., 7:30am- 11pm Apr. and Oct., 7:30am-midnight May, 7:30am-1am June-Sept.

Just beyond the Chiesa di San Francesco, this small square is a popular spot, primarily for the panoramic view it offers across the Gulf of Naples. With shady spots to sit beneath the trees, you can relax a moment and savor the view across to Naples and Vesuvius. Walk right to the edge of the park and peer down the sheer cliff to Sorrento's beach area below. You can get down to the beach via a zigzag staircase or pay a small fee to take the available elevator (Sorrento Lift, Villa Comunale; tel. 081/807-2543; www.sorrentolift.it; hours same as Villa Comunale; €1 each way or €1.90 return).

1: Piazza Tasso **2:** Basilica di Sant'Antonino dedicated to Sorrento's patron saint **3:** beautiful frescoed entrance to the Sedil Dominova

1

2

3

The Intarsia of Sorrento

Sorrento's tradition of intarsia (wood inlay or marquetry) dates back centuries and is kept alive today by the town's artisans. The craft has been associated with Sorrento since at least the 16th century and flourished in the 19th century; an intarsia school was even founded here in the 1880s. The process is labor-intensive and involves creating mosaic-type designs by inlaying thin slivers of wood into a base. Different types of wood provide different colors, and the tiny pieces are hand cut to create elaborate designs, including landscapes and ornate floral and geometric patterns. Popular items that feature intarsia today include music boxes, decorative boxes and trays, frames, and tables. Classic motifs include lemons and images of Sorrento and its surrounding landscape, and these pieces make lovely keepsakes from your visit to Sorrento. You'll find fine examples of intarisa in many places around Sorrento, but here's a guide to the highlights around town.

WHERE TO SEE AND BUY INTARSIA

- **Museobottega della Tarsialignea:** This museum is entirely devoted to intarsia and the contribution Sorrento's artisans have made over the centuries. Here, you can learn about the process and explore an impressive collection spread across five levels.
- **Museo Correale di Terranova:** While not exclusively focused on intarsia like the Museobottega della Tarsialignea, this museum has many inlaid woodwork pieces, including especially fine examples of tables and other furniture.
- **Cattedrale di Sorrento:** Look at the panels surrounding the portal on the inside of Sorrento's Cathedral, as well as the early-20th-century choir stalls and the stations of the cross.
- **Stinga Tarsia:** Brothers Franco and Roberto Stinga are third-generation woodworkers whose music boxes, frames, and furniture feature inlaid designs that range from delicate floral motifs to modern geometric patterns.
- **A. Gargiulo & Jannuzzi:** Located just off Piazza Tasso, this family-run store has offered fine crafts, including intarsia, for six generations. Sometimes you can even see artisans at work creating inlaid woodwork designs.

★ Museo Correale di Terranova

Via Correale 50; tel. 081/878-1846; www.museocorreale.it; 9:30am-6:30pm Tues.-Sat., 9:30am-1:30pm Sun., closed Mon.; €8

Set in the historic residence of the noble Terranova family, this museum opened in 1924 thanks to the donation of the collection and residence by Alfredo and Pompeo Correale, counts of Terranova. The museum offers an incredible glimpse into Sorrento's history through a broad range of exhibits, from archaeological finds uncovered in the town to an extensive collection of paintings from the 15th-19th centuries and an extraordinary collection of porcelain and ceramics. The museum occupies four floors and starts on the ground level with a gallery dedicated to the Correale family, followed by a gallery dedicated to the inlaid woodwork tradition of Sorrento. The final gallery on the ground level displays fascinating archaeological finds, including Greek and Roman statues and two sculptures from Egypt that were uncovered near the Sedil Dominova, which arrived in Sorrento during Roman times.

On the upper floors, paintings are displayed among fine examples of furniture, ceramics from China and Japan, and historic clocks, many of which are ticking away and periodically fill the galleries with their chimes. The Room of Mirrors is resplendent with its late 18th-century gold-embellished mirrors and consoles. The extensive collection of 18th- and 19th-century landscape paintings from the Posillipo School brings to life this important Neapolitan school of painting. On the upper level, the ceramics exhibits include majolica from Italy and France as well as porcelain dishes, vases, and figurines from significant European producers, such as Meissen and Sèvres, as well as Capodimonte pieces made by the Real Fabbrica di Napoli.

After visiting the museum, take time to explore the extensive gardens, an unexpected oasis right in the heart of Sorrento. The large gardens include a citrus grove that was first planted in the 17th century and a pathway that leads to the Terrazza Belvedere, a large terrace with a fabulous view of the Gulf of Naples.

BEACHES

MARINA PICCOLA

Spiaggia San Francesco

Located just west of Marina Piccola and directly below the Villa Comunale, Sorrento's main beach area is not like most beaches in that there is a distinct lack of beach. While there is a small sandy area nearest the port and shoreline, most sunbathing space consists of specially built beach club establishments (*stabilimente balneare)* that are constructed on a series of jetties. The platforms have sun bed loungers, umbrellas, facilities like changing rooms and showers, and access to the sea via steps. Located on the western side of the beach area, **Bagni Salvatore** (tel. 081/878-1214; www.bagnisalvatore.com; Apr. 25-mid Oct.; sun beds €13 and umbrellas €6) offers friendly service, tranquil water for swimming, and a unique glimpse of Roman ruins as a backdrop. Marina Piccola can be reached via the port area directly, or from the Villa Comunale if you follow the zigzag staircase or take the elevator down.

TOP EXPERIENCE

★ MARINA GRANDE

Via Marina Grande

Only a short walk from the center of Sorrento, the Marina Grande harbor feels worlds away from the hustle and bustle of the city center. Here, you can stroll along the water's edge, enjoy a peaceful swim, or dine by the sea at a number of different restaurants. Fishing is still an important local activity as well, as the piles of nets, colorful fishing boats, and fishermen at work would attest. For swimmers, there's a small sandy beach area in the middle of the harbor, or opt for one of the sunbathing platforms built out into the harbor like **Ristorante Bagni Sant'Anna** (Via del Mare; tel. 081/807-4178; www.

sunbathing and swimming plaftorms near Marina Piccola

ristorantebagnisantanna.com; Mar.-Nov.; sun bed and umbrella €13), which offers sun beds, umbrellas, hot showers, and changing rooms. With sea access from the platform, you can swim with stunning views of the Gulf of Naples. You can reach the Marina Grande by car or bus along Via del Mare. However, if you opt to go on foot, a pleasant walk leads you down Via Marina Grande near Piazza della Vittoria. As you near the sea, you'll pass through a stone arch that dates to the third century BC and the Greek origins of the city.

BAGNI DELLA REGINA GIOVANNA

Traversa Punta Capo

West of Sorrento, you'll see verdant mountain slopes running down the rugged coastline all the way to Capo di Sorrento, the cape that juts out west of the city. Here tucked into a little cove in a particularly scenic spot is the Bagni della Regina Giovanna, a tiny lagoon with an arched entrance opening to the sea. The beautiful natural pool is named after Giovanna II, the Queen of Naples in the 15th century, who legend says loved to swim here. Entrance to the sea is rocky, but the water is splendid. Note that there are no beach facilities here. The beach can be reached by taking the Line A bus from Salerno to Capo di Sorrento and following signs to Ruderi della Villa Romana di Pollio (Ruins of the Roman Villa of Pollio) for about 15 minutes down to the lagoon. Not far beyond the Bagni della Regina Giovanna you'll find the ruins of an ancient Roman villa.

WATER SPORTS

SORRENTO DIVING FUTURO MARE

Via Marina Piccola 63; tel. 349/653-6323; www.sorrentodiving.it; Mar.-Nov.; small group snorkeling excursions from €35 per person, scuba diving excursions from €90 per person

For snorkeling and diving excursions, head to Marina Piccola, where the experienced team at Futuro Mare can help you plan a variety of underwater explorations. Options include daily small group excursions (10 people maximum) that leave from Sorrento and go out to the scenic **Baia di Mitigliano** or a tour that covers the Sorrento coast as well as the beautiful marine-protected area of the **Baia di Ieranto.** Private tours and excursions are also available and start at €600 for groups of 1-8 people.

CAPITANO AGO

Via del Mare 92; tel. 081/188-62797; www.capitanoago.com; Mar. 15-Oct. 31; group tour starting at €68 per person, private tour from €550 for up to 6 people

See the Sorrento coastline up close, or enjoy seeing Capri or the Amalfi Coast by boat from Sorrento, with Capitano Ago's small group and private boat excursions. Small group excursions have room for a maximum of 13 people and include options like a Capri tour, an Amalfi Coast tour with stops for free time ashore at Positano and Amalfi, and sunset or fishing excursions. Private tours are available to the Amalfi Coast, Capri, Ischia, and Procida.

KAYAK SORRENTO

Via Marina Grande 90; tel. 328/702-1422; www.kayaksorrento.com; Mar.-Nov.; group tours from €40 per person, private tours from €70 per person

Spend time immersed in the natural beauty of the Sorrento coastline with a guided kayak excursion starting from Marina Grande. Guided 2-3-hour excursions are available following the coastline west toward the Bagni della Regina Giovanna past caves, beautiful coves, and historic sites. Learn about the landscape with its legends and history while gliding along the sea. Group tours are available daily, usually departing at noon, or you can take a sunset tour starting at 4:30pm. Group tours can accommodate up to 30 people, or you can opt for a private guided excursion.

ENTERTAINMENT AND EVENTS

The Arts

SORRENTO MUSICAL AND TARANTELLA SHOW

Corso Italia 219; tel. 081/878-1470; www.cinemateatroarmida.it; Mar.-Dec.; €25 per person, including welcome drink

Be swept away to the Sorrento of bygone days with a vibrant and entertaining Sorrento Musical Show that brings to life moments of Sorrento's history and tradition. Classic songs like "O Sole Mio" ("My Sunshine") and "Torna a Surriento" ("Return to Sorrento") are highlights. For a more in-depth focus on traditional Neapolitan song and dance, opt for the Tarantella Show. Check in advance for show schedules. Most performances are staged April-June and September-October.

VILLA FIORENTINO

Corso Italia 53; tel. 081/878-2284; www.fondazionesorrento.com

Set back from Corso Italia, the Villa Fiorentino was constructed at the beginning of the 1930s for Antonino Fiorentino and his wife Lucia Cuomo, who had a successful business producing and selling fine embroidered fabrics. Surrounded by gardens with many varieties of roses and camelias, the villa is now home to the Fondazione Sorrento, a center for exhibits, concerts, and cultural events throughout the year.

Festivals

EASTER HOLY WEEK

Historic center; Holy Week and Easter Sunday

Easter is one of the most important religious holidays of the year in Italy, and in most towns, it is celebrated with processions, especially during Holy Week (the week leading up to Easter Sunday). Sorrento has a series of processions that are among the largest and most moving in the region. The procession that takes place on Good Friday starts with the *Processione Bianca* (White Procession) that begins before dawn: Hundreds of people dressed in hooded white costumes carry the statue of the Madonna Addolorata (Our Lady of Sorrows) and other elements that commemorate the Passion of Christ. The candlelit procession moves through the streets of the historic center and finishes around dawn. That same night the *Processione Nera* (Black Procession), a tradition dating back to the 1300s, takes place after dark and represents the final moments of the Passion of Christ, with statues of Christ—after being taken down from the cross—and the Madonna Addolorata carried through the streets of Sorrento by people dressed all in black. With the torches flickering, sorrowful music, and thousands of faithful, the processions are incredibly poignant to witness.

FESTIVAL OF SANT'ANTONINO

Basilica di Sant'Antonino and various locations; Feb. 14

Sorrento's patron saint is celebrated every year on February 14 with a festival commemorating the day of his death in AD 625. Special Masses and a procession are held, where a silver statue of the saint is borne through the historic center. The procession, which usually takes place at about 9am, not only is an important event for the town's faithful, but also is seen as a harbinger of spring weather and a good year to come. Festival lights, stalls selling food and toys, and crowds of people coming to honor the saint create a lively atmosphere in Piazza Sant'Antonino and the historic center of Sorrento.

FESTIVAL OF SANTI ANNA E GIOACCHINO

Marina Grande; July 26-30

Taking place right at the peak of summer, the Festival for Sant'Anna and San Gioacchino in Marina Grande is an eagerly anticipated summer festival for the town's faithful, and a fun event to experience for visitors. Centering around the Chiesa di Sant'Anna along the waterfront in Marina Grande, the religious and traditional events take place over several days, including a procession on July 26, musical concerts by the sea, games, and a fireworks display over the harbor on July 30.

LEMONJAZZ FESTIVAL

Corso Italia 53; tel. 333/220-2242; www.lemonjazz.it; usually first week of July but varies; €20

For jazz enthusiasts, the Lemonjazz festival offers a program of musical events hosted in the beautiful setting of Villa Fiorentino. Dates vary from year to year, but the festival schedule is announced online well in advance. Some concerts are free while others are ticketed, so check the website for details.

NIGHTLIFE

Clubs

FAUNO NOTTE CLUB

Piazza Torquato Tasso 13; tel. 081/878-1021; www.faunonotte.it; 11:30pm-3:45am daily Apr.-Oct.; €10-25

For the nightclub scene in Sorrento, head to Fauno Notte Club right in Piazza Tasso. There's always something going on here after dark, as the club hosts visiting DJs, live music, and themed dance nights. During the week entrance is free and you pay only for drinks, which cost about €10. On Saturdays and for special events the cover charge goes up to €15-25.

Bars

FUORO51

Via Fuoro 51; tel. 081/878-3691; www.fuoro51winebar.com; 11am-midnight daily Apr.-Oct., closed Mon. Nov.-Mar., closed Jan.; starting at €5

For a relaxed setting and a selection of more than 300 wines, head to this *enoteca* (wine bar) in the historic center. There's an excellent choice of wines with a special focus on Italian producers, especially those of Campania. If you're interested in wine, this is a great place to try many Campanian wines that are challenging to find outside of the area. A selection of cured meats, salami, and cheese trays are available to enjoy along with your wine.

LA BOTTEGA DELLA BIRRA

Via San Nicola 13; tel. 340/591-6221; labottegadellabirra-@libero.it; noon-2am daily Apr.-Oct., 6pm-1am Nov.-Mar.; €5-6.50

Beer enthusiasts will enjoy this welcoming spot in the historic center. Created by Nunzio Manna to cultivate his passion for discovering the best beers, La Bottega della Birra offers a vast selection of artisan beers from across Italy, as well as international beers from Belgium, England, America, and more. A variety of local dishes, cheese and meat plates, and bruschette designed to pair well with beer are also available.

SHOPPING

Woodwork and Artisan Crafts

A. GARGIULO & JANNUZZI

Viale Enrico Caruso 1; tel. 081/878-1041; www.gargiulo-jannuzzi.it; 9am-8pm daily

For six generations this store has been a source of artisan crafts right on Piazza Tasso in the heart of Sorrento. There's a fine and large selection of inlaid woodwork, including enchanting music boxes, gorgeous furniture, and even chess sets. You'll also find other local crafts, such as ceramics, hand-embroidered linens, and laces. Occupying three floors, this shop invites you to take time to browse, and you might just see artisans at work. Check the open hours in advance, as the store may close later in the summer and slightly earlier in the winter.

STUDIO D'ARTE DI MARCELLO AVERSA

Via Sersale 3; tel. 081/877-1535; www.marcelloaversa.it; 9:30am-1:30pm and 5:30pm-9:30pm Apr.-Oct., 9:30am-1:30pm and 4:30pm-8:30pm Nov.-Mar., closed Jan.

Tucked away on a small street behind the Cattedrale di Sorrento, you'll find the workshop and showroom of artist Marcello

1: Fauno Bar in Piazza Tasso is the best spot for people watching anytime of the day or night.
2: Villa Fiorentino serves as the cultural and arts center of Sorrento.

PALAZZO
JANNUZZI
FAUNO BAR
FAUNO BAR
1
2
TRANSFORMATIONS

Aversa. Born in nearby Sant'Agnello, Marcello began work in his family's business, which has made bricks for wood-fire ovens since the 16th century. However, at a young age he discovered his passion for sculpting with terra-cotta, especially in the Neapolitan *presepe* (nativity) tradition. From impossibly tiny figurines to entire large grottoes filled with sculptures, his creations suggest captivating landscapes full of movement, intricate detail, and hours upon hours of passionate work. Stop by and you'll often find Marcello at his work bench, focused on his next creation.

STINGA TARSIA

Via Luigi de Maio 16; tel. 081/878-1165; www.stingatarsia.com; 9:30am-10pm daily Apr.-Oct., 9:30am-1:30pm and 4pm-8:30pm Nov.-Mar.

As third-generation woodworkers, brothers Franco and Roberto Stinga are passionate about continuing the family tradition of creating finely handcrafted furniture, decorative items, and their particularly fine music boxes. In addition to the intricate carved patterns in a style dating back to the 19th century, a selection of contemporary inlaid pieces with creative geometric designs bring a new look to Sorrento's traditional artisan craft.

Shoes

BALLERÌ

Corso Italia 187; 081/224-8970; www.ballerisorrento.com; 10am-10pm daily June-Sept., 10am-1:30pm and 4:30pm-9pm daily Oct.-May

Just a few steps from Piazza Tasso you'll find this cheerful shop with a collection of shoes designed by Gaia de Lizza and inspired by Neapolitan musical traditions, fine craftsmanship, and Gaia's family's heritage. Ballerì is a family affair, created by Gaia and her siblings Sergio and Solange. The classic ballerina flats are finely made, and the designs inspired by Sorrento with hand-embroidered lemons will add a sunny bounce to your step, as you're reminded of beautiful moments in Sorrento.

SANDALI CORCIONE

Corso Italia 28; tel. 338/349-3632; www.sandalicorcione.com; 8:30am-1pm and 4pm-6pm daily year-round

This lovely boutique is located along the pedestrian-only part of Corso Italia near the Villa Fiorentino and has specialized in handmade sandals and shoes since 1925. Quality Italian leather is used, and everything from classic designs to Swarovski crystal-decorated sandals are on display. The sandals and shoes can all be custom-made for your feet.

Speciality Foods

LIMONORO

Via San Cesareo 49; tel. 081/878-5348; www.ninoandfriends.it; 9am-10pm daily

If you're strolling down the Via San Cesareo through the historic center, you'll notice that this bright shop seems to be permeated with lemons. Stop in to sample their locally made *limoncello* (lemon-infused liqueur) and a variety of other tempting products. The *limoncello* comes in many different bottle shapes and sizes, and there are lemon-filled candies and cookies, candied lemon and citrus peels dipped in chocolate, and so much more. For even more chocolate temptations, continue down the street to the **Nino & Friends Chocolate Store** at Via San Cesareo 67c (tel. 081/877-1693; 9am-10pm daily).

FOOD

Seafood

PORTA MARINA

Via Marina Grande 25; tel. 349/975-4761; anna.sorrento@alice.it; noon-3:30pm and 6pm-10:30pm daily Apr.-Oct.; €15-25

Set right along the water's edge in Marina Grande, this small and casual seafood restaurant is run by six fishermen brothers who bring in the daily catch. The menu is determined by what they've caught and is written up on a board. You might find fried calamari or grilled octopus, spaghetti with clams, or grilled fresh local fish. With a glass of crisp white Campania wine and the view of Marina Grande harbor, it just can't be beat.

Regional Cuisine

FAUNO BAR

Piazza Tasso 13/15; tel. 081/878-1135; www.faunobar.it; 7am-2am daily year-round; €8-18

With a large terrace on Piazza Tasso, this bar and restaurant is right in the middle of it all. Open from early in the morning until late at night, it's a great spot to stop for cappuccino in the morning to watch the busy piazza scene. Later in the day, choose a light meal from their excellent selection of salads or full-menu dishes. Gluten free, vegetarian, and vegan menus are also available. With its central location, this is also a popular spot for *aperitivo* or after-dinner drinks.

TAVERNALLEGRA

Via della Pietà 30; tel. 081/878-4221; www.tavernallegra.com; 11am-11pm daily, closed Jan. 10-Feb.28; €12-25

You'll find this cheery restaurant tucked away in a side street not far from the Cattedrale di Sorrento. Here you can enjoy traditional dishes like linguine with lobster, handmade *scialatielli* pasta with clams and zucchini, or other fresh seafood options. There's also a rich selection of seasonal vegetable choices, as well as an excellent chateaubriand steak. Live music and a festive atmosphere bring local traditions to life.

IL BUCO

2a Rampa Marina Piccola 5; tel. 081/878-2354; www.ilbucoristorante.it; 12:30pm-2:30pm and 7:30pm-10:30pm, closed Wed. and Jan.-Feb.; €22-30

Located just off Piazza Sant'Antonino, this restaurant is a gourmand's dream. Here Sorrentine traditions and quality ingredients are celebrated as the artistic treasures they truly are, and the menu reflects the seasons as well as inspiration from the sea and from locally produced vegetables, meats, and cheeses. Specialties include a delightful linguine pasta with lemon-scented scorpion fish on a sauce of roe and sundried tomatoes. A variety of tasting menus are available, and you can't go wrong with the Mi Fido di Te (I Trust You) tasting menu personally selected by chef Peppe Aversa. Just save room for the creamy lemon dessert with a *limoncello* froth. Reservations are suggested.

L'ANTICA TRATTORIA

Via Padre Reginaldo Giuliani 33; tel. 081/807-1082; www.lanticatrattoria.com; noon-11:30pm daily, closed Jan. 7-Mar. 20; €25-35

With beautiful seating areas, including a bougainvillea-covered pergola terrace, this is a welcoming spot with a familial atmosphere for excellent dining in Sorrento. The menu has many tempting choices, but a favorite is the Tagliolini Antica Trattoria, a pasta dish served with a lemon cream sauce, red prawns, and lumpfish on creamed spinach. The large wine cellar, stocked with more than 30,000 bottles, is the work of owner Aldo D'Oria and his son Luca, both of whom are passionate about wine and fine dining.

RISTORANTE TASSO

Via Correale 11d; tel. 081/878-5809; www.ristorantetasso.com; noon-midnight daily; €30-60

Enter through an archway not far from Piazza Tasso to find an elegant and bright dining room with an outdoor patio and garden area that's refreshing in the summer. The menu is varied with plenty of tempting options for seafood and non-seafood lovers. Plus there's excellent pizza, homemade pasta, and local mozzarella.

TERRAZZA BOSQUET

Piazza Tasso 34; tel. 081/877-7836; www.exvitt.it; 7:30pm-11pm daily Apr.-Jan. 7; €32-38

The Michelin-starred restaurant at the Grand Hotel Excelsior Vittoria is the perfect spot in Sorrento for a gourmet meal with impeccable service and spectacular views of the Gulf of Naples. A variety of excellent tasting menus are available. While the menu changes seasonally, the Terra Mater pasta made with Sorrento lemons, anchovies, snap peas, and a touch of thyme combines the classic flavors of Sorrento in a refreshing dish. Smart casual attire and reservations highly recommended.

SEMOLA PASTA BAR

Via Torquato Tasso 53/55; tel. 081/1900-4857; https://semola-pasta-bar.business.site; noon-midnight daily Apr.-Jan.; €8-16

While pasta is a fixture on nearly every menu in Italy, Semola Pasta Bar focuses on handmade pasta served in a variety of traditional and creative dishes. Try the classic ravioli or the *gnocchi alla sorrentina* (potato and flour dumplings served with a tomato sauce enriched with mozzarella and basil). Or look for seasonal options like the pasta with pumpkin and shrimp. The restaurant is located on a quiet street in the historic center with nice outdoor seating. Takeaway service is also available.

D'ANTON DESIGN & BISTROT

Piazza Sant'Antonino; tel. 333/154-3706; info@dantonsorrento.com; 10am-1am daily May-Sept., 10am-11pm daily Mar.-Apr. and Oct.-Jan.6, closed Jan.7-Feb.; €6-20

A family interior design boutique transformed into a cocktail bar and bistrot, D'Anton reflects one family's passion for good fresh fare and design. Stop in for coffee and you'll likely leave with the coffee cup or something else tempting. Enjoy brunch in the morning or a light lunch or dinner, or simply stop by for drinks. The *limoncello* cocktail is a signature, made with a touch of Sorrento's famous lemon liqueur.

Gelato

GELATO RAKI

Via San Cesareo 48; tel. 081/1896-3351; www.rakisorrento.com; 11am-12:30am daily; €2.50-6

There's certainly no shortage of gelato options in the historic center, but Raki stands out because of the owners' focus on top-quality fresh and all-natural ingredients. The artisan gelato is made on-site, and the mouthwatering selection often includes a refreshing *limone* gelato made with Sorrento's lemons. Cash only.

ACCOMMODATIONS

Under €100

B&B IL ROSETO

Corso Italia 304; tel. 081/878-1038; www.ilrosetosorrento.com; Feb.-Dec.; €60 d

Surrounded by lemon trees, this friendly B&B has five comfortable rooms with sea or garden views. All rooms include either a balcony or terrace, and there's a nicely landscaped pool area for relaxing, The train station is a 10-minute walk away, and Piazza Tasso is about 15 minutes' walk. Free parking is available on-site.

€100-200

RESIDENZA IL CAMPANILE

Corso Italia 103; tel. 081/807-1886; www.ilcampanilesorrento.it; open Mar.-Dec.; €100 d

It doesn't get more central or characteristic than this residence with six double rooms overlooking Corso Italia and the Cattedrale di Sorrento. The building dates to the 1800s, and the rooms are set on two levels. Breakfast is served on the rooftop terrace from April to September, and served in your room during colder months. Note that there is no elevator due to the historic nature of the building.

ULISSE DELUXE HOSTEL

Via del Mare 22; tel. 081/877-4753; www.ulissedeluxe.com; closed Jan. 7-14; dorm rooms from €35, €120 d

Located not far from Corso Italia on the road down to Marina Grande, this hostel offers a variety of cheery accommodations, including double, triple, and quadruple rooms, as well as men's and women's dormitory-style rooms. Besides the dorm rooms, all rooms have en suite bathrooms. Free Wi-Fi is available throughout the hostel.

RELAIS VILLA ANGIOLINA SORRENTO

Via Parsano 12; tel. 081/878-4523; www.villangiolina.com; open Apr.-Dec.; €159 d

Located in a nice residential area south of Piazza Tasso, this B&B is set in a historic farmhouse surrounded by a large citrus grove. Though the surrounding landscape has changed, the owners' respect for tradition is evident in the 11 large double rooms that are decorated in natural tones, with hand-painted ceramics adding a touch of color to the bathrooms. Note that some rooms have steps to access the bathroom, so inquire when booking if this is a concern. Apartments and suites are also available in the center of Sorrento.

LA PIAZZETTA GUEST HOUSE

Via San Francesco 1; tel. 081/878-1736; www.lapiazzettasorrento.com; open Dec.-Oct.; €160 d

With an excellent location overlooking the pretty green park area of Piazza Sant'Antonino, this beautifully remodeled guest house offers nine rooms and three apartments with mezzanines. The style is clean, modern, and above all bright. This is an excellent choice, especially if you're looking for the convenience of an apartment setting.

★ MAISON TOFANI

Via San Cesareo 34; tel. 081/878-4020; www.maisontofani.com; open Feb. 13-Jan. 7; €189 d

Right in the historic center, not far from Piazza Tasso, this gorgeous hotel is set in an 18th-century building that is full of historic charm. Each of the 10 rooms is different, with some featuring unique touches like exposed wood beams. Traditional terra-cotta floors with majolica tiles add a warm touch that's perfectly complemented by contemporary furnishings and colorful accents. Some rooms have balconies overlooking the town center. Breakfast is served in a beautiful room full of historic charm, with ornate doors and a frescoed ceiling.

TASSO SUITES

Via Luigi de Maio 13; tel. 081/011-2802; www.tassosuites.it; open year round; €190 d

Just a few steps from Piazza Tasso in the historic center, this hotel offers modern rooms as well as apartments decorated in a contemporary style, with crisp white furniture and contrasting pops of color. The on-site spa offers a host of services for relaxation and well-being, including steam baths, Finnish sauna, Jacuzzi hydro-massage, massages, and beauty services.

€200-300

HOTEL DEL MARE

Via del Mare 30; tel. 081/878-3310; www.hoteldelmare.com; open Apr.-Oct.; €230 d

Located just around the corner from the beach, this small hotel is a comfortable option in the charming setting of Marina Grande. The rooms are not large, but they're cozy and clean. Choose from standard rooms with no view to balcony rooms overlooking Marina Grande and sea-view rooms. Breakfast can be enjoyed in your room or in the breakfast room, which is literally carved into the rocks. Atop the hotel you can lounge on the roof terrace with a view of the sea.

PALAZZO MARZIALE

Piazza Francesco Saverio Gargiulo 2; tel. 081/807-4406; www.palazzomarziale.com; open Dec. 27-Oct.; €230 d

Overlooking the Villa Comunale gardens, this boutique hotel is set in the 15th-century residence of the Savarese family. The secluded atmosphere here blends historic charm with modern conveniences, contemporary decorative touches, and first-class guest service for an exclusive stay right in the heart of Sorrento. The rooms range from classic doubles to larger superior and deluxe rooms, as well as suites. The Junior Suite is particularly lovely with its terrace overlooking the Chiesa di San Francesco.

Over €300

★ HOTEL LA MINERVETTA

Via Capo 25; tel. 081/877-4455; www.laminervetta.com; closed for 20 days in Jan.; €350 d

While located a bit outside of Sorrento's historic center, the position of this extraordinary boutique hotel affords enviable views of Marina Grande and all of Sorrento. Stepping inside is like seeing the pages of a design magazine come to life. Every angle and detail is beautifully curated with crisp modern design in a palette of predominately blue, red, and white. There are large windows with panoramic views, and contemporary ceramics and art on display. The 12 rooms all have sea views, and each one is wonderfully unique. Follow the steps down to find a pool clinging to the cliffside and continue down the zigzag steps to reach Marina Grande.

HOTEL BELLEVUE SYRENE

Piazza della Vittoria 5; tel. 081/878-1024; www.bellevue.it; open mid-Mar.-Jan. 3; €560 d

Situated along the cliffside of Sorrento where there was a Roman villa in the 2nd century BC, this hotel is set in an 18th-century villa that was transformed into a hotel in 1820. The historic character has been finely preserved while at the same time the property has been updated to offer a thoroughly luxurious stay. Sea-view rooms come in a variety of sizes and are worth the splurge. If you're looking for a truly special stay, check out their extraordinary suites. The hotel has excellent dining options as well as its own private bathing platform, which is reached by elevator or via a long staircase, carved into the rocks, that passes by Roman ruins.

GRAND HOTEL EXCELSIOR VITTORIA

Piazza Tasso 34; tel. 081/877-7111; www.exvitt.it; open Apr.-Jan. 7; €606 d

A bastion of Sorrento hospitality since its founding in 1834, the Grand Hotel Excelsior Vittoria commands prime real estate overlooking the sea above Marina Piccola, with a beautifully landscaped entrance from Piazza Tasso. Many notable guests have enjoyed this hotel, and the Neapolitan tenor Enrico Caruso's stay has been memorialized with the spectacular Caruso Suite, which includes the singer's piano. The hotel has retained old-world charm while offering all the modern comforts expected at a five-star hotel. The pool is set in landscaped gardens, and with the Michelin-starred Terrazza Bosquet restaurant for dining and a spa on-site, this could be your address for a luxurious escape right in the center of Sorrento.

INFORMATION AND SERVICES

Tourist Information

AZIENDA AUTONOMA DI SOGGIORNO E TURISMO DI SORRENTO-SANT'AGNELLO

Via Luigi de Maio 35; tel. 081/807-4033; www.sorrentotourism.com; 9am-7pm Mon.-Sat. and 9am-1pm Sun. Apr.-Oct., 9am-4pm Mon.-Fri. Nov.-Mar.

In addition to its office on Via Luigi de Maio, the Sorrento tourist office has a main information point located conveniently in the center of town at Piazza Tasso (Piazza Tasso; 10am-noon and 4pm-8pm daily Apr.-Dec.). Piazza Tasso is large and busy, so look for the yellow baroque-style church on the eastern edge and the info point is located just before the entrance to the church.

Medical Services

For emergency services in Italy, dial 118 for ambulance and urgent care. The ***ospedale* (hospital)** in Sorrento is located at the western end of Corso Italia and has a *pronto soccorso* (emergency room) open 24/7 (Corso Italia 1; tel. 081/533-1111). You'll find several **pharmacies** along Corso Italia and right in Piazza Tasso for non-emergency assistance.

GETTING THERE

By Train

From Naples, you can take the **Circumvesuviana** train line operated by **EAV** (www.eavsrl.it) from **Piazza Garibaldi** at the **Napoli Centrale** train station to **Sorrento's train station.** There are departures about every 30 minutes, and the trip takes about 60 minutes from Naples to Sorrento. Tickets cost €3.90 and can be purchased at the station. Keep in mind that the Circumvesuviana trains are primarily commuter- or metro-style trains, so there are many stops in between Naples and Sorrento, including Vico Equense and Castellammare di Stabia on the Sorrentine Peninsula, as well as Pompeii and Herculaneum. The train can get quite busy, so don't be surprised if you have to stand for part of the journey during peak hours in the morning and evening.

By Bus

From the **Aeroporto Internazionale di Napoli** (also called Capodichino Airport), **Curreri Service** (tel. 081/801-5420; www.curreriviaggi.it) offers bus service from the airport to Sorrento with various stops along the way, including Pompei and Vico Equense, before arriving at the **Sorrento train station.** The bus departs from Capodichino every 1-1.5 hours from 9am to 7:30pm, and tickets cost €10. At the airport, tickets are available from an automatic vending machine just outside the Arrivals area and buses depart from the bus terminal outside the arrivals area near the P1 parking area. Advance booking and payment can be made online.

To reach Sorrento from the Amalfi Coast, **SITA SUD** (tel. 089/386-6701; www.sitasudtrasporti.it, from €1.30) has a bus line connecting Amalfi to Sorrento with stops along the coastline, including Positano. Buses depart roughly every hour 6:20am-9:20pm from Amalfi (fewer buses Sun. and holidays). Travel time from Amalfi to Sorrento is about an hour and 40 minutes; it's about 1 hour from Positano to Sorrento. Buses arrive in Sorrento at the Piazza Giovanni Battista de Curtis in front of the train station. Tickets can be purchased at local *tabacchi* (tabacco) stores or sometimes right at the bus departure point in Piazza Giovanni Battista de Curtis from a small booth.

The **City Sightseeing** (081/1825-7088; www.city-sightseeing.it/it/sorrento) Sorrento Coast to Coast line will take you from Positano and Amalfi to **Sorrento's train station.** Buses run roughly every hour 8:50am-5:45pm, and the journey from Amalfi to Sorrento takes 1 hour 25 minutes. From Positano, the ride takes 40 minutes. Unlike other City Sightseeing routes, this one doesn't follow the hop-on hop-off format. The first ticket costs €10, but if you get off at a midway point and get back on the same route you will need to pay again. Each subsequent ride costs €6 if you present your first full-price ticket. Tickets for all City Sightseeing buses are purchased onboard.

From Rome, **Autolinnee Marozzi** (tel. 080/579-0111; www.marozzivt.it; daily; €19) offers a 4-hour bus trip from outside the Roma Tiburtina train station to Sorrento, with a stop at Corso Italia 259b (near Piazza Giovanni Battista de Curtis, near the train station). Departures are once or twice daily, depending on the day of the week and season. Tickets can be booked in advance online, but the website is only available in Italian. You can purchase tickets onboard for a surcharge of €5 per ticket.

By Ferry

Ferries arrive at Sorrento's **Marina Piccola** from destinations around the Gulf of Naples. There are many companies to choose from that offer transportation on vessels from high-speed jet boats to *aliscafo* (hydrofoil) and slower *traghetti* (ferries) that transport passengers and vehicles.

Alilauro (tel. 081/878-1430; www.alilaurogruson.it; starting at €13.11 per person) offers routes connecting Sorrento to Naples, Capri, Ischia, Procida, and the Amalfi Coast seasonally from Apr.-Oct. From Capri, **Gescab** (tel. 081/428-5259; www.gescab.it; from €18) offers many daily trips for the quick 30-minute journey. **Caremar** (tel. 081/189-66690; www.caremar.it; from €16.90 for passengers and €28.50 for vehicles) also offers passenger and car ferries from Capri. **NLG** (tel. 081/807-1812; www.navlib.it; starting at €13.10 per person) operates jet routes from Capri and Naples to Sorrento, with the trip taking about 30 minutes from Capri and 40 minutes from Naples. **SNAV** (tel. 081/428-5555; www.snav.it; from €20.30) operates a Capri-to-Sorrento line as well, with a journey of about 30 minutes. From Easter through October, **Alicost** (tel. 089/871-483; www.alicost.it; €15.00-20.80 per person) offers ferry service from Positano and Amalfi to Sorrento. The ferry ride from Positano to Sorrento takes about 50 minutes, while from Amalfi it is about 1 hour 15 minutes. Gescab, Caremar, NLG, and SNAV all offer year-round service to Sorrento, but with a more limited schedule off season from Nov.-Mar.

By Car and Scooter

From Naples, follow the **A3** autostrada out of Naples south to Castellammare di Stabia where you'll continue on the **Strada Statale della Penisola Sorrentina (SS145)** along the coastline all the way to the center of Sorrento. Drive time from Naples to Sorrento is about 1 hour and 30 minutes, but expect a slightly longer drive when there's traffic during the summer months.

From the Amalfi Coast, follow **SS163** (the Amalfi Coast road) until it meets **SS145,** at which point you can continue straight along SS145 into Sorrento from the east. Or take a left on SS145 and follow a route about 5 miles (8 km) longer via Sant'Agata sui Due Golfi to arrive in Sorrento from the west. Either way, the drive from Amalfi to Sorrento takes about 1 hour and 30 minutes with no traffic, and about 45 minutes from Positano to Sorrento.

Paid parking lots are available in many places around town, including at Marina Piccola harbor, near Piazza Tasso on Via Fuorimura, on Via Correale not far from the Museo Correale di Terranova, and on Via del Mare near Corso Italia. Expect parking to cost about €2 an hour or more.

GETTING AROUND

Sorrento's historic center and main sights are quite easy to explore on foot. Local buses run through town and provide a good way to ride between the center of town and Marina Piccola or Marina Grande because they are located beneath the rest of Sorrento.

By Bus

To get around, **EAV** (www.eavsrl.it; departures every 20-30 minutes; starting at €1.30) offers four lines that cover the town with buses passing about every 20 minutes. Bus schedules are not available online from EAV, so the tourist office and info points are the best places to find out the latest schedules and information. Linea A (Line A) runs from Sorrento to Capo di Sorrento 5:20am-1am (and 5:50am-12:20am the opposite direction). Linea B and Linea C run from Marina Piccola to Piazza Tasso and the train station 7am-11:30pm (7:30am-10:45pm in the opposite direction). Linea D and Linea E circulate around town with various stops including Marina Grande, Piazza Tasso, and the train station (7:10am-11:35pm). Tickets must be purchased before boarding and can be bought at *tabacchi* (tobacco) shops and news agents.

Sorrentine Peninsula

While Sorrento draws the most visitors along the Sorrentine Peninsula, there are many beautiful spots and interesting towns to discover. The area covered here is the northern coastline of the Sorrentine Peninsula located on the Gulf of Naples. It is distinct from the Amalfi Coast, which is located along the southern part of the peninsula on the Gulf of Salerno. Given its proximity to Naples, this coastline is definitely on the radar of Italian travelers, especially during the summer months. However, many of the sights included here are lesser known by international travelers, which gives them a charm well worth discovering. Climb to the highest point on the Sorrentine Peninsula, dine with stellar views of Capri, swim in little coves, and experience all the Sorrentine Peninsula offers.

VICO EQUENSE

Leaving the dense urban area south of Naples and following the cliff-hugging road along the Sorrentine Peninsula, you'll come to Vico Equense, one of the first cities you'll meet along the coastline. Situated on a promontory with steep cliffs dropping down to the

Hop-On, Hop-Off

City Sightseeing (tel. 081/1825-7088; www.city-sightseeing.it/it/sorrento; Apr.-Oct.; €10-12) offers a relaxed way to explore the Sorrento coastline if you don't have a car. The **Sorrento alla Scoperta dei due Golfi** route starts right in front of the Sorrento train station and travels through Sant'Agnello, Massa Lubrense, Termini, and Sant'Agata sui Due Golfi with the chance to hop on and off as many times as you would like. There are four departures daily (9:40am, 11:40am, 1:40pm, 3:40pm). The entire circuit takes 1 hour 40 minutes, and offers views of both the Gulf of Naples and Salerno.

WHAT TO DO IN MASSA LUBRENSE

Hop off in Massa Lubrense where the bus stops in Largo Vescovado. There you'll find the **Chiesa di Santa Maria delle Grazie,** which has a lovely ceramic-tiled floor based on an 18th-century design, with elements of the original still present. Nearby is a nice overlook where you'll find the **Ristorante Il Cantuccio,** which is a great spot to enjoy the views over lunch.

WHAT TO DO IN SANT'AGATA SUI DUE GOLFI

This small town has a cute little center to explore if you hop off here. Stroll down **Corso Sant'Agata,** lined with shops, to a small piazza and the town's church dedicated to Santa Maria delle Grazie. Stop for coffee or walk to the nearby **Monastero di San Paolo al Deserto** for a spectacular view over both the Gulf of Naples and Gulf of Salerno.

sea below and deep green forested mountain slopes above, the city has ancient origins going back to Italic tribes, Etruscans, Greeks, and Romans. Sitting at the edge of the cliff, the **Castello Giusso** (Giusso Castle), built in the 13th century, overlooks the picturesque Marina di Vico harbor. The heart of the city is **Piazza Umberto I** with the Fontana dei Delfini (Fountain of the Dolphins) from 1844. Around the city you'll find beautiful churches, including the **Chiesa della Santissima Annunziata** from the 14th century, an interesting science museum, and the city's famous meter-long pizza. For nature enthusiasts, hiking atop one of the highest points on the Sorrento coast at **Monte Faito** is a reason to add Vico Equense to your itinerary.

Sights

CHIESA DELLA SANTISSIMA ANNUNZIATA

Via Vescovado; tel. 338/997-0877; 9:30am-11am Mon., Thurs., and Sat., 10am-12:30pm Sun.

Set right at the edge of a cliff dropping about 295 feet (90 m) to the sea, this church is quite a sight, especially when seen from the overlook along Corso Filangieri nearby, with the Gulf of Naples and Mount Vesuvius in the distance. The first cathedral in Vico Equense was built on the beach at Marina di Aequa, but was later pillaged during pirate attacks. In the 14th century, this beautiful cathedral was built in a more protected high point atop the ruins of an ancient Roman temple. The church was later remodeled in the late 18th century, including its baroque pink facade with white decorative elements. A cathedral until 1818 when it was incorporated into the diocese of Sorrento, the church was damaged in 1980 by an earthquake and reopened in 1995. The interior is a rare example of Gothic architecture on the Sorrentine Peninsula. Though it was also remodeled in the baroque style, the apse reveals traces of the Gothic-era stone arches and vaulting.

MUSEO MINERALOGICO CAMPANO

Via San Ciro 38/Viale Rimembranza 1; tel. 081/801-5668; www.museomineralogicocampano.it; 10am-1pm and 5pm-9pm Tues.-Sat. Mar.-Sept., 10am-1pm Tues.-Sun. Oct.-Feb.; €5

The Campanian Mineralogical Museum has

an extensive collection of fossils, minerals, precious stones, stone tools, and shells from around the world. From dinosaur eggs to mammoth hair, more than 500 gemstones, and 3,500 minerals of 1,400 different varieties, the collection is an extensive one. Housed in a former convent from the 17th century, the displays are well presented, including information in English.

ANTIQUARIUM SILIO ITALICO

Corso Filangieri 98; tel. 081/802-7551; www.vicotourism.it; 9am-1pm Mon.-Fri., 3:30pm-6:30pm Tues. and Thurs., 9:30am-12:30pm Sat., closed Sunday; free

Located in the *Comune* (city hall) of Vico Equense, this small museum has three rooms displaying about 200 artifacts discovered in the area from a variety of different civilizations, from the seventh to the third century BC, including the earliest Italic tribes, Etruscans, and Greeks. You'll see Etruscan bronzes, Greek vases with black and red figures, jewels, and weapons. Information on the collection is in Italian only. However, for more information you can visit the **Azienda Autonoma Cura Soggiorno e Turismo Vico Equense,** the city's tourist office, which is also located in the *Comune* because they manage the museum.

MONTE FAITO

Villaggio Monte Faito; tel. 081/930-247; www.parcoregionaledeimontilattari.it

From Vico Equense, the mountains soar to some of the highest peaks of the Monti Lattari (Lattari Mountains) along the Sorrentine Peninsula. The Parco Regionale dei Monti Lattari covers a vast area of 39,537 acres (160 square km) and Monte Faito is among the highest points. It is one of the easiest peaks to reach, thanks to a **cable car** and offers some of the best panoramic views over the peninsula and entire Gulf of Naples. The peak of the mountain is 3,711 feet (1,131 m), but there are excellent view points near the cable car station at 3,583 feet (1,092 m). Some of the best views are to be had from the cable car on the ride up. After exiting the station, you'll find a small square with cafés and signposts indicating walks in the area. For a lovely view, follow signs to the Ristorante Sant'Angelo, a short walk along the wooded pathway and narrow street below, to reach the Piazzale dei Capi with more food shops and café options. Just beyond is a rocky area where you can climb up to enjoy fantastic views. It's a great spot to enjoy a break before taking the cable car back down.

The best and most scenic way to reach Monte Faito is via the **Funivia,** or cable car, line that runs from the **Castellammare di Stabia Circumvesuviana train station** east of Vico Equense. The cable car is operated by **EAV** (tel. 081/200-991; www.eavsrl.it; 8:25am-8:15pm July-mid-Sept., 9:35am-4:25pm Apr.-June and Oct.-Nov.; €5.50 one way, €8 return). Cable cars depart about every half hour and the journey takes about 10 minutes.

If you'd rather not take the cable car, EAV also operates **buses** connecting Vico Equense and Monte Faito, departing from the Vico Equense Circumvesuviana train station and arriving at the Funivia station on Monte Faito. There are only 5-7 departures daily, so check the schedule in advance and plan for a 45-minute journey. You can also reach Monte Faito by car from Vico Equense following **Via Raffaele Bosco (SS 269)** to the village of Moiano, where signs indicate to continue along Via Faito. Follow the narrow and twisty road to the top where there is parking, along with cafés and restaurants.

Vineyards

ABBAZIA DI CRAPOLLA

Via San Filippo; tel. 339/623-8238; fulvio.alifano@gmail.com; Apr.-Oct.; tastings and tours from €40 per person

Founded in 2007, this vineyard is located on the mountain slopes above Vico Equense, where grapes have been grown for centuries.

1: The Chiesa della Santissima Annunziata sits right at the edge of a cliff in Vico Equense. **2:** The Fontana dei Delfini is in Piazza Umberto I in the center of Vico Equense.

1

2

In the Middle Ages this area was a rural monastic center connected with the Benedictine abbey near the Crapolla fjord on the southern side of the Sorrentine Peninsula. In an area known for its gastronomic treasures, the Abbazia di Crapolla is dedicated to bringing back the ancient wine tradition of the area. Fulvio Alifano and Peppe Puttini have transformed this scenic setting into a first-class vineyard, planting traditional local grapes like fiano and falanghina along with pinot nero and merlot. Set at 984 feet (300 m) above the sea, this vineyard offers an excellent way not only to enjoy the natural landscape of the Sorrentine Penninsula, but also to sample some of the prized wines from this very special vineyard.

Beaches

MARINA DI VICO

Via Cristoforo Colombo

The small harbor of Marina di Vico is a scenic spot surrounded by green mountain slopes where you'll find a castle, little houses, turquoise water, and beautiful views of the Gulf of Naples. Dating back to the late 13th century, the **Castello Giusso** (Giusso Castle) took on its current design starting with modifications and expansions in the 16th century. Although privately owned, it is one of the elements of Marina di Vico that help to create a scenic setting for swimming. There are several beach clubs (*stabilimenti balneari*) along the sandy beach area on the western side of the harbor. **Lido Da Vittorio** (tel. 334/947-8782; open Easter-Oct.; starting at €12 for sun bed and umbrella) has a particularly nice spot on the western side of the beach.

Food

TORRE DEL SARACINO

Via Torretta Marina d'Aequa 9; tel. 081/802-8555; www.torredelsaracino.it; 7:45pm-10pm Tues., 12:45pm-2pm and 7:45pm-10pm Wed.-Sat., 12:45pm-2pm Sun., closed Monday; tasting menus from €155 per person

Set by a historic watchtower overlooking Marina di Aequa, Gennaro Esposito's Michelin two-starred restaurant offers a one-of-a-kind dining experience. Keeping true to his roots, Esposito has created a menu dedicated to traditional and locally sourced ingredients of the highest quality; both seafood and other options are beautifully done. Menus change seasonally, but among the classics are dishes with *pesce bandiera*, a local fish with a compact white texture and delicate flavor, or wide tagliatelle pasta with broccoli and sea urchin. Another highlight is the beautifully balanced zucchini soup with poached egg and red prawns. Tasting menus are available and highly recommended. Reservations are recommended and are required at least two days in advance for groups of more than four people.

★ PIZZA A METRO DA GIGINO

Via Giovanni Nicotera 15; tel. 081/879-8309; www.pizzametro.it; 10am-midnight daily; €28-34 for a meter of pizza

Vico Equense is a frequent stop for foodies to try the famous *pizza a metro* (meter-long pizza) that was created in the 1950s by local pizza maker Gigino Dell'Amura. His iconic restaurant is now run by his children and extended family, who continue to make the traditional long pizzas—rich with toppings like broccoli, sausage, and roasted vegetables—that are perfect for sharing, with each meter suggested for about five people.

GELATERIA GABRIELE

Corso Umberto I, 8; tel. 081/879-8744; www.gabrieleitalia.com; 9am-2pm and 4pm-midnight, closed Tuesday and from Jan. 7-Feb. 7; €2-5

Famous in the area for gelato and pastries, this is a classic spot to stop and enjoy a sweet break right in the heart of Vico Equense near the central Piazza Umberto I. With 70 years of tradition and considered among the top *gelaterie* in Italy, Gelateria Gabriele specializes in flavors that highlight locally grown products like Sorrento's lemons, walnuts, figs, and more.

Accommodations

ASTAPIANA VILLA GIUSSO

Via Camaldoli 51; tel. 081/802-4392; www.astapiana.com; Apr. 15-Nov. 2; €120 d

Located on the slopes of the mountains above Vico Equense, this *masseria* (farmhouse) offers seven double bedrooms with private bathrooms and a family suite decorated with antique furnishings that add to the historic charm of the natural setting. This *agriturismo* is surrounded by olive groves, vineyards, citrus groves, and chestnut tree forests that you can enjoy on a guided visit. The on-site restaurant largely uses its own farm-fresh ingredients, including homegrown olive oil.

LE ANCORE

Via Marina d'Aequa 39; tel. 081/802-8896; www.leancorehotel.com; open year round except closed Jan. 7- Feb. 10; €140 d

Set right across from the beach in the Marina d'Aequa harbor, this small hotel offers a true seaside experience with its bright and inviting rooms, all with views of the sea and across the gulf to Mount Vesuvius. All eight rooms are decorated in vibrant colors, including colorful ceramics in the local style.

Information and Services

AZIENDA AUTONOMA CURA SOGGIORNO E TURISMO VICO EQUENSE

Corso Filangieri 100; tel. 081/801-5752; www.vicotourism.it; 8am-6pm Mon.-Fri., 9am-1pm Sat., closed Sun.

Just a couple of blocks from Piazza Umbero I, the town's tourist office has a small side entrance in the elegant building that houses the *Comune* (city hall). Stop in for detailed information on opening hours for local churches and other sights, as they can change or vary throughout the year.

Getting There

BY TRAIN

Located about 25 miles (40 km) southeast of Naples, Vico Equense is the first city you'll encounter on the Sorrentine Peninsula if you're coming from the Naples area. It is 6.8 miles (11 km) east of Sorrento, and because it is situated between two popular destinations, it is well connected with various transportation options. The **Circumvesuviana** train line, operated by **EAV** (www.eavsrl.it) connecting Naples with Sorrento stops at Vico Equense for the center of town and Seiano for the Marina di Aequa harbor, even though it's only a little more than a mile (1 km) from town to the harbor. The train runs about every 30 minutes, and costs €3.40 per person from Naples and €2.00 from Sorrento. The journey from Naples to Vico Equense takes about 55 minutes, while the trip from Sorrento takes about 10 minutes.

BY CAR

To reach Vico Equense from Naples, follow the **A3** autostrada south out of Naples and exit at Castellammare di Stabia, where you'll continue on the **Strada Statale della Penisola Sorrentina (SS145)** to Vico Equense. From Sorrento, drive east on the SS145 to reach Vico Equense. The drive takes about 45 minutes from Naples and 30 minutes from Sorrento.

BY FERRY

Vico Equense has two ports, **Marina di Aequa** (also known as the **Porto di Seiano**), and the smaller **Marina di Vico.** Ferries operated by **Gescab** (tel. 081/428-5259; www.gescab.it; starting at €18.60) depart from Capri to the Porto di Seiano, a trip that takes about 30 minutes. **Alilauro** (tel. 081/497-2238; www.alilauro.it; starting at €2.50 per person) has a seasonal Archeolinea route connecting the Porto di Seiano with Naples, Sorrento, Positano, and Amalfi that runs Tuesday-Friday. The ferry ride from Naples to Seiano is 30 minutes, from Sorrento to Seiano takes about 15 minutes, from Positano to Seiano it's about 45 minutes, and from Amalfi 1 hour 20 minutes.

Getting Around

The center of Vico Equense is small and easy to explore on foot. To walk from the Vico

Equense train station to the Piazza Umberto I only takes about five minutes along Corso Filangieri. The Vico Equense train station is the hub for local buses operated by **EAV** (www.eavsrl.it; departures every 20-30 minutes; starting at €1.30) that offer service to Sorrento, Marina di Aequa, Marina di Vico, and Monte Faito.

MASSA LUBRENSE

The tip of the Sorrentine Peninsula is one of the most remarkable parts of the entire region with its sparsely populated mountain slopes, rugged coastline, large marine protected zone, and rural villages. Large parts of the peninsula in this area remain unspoiled, and a tranquil natural beauty reigns. Technically, the administrative area of Massa Lubrense covers much of the tip of the peninsula from west of Sorrento along the coastline to **Punta Campanella,** and along the southern side of the peninsula to **Nerano** and its harbor area of Marina del Cantone. This includes a number of *frazioni* (small villages), that are very spread out and are quite distinct from the city of Massa Lubrense. To spend time exploring this area means getting off the beaten path and discovering small mountain farms, a rural lifestyle, and seaside villages where fishing continues to be a mainstay. The town of Massa Lubrense is a good jumping-off point to see the area, with a sleepy city center and tiny harbor at **Marina della Lobra.** Just beyond Massa Lubrense toward the tip of the Sorrentine Peninsula, the natural setting is stunning with the island of Capri in the distance. It's a place where land, sea, and sky blend into one breathtaking panorama.

Sights

CHIESA DI SANTA MARIA DELLE GRAZIE

Largo Vescovado 1; tel. 081/878-9274; www.excattedrale.it; 7:30am-12:30pm and 5pm-7pm Mon.-Fri., 7:30am-12:30pm Sat.-Sun.; free

In the center of Massa Lubrense, the city's former cathedral sits on a piazza next to a small park and not far from an overlook along the coastline that takes in views of Capri and Ischia across the Gulf of Naples. To the left of the church entrance is Palazzo Vesçovile, dating back to the 15th century, where the bishops of Massa Lubrense once lived. Beyond the rather simple baroque facade is a beautiful church constructed from 1512-1542 as a proper seat for the bishops within this rural area. After an earthquake in 1687, restoration took place, incorporating the baroque elements we see today.

Most notable is the elaborate majolica tiled floor with baroque flourishes that was originally designed in 1780 by Ignazio Chiajese, son of ceramic artist Leonardo Chiajese, who designed the extraordinary ceramic floor at the Chiesa Monumentale di San Michele in Anacapri. Much of the floor today is a later copy of the original, parts of which can still be seen in the church, especially in the chapels on either side of the altar. The tall bell tower to the right of the church entrance was remodeled in the early 1900s when the clock and dome were added to the top.

Beaches

MARINA DI PUOLO

Via Marina di Puolo

Located between Sorrento and Massa Lubrense, this little harbor with traditional fishermen's houses and a beach is a popular spot in the summer. The beach has sandy sections as well as areas with small rocks and the water is excellent for swimming. The beach is a designated Blue Flag Beach, a ranking by the Foundation for Environment Education for the finest water quality. You'll find free areas where you can just throw down a towel also in addition to several beach clubs (*stabilimenti balneari)* offering sun bed and umbrella rentals, and services like showers, changing rooms, and seaside bars or restaurants. Head to **Cinque Mare** (tel. 334/746-2783; www.cinquemareservice.it; May-Oct.) to rent a

1: Torre Cangiani **2:** Chiesa di Santa Maria delle Grazie in the center of Massa Lubrense

1

2

sun bed and umbrella for a relaxing day at the beach. Beyond the small jetty is a rockier beach where the turquoise water is lovely for swimming.

Water Sports

PUNTA CAMPANELLA DIVING

Via Fontanella; tel. 338/471-2360; www.puntacampanelladiving.com; open end of Apr.-Oct.; snorkeling from €50 per person, diving €120 per person

Based in Marina della Lobra, this is one of the premier diving centers on the Sorrentine Peninsula. This provider offers scuba diving and snorkeling excursions along the Sorrento coastline, Amalfi Coast, Capri, and surrounding areas. It also specializes in excursions in the **Area Marina Protetta di Punta Campanella** (Protected Marina Area of Punta Campanella), which stretches along the northern and southern sides of the Sorrento Peninsula around the tip of Punta Campanella, covering nearly 25 miles (40 km) of coastline and the sea. The diving center itself is well equipped, and the team members are highly experienced in sharing the underwater beauty of the area. They also have a passion for underwater photography and offer courses and themed photography excursions as well.

Food

RISTORANTE IL CANTUCCIO

Largo Vescovado, Via Pennino 1; tel. 081/878-9300; www.ilcantucciomassalubrense.com; noon-4pm and 6pm-11:30pm daily Dec. 15-Oct. 31; €9-22

Just beyond the Chiesa di Santa Maria delle Grazie, this family-run restaurant has a beautiful terrace with views of Capri and the Gulf of Naples. The menu highlights typical dishes of the area; the zucchini flowers stuffed with ricotta and pesto sauce are an excellent place to start. Seafood is done very well here, too; the spaghetti with fresh seafood is a good choice as well as the seared tuna with pistachio.

RISTORANTE DON VITO

Marina di Puolo 16; tel. 081/533-9819; www.ristorantedonvito.com; noon-3:30pm and 7pm-11:30pm daily Mar. 16-Nov. 14, closed Wed. Nov. 15-Mar. 15; €8-20

Brothers Salvatore and Francesco Stinga have created a gastronomic gem in the enchanting setting of Marina di Puolo, only a few steps from the sea. After spending time working in the best kitchens around Sorrento and Capri, they decided to come together to open their own restaurant, dedicated to traditional cooking and their family recipes. Seafood is the highlight here, but there are plenty of options on the menu. Seafood enthusiasts should try their risottos or the *zuppiera di spaghetti alla pescatora*, a pasta dish so rich with seafood that it is served in a large soup bowl.

Accommodations

TORRE CANGIANI

Via Vigliano 1/A; tel. 081/532-7825; www.torrecangiani.com; closed Dec. 24-26; €120 d

Immersed in a peaceful natural setting between Sorrento and Massa Lubrense, this *agriturismo* offers a true farm-stay experience and unique accommodations in a 16th-century watchtower. The Torre Cangiani tower overlooks the country house, with lemon and olive groves planted on the steep terraced hills. There are four different room locations, with the Tower room and Guestroom offering splendid views of the gulf.

ART HOTEL VILLA FIORELLA

Via Vincenzo Maggio 5; tel. 081/878-9832; www.arthotelvillafiorella.com; open mid Apr.-Dec.; €334

Set below the center of Massa Lubrense on the road leading down to Marina della Lobra, this boutique hotel is surrounded by olive trees and includes a heated infinity pool with stellar views of Capri and the Gulf of Naples. The rooms are full of light, beautifully finished with a contemporary design, and true to the hotel's name with an artistic touch. This is a great place to opt for a sea-view room because you can savor the remarkable views day and night. With the onsite Fiorella Restaurant, Scirocco Pool Bar & Restaurant, and the Cielo Sky Lounge, everything from poolside snacks to a relaxed yet elegant dinner or sunset drinks is right at your fingertips.

Information and Services

PRO LOCO MASSA LUBRENSE

Viale Filangieri 11; tel. 081/533-9021; www.massalubrenseturismo.it; 9:30am-1pm and 4:30pm-8pm daily May-Oct., 9:30am-1pm daily Nov.-Apr.

The Massa Lubrense tourist office is located in the center of town near the Chiesa di Santa Maria delle Grazie in a well marked office that is easy to spot. They are open year-round in the morning, and in the evening as well from May to October. Staff can help answer any travel questions about the area.

Getting There and Around

BY CAR OR SCOOTER

As Massa Lubrense and its surrounding *frazioni* are quite spread out, this area is best explored by car or scooter. From Sorrento, follow SS145 west out of the city and bear right onto Via Capo, following signs to Massa Lubrense. After about 15 minutes, the road runs right through the center of Massa Lubrense at Largo Vescovado. From Nerano, the most scenic drive to Massa Lubrense follows Via Capo d'Arco northwest to Termini and follows Via Nastro d'Oro along the coastline until it becomes Via IV Novembre and leads to Largo Vescovado in Massa Lubrense after a 25-minute drive.

BY PUBLIC TRANSIT

The closest train station is the **Circumvesuviana** station in Sorrento where you can catch the Linea A bus operated by **EAV** (www.eavsrl.it; departures every 20-30 minutes; starting at €1.30) connecting Sorrento to Massa Lubrense. **SITA SUD** (tel. 089/386-6701; www.sitasudtrasporti.it, from €1.30) also operates a bus that runs from the train station to Massa Lubrense and Marina della Lobra, as well as Nerano, Marina del Cantone, and Sant'Agata sui Due Golfi. The bus ride from Sorrento to Massa Lubrense is about 20 minutes.

NERANO AND MARINA DEL CANTONE

Very near the tip of the Sorrentine Peninsula along the southern coastline, the small town of Nerano and its seaside village of Marina del Cantone seem worlds away from the busy streets of Sorrento and the popular Amalfi Coast. A narrow and winding road zigzags down the mountain through the sleepy town of Nerano, where you can catch a glimpse of the turquoise sea as the road makes its way down to Marina del Cantone. Here you can enjoy a true escape surrounded by nature while relaxing on the beach, kayaking to isolated and beautiful coves, or savoring a beautiful meal by the sea as little boats putter back and forth to the seaside restaurants.

Beaches

★ MARINA DEL CANTONE

Marina del Cantone

Set in a beautiful bay, Marina del Cantone has a secluded atmosphere at once natural and exclusive. The beach is lined with hotels and restaurants that are among the most popular spots in the area for VIP and celebrity travelers. The long and pebbly beach gently slopes down into the sea, which is clear and calm here, so it's a particularly good beach for swimming. The beach is one of the few Blue Flag-classified beaches along the southern coastline of the Sorrentine Peninsula. You'll find free areas as well as sun bed rentals and beach services offered by beach clubs like **Bar Bagni Mimì** (tel. 081/808-1174; www.bagnimimi.it; Apr.-Oct.).

TOP EXPERIENCE

Kayaking

The best way to experience the natural landscape and beautiful coastline surrounding Marina del Cantone is by kayak.

CHASING SYRENS

Marina del Cantone; tel. 333/277-2987; www.chasingsyrens.com; Apr. 1-Oct. 31; hourly rentals from €18, tours from €30 per person

Your experience of these scenic waters will be even better with the clear kayaks from Chasing Syrens. Hourly rentals are available, but consider joining one of their small-group tours to explore the area with a local guide. The four-hour Jeranto Tour starts at 9am and includes stops at caves, small coves, and the Bay of Jeranto, as well as breaks for swimming, snorkeling, or relaxing. For a shorter jaunt, join the 90-minute East Tour in the afternoon. Groups top out at 10 people for the morning tour and 14 for the afternoon tour.

Food and Accommodations

RISTORANTE LO SCOGLIO

Piazza delle Sirene 15, Marina del Cantone; tel. 081/808-1026; www.hotelloscoglio.com; 12:30pm-4:30pm daily Apr. 1-Nov. 5, until 5:30pm June-Aug., 12:30pm-4:30pm Sat.-Sun. only Nov. 6-Mar. 31; restaurant €16-40; rooms from €159 d

Much loved by travelers from around the world who come to enjoy the incredibly simple yet fresh fare overlooking the sea in Marina del Cantone, the De Simone family's restaurant is a gastronomic haven. Whether you're enjoying fresh vegetables from the family garden prepared in traditional styles, or the popular local Nerano dish spaghetti with zucchini, or ravioli with yellow tomatoes, the light, fresh flavors are divine. Seafood is exquisite here; try the linguine with sea urchin, grilled lobster, or locally caught pezzogna, a flaky white fish. If you're like most visitors to Lo Scoglio who arrive and never want to leave this enchanting spot, there are also 14 simple yet stylish double or triple rooms with sea views (hotel open from Apr. 1-Nov. 5).

RISTORANTE QUATTRO PASSI

Via Amerigo Vespucci 13N, Nerano; tel. 081/808-1271; www.ristorantequattropassi.it; noon-3:30pm and 7pm-11:30pm Thurs.-Mon., noon-3:30pm Tues., closed Wed. Mar 15-Oct. 30; €25-50, tasting menus from €180 per person; rooms from €250 d

For chef Antonio Mellino, the beauty of Nerano and Marina del Cantone means home. Although born in Argentina, at only

Marina del Cantone

six years old, he came with his family to Nerano. Founded in 1983, this family-run restaurant has evolved over the years to become one of the most celebrated restaurants on the Sorrentine Peninsula. The Michelin two-starred restaurant offers a unique blend of traditional cooking and innovation. In addition to the artfully designed dining areas, there's a boutique hotel offering luxury stays. The six large rooms and two suites feature modern decor, bright pops of color, and gorgeous views over Marina del Cantone.

CONCA DEL SOGNO

Via Amerigo Vespucci 25, Nerano; tel. 081/808-1036; www.concadelsogno.it; 12:30pm-4:30pm and 8pm-9:30pm daily Easter-mid-Oct.; restaurant €25-100, rooms from €200 d

Set along the rocky cove overlooking the beautiful Baia di Recommone with its Blue Flag beach, Conca del Sogno offers beach club services as well as a top-notch restaurant and a small hotel with five charming rooms. With its seaside location, naturally seafood is excellent here; the lobster pasta and salt-crusted freshly caught fish are fine choices. You could also opt for the classic Nerano dish spaghetti with zucchini. The hotel rooms are bright and fresh, and feature private terraces overlooking the sea for a romantic holiday stay.

Getting There and Around

BY CAR

Nerano and Marina del Cantone are quite secluded areas along the Sorrentine Peninsula and are most easily reached by car or scooter. From Massa Lubrense it's about a 30-minute drive following Via IV Novembre and Via Nastro d'Oro southwest through Termini, and then continuing along Via Capo d'Arco down to Nerano and through Nerano for about five more minutes to reach Marina del Cantone. From Sant'Agata sui Due Golfi, follow Via dei Campi southwest out of town; that road becomes Via Santa Maria della Neve, then Via Leucosia, and Via Capo D'Arco. Follow signs for Nerano and stay on Via Capo D'Arco as it winds down through Nerano and then to Marina del Cantone. It's a 15-minute drive to Nerano and about 20 minutes to Marina del Cantone. Parking is available in parking lots and along the road in Marina del Cantone.

BY BUS

If you're traveling by public transportation, the closest train station is in Sorrento, where you can continue by **SITA SUD** (tel. 089/386-6701; www.sitasudtrasporti.it; from €1.30) bus. Catch the bus heading to Nerano in the piazza in front of the train station; the bus stops at both Nerano and Marina del Cantone; the ride will take about one hour. The bus first passes through Massa Lubrense and Sant'Agata sui Due Golfi before reaching Nerano.

SANT'AGATA SUI DUE GOLFI

Nestled along the Lattari Mountains, the town of Sant'Agata sui Due Golfi takes its name from its setting, which offers views of the Gulf of Naples to the north and Gulf of Salerno to the south. It's a rural and quiet place, noted for its agricultural and culinary traditions, and many visitors zip right through when traveling between Sorrento and the Amalfi Coast. Stop for a visit in town to stroll down the lovely Corso Sant'Agata, which leads to a small piazza and the town's church dedicated to Santa Maria delle Grazie, or to take in the panoramic views from the monastery nearby. Don't miss dining at Don Alfonso 1890, a true gastronomic gem on the Sorrentine Peninsula.

Sights

MONASTERO DI SAN PAOLO AL DESERTO

Via Deserto 23; tel. 081/878-0199; www.monachedeserto.altervista.org; 10am-12pm and 3pm-5pm daily; free

One of the best views in Sant'Agata sui Due Golfi is from the peaceful setting of this monastery and its panoramic Belvedere terrace, where you can admire views toward Capri, Ischia, Procida, and Vesuvius. Founded in 1679, the monastery has housed diverse religious communities and was abandoned multiple times. Since the early 1980s, it has been home to Benedictine nuns who completely restored the monastery. You can reach the monastery easily by car from the center of Sant'Agata sui Due Golfi or on foot with a 15-minute uphill walk along Via Deserto. If the entrance marked Belvedere isn't open, ring the doorbell at the door to the left and ask the nuns for the key to visit.

Food and Accommodations

LO STUZZICHINO

Via Deserto 1A; tel. 081/533-0010; www.ristorantelostuzzichino.it; noon-3pm and 7pm-11pm closed Wed. Sept.-June and closed mid-Jan.-mid Feb.; €8-20

A warm welcome and traditional cooking have been the hallmarks of this *osteria* run by the De Gregorio family since 1989. You can't go wrong with their signature dish of pasta and potatoes with the local *provolone del Monaco* cheese. The ravioli with ricotta and clams with a lemon sauce is a unique and tasty option as well.

★ REGIONAL RISTORANTE DON ALFONSO 1890

Corso Sant'Agata 11/13; tel. 081/878-0026; www.donalfonso.com; 12:30pm-2:30pm and 7:30pm-10:30pm daily Apr.-Oct.; €34-45, tasting menu from €150 per person; rooms from €300 d

Set in a historic building right in the center of Sant'Agata sui Due Golfi is one of the finest restaurants on the entire Sorrentine Peninsula. It's here, in the rural setting at the tip of the peninsula, that the Iaccarino family creates exquisite dishes that use local traditions as a firm foundation for innovation. The menu changes seasonally based on the fresh produce grown at the family's terraced organic farm in Termini. The tasting menus let you sample the finest of the season, or try a classic like *strascinati* (cannelloni pasta on a light tomato sauce with basil and mozzarella). At Ristorante Don Alfonso 1890, you'll experience fine dining that is well worth the splurge.

For a peaceful stay in Sant'Agata sui Due Golfi, Don Alfonso 1890 also has eight lovely rooms and suites available in its **boutique hotel.** The decor blends historic furnishings from the 1700-1800s with modern design and all the services and details of a luxury hotel.

Getting There and Around

BY CAR

Sant'Agata sui Due Golfi is located just off the **SS145** road that connects Sorrento with the Amalfi Coast Road (SS163). The town is set in the mountains about 6.2 miles (10 km) from Sorrento, 3.4 miles (5.5 km) from Massa Lubrense, and 10.5 miles (17 km) from Positano. Plan for a drive of about 25 minutes from Sorrento, 15 minutes from Massa Lubrense, and about 30 minutes from Positano.

BY BUS

The town can be reached by buses operated by **SITA SUD** (tel. 089/386-6701; www.sitasudtrasporti.it, from €1.30) from Sorrento, Amalfi, and Positano. However, not every bus on the line connecting Amalfi and Sorrento travels via Sant'Agata sui Due Golfi, so it's best to check with the driver in advance. SITA SUD also operates a bus line that circulates between Sorrento, Massa Lubrense, and Sant'Agata sui Due Golfi about every hour, 5:15am-9:40pm. The bus ride to Sant'Agata sui Due Golfi from Sorrento takes about 35 minutes, while from Positano it's about 30 minutes and from Amalfi it's about an hour and 20 minutes.

1: the garden at Ristorante Don Alfonso 1890 **2:** the charming town center of Sant'Agata sui Due Golfi

1

2

Capri

Itinerary Idea 228
Sights 229
Beaches 240
Sports and Recreation . . 242
Entertainment and Events 246
Shopping 248
Food 251
Accommodations 255
Information and Services 258
Transportation 258

With a natural beauty that's famous around the world, the island of Capri is one of Italy's most popular travel destinations. What this small island lacks in size it easily makes up for with its mesmerizing blue sea, soaring cliffs, and Mediterranean charm. In this place of stunning scenery, there is so much to discover beyond the breathtaking views… but you won't want to miss those views!

Split between two towns and two harbors, Capri's sights spread from rocky beaches to mountain peaks, with historic sights and, of course, shopping to enjoy along the way. Visit the bustling Piazzetta, enjoy iconic views of the Faraglioni rock formations off the coastline, and stroll along the chic shopping streets. Then get away from it all by exploring the island's quieter side. Hike to incredible overlooks, ride a

Highlights

Look for ★ to find recommended sights, activities, dining, and lodging.

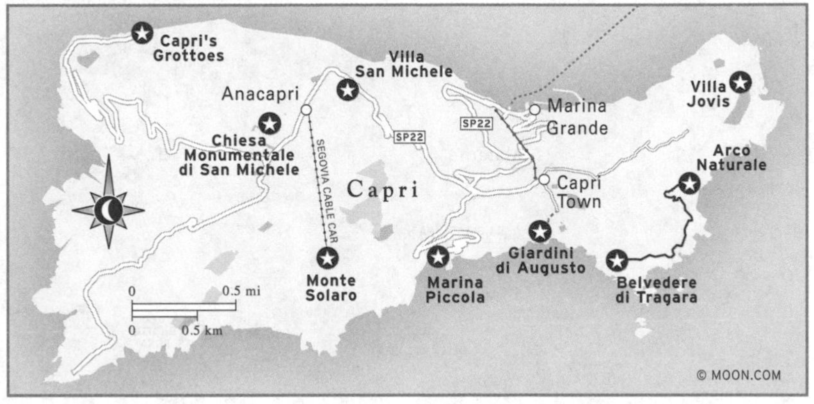

★ **Giardini di Augusto:** Visit these beautifully curated gardens to enjoy one of the best views of the Faraglioni rocks and peer down over the zigzagging Via Krupp (page 231).

★ **Villa Jovis:** Hike to the top of Monte Tiberio to explore the ruins of the once palatial villa of Roman Emperor Tiberius. Stunning views are an added bonus (page 232)!

★ **Capri's Grottoes:** Enjoy a private or group boat tour around the island to see Capri's natural grottoes, including the Grotta Azzurra (Blue Grotto), up close (page 236).

★ **Villa San Michele:** Stunning views and gardens blend beautifully at this museum located in what was once the home of Swedish doctor and writer Axel Munthe (page 236).

★ **Monte Solaro:** Ride the chairlift to Capri's highest point for unforgettable views across the island and Gulf of Naples (page 237).

★ **Chiesa Monumentale di San Michele:** The remarkable floor in this church is completely covered with an 18th-century hand-painted majolica tile scene of the Garden of Eden (page 238).

★ **Marina Piccola:** Capri's smaller harbor is a picturesque spot to swim on the rocky beach or dine overlooking the turquoise sea (page 241).

★ **Arco Naturale to Belvedere di Tragara Walk:** A pleasant walk through Capri town leads to a large natural arch, immersed in a quiet spot of immense beauty, and continues to the Belvedere di Tragara, a beautiful overlook above the Faraglioni (page 242).

Capri

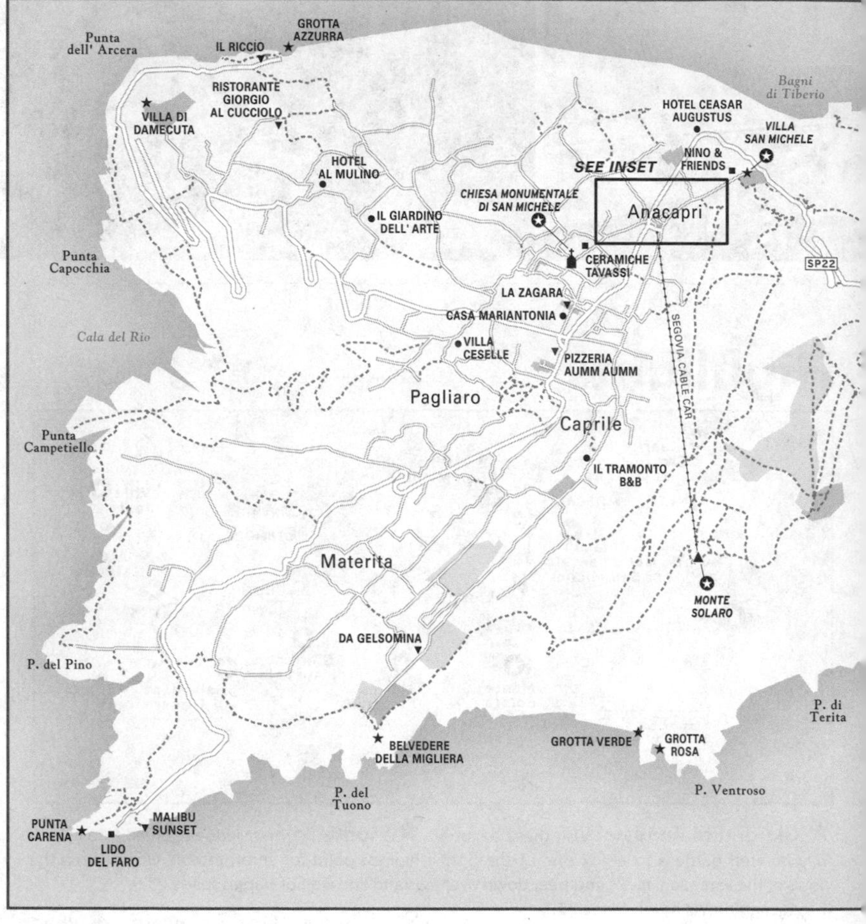

chairlift to the top of Monte Solaro, and meander down pedestrian-only pathways past bougainvillea-draped villas. Once you've enjoyed the top sights on land, get out on the water to take in the landscape from the sea, explore the island's grottoes, and find tiny coves where you can dive into the sea for a swim.

While its popularity means plenty of crowds during the busy season, Capri should still be on every traveler's must-see list. Whether you're planning a day trip or staying longer, there are plenty of ways to enjoy Capri's beauty that will take you from the most popular spots to tranquil corners of the island immersed in nature. Find those quiet moments, and Capri will surely capture your heart just as it has so many travelers for ages.

Previous: For the best view of the Faraglioni, head to the Giardini di Augusto; the port of Marina Grande; the Grotta di Matromania.

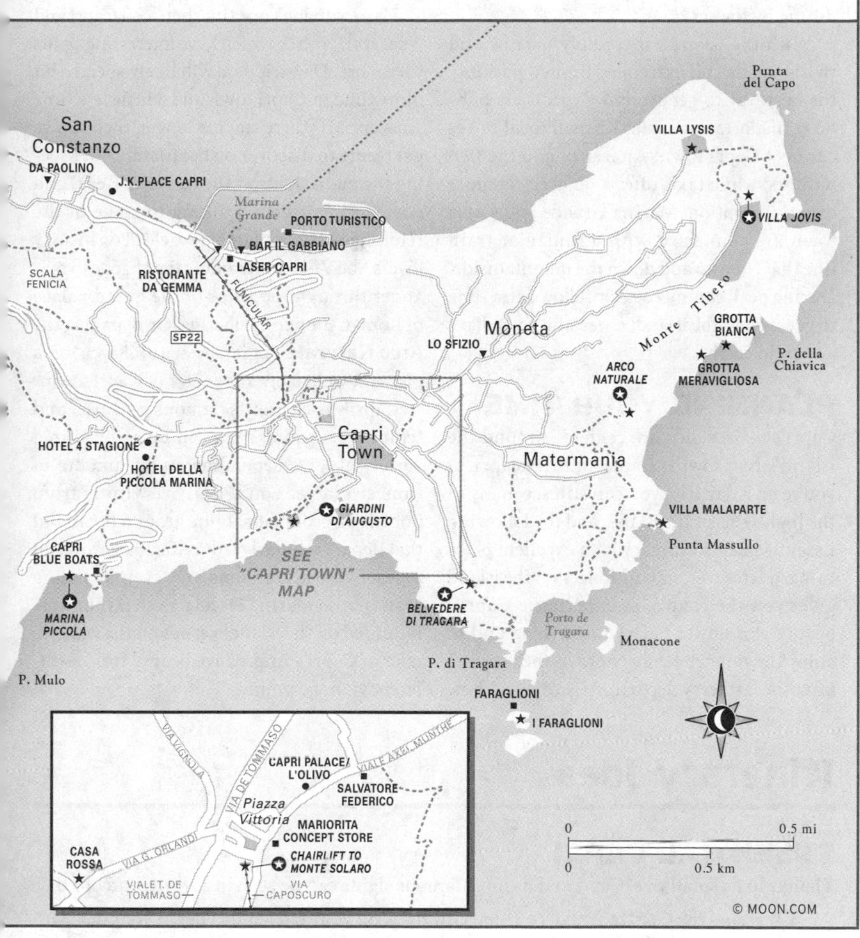

ORIENTATION

Located just off the tip of the Sorrentine Peninsula, Capri is the best-known island in the Gulf of Naples. Measuring only about 4 square miles (10.4 square km), it packs an intense amount of beauty into its small size. **Monte Solaro** soars to 1,932 feet (589 m) on the western side of the island, while on the northeastern side **Monte Tiberio** rises to 1,095 feet (334 m). The island's largest town, also called **Capri,** is situated along the dip between the two mountains just east of the middle of the island, while **Anacapri** spreads out around the base of Monte Solaro on the higher western side.

Capri has two harbors with the main ferry harbor and tourist port of **Marina Grande** on the northern side of the island. This is where ferries arrive and depart, and where you'll find the main transportation hub of the island. On the southern side of the island, **Marina Piccola** is a beautiful little area with lovely albeit rocky swimming spots and plenty of excellent beach clubs for swimming and dining by the sea.

With the island's incredibly narrow and twisty roads and extremely limited parking, the best way to get around Capri is via public transportation or taxi. Small local buses connect Capri town, Anacapri, and the two harbors, while taxis offer a quicker yet more expensive option. Marina Grande and Capri town are connected with a funicular train line that runs up and down the mountainside. During peak summer season, allow extra time to get around the island, especially if you have a ferry to catch.

PLANNING YOUR TIME

Capri's main sights are centered around the island's two towns: Capri and Anacapri. If you're on a day trip, you can still see many of the highlights of the island, and the following Essential Capri itinerary is an excellent place to start. However, staying longer on the island gives you the chance to experience Capri's beauty at a slower pace while hiking and to enjoy the quieter atmosphere in the evening after the last ferry departs. Regardless of how much time you have, Capri is a captivating place to visit.

Plan to divide your time between Capri and Anacapri, both of which have interesting sights to explore. Day-trippers will likely spend a bit more time in Capri town and a little less time Anacapri. If you're staying longer, then you've got plenty to discover on the island. After seeing the main sights in the center of Capri and Anacapri, consider walking to some of the remarkable sights farther afield. For history lovers, the **Villa Jovis** offers the chance to meander through the ruins of the grand palace of Roman Emperor Tiberius. Or marvel at the **Arco Naturale,** a massive natural arch, on a pleasant walk from the center of Capri town.

Capri's rocky cliffs, famous grottoes, and tempting turquoise sea can be enjoyed in a variety of ways depending on the amount of time available. You'll find everything from hour-long group boat tours around the island that depart regularly from Marina Grande to private boat excursions and even kayaking rentals from Marina Piccola. Even if your time is limited on the island, get out on the water to take in Capri's impressive beauty from a different vantage point.

Itinerary Idea

ESSENTIAL CAPRI

Thanks to its small size, Capri and its most famous sights can be seen in a whirlwind of a day.

1 If seeing the **Grotta Azzurra** (Blue Grotto) is on your bucket list, begin your day with an early visit before all the crowds arrive. There are a number of group and private tour options readily available from Marina Grande, where your ferry to Capri docks.

2 After seeing the grotto, take a local bus or taxi up to Piazza Vittoria in Anacapri and hop on the chairlift to the top of **Monte Solaro** to enjoy the view from the island's highest point.

3 Stroll through Anacapri to the **Chiesa Monumentale di San Michele** to see the remarkable 18th-century hand-painted ceramic floor.

4 Head to Capri and enjoy a leisurely lunch of *Caprese* (Capri-style) specialties like the traditional *ravioli caprese* at **Ristorante Michel'angelo.**

5 Take a walk from the Belvedere di Tragara in the center of town out to the **Arco Naturale** and back to get a sense of the landscape and life in Capri.

Itinerary Idea

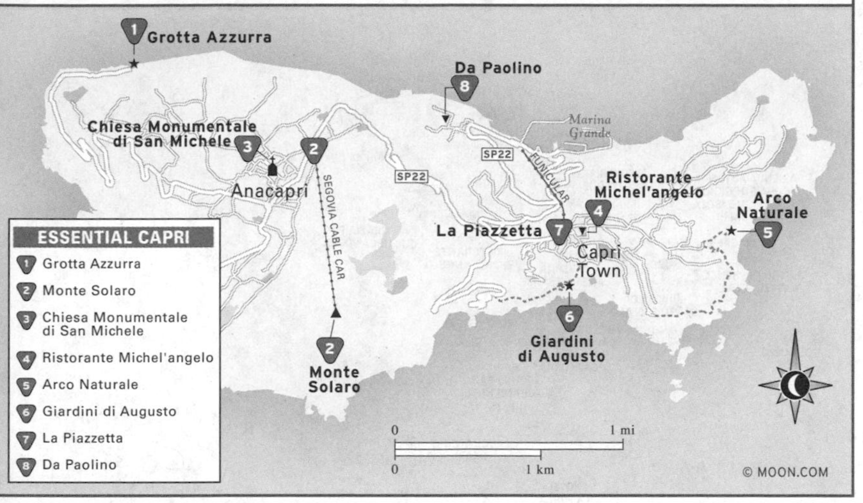

6 Visit the **Giardini di Augusto** for a remarkable view overlooking the Faraglioni rocks and the zigzagging Via Krupp.

7 Back in Capri town, head to **La Piazzetta** for an afternoon coffee and a little window shopping.

8 Dine on freshly caught seafood in an unforgettable setting under the lemon trees at **Da Paolino.**

Sights

CAPRI TOWN

La Piazzetta

Piazza Umberto I, Capri

Its official name is Piazza Umberto I, but this busy little piazza is more commonly known as La Piazzetta. It has a long history as the nucleus of the community since Roman times, and probably even dating back as far as the early Greek settlement on the island. Starting in the 16th century, the piazza's shape we see today began to take form. The area was used for occasional markets and was the hub of religious celebrations until the 1930s when the first café opened on the square. This is when the Piazzetta as a center of socialization truly began. Many more cafés followed and the Piazzetta was transformed into the place to see and be seen. Known as the *salotto del mondo* (theater of the world), the Piazzetta welcomes travelers from around the globe.

Today the piazza is lined on three sides by buildings and cafés and on the fourth by the **Chiesa di Santo Stefano.** The distinctive *Torre dell'Orologio* (Clock Tower) has the form today of a bell tower. It is thought to have been a part of the defensive walls of the medieval city, but also is considered the only remaining piece of a large church and monastery that once occupied the site where the Chiesa di Santo Stefano stands today. Whatever its

Capri Town

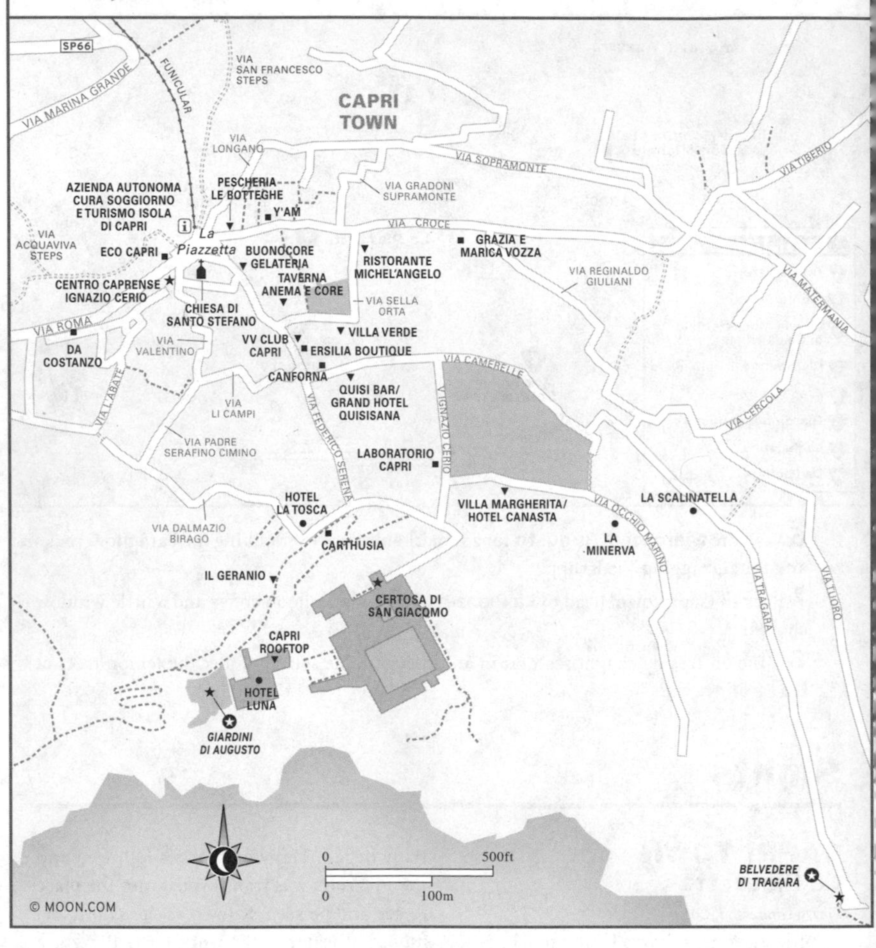

origins, the tower with its colorful majolica tile design dating from the 1800s is considered by locals to be the symbol of Capri.

Beyond the Piazzetta and through the arch to **Via Longono** and **Via le Botteghe** is the **medieval quarter** of the city with its maze of little streets and courtyards. This is an intriguing area to explore because it is also home to lovely little boutiques and restaurants. Following Via Vittorio Emanuele from the Piazzetta leads to the high-end shopping area of **Via Camerelle** and the **Giardini di Augusto.**

As Capri's transportation hub, with buses and taxis nearby and the funicular to Marina Grande, all life seems to pass through the Piazzetta. Stop for a coffee or *aperitivo* during the day to watch the world go by or find a table after dark to watch the Piazzetta truly come to life.

Chiesa di Santo Stefano

Piazza Umberto I, Capri; tel. 081/837-0072; 8am-1pm and 4pm-9pm daily, closes at 7pm Nov.-Mar.

Located at the top of a small flight of steps

from the Piazzetta, the facade of Capri's largest church feels squeezed into an impossibly narrow passageway. In fact, you'll need to look from a few different angles to take in the baroque design and spot the even more interesting series of small lantern-shaped domes that run along each side of the nave. The luminous white baroque interior is filled with light from the windows and domes along the nave and the large dome over the crossing. The church was built in the late 17th century on the site of an earlier church and is dedicated to Santo Stefano (St. Stephen). However, there's also a special reverence here for San Costanzo (St. Constantius), Capri's patron saint. The church holds an important silver bust reliquary statue of the saint from 1715, and that statue is carried during the procession for the saint's festival on May 14. Don't forget to look down when exploring the church, for in the main altar area you'll find a multicolored marble floor that was uncovered at the Villa Jovis, and in the side chapel to the left of the altar there's another Roman-era marble floor, likely from ruins near Punta Tragara.

Centro Caprense Ignazio Cerio

Piazzetta Cerio 5; tel. 081/837-6681; www.centrocaprense.org; 10am-1pm Mon., 10am-4pm Tues.-Wed. and Fri., 11am-4pm Thurs. and Sat, closed Sun.; €3

Situated opposite the Chiesa di Santo Stefano, the Palazzo Cerio—also known as the Palazzo Arcucci—is one of the most historic buildings around the Piazzetta. It was built in the 14th century for Giacomo Arcucci, the founder of the Certosa di San Giacomo. Today it houses the Centro Caprense Ignazio Cerio, a cultural center dedicated to Capri history and home to a library and museum displaying archaeological, paleontological, and naturalistic finds. The center was founded in 1949 by Edwin Cerio, a noted writer and engineer, in honor of his father, Ignazio Cerio, a doctor and naturalist. The museum's collection and role in preserving Capri's history in many forms makes this a fascinating spot to explore. Don't leave without heading up to the rooftop terrace for a bird's-eye view overlooking the Piazzetta. The center also organizes cultural events, meetings, and concerts throughout the year.

★ Giardini di Augusto

Via Matteotti 2, Capri; tel. 081/837-0686 (tourist office); www.cittadicapri.it; 9am-7:30pm daily Apr.-Sept., until 4pm in winter; €1

The beautiful Giardini di Augusto (Gardens of Augustus) were created on land purchased at the end of the 1800s from the nearby Certosa di San Giacomo Carthusian monastery by German Industrialist Friedrich Alfred Krupp. While there is a strong connection between Capri and ancient Rome, the gardens didn't receive their name in honor of Augustus until after World War I. Spread across several terraces, the lush gardens are full of seasonal flowers as well as plant and flower species that are typical of Capri, like *ginestra* (broom), bougainvillea, cacti, and bird of paradise. The terraced garden offers shaded spots with ceramic-tiled benches, giving you a relaxing spot to sit and rest. However, the main draw here is the sweeping view from the edge of the garden of the Faraglioni rocks and the Certosa di San Giacomo in one direction, and the bay of Marina Piccola in the other.

Look down from the highest terrace of the garden to see the famous Via Krupp, a zigzagging pathway down the mountain connecting Capri with Marina Piccola below. Excavated out of the mountainside, this remarkable pathway was created at Krupp's expense by the engineer Emilio Mayer. Unfortunately, the scenic pathway has been closed for some time due to the danger of falling rocks. Yet, the view looking down on Via Krupp with the bright turquoise sea just beyond is not to be missed.

Certosa di San Giacomo

Via Certosa 1, Capri; tel. 081/837-6218; www.polomusealecampania.beniculturali.it/index.php/la-certosa-sangiacomo; 10am-6pm May, 10am-7pm June-Aug., 10am-5pm Sept.-Oct., 9am-2pm Nov.-Dec., 10am-2pm Jan.-Apr., closed Mon. year-round; €6

Easy to spot on the way to the Giardini

di Augusto, the Certosa di San Giacomo was built starting in 1371 by the nobleman Giacomo Arcucci as a Carthusian monastery. The complex included a series of buildings and gardens organized around two cloisters, a large one and a small one, much of which can be visited today. The church off the small cloister has an impressive vaulted ceiling that reveals its Gothic origins amid the remains of the late 17th-century decor. Walking around the cloisters offers a chance to enjoy a shady and peaceful moment, an especially appealing break from the summer sun.

Since 1974, the former refectory of the monastery has housed a museum dedicated to the works of German painter Karl Wilhelm Diefenbach, who arrived on Capri in 1900 and remained until his death in 1913. The collection contains 31 of his paintings—many of them impressively large, dramatic, and dark—along with five plaster sculptures and one portrait.

I Faraglioni

Punta Tragara

Perhaps Capri's most iconic symbol, the Faraglioni are three large rocks located just off the Punta Tragara. With sheer cliffs and only a scattering of vegetation along the top, the three Faraglioni are majestic to behold. The rock closest to the land is connected to the island and rises to 358 feet (109 m), while the center rock with the hole in the middle rises to 266 feet (81 m), and the farthest one out is 341 feet (104 m) high. On the outer rock and the nearby rock formation called Monacone lives a rare type of lizard called the *lucertola azzurra* (blue lizard), which has an incredible blue tint, the color of the deep sea surrounding the Faraglioni. The rocks can be admired from many vantage points around the island, including the Giardini di Augusto and Belvedere di Tragara, and from high above in Anacapri from the top of Monte Solaro. You can also see the Faraglioni close up from the sea, as small boats can cruise right through the opening in the center rock.

Arco Naturale

Via Arco Naturale, Capri

For an experience immersed in Capri's natural beauty, take a walk to the Arco Naturale (Natural Arch) from the Piazzetta. Located about 656 feet (200 m) above sea level, the craggy natural arch is about 66 feet (20 m) tall and 39 feet (12 m) wide. Located in a peaceful setting surrounded by pine trees, the outside part of the arch is thick and massive and tapers to only a narrow connection on the side closest to the island, creating a naturally framed view of the sea. The walk to the arch through Capri town becomes quieter and more secluded as you go, and leads to a set of steps down to a series of small overlooks where you can admire the arch from a variety of different view points. In the distance, you'll spot the **Sorrentine Peninsula** and beyond to the right the **Li Galli islands** off Positano. The setting is nearly untouched nature where you can listen to the wind blowing through pine trees and catch the scent of the sea far below as boats pass by. You can also spot the Arco Naturale from the sea on a boat tour around the island.

★ Villa Jovis

Via Tiberio, Capri; tel. 081/837-0381; www.polomusealecampania.beniculturali.it/index.php/la-villa; 10am-7pm daily June-Sept., 10am-6pm Oct. and Apr.-May, 10am-4pm Nov.- Dec. and Mar., closed Jan.-Feb.; €6

Sitting atop the highest point of Monte Tiberio on the northeastern point of Capri are the ruins of a lavish villa built for Emperor Tiberius. From this perch atop Capri, Tiberius ruled the Roman Empire from AD 27 to 37. The largest of Tiberius's villas on the island, Villa Jovis was a massive estate that functioned as a fortress yet included all the modern comforts of a Roman imperial residence. Exploring the site, you'll find four large cisterns used to collect rainwater, which was

1: the ruins of the palace were Roman emperor Tiberius once lived at Villa Jovis **2:** beautiful view from the Centro Caprense Ignazio Cerio **3:** the Arco Naturale

1
2
3

fundamental because Capri has no natural water sources. Given the limited surface area near the top of Monte Tiberio, the villa occupied many levels rather than following the more traditional sprawling layout of Roman imperial villas.

Though it's hard to look at the state of the ruins and envision the original design, visiting the Villa Jovis offers the chance to wander through what was once a splendid example of Roman architecture and imagine the ancient Roman lifestyle on Capri. Exploring the site and walking through multiple levels, you can see parts of the imperial residence as well as the servant's quarters, baths, and even the ingenious series of large cisterns that held the villa's water supply. Although there is not a lot of historical information offered throughout the site, you'll see enough to gain some insight from this ancient site. The villa's setting is dramatic, overlooking a sheer cliff that drops straight to the sea; this is sometimes called Tiberius's Leap, where it's said people the emperor wasn't pleased with were shown the exit. Take your time admiring the sweeping views across the Gulf of Naples and the Sorrentine Peninsula. Adjacent to the ruins you'll find a small church with a plain gray facade and arched entrance. It is dedicated to Santa Maria del Soccorso and dates from around the 16th century, but it's most popular for the large terrace in front with panoramic views over the ruins, the island, and the Gulf of Naples and Gulf of Salerno.

Located at the extreme northeastern tip of the island at the highest point of Monte Tiberio, the walk to reach Villa Jovis is almost entirely uphill from the center of Capri. Starting from La Piazzetta, look for the signs to Villa Jovis and follow Via Longono, Via Sopramonte, and Via Tiberio. Comfortable shoes are recommended, and during the summer months don't forget to bring water as there are limited opportunities to purchase refreshments as you near Monte Tiberio. The walk takes about 45 minutes each way.

Villa Lysis

Via Lo Capo 12, Capri; tel. 081/838-6111; www.villalysiscapri.com; 10am-6pm Apr.-May and Sept.-Oct., 10am-7pm June-Aug., 10am-4pm Nov.-Dec., closed Wed.; €2

Along the pathway leading through the rugged mountainous landscape up to the summit of Monte Tiberio lies one of Capri's most curious villas. Set in an extraordinarily scenic spot at the edge of the cliff overlooking the Gulf of Naples and Marina Grande below, the secluded and inaccessible location was exactly what the villa's owner, the French writer Jacques d'Adelswärd-Fersen, was looking for when he built the villa starting in 1904. After being arrested in Paris the previous year for scandalous behavior, he fled to Capri, a place he had visited at a young age, where he built a refuge from the world. And quite a refuge it was: Villa Lysis defies any one architectural style and rather blends everything—from Louis XVI to art nouveau and Asian influences—from his travels around the world. The Villa Lysis became a meeting point for d'Adelswärd-Fersen, his companion Nino Cesarini, and the many artists and writers who visited Capri at the beginning of the 20th century.

After d'Adelswärd-Fersen's death, the villa eventually fell into disrepair and has gone through subsequent restorations. While much has been lost, the romantic and decadent atmosphere is still captivating. The villa and gardens are open to explore for only a small admission fee. Though the rooms are not decorated in the lavish style they once were, there is an air of the original elegance and flair, especially in the large salon with its columns decorated with gold mosaic details. The gardens are the highlight, with many terraces and picturesque spots to enjoy the fine views over Marina Grande below. During the summer the villa often hosts concerts, theatrical performances, and exhibitions. To reach Villa Lysis, follow the same directions for Villa Jovis. The walk takes approximately

45 minutes from the Piazzetta and is mostly uphill. Especially if you enjoy architecture, it's a pleasant stop on the way to or from visiting Villa Jovis.

ANACAPRI

Grotta Azzurra

Grotta Azzurra, Anacapri; tel. 081/837-5646; 9am-5pm daily Apr.-Oct., 10:30am-12:30pm daily Nov.-Mar., weather permitting; €14

Synonymous with Capri's fame around the world, the Grotta Azzurra (Blue Grotto) is one of the island's most popular sights. This natural cavern is about 197 feet (60 m) long and 82 feet (25 m) wide. The catch is that the entrance to the grotto is very small and can only be accessed by small rowboats that hold up to four people. To visit the grotto you have to transfer to one of these smaller rowboats and lie nearly flat as your skipper carefully pulls the boat into the grotto to row you around. Inside, you'll see the famous deep electric blue water that shimmers with a silvery glow thanks to the refraction of light from an opening below sea level. This magical space led to a Roman nymphaeum where statues have been uncovered. For ages it was largely forgotten and mostly feared by local fishermen until it was rediscovered by German travelers August Kopisch and Ernst Fries in 1826.

Given its popularity and limited access, the Grotta Azzurra can be a bit challenging to visit, especially during the busy summer season. Before you can enter, be prepared for a lengthy wait, which for some travelers can seem disproportionate to the limited amount of time you actually get to stay inside (about 10 minutes). However, if seeing the Grotta Azzurra is on your bucket list, it is quite a unique experience and the colors certainly don't disappoint.

The entrance to the Grotta Azzurra can be reached by land or sea, but you can only enter the grotto by boat. Several boat companies, including **Motoscafisti Capri** (Marina Grande; tel. 081/837-5646; www.motoscaficapri.com; from €15 per person) and **Laser Capri** (Via Cristoforo Colombo 69; Marina Grande; tel. 081/837-5208; www.lasercapri.com; from €15 per person) offer group boat service from Marina Grande to the Grotta Azzurra, with the option to add on a boat tour around the island for an additional fee. By land, you can reach the grotto by taxi or via the local Capri bus to the Grotta Azzurra, but you'll need to walk down some

Grotta Azzurra

★ Cruising Around Capri's Sea Grottoes

Though the Grotta Azzurra, the Blue Grotto, gets most of the attention, Capri has many beautiful, colorful grottoes, and the best way to see them all is on a boat tour around the island. Pack a picnic for the day, and remember to wear or bring your swimsuit and plenty of sunscreen! While there are many small grottoes, here are the largest and most impressive ones to visit around the island.

GROTTA AZZURRA

Capri's most famous grotto is also its most secluded. Compared to the other grottoes that can be enjoyed easily on a boat cruise around the island, the Grotta Azzurra and its stunning electric-blue water can only be seen if you climb aboard a small rowboat and lie flat to be taken inside. Even though the time inside the grotto is quite limited (about 10 minutes), it's an exhilarating experience.

GROTTA BIANCA AND GROTTA MERAVIGLIOSA

Located on the eastern side of the island, the Grotta Bianca (White Grotto) is one of the most impressive when seen from the sea. This large cave is divided into two areas and gets its name from the white hue of the calcareous material on the cliffside. Stalactites frame the upper ridge of the opening, and peering deeper inside reveals the Grotta Meravigliosa (Marvelous Grotto) high above. Small boats can enter close to the Grotta Bianca, offering a better view into the dark cavern above where there's a stalagmite that resembles a statue of the Madonna praying.

GROTTA VERDE

Along the southern side of the island, the Grotta Verde (Green Grotto) is noted for its intensely green water. It's a popular spot to stop and swim in the beautiful water on private boat excursions. You can swim right through a natural arch in the water at the entrance of the grotto and explore little caves in the area.

GROTTA ROSSA

Not far from the Grotta Verde, the Grotta Rossa (Red Grotto) gets its name from the brilliant red hue of the coral that grows just below the water line of the large cave. This can easily be enjoyed on a boat tour around the island as the opening is large enough for small boats to get quite close.

steps to the spot near the entrance where you can board the rowboats to enter.

If you're on a day trip, it's a good idea to visit the grotto in the morning, as occasionally wind or weather changes can require the grotto to close in the afternoons. A visit is not guaranteed, as even on days when the weather seems nice the sea conditions near the grotto might make it unsafe to enter. Though the Grotta Azzurra is often closed during the winter from November to March, if the weather and sea conditions are appropriate it can occasionally be open. Throughout the year, if the Motoscafisti Capri ticket booths are open in Marina Grande, that means the grotto is open.

★ Villa San Michele

Viale Axel Munthe 34, Anacapri; tel. 081/837-1401; villasanmichele.eu; 9am-4:30pm Mar., 9am-5pm Apr. and Oct., 9am-6pm May-Sept., 9am-3:30pm Nov.-Feb.; €8

Immersed in nature, Villa San Michele was the home of noted Swiss doctor and writer Axel Munthe (1857-1949). In his will, he bequeathed the estate to the Swiss government to welcome and promote ties between Switzerland and Italy and to inspire Italian artists, writers, and researchers. Munthe is largely known today for his autobiographical work *The Story of San Michele,* first published in 1929. Admission includes a visit to

SELF-BOATING TOUR

- Head out from Marina Piccola west toward the **Grotta Verde** (Green Grotto), where you can stop for a swim.
- Continue along the coastline to the westernmost tip of the island at **Punta Carena,** which is marked by a pink and white lighthouse.
- Cruise along the rugged western coastline of the island past old **watchtowers** and **forts** perched at the edge of the cliffs.
- On the northwestern side of the island you'll find the famous **Grotta Azzurra** (Blue Grotto). Stop for a visit inside to see the light shimmering across the electric blue water. Here, you'll have to pay an entrance fee and transfer aboard a rowboat to be taken inside the grotto.
- Enjoy the views of Marina Grande while continuing east past the port. Look up high to catch a glimpse of the **Villa Lysis,** and around the northeast corner of the island the setting of the ruins of Villa Jovis.
- Cruising along the eastern coastline, stop to see the **Grotta Bianca** (White Grotto). From your boat perch, you're getting the best view of it.
- Not far from the White Grotto, keep gazing up to the mountain to look for the **Arco Naturale,** a large natural arch located high above the sea. This is a beautiful area to drop anchor for a swim, with soaring cliffs of unspoiled natural beauty and incredible turquoise water.
- Soon you'll see the striking red **Villa Malaparte,** a modern villa nestled right on top of the Punta Massullo promontory.
- Just beyond the villa, stop to look closely at the **Grotta Rossa** (Red Grotto), also called the Grotta del Corallo. If your boat is small enough, get a close look at the coral.
- End the day with a spectacular cruise right through the hole in the middle **Faraglioni** rock before returning to Marina Piccola.

his home, which has been transformed into a museum, and the chance to explore the gorgeous garden dotted with statues. Stroll along the pergola-covered walkway to the very end to find a loggia with an Egyptian sphinx and you will enjoy an extraordinary view overlooking Marina Grande below and the Gulf of Naples. Nearby is a little chapel dedicated to San Michele. Above the villa rises Monte Barbarossa, where birds rest during spring and autumn migrations. In 1904, Munthe bought the entire mountain to protect the birds from local hunters, and in the garden you can visit a small building with information on migratory birds. Atop the Villa San Michele is a café with a serene outdoor terrace. The Villa San Michele also hosts concerts and cultural events during the summer season.

TOP EXPERIENCE

★ Monte Solaro

Chairlift: Via Caposcuro 10, Anacapri; tel. 081/837-1438; www.capriseggiovia.it; 9:30am-4pm Mar.-Apr., 9:30am-5pm May-Oct., 9:30am-3:30pm Nov.-Feb.; €11

At 1,932 feet (589 m), Monte Solaro is Capri's highest point and offers a splendid bird's-eye view overlooking the island. From here you'll also enjoy an excellent vantage point to take in the entire area from the Sorrentine Peninsula to Ischia, Procida, and Mount

Best Views on Capri

If there's one thing Capri has in abundance, it's beautiful views: the kind you never forget. The island's small size seems only to enhance the captivating views of the soaring mountains, sheer cliffs, and impossibly blue sea that changes from brilliant turquoise to electric blue. Whether you're looking for the best views in Capri town to explore on a day trip, fine dining with a view, or the most picturesque beach, here are the top spots on the island to savor Capri's views.

BEST CAPRI VIEWS

- **Giardini di Augusto:** Only a short stroll from the central Piazzetta, these gardens are easy to reach to enjoy a view of the Faraglioni rocks. The beautiful garden setting is an extra perk.
- **Villa Jovis:** If you have time for a longer walk, visit the ruins of Villa Jovis, set atop the island's second highest point. This location offers spectacular views over the island as well as toward the Sorrentine Peninsula and Gulf of Naples, and the villa will be especially interesting to history lovers.
- **Arco Naturale to Belvedere di Tragara Walk:** This walk in Capri town takes less time than it takes to reach Villa Jovis, but you'll enjoy views of exceptionally beautiful, unspoiled nature, including a large natural arch and overlook near the Faraglioni rocks.

BEST ANACAPRI VIEWS

- **Villa San Michele:** The gardens of this villa in Anacapri offer a scenic view overlooking Marina Grande and the Gulf of Naples. If time is limited, however, a similar view can be found from the end of Via Axel Munthe below the villa.
- **Monte Solaro:** Hands down, the finest view on Capri is from the island's highest point atop Monte Solaro. Hop on the chairlift for a scenic ride to the top to enjoy the 360-degree views over the island.
- **Belvedere della Migliera Walk:** This relatively easy and flat walk from the center of

Vesuvius, all located across the Gulf of Naples. Standing at the edge of the cliff, the yachts below seem so far away yet the turquoise sea so temptingly close. With the sound of the wind blowing through ragged pine trees, the sun-baked Mediterranean vegetation, and the call of seagulls in the air, this is one of Capri's most majestic spots and simply must be experienced.

Getting to the top of Monte Solaro is an experience in itself, thanks to the **Seggiovia Monte Solaro,** a chairlift that runs from Piazza Vittoria to the summit. Simply hop on one of the 156 single seats that run continuously and enjoy the 13-minute ride to the top. Along the way, you'll pass over a quiet residential area of Anacapri, and as the climb continues up the steep slope, everything drops away and you're surrounded by nature. On the way down, there's an excellent view from the chairlift across the gulf, especially on a clear day. Purchase only a one-way ticket for €8 if you would like to hike up or down, which takes about an hour.

★ Chiesa Monumentale di San Michele

Piazza San Nicola, Anacapri; tel. 081/837-2396; www.chiesa-san-michele.com; 9am-7pm Apr.-Sept., 10am-3pm Oct.-Mar.; €2

One of Anacapri's gems, this baroque church dedicated to San Michele Arcangelo was constructed from 1698 to 1719 and features a central floor plan with an octagonal shape and a large dome. The entire floor of the church is covered with marvelous hand-painted majolica tiles depicting Adam and Eve in the Garden of Eden. Created by master majolica

Anacapri leads to a panoramic overlook where you can enjoy gorgeous views of the southern side of the island from the Faraglioni to Punta Carena.

BEST SEA VIEWS

- **Boat Tour Around the Island:** Capri is perhaps even more breathtaking when seen from the sea. Choose from private or group tours, or rent a boat and cruise around on your own. However you go, you'll see grottoes up close and enjoy spotting Capri's mountain goats along the cliffs.
- **Marina Piccola:** Of Capri's beaches, one of the most enjoyable and beautiful is the island's Marina Piccola with its turquoise water and view of the Faraglioni in the distance.
- **Faraglioni Beach:** For an even closer look at the Faraglioni, head to this beach located right at the base of the three large rock formations. Here you'll find chic beach clubs like **La Fontelina,** where VIP Capri visitors from the mega yachts tend to go for seaside dining.

A TABLE WITH A VIEW

- **Capri Rooftop, Capri:** Perfect for a relaxed drink anytime of the day, this bar situated next to the Giardini di Augusto in Capri town has picture-perfect views of the Faraglioni.
- **Maliblu Sunset, Anacapri:** Located on Punta Carena at the westernmost tip of the island, this beach club offers a stunning setting, surrounded by the natural beauty of Capri, to enjoy drinks and live music during their summer sunset parties.
- **Il Geranio, Capri:** Tucked away in a peaceful spot above the Giardini di Augusto, this is a lovely place to dine with a view over the Faraglioni.
- **Il Riccio, Anacapri:** For fine seaside dining with equally nice views, head to this exclusive beach club, situated on the rocky coastline near the Grotta Azzurra.

artist Leonardo Chiaiese in 1761, the floor is a remarkable work of art and visitors are not allowed to walk on it. From a narrow platform along the edge, you can examine the garden scene with its 18th-century images of exotic animals and the serpent wrapped around the tree of life. Climb the spiral staircase to the upper level near the organ for an even better view looking down on the scene.

Casa Rossa

Via Giuseppe Orlandi 78, Anacapri; tel. 848/800-288; www.comunedianacapri.it/pagina89_casa-rossa.html; 10am-2pm and 5pm-8pm June-Sept., 10am-4pm Oct.-May, closed Mon. all year; €3.50

It's impossible to miss this eccentric house, with its distinctive red color, located on Via Giuseppe Orlandi not far from Piazza Vittoria. It's not only the red color that grabs attention, but also its eclectic architectural style. Built between 1876 and 1899 for American colonel John Clay MacKowen, the house is a treasure trove of architectural elements and is home to a museum featuring paintings of Capri from the 1800s to 1900s. MacKowen was keenly interested in archaeology; he was the first to recover Roman statues from the Grotta Azzurra, and four of these sculptures are on display in the Casa Rossa. Climb to the top level for a view overlooking Anacapri. Guided visits in English are offered throughout the day, starting on the hour. Choose a tour because explanatory information is not available.

Villa di Damecuta

Via Antonio Maiuri, Anacapri; tel. 081/838-7111 (Anacapri town hall); www.comunedianacapri.

it/pagina75_villa-damecuta.html; 10am-noon and 4pm-7pm Apr.-mid-Oct., 10am-1pm and 2:30pm-4:30pm mid-Oct.-Mar.; closed Mon. year-round; free

Set in a secluded area on the western edge of the island, the Villa di Damecuta is something of a mystery. All we know is that it was once a grand imperial Roman villa that was used by Augustus or Tiberius, or perhaps by both emperors. Only a few remnants of the buildings remain, as the sight was poorly preserved over the centuries. It even served as a military training ground at the beginning of the 19th century as the French and English battled over control of the island. Little is left of the ruins other than a general idea of the footprint of the imperial palace, outlined by the walls that are barely visible above ground level. Yet, you can make out a long path leading to a semicircular terrace situated to make the most of the views across the Gulf of Naples to Ischia and Procida in the distance.

Beaches

With gorgeous colors ranging from deep cobalt blue to shockingly bright turquoise, the sea around Capri just beckons for a swim. However, be prepared for higher prices compared to other towns in the area. For private beach clubs, there's usually a set price per person that includes a chair and access to a shower and changing rooms; there's often an additional cost to rent umbrellas. Given that the beaches are very rocky, it is generally worth the splurge for a comfortable beach experience.

MARINA GRANDE

Marina Grande, Capri

Just steps beyond the Marina Grande port to the west is a long, narrow stretch of beach that's a good spot if you only have time for a quick swim. **Le Ondine Beach Club** (Via Marina Grande; tel. 081/837-4014; www.dagemma.com; 9:30am-6pm daily mid Apr.-mid-Oct.; sunbed €15 and unbrella €7) offers sun bed and umbrella rentals along with changing rooms and showers. Or head to the westernmost side of the beach for a free area where you can just throw down a towel. The water is clear and pleasant for swimming, with the western side offering finer pebbles and gentler slope into the sea. It's a popular and busy beach with tourists, but you'll find the western side has a more local scene.

Small boats depart from the eastern side of the beach for the nearby **Bagni di Tiberio** (Via Palazzo a Mare 41; tel. 081/837-0703; www.bagnitiberio.com; May 1-Sept. 30; from €12 per person), a beach club located west of Marina Grande. With incredible water and set in an area rich with Roman history, Bagni di Tiberio offers a more secluded beach experience compared to Marina Grande. The beach can also be reached on foot after a 25-minute walk from Marina Grande; follow Via Marina Grande to Via Palazzo a Mare and continue along to reach the beach.

FARAGLIONI

Punta Tragara, Capri

One of Capri's most dramatic and exclusive beach experiences is right at the foot of the Faraglioni rocks. Two notable beach clubs are located on the rocky stretch connecting the island with the first Faraglioni. The beach clubs are nestled right into the rocks with platforms and ladders for sea access. **Da Luigi ai Faraglioni** (Via Faraglioni 5; tel. 081/837-0591; www.luigiaifaraglioni.com; late Apr.-Oct. 1; from €22 per person) is located right at the base of the Faraglioni, while just to the west with a spectacular view is **La Fontelina** (Località Faraglioni; tel. 081/837-0845; www.fontelina-capri.com; Apr. 21-Oct. 14; from €26 per person), a popular spot with VIP travelers. Both beach clubs have excellent restaurants where you can dine steps from the sea.

They are also popular spots, so a reservation is an excellent idea, especially June-August. The setting is rocky and beautiful, so expect to access the sea by ladders and steps. Yet once you're in the water it's exquisite for swimming.

To reach the Faraglioni beach clubs, follow the pathway from the **Belvedere di Punta Tragara** that leads down steeply about 984 feet (300 m) to sea level. The beach clubs also offer a pickup or drop-off boat shuttle service from Marina Piccola; the service is complimentary for Da Luigi ai Faraglioni clients and starts at €20 for up to four La Fontelina clients.

TOP EXPERIENCE

★ MARINA PICCOLA

On Capri's southern side between the Faraglioni to the east and the rugged coastline below Anacapri is the island's very charming Marina Piccola. It's a buzzing seaside spot during the summer months thanks to the beautiful, albeit rocky, beaches and restaurants that are popular with locals and tourists alike. The marina is split in two by the Scoglio delle Sirene, a small, rocky promontory that juts out into the bright turquoise sea, with swimming areas, beach clubs, and small, free beach areas on both sides.

Given the rugged setting, a sun bed is a good idea here, and you'll find plenty of options to rent one from the restaurants and *stabilimenti balneari* (beach clubs) along the little marina. Try **Bagni Internazionali** (Via Marina Piccola 95; tel. 081/837-0264; www.bagninternazionali.com; May-Oct. daily) for a sunny spot. Or head to **La Canzone del Mare** (Via Marina Piccola 93; tel. 081/837-0104; www.lacanzonedelmare.com; end of Apr.-Oct.1; entrance and sun bed €30) for elegant dining in the iconic hotel founded by English actress and singer Gracie Fields.

Beyond Marina Piccola, in a tiny cove, the water at the **Torre Saracena** beach is an impossibly bright shade of turquoise. It's a secluded spot with beach access available via the **Torre Saracena Beach Club** (Via Marina Piccola; tel. 081/837-0646; May-Oct. daily). They offer clients complimentary boat service from Marina Piccola to the Torre Saracena Beach Club. You can also walk there by taking Via Krupp off of Via Marina Piccola and following the signs to Spiaggia Torre Saracena.

Marina Piccola can be reached by bus or taxi from all the main points on the island. You can also enjoy a pleasant walk down from Capri town by following Via Roma from the Piazzetta to the roundabout where

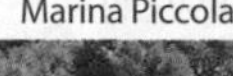

Marina Piccola

the road splits to go up to Anacapri or down to Marina Grande. Continue along Via Mulo, which leads through the quiet residential area of Marina Piccola. It's a more direct and enjoyable walk compared to following the zigzagging road connecting Marina Piccola and Capri town. The walk takes about 25 minutes from the Piazzetta and is largely downhill once you start along Via Mulo, so a bus is a good option for the return.

PUNTA CARENA

Str. Faro di Carena, Anacapri

The pink and white striped lighthouse that sits on the Punta Carena is one of the prettiest sights associated with Capri. This spot marks the southwesternmost point on the island and is surrounded by impressive craggy mountains. Easily spotted from the sea on a boat trip around the island, the **Lido del Faro** (Str. Faro di Carena; tel. 081/837-1798; www.lidofaro.com; 9:30am-sunset daily mid-Apr.-Oct.; entrance and sun bed €30) beach makes this a popular area for swimming in the summer months. This area is about as rugged as swimming gets on Capri, so be prepared for rocky entrances to the sea and a higher price tag in the peak of summer, due to the isolated and exclusive setting. From Anacapri, local buses on the Anacapri-Faro route run back and forth about every 30 minutes and provide a convenient way to reach the beach.

Sports and Recreation

With its remarkably varied landscape from rugged mountains to sea grottoes, Capri is a fun destination for active travelers.

WALKS

Exploring Capri on foot is one of the best ways not only to enjoy the island's natural beauty but also to get away from the crowds. You won't have to wander very far off the well-beaten path to find quiet spots, residential streets lined with beautiful villas, and incredible views. Here are two walks to enjoy while visiting Capri town and Anacapri.

★ ARCO NATURALE TO BELVEDERE DI TRAGARA WALK

Start in the Piazzetta, Capri

Explore Capri's quieter side on this enjoyable walk that leads from the busy Piazzetta through peaceful side streets to a large natural arch and scenic overlook above the Faraglioni rocks. This walk is a loop that starts in the center of town and returns to the Via Camerelle. Much of the walk doesn't involve too many steps, but there is a stretch that requires a good number. If stairs are an issue, consider either doing the first part leading to the Arco Naturale and then turning back, or starting on the Via Camerelle, walking to the Belvedere di Tragara, and returning without doing the entire loop. To walk the entire loop takes about two hours, depending on the number of times you stop to take photos, of course.

Start off in the Piazzetta opposite the **Chiesa di Santo Stefano** and look for an arched walkway and signs pointing to the Arco Naturale. The walk is well-marked as it leads through the narrow streets and begins to head east out of the center of town along Via Matermania; keep following signs along Via Arco Naturale. As you approach the natural arch, there's a series of terraces and steps you can follow down to enjoy various view points of the arch and the turquoise sea.

Walk back up the steps from the Arco Naturale and look for the signs nearby for the **Grotta di Matermania.** From there a steep staircase called Via del Pizzolungo leads down the forested mountainside past the Grotta di Matermania, a large cavern that the Romans once used as a luxurious nymphaeum (a monument dedicated to nymphs). Continue along Via del Pizzolungo, which becomes a more level and well maintained walkway hugging the cliffside. Along the way you'll pass above the **Villa Malaparte,** a striking red villa that stands out against the natural setting. This private home was created by Italian writer Curzio Malaparte and is an intriguing example of Italian modern architecture. With its intense red hue and clean lines, the building stands out vividly atop Punta Massullo with its steep cliffs dropping straight to the sea. The villa was donated to the Giorgio Ronchi Foundation in 1972 and is not open to the public for visits.

Not far beyond the Villa Malaparte, the captivating Faraglioni rocks come into view. The landscape along this section of the Via del Pizzolungo is rugged cliffs and untouched nature; the only sounds are birds singing and boats puttering by in the sea below. When you reach the **Belvedere di Tragara,** you'll find a shady spot with an incredible view overlooking the Faraglioni rocks. From here, continue along Via Tragara, which leads to Via Camerelle and takes you right back into the heart of Capri town.

BELVEDERE DELLA MIGLIERA WALK

Start at Piazza Vittoria, Anacapri

One of Capri's most peaceful and easy walks leads to a remarkable view at the **Belvedere della Migliera** (Via Migliera, Anacapri), where you can see all the way from the Faraglioni to the tip of the Punta Carena with its pink and white lighthouse. Starting in **Piazza Vittoria,** look for the chairlift to Monte Solaro. To the left of the chairlift, follow **Via Caposcuro** until it bends to the left and becomes **Via Migliera.** Continue along this road to the viewpoint at the very end. The relatively level walkway leads you through a rural landscape with terraces of grape vines, gardens, and a view in the distance across the Gulf of Naples to Ischia. The walk takes about 30 minutes each way.

HIKING

Capri is excellent for hiking because the island's small size and public transportation routes make hikes relatively accessible. If you're looking to explore the natural landscape of Capri away from the crowds, there are plenty of options that feel very much off the tourist path and take you along rugged dirt trails and beautiful cliffs, and offer spectacular views. There will be plenty of steps and altitude changes during hikes, so sturdy, comfortable walking shoes are recommended. Because much of the landscape is exposed to the strong Mediterranean sunshine, a hat, sunscreen, and plenty of water are also strongly recommended.

Trails are generally well marked with signs throughout the island, with the more rugged and rural hikes located in Anacapri. Along with the easier walk to the Belvedere della Migliera, popular hikes in Anacapri include hiking up and around the mountainside of **Monte Solaro** or following the **Sentiero dei Fortini** (Pathway of the Forts) that leads along the western coast of Capri from Punta Carena in the southwest to the Grotta Azzurra in the northwest. The Scala Fenicia (Phoenician Steps) leading from Anacapri to Marina Grande is also a popular hike for travelers who are not afraid to take 921 steps down an ancient staircase that was once the only path connecting the port to Anacapri.

HIKING TO MONTE SOLARO

Piazza Vittoria, Anacapri

While the chairlift to the top of Monte Solaro is a fun and easy way to reach Capri's highest point, the hike up the mountain to reach the summit is an equally beautiful experience. From Anacapri's central Piazza Vittoria, head down Via Capodimonte and after a few minutes' walk, look for signs indicating Monte Solaro and a staircase leading up on the right. Follow Via Monte Solaro as it climbs up the mountainside; you'll traverse stone steps as well as concrete and dirt pathways. It's a steep walk that takes about an hour. At the top of the climb, you'll be rewarded with spectacular 360-degree views over the island. Enjoy a well-deserved rest

1
2
3

before returning back down, or hop on the chairlift for the ride back to Piazza Vittoria.

CAPRI TRAILS

tel. 347/368-1699; www.capritrails.com; year-round; starting at €140 for 3-hour private hike

Experience Capri's most beautiful hikes with Luigi Esposito, a local Capri hiking guide, who is passionate about sharing the island's natural treasures and scenic spots. Luigi can organize private guided hikes around Capri based on your experience and time allowance, from shorter three-hour hikes to full-day (6-8 hours) hikes. Contact him in advance to find out which of Capri's hikes is the best one for your time on the island.

BOAT TOURS AND RENTALS

Seeing Capri from the water is one of the best ways to enjoy the island's natural beauty up close. There are a number of different options readily available, from group boat tours that depart regularly from Marina Grande to private boat excursions. Marina Grande offers the most options for last-minute booking of group tours, which can be purchased right before boarding. If you're traveling during the summer season, especially in July and August, it's a good idea to book a private boat excursion in advance.

★ LASER CAPRI

Via Cristoforo Colombo 69, Marina Grande; tel. 081/837-5208; www.lasercapri.com; 9am-5pm daily; from €15-18 per person

For an easy and affordable way to see Capri by sea and visit the Grotta Azzurra (Blue Grotto), check out the offerings from Laser Capri right in Marina Grande. This provider offers a variety of group boat tour options. The classic boat tour highlights the most popular grottoes and cruises through the Faraglioni rocks. If you would like to visit the Grotta Azzurra, take an island tour that includes a visit (admission to Blue Grotto paid separately). The boats are medium-sized and can be spotted easily as they're marked "Grotta Azzurra." Tours depart about every 30 minutes 9am-4pm from Pier 23 in Marina Grande with the ticket office just opposite the pier.

CAPRI BLUE BOATS

Via Mulo 72, Marina Piccola; tel. 339/619-2151; www.capriblueboats.com; Apr.-Oct.; starting at €80

Located in Marina Piccola, which is more tranquil than busy Marina Grande, Capri Blue Boats offers smaller self-drive boats that can be rented without a license, as well as private boat excursions with captains. For both options, Capri Blue Boats uses wooden boats that are very traditional in the area. Self-drive rentals can be 2-7 hours, and excursions with a captain range from a 2.5-hour tour of the island all the way up to full-day excursions or sunset cruises.

CAPRI EXCURSIONS

Marina Grande; tel. 366/317-0573; www.capriexcursions.com; Apr.-Oct.; from €150

Local captain Vittorio De Martino offers a variety of private boat excursions around the island aboard a comfortable Sorrento-style wooden boat. Tour guests meet in Marina Grande, and excursions can be customized or themed to include activities such as snorkeling, fishing, or photography experiences.

COOKING CLASSES

★ RISTORANTE MICHEL'ANGELO

Via Sella Orta 10; tel. 081/837-7220; www.caprimichelangelo.com; 9:30am or 4pm Thurs.-Tues.; Apr.-mid-Nov.; from €125 per person

Take a break from swimming and hiking to delve deeper into Capri's culinary traditions with a cooking class led by Capri local Gianluca D'Esposito and his Australian-born wife, Holly Star. Learn hands-on how to make *Caprese* (Capri-style) recipes passed down through Gianluca's family for generations, so you can enjoy a taste of Capri even

1: path atop Monte Solaro **2:** The chairlift to Monte Solaro is fun and offers stunning views. **3:** view of the Faraglioni rocks from the top of Mount Solaro

after you've gone home. Both private and small group classes are available, and you can choose from a variety of master classes, including a popular Lemon Twist class. Classes are offered in the morning or afternoon and are followed by lunch or dinner. Advance booking is required.

Ristorante Michel'angelo also offers delicious picnics that are perfect for hikes in the area around Capri town. Menus highlight local specialties and Ristorante Michel'angelo provides everything you need, including suggestions for the best local spots to enjoy your picnic.

Entertainment and Events

Whether you're relaxing with a prosecco in a rooftop bar or watching a religious procession weaving through the narrow streets of the island, you'll find that Capri's beauty is a stunning backdrop to some of the island's most memorable moments. If you enjoy the nightlife scene, stay in Capri town where you'll find the island's hottest nightclubs.

NIGHTLIFE

Capri town is the center of the island's chic nightlife scene and offers a variety of lively spots to sip cocktails or dance until the early hours of the morning.

Capri

TAVERNA ANEMA E CORE

Via Sella Orta 1, Capri; tel. 081/837-6461; www.anemaecore.com; 10:30pm-3am Thurs.-Sun. Apr.-Jun., 10:30pm-3am Thurs.-Tues. Jul.-Oct.; entrance starts at €40 per person

A Capri nightlife institution in the best possible way, Guido Lembo is the heart and soul of Taverna Anema e Core. Born and raised on Capri, Guido has a passion for music and an engaging style of performing that brings the audience into the experience and has made his nightclub one of the most famous in the world. This is the spot where you might catch sight of international movie stars, musicians, athletes, and VIP visitors to Capri. This is a truly unique Capri hot spot that stands apart from other clubs. Entrance is €40 per person, but for a table prices start at €100. Reservations for tables are highly recommended Jul.-Aug.

CAPRI ROOFTOP

Via Matteotti 7, Capri; 081/837-8147; www.caprirooftop.com; 10am-2am daily mid-May-mid-Sept., and 9am-midnight mid-Apr.-mid-May and mid-Sept.-Nov., closed Dec.-mid-Apr.; €18

If your idea of evening entertainment is a cocktail and gorgeous view, head to Capri Rooftop. Set above the Hotel Luna next to the Giardini di Augusto, this rooftop bar affords spectacular views of the Faraglioni in the distance. Choose from a tempting selection of classic cocktails and signature creations like the *Luna Caprese* made with *limoncello*, vodka, citrus, and soda.

VV CLUB CAPRI

Via Vittorio Emanuele 45, Capri; tel. 329/064-4576; www.vvclubcapri.com; 10:30pm-5am daily June-Sept, 10:30pm-5am Fri.-Sun. Apr.-May and Oct.; from €20

On Capri's stylish Via Vittoria Emanuele shopping street, just moments from the Piazzetta, VV is a fashionable nightclub that attracts an international crowd. The scene gets started around midnight and goes late into the night. The cover charge starts at €20 and includes a drink, but can go higher for some events. Tables can be booked without a cover charge. Reservations are a good idea, especially during the weekends in July and August.

QUISI BAR

Via Camerelle 2, Capri; tel. 081/837-0788; www.quisisana.com; 10am-2am daily Apr.-Oct.; €8-26

As a bastion of style on Capri, the Grand Hotel Quisisana's outdoor bar, set on chic Via

Camerelle, is one of the island's iconic places to see and be seen. It's an elegant yet relaxed setting to watch the glamorous crowds pass by, especially in the evenings with live piano music 6pm-2am.

Anacapri

MALIBLU SUNSET

Faro Punta Carena, Anacapri, 80071; tel. 081/837-2560; www.maliblusunset.com; 11am-sunset daily Apr.-Oct.; €10-12

With a gorgeous setting on Punta Carena at the southwest tip of Capri, this beach club is popular for sunbathers during the day, and the fun kicks up a notch as the sun begins to set. Summer events include sunset parties with DJs and live music.

FESTIVALS AND EVENTS

Capri has a vibrant cultural scene with festivals and concerts throughout the summer season. In addition, the Villa San Michele in Anacapri and the Centro Caprense Ignazio Cerio and Villa Lysis in Capri host concert programs and events throughout the season.

ROLEX CAPRI SAILING WEEK

Capri; www.rolexcaprisailingweek.com; info@rolexcaprisailingweek.com; early May

For a week every year in May, Capri is a top sailing hub of the Mediterranean. The Rolex Capri Sailing Week includes a variety of races and the celebrated sailing Regata dei Tre Golfi that starts dramatically at midnight in Naples and ends in Capri. Activity centers around Marina Grande, but a good viewpoint from high on the island is the panoramic terrace below the bell tower in the Piazzetta with views over the Gulf of Naples.

FESTA DI SAN COSTANZO

Piazzetta and Marina Grande, Capri; May 14

Celebrations for Capri's patron San Costanzo take place May 14 and include a grand procession that starts from the Chiesa di Santo Stefano in the Piazzetta and leads down to the Chiesa di San Costanzo along the road to Marina Grande. The heart of the procession is a large and very precious silver reliquary of the saint dating from 1715. Carried on a flower-covered platform and accompanied by music and the town's faithful, the statue is kept in the Chiesa di San Costanzo for a week before being returned to the Chiesa di Santo Stefano with another procession.

FESTA DI SANT'ANTONIO

Chiesa di Santa Sofia, Anacapri; June 13

Anacapri honors Sant'Antonio every year on June 13 with a colorful summer festival. Every neighborhood along the procession route is adorned with elaborate altars and designs created with flower petals on the ground. Balconies are draped with flowers and brightly colored blankets, and onlookers shower the statue of the saint with flowers as the procession passes. The procession begins at the Chiesa di Santa Sofia in Anacapri and leads through the streets of town before returning to the church.

SETTEMBRATA ANACAPRESE

Anacapri; www.comunedianacapri.it; starts last Sun. in Aug.

Beginning the last Sunday of August and lasting several days, this festival celebrates Anacapri's culture and cuisine with parades, music, local crafts, and, of course, good food. Each year the festival has a special theme, and the four areas of Anacapri compete to make the best floats and costumes for the parade.

Shopping

Famous around the world for fashion, Capri truly is a dream for shoppers, whether you're picking out a perfume made with flowers on the island, enjoying the iconic Capri experience of having sandals custom made, or splurging at a big-name designer boutique. Even if you're not big on shopping, it's still quite fun window shopping while strolling through Capri town or Anacapri.

CAPRI

Capri town is known for fine shopping, and you'll see why as soon as you arrive. The main shopping spots include the areas immediately surrounding the Piazzetta, **Via Vittorio Emanuele** and elegant **Via Camerelle**. This is where you'll find boutiques from top Italian and worldwide fashion designers, including Dolce & Gabbana, Salvatore Ferragamo, Valentino, Dior, Chanel, and more. Because those powerhouse brands speak for themselves, the selection of shopping spots below are more unique stores that represent Capri's artistic heritage, traditions, and style. Many are also smaller spots you might miss if you don't know where to look.

Perfume

★ CARTHUSIA

Viale Matteotti 2d, Capri; tel. 081/837-5393; www.carthusia.it; 9am-8pm daily Apr.-Sept., 9am-4:30pm Oct.-Mar.

The air in Capri seems extra sweet, especially when you walk by one of the many Carthusia shops on the island. Legend has it that the first Carthusia perfume dates back to 1380 when a prior of the Carthusian monastery, Certosa di San Giacomo, noticed that the water from a special floral bouquet made for a visit by Queen Giovanna d'Angiò had been infused with a captivating scent.

Carthusia produces perfumes, soaps, lotions, and home products inspired by the flowers of Capri, and here you'll find distinctive souvenirs that reflect the island's history and capture its natural scents so you can take them home. Craftsmanship is this provider's top priority, and every step of the production is done by hand and with great care. Each scent is inspired by the island's native plants, featuring the sweet fragrances of geranium and lily of the valley, the woody scent of cedarwood, and the fresh smell of citrus blossoms. You can watch fragrances being produced here, in Carthusia's factory and main store.

You'll also find stores in **Marina Grande** (Via Marina Grande), **Anacapri** (Viale Axel Munthe 26), at **Via Camerelle 10** in Capri, **Sorrento** (Corso Italia 117), and **Positano** (Via della Tartana).

Sandals

CANFORA

Via Camerelle 3; tel. 081/837-0487; www.canfora.com; 9:30am-11pm Apr.-Oct., 10:30am-5pm Nov.-Mar.

One of Capri's historic sandal boutiques, Canfora tells the story of how handmade sandals became synonymous with the jet-set life on Capri. In 1946, Amedeo Canfora decided to open a sandal shop across from the elegant Grand Hotel Quisisana. It was a small storefront with soles of shoes and decorative strips of leather lining the walls, and a workbench to create the shoes. The measurements of regular clients were kept in special books. Before long, word spread about the exquisite sandals created by Amedeo Canfora and famous clients, including Princess Margaret, Grace Kelly, Maria Callas, and Jackie Kennedy, came to have custom-fitted sandals made.

The Canfora boutique has always been a cornerstone for tradition, quality, and

---

1: Eco Capri **2:** Taverna Anema e Core **3:** Carthusia **4:** Canfora sandal boutique on Via Camerelle

ECOCAPRI
Eco Capri
1
2
AVERNA
ANEMA
E
CORE
Carthusia
3
4
CANFORA
CANFORA
50%

creativity. Whether you're looking for something classic or glam, you'll find it here. Amedeo Canfora passed his skills down to his children, and then to his grandsons Fabrizio and Costanzo, who now can be found making sandals and running the shop in Capri. For a unique piece of Capri history you can wear and enjoy, have a pair of sandals custom made to fit while you wait.

DA COSTANZO

Via Roma 49, Capri; tel. 081/837-8077; caprimania@supereva.it; 9am-8:30pm daily Mar.-Nov.

A classic spot for handmade sandals since 1963, this little boutique is not far from the Piazzetta. Inside, there's a huge selection of beautiful sandals in a tiny space where you can choose just the style you want and enjoy watching them be made right before your eyes.

Clothing and Accessories

★ ECO CAPRI

Piazetta Ignazio Cerio 11, Capri; tel. 081/837-4510; www.ecocapri.com; 10am-8pm daily Apr.-Oct., closed Nov.-Mar.

Tucked away through a tiny passageway just off the Piazzetta, this remarkable boutique captures the style and beauty of Capri with custom clothing, accessories, and home decor inspired by the incredibly creative Cerio family. Fernando Cerio, the grandson of artist Letizia Cerio, has created a shop that is imbued with the spirit of Capri. Look for the stunning scarves, clothing, and decorative pieces made with Letizia's prints and designs inspired by Capri.

GRAZIA E MARICA VOZZA

Via Fuorlovado 38, Capri; tel. 081/837-4010; www.graziaemaricavozza.com; 10am-9pm Apr.-Oct.

Twins Grazia and Marica opened their first studio and boutique in Capri in 1999, and their striking and creative jewelry designs evoke the allure of Capri. The offerings here are truly pieces of wearable art.

Y'AM

Via Madonna delle Grazie 7, Capri; tel. 081/837-5510; www.yamcapri.it; 10:30am-8:30pm daily Apr. and Sept.-Oct., 10:30am-10pm daily May and Jun.-Aug., closed Nov.-Mar.

Capri-born designer Valeria De Gregorio launched this label in 2016 and created a clothing line inspired by Capri's fashion history and local style. The dresses and kaftans are uniquely Capri with their colors and simple elegance, and the T-shirts with fun Neapolitan sayings make great souvenirs.

ERSILIA BOUTIQUE

Via Vittorio Emanuele 53, Capri; tel. 081/837-7127; www.ersiliacapri.com; 10am-10pm daily Apr.-Oct.

This is the spot to head for iconic Capri linen in a tempting array of Mediterranean blues and classic crisp white. There are plenty of styles to choose from, from tailored shirts to light summery dresses. The quality is top-notch and the linen wears beautifully.

LABORATORIO CAPRI

Via Ignazio Cerio 6, Capri; tel. 081/837-6296; www.laboratoriocapri.it; 10am-10pm daily Apr.-Oct.

Stroll down this quiet street a bit off the beaten path to find this treasure trove of Capri fashion and design. From classic to whimsical, you'll find an appealing selection of locally made clothing, bags, and accessories that recall the elegance of Capri in the 1950s and '60s.

ANACAPRI

Though you won't find as many high-fashion designer names in Anacapri as there are in Capri town, Anacapri is a lovely area for shopping with many wonderful small boutiques, local artisans, and a quieter pace. The best shopping area centers around the busy **Piazza Vittoria, Via Giuseppe Orlandi,** and **Via Capodimonte.** You'll find shops selling ceramics, linen clothing, sandals, and jewelry. These streets are also home to the top sights in town, which means you can enjoy a bit of shopping while strolling to the

Chiesa di Monumentale di San Michele or Villa San Michele.

CERAMICHE TAVASSI

Via Giuseppe Orlandi 129, Anacapri; tel. 081/838-2067; ceramichetavassi@virgilio.it; 9am-9pm daily Apr.-Dec.

This shop is as bright and beautiful as the ceramics on display, featuring traditional design elements like decorative tiles, coral, lemons, and fish, with a creative touch. Walk to the back of the shop to see new designs being hand-painted in the little studio right in the shop.

NINO & FRIENDS

Via Axel Munthe 16, Anacapri; tel. 081/837-3967; www.ninoandfriends.it; 10am-4pm daily Apr.-Oct.

The delicious scent from this large shop will lure you in as you walk along the tree-lined Via Axel Munthe. Selling chocolates, *limoncello*, coffee, and candies, the owners share a firm belief that you must sample their products to savor the flavors; this truly is a sweet stop. You'll find Capri-inspired perfumes and elegant sandals as well.

SALVATORE FEDERICO

Via Capodimonte 58, Anacapri; tel. 081/837-3061; fabio@capri.it; 10am-7pm daily Apr.-Oct.

An Anacapri native with a grand passion for painting and music, Salvatore Federico has been capturing the ever-changing beauty of the island in his paintings and drawings since he was seven years old. Along the walkway to Villa San Michele, you'll find his gallery full of captivating pieces, from large oil paintings down to delicate watercolors and charcoal sketches. Whatever your budget or space allows, you'll find a unique view of Capri by Salvatore to help you remember your visit.

MARIORITA CONCEPT STORE

Via Capodimonte 2, Anacapri; tel. 081/978-0540; www.mythahotels.com; 9am-8pm daily Feb.-Dec.

Sitting at the top of Piazza Vittoria, this large concept store is an icon when it comes to high-end shopping in Anacapri. Connected to the stylish Capri Palace hotel next door, the shop offers a well curated selection of designer labels, as well as the custom Capritouch collection with pieces inspired by the island's colors and a relaxed yet chic style.

Food

MARINA GRANDE

Seafood

RISTORANTE DA GEMMA

Via Cristoforo Colombo, Capri; tel. 081/837-4014; www.dagemma.com; 9:30am-6pm daily (with lunch served noon-3:30pm) mid-Apr.-mid-Oct., 8pm-11pm Fri.-Sun. Jul.-Aug.; €15-30

Located just beyond the harbor at Marina Grande, this restaurant has a seafront terrace along with a lounge bar and **Le Ondine** beach club. Family run for more than 80 years, this iconic Capri restaurant moved to its current location in 2017. With its setting overlooking the sea, the natural choice here is seafood. Each dish is as beautiful as it is delicious, with the focus on freshness and tradition. From an appetizer with raw tuna, watermelon, and mint to the pasta with zucchini flowers, you'll find new and interesting flavors to tempt your palate.

Regional Cuisine

DA PAOLINO

Via Palazzo a Mare 11, Capri; tel. 081/837-6102; www.paolinocapri.com; 7pm-11:30pm daily late Apr.-late Oct. (open also for lunch 12:30pm-2:15pm Apr.-May only); €22-50

One of Capri's most romantic spots, this restaurant has an enchanting dining terrace nestled into a lemon grove. The menu is varied but very traditional, and includes beautiful pasta dishes, as well as meat and fish main courses. The fresh pasta or ravioli with lemon sauce is a classic choice while dining under the lemon trees. Sautéed mussels and clams are divine, and the catch of the day is grilled to perfection. Booking in advance is necessary to secure a table.

Cafés

BAR IL GABBIANO

Via Cristoforo Colombo 76, Capri; tel. 081/837-6531; bargabbiano@gmail.com; 7am-8pm daily Mar.-Nov.; €3-10

Whether you need a strong espresso after getting off the ferry or a *spritz* and a rest at the end of a day of sightseeing before leaving Capri, this friendly family-run bar along the harbor is a good choice. This spot is great for drinks and pastries, just steps from where the ferries arrive and depart.

CAPRI

Seafood

PESCHERIA LE BOTTEGHE

Via le Botteghe 19, Capri; tel. 081/837-6942; www.pescherialebotteghe.it; 1pm-3pm and 7pm-11pm daily Apr.-Oct.; €5-20

Tucked away on a narrow street very near the Piazzetta, this local fish shop transforms into an excellent seafood diner for lunch and dinner with casual, bar-style seating. You'll enjoy only the freshest fish, oysters, *crudo di pesce* (raw seafood), and outstanding fried calamari and *alici* (anchovies).

Regional Cuisine

★ RISTORANTE MICHEL'ANGELO

Via Sella Orta 10, Capri; tel. 081/837-7220; www.caprimichelangelo.com; 11:30am-3pm and 6:30pm-midnight Thurs.-Tues. Apr.-mid-Nov.; €18-35

For authentic *Caprese* cooking and a setting that will make you feel like family, head to this restaurant in the heart of Capri town, tucked away on a peaceful side street. Owners Gianluca D'Esposito and his Australian wife, Holly Star, met and fell in love in the restaurant in 2013, and they put their passion into their food. The flavors of traditional Capri dishes come through because ingredients are carefully and locally sourced, and the pasta is made fresh daily. You'll want to visit more than once to try everything on the menu, from the tempting Mozzarella Bar and wood-fire oven pizzas to beautifully prepared pasta dishes like the *linguine al limone "Marina Piccola,"* lemon linguine pasta with fresh seafood. The wine list is exclusively Italian and very carefully selected by Gianluca. During the summer, enjoy live piano bar music starting at 7:30pm by local Capri musician Bruno Lembo. You can even learn how to re-create some of the couple's family recipes with a **cooking class** by Gianluca and Holly (starting at €125 per person).

IL GERANIO

Viale Giacomo Matteotti 8, Capri; tel. 081/837-0616; www.geraniocapri.com; 12pm-3pm and 7pm-11pm daily Apr.-Oct.; €14-30

Situated above the Giardini di Augusto, with the same gorgeous view overlooking the Faraglioni, this is one of Capri's most romantic dining spots. Whether you're looking for lunch with a view or a peaceful candlelit dinner under the pine trees, this is a great choice. Try the *pappardelle* (thick noodles) with fresh prawns followed by the grilled seafood platter. There's an excellent wine selection, and great desserts to finish off a delicious meal in an unforgettable setting.

VILLA VERDE

Via Sella Orta 6, Capri; tel. 081/837-7024; www.villaverde-capri.com; noon-3pm and 7pm-11pm daily Apr.-Oct.; €16-30

Located just off Via Vittorio Emanuele, not far from the Piazzetta, this restaurant is a convenient choice in the center of town. The dining garden terrace is an elegant spot for lunch or dinner. The menu offers a gourmet take on traditional dishes, including a delicious *burrata* (rich, creamy cheese) appetizer, as well as pizza cooked in a traditional wood-fire oven.

Pizzeria

LO SFIZIO

Via Tiberio 7/e, Capri; tel. 081/837-4128; www.losfiziocapri.com; noon-3pm and 7pm-midnight Wed.-Mon., closed Tues.; Apr.-Nov.; pizzas from €6-15 and pasta dishes from €10-19

This casual dining spot is located halfway between the Piazzetta and Villa Jovis. With both indoor and outdoor dining options, this pizzeria offers fresh pasta, and meat and fish options, as well as delicious pizza from the wood-fire oven. Popular with locals, this is a great and affordable option, away from the crowds, as long as you don't mind the 15-minute walk from the town center.

Gelateria

GELATERIA BUONOCORE

Via Vittorio Emanuele 35, Capri; tel. 081/837-7826; buonocore.capri@libero.it; 8am-11pm daily Apr.-Oct.; €3-6

Stroll down Via Vittorio Emanuele from the Piazzetta to Via Camerelle, and the divine scent of this gelateria and bakery will stop you in your tracks. It's a popular spot offering excellent quality. There's a selection of gelato you can buy at the window right off the street, but go inside to find baked goods like their *caprilù* (lemon and almond cookies).

ANACAPRI

Seafood

IL RICCIO

Via Gradola 4, Anacapri; tel. 081-837-1380; www.capripalace.com; 12:30pm-3:30pm daily, 7:30pm-11pm Thurs.-Sun.; May-Oct.; €30-60

Capri's most exclusive seaside dining address is the Il Riccio beach club on the rugged northwest tip of the island near the famed Blue Grotto. Part of the elegant **Capri Palace,** this is no ordinary beach club. Boasting a Michelin star, this is the spot for fine dining, especially seafood, overlooking the sea. Start with their divine *plateau royal* with assorted raw fish, and the curious should try the spaghetti with sea urchins: a local specialty. Just save room for dessert and a visit to the Temptation Room full of traditional Neapolitan and *Caprese* desserts.

Regional Cuisine

★ DA GELSOMINA

Via Migliara 72, Anacapri; tel. 081/837-1499; www.dagelsomina.com; 12:30pm-3:30pm and 7pm-11pm mid-Apr.-mid-Oct., closed Nov. 15-Mar. 31; €12-26

Escape from the crowds at this restaurant near the beautiful Belvedere Migliera overlook, which is a pleasant walk from the center of Anacapri. (The restaurant also offers a

Gelateria Buonocore

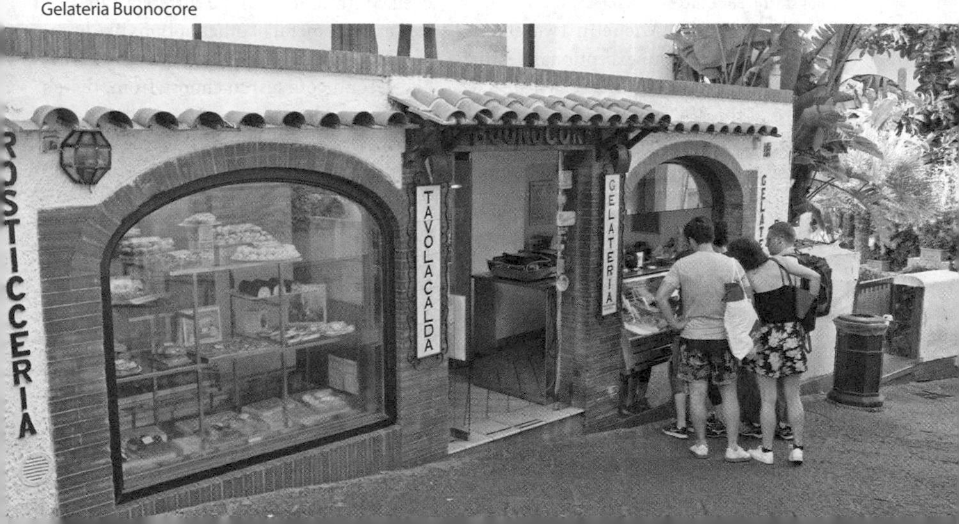

complimentary shuttle service from the center of town if you call ahead.) This family-run restaurant has a welcoming atmosphere and serves up local favorites like ravioli filled with *caciotta* cheese, as well as traditional chicken and rabbit dishes. If you're looking for a quiet escape, the restaurant also has a small B&B (rooms from €180) and a large pool nearby.

RISTORANTE GIORGIO AL CUCCIOLO

Via La Fabbrica 52, Anacapri; tel. 081/837-1917; www.cucciolocapri.com; 12pm-3:30pm and 7pm-midnight daily Apr.-Oct.; €15-30

Traditional *Caprese* dishes are the heart of this family-run restaurant with a remarkable view overlooking the Gulf of Naples. Located along the road to the Grotta Azzurra (Blue Grotto) and surrounded by a peaceful natural setting, this eatery celebrates local fare that exudes simplicity and freshness. There's excellent seafood as well as other options if you're looking for a break from fish. With reservation, a shuttle service is available from the center of Anacapri.

L'OLIVO

Via Capodimonte 14, Anacapri, 80071; tel. 081/978-0560; www.capripalace.com; 7:30pm-10:30pm; May-Oct.; €50-60 or tasting menus starting at €140 per person

The Capri Palace's Michelin two-starred L'Olivo restaurant is an exceptional destination for fine dining on the island. The relaxed elegance of the dining room, with a view of the sea in the distance is the perfect setting to enjoy the creative interpretations of regional dishes by executive chef Andrea Migliaccio and chef Salvatore Elefante. Specialties include a delicate lemon-scented homemade pasta with creamy *burrata* cheese, red prawns, and sea asparagus, or choose the Gourmet Menu to sample top choices from the chefs. Reservations are highly recommended.

LA ZAGARA

Via Giuseppe Orlandi 180, Anacapri; tel. 081/837-2923; www.casamariantonia.com; 12:30pm-3pm and 7pm-midnight daily end of Mar.-early Nov.; €12-25

Located at the serene Casa Mariantonia right in the center of Anacapri, this lovely restaurant is set among the villa's lemon grove where citrus scents blend perfectly with the Mediterranean flavors and creations of chef Flavio Astarita. The menu options are well balanced between seafood specialties like pasta with octopus ragu or fresh grilled tuna and the excellent grilled beef tenderloin.

Pizzeria

PIZZERIA AUMM AUMM

Via Caprile 18, Anacapri; tel. 081/837-3926; www.pizzeriacapriaummaumm.it; 11:30am-3:30pm and 7pm-1am daily, closed Jan. 6-Mar. 30; €8-18

Head to this popular pizzeria for traditional Neapolitan-style pizza cooked in a wood-fire oven. With more than 30 different types, as well as a full menu of other options like burgers, salads, and Italian *primi* and *secondi* (first and second courses) to choose from, there's something for everyone. If you like sports, head here to join the locals cheering on a soccer match on the big-screen TV.

Accommodations

Although not a very large island, Capri has an abundance of accommodations. Yet, because it's one of the most popular destinations in the Campania region, it's not unusual for hotels to be fully booked for much of the season. It's always a good idea to book in advance for Capri, especially if you have a certain hotel or experience in mind. Capri isn't exactly cheap when it comes to accommodations, so that gives you even more reason to book an affordable room well in advance.

CAPRI

Capri town is very much the hub of activity on the island and is a good place to base your stay, especially if you enjoy the shopping scene, nightlife, and easy access to the beach at Marina Piccola.

Under €100

HOTEL 4 STAGIONE

Via Marina Piccola 1, Capri; tel. 081/837-0041; www.4-stagioni.hotelsinamalficoast.com; open year-round; €85 d

This small hotel is located right at the roundabout that is the hub for buses connecting to all parts of the island. You can hop on a bus, follow the scenic Via Mulo down to Marina Piccola, or walk about 10 minutes to the Piazzetta nearby. The 13 rooms range from double to quadruple occupancy, and many have sea views. For relaxation, the hotel also includes a sun terrace and garden.

€100-200

HOTEL LA TOSCA

Via Dalmazio Birago 5, Capri; tel. 081/837-0989; www.latoscahotel.com; open mid-Mar.-early Nov.; €165 d

Set in one of the loveliest areas of Capri, yet at a price point that's easy on the wallet, this small hotel has been created in a traditional home with a pretty setting, surrounded by gardens with views of the Certosa di San Giacomo monastery and the Faraglioni beyond. The 11 large rooms are peaceful and some even have little terraces with sea or garden views. Breakfast is served on the terrace with a view of the sea, or in your room for no extra charge. This is a top affordable option in the heart of Capri town.

★ HOTEL CANASTA

Via Campo di Teste 6, Capri; tel. 081/837-0561; www.hotelcanastacapri.it; closed Dec. 9-Feb. 28; €180 d

Set in a peaceful spot not far from the Certosa di San Giacomo monastery, this boutique hotel is a little Capri gem. Inside you'll find only 15 rooms, but all are nicely appointed and very welcoming. Standard rooms have a patio with internal view while Medium rooms offer a terrace with garden view. For a sea view, try to score one of the two superior double rooms with a terrace and sea view. There's also a top-notch restaurant, **Villa Margherita** (tel. 081/837-7532; www.ristorantevillamargheritacapri.com; noon-2:30pm and 7pm-12am daily Apr.-Oct.; €20-35), which serves a lovely raw seafood starter and their specialty Fettuccine Villa Margherita, lemon fettuccine with shrimp infused with lemon peels. Recently remodeled and offering a swimming pool with lovely outdoor lounge areas, this is a place you will love to call home on Capri.

Over €300

HOTEL DELLA PICCOLA MARINA

Via Mulo 14/16, Capri; tel. 081/837-9642; www.hdpm.it; open mid-Apr.-mid-Oct.; €310 d

Set along the walkway down to Marina Piccola yet not far from the Piazzetta, this four-star hotel offers 40 rooms decorated in muted tones and colorful accents. Superior rooms open to patios that lead to the pool, while Deluxe rooms offer private balconies with sea views. With a pool surrounded by sun beds, a small fitness center, Turkish bath, and massage room, the hotel offers a relaxing escape in Capri.

HOTEL LUNA

Viale Giacomo Matteotti 3, Capri; tel. 081/837-0433; www.lunahotel.com; closed Nov.-Apr.; €320 d

With a dream location tucked away between the Giardini di Augusto and the Certosa di San Giacomo, this hotel boasts stellar views of the Faraglioni as well as a large pool, gym with sea view, small spa, and beautifully landscaped grounds. The rooms are all classically furnished with Mediterranean accents. Rooms range from Standard to Deluxe, but here you'll want to go for one of the 20 Camera Deluxe or 4 Suites to have a private terrace with a view of the sea and Faraglioni. Dining well is right at your fingertips with two restaurants and two bars on-site, including the Capri Rooftop bar.

GRAND HOTEL QUISISANA

Via Camerelle 2, Capri; tel. 081/837-0788; www.quisisana.com; Mar.-Oct.; €450 d

The Grand Hotel Quisisana has been a bastion of style in the heart of Capri town since it opened in 1845. Exuding a timeless sense of elegance with a touch of old-world glamour, the hotel's rooms and suites are as stylish as every detail you'll find throughout the hotel's beautiful grounds, large pool, world-class spa, and dining experiences. Proudly owned by the Morgano family from Capri, the hotel is one of Capri's largest, yet every detail has a personal touch to make you feel at home.

LA SCALINATELLA

Via Tragara 8, Capri; tel. 081/837-0633; www.scalinatella.com; open Apr.-Oct.; €530 d

A picture of pure luxury and elegance, this small boutique hotel offers 20 rooms and villas overlooking Capri and the sea. Crisp white decor and hand-painted ceramic tile floors in striking patterns of white and blue perfectly complement the sea and sky view beyond. This property is ideal for romance or a honeymoon in a tranquil setting surrounded by nature and with plenty of spaces to relax, including two outdoor pools facing the sea. No children.

★ LA MINERVA

Via Marino Occhio 8, Capri; tel. 081/837-7067; www.laminervacapri.com; closed Nov.-early Mar.; €590 d

This boutique hotel captures all of Capri's chic charm and beautiful sea views in an intimate setting. Its 19 rooms offer a refreshing blend of contemporary decor and classic elements like colorful ceramic tiles, vaulted ceilings, and a pool set in a garden. Brothers Luigi, Antonino, and Marco are your hosts and the third generation to welcome guests in this former house, where their grandparents first opened the hotel in the early 20th century.

ANACAPRI

Anacapri's setting, higher on the island than Capri town, lends it a sense of calm that makes it a quieter spot for a holiday stay. You'll find secluded B&Bs, luxury five-star hotels, and everything in between in Anacapri.

€100-200

IL TRAMONTO B&B

Via Migliera 30/b, Anacapri; tel. 334/712-5862; www.iltramonto.it; open year-round; €120 d

Immersed in the natural landscape of Anacapri along the walk to Belvedere della Migliera, this welcoming B&B is aptly named with the Italian word for sunset because the views are extraordinary from the peaceful garden. The four lovely rooms all open to the sun terrace, which is well equipped with chairs, umbrellas, and comfortable places to lounge.

IL GIARDINO DELL' ARTE

Traversa la Vigna 32b, Anacapri; tel. 081/837-3025; www.giardinocapri.com; open Apr.-Oct.; €150 d

Enjoy a peaceful escape at this B&B with a luxurious and artistic air. The garden area includes plenty of space to relax as well as a small hydromassage pool and sun beds. The five rooms are decorated with beautiful local ceramics and a bright style, and each has a terrace with panoramic views. Enjoy fine sunset views across the Gulf of Naples toward Ischia. Complimentary pick up and drop off service from the Marina Grande port is offered to guests.

VILLA CESELLE

Via Monticello 1/D, Anacapri; tel. 081-838-2236; www.villaceselle.com; open Apr.-Nov.; €150 d

This boutique hotel is set in a garden in a residential area of Anacapri that has been a retreat for artists, writers, and travelers since the early 1900s. It includes 10 rooms, 2 suites, and an independent annex, along with a relaxing garden area and hot tub. Owned by the same family as Da Gelsomina, the hotel also offers a large pool with panoramic views near the Belvedere della Migliera. The walk to the pool is beautiful or there is also a transfer service available.

HOTEL AL MULINO

Via La Fabbrica 11, Anacapri; tel. 081/838-2084; www.mulino-capri.com; open Easter-Oct.; €160 d

Located in a former a farmhouse, this small hotel run by the grandchildren of the original owners has a beautiful setting surrounded by fruit trees, olive trees, and charming gardens. The nine rooms are bright and cheerfully decorated. All open onto private terraces surrounded by nature. The pool is perfect for a refreshing dip while relaxing on the sun terrace.

€200-300

★ CASA MARIANTONIA

Via Giuseppe Orlandi 180, Anacapri; tel. 081/837-2923; www.casamariantonia.com; open end of Mar.-early Nov.; €300 d

One of the prettiest spots on the island, this boutique hotel is set in a lemon grove and offers a peaceful escape right in the center of Anacapri. Named after the grandmother of the current hosts, the hotel has a welcoming family feel and the service is as warm and inviting as the nine rooms and relaxing pool. Dine under lemon trees at the hotel's restaurant **La Zagara** or enjoy an evening *aperitivo* at the well stocked Wine Bar.

Over €300

HOTEL CEASAR AUGUSTUS

Via Giuseppe Orlandi 4, Anacapri; tel. 081/837-3395; www.caesar-augustus.com; open mid-Apr.-Oct; €435 d

Perched on the edge of a cliff overlooking Marina Grande with the Sorrentine Peninsula and Gulf of Naples beyond, this remarkable property began as a private home two centuries ago. It later became an exclusive retreat for artists and intellectuals from around the world, and today it's a popular spot for travelers looking for a luxurious and calm oasis on Capri. The double infinity pool is a place of dreams, and just beyond is a 2-acre garden where the majority of produce used in the onsite restaurant is grown. There are 49 finely appointed rooms and 6 exclusive suites, each one more beautiful than the last. This is where you definitely want to splurge on a sea view.

CAPRI PALACE

Via Capodimonte 14, Anacapri; tel. 081/978-0111; www.capripalace.com; open mid-Apr.-late Oct.; €600 d

One of the exclusive Mytha Hotel Anthology properties, the Capri Palace is a haven of modern art and design right in the heart of Anacapri. Located at the top of Piazza Vittoria, the hotel is central but still feels hidden away. That secluded atmosphere flows through every gorgeous nook of the hotel's 49 immaculate rooms and 19 suites, the beautiful pool area, the world-class spa, and Michelin two-starred restaurant **L'Olivo.** For time by the sea, simply head to the hotel's Michelin-starred Il Riccio beach club.

MARINA GRANDE

Not far from the harbor and Marina Grande Beach, enjoy a secluded stay with convenient access to ferry service from the port if you're interested in exploring the surrounding area during your time on the island.

J. K. PLACE CAPRI

Via Marina Grande 225, Capri; tel. 081/838-3001; www.jkcapri.com; open mid-Apr.-late Oct.; €1,300 d

This historic hotel has hosted travelers since the late 1800s and is still one of the island's most stylish addresses. Perched in a scenic spot overlooking Marina Grande harbor, with steps leading down to the beach below, this property has the refined elegance of a luxury home and a sea view that will make your heart sing. The deluxe rooms are particularly tempting thanks to the crisp blue and white decor and the private balconies with sun beds. With a peaceful pool area, spa, gym, and restaurant, you'll have all you need for a relaxing stay.

Information and Services

TOURIST INFORMATION

AZIENDA AUTONOMA CURA SOGGIORNO E TURISMO ISOLA DI CAPRI

Piazza Umberto I, Capri; tel. 081/837-0686; www.capritourism.com; 8:30am-8:15pm Mon.-Sat., 9:30am-1:30pm and 2pm-5:15pm Sun. June-Sept., 8:30am-4:15pm Mon.-Fri. Nov.-May

Capri's tourist office has information points in the three main areas of the island. Upon arrival at Marina Grande, you'll find an info point at the western end of the port across from the ferry and bus ticket booths (tel. 081/837-0634). In Capri town, the info point is in an easy-to-spot location in the Piazzetta directly below the bell tower (tel. 081/837-0686). In Anacapri, the info point is not far from Piazza Vittoria at Via Giuseppe Orlandi 59 (tel. 081/837-1524).

HEALTH SERVICES

Should medical services be needed or an emergency arise, Capri's hospital, **Ospedale Capilupi** (Via Provinciale Anacapri 5, Capri; tel. 081/838-1227), is located at the roundabout intersection of the road to reach Capri town's center and the road up to Anacapri. In an emergency, head to the emergency room (*pronto soccorso*) or dial 118.

Transportation

Capri is reachable by boat year-round from Naples and Sorrento, and seasonally from other locations in the Gulf of Naples and Amalfi Coast. Capri is a small island with two towns that are easy to reach from the Marina Grande harbor where all boats arrive. Transportation options are readily available near where ferries dock, including taxis, buses, and the funicular train to Capri town.

GETTING THERE

By Boat

All ferries to Capri arrive at **Marina Grande,** which makes this small harbor a very busy spot as it's also the island's **Porto Turistico** (www.portoturisticodicapri.com). Cruise ships drop anchor off of Marina Grande and tender passengers in to the port. In the Gulf of Naples, there's a variety of ferry companies offering year-round, regular connections to Capri from Naples and Sorrento, and seasonally service from Ischia and Procida. Prices and speed vary depending on the type of ferry, with options ranging from faster jets and hydrofoils to slower ferries that also transport cars. The faster the boat the higher the price, but they all arrive in Marina Grande on Capri. All are comfortable options, and the departure port and time usually determine which company to use, as nearly all providers offer a variety of boats. Tickets from most companies can be purchased online in advance or at ticket booths at the departure port. For peak summer travel, buying tickets in advance is a good idea, if only to avoid long ticket queues.

If you're looking for speed, opt for a jet or *aliscafo* (hydrofoil) from **NLG** (tel.

081/552-0763; www.navlib.it; starting at €18 per person), **Gescab** (tel. 081/704-1911; www.gescab.it; starting at €18), **SNAV** (tel. 081/428-5555; www.snav.it; from €16.90), or **Alilauro** (tel. 081/497-2238; www.alilaurogruson.it; from €19.30 per person). If you're transporting a car, you'll need to book on a *traghetto* or *motonave* (ferries) operated by **Caremar** (tel. 081/189-66690; www.caremar.it; from €12.30 for passengers and €28.50 for vehicles), which offers faster options as well. Crossing to Capri takes about an hour from Naples and Ischia, and about 30 minutes from Sorrento. From the Amalfi Coast, ferries to Capri take just under 2 hours from Salerno, about an hour and 30 minutes from Amalfi, and a little under an hour from Positano.

While ferry service to Capri runs year-round from Naples and Sorrento, ferries from the Amalfi Coast only run from about Easter through early November. **Alicost** (tel. 081/837-0819, www.alicost.it, €19.80-21.30 per person) offers regular ferry service from Salerno, Cetara, Maiori, Minori, Amalfi, and Positano on the Amalfi Coast. From Salerno there are usually 1-3 ferry services in the morning, and the journey is a little over 2 hours. From Cetara, there is one ferry departure in the morning and it takes just under 2 hours to reach Capri. From Maiori and Minori there's usually only one departure in the morning for Capri and it takes about 1 hour 40 minutes from Maiori, and 1 hour 30 minutes from Minori. From Amalfi and Positano, there are 1-4 departures daily for Capri and the journey takes about 1 hour 20 minutes from Amalfi and 45 minutes from Positano. From Positano, **Lucibello** (tel. 089/811-164; www.lucibello.it; €18.50-21 per person) also offers a ferry service to Capri; it runs 3 times a day and takes 30 minutes.

Car Restrictions

Due to its small size and narrow roads, the island of Capri limits the number of cars on the island during the busiest times of the year. From March until the end of October and December 20-January 7, nonresidents are not permitted to bring a car to Capri. So if you're traveling around Italy by car, you'll need to leave your car in a garage in Naples or Sorrento before continuing on to Capri via ferry. If you're visiting outside of those dates, you will be able to bring your car on one of the larger ferries, usually called a *traghetto*. However, even off-season, navigating Capri by car isn't recommended as parking is extremely limited, and the island is quite small and fairly easy to navigate by public transportation.

GETTING AROUND

With plenty of transportation options and the island's small size, Capri is easy to navigate—in theory. The challenge comes when the island gets crowded, especially during peak summer season. Be prepared for lines, and allow extra time to get around on public transportation. The good news is that, although it can be busy, Capri is full of inexpensive ways to get around.

By Bus

Capri's public buses are pint-sized to match the island and connect all the main points on Capri, including Marina Grande, Capri town, Anacapri, Marina Piccola, Punta Carena, and the Grotta Azzurra. Buses are operated by **A.T.C.** (tel. 081/837-0420) and the cost is €2 per ride if you purchase tickets before boarding at the bus terminals or €2.50 if you buy them onboard. Buses run every 15-30 minutes about 6am-12am, but the buses are small and they can be very crowded in the summer. The bus lines on Capri run between Marina Grande and Capri town, Marina Grande and Anacapri, Capri town and Anacapri, and Capri town and Marina Piccola, as well as from Anacapri to Punta Carena and Anacapri to the Grotta Azzurra. The bus from Marina Grande to Capri town and from Capri town to Anacapri takes about 15 minutes, while from Marina Grande to Anacapri takes about 20 minutes.

In Marina Grande, the bus terminal is located on the western side of the port next to the ticket booths. In Capri town, the main bus terminal is on Via Roma very near the Piazzetta. In Anacapri, buses pick up in Piazza Vittoria and the nearby terminal at Viale T. De Tommaso 22. Given the high demand, there are usually points indicating where to wait for each bus line.

By Funicular

Capri's ***Funicolare*** (Servizio Funicolare S.I.P.P.I.C.; Piazza Umberto I, Capri; tel. 081/837-0420; www.funicolaredicapri.it; €2 each way) is a train line connecting Marina Grande with Capri town at the Piazzetta. The cable car train runs diagonally up the side of the mountain and offers an inexpensive and relatively quick way to travel between the port and Capri town. Tickets can be purchased before boarding in the office at the entrance in the Piazzetta or across the street from the large entrance marked Funicolare in Marina Grande. During the busy season, there can be long lines at Marina Grande in the morning to go up to Capri town as well as to return to the port later in the day. Plan accordingly to avoid stress or rushing, especially if you are going down to Marina Grande to catch a ferry. The funicular runs about every 15 minutes 6:30am-8:30pm or 9pm.

By Taxi

Certainly the most comfortable way to get around Capri is by taxi, especially if you opt for one of the classic open-top taxis. You'll find taxis in Marina Grande near where the ferries arrive and depart, in Capri town at Piazza Martiri d'Ungheria near the Piazzetta, and in Piazza Vittoria in Anacapri. Keep in mind that rates are higher than in some other locations, with a minimum rate of €9 and set rates starting at €17 for the short jaunt between Marina Grande and Capri town, and going up to €40 for a trip from Marina Grande to the Grotta Azzurra (Blue Grotto). There are predetermined rates, but it's still essential to agree on the rate with the driver before departing. One reliable company is the **Cooperative Taxi Capri** (tel. 081/837-6464; www.capritaxi.it), which offers round-the-clock service.

By Scooter

If you'd like more freedom to move about the island and have a sense of adventure, renting a scooter on Capri could be a good choice. Keep in mind that the roads are very narrow and twisty and busy with traffic during the season from early spring through October. Parking is difficult to find, too, which can make things a little tricky. However, a scooter does offer the chance to explore the entire island relatively quickly and at your own pace. There are multiple options to rent one on the island, but **Oasi Motor** (Via Cristoforo Colombo 47; tel. 081/837-7138; www.noleggioscooter-oasi.it; 9am-8pm daily Mar.-Oct., 9am-1:30pm and 3pm-6:30pm Mon.-Sat. Nov.-Feb.; starting at €25) is conveniently located right in Marina Grande.

Ischia and Procida

An island with volcanic origins, Ischia offers an exquisite blend of verdant mountain slopes, turquoise sea, thermal spas, and fishing villages. Around every corner, there's a varied landscape to discover, from bubbling hot thermal springs to steeply sloped vineyards and historic castles. Though this island is not on every day-tripper's radar, Ischia is an oasis that is ideal for a relaxing holiday surrounded by nature.

Called the *Isola Verde* (Green Island), Ischia centers around Monte Epomeo, which soars to 2,589 feet (789 m) and is largely covered by thick vegetation and forests. Although its volcanic history has made the island incredibly lush, its name is thought to refer to the unusual

Itinerary Ideas 268
Ischia Town 272
Casamicciola Terme . . . 283
Lacco Ameno 289
Forio 296
Serrara Fontana, Sant'Angelo, and Barano d'Ischia 303
Procida 310

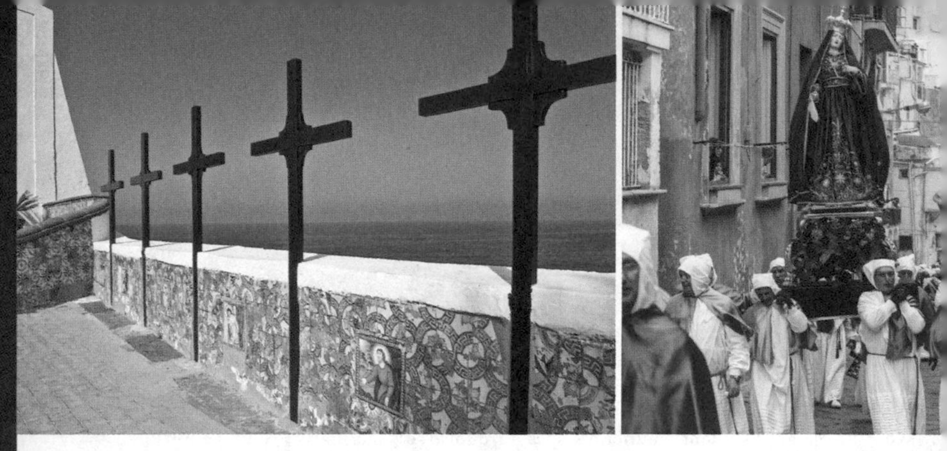

Highlights

Look for ★ to find recommended sights, activities, dining, and lodging.

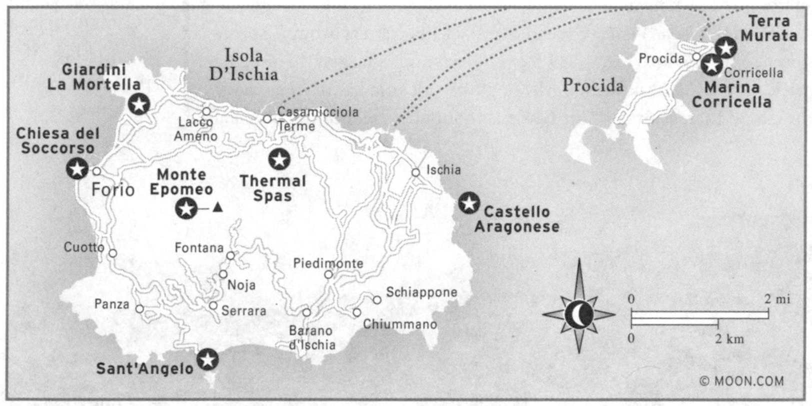

★ **Castello Aragonese, Ischia:** Enjoy panoramic views while exploring the medieval castle, churches, and ruins perched atop a rocky islet (page 272).

★ **Thermal Spas on Ischia:** Spend time relaxing in one of the island's many thermal spas that have been famous since ancient times for the healing properties of their waters (page 286).

★ **Giardini La Mortella, Ischia:** Visit the sprawling gardens of English Composer Sir William Walton and his wife (page 296).

★ **Chiesa del Soccorso, Ischia:** With its simple white facade, this small church is set on a picturesque promontory overlooking the sea (page 297).

★ **Sant'Angelo, Ischia:** This quaint fishing village on Ischia's southern coast is one of the island's most chic spots (page 304).

★ **Monte Epomeo, Ischia:** Hike up to the island's highest point on the mountain that forms the green heart of Ischia (page 305).

★ **Marina Corricella, Procida:** Dine seaside in this colorful and much-photographed village on Procida (page 310).

★ **Terra Murata, Procida:** Explore the narrow streets and historic churches of Procida's medieval town and take in the views from Procida's highest point (page 311).

green-hued tufa stone that is found on Ischia, especially on the southern side of the island.

Spilling down the slopes to the rugged coastline, the island's towns have a rich history to discover, dating back to early Greek settlers. Yet, while the island's natural beauty and quaint villages are alluring, what has attracted visitors to the island since ancient times is the abundance of thermal springs dotted around the island. Known for their healing properties for over 2,000 years, more than 100 springs and hydrothermal basins offer a variety of temperatures and chemical properties. Whether you're looking for pure relaxation or therapeutic treatments, Ischia's spas are good for the body and soul.

A short ferry ride from Ischia is the smallest of the Phlegraean Islands in the Gulf of Naples, Procida, which can easily be explored on a day trip from Ischia or Naples. However, there's a relaxed allure to Procida that begs a longer visit if your travels allow. Stay and meander through the medieval Terra Murata village at the island's highest point, enjoy leisurely lunches among the pastel-hued buildings and fishing boats of Marina Corricella, and experience your own *Il Postino* movie moments biking around the island's residential streets.

ORIENTATION

Located in the Gulf of Naples about 20.5 miles (33 km) west of Naples, Ischia is the largest island in the gulf with the tiny neighboring island of Procida sitting closer to the Italian mainland not far off the tip of Capo Miseno, the point that defines the northern edge of the Gulf of Naples. Procida sits only about 5 miles (8 km) east of Ischia and about 8.1 miles (13 km) west of Capo Miseno. It's a small island measuring only 1.4 square miles (3.7 square km), compared to the much larger island of Ischia, which covers 18.1 square miles (47 square km).

Ischia

Ischia is a large island comprising six towns located along the coastline and spread out on the slopes of **Monte Epomeo,** the mountain that rises up from the center of the island. Ischia's largest port where the majority of ferries arrive and depart is located in the town also called Ischia, which covers the northeastern part of the island from the port area, called **Ischia Porto,** down to the Castello Aragonese area called **Ischia Ponte.** Near Ischia's port, you can catch the SP270, the main road on the island that weaves through all of the towns and circles back to Ischia town. The towns of **Casamicciola Terme** and **Lacco Ameno** are located on the northern side of the island while Forio covers most of the western coastline. Along the southern side of the island, which is more rugged, you'll find Serrara Fontana with its charming fishing village of **Sant'Angelo,** and Barano d'Ischia with the popular beach **Spiaggia dei Maronti.**

From Ischia Porto, the SP270 hugs the coastline to Casamicciola Terme, located only about 2.5 miles (4 km) west of Ischia Porto. Here you'll find another important ferry arrival and departure port. Continuing west about 1.2 miles (2 km) on SP270 along Ischia's north coastline leads to Lacco Ameno. This town stretches from its charming port west to the hilly area at the northwestern tip of the island where you'll find the secluded **Baia di San Montano** and the **Giardini La Mortella** gardens. Following the SP270 road southwest out of Lacco Ameno leads to Forio, located about 2.4 miles (3.8 km) away. Forio spreads out over much of the western coastline of Ischia and the road leads down from the slopes of Monte Epomeo to the coastline at the town's port, which offers limited ferry service.

Continuing the circuit around the island on the SP270, leave Forio and the road climbs

---

Previous: view of Ischia from the Castello Aragonese; the Chiesa del Soccorso church in Forio; Procida's Good Friday procession.

Ischia and Procida

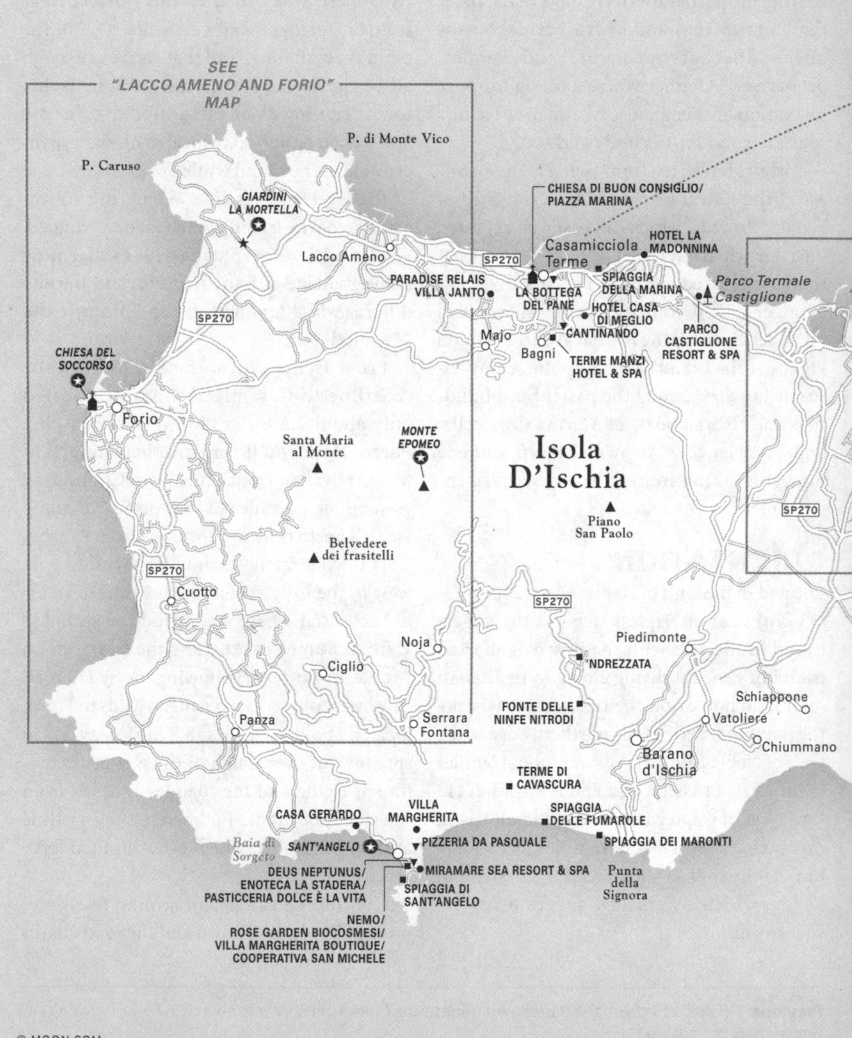
SEE "LACCO AMENO AND FORIO" MAP
P. di Monte Vico
P. Caruso
GIARDINI LA MORTELLA
Lacco Ameno
CHIESA DI BUON CONSIGLIO/ PIAZZA MARINA
Casamicciola Terme
HOTEL LA MADONNINA
SP270
PARADISE RELAIS VILLA JANTO
LA BOTTEGA DEL PANE
SPIAGGIA DELLA MARINA
Parco Termale Castiglione
HOTEL CASA DI MEGLIO
CANTINANDO
Majo
Bagni
PARCO CASTIGLIONE RESORT & SPA
TERME MANZI HOTEL & SPA
CHIESA DEL SOCCORSO
Forio
Santa Maria al Monte
MONTE EPOMEO
Isola D'Ischia
Piano San Paolo
Belvedere dei frasitelli
Cuotto
Piedimonte
Noja
'NDREZZATA
Ciglio
Schiappone
FONTE DELLE NINFE NITRODI
Vatoliere
Panza
Serrara Fontana
Chiummano
Barano d'Ischia
TERME DI CAVASCURA
CASA GERARDO
VILLA MARGHERITA
SPIAGGIA DELLE FUMAROLE
Baia di Sorgeto
SANT'ANGELO
PIZZERIA DA PASQUALE
SPIAGGIA DEI MARONTI
DEUS NEPTUNUS/ ENOTECA LA STADERA/ PASTICCERIA DOLCE È LA VITA
MIRAMARE SEA RESORT & SPA
Punta della Signora
SPIAGGIA DI SANT'ANGELO
NEMO/ ROSE GARDEN BIOCOSMESI/ VILLA MARGHERITA BOUTIQUE/ COOPERATIVA SAN MICHELE
© MOON.COM

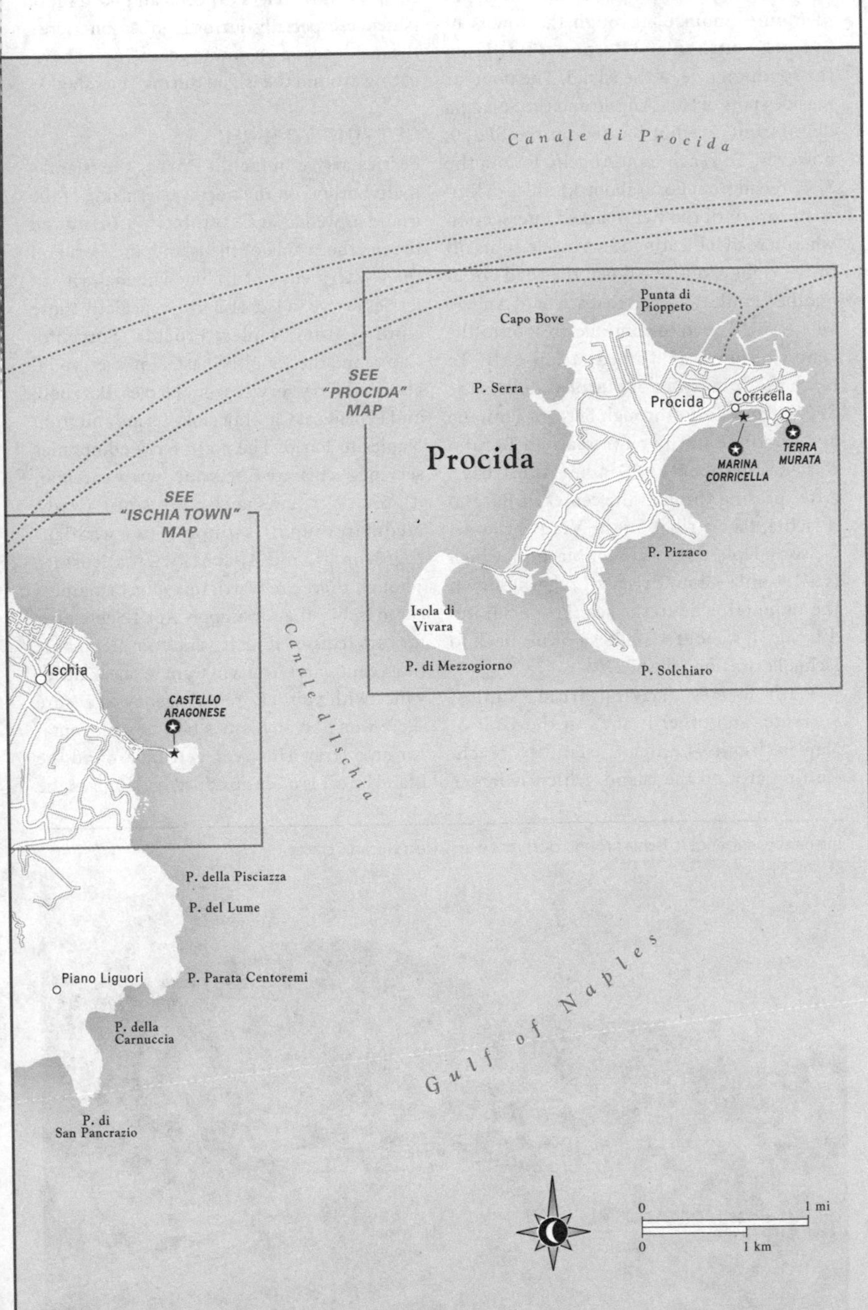

Canale di Procida
Punta di Pioppeto
Capo Bove
SEE "PROCIDA" MAP
P. Serra
Procida
Corricella
Procida
MARINA CORRICELLA
TERRA MURATA
SEE "ISCHIA TOWN" MAP
P. Pizzaco
Isola di Vivara
P. di Mezzogiorno
P. Solchiaro
Canale d'Ischia
Ischia
CASTELLO ARAGONESE
P. della Pisciazza
P. del Lume
Piano Liguori
P. Parata Centoremi
P. della Carnuccia
Gulf of Naples
P. di San Pancrazio
0
1 mi
0
1 km

away from the coastline and up into the slopes of Monte Epomeo, through the towns of **Serrara Fontana** and **Barano d'Ischia** on the southern side of the island. The popular seaside spots of Sant'Angelo and the Spiaggia dei Maronti are not located on the SP270, however. To reach Sant'Angelo, follow the SP270 road from Forio about 3.1 miles (5 km) southeast until the well-marked intersection where a road indicating Sant'Angelo splits off to the right. Continue down the road about another 2 miles (3.2 km) to reach Sant'Angelo where you'll need to continue on foot to the center of town, as it's pedestrian-only. To reach the **Spiaggia dei Maronti,** follow the SP270 from Forio through Serrara Fontana and continue until you've reached Barano d'Ischia after about an 8.7-mile (14km) drive. After passing through the center of Barano d'Ischia, take a right on the Via Pendio del Gelso and follow the signs for Maronti, which is a 1.9-mile (3km) drive, zigzagging down the mountainside to the sea. From Barano d'Ischia, it's about 4.3 miles (7 km) back to Ischia Porto along the SP270.

With ferries arriving from Naples, Sorrento, and other islands in the Gulf of Naples, Ischia is an easy island to reach. Getting around the island, which is larger than many travelers expect, can take a bit of patience, especially during high season. Here's the inside scoop on how to get there and navigating around the island during your stay.

GETTING TO ISCHIA

Ferries arrive in **Ischia Porto,** the island's main harbor, on the northeastern side of the island as well as at **Casamicciola Terme** on the northern side of the island and Forio on the western edge of Ischia. The majority of ferries arrive in Ischia Porto, especially those coming from Naples, Procida, Sorrento, Capri, and the Amalfi Coast. However, you'll also find ferry service from Naples, Pozzuoli, and Procida at Casamicciola Terme and from Naples to Forio. The main ferry companies serving Ischia are **Caremar** (www.caremar.it), **SNAV** (www.snav.it), **Medmar** (www.medmargroup.it), **Alilauro** (www.alilaurogruson.it), and **Alicost** (www.alicost.it). Though there are restrictions for bringing a car to Ischia, they only apply April-September for cars registered to drivers from Campania (not rental cars). You will want to check in advance with your car rental agency to ensure there won't be any issues taking your rental car on a ferry. However, getting around the island by car is often an added hassle given the

the narrow entrance to Ischia's round port that was once a volcanic crater

traffic on the narrow roads and parking challenges during the summer. It's often easier to hop around the island by taxi or on the many public buses that circle Ischia.

BUSES AROUND ISCHIA

Getting around the island is relatively easy thanks to a series of bus lines. Regular bus service is operated by **EAV** (www.eavsrl.it), offering an inexpensive option for exploring the island. The main lines circulating the island are the CS (Circolare Sinistra) and the CD (Circolare Destra). The CS runs from Ischia Porto west to Casamicciola Terme, Lacco Ameno, Forio, Panza, Sant'Angelo, Serrara Fontana, Barano d'Ischia, and back to Ischia Porto. The CD runs the same route in the opposite direction. Bus Line 1 connects Ischia Porto, Casamicciola Terme, Lacco Ameno, Forio, and Sant'Angelo, while Line 2 follows the same route but goes only as far as Forio. Within Ischia town, Line 7 runs between Ischia Porto and Ischia Ponte.

Buses start about 4:30am and run continuously until about 2:30am (sometimes lines end service around midnight) with service every 15-30 minutes for the CD and CS lines and most other main lines around the island. Tickets start at €1.50 for a single ride, and there are one-day passes available for €4.50, three-day passes for €11.00, and seven-day passes for €14.50. Tickets need to be validated at the machine near the driver when you board, but passes are validated on the first ride only. Tickets can be purchased in local *tabacchi* (tobacco shops) or in Ischia Porto at the bus terminal in Piazza Trieste near the ferry terminal.

HIRING A TAXI

Taxis in Ischia are all privately owned and the best way to catch one is to head to a taxi stand, located in all of the towns around Ischia. If you're arriving by ferry in Ischia Porto, Casamicciola Terme, or Forio, you'll find taxi stands right by the ports. Taxi stands are also located in the center of most towns or along the waterfront and are marked with orange Taxi signs. There's a variety of taxi sizes in Ischia, from sedans to minivans and the very characteristic micro taxis. These four-, or sometimes even three-wheeled vehicles are tiny and can zip around the narrow streets of the island with ease. Some are even open on the sides or top for a breezy ride on a summer day. There are established set fares between towns on the island, but you'll often find prices are higher during peak periods. Be sure to ask for the fare to your destination and agree upon a price before leaving.

Procida

All ferries to Procida arrive in the island's **Marina Grande** port on the northeast side of the island. From there it's a pleasant walk to reach **Marina Corricella,** a small seaside village with pastel-hued buildings, and the oldest settlement on the island called **Terra Murata** on the highest point of Procida. On the southwest side of the island is the **Marina Chiaiolella,** a small harbor, and beyond the islet of **Vivara,** which is now a nature reserve.

PLANNING YOUR TIME

Ischia is an ideal setting for relaxation and restoration. The island has a wealth of thermal spas, water parks, and beaches to explore. Each spa boasts different healing aspects thanks to the unique properties of the thermal waters found around the island. There are also plenty of opportunities to get out in nature to hike along the rugged slopes of Monte Epomeo. Given its size and variety of experiences, Ischia warrants more than just a day trip.

If you're looking for a relaxed holiday that will take full advantage of Ischia's charms, plan to spend at least 3 days on Ischia to take in the main sights, spend some time relaxing on the beaches, and experience a thermal spa or two. However, you could easily fill 5-7 days exploring and taking day trips beyond the island. If your holiday is based on Ischia, Procida makes an ideal day trip from Ischia thanks to its close proximity and small size.

Itinerary Ideas

TWO DAYS ON ISCHIA

With beautiful vistas, tempting beaches, and soothing thermal spas, Ischia beckons for a leisurely stay. However, if your time is limited, you can still spend a fun couple of days exploring a few of the highlights and getting in a little time at a thermal spa.

Day One

1 Begin the day in Ischia Porto where the majority of ferries arrive. Head along the northern coastline of the island to the town of **Casamicciola Terme.** Enjoy a walk along the waterfront lined with shops and cafés.

2 Hop over to the next town west on the coastline, **Lacco Ameno.** Stroll along the waterfront of the lovely harbor with a view of the Il Fungo rock. Enjoy a bit of shopping for locally made linens at De Vivo, or perhaps have a pair of sandals made to fit at Mario D'Ischia Sandali.

3 Stop for a light and fresh lunch at **Terra Madre** along the waterfront in Lacco Ameno.

4 Visit the **Giardini La Mortella** between Lacco Ameno and Forio to explore the remarkable terraced gardens.

5 See the **Chiesa del Soccorso** in Forio with its stark white facade and sweeping view overlooking the town.

6 Head back to Ischia Porto to enjoy an evening stroll along the lively shop-lined **Corso Vittoria Colonna** for a great evening atmosphere.

7 Enjoy a delicious dinner with local seafood specialties at **Cap' e' Fierr** right on the beach in Ischia town.

Casamicciola Terme with its harbor and historic thermal spas

Day Two

1 Start the morning by exploring the charming **Ischia Ponte** area and admire the view out to the **Castello Aragonese.** Take the elevator to the top of the castle to explore the fascinating medieval site.

2 Head up into the mountains southwest of Ischia Ponte to the **Fonte delle Ninfe Nitrodi** thermal spa for some relaxation time. Enjoy lunch at their on-site restaurant, which serves healthy dishes inspired by the natural setting.

3 Meander down to the pedestrian-only area of **Sant'Angelo** and enjoy an evening stroll along the water's edge in this picturesque fishing village.

4 Enjoy romantic views overlooking Sant'Angelo and dine on fresh seafood at **Deus Neptunus.**

ESSENTIAL PROCIDA

Procida's small size makes it easy to explore on a day trip.

1 Stroll along the harbor in **Marina Grande** on Via Roma. Stop for coffee and try *la lingua,* a traditional Procida cream-filled pastry at **Bar dal Cavaliere.**

2 Head to explore **Terra Murata,** the medieval fortified old town on the highest point of Procida.

3 Visit the 16th-century **Abbazia di San Michele Arcangelo** and admire the views of the Gulf of Naples.

4 Follow the steep steps and narrow passageways down to Marina Corricella. Stop for lunch at **Il Pescatore** just steps from the colorful fishing boats lining the harbor.

5 After lunch, take a leisurely walk around the pastel-hued **Marina Corricella** and stop for a gelato at Chiaro Di Luna.

6 For time at the beach, head to the nearby **Spiaggia della Chiaia.** Rent a sun bed from La Conchiglia and spend the afternoon relaxing.

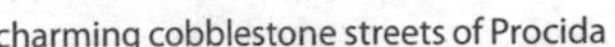

charming cobblestone streets of Procida

Itinerary Ideas

TWO DAYS ON ISCHIA
DAY ONE
1 Casamicciola Terme
2 Lacco Ameno
3 Terra Madre
4 Giardini La Mortella
5 Chiesa del Soccorso
6 Corso Vittoria Colonna
7 Cap' e' Fierr
DAY TWO
1 Ischia Ponte
2 Fonte delle Ninfe Nitrodi
3 Sant'Angelo
4 Deus Neptunus
P. Cornacchia
P. di Monte Vico
P. Caruso
Giardini La Mortella
Terra Madre
Lacco Ameno
SP270
Casamicciola Terme
Majo
Bagni
Chiesa del Soccorso
Forio
Isola D'Ischia
Santa Maria al Monte
Monte Epomeo
Piano San Paolo
Belvedere dei frasitelli
Cuotto
Fontana
Noja
Ciglio
Piedimonte
Schiappone
Vatoliere
Chiummano
Panza
Serrara
Fonte delle Ninfe Nitrodi
Barano d'Ischia
Sant'Angelo
Deus Neptunus
Punta della Signora

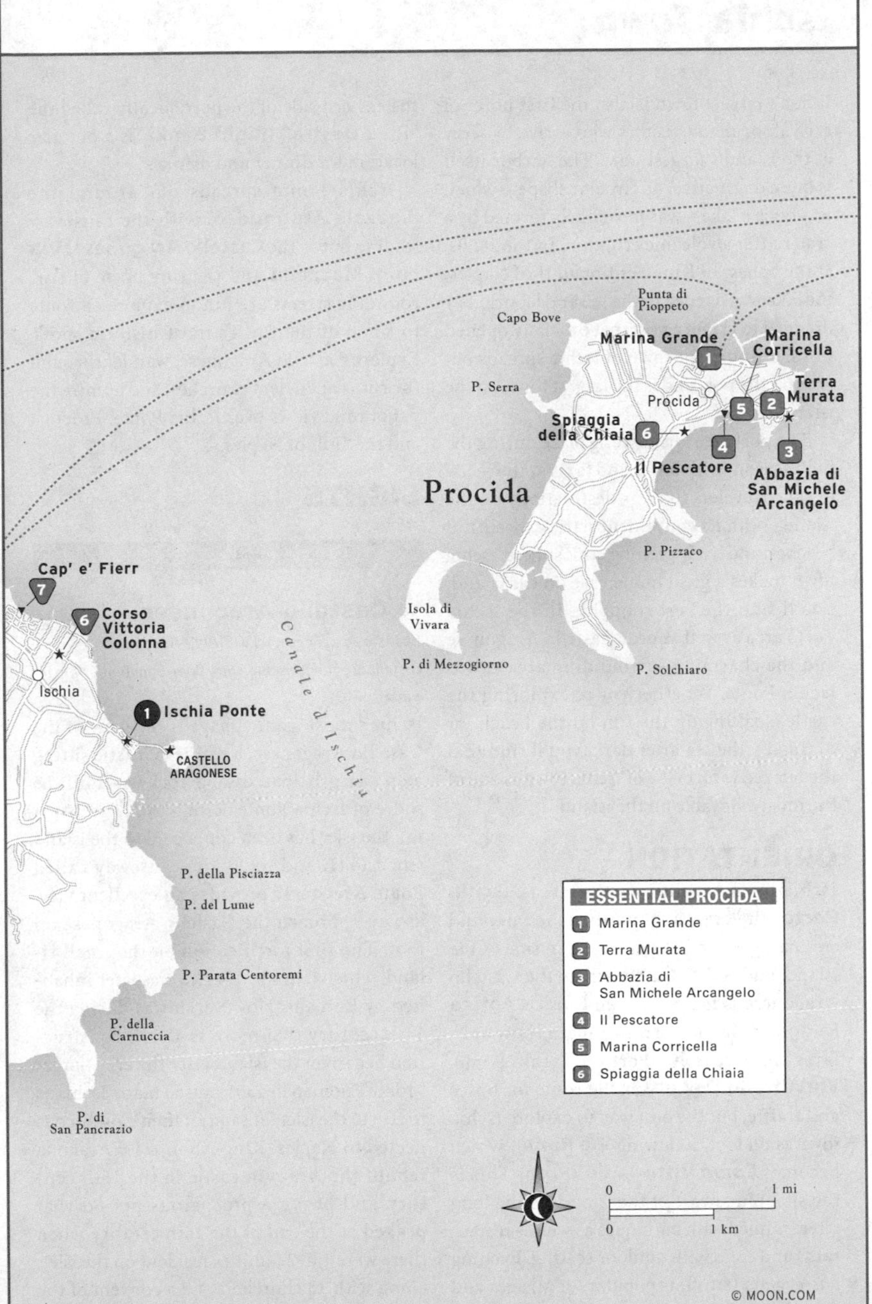
Punta di
Pioppeto
Capo Bove
Marina Grande
Marina
Corricella
Terra
Murata
P. Serra
Procida
Spiaggia
della Chiaia
Il Pescatore
Abbazia di
San Michele
Arcangelo
Procida
P. Pizzaco
Isola di
Vivara
P. di Mezzogiorno
P. Solchiaro
Cap' e' Fierr
Corso
Vittoria
Colonna
Ischia
Ischia Ponte
CASTELLO
ARAGONESE
Canale d'Ischia
P. della Pisciazza
P. del Lume
P. Parata Centoremi
P. della
Carnuccia
P. di
San Pancrazio
ESSENTIAL PROCIDA
1 Marina Grande
2 Terra Murata
3 Abbazia di San Michele Arcangelo
4 Il Pescatore
5 Marina Corricella
6 Spiaggia della Chiaia
0
1 mi
0
1 km
© MOON.COM

Ischia Town

Ischia's largest town is also the first point of arrival for many visitors who arrive by ferry at the island's largest port. The harbor itself is quite distinctive; its circular shape—which was once a lake—was most likely formed by a crater after a volcanic eruption. In the 1850s, at the behest of King Ferdinand II of Naples, the lake was opened to the sea and laboriously dredged to create a port that officially opened in 1854. Today the town of Ischia spreads out around the port and is the largest town on the island.

The port area is a bustling place during the high season, with buses and taxis at the ready to take travelers to their destinations on the island. With its convenient setting, beautiful beaches, and lively evening atmosphere, Ischia town makes a great home base on the island. You'll find the best shopping in the Ischia Porto area as well as near Castello Aragonese and the charming surrounding area called Ischia Ponte. Whether you're exploring the castle, soaking up the sun on the beach, or dining by the sea after dark, you'll find that the relaxed resort vibe of Ischia town is one of the most enjoyable on the island.

ORIENTATION

Ischia town is split into two areas: **Ischia Porto,** the area surrounding the port and stretching down the northeastern side of the island, and **Ischia Ponte** where the Castello Aragonese is located. From **Piazza Antica Reggia** near the port, two main thoroughfares connect Ischia Porto to Ischia Ponte. **Via Alfredo De Luca** is the route for buses and traffic, but the best way to explore Ischia town is on foot, following **Via Roma,** which becomes **Corso Vittoria Colonna.** This is the shopping heart of the island, as the long street is lined with boutiques as well as restaurants and cafés with outdoor seating. Evening *passeggiata* (stroll) is popular for all ages and a traditional local experience. After dark, the eastern side of the port, locally called the **"Riva Destra" (Right Bank),** is a popular location for dinner and drinks.

Ischia Ponte spreads out around the **Piazzale Aragonese,** with the causeway leading out to the **Castello Aragonese. Via Luigi Mazzella** and the tiny maze of surrounding streets are fun to explore en route to some of the town's most historic spots. Explore Castello Aragonese, wander through the ruins of ancient churches, and admire the panoramic views over Ischia Ponte, Procida, and the Gulf of Naples.

SIGHTS

TOP EXPERIENCE

★ Castello Aragonese

Castello Aragonese; tel. 081/992-834; www.castelloaragoneseischia.com; 9am-8pm (until 4pm in winter); €10

Ischia's most iconic image is the view of the Castello Aragonese, a medieval castle sitting atop a largely inaccessable rocky islet off the shore of Ischia Ponte. Rising to 371 feet (113 m), the islet has been connected to the island since 1441, and today the causeway called Ponte Aragonese provides an excellent view as you approach the Castello Aragonese on foot. The first fortification on the small island, which dates to 474 BC, was later inhabited by Romans. However, it was during the 14th century that more in-depth construction began on the island after the eruption of Monte Epomeo in 1301 caused many Ischians to flee to the islet for safety. Often closely connected to Naples, King Alfonso I d'Aragona rebuilt the Angevin castle in the 15th century and began a prosperous period that peaked at the end of the 16th century when there were 1,892 families resident on the islet, along with 13 churches, and a convent of the Monache Clarisse (Poor Clares). During the

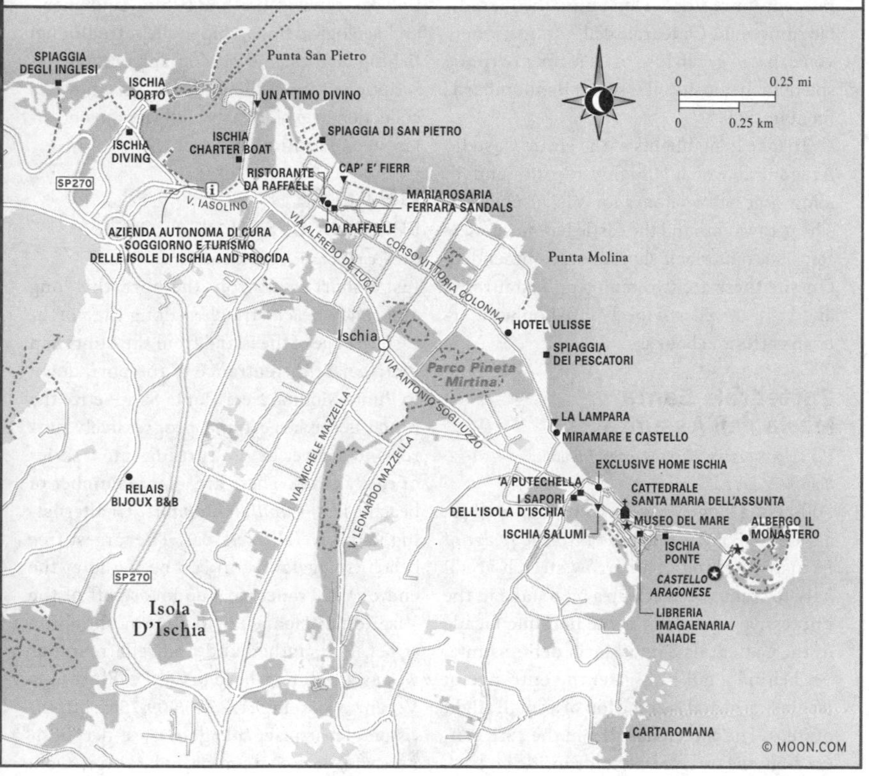

18th century, Ischians began to move ashore to more comfortable dwellings, and in 1809 the castle was significantly damaged during the battles between the Bourbon rulers of Naples, with the help of the English navy fighting against the brief French control of Naples and the surrounding area in the early 19th century. By 1823, King Ferdinand I of Naples expelled the last 30 residents of the island and transformed the castle into a prison, which remained in use until 1860. Since 1911, the island has been privately owned, but it is possible to visit and explore by paying an entrance fee of €10.

When you visit Castello Aragonese, an elevator tunneled out of the rock makes reaching the top quick and easy. A well-marked pathway leads around the Castello Aragonese through all the top spots to visit along with panoramic view points. Highlights include the views over Ischia Ponte from the **Terrace of the Immacolata** next to the 18th-century **Chiesa dell'Immacolata,** where art exhibitions are often held under the soaring dome in its beautiful, bright white baroque interior. Nearby is the **Convento di Santa Maria della Consolazione,** which was the convent of the cloistered nuns of the Poor Clares, along with the cemetery below the church. Here you can imagine (or try not to) the macabre scene in the dark crypt where the corpses of the nuns were placed on draining seats to decompose. Moving on, the pathway leads past ruins of churches and terraces now planted with gardens, olive trees, and grapevines, where the houses of the island's many residents once stood. Don't miss the incredible ruins of the Cattedrale dell'Assunta, where you can still get an idea of its former baroque splendor, before it collapsed under bombardment in 1809.

To take in highlights of the entire Castello Aragonese, which is highly recommended, allow at least two hours for a leisurely visit. The pathway around the castle has quite a few steps, so comfortable shoes are recommended. On-site there are two tempting restaurants and bars, as well as a lovely giftshop with artisan crafts and books.

Cattedrale Santa Maria dell'Assunta

Via Luigi Mazzella 72; www.chiesaischia.it; 8am-12:30pm daily; free

Follow Via Luigi Mazzella from the small piazza near Ponte Aragonese into the heart of Ischia Ponte, and in a narrow stretch you'll have to crane your neck up a bit to take in the impressive yellow and white baroque facade of the Cattedrale Santa Maria dell'Assunta. Set behind a tall iron gate, the entrance of Ischia's cathedral is at the top of a small flight of steps. The church dates from the 18th century, but the treasures it holds inside go back much further. Highlights include a baptismal font supported by three caryatids from the late Renaissance, and a treasured wooden cross from the 13th century.

Museo del Mare

Via Giovanni da Procida 3; tel. 081/981-124; www.museodelmareischia.it; 10:30am-12:30pm and 4pm-8pm Tues.-Sun. Apr.-Jun. and Sept.-Oct., 10:30am-12:30pm and 7pm-11pm Tues.-Sun. Jul.-Aug., 10:30am-12:30pm Tues.-Sun. Nov.-Jan., closed Feb.; €2.50

Opposite the cathedral stands the **Palazzo dell'Oroglogio** (Clock Palace), an 18th-century building that takes its name from the clock at the top. Around the corner is the small yet fascinating Museo del Mare (Museum of the Sea), dedicated to the island's rich nautical history. Spread across three floors, the collection covers navigation and fishing equipment, archaeological finds, ship models, traditional fishing clothes, and photographs. Many descriptions are in Italian, but it's an enjoyable collection to explore, especially for anyone interested in nautical history.

BEACHES

SPIAGGIA DI SAN PIETRO

Between Punta San Pietro and Punta Molina

Just a short stroll from the port, this long and sandy beach stretches along the northeastern edge of the island from the Punta San Pietro, near the entrance to the port, down to Punta Molina. Near Punta San Pietro, the beach is the largest and progressively narrows to a sliver before turning into a series of rocky coves. There are a large number of beach clubs (*stabilimenti balneari*) alternating with several free areas. The largest free beach (*spiaggia libera*) can be found at the end of Via Francesco Buonocore off of the Via Roma: Ischia Porto's main shopping street. For sun bed and umbrella rental as well as fine dining, head to **Cap' e' Fierr** (Via Venanzio Marone 9; tel. 340/009-7505; https://ristorantebarspiaggia-bagno-cap-e-fierr.business.site; 8am-6:30pm daily late Apr.-Oct.; two sun beds and umbrella starting at €12).

SPIAGGIA DEI PESCATORI

Via Spiaggia dei Pescatori

Located on the eastern side of the island between Ischia Porto and Ischia Ponte, the Spiaggia dei Pescatori is a popular sandy beach with a view of Procida in the distance. The beach is named after the small houses that line the beach and once belonged to fishermen (*pescatori*). Both free areas and beach clubs (*stabilimenti balneari*) are available. **Bagno Francesca Lido & Snack Bar** (Via Spiaggia dei Pescatori 7; tel. 347/077-4897;

1: Castello Aragonese **2:** Beach clubs line the Spiaggia di San Pietro in Ischia town. **3:** vintage Vespa scooter on the beach **4:** a colorful street in Ischia

1
2
3
4

Best Beaches on Ischia and Procida

The islands of Ischia and Procida are a haven for sunbathing and swimming. The sea is temptingly clear, and most beaches are sandier than you'll find on Capri and the Amalfi Coast. With so many beaches to choose from, here's a head start to finding your favorite spot on Ischia and Procida.

Spiaggia di Sant'Angelo

BEST BEACHES FOR SWIMMING AND WATER SPORTS

- **Spiaggia Citara, Forio (Ischia):** Located on the western coastline of Ischia, this is a beautiful spot for long summer-day swims. The fine sandy beach, clear water, and beautiful setting make it one of the best beaches for swimming.
- **Spiaggia di Sant'Angelo (Ischia):** Not only is this one of the prettiest towns on Ischia, but Sant'Angelo is also a fine area for swimming as well as snorkeling and kayaking.

BEST BEACHES FOR VIEWS

- **Spiaggia dei Pescatori, Ischia Ponte (Ischia):** From this long sandy beach you can enjoy a picture-perfect view of the Castello Aragonese as well as the island of Procida in the distance.
- **Spiaggia della Chiaia (Procida):** Spend a peaceful day on this stretch of beach with a view across to the pastel-colored buildings of Marina Corricella.

BEST BEACHES FOR FAMILIES

- **Spiaggia dei Maronti, Barano d'ischia (Ischia):** The longest beach on Ischia, this spot offers fine sand, clear turquoise water, and a host of beach services from the beach clubs (*stabilimenti balneari*), making it one of the most popular beaches on the island.
- **Spiaggia di San Francesco, Forio (Ischia):** This sandy beach is a great choice for families with its easy grade into the sea, calm water, and plenty of beach clubs.

MOST ROMANTIC BEACHES

- **Baia di San Montano, Lacco Ameno (Ischia):** This gorgeous beach set in a horseshoe-shaped bay is one of the most romantic on Ischia as it's truly immersed in the island's natural beauty.
- **Spiaggia del Pozzo Vecchio (Procida):** Also called the *Spiaggia del Postino* for the 1994 movie *Il Postino* that was filmed here, it's an appealing spot for a romantic day at the beach.

HIDDEN GEMS

- **Cartaromana, Ischia Ponte (Ischia):** This is a tiny beach tucked away south of the Castello Aragonese. Just hop on a boat near the Piazzale Aragonese, close to the causeway leading out to the castle, to reach this secluded beach.
- **Baia di Sorgeto (Ischia):** This rocky beach set in a small remote bay on the southwest coast of Ischia is famous for its hot springs that bubble up below the water's surface, creating natural hot pools.

9am-7pm daily May-Oct.) is a friendly spot to spend a day at the beach.

CARTAROMANA

Via Cartaromana

This secluded beach has a picturesque view of a small bay with the Scogli di Sant'Anna rocks and the Castello Aragonese in the distance. Just offshore in the bay are the ruins of a Roman town called Aenaria, which was founded in the first century BC. The beach can be reached by a pathway and about 100 steps down from Via Cartaromana, or more easily in a taxi boat from Ischia Ponte run by **IschiaBarche** (Via Pontano 3; tel. 081/984-854; www.ischiabarche.it; €4.50 per person one way, €7.50 return).

SPIAGGIA DEGLI INGLESI

Spiaggia degli Inglesi

This small beach is only accessible via a pathway that starts near Ischia's port. To find it, follow Via Iasolino to the western side of the port to where it ends at Via Svincolo Porto. Across the street, follow the pedestrian pathway marked Via S. Alessandro. Continue along as it leads uphill and then down a steep staircase for about 15 minutes. While small, the beach has a secluded feel and lovely clear water. Much of the fine sand here has eroded, but there is still a small public beach area with a mix of sand and pebbles and a sunbathing platform that is part of a small beach club and restaurant. With its secluded setting and position, this beach doesn't get as much sun as some others, but it's a good choice if you enjoy hiking and a bit of an adventure.

SPORTS AND RECREATION

Boat Trips and Water Sports

ISCHIA DIVING

Via Iasolino 106; tel. 081/981-852; www.ischiadiving.net; Easter-Oct.; dives from €40 per person

With an underwater landscape just as remarkably varied as what you'll find on land, Ischia is an excellent spot for scuba diving. Ischia Diving is located very near Ischia's port and offers guided dives for travelers with an international diving certification in the best spots around Ischia and Procida. Equipment rental is also available.

ISCHIA CHARTER BOAT

Via Porto 40; tel. 340/195-5385; www.ischiacharterboat.it; Apr.-Oct.; from €900 for up to 8 people

See Ischia's coastline from the sea on a private boat excursion that offers you the chance to stop and swim in beautiful little spots and take in the entire island in comfort. Ischia Charter Boat offers a number of different boats to choose from for excursions around the island, to nearby Procida, or to Capri, Sorrento, and the Amalfi Coast.

ENTERTAINMENT AND EVENTS

ISCHIA FILM FESTIVAL

Castello Aragonese; tel. 081/181-66810; www.ischiafilmfestival.it; last Sat. in June to first Sat. in July; daily tickets €10

With events held in various evocative settings at Castello Aragonese, the Ischia Film Festival attracts the top players in Italy's film industry and from around the world. Also called the International Film Location Festival, the Ischia Film Festival celebrates international films that create a captivating sense of place. Film screenings take place throughout the week along with panels and presentations.

FESTA A MARE AGLI SCOGLI DI SANT'ANNA

Ischia Ponte; tel. 081/333-3206; www.festadisantanna.it; July 26

Since 1932, this popular local festival has combined history, tradition, and folklore. Every year on July 26, Ischia Ponte is transformed into a festival setting surrounding the Castello Aragonese to the Baia di Cartraromana with its Scogli di Sant'Anna rock formations. Centered around the day honoring Sant'Anna (St. Anne) and the small Chiesa di Sant'Anna overlooking the bay, the festival includes a boat procession, floats decorated in different themes, and a spectacular fireworks display over the Castello Aragonese and Scogli di Sant'Anna. The festival often includes concerts, processions, and other events.

FESTA DI SAN GIOVAN GIUSEPPE DELLA CROCE

Chiesa Collegiata dello Spirito Santo, Via Luigi Mazzella 70; tel. 081/333-4556; www.lafontanadelvillaggio.it; Sept. 3

Celebrating Ischia's patron San Giovan Giuseppe della Croce, this multiday festival is centered around the Chiesa dello Spirito Santo near the cathedral in Ischia Ponte. The peak of celebrations takes place September 3 with a sea procession from Ischia Ponte to Ischia Porto and back, along with a food festival, concerts, and fireworks near the Castello Aragonese.

SHOPPING

Spa and Beauty Products

NAIADE

Via Mazzella Luigi 32; tel. 328/318-3244; www.fonteninfenitrodi.com; 9am-1pm and 3pm-9pm daily Mar.-mid-Jun. and mid-Sept.-Dec., 9am-1pm and 3pm-10:30pm daily mid-Jun.-mid-Sept., 9am-1pm daily Jan.-Feb.

Not far from Castello Aragonese in Ischia Ponte, this sliver of a shop sells beauty products created on Ischia with a special focus on the Ischia Spaeh line of products made with the thermal waters from the Fonte delle Ninfe Nitrodi. The water has been noted for its healing properties since ancient times, and the products are designed to replenish and refresh the skin.

Clothing and Accessories

MARIAROSARIA FERRARA SANDALS

Via Venanzio Marone 2; tel. 081/985-418; www.mariarosariaferrara.com; 9:30am-11pm daily Mar.-Dec., 9:30am-9pm daily Jan.-Feb.

Tucked away just off of Via Roma not far from Ischia's port, this little boutique is home to Mariarosaria Ferrara and her gorgeous handmade sandals. Born and raised in Ischia, Mariarosaria came back home after studying fashion and she has mastered the art of sandal making. Stop in for a friendly chat and beautiful custom-fitted sandals while you wait.

'A PUTECHELLA

Via Luigi Mazzella 151; tel. 081/333-4537; www.aputechella.it; 9am-midnight daily Easter-Nov.

The tempting window displays are enough reason to step inside this lovely boutique, and once inside you'll be rewarded with a treasure trove of clothing, shoes, and jewelry all beautifully curated by owner Alessandra Panzini.

Books

LIBRERIA IMAGAENARIA

Palazzo dell'Orologio, Via Luigi Mazzella 46/50; tel. 081/985-632; www.imagaenaria.com; 9am-12am daily Jun.-Aug., 9am-9pm daily Sept.-May

Though perhaps unexpected just a few steps from the sea in Ischia Ponte, this independent bookshop and publishing house is a dream for book lovers. Books in multiple languages are available, as well as an extensive and fine collection of antique prints.

FOOD

Seafood

CAP' E' FIERR

Via Venanzio Marone 9; tel. 340/009-7505; https://ristorantebarspiaggia-bagno-cap-e-fierr.business.site; 12:30-4:30pm and 7pm-10:30pm daily late Apr.-Oct.; €7-30

Situated along the Spiaggia di San Pietro, this restaurant and beach club is an excellent spot to dine near the popular Via Roma shopping street. Seafood is the specialty here. Start with the fish parmigiana, a variation of the classic dish made with fried eggplant, tomatoes, buffalo mozzarella, and a fish fillet. The linguine with capers, black olives, and king red prawns is an excellent choice, as is the fresh catch of the day prepared in seasonal variations. Relaxed at lunch and romantic for dinner, make a day of it by renting a sun bed and soaking up the sun.

UN ATTIMO DIVINO

Vua Porto 103; tel. 081/1952-8411; unattimodivino@libero.it; 11am-3pm and 7pm-12am daily Apr.-Jun. and Sept.-Oct., 7pm-12am daily Jul.-Aug., 11am-3pm and 7pm-12am Wed.-Mon. Nov.-Mar.; three-course menu €40-50 per person

Nearly at the end of the *Riva Destra* along Ischia's port, this small restaurant and wine bar offers a unique dining experience. Here there is no fixed menu, and the specialties change daily, depending on the catch of the day. The real specialty here is a creative fixed-price three course menu that includes an appetizer, first, and second course, all prepared with the fish caught that day. Once you select the fish, chef Raimondo Triolo will set to work creating the menu just for you. Ask the waiters to suggest a bottle of wine from the restaurant's excellent selection. The setting is friendly and relaxed, yet limited, so reservations are a good idea.

Regional Cuisine

ISCHIA SALUMI

Via Luigi Mazzella 100; tel. 081/992-411; info@ischiasalumi.it; 9am-12am daily Mar.-Jan.; sandwiches from €5 and platters from €15

This popular spot is the place for locally made salami and an excellent selection of cured meats and cheeses. You can enjoy meat and cheese platters or delicious sandwiches. Try their unique rabbit salami, reflecting the island's long tradition of rabbit dishes. A small seating area outside is a great spot to sit and enjoy local specialties accompanied by local beer and drinks, just a short stroll from Castello Aragonese.

RISTORANTE DA RAFFAELE

Via Roma 29; tel. 081/991-203; www.daraffaele.it; 11:30am-3:30pm and 6pm-midnight daily Apr.-Oct.; €6-30

Stop in this family-run restaurant on Ischia's main shopping street for a great choice of local specialties as well as delicious Neapolitan-style pizza. Though there are plenty of options, you can't go wrong with the grilled fish or meat, and the local Ischia-style rabbit stewed in wine, tomatoes, and herbs is also a popular choice.

LA LAMPARA

Via Pontano 5; tel. 081/991-333; www.lalamparaischia.com; 1pm-3pm and 8pm-11pm Thurs.-Tues.; €27-40, tasting menu €95 per person

Situated on the rooftop of the Miramare e Castello hotel, this elegant restaurant is a favorite for refined dining on Ischia. Created by top chef Ciro Calisé, the menu is dedicated to local specialties with a creative interpretation and elegant presentation. The menu changes seasonally, but be sure to try the linguine with sea urchin if it's offered. The view of Castello Aragonese and Procida provides a perfectly romantic backdrop and is equally appealing at lunch or dinner.

ACCOMMODATIONS

DA RAFFAELE

Via Roma 29; tel. 081/991-203; www.daraffaele.it; open Apr.-Oct.; €70 d

Set along Ischia's bustling shopping street, this cheery hotel has large, very clean rooms and friendly service. The location is conveniently close to the port as well as Spiaggia San Pietro, making it a great home base to get around the island and to enjoy leisurely beach time. The hotel has an on-site restaurant and pizzeria, so excellent dining is only steps away. This is the best deal on Ischia for a comfortable room at great rates.

ALBERGO IL MONASTERO

Castello Aragonese; tel. 081/992-435; www.albergoilmonastero.it; open Apr.-Oct.; €145 d

This extraordinary hotel offers the chance to stay at the Castello Aragonese in the historic monastery, which has been transformed into an exclusive and truly one-of-a-kind hotel. Dating back to the 16th century, the property offers a tranquil atmosphere and architectural details that remain very much intact while the hotel has been created to offer every modern comfort. The rooms are fittingly austere in way that captures the hotel's heritage, and with a setting like the Castello

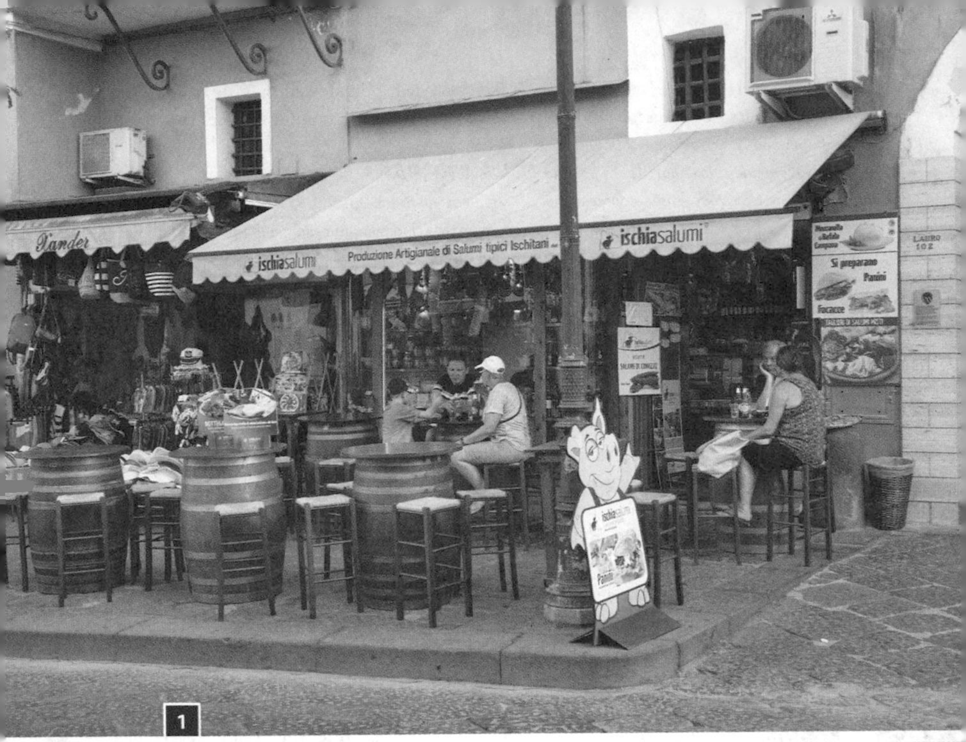
ischiasalumi
Produzione Artigianale di Salumi tipici Ischitani
ischiasalumi
Si preparano
Panini
Focacce
LAURO
102
1

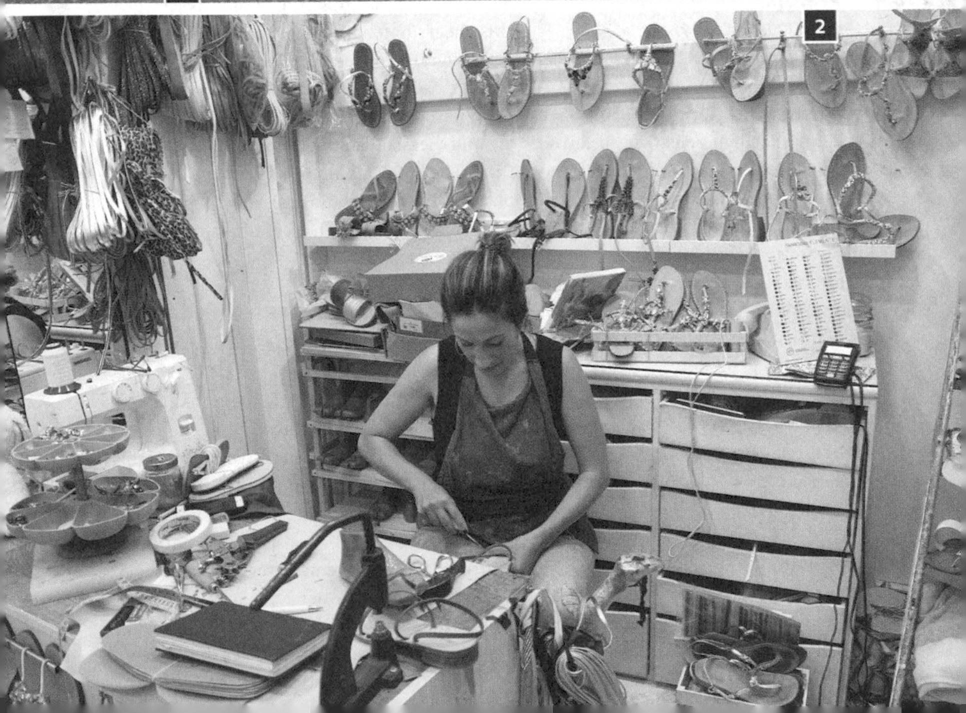
2

Aragonese, this is the spot to splurge for a sea view room. This hotel is not recommended for children.

HOTEL ULISSE

Via Champault 9; tel. 081/991-737; www.hotelulisse.com; open mid-Apr.-Oct.; €169 d

Halfway between Ischia's port and Ischia Ponte, this small hotel is tucked away in a quiet spot near the Spiaggia dei Pescatori. Many of its simple yet bright rooms feature balconies or terraces with a view of the Castello Aragonese in the distance. With two pools, a restaurant, and a rooftop terrace with grand views, this is a tempting option, especially for families.

RELAIS BIJOUX B&B

Via Pendio di Lapillo 1b; tel. 081/333-1034; www.relaisbijouxischia.it; open Apr.-Oct.; €250 d

Situated in the hills above Ischia town, this gorgeous B&B is a gem with its stylish rooms, landscaped gardens, and sweeping views over Ischia to Castello Aragonese, Procida, and the Gulf of Naples. Indoor and outdoor spaces flow together, and both are equally well curated. Your day starts with an extensive breakfast, and the pool invites for sunbathing. This property is ideal for a relaxed escape surrounded by nature.

MIRAMARE E CASTELLO

Via Pontano 5; tel. 081/991-333; www.miramarecastello.com; open mid-Apr.-Oct.; €250 d

Located right on the sea near Castello Aragonese, this luxury hotel is an icon of style and fine dining on Ischia. The views are captivating, whether you're relaxing on your own terrace, on the private beach, or by the seaside swimming pool. A heated indoor pool and top-notch spa complete the relaxed setting. Of the hotel's 41 bright and inviting rooms, the 23 superior and deluxe rooms have the coveted sea views.

1: Ischia Salumi **2:** Owner and designer Mariarosaria Ferrara creating handcrafted sandals.

EXCLUSIVE HOME ISCHIA

Via Stradone 14; tel. 335/664-1896; www.exclusivehomeischia.it; open Apr.-Oct.; €428 d

With an enviable position steps from the sea in Ischia Ponte, these stunning apartments offer incredible views of the nearby Castello Aragonese. Exquisitely remodeled and decorated, the apartments let you enjoy an Ischia stay with the comforts of home, as you'll have access to your own kitchen and a terrace for relaxed evening dining with a view. The apartments have a minimum stay of four nights, except in July and August when the minimum stay is seven nights.

INFORMATION AND SERVICES

Tourist Information

AZIENDA AUTONOMA DI CURA, SOGGIORNO E TURISMO DELLE ISOLE DI ISCHIA AND PROCIDA

Via Iasolino 7; tel. 081/507-4231; www.infoischiaprocida.it; 9am-1:30pm and 3pm-8pm daily May-Oct., 9am-1:30pm Mon.-Fri. Nov.-Apr.

This is the main tourist office serving all of Ischia and Procida and is conveniently located right in the port where ferries arrive. Stop in for friendly help in English and assistance with any questions you may have about the islands, getting around, or tours or excursions, as well as the latest information on upcoming special events.

GETTING THERE

By Boat

Frequent ferry service is available from Naples to Ischia and is operated by several different companies offering both high-speed hydrofoils and slower ferries for passengers and vehicles. **Caremar** (tel. 081/189-66690; www.caremar.it; 13-14 departures daily; from €17.90 for hydrofoil, €12.30 for the ferry for passengers, and from €37.20 for vehicles) has the most departures daily with hydrofoils leaving from Molo Beverello and slower ferries departing from the Calata Porta di Massa ferry terminal. Also from the Calata Porta di Massa, **Medmar** (tel. 081/333-4411; www.

medmargroup.it; 3-6 departures daily; from €11 for passengers and €43 for vehicles) operates passenger and vehicle ferries to Ischia. **Alilauro** (tel. 081/551-3236; www.alilaurogruson.it; 10-11 departures daily; from €18.60 per person) also runs frequent hydrofoil service from Molo Beverello to Ischia. The ferry ride from Naples to Ischia takes about 1 hour with hydrofoil, and 1.5 hours by ferry.

To reach Ischia Porto from Procida, many ferries stop at Procida on the way from Naples to Ischia. **Caremar** (tel. 081/189-66690; www.caremar.it; about 13 departures daily; from €8.70 for hydrofoil, or €7.80 for ferry for passengers and €28.50 for vehicles) runs both hydrofoils as well as ferry service for passengers and vehicles. The ferry ride from Procida takes about 20 minutes with hydrofoil and 30 minutes on the slower ferries.

Ferry service is operated from Sorrento to Ischia by **Alilauro** (tel. 081/551-3236; www.alilaurogruson.it; 2-3 departures daily; from €22.90 per person) seasonally April-October. The ferry ride from Sorrento to Ischia takes about 1 hour.

From Salerno, the Amalfi Coast, and Capri, ferry service is run seasonally by **Alicost** (tel. 089/871-483 weekdays; 089/948-3671 weekends; www.alicost.it; 1 departure daily; from €22.10 per person) from June to September with departures from Salerno, Amalfi, Positano, and Capri. The ferry ride from the Amalfi Coast to Ischia takes nearly 3 hours from Salerno, 2.5 hours from Amalfi, 2 hours from Positano, and 1.5 hours from Capri. **Alilauro** (tel. 081/551-3236; www.alilaurogruson.it; 1-2 departures daily; from €19.60 per person) also runs seasonal ferry service April-September connecting Capri to Ischia.

By Bus

The local buses on Ischia are operated by **EAV** (www.eavsrl.it; daily 6:30am-midnight; every 15-30 minutes; from €1.50) and circulate the island, connecting all of the towns. From Casamicciola Terme it's a 10-minute ride and you'll want to catch the CD, Line 1, 2, or 3 buses. From Lacco Ameno and Forio, catch the CD, Line 1 or 2 buses. The ride from Lacco Ameno to Ischia Porto is about 15 minutes, and from Forio it's 25-30 minutes. From Sant'Angelo, catch the Line 1 bus, or either the CD or CS bus to reach Ischia Porto, and the journey is 45-55 minutes. From the Serrara Fontana and Barano d'Ischia areas, you'll want to catch the CS bus; the journey is about 40 minutes from Serrara Fontana and 20 minutes from Barano d'Ischia.

By Car

To reach Ischia by car from Casamicciola Terme and Lacco Ameno, follow the SP270 road (the main road that runs around Ischia) along the waterfront east to reach Ischia Porto. It's about a 10-minute drive from Casamicciola Terme to Ischia and about 15 minutes from Lacco Ameno. From Forio, catch the SP270 heading northeast from near the port and continue along through Lacco Ameno and Casamicciola Terme to reach Ischia Porto, which is about 30 minutes away. From the Serrara Fontana and Barano d'Ischia areas on the southern side of the island, you'll again want the SP270 heading east, but the road will lead through the mountains on the southeastern side of the island and up to Ischia Porto. From Serrara Fontana the drive is about 30 minutes, and from Barano d'Ischia it's 15-20 minutes.

GETTING AROUND

Ischia town is highly walkable, and to get between the port area and Ischia Ponte, the most pleasant walk is along Corso Vittoria Colonna because it is largely pedestrian-only. Yet, from the port to Ischia Ponte it does take 40-45 minutes to walk at a comfortable pace. You can also catch the Line 7 local bus operated by **EAV** (www.eavsrl.it; 6:30am-midnight daily; departures every 15-30 minutes; 10-minute ride; from €1.50) that connects the Ischia Porto bus terminal to Ischia Ponte near the Castello Aragonese.

Taxis also provide a convenient way to get

around Ischia town and a stand is located along Via Iasolino right at the ferry terminal. A taxi stand is also located in Piazza degli Eroi in Ischia Town and Piazzale Aragonese in Ischia Ponte. The set fare for a ride within Ischia is €12, or you could go for the metered rate starting at €3 and with a set minimum of €10.

Casamicciola Terme

Only a short jaunt from Ischia town, Casamicciola Terme cascades down the mountainside to the sea and is an area of unique thermal sources on the island's northern edge. In the hills over the town's harbor is an area of underground activity that has created many hot springs with thermal water. Home to some of Ischia's most historic thermal spas, this has been a popular destination for wellness since the 1600s. However, that same underground activity has also brought its share of tragedy to the town. In 1883, Casamicciola Terme was at the epicenter of a massive earthquake that nearly destroyed the entire town and caused a significant number of deaths. In 2017, the town had a reminder that Ischia is indeed a volcanic island when another earthquake struck the area.

If you're looking for the quintessential Ischia spa experience, plan to spend some time in Casamicciola Terme, especially in the peaceful hilly area around **Piazza Bagni** or at the **Parco Termale Castiglione** set along the sea between Casamicciola Terme and Ischia Porto. The Casamicciola port is one of the larger ones on the island after Ischia Porto, which makes it convenient to reach Procida, Naples, and other destinations direct by ferry. With cute shops, cafés, and restaurants, the waterfront by the harbor is a pleasant place to stroll along the tree-lined pedestrian area and the shady Piazza Marina.

SIGHTS

Piazza Marina

Just opposite the harbor, this piazza sits between the busy SP270 road and the pedestrian Corso Luigi Manzi. It's a popular spot for locals to relax and kids to run around the large central fountain. Take a closer look around the edge of the fountain at the series of colorful ceramic tiles created in 2016. The panels depict a variety of the town's historic spots, seasonal activities, scenes of daily life, important visitors, and local festivals and traditions. You'll see Henrik Ibsen, who spent time in Casamicciola Terme in 1867 when he was writing his iconic work *Peer Gynt*. Among historic scenes of the town's piazzas and churches, Giuseppe Garibaldi, the great Italian general, who contributed to the unification of Italy in the 19th century, also appears in honor of his visit to the area's thermal spas in 1864. Nearby a panel depicts the Osservatorio Geofisico (Geophysical Observatory) with a portrait of Giulio Grablovitz (1846-1928), an important Italian scientist, seismologist, and volcanologist who founded the observatory above town after the 1883 earthquake.

Chiesa di Buon Consiglio

Piazza Marina

This little church just off Piazza Marina is dedicated to the Madonna di Buon Consiglio (Our Lady of Good Counsel) and was founded in 1821 by a group of local fishermen. As a result, it is also sometimes referred to as the *Chiesa dei Marinai* (Church of the Fishermen). The pale pink and white facade is topped with a distinctive design with two bells flanked by a clock on the left and an anchor on the right. Inside, the altar is the main focal point and is decorated with colorful marble and a painting of the Madonna di Buon Consiglio.

SPAS AND BATHS

PARCO CASTIGLIONE RESORT & SPA

Via Castiglione 62; tel. 081/982-551; www.termecastiglione.it; 9am-7pm daily mid-Apr.-mid-Oct.; from €28

Located along the rugged coastline between Casamicciola Terme and Ischia Porto, this thermal spa is a green oasis cascading down to the sea. Enjoy 10 thermal swimming pools along with a natural sauna set inside a grotto, a Turkish bath, plenty of outdoor space for relaxing, dining options ready at hand, private sea access, and an abundance of beauty and wellness treatments. Admission includes access to the sea and thermal pools, changing rooms, sauna, whirlpool, and sun beds. There's also a hotel on-site for a complete spa escape.

TERME MANZI HOTEL & SPA

Piazza Bagni 4; tel. 081/994-722; www.termemanzihotel.com; spa open year-round, hotel open Apr.-mid Oct.; spa entry from €50, hotel €300 d

This elegant hotel and thermal spa offers a five-star luxury experience in every sense. Built in the 19th century around the Gurgitello Springs, this is one of the most important hot springs on the island and has been noted for its healing and regenerative properties since antiquity. It was here that Italian general Giuseppe Garibaldi came in 1864 to heal wounds he received in battle. The hyper thermal waters in the spa and the thermal mud treatments are a specialty. The hotel offers a relaxed first-class experience, but daily access to the spa is available for non-guests with advance reservation. The spa is an elegant affair with classically inspired elements, including a Roman-themed spa experience inspired by the ancient approach to bathing in a variety of pools heated to different temperatures. The spa includes two thermal pools—one indoors and one outdoors—as well as a sauna, Turkish bath, relaxing showers, and excellent on-site dining options.

BEACHES

SPIAGGIA DELLA MARINA

Via Salvatore Girardi

Even with its harbor and long waterfront, there aren't a lot of large beach areas right in Casamicciola Terme. However, there are a few spots to swim while you're visiting the town. There's a little beach to the west of the port and tiny beach clubs (*stabilimenti balneari*) along the rocky coastline east and west of town. However, your best swimming option is the Spiaggia della Marina located just east of the port. This small beach area is protected by a manmade jetty and has direct access to the sea from the beach or via a platform built over the jetty.

SHOPPING

While strolling along the waterfront and especially Corso Luigi Manzi to Piazza Marina, you'll pass by the town's main shopping area, which also has plenty of café and restaurant options.

FISCHI D'ISCHIA

Corso Luigi Manzi 11; tel. 081/994-141; www.fischidischia.it; 9am-1pm and 4pm-10pm daily Apr.-Oct, 10am-1pm and 4pm-8pm Mon.-Sat. Nov.-Mar.

This colorful ceramic shop is an Ischia classic thanks to the unique whistles handmade by owner Luigi Mennella. Why whistles? There's an old rhyming expression in Italian that goes: *Ad Ischia si mangia, si beve e si fischia* ("On Ischia, you eat, you drink, and you whistle"). Here the whistles have a variety of different shapes and purposes. The horn-shaped whistles are inspired by a Neapolitan legend that they ward off evil spirits; different colored whistles are supposed to combat a variety of issues, from solving problems with bad neighbors to finding true love.

1: Chiesa di Buon Consiglio **2:** boats moored in the harbor of Casamicciola Terme **3:** Stop in Fischi d'Ischia for traditional handmade whistles.

1

2

3

FISCHI ISCHIA
La fischietteria del corso
D'ISCHIA
FISCHI D'ISCHIA

TOP EXPERIENCE

Ischia's Thermal Spas

Visiting a thermal spa in Ischia is a relaxed experience and there may be a variety of options available, from soaking in heated pools to skin and beauty treatments, massages, and highly specialized healing treatments. All spas are mixed-gender with men and women using the same thermal pools and zones.

WHAT TO EXPECT

What To Bring

You'll need comfortable beachwear, bathing suits, flip-flops, and sun protection if you're visiting an outdoor spa. No particular type of bathing suit is required, but you can expect to see most women in bikinis and men in Speedo-style swimwear. A bathing cap is required for swimming in most pools at thermal spas; caps are usually available to purchase if you don't have one. Though it's not required, a beach coverup is nice to have for women.

Rules and Etiquette

Individual spas will detail the rules before entering, but do note that it is common practice to shower before entering thermal pools.

Thermal spas are places of relaxation and rest, so music played without headphones is not permitted, and in certain areas of some spas—such as the **Regina Isabella Terme & Spa** in Lacco Ameno—cell phones and electronic devices are not permitted.

Children

Children are welcome in most thermal spas on Ischia, but often with some restrictions as to what ages are allowed in certain areas like the heated thermal pools, depending on the temperature of the water. Many spas offer a discounted or free entry for children and infants. Check with the spas in advance for specific restrictions or guidelines. Certain spas are better suited than others for an enjoyable day for the whole family. For example, **Negombo,** in Lacco Ameno, has no restrictions on children if they are accompanied by parents, and children will enjoy the two saltwater pools and the beach facilities. Likewise, the **Giardini Poseidon Terme** (Forio) has three saltwater pools and beach areas that children 12 and younger can use, but kids are not allowed in the thermal zone.

BEST SPAS ON ISCHIA

With so many thermal spas to choose from on Ischia, it can be hard to know where to start. The good news is that the standards of service and quality are very high, so you truly can't go wrong. If your time is limited or you're searching for the perfect fit, here's a good starting place to find the right spa for your holiday on Ischia.

Best Spa for a Day Trip

If you have limited time on Ischia but still want the spa experience, head to **Parco Castiglione Resort & Spa.** Located in Casamicciola Terme, it's the closest thermal park to the ferry terminals in Ischia Porto and Casamicciola Terme, so you'll have more time to relax in one of the 10 thermal pools or the sauna, or to swim in the sea.

Best Bang for Your Buck

As Ischia's largest thermal park, the **Giardini Poseidon Terme** offers the most options. You'll enjoy 20 thermal spring and saltwater pools, private beach access, and beautiful gardens, all included in one entrance fee.

Giardini Poseidon Terme

Most Luxurious

For an elegant and utterly tranquil experience, head to the **Regina Isabella Terme & Spa** in Lacco Ameno. Part of a luxury five-star hotel, the spa specializes in treatments using the hyperthermal spring waters right from the source.

Best Spas for Healing

For more than 2,000 years, the water at the **Fonte delle Ninfe Nitrodi** spa has been appreciated for its healing properties, especially for skin. A day spent in the water and drying naturally in the sun leaves your skin feeling wonderfully fresh. Set in the hills above the Spiaggia dei Maronti, the **Terme di Cavascura** is popular for its thermal vapors and mud treatments using hot thermal water from the source on-site.

Best Spas for Beauty Treatments

Set in the natural oasis of the Baia di San Montano, **Negombo** offers a wide selection of beauty treatments, relaxing or therapeutic massages, skin and bodycare treatments, and an extensive selection of Ayurvedic treatments. With luxurious surroundings, the **Terme Manzi Hotel & Spa** in Casamicciola Terme has a fine selection of thermal mud and other treatments available.

Most Unique Setting

A truly natural spa experience on Ischia can be found in the **Baia di Sorgeto,** where thermal water bubbles up from below the sea along the rocky shoreline and you can soak in natural hot-water pools.

I SAPORI DELL'ISOLA D'ISCHIA

Via Luigi Mazzella 148; tel. 081/996-524; www.saporischitani.it; 9am-11pm daily Apr.-Oct.

Stop in here for a nice selection of Ischia's traditional products, including liqueurs, spices, marmalades, and sweets. This is a good spot to try the local liqueur made with *rucola* (arugula), which has a spicy and strong kick.

FOOD

Regional Cuisine

CANTINANDO

Via Monte della Misericordia, 81; tel. 081/994-379; https://cantinando.business.site; 7:30pm-11pm daily Easter-Oct.; €10-20

Set in the upper part of Casamicciola Terme not far from Piazza Bagni, this restaurant has a welcoming rustic atmosphere that pairs perfectly with its traditional dishes and wine selection. This is an excellent spot to try *coniglio all'Ischitana* (Ischia-style rabbit) as well as fish specialties.

Light Bites

LA BOTTEGA DEL PANE

Corso Luigi Manzi 33; tel. 081/996-777; www.bottegapane.it; 7am-9:30pm daily year-round; €2-8

This popular little bakery is the place for everything from freshly baked *cornetti* (croissants) in the morning to a variety of breads as well as sandwiches, snacks, and pizza takeaway. Their products are made with *lievito madre* (natural yeast), making them light and incredibly fresh.

ACCOMMODATIONS

PARADISE RELAIS VILLA JANTO

Via Grande Sentinella 32; tel. 081/900-579; www.villajanto.com; €92 d

Set in the hills above Casamicciola Terme's harbor, this is a little oasis of hospitality and comfort surrounded by Ischia's natural beauty. The rooms are comfortably decorated in a simple style, and some feature sea views. At the restaurant you'll find wonderfully fresh dishes made with organic, garden-fresh ingredients by the owners. For relaxation, there's an outdoor and indoor pool as well as free shuttle service to the thermal spas at Piazza Bagni nearby.

HOTEL CASA DI MEGLIO

Corso Vittorio Emanuele 46; tel. 081/994-940; www.casadimeglio.it; mid-Apr.-late Oct.; €140 d

This hotel was founded in 1960 by Antonio Di Meglio, who has a passion to create welcoming accommodations with a home-like atmosphere. Still family-run by Antonio and his children, the hotel offers 35 comfortable rooms, and guests can also enjoy the outdoor thermal pool, beauty and wellness center, on-site restaurant, free shuttle service to the beach, and excursions organized by the owners.

HOTEL LA MADONNINA

Via Salvatore Girardi 8; tel. 081/333-0170; www.hotellamadonnina.it; €169 d

With a secluded setting along the rocky coastline east of Casamicciola Terme, this lovely hotel has 21 bright rooms, all with balconies or terraces to admire the sea view. An elevator goes down to the rocky beach area where you'll find sea access, a solarium, and sun beds. There's also an indoor pool and spa and an on-site restaurant that is particularly romantic at sunset.

GETTING THERE

By Ferry

Casamicciola Terme has the second largest port on the island, and ferries arrive here from Naples and Procida. **SNAV** (tel. 081/428-5555; www.snav.it; 4 departures daily; from €20.20) offers fast hydrofoil service from both Procida and the Molo Beverello in Naples to Casamicciola. **Caremar** (tel. 081/189-66690; www.caremar.it; 1 departure daily; from €17.90 for hydrofoils, €12.30 for ferries, and €37.20 for vehicles) runs ferries to transport passengers and vehicles, departing from the Calata Porta di Massa ferry terminal in Naples and from Procida. The ferry ride from Naples to Casamicciola Terme is approximately 1.5 hours, and from Procida it's 20-30 minutes depending on the type of hydrofoil or ferry.

By Bus

Ischia's local bus service operated by **EAV** (www.eavsrl.it; daily 6:30am-midnight; departures every 15-30 minutes; from €1.50) provides an excellent way to reach Casamicciola Terme. From Ischia Porto, catch the Line 1, Line 2, or CS bus and it's only a 10-minute ride. From Lacco Ameno and Forio, you'll want the CD, Line 1, or Line 2 bus, and the journey takes about 5 minutes; from Forio it's about 15 minutes. To reach Casamicciola Terme from Sant'Angelo, the Line 1 or CD bus is the best option, and the journey takes 35 minutes. From the Serrara Fontana and Barano d'Ischia areas on the southern part of the island, you'll want to catch the CD bus and the ride takes about an hour.

By Car

Located on the northern side of the island, Casamicciola Terme is only a little over 3 miles (5 km) from Ischia Porto to the east and even closer to Lacco Ameno, a little more than a mile (2 km) to the west. To drive to Casamicciola Terme from Ischia Porto, follow the SP270 road west for about 10 minutes. From Lacco Ameno, head east on SP270 and it's only a 5-minute drive. From Forio, follow SP270 east and it's a 20-minute drive. From Sant'Angelo, you'll want to reach the SP270 road to head west, and it will lead through Forio and Lacco Ameno before arriving in Casamicciola Terme in 35-40 minutes. From Serrara Fontana, Barano d'Ischia, and points on the southeastern side of the island, you can follow SP270 east to take a left onto Via Duca Abruzzi, which meanders over the mountain slopes, becoming Via Vicinale Cretaio and arriving down into Casamicciola Terme after a 40-minute drive.

GETTING AROUND

The main circle road around Ischia (SP270) runs right along the waterfront and harbor of Casamicciola Terme while the hilly upper part of town is reached by Via Monte della Misericordia from near the port or by a series of other windy roads along the mountain slopes. The town is small and easily walkable, but you will need to take a bus or taxi to get between the thermal area around Piazza Bagni and the waterfront. The **EAV** bus Line 3 runs from Piazza Marina on the waterfront to Piazza Bagni. Taxis can be found at the stand right by the ferry terminal. Parking is available in a small paid parking lot on the waterfront by the eastern side of the port.

Lacco Ameno

Situated at the northwestern tip of the island, Lacco Ameno has a picturesque setting with its harbor nestled between the slopes of **Monte Epomeo** and the hill of **Monte Vico.** Just beyond the harbor and tucked away below Monte Vico is the **Baia di San Montano,** a semicircular bay surrounded by lush greenery and cliffs. A chic resort since the 1950s, the town has a relaxed yet elegant atmosphere and is one of the island's loveliest spots for a holiday. With a beach right in town and the **Negombo hydrothermal water park** and **Terme della Regina Isabella** with its unique thermal water, there's a great combination of wellness and relaxation right at hand.

While Lacco Ameno is a picture of resort charm today, the town has a long and somewhat unexpected history. It was here on the hill of Monte Vico that Greek settlers arrived onshore and founded the first colony of Magna Graecia in what is now modern-day Italy. That first settlement was established around 775 BC, when the island of Ischia was called Pithecusa, and it quickly became an important merchant community thanks to its strategic location in the Gulf of Naples. Ischia's ancient history can be explored at

Lacco Ameno's **Museo Archeologico di Pithecusae.**

The heart of Lacco Ameno is the **waterfront area** stretching from the beginning of the harbor in the east to **Piazza Santa Restituta** near the base of the steep Monte Vico hill. In the center of the harbor is the distinctive mushroom-shaped rock called Il Fungo.

SIGHTS

Chiesa di Santa Restituta

Piazza Santa Restituta; tel. 081/994-774; www.parrocchialacco.it

Just off Piazza Santa Restituta, this church dedicated to Santa Restituta dates from 1886 after the earlier baroque church was destroyed during the 1883 earthquake. The neoclassical-style facade in pink and white features four pilasters and a small bell tower on the right. Inside, the church has a striking design with ornate wooden details and an impressive coffered ceiling.

Santa Restituta has a strong connection with the community of Lacco Ameno. Legend says that the body of this African martyr arrived by boat from Carthage and landed on the Spiaggia di San Montano. A church has stood on this site since 1036, and excavations below the church have found that it was built on the site of an early-Christian basilica. The complex also houses a museum with a collection of important Greek and Roman archaeological finds. However, the museum and archaeological site below Santa Restituta are currently closed, awaiting renovation work with no definite reopening date.

Complesso Museale di Villa Arbusto

Villa Arbusto, Corso Angelo Rizzoli 210; tel. 081/996-103; www.pithecusae.it or www.museoangelorizzoli.it; 9:30am-1:30pm and 3pm-6pm Tues.-Sun.; €5

Located on the hill above town, Villa Arbusto is a sprawling 18th-century villa that was once the home of Angelo Rizzoli (1889-1970), the noted Italian film producer and editor. In the 1950s, thanks to his film connections, Rizzoli put Lacco Ameno on the map, drawing chic visitors to his villa and thermal spas in town. The villa was eventually sold to the town of Lacco Ameno and in 1999 the main buildings were opened as the **Museo Archeologico di Pithecusae.** Dedicated to the island's fascinating heritage, the museum's collection covers prehistory through Greek and later Roman settlements. There's a particularly good collection of rare objects from Ischia's first Greek settlement from the 8th century BC. Don't miss the *Coppa di Nestore* (Nestor's Cup), a ceramic cup from c. 725 BC that has a Greek inscription referencing Homer's *Iliad*; the cup is the oldest object to have been found in the western Mediterranean and is one of the indications that ancient Pithecusae was the earliest Greek settlement of Magna Graecia.

Also in Villa Arbusto is the **Museo Angelo Rizzoli,** a small museum highlighting Rizzoli's life, work, and contributions to Lacco Ameno. Rizzoli's story is told through historic newspaper clippings, photos, and documents. It's a fine testament to the man who did so much to benefit Lacco Ameno. Stroll through the villa's gardens, dotted with citrus trees and tropical plants, and enjoy the view from the pergola; it's easy to see why Rizzoli was so drawn to this picturesque spot on Ischia.

SPAS AND BATHS

NEGOMBO

Via San Montano; tel. 081/986-152; www.negombo.it; daily Apr. 20-Oct. 7; from €33 per person

Set in the beautiful Baia di San Montano, Negombo is a natural oasis offering thermal and saltwater pools, lush gardens, grottoes, and tranquility. The park's 13 pools have a variety of water sources and temperatures, each one with different benefits to the body for rejuvenation and relaxation. The price of admission also includes access to the Turkish bath, and the Spiaggia di San Montano beach with sun beds and umbrellas, showers, and changing rooms. The spa offers a wonderful variety of skincare and body treatments, including

Lacco Ameno and Forio

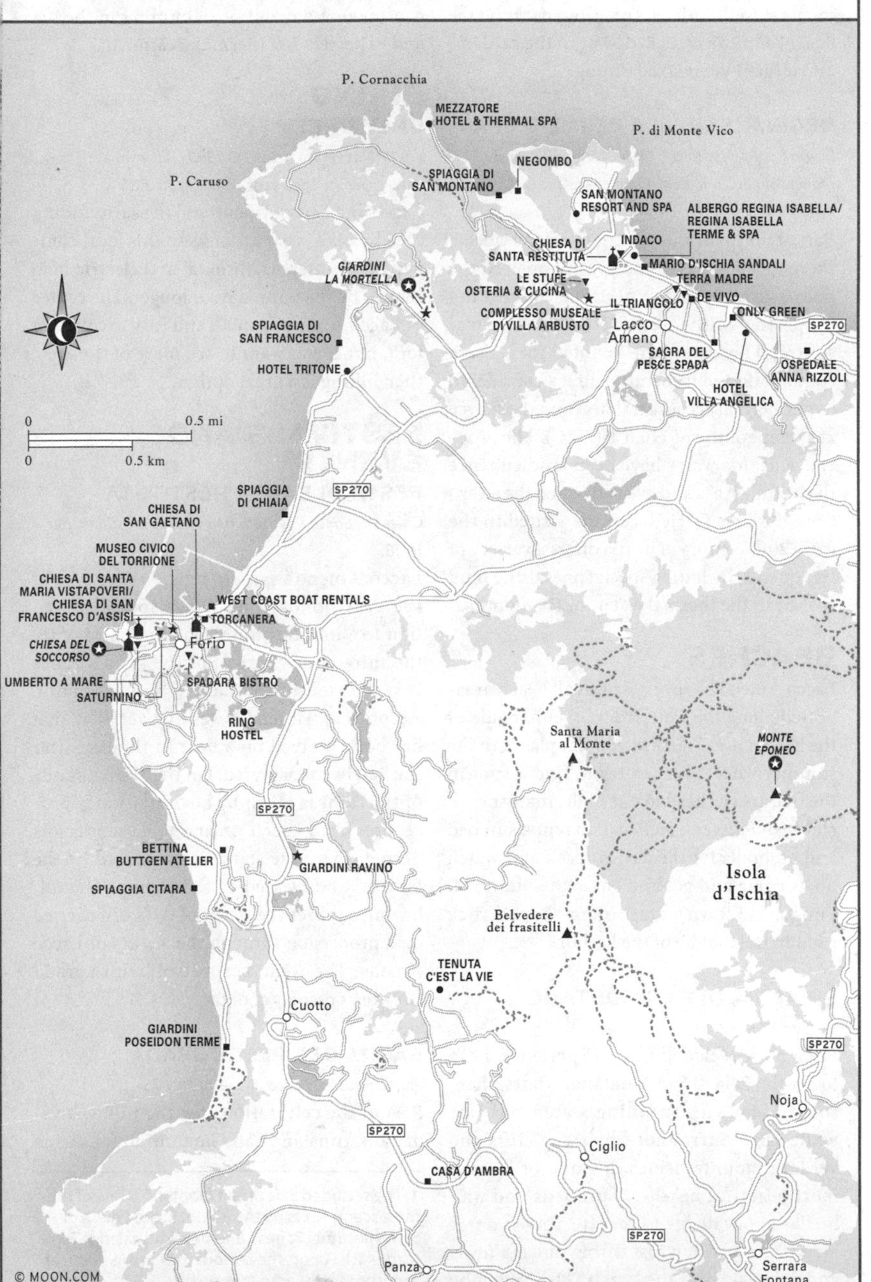
P. Cornacchia
MEZZATORE HOTEL & THERMAL SPA
P. di Monte Vico
NEGOMBO
P. Caruso
SPIAGGIA DI SAN MONTANO
SAN MONTANO RESORT AND SPA
ALBERGO REGINA ISABELLA/ REGINA ISABELLA TERME & SPA
CHIESA DI SANTA RESTITUTA
INDACO
GIARDINI LA MORTELLA
MARIO D'ISCHIA SANDALI
LE STUFE
TERRA MADRE
OSTERIA & CUCINA
DE VIVO
IL TRIANGOLO
COMPLESSO MUSEALE DI VILLA ARBUSTO
ONLY GREEN
Lacco Ameno
SP270
SPIAGGIA DI SAN FRANCESCO
SAGRA DEL PESCE SPADA
OSPEDALE ANNA RIZZOLI
HOTEL TRITONE
HOTEL VILLA ANGELICA
0 0.5 mi
0 0.5 km
SPIAGGIA DI CHIAIA
CHIESA DI SAN GAETANO
MUSEO CIVICO DEL TORRIONE
CHIESA DI SANTA MARIA VISTAPOVERI/ CHIESA DI SAN FRANCESCO D'ASSISI
WEST COAST BOAT RENTALS
TORCANERA
CHIESA DEL SOCCORSO
Forio
UMBERTO A MARE
SPADARA BISTRÒ
SATURNINO
RING HOSTEL
Santa Maria al Monte
MONTE EPOMEO
BETTINA BUTTGEN ATELIER
GIARDINI RAVINO
SPIAGGIA CITARA
Isola d'Ischia
Belvedere dei frasitelli
TENUTA C'EST LA VIE
Cuotto
GIARDINI POSEIDON TERME
Noja
Ciglio
CASA D'AMBRA
Panza
Serrara Fontana

massages, facials, and Ayurvedic treatments. There's a variety of on-site options for refreshments as well, with bars offering snacks on the beach, a trattoria tucked away in the gardens, and elegant yet relaxed dining.

REGINA ISABELLA TERME & SPA

Piazza Santa Restituta 1; tel. 081/994-322; www.reginaisabella.com; 8am-8pm; open Apr.-Oct.; from €40

Part of the luxurious Albergo Regina Isabella, these thermal baths and spa are open to the public to visit and experience the healing properties of the waters from the thermal source. The water here is noted for its rare combination of minerals, and it's considered hyperthermal because it flows from the source at a temperature of 170.6°F (77°C). The properties of this water have been studied since the Middle Ages and even attracted the attention of Marie Curie when she visited in the early 20th century. The spa offers a variety of treatments, including special ones using mud soaked in the thermal water for six months.

BEACHES

Lacco Ameno has a series of small beach areas dotted along the waterfront on either side of the harbor area. They're popular places in the summer where you can try to find a spot in the free area or head to one of the many beach clubs (*stabilimenti balneari*) to rent a sun bed and umbrella for the day. Sit back and watch boats come and go, and enjoy the view of Il Fungo, the town's mushroom-shaped rock right in the middle of the harbor.

SPIAGGIA DI SAN MONTANO

Via San Montano

For a more secluded beach experience, head to nearby Baia di San Montano, a horseshoe-shaped bay with stunning water and fine white sand. Surrounded by steep cliffs and verdant mountainsides, it's one of Ischia's most beautiful beaches. Sun beds and umbrellas are available to rent, or there's a free area where you can just throw down a towel and enjoy a day at the beach. The Negombo thermal park has a large beach area with sun bed and umbrella rentals, which means you can make a day out of swimming in the sea and experiencing thermal treatments.

BIKING

ONLY GREEN

Via IV Novembre 6; tel. 081/996-313; www.only-green.it; open year-round; from €35

Exploring Lacco Ameno and the surrounding area by bike is easy thanks to this local company that offers traditional and electric bike rentals by the hour, day, or longer. The center of Lacco Ameno is small and easy to cover on foot, but if you want to see more of the area, then biking is a great option.

FESTIVALS AND EVENTS

FESTA DI SANTA RESTITUTA

Chiesa di Santa Restituta and various locations; May 16-18

Lacco Ameno's largest religious festival of the year honors the town's special devotion to Santa Restituta. Starting on May 16, the miraculous arrival of the saint's relics is re-created in the Baia di San Montano. According to legend it was that very day that her body arrived on a boat in the bay after she had been martyred. On the 17th, a statue of the saint is taken by boat in a water procession from Lacco Ameno to Casamicciola Terme where the statue is welcomed by the faithful and blessed by the bishop. The following day sees the statue of the saint carried on a procession through the streets of Lacco Ameno. The event is capped off with a grand fireworks display at night.

SAGRA DEL PESCE SPADA

Piazza Rosaria, Lacco di Sopra; July 25

Part of the celebrations for the July festival of Sant'Anna and San Gioacchino (St. Anne

1: The secluded Baia di San Montano is one of the most scenic spots on the island. **2:** the Chiesa di Santa Restituta **3:** fresh and delicious salad at Terra Madre **4:** Il Fungo, the famous rock in the shape of a mushroom in Lacco Ameno bay

1
2
3
4

and St. Joachim) in a small church above the harbor, this is a much-anticipated food festival dedicated to swordfish. Enjoy traditional dishes made with seafood, as well as music and fireworks over the harbor after dark.

SHOPPING

Lacco Ameno's main shopping area includes the Corso Angelo Rizzoli, which runs along the waterfront, as well as the small streets nearby and Piazza Santa Restituta.

DE VIVO

Via Roma 34-36; tel. 081/900-086; www.devivotessilericami.com; 9:30am-1pm and 4pm-9pm Apr.-Oct.

An Ischia essential, De Vivo has been producing fine fabric clothing and household linens for more than 50 years. Salvatore De Vivo and his sons are passionate about selecting the finest cotton, linen, and hemp fabrics. Along Via Roma you will find three of the family's shops. Stop in **Tessile Ricami** for beautiful sheets, towels, and fabric. **Veste la tua Notte** specializes in pajamas and lingerie, while the little **Casa De Vivo** has cute gifts and decor items.

MARIO D'ISCHIA SANDALI

Corso Angelo Rizzoli 57; tel. 081/900-153; www.mariodischia.com; 10am-1pm and 5pm-10pm daily Jun.-Sept., 10am-1pm and 4:30pm-8pm daily Oct.-May, closed Sun. Nov.-Mar.

Stop in here for fine handmade sandals custom-fit to your feet. Since 1958, this has been the go-to address in Lacco Ameno for high-quality and stylish all Italian leather sandals made by hand. Choose from a variety of styles, from simple and classic to elegant sandals glittering with embellishments.

FOOD

TERRA MADRE

Corso Angelo Rizzoli 22; tel. 081/995-082; www.terramadreischia.it; 11am-5pm and 6pm-1am daily Mar. 25-Oct.; €12-24

With a bistro feel and specializing in typical island cuisine and fresh ingredients, this restaurant is a great spot to stop near the waterfront in Lacco Ameno. Grab one of the outdoor tables for a relaxed lunch or dinner. The menu includes a good selection of first and second courses as well as hearty salads.

IL TRIANGOLO

Corso Angelo Rizzoli; tel. 081/994-364; https://triangoloischia.business.site; 7am-1am daily; €7-30

This restaurant, pizzeria, and bakery is a popular spot along the waterfront of Lacco Ameno, with its large covered outdoor and indoor dining areas. There's a full range of options, from coffee and pastries in the morning to a broad menu of lunch and dinner options, including classic Neapolitan-style pizzas.

LE STUFE OSTERIA & CUCINA

Corso Angelo Rizzoli 210; tel. 328/625-0584; lestufeosteriaecucina@gmail.com; 7pm-11:30pm Thurs.-Tues.; €14-35

Set in a secluded area not far from the Museo Archeologico di Pithecusae, this restaurant feels like a hidden gem once you arrive. The setting and service are both welcoming, and the view overlooking Lacco Ameno is especially fine from the outdoor seating area. Ingredients are fresh and seasonal, which means the specialties change throughout the year. However, if available, don't miss the pasta made with *cicale di mare*, a type of locally caught crustacean.

INDACO

Piazza Santa Restituta; tel. 081/994-322; www.reginaisabella.com; 7:30pm-10:30pm daily late Apr.-late Oct.; tasting menu from €120

The Michelin-starred restaurant of the Albergo Regina Isabella is the place for a romantic or special dinner on Ischia. Headed by chef Pasquale Palamaro, the restaurant highlights seafood and locally sourced ingredients from the island, some from as close as the hotel's garden. The dining room and outdoor seating area afford a charming view overlooking Lacco Ameno. A variety of masterfully created tasting menus are available. Reservations are highly recommended.

ACCOMMODATIONS

HOTEL VILLA ANGELICA

Via IV Novembre 28; tel. 081/994-524; www.villaangelica.it; €75 d

Situated only a short stroll from the waterfront, this small hotel is set in a Mediterranean-style villa with welcoming communal spaces, lush greenery, and a lovely pool area. The 20 rooms are decorated with a simple style and colors that complement the natural setting. Most of the rooms feature a balcony or terrace with views toward the sea or Monte Epomeo.

SAN MONTANO RESORT AND SPA

Vico I Torre; tel. 081/994-033; www.sanmontano.com; open Apr. 10-Oct.20; €350 d

With an incredibly scenic location atop Monte Vico, this luxurious resort and spa offers a peaceful stay with expansive views overlooking both the Baia di San Montano and the harbor of Lacco Ameno below. A drive up a steep and twisty road leads to this oasis that sprawls across the top of Monte Vico, with multiple pools, beautifully landscaped grounds, and restaurants with gorgeous views. The rooms are elegant and offer a variety of configurations from garden to sea views. The Exclusive Vista Mare suites have direct access to an infinity pool accessible only to guests in these stunning rooms. There's a complimentary shuttle to Lacco Ameno or the Spiaggia di San Montano, where sun beds are available for guests.

ALBERGO REGINA ISABELLA

Piazza Santa Restituta; tel. 081/994-322; www.reginaisabella.com; open Apr.-early Nov.; €583 d

One of Ischia's most elegant addresses since it opened in the 1950s, this remarkable five-star property was built by Angelo Rizzoli, the noted Italian editor and film producer. Rizzoli was enamored with Lacco Ameno and had this hotel built to enhance the region. The luxurious rooms are warmly decorated with elegant touches, many with striking majolica tiles. Located in three separate buildings set directly on the sea, the hotel rooms vary from singles to superior doubles, with garden and sea views available. The suites are impeccable in every detail. The hotel's Michelin-starred **Ristorante Indaco** offers a top Ischia dining experience, and two more restaurants and several bars add to an unforgettable dining experience during your stay.

INFORMATION AND SERVICES

Tourist and local information is available at the **Info Point** (Comune di Lacco Ameno; tel. 081/189-04168; 8:30am-1:30pm and 2pm-7pm daily) in **Piazza Santa Restituta** in the 16th-century tower to the right of the Chiesa di Santa Restituta.

Medical and Emergency Services

OSPEDALE ANNA RIZZOLI

Via Fundera 2; tel. 081/507-9111; www.aslnapoli2nordservizionline.it/en/anna-rizzoli-ischia; open 24 hours

The only hospital on Ischia is in Lacco Ameno and offers a 24-hour emergency room (*pronto soccorso*). For **emergency services** anywhere on the island, the number to dial in Italy is 118 for ambulance and urgent care.

GETTING THERE

Lacco Ameno is located on the northwest corner of Ischia about 1 mile (2 km) west of Casamicciola Terme and 2.5 miles (4 km) from the historic center of Forio on the western side of the island. Although Lacco Ameno has a picturesque port, there is no ferry service direct to the town. The nearest ports are in Casamicciola Terme or Forio.

By Bus

Local buses operated by **EAV** (www.eavsrl.it; daily 6:30am-midnight; departures every 15-30 minutes; from €1.50) connect Lacco Ameno with all parts of the islands and drop off in town along the waterfront by the harbor. To reach Lacco Ameno from Ischia Porto and Casamicciola Terme, take the Line 1, Line 2, or CS bus and it's only a 15-minute ride from

Ischia Porto and 5 minutes from Casamicciola Terme. From Forio, you'll want the CD, Line 1, or Line 2 bus and the ride is about 10 minutes. From Sant'Angelo, catch the Line 1 or CD bus, and the ride takes about 30 minutes. From the Serrara Fontana and Barano d'Ischia areas, the best option is the CD bus and the trip is about 50 minutes.

By Car

To reach Lacco Ameno by car from Ischia Porto and Casamicciola Terme, follow the SP270 road west. It's about a 15-minute drive from Ischia Porto and only about 5 minutes from Casamicciola Terme nearby. From Forio, follow SP270 east and it's a 15-minute drive. From Sant' Angelo, first reach the SP270 road and follow it west as it passes through Forio and reaches Lacco Ameno in about 30 minutes. To reach Lacco Ameno from Serrara Fontana and Barano d'Ischia on the southeastern side of the island, again follow SP270 west through Forio to Lacco Ameno and plan on a drive of about 40 minutes.

GETTING AROUND

Lacco Ameno's waterfront and town center are small and enjoyable to walk along. You may, however, want to catch a taxi to reach the Baia di San Montano beach. The taxi stand in town is located near the harbor at the beginning of Corso Angelo Rizzoli, where the SP270 ring road turns inland and passes through the upper part of Lacco Ameno on the way to Forio. There's parking in a small paid lot located along the harbor, just east of the intersection of SP270 with Corso Angelo Rizzoli.

Forio

Covering the entire western side of Ischia, Forio is the second-largest town on Ischia and is one of the island's most popular tourist destinations. The town spreads out along the coastline up into the slopes of **Monte Epomeo,** from the northwestern corner of the island down to the southwestern part where the *frazione* (hamlet) of **Panza** is located. About midway down the western coastline, the **Punta del Soccorso** promontory juts out where the stark white **Chiesa del Soccorso** church sits in a picturesque spot. To the north lies Forio's historic center, the port, and the popular and long stretch of sandy beaches from the **Spiaggia di Chiaia** to the **Spiaggia San Francesco.** Farther south, where the coastline becomes more rugged and rural, is the **Spiaggia di Citara** where the popular **Giardini Terme Poseidon thermal park** is located.

With such an expansive footprint, Forio offers the chance to experience the best that Ischia has to offer, from lush green spaces and a historic town center to thermal spas and sunny beaches. Forio's setting along the west coast of Ischia makes it an exceptional spot to enjoy the sunset, and the waterfront and historic center of Forio hum with people out and about for the traditional *passeggiata* (stroll) or a relaxed *aperitivo* (happy-hour drink).

SIGHTS

★ Giardini La Mortella

Via Francesco Calise 45; tel. 081/986-220; www.lamortella.org; 9am-7pm Tues., Thurs., Sat., Sun. Apr.-Oct.; €12

Set on a lush green promontory above Spiaggia di San Francesco, these incredibly landscaped gardens were once the private oasis and creative home of English composer **Sir William Walton** (1902-1983) and his Argentinian-born wife **Susana Walton** (1926-2010). Spreading over about 5 acres (2 hectares), the gardens were lovingly created starting in 1958 by Susana. She worked with passion to expand and develop the gardens for the next 50 years. The garden is divided into two parts that flow together. The plan for the valley garden was originally laid out by British garden designer Russell Page (1906-1985) while the sunnier hill gardens were developed over time.

A well-marked pathway leads through the Mediterranean and subtropical gardens, which feature ponds, little waterfalls, and unique buildings, pavilions, and glasshouses. Stop to admire the large fountain with giant Victoria Amazonica water lilies. Nearby a small greenhouse is home to more giant lilies and a wall fountain with a large mask inspired by Sir William Walton's piece *Facade*. Exploring the gardens is like a treasure hunt with hidden surprises to discover. There's a cascade with sculpted crocodiles, a Thai-inspired garden with bamboo and lotus flowers, a Greek-style theater where concerts take place in the summer, a stone memorial to William Walton where his ashes are preserved, and many more treasured spots. One of the most artistic is the *Tempio del Sole* (Temple of the Sun), a small building dedicated to Apollo and decorated with plants, fountains, and phrases from William Walton's compositions. A small museum and recital hall shows a film about Sir William Walton and La Mortella. Stop for a pleasant respite at the lovely tearoom that also serves light lunches.

Allow at least an hour or two to explore the gardens at a leisurely pace, leaving time to stop and rest on one of the many benches dotted throughout the gardens and to take in the incredible views overlooking Forio. The gardens are accessible for disabled visitors. Free parking is available at the upper entrance off Via Zaro.

★ Chiesa del Soccorso

Via del Soccorso

One of Ischia's most iconic landmarks, the Chiesa del Soccorso sits at the tip of the Punta del Soccorso promontory surrounded by a large piazza. Although this is a small church, its bright white facade stands out brilliantly against the blue of the sky and sea beyond. It's a scene evocative of Greece, and its unusual style is part of what makes this such an architectural gem. The church has always been connected with the sea, and its setting and stark color are a point of reference for sailors and fishermen. A church has stood on this sight since 1350, but the structure was later remodeled and expanded in the 18th century. The church is accessed via a small flight of stairs with five crosses on the right and ceramic tiles from the 1700s decorating the double staircase entrance to the church. Inside,

Giardini La Mortella

the single nave church is moving in its simplicity with its cross-vaulted ceiling chapels lining both sides. One of the most distinctive features of the church is a collection of ship models that were ex-votos from fishermen in thanks for being saved from shipwrecks.

Chiesa di Santa Maria Visitapoveri and Chiesa di San Francesco d'Assisi

Piazza Municipio

Near the Chiesa del Soccorso on Piazza Municipio are two more interesting churches side by side. On the right, the unusual double-facade entrance leads to the Chiesa di Santa Maria Visitapoveri, which was founded in the early 1600s. Inside, the single-nave church is lined on each side with large wooden stalls with a series of grand oval paintings just above on both sides of the nave. The rich decoration and small size create a unique closeness rarely felt in baroque architecture. Next door to the left, the Chiesa di San Francesco d'Assisi dates from 1646 and once included a convent and cloister. The plain white facade is in stark contrast to the rich baroque yellow and white decor and elegant marble altar inside the church.

Museo Civico del Torrione

Via del Torrione 32; tel. 081/333-2126; www.iltorrioneforio.it; 10am-12:30pm and 7:30pm-10:30pm Apr.-Oct., 9:30am-12:30pm and 5pm-7pm Nov.-Mar., closed Mon.; €2

Set in a round stone watchtower dating from around 1480, this civic museum is set on two levels and offers an interesting look inside a historic watchtower. The museum hosts temporary art exhibits, and on the upper level you can see paintings and sculptures by the local artist Giovanni Maltese (1852-1913) who transformed the tower into his studio and home for nearly 30 years.

Chiesa di San Gaetano

Piazza San Gaetano

Along with the tower of the nearby Museo Civico del Torrione, the other easy to spot sight in Forio is the pale orange and white dome of the Chiesa di San Gaetano. Built in 1655 for the town's fishermen, the church was completely redone in 1857, maintaining the structural lines of the exterior and preserving the rich baroque-style interior from the 18th century, with its pale blue color and elaborate white stucco accents and artistic touches. Look for the sundial on the side of the dome that tells time accurately.

Giardini Ravino

Via Provinciale Panza 140b; tel. 081/997-783; www.ravino.it; 9am-7pm, closed Tues. and Thurs.; open Mar. 10-Nov. 15; €9

In the hills above Forio lies a fascinating tropical Mediterranean park that is home to the largest and most varied collection of cacti and succulents in Europe. Founded by Giuseppe D'Ambra, who has collected plants from around the world, the gardens are beautifully landscaped and dotted with creations by local artists. After exploring the gardens, stop for a rest at the **Cactus Lounge Café,** which serves drinks and light lunch options.

SPAS AND BATHS

GIARDINI POSEIDON TERME

Via Giovanni Mazzella 338; tel. 081/908-7111; www.giardiniposeidonterme.com; 9am-7pm mid-Apr.-Oct. 1, 9am-6:30pm Oct. 2-31; from €33 per person

Set at the tranquil southern end of the Spiaggia di Citara and completely immersed in nature, Giardini Poseidon Terme is the island's largest thermal park. Spreading over nearly 15 acres (6 hectares), the park's 20 pools are thermal spring-fed or saltwater, and vary in temperature. Following the suggested route through the park emphasizes the therapeutic effects of the thermal and hyperthermal volcanic spring water. The gardens also include private beach access with sun beds and umbrellas, a wellness center for specialized spa treatments, and three dining areas.

1: cacti in the Giardini Ravino **2:** The brilliant white Chiesa del Soccorso is an iconic image of Ischia. **3:** a souvenir shop in Forio **4:** deck chairs and straw sunshades at the Giardini Poseidon Terme

1

2

Everything you need for a relaxing day absorbing Ischia's natural healing properties of sun, thermal waters, and tranquil beaches is right at your fingertips.

BEACHES

SPIAGGIA DI SAN FRANCESCO

Via Tommaso Cigliano

Stretching out below the mountain slopes of Punta Caruso, the Spiaggia di San Francesco is a long and sandy beach in the northern part of Forio. As it's not in the town center and is surrounded by a primarily residential area, it's a quiet spot that's also popular with families with young children. The beach is lined with free areas and a selection of *stabilimenti balneari* (beach clubs) where you can rent sun beds and umbrellas, use the shower and changing room facilities, and dine by the sea.

SPIAGGIA DI CHIAIA

Via Spinesante

Just north of the port and running along the historic center of Forio, this beach is a popular and often quite crowded spot in the summer. Yet the fine sand and *stabilimenti balneari* like **Lido Mattera** (Via Spinestante 90; tel. 081/333-2530; www.lidomattera.it; daily May-Oct.; from €20 per day for two sun beds and umbrella) lining the beach make this an appealing spot for a swim if you're staying in the historic center. There are free areas where you can just throw down your towel and enjoy a swim toward the northern and southern edges of the beach.

SPIAGGIA CITARA

Via Giovanni Mazzella

Along the southwestern coastline of Ischia, the Spiaggia di Citara is a beautiful fine sandy beach that stretches south to the verdant Punta Imperatore. It's a lovely natural setting that is also home to the Giardini Poseidon Terme, the largest thermal park on the island. There are free beach areas as well as beach clubs (*stabilimenti balneari*) to choose from, such as **Bagno Teresa** (Via Giovanni Mazzella 87; tel. 081/908-517; www.bagnoteresabeach.it; daily Apr.-Oct.; from €10 per day for two sun beds and umbrella).

BOAT RENTALS

WEST COAST BOAT RENTALS

Via Giacomo Genovino 6; tel. 339/613-7491; www.westcoastischia.it; Apr. 10-Nov. 15; from €100 for self-drive boats and €220 for boat with captain

Located right in Forio's port, this friendly company offers small boat rentals without a skipper (no license required), or excursions with skipper on a variety of different motorboats and traditional wooden Sorrentine-style boats. Excursions are available to survey the most beautiful spots around the island, or to visit Procida.

VINEYARDS

CASA D'AMBRA

Via Mario D'Ambra 30; tel. 081/907-246; www.dambravini.com; May-Oct., reservation required; from €27 per person

Founded in 1888 by Francesco D'Ambra, Casa D'Ambra is Ischia's leading wine producer and offers visitors the chance to visit the family's museum, cantina, and vineyards, and to sample their excellent wines. Situated on the slopes of Monte Epomeo high above Forio, this winery has a truly spectacular natural setting. The master enologist behind Casa D'Ambra's award-winning wines is Andrea D'Ambra, the great grandson of the vineyard's founder. A wine tour experience is available with advance booking and includes a visit to the vineyard, winery, and wine tasting in the cellar tasting room.

FESTIVALS AND EVENTS

FESTA DI SAN VITO

Chiesa di San Vito Martire, Piazza Municipio, and various locations; June 14-17

Every summer the town of Forio celebrates its patron and protector San Vito with a four-day festival. Religious celebrations are centered around the beautiful **Chiesa di San Vito Martire** (Via San Vito 62) located above the center of Forio. Festival events include concerts and performances in Piazza Municipio, in front of the Chiesa di Santa Maria Vistapoveri, processions through town and on the sea, and a big fireworks display over the water.

SHOPPING

Forio's main shopping area starts near the **Via del Soccorso** in the historic center. The long street **Via Avvocato Francesco Regine** turns into **Corso Matteo,** and along this street you'll find the best shopping area as well as the cross street **Via Erasmo di Lustro** leading to Piazza Balsofiore Luca near the Chiesa di San Gaetano.

TORCANERA

Via Erasmo Di Lustro 5; tel. 081/997-262; www.torcanera.it; 9am-7pm daily

For local specialties, stop in this well-stocked shop close to Piazza Balsofiore Luca where you'll find tempting options lining the shelves and spilling out into displays along the street. Try something new from the variety of *amaro* (bitter) herbal liqueurs, such as the *amaro torcanera alla portulaca*, made with purslane, a native plant to Ischia, mixed with aromatic herbs. Other unique Ischia liqueurs include those made with thyme and arugula. The selection of local sweets, wines, and food products is large and varied.

BETTINA BUTTGEN ATELIER

Via Giovanni Mazzella 210; tel. 338/573-1242; www.bettinabuttgen.com; 9am-1pm Tues.-Sat. Mar.-Dec.

South of Punta del Soccorso on the road toward the Spiaggia di Citara, stop in this beautiful boutique that is also the workshop of textile designer Bettina Buttgen. Her clothing and jewelry creations are visually captivating pieces of wearable art. With incredible attention to detail, the pieces are woven, dyed, painted, and designed all by hand.

FOOD

Seafood

UMBERTO A MARE

Via del Soccorso 2; tel. 081/997-171; www.umbertoamare.it; noon-3pm and 6:30pm-11pm daily late Apr.-Oct.; €18-30

With a gorgeous setting below the Chiesa del Soccorso, this is an iconic spot for dining by the sea in Ischia. Seafood is prepared exceptionally well here. Wine enthusiasts will enjoy the large wine selection available. Though the indoor dining rooms offer beautiful views, book in advance to dine at one of the 10 exclusive tables outside by the sea.

SATURNINO

Via Soprascaro 17; tel. 081/998-296; www.ristorantesaturnino.it; 12:30pm-2:30pm and 7:30pm-11:30pm daily from Apr.-Oct.; €18-22

This restaurant offers a rare gastronomic experience for travelers who enjoy discovering the authentic and creative. Chef Ciro Mattera and his wife Stefania Coletta have combined their passions for traditional cooking and friendly service in this restaurant, just a few steps from Forio's port. Choose the fish or traditional menu options and let Stefania guide you through the meal as Ciro prepares dishes based on the freshest ingredients available. If you're not keen on seafood, the rabbit-themed menu is an excellent way to try another side of Ischia's local cuisine.

Regional Cuisine

SPADARA BISTRÒ

Piazza Giacomo Matteotti 11; tel. 333/132-2249; spadarabistro@gmail.com; noon-2:30pm and 7pm-midnight daily Apr. 15-Jun. 12 and Sept. 11-Nov. 3, noon-2:30pm daily Jun. 13-Sept. 10, 6pm-midnight Wed.-Mon. Nov. 4-Jan. 31 and Mar. 1-Apr. 14, closed Feb.; €9-18

Located in a charming piazza in the historic center, this bistro infuses every dish with high-quality ingredients, many grown on the Villa Spadara farmhouse on Ischia, whether it's delicious *bruschette* or salads for a light lunch, an *aperitivo*, gourmet burgers, or traditional pasta dishes. Try their version of the popular Ischia *la zingara* sandwich made with prosciutto crudo, mozzarella, tomatoes, lettuce, and mayonnaise. The outdoor seating area in the piazza is great for people-watching and atmosphere.

ACCOMMODATIONS

RING HOSTEL

Via Gaetano Morgera 80; tel. 339/470-2996; www.ringhostelischia.com; open year-round; dorms from €20, private rooms from €35

Located about 10 minutes up from the center of Forio, this friendly hostel offers both dormitory and private rooms. Shared spaces include a rooftop terrace with views over town as well as a kitchen, dining room, and social lounge with TV. Private rooms range from single to quadruple and include private bathroom and shower. Hiking excursions, hot spring visits, cooking classes, and other experiences can be arranged by the hostel. All rooms include Wi-Fi.

HOTEL TRITONE

Via Tommaso Cigliano 88; tel. 081/987-471; www.hoteltritoneischia.it; open Apr.-Oct.; €125 d

Set on the Spiaggia di San Francesco, this hotel offers a complete Ischia experience thanks to its pools, garden setting, thermal spa, beach access, and lovely restaurants. The rooms are decorated with a warm Mediterranean style and all feature a balcony or terrace. Both sea- and garden-view rooms are available and are located in the central hotel, a bungalow-style building closer to the sea, or in the Villa Quisisana in a garden setting.

TENUTA C'EST LA VIE

51/BIS Via Pietra Brox; tel. 338/394-4341; www.tenutacestlavie.it; open Apr.-Oct.; €200 d

Enjoy a peaceful rural setting with all the modern comforts at this vineyard estate in the hills above Forio. Called *rustici*, the four independent homes offer a variety of styles, from the Chiesetta Rosa with its traditional tufa stone walls to the soft blues of the Belvedere. There's outdoor space to enjoy the sun, as well as private mini wellness pools or hot tub just outside your door. Meals are available at the Bistrot, where fresh ingredients and local recipes are served with the estate's locally grown and produced wines.

MEZZATORE HOTEL & THERMAL SPA

Via Mezzatorre 23; tel. 081/986-111; www.mezzatorre.it; open mid-Apr.-mid-Oct. 14; €520 d

Overlooking the Baia di San Montano, this remarkable resort is set in a secluded spot surrounded by a lush forest and the tempting blue sea. The hotel includes private sea access, four pools, and an excellent thermal spa situated in the 16th-century tower, for complete relaxation. For gourmet dining visit the hotel's Chandelier restaurant, or enjoy a more relaxed setting at the **Sciuè Sciuè** restaurant. From lovely single rooms to luxurious suites, the 45 rooms and 12 suites are all beautifully decorated and offer a variety of sea or garden views.

GETTING THERE

By Ferry

Located on the western side of the island, Forio's port offers limited ferry service from Naples operated by **Alilauro** (tel. 081/551-3236; www.alilaurogruson.it; about 5 departures daily; from €20.40 per person). The hydrofoil service from Molo Beverello in Naples to Forio takes about an hour.

By Bus

The local buses in Ischia are operated by **EAV** (www.eavsrl.it; 6:30am-midnight daily; departures every 15-30 minutes; from €1.50) and provide service from all towns on the island to Forio. To reach Forio from Ischia Porto, Casamicciola Terme, or Lacco Ameno, catch the Line 1, Line 2, or CS bus. The ride from Ischia Porto is about 25 minutes, from Casmicciola Terme about 15 minutes, and from Lacco Ameno about 10 minutes. From Sant'Angelo, you'll want the CD or Line 1 bus, and it's a 10-15 minute ride. From Serrara Fontana and Barano d'Ischia, take the CD bus and the trip is about 40 minutes.

By Car

To get to Forio by car from Ischia Porto, Casamicciola Terme, and Lacco Ameno, follow the SP270 road west. Expect a 30-minute drive from Ischia Porto, 15-20 minutes' drive from Casamicciola Terme, and about 10 minutes from Lacco Ameno. From Sant'Angelo, you'll need to take the SP270 road west and the drive is 10-15 minutes. To reach Forio from Serrara Fontana and Barano d'Ischia on the southeastern side of the island, follow SP270 west for about 20-30 minutes.

GETTING AROUND

The historic center of Forio is easily explored on foot, but the town's footprint is large and covers the western side of the island. You'll want to catch a bus or taxi to reach areas outside of the town center. A taxi stand is located right at the port where SP270 passes through Forio, and all buses can be caught in this area as well.

Serrara Fontana, Sant'Angelo, and Barano d'Ischia

Ischia's rugged southern coastline is not nearly as developed as the northern side of the island; this is especially true in the southeastern part of the island where mountains drop straight down to the sea. Along the southern slopes of Monte Epomeo are the towns of **Serrara Fontana** and **Barano d'Ischia,** two of Ischia's six official towns. Yet, because the towns are spread out along the mountainside, each comprises many smaller *frazioni* (hamlets). Though Serrara Fontana and Barano d'Ischia are both set in Ischia's famous green landscape and have a rustic charm, each one has a connection to the sea that is a major lure for travelers.

One of Serrara Fontana's *frazioni* is **Sant'Angelo,** one of the most secluded and picturesque seaside villages on Ischia. Here you can relax in a tranquil setting by the sea or take a boat west to the nearby **Baia di Sorgeto** where hot thermal water bubbles up in rock pools along the beach. In the other direction you'll find the famous **Spiaggia dei Maronti,** which is a part of Barano d'Ischia.

Whether you enjoy hiking to the top of **Monte Epomeo** or relaxing in the healing waters of the island's oldest spa at the **Fonte delle Ninfe Nitrodi,** a visit to Ischia isn't complete without time exploring the captivating southern coastline.

SIGHTS

Serrara Fontana Belvedere

Piazza Pietro Paolo Iacono, Serrara Fontana

The least populated of Ischia's six towns, Serrara Fontana is made of seven *frazioni* and is named after the two largest. It is unique on the island because of the way it is scattered across the slopes of the mountain, from the seaside in Sant'Angelo all the way up to Fontana, which sits at about 1,181 feet (360 m) above sea level. The area has a strong agricultural heritage that is still important today. The charming fishing village of Sant'Angelo is the most popular attraction in the area, but a stop in the center of Serrara offers a beautiful view of Sant'Angelo below from the belvedere in Piazza Pietro Paolo Iacono. This scenic overlook on the side of the road through Serrara Fontana has benches where you can sit and take in the view of Sant'Angelo, and on a clear day you can see across the Gulf of Naples the island of Capri and the Sorrentine Peninsula.

★ Sant'Angelo

Jutting out into the Gulf of Naples at Ischia's southernmost post, Sant'Angelo is a seaside village famous for its colorful jumble of houses that used to belong to the town's fishermen. The little village is now a chic holiday setting with a secluded atmosphere, thanks in large part to the fact that the town is pedestrian-only. From the nearest road, a narrow walkway leads down to the Piazzetta Sant'Angelo by the sea where a small isthmus leads out to the **Torre di Sant'Angelo.** This massive tufa rock is a distinctive symbol of the town, though it is largely inaccessible today. You can walk out to it along the isthmus, which has beach clubs (*stabilimenti balneari*) for swimming on one side and a small harbor on the other side where boats depart to reach the Spiaggia dei Maronti and Baia di Sorgeto springs nearby. Above the beach, the seaside village with its multihued buildings are all connected by steps and narrow pathways where you'll find little wine bars, restaurants overlooking the sea, and lovely boutiques as you explore. With its tranquil and exclusive setting, Sant'Angelo is one of the finest spots on the island for a relaxing holiday.

Barano d'Ischia

Piazza San Rocco

Spreading over the hills in the southeastern part of the island, the town of Barano d'Ischia sits between Ischia town and Serrara Fontana. Home to some of the oldest thermal springs on Ischia as well as the island's most popular beach, this town encompasses not only the agricultural traditions of the island but also the spas and beaches that Ischia is known for. The entrance to the town from the east is marked by a 16th-century Roman-style aqueduct called Pilastri that was used to carry water from the hills down to Ischia Ponte. The center of town is **Piazza San Rocco,** which is home to the Chiesa di San Sebastiano Martire from the 17th century. Next to the church, an overlook offers a panoramic view of the coastline including Sant'Angelo. In the *frazione* of Buonopane above the town center of Barano d'Ischia, the **Fonte delle Ninfe Nitrodi** is this island's most historic thermal spa. However, what has put Barano d'Ischia on the map since the 1960s is the popularity of the **Spiaggia dei Maronti.** This long, sandy beach is popular not only for its beautiful setting and view of Sant'Angelo in the distance but also for the Cavascura thermal springs nearby.

SPAS AND BATHS

FONTE DELLE NINFE NITRODI

Via Pendio Nitrodi, Barano d'Ischia; tel. 081/990-528; www.fonteninfenitrodi.com; 9am-7pm daily May-Sept., 9:30am-6:30pm daily Mar.-Apr. and Oct., 10am-5:30pm daily Nov.; from €12 per person

With more than 2,000 years of history, this unique thermal spa in the mountains northeast of Sant'Angelo is known as one of the oldest in the world, thanks to some very special archaeological finds. A series of carved Roman tablets depicting Apollo and nymphs indicates that even the earliest Roman settlers on the island had discovered the healing power of the waters from the Nitrodi source. The water's properties are especially beneficial to the skin.

The spa is organized around a series of showers and sun beds, as the effect is stronger if you dry naturally in the sun. The spa is ensconced in beautiful gardens full of herbal plants that create a natural aromatherapy effect. Enjoy herbal infusions to cleanse the body, or opt for treatments from the wellness center. The finishing touch to the experience is to relax in the sun while taking in the sweeping views over the island.

TERME DI CAVASCURA

Via Cavascura, Sant'Angelo; tel. 081/905-564; www.cavascura.it; 8:30am-6pm Apr. 20-Oct. 20; from €12 per person

Carved into a gorge above the Spiaggia dei Maronti, these unique thermal baths have been noted for healing properties since the earliest Greek settlers arrived on Ischia. The hot thermal waters and vapors can be experienced in a natural setting because the spa's outdoor rooms are caverns dug out of the living stone. Take a hot shower in a waterfall coming down from the mountain and spend time relaxing in the sauna carved out of the mountainside. Mud treatments are a popular option here. Cavascura has also created a line of skincare products produced with thermal water from the source. The spa is accessible from the Spiaggia dei Maronti if you walk uphill into the gorge about five minutes. A taxi boat is also available from Sant'Angelo by the **Cooperativa San Michele** (Via Sant'Angelo 87; tel. 081/904-460; www.cooperativasanmichele.net; €4 per person).

BEACHES

SPIAGGIA DI SANT'ANGELO

Via Nazario Sauro, Sant'Angelo

Located on the western side of the walkway opposite the small port, this is a beautiful beach right in the center of Sant'Angelo, offering lovely views and spots to swim and sunbathe. The area closest to town is a small free beach, while the rest is lined with very small beach clubs (*stabilimenti balneari*) offering sun bed and umbrella rentals. **Lido del Sole** (Spiaggia Sant'Angelo; tel. 338/826-0856) is a good choice for a comfortable day at the beach.

SPIAGGIA DEI MARONTI

Barano d'Ischia

East of Sant'Angelo, the Spiaggia dei Maronti stretches out nearly 2 miles (about 3 km) and is the longest beach on the island. It's also one of the most beautiful, thanks to its protected natural setting, view of Sant'Angelo in the distance, and clear turquoise sea. The sandy golden beach is lined with rows of colorful sun beds and umbrellas. Many restaurants and *stabilimenti balneari* are interspersed with free swimming areas along the beach. A great spot to stop is **Bar Ristorante Ida** (tel. 081/990-163; Easter-Oct.; €10 for two sun beds and umbrella), which is equipped with everything you'll need for a comfortable day at the beach. Fans of **Elena Ferrante's Neapolitan Novels** will enjoy a stroll down **Maronti** where so many key scenes took place in the second novel *The Story of a New Name*. The beach is accessible by car or bus, and parking is available in various lots near the beach. A comfortable and easy option is to arrive from Sant'Angelo on a **water taxi** operated by **Cooperativa San Michele** (Via Sant'Angelo 87; tel. 081/904-460; www.cooperativasanmichele.net; €4 per person).

BAIA DI SORGETO

Via Sorgeto, Panza, Forio

West of Sant'Angelo, this gorgeous bay is home to one of Ischia's most unusual thermal water experiences. Below the sheer cliffs, this rocky beach has thermal springs underneath the surface of the water near the shoreline that bubble up with hot water. A swim here in the hot rock pools offers the rare chance to enjoy a thermal spring experience surrounded by immense natural beauty. Even better? It's free. That is, if you're willing to dare the steep 214 steps from Via Sorgeto down to the beach. Arriving by boat is definitely recommended. Although this bay technically falls in Forio, it's only a short boat ride from Sant'Angelo, and regular taxi boat service is operated by **Cooperativa San Michele** (Via Sant'Angelo 87; tel. 081/904-460; www.cooperativasanmichele.net; €6 per person) during the summer months. A small restaurant **La Sorgente** (Baia di Sorgeto; tel. 081/907-837; www.sorgeto.it; May-Oct.) right on the rocks offers sun bed rentals as well as dining options.

SPIAGGIA DELLE FUMAROLE

Sant'Angelo

Just a short walk between Sant'Angelo and Spiaggia dei Maronti, this small beach is notable for its fumaroles. Hot vapors are caused by volcanic activity, and the steam has created a naturally hot sand beach. As an added bonus, the sea here is beautifully clear for a swim.

HIKING

★ MONTE EPOMEO

Via Epomeo, Frazione of Fontana

Rising up in the center of Ischia, Monte Epomeo is the island's highest point, reaching

2,589 feet (789 m). From the craggy top of the mountain, there's a truly breathtaking 360-degree view of the entire island. Though there are pathways from various spots on the island, one of the easiest and best marked routes starts in the *frazione* of Fontana in the mountains above Sant'Angelo. You can reach the village by catching the CD or CS bus, as both pass through Fontana. A sign pointing toward Monte Epomeo is marked off the SP270 road at Via Epomeo. From here, follow an uphill paved road that winds up the mountains surrounded by forest on both sides and occasional secluded houses, which become even more sparse as you get higher and higher. Continue uphill as the road becomes Via Militare. Follow it up until you reach an intersection where signs point off to the left to a pathway. Here, the hike becomes especially beautiful, as vistas begin to open up over the island. The last part of the hike is steep and rocky but well worth the climb for the views at the top. There are some spots near the top to stop for refreshments, such as **La Grotta da Fiore** (Via Epomeo 21; tel. 081/999-521; www.epomeolagrotta.com; daily Feb.-Nov.). The distance of the hike is about 3.1 miles (5 km) round-trip and takes about 2.5 hours.

BOAT TRIPS AND WATER SPORTS

COOPERATIVA SAN MICHELE

Via Sant'Angelo 87, Sant'Angelo; tel. 081/904-460; www.cooperativasanmichele.net; Apr. 20-Oct.; from €3 per person

Located right in Sant'Angelo, this local cooperative offers boat taxi service to many beaches and springs in the area, including Sorgeto, Fumarole, Cavascura, and Spiaggia dei Maronti for a small fee (€3-6 per person). For up to 6 people (starting around €100), this provider offers taxi boat service to other destinations around the island like Forio, Lacco Ameno, Castello Aragonese, and more. Boat excursions around the island are also available.

NEMO

Via Sant'Angelo 85, Sant'Angelo; tel. 366/127-0197; www.nemoischia.it; 9am-6:30pm daily Jul.-Sept. 15; from €25 per person

Explore Ischia's remarkable seascape with an experience snorkeling or kayaking with the team at Nemo in Sant'Angelo. Dedicated to sharing and respecting the sea, a passionate team is on hand to help you discover the marine treasures of Ischia firsthand during your stay. All experiences are tailored to your ability and time available, but must be booked in advance. Snorkeling experiences can start right from the beach in Sant'Angelo or by boat around the island. Hiking excursions with environmental guides are also available.

FESTIVALS AND EVENTS

FESTA SAN MICHELE ARCANGELO

Sant'Angelo, Sept. 29-30

The fishing village of Sant'Angelo takes its name from its patron San Michele Arcangelo, and every year at the end of September the saint is celebrated with a festival centered around the little **Chiesa di San Michele.** On the first day after a celebratory Mass, a statue of the saint is carried through the maze of streets in town. On the second day, another procession carries the statue of the saint to the town's small piazza by the sea, where it is displayed until the evening procession on the sea heads first toward the Baia di Sorgeto and then returns to the Spiaggia dei Maronti. The evening is capped off with concerts and a spectacular fireworks display over the sea.

'NDREZZATA

Buonopane, Barano d'Ischia; www.gruppofolkndrezzata.com; Easter Monday and June 24

In the mountains of Barano d'Ischia, the frazione of Buonopane is home to one of the island's most interesting folklore traditions. The 'Ndrezzata is a local dance performed

1: hiking Monte Epomeo **2:** beautiful sea view from Sant'Angelo **3:** Sant'Angelo is a jumble of colorful buildings right by the sea.

1

2

3

by a group of men in the small piazza near the **Chiesa di San Giovanni Battista.** The folk dance may have ancient origins, although the exact lineage is unknown. It features 18 men dressed in traditional fishermen costumes from the 17th century, each carrying wooden sticks. The dance is accompanied by a song and rhythmic beating of the wooden sticks and swords, and as the story unfolds the pace becomes more energetic. The tradition is passed down from one generation to the next and is a unique local experience to witness. The dance traditionally takes place for the festival of San Giovanni Battista on June 24 and on the Monday following Easter.

SHOPPING

VILLA MARGHERITA BOUTIQUE

Piazza Sant'Angelo 5, Sant'Angelo; tel. 335/725-5878; www.villamargheritaboutique.com; 10am-11:30pm daily early Apr.-Oct.

This gorgeous boutique is infused with an air of chic island elegance, and it's a pleasure to explore the diverse collection of clothing, gifts, and homeware on display. The setting is warm and inviting. This is a concept store that captures the true essence of Ischia in the colors and traditional items on display.

ROSE GARDEN BIOCOSMESI

Via Chiaia di Rose 10, Sant'Angelo; tel.081/904-367; rosegardenischia@gmail.com; 9:30am-1pm and 3:30pm-8pm daily Apr.-Oct.

This cute shop has an excellent selection of natural and organic skincare lines and makeup. A charming selection of all-natural gifts, candles, perfume, home scents, and jewelry is also on display.

FOOD

Seafood

DEUS NEPTUNUS

Via Chiaia delle Rose, Sant'Angelo; tel. 081/999-135; www.deusneptunus.it; 12:30pm-3:30pm and 7pm-11pm daily Mar.-Oct.; €10-60

Set in a scenic spot overlooking Sant'Angelo, this restaurant is a dream combination of fine views and excellent dining. Seafood is the specialty here, with fresh ingredients and the local catch top of the menu. The pasta sautéed with mussels and pecorino cheese is outstanding, but you can't go wrong with any of the options. The family-run atmosphere as well as the fine views from the dining terrace create the perfect setting.

Regional Cuisine

ENOTECA LA STADERA

Via Comandante Maddalena 15, Sant'Angelo; tel. 081/999-893; lvoiacono@gmail.com; 6:30pm-2am daily Easter-mid-Nov.; wine from €5-15

Meander through Sant'Angelo's streets and staircases to find this wine bar with an excellent selection of wines and spirits, and a menu with themes throughout the week, such as a mozzarella, grilled meats, bruschetta, and more. With a small indoor and courtyard dining areas, this is a great spot to try local wines from Ischia.

Pizzeria

PIZZERIA DA PASQUALE

Via Sant' Angelo 79, Sant'Angelo; tel. 081/904-208; www.dapasquale.it; 12:30pm-3pm and 7pm-midnight Apr.-Nov.; €10-15

A family-run pizzeria full of local charm, this is the place to enjoy Neapolitan-style pizza cooked in a traditional wood-fire oven. Seasonal ingredients are key to the fresh flavors. Try their pizza with zucchini flowers or cherry tomatoes and *mozzarella di bufala*.

Bakery and Gelateria

PASTICCERIA DOLCE È LA VITA

Via Nazario Sauro 10, Sant'Angelo; tel. 081/999-120; www.pasticceriadolceelavita.it; 8am-midnight daily; €2-6

Just steps from Sant'Angelo's seaside piazza, this is a sweet spot to try local desserts and gelato. Head inside and steps lead up to a nice terrace where you can sit and enjoy an equally sweet view.

ACCOMMODATIONS

CASA GERARDO

Via Cava Grado, Sant'Angelo; tel. 081/907-790; www.casagerardo.it; open Mar.-Nov.; €100 d

This lovely little hotel has a panoramic view of Sant'Angelo and plenty of shady terraces to take it all in during your stay. The rooms are bright and all feature balconies or terraces that are perfect for relaxing moments enjoying the stunning sea views. Nearly all the rooms have sea views, so check in advance because this is a sea view you will want to savor.

MIRAMARE SEA RESORT & SPA

Via Comandante Maddalena 55, Sant'Angelo; tel. 081/999-219; www.miramareresort.it; open late Apr.-Oct; €400 d

Just steps from Sant'Angelo's pretty seaside piazza, this elegant hotel offers a complete Ischia experience with its 55 modern and well-designed rooms, great sea views, private beach access, and a connection to the nearby Apollon Club hotel with its **Aphrodite Apollon Thermal Park and Spa.** The hotel's fine restaurant has a dining area with an unbelievably romantic outdoor terrace.

VILLA MARGHERITA

Via Sant' Angelo 41, Sant'Angelo; tel. 335/725-5878; www.villamargheritasantangelo.com; open mid-Apr.-Dec.; €500 d

Located just above the center of Sant'Angelo, this charming property offers guests a peaceful retreat surrounded by a carefully curated decor and sweeping views of the Spiaggia dei Maronti. Divided into two areas—each one welcoming up to three guests—this hotel will make you feel at home with attentive service and a warm environment.

GETTING THERE

By Bus

The Serrara Fontana, Sant'Angelo, and Barano d'Ischia areas are served by buses operated by **EAV** (www.eavsrl.it; 6:30am-midnight daily; departures every 15-30 minutes; starting at €1.50). The CS and CD buses circulate around the island in both directions and pass through all three areas. From Ischia Porto, take the CD bus and it's about 20 minutes to Barano d'Ischia, 40 minutes to Serrara Fontana, and about 60 minutes to Cavo Grado, the stop for Sant'Angelo. If Sant'Angelo is your destination, you can also take the CS from Ischia Porto and the ride is a little shorter, about 45 minutes. From Casamicciola Terme, Lacco Ameno, and Forio, hop on the CS or the Line 1 bus to reach Sant'Angelo, or take the CS to reach Serrara Fontana or Barano d'Ischia. The ride from Casamicciola to Sant'Angelo is about 35 minutes, from Lacco Ameno about 30 minutes, and from Forio about 20 minutes.

By Car

The SP270 road that circles Ischia passes right through both Serrara Fontana and Barano d'Ischia, making it easy to reach both of these areas by car. From Ischia Porto, head southwest on SP270 and plan for a 20-minute drive to Barano d'Ischia and 30 minutes to Serrara Fontana. From Casamicciola Terme, on the north side of the island, you can take the SP270 road in either direction to reach the south side of the island. Either head east and pass through Ischia Porto before reaching Barano d'Ischia and Serrara Fontana or head west and pass through Lacco Ameno and Forio before reaching first Serrara Fontana and then Barano d'Ischia. Either way it's a 30- or 40-minute drive. From Lacco Ameno, follow the SP270 road and it's a 30- to 40-minute drive, while from Forio you'll follow the same road and the drive is 20-30 minutes.

To reach Sant'Angelo by car, from the SP270 southwest of Serrara Fontana, look for signs for Sant'Angelo and follow Via Provinciale Panza-Succhivo, which leads down to the Cavo Grado area above Sant'Angelo after about a 10-minute drive. There is a paid parking lot near the pedestrian-only pathway down into the village.

GETTING AROUND

Though the seaside village of Sant'Angelo is a pedestrian-only zone and easily walkable, the towns of Serrara Fontana and Barano d'Ischia are very spread out along the mountain slopes on the southern side of the island. To get around these three areas you'll need to take a bus or taxi. The CD or CS buses all pass through Serrara Fontana, Barano d'Ischia, and the Cavo Grado bus stop, which is the closest to Sant'Angelo. From there a walkway leads down to the village. There's also a taxi stand located at Cavo Grado.

Procida

In a region full of beautiful colors like the pastel-hued cascade of buildings in Positano or the many shades of turquoise and blue sea of Capri, there's one place that is easily the most colorful, the island of Procida. This small island is located between Ischia and Capo Miseno in the Campi Flegrei west of Naples. With an area of only 1.4 square miles (3.7 square km) and about 10 miles (16 km) of rugged coastline, Procida is the perfect size for exploring. Though you can see all the sights in a day trip, it's a dreamy spot to make your home base for a relaxed holiday by the sea.

Ferry service frequently connects Procida with Ischia and Naples throughout the year, with ferries arriving in the island's **Marina Grande** harbor. Lined with brightly colored buildings and boats, **Via Roma,** which runs along the waterfront, is a pleasant place to stroll and shop. The rest of Procida's top sights are located above the Marina Grande area to the south where you'll find the pastel dream harbor of **Marina Corricella** and above that the **Terra Murata,** the oldest settled area on the highest spot of the island. From Via Roma in Marina Grande, follow Via Vittorio Emanuele uphill and take a left on Via Principe Umberto to reach Piazza dei Martiri where you can continue down to Marina Corricella or up to Terra Murata; each is about a 20-minute walk from Marina Grande.

To reach the southern points on the island like the **Marina Chiaiolella,** beautiful beaches, and the small island nature reserve of Vivara, you'll need to take a bus or taxi, or travel like many locals and the lead character in the 1994 movie *Il Postino,* filmed on Procida: go by bike. Just be prepared to fall in love with Procida, as it truly is an enchanting place that captures the heart.

SIGHTS

TOP EXPERIENCE

★ Marina Corricella

Via Marina di Corricella

With its jumble of pastel yellow, pink, and blue houses and colorful wooden fishing boats lining the harbor, Marina Corricella is perhaps the prettiest spot in all of Campania. The oldest harbor on Procida, it was a village of fishermen, and the piles of nets and boats in the harbor are signs that the tradition is still going strong. Via Marina di Corricella is a small and sometimes narrow walkway along the harbor that, like all of Marina Corricella, is pedestrian-only. To reach it you must walk down gently sloped steps from Via San Rocco, not far from Piazza dei Martiri, or a zigzag staircase from Via Marcello Scotti that leads down to the western end of the harbor.

Now lined with restaurants, cafés, and shops, Marina Corricella is a romantic spot to dine by the sea or enjoy a leisurely stroll. If you've watched the movie *Il Postino*, you'll enjoy picking out some of the locations where it was filmed. Although a popular spot, especially in the summer, there's an air of tranquility in this beautiful setting with the pastel colors of the buildings reflected in the harbor and the salty scent of the sea filling the air.

Procida

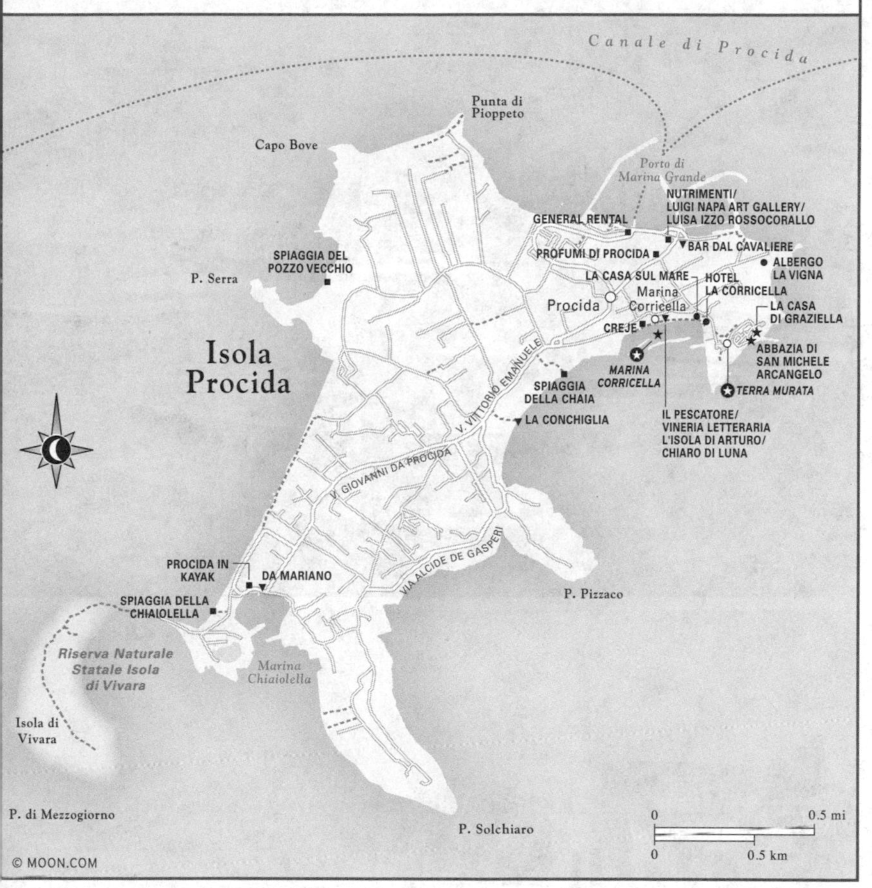

★ Terra Murata

Salita Castello to Via Borgo

Set atop the highest point of Procida, Terra Murata is one of the oldest settled areas of the island and also one of its most intriguing. This fortified area is set right into the rocky cliffs and its name, Terra Murata, meaning "walled land," reflects the fortified setting, which was created when the island's residents fled here in the 9th century for safety from barbarian and pirate attacks. The oval-shaped walled village is home to the impressive **Abbazia di San Michele Arcangelo** and a small museum called **La Casa di Graziella** where you can learn more about Procida's history.

Just outside the fortified walls of the Terra Murata, also atop the highest point of the island, is the Palazzo D'Avalos. Built in the 16th century as a defensive castle and stately home, it later became a royal residence for the Bourbon kings of Naples in the 18th century before being transformed into a prison in 1830. The prison was closed in 1988, but the buildings stand, now a place of silence.

Along the way up to or down from the Terra Murata, stop at the overlook near Punta

1

2

dei Monaci (Point of the Monks), where you'll find excellent views over Marina Corricella. The **Chiesa di Santa Margherita Nuova** set in this scenic spot hosts periodic art exhibits and events.

Abbazia di San Michele Arcangelo

Terra Murata; tel. 081/896-7612; www.abbaziasanmicheleprocida.it; 10am-12:30pm Mon.-Sat.; free guided visits available

Dedicated to San Michele Arcangelo (St. Michael the Archangel), the patron saint of Procida, this remarkable abbey holds a rich history that reflects the island's strong religious traditions. Situated at the edge of the Terra Murata with a sheer drop to the sea 299 feet (91 m) below, the abbey dates to the 15th century and has many layers of architectural styles that parallel its past. For example, it has two facades, one being the traditional entrance leading into the nave of the church and the other on the back of the church, which is the main entrance used today and leads into the nave just to the right of the main altar.

The church has a Latin cross shape with 3 naves and 17 altars. The main altar is richly decorated in marble and paintings, and dates from the 18th century. Above the altar are paintings by the Neapolitan painter Nicola Russo from 1690, with one much beloved by the island's faithful showing San Michele protecting the island of Procida. Above the central nave is a richly decorated 17th-century coffered wood ceiling with carved rosettes all gilded in pure gold. In the center of the ceiling is a fine painting by Roman artist Luigi Garzi from 1699, showing San Michele defeating Satan's angels. The abbey offers free guided tours as well as information in English for visitors. Just stop and ask at the information desk located right inside the entrance.

1: Fishing boats line the Marina Corricella with an excellent view of Terra Murata. **2:** remarkable views from atop Terra Murata—Procida's highest spot

La Casa di Graziella

Palazzo della Cultura, Terra Murata; tel. 333/373-9076; lacasadigraziella@gmail.com; 10am-1pm Tues.-Sun.; €3

This small museum re-creates a typical house in Procida from the 1800s and is set high atop Terra Murata in one of the oldest buildings that dates back to before the 16th century. In 1656, the palazzo was turned into an orphanage. The name of the museum, which means The House of Graziella, refers to the book *Graziella* by the French writer Alphonse de Lamartine, about his personal experience visiting the island in 1812 and falling in love with a young orphan woman named Graziella. Though the house is a reconstruction and nothing belongs to Graziella of the popular romantic tale, it is a fascinating small museum well worth a visit. The collection is spread across several rooms of the house, each one rich with historical objects from daily life, from the kitchen walls covered in pots, pans, and cooking utensils to traditional furniture, clothing, and decor in the sitting room and bedroom. There's also a terrace with incredible views. The small entrance fee includes a guided visit, also in English, that offers excellent context for the items on display.

BEACHES

SPIAGGIA DELLA CHIAIA

Via dei Bagni

Located west of Marina Corricella, this beautiful beach overlooks the bay from Punta dei Monaci and the Terra Murata across to Punta di Pizzaco. The Spiaggia della Chiaia is a long and narrow beach with fine dark sand and very clear water for swimming. The beach is reached only on foot with access from Via Vittorio Emanuele by following the steps down along Via dei Bagni to the eastern side of the beach. Another pathway and steps called Via Pizzaco starts from Piazza Olmo and leads down about 180 steps to the western side of the beach where the restaurant **La Conchiglia** (Via Pizzaco 10; tel. 081/896-7602; www.laconchigliaristorante.com; daily Apr.-mid-Nov.; sun beds from €8) offers sun bed and umbrella rentals along with a boat service from Marina Corricella. Much of the beach is a *spiaggia libera* (free beach) and it's popular with locals and visitors alike for its natural setting surrounded by rocky cliffs and fine views.

SPIAGGIA DEL POZZO VECCHIO

Via Cesare Battisti

Also referred to as the *Spiaggia del Postino* in honor of the 1994 movie *Il Postino,* which was filmed here, this beautiful horseshoe-shaped beach is located along the northwestern side of the island. Sheer cliffs around the beach provide a secluded setting, which has fine dark sand. A large part of the beach is a *spiaggia libera*, but there are also and sun bed and umbrella rentals from a small beach club, **Spiaggia Pozzovecchio de Il Postino** (Via Cesare Battisti; tel. 333/872-0525; spiaggiapozzovecchio@libero.it; daily May-Sept.). To reach this beach, follow Via Cesare Battisti and to the right of the entrance to the island's cemetery is a narrow and inclined walkway—marked with signs saying *Spiaggia*—that leads down to the beach. Given the setting facing the northwest, this beach gets the best sun in the afternoons and evenings in the summer.

SPIAGGIA DELLA CHIAIOLELLA

Lungomare Cristoforo Colombo

Located at the southwestern tip of the island, this long beach offers free areas interspersed with beach clubs (*stabilimenti balneari*) for sun bed and umbrella rentals. **Lido di Procida** (Lungomare Cristoforo Colombo 6; tel. 081/896-7531; www.lidodiprocida.com; daily May-Oct.) is a classic option for sun beds, umbrella rental, and beach services. Here the sand is also fine and dark, and the water is calm and clear for swimming. The beach is also close to the charming Marina Chiaiolella, a small harbor lined with boats, and the bridge leading out to the Vivara island nature reserve. The beach has sun all day, but the sunsets are particularly gorgeous from this beach.

SPORTS AND RECREATION

Water Sports

PROCIDA IN KAYAK

Via Marina Chiaiolella 30; tel. 348/348-7880; www.procidainkayak.it; excursions daily July-Sept. and Sun. only Jan.-July; from €35 per person

Set out from the Marina Chiaiolella on a guided kayak excursion led by locals familiar with all of the beautiful places and history of the island. Excursions range from a 1.5-hour trip to the Spiaggia del Pozzo Vecchio to a 3-hour tour focusing on Marina Corricella or a 4-hour *Il Postino*-themed excursion highlighting movie locations, and a complete tour around the island that also takes about 4 hours.

Parks

ISOLA DI VIVARA RISERVA NATURALE STATALE

Ponte di Vivara; tel. 081/283-388; www.vivarariservanaturalestatale.it; guided visits only, advance booking required; €10

Located off the southwest coast of Procida is a small and lush green island called Vivara that is connected to Procida by a small footbridge built in 1956. Covering 79 acres (32 hectares), with 1.9 miles (3 km) of coastline, this reserve is of considerable interest from a geological, historical, and archaeological point of view as well as for its flora and fauna. Since 1974, this has been a protected area and in 2002 it became a *Riserva Naturale Statale* (State Nature Preserve) and visits to the island became limited to guided tours. It is a remarkably unspoiled place of natural beauty in the Gulf of Naples that is home to hundreds of species of flora and fauna, as well as resident and migratory birds.

To visit the nature reserve and discover its many natural features, you must book a tour in advance via the **Vivara Riserva Naturale Statale booking website** (www.studio3c.com/vivara). Guided tours are usually given at 10am Friday to Sunday. Led by authorized nature guides, the tours last about two hours. You'll need to pay in advance with credit card (no cash) and arrive about 20 minutes before the scheduled time with your payment receipt and identification. Closed shoes are required (no sandals or flip-flops) for the walk. Tours accommodate up to 25 people, and at least 8 people are needed for a tour to take place. Note that there are no bathroom facilities and no potable water on the island, so visitors should bring water. Glass bottles and food are not allowed on the island.

FESTIVALS AND EVENTS

FESTA DI SAN MICHELE ARCANGELO

Abbazia di San Michele Arcangelo, various other locations; May 8 and Sept. 29

Twice a year Procida celebrates its patron saint San Michele Arcangelo with a religious festival centered around the Abbazia di San Michele Arcangelo in Terra Murata. The festival is held in memory of an apparition of the saint that is said to have appeared above the island in 1535. Both festival days include special Masses and processions carrying a precious silver and gold statue of San Michele Arcangelo from 1727. On May 8 the statue is carried through the streets of Procida, and during the September 29 celebration it is carried to a small overlook near the Chiesa di Santa Margherita Nuova. From there a benediction is given protecting the island and the mariners who fill the harbor below with boats of all shapes and sizes.

SETTIMANA SANTA

Various locations; Easter week

In Italy, Easter is celebrated in most towns with religious processions during the week before Easter called Settimana Santa (Holy Week). Easter processions in Procida are spiritual, intense, and extremely moving. Among the most impressive religious events of the week are the Processione degli Apostoli on Holy Thursday (the one before Easter Sunday) and the Venerdì Santo (Holy Friday) processions. On the evening of Holy Thursday, a procession takes place where members of various confraternities, completely shrouded in white robes and carrying wooden crosses, walk slowly through the dark streets of Procida, only illuminated by candles. On Holy Friday, an elaborate morning procession departs from the Abbazia di San Michele Arcangelo and follows the streets of Procida down to Marina Grande. Carried in the procession is a statue from 1728 depicting the body of Christ after being taken down from the cross and a statue of the Madonna Addolorata (Our Lady of Sorrows). Both processions offer a meaningful way to experience the Easter holiday in Italy.

SHOPPING

Procida is a lovely place to shop, with many locally owned small stores lining the most frequented streets from Marina Grande to Marina Corricella. There's no need to go out of your way to find the best shops because you'll stroll right by them while visiting the top sights on the island.

Marina Grande

NUTRIMENTI

Via Roma 54; tel. 081/896-7440; www.nutrimenti.net; 10am-1pm and 4pm-8pm Mon.-Sat.

Along Via Roma, stop in Nutrimenti, a marvelous bookstore and independent publisher; you'll find an excellent selection of books and gifts about Procida.

LUIGI NAPPA ART GALLERY

Via Roma 50; tel. 081/896-0561; www.luiginappa.com; 8:30am-noon and 4pm-10:30pm daily May-Oct.

Nearby, the colorful artwork on display at the Luigi Nappa Art Gallery is created by Procida-born artist Luigi Nappa and capture the joy and explosion of colors of a summer's day on the island.

Via Vittorio Emanuele

LUISA IZZO ROSSOCORALLO

Via Vittorio Emanuele 6; tel. 081/896-9356; luisaizzorossocorallo@gmail.com; 10am-1pm and 4pm-11pm daily June-Sept., 10am-1pm and 5pm-7pm Tues.-Sun. Oct.-May

Located just at the start of Via Vittorio Emanuele near Via Roma on the left, Luisa Izzo RossoCorallo sells handmade coral jewelry.

PROFUMI DI PROCIDA

Via Vittorio Emanuele 53-55; tel. 081/896-0233; www.profumidiprocida.it; 9am-10pm daily June-Aug., 9am-6pm Tues., Thurs., and Sat. Sept.-May

Stop in here for locally made perfumes and home fragrances inspired by the natural scents of Procida.

Marina Corricella

CREJE

Via Marina Corricella 60; tel. 081/810-1865; creje.procida@gmail.com; 10:30am-midnight daily June-Aug., 10:30am-8pm Mar.-May and Sept.-Oct., closed Nov.-Feb.

Creje has a beautiful selection of clothing, handmade leather bags, accessories, and home decor.

FOOD

Seafood

LA CONCHIGLIA

Via Pizzaco 10; tel. 081/896-7602; www.laconchigliaristorante.com; noon-3:30pm and 7pm-10:30pm daily Apr.-mid-Nov.; €12-20

Situated right on Spiaggia della Chiaia, this restaurant is a top choice for relaxed dining and excellent seafood. Try the fresh pasta served with mussels and zucchini or mussels and broccoli. Enjoy a view across the bay to Marina Corricella, where the restaurant offers boat pickup during the season. Make a relaxing day of it by renting a sun bed and umbrella from the restaurant and enjoying the beach just steps from the restaurant. Boat service is available from Marina Corricella to the restaurant. Call in advance to find out the schedule or to arrange a pickup.

DA MARIANO

Via Marina Chiaiolella 32; tel. 081/896-7350; marianolanzuise@libero.it; 5pm-midnight Mon.-Fri., 1pm-4pm and 5pm-midnight Sat.-Sun., open Easter-Nov.; €8-25

Seafood enthusiasts will love this restaurant right on the Marina Chiaiolella harbor, a tranquil location away from the hustle and bustle of the Marina Grande. The setting, with an outdoor covered dining terrace just steps from the sea, is the ideal place to enjoy the freshly prepared traditional Procida seafood dishes, such as pasta with fresh anchovies, tomatoes, and pecorino cheese; excellent fried calamari and shrimp; or baked fresh fish with the flavor of lemons grown on Procida.

IL PESCATORE

Via Marina di Corricella 63; tel. 081/1972-1905; www.sanmicheleprocida.com; noon-4pm and 7pm-midmight daily June-Sept., noon-4pm and 7pm-midnight Tues.-Sun. Mar.-May and Oct., closed Nov.-Feb.; €12-15

Set right along Marina Corricella by the edge of the harbor, this restaurant is an excellent choice for seafood and incredibly fresh ingredients, often straight from the sea. The menu highlights classic flavors of Procida and the Gulf of Naples, including a refreshing pasta with lemon pesto and a fine pan-seared tuna.

Wine Bar

VINERIA LETTERARIA L'ISOLA DI ARTURO

Via Marina di Corricella 40; tel. 333/657-0399; tarcisio13@hotmail.com; 10am-10pm daily Mar.-May and Oct.-Nov., 8am-2am daily June-Sept.; €5-10

A beautiful blend of wine bar, bookstore, and gift shop, this is a great place for a glass of wine or a light meal, or simply to peruse the books and selection of clothing and accessories on display. Find a spot at one of the tables outside along the waterfront in Marina Corricella to try local wines or choose from their menu of artisan beers, liqueurs, or cocktails.

Bakeries and Gelato

BAR DAL CAVALIERE

Via Roma 42; tel. 081/810-1074; bardalcavaliere@gmail.com; 6:30am-3am daily June-Aug., 6:30am-1am Tues.-Sun. Sept.-May; €2.50-5

Stop in this bakery and coffee shop overlooking the harbor in Marina Grande to try the island's local dessert called *lingue di bue* (ox tongues), a name that mercifully refers to the pastry's long, oval shape. Traditionally served warm, this is made with puff pastry with a lemon cream filling, or sometimes with pastry cream or chocolate, although the lemon is the most typical. With its pleasant outdoor dining terrace and late hours, it's also a popular spot for *aperitivo* or cocktails at night.

CHIARO DI LUNA

Via Marina di Corricella 87; tel. 333/770-0776; chiarodilunabargelateria@gmail.com; 10am-8pm daily Mar. 15-Apr. and Nov. 3, 10am-11pm daily May-June and Sept., 9am-2am daily July-Aug.; €2.50-4 take away, €4-8 table by sea

Set right along Marina Corricella with seating beside the sea, this gelato bar creates only handmade artisan gelato and sorbet using fresh ingredients, many homegrown in the family's garden. A great spot to stop for gelato or cocktails to enjoy the atmosphere of Marina Corricella.

ACCOMMODATIONS

LA CASA SUL MARE

Via Salita Castello 13; tel. 081/896-8799; www.lacasasulmare.it; open Mar.-early Nov.; €180 d

Ideally situated near Piazza dei Martiri and only a short walk from Marina Corricella and Terra Murata, this hotel is located in a lovely 18th-century palazzo with 10 rooms all boasting incredible views over the bay of Marina Corricella. The rooms are simply yet elegantly decorated with ceramic tile floors, Mediterranean colors, and private balconies where you can soak up the sun and the fine views.

ALBERGO LA VIGNA

Via Principessa Margherita 46; tel. 081/896-0469; www.albergolavigna.it; open mid-Feb.-early Nov.; €195 d

Set in a vineyard and peaceful residential area near the northeastern tip of the island, this hotel is a great option for a peaceful stay in Procida, surrounded by nature and beautiful design. Although the setting is secluded, it is not remote and you'll find Piazza dei Martiri only a short stroll away with Marina

Try the traditional desserts at Bar dal Cavaliere.

Corricella and Terra Murata just beyond. Accommodations vary from standard rooms, some featuring sea views, to spacious superior rooms with loft sleeping areas, a dreamy view suite with sea views, and a special standard room decorated with works by Procida artist Luigi Nappa. The hotel features an on-site spa with a Jacuzzi and Turkish bath, massage, and beauty treatments.

HOTEL LA CORRICELLA

Via Marina di Corricella 88; tel. 081/896-7575; www.hotelcorricella.it; open Apr.-Oct.; €150 d

Set right in Marina Corricella at the eastern end of the seafront walkway Via Marina di Corricella, this is the perfect place to soak up the atmosphere of Procida's most iconic spot. The rooms are decorated with terracotta floor tiles, and warm decor in soft Mediterranean colors that blend with the pastel hues of Marina Corricella. All rooms open to a terrace with a view of Marina Corricella, but note that the eight standard rooms share a common terrace while the one superior room has a private terrace. Whatever room you choose, you'll fall in love with the views.

TOURIST INFORMATION

For information on Procida, you'll find an **Info Point** (Via Roma; tel. 344/116-2392; www.prolocodiprocida.it; 10am-1pm daily) at the ferry terminal on Via Roma at the western end of the port in Marina Grande next to where ferry tickets are sold. The staff can provide information in English about getting around the island and available guided tours.

GETTING THERE

By Boat

Procida is well connected to other destinations in the region by ferries from Ischia and Naples that arrive in the island's Marina Grande harbor. To reach Procida from Ischia Porto, there are many ferry options each day. **Caremar** (tel. 081/189-66690; www.caremar.it; about 14 departures daily; from €7.80 for passengers and €28.50 for vehicles) offers passenger hydrofoil service as well as ferry service for passengers and vehicles. **Medmar** (tel. 081/333-4411; www.medmargroup.it; 1-2 departures daily; starting at €12.40 for passengers) runs service from Ischia Porto to Procida, which takes about 20 minutes by hydrofoil and 30 minutes by ferry.

From the port at Casamicciola Terme on Ischia, you can also take the ferry direct to Procida with service provided by **SNAV** (tel. 081/428-5555; www.snav.it; 4 departures daily; from €10.30) and Caremar (tel. 081/189-66690; www.caremar.it; 2 departures daily; from €7.80 for passengers and €28.50 for vehicles). The ferry ride from Casamicciola Terme to Procida takes 20-30 minutes, depending on the type of hydrofoil or ferry.

From Naples, ferries depart from the port at **Molo Beverello** and at **Calata Porta di Massa.** During the summer season, especially July-August, it's a good idea to book your ticket online in advance. The faster hydrofoils depart from Molo Beverello and take about 45 minutes to cross over to Procida. Both Caremar (tel. 081/189-66690; www.caremar.it; 8 departures daily; from €14.40) and SNAV (tel. 081/428-5555; www.snav.it; 4 departures daily; from €17.50) offer frequent ferry service throughout the year. The slower ferries for passengers and vehicles depart from Calata Porta di Massa and take about an hour to reach Procida. Caremar (tel. 081/189-66690; www.caremar.it; about 7 departures daily; from €10.60 for passengers and €29.50 for vehicles) is the company to use if you're traveling with a vehicle to Procida.

Car Restrictions

If you're traveling to Procida with a car, you'll want to make sure there aren't any issues with your car rental agency for taking the car on a ferry. Restrictions for bringing a car to Procida only apply to residents of the region of Campania. Yet, during the summer the island does often enforce a variety of different traffic regulations and restrictions. This combined with the island's small size, very narrow streets, and limited parking make a car truly unnecessary and not recommended for Procida.

GETTING AROUND

Procida is a small island and best explored on foot, via bike, scooter, or taxi. Walking around Procida's main sights does involve some uphill and downhill slopes and some steps to reach Marina Corricella. Don't expect sidewalks along the narrow streets, and do be aware of scooters and bikes as they tend to zip up and down the streets. Streets are generally cobblestoned throughout Procida, so if you're arriving with luggage you may want to opt for a taxi transfer if you need to move luggage.

Electric bikes, scooters, and even cars can be rented from **General Rental** (Via Roma 134, tel. 339/716-3303; www.generalrental.it; 8:30am-8pm daily; from €20). Electric bikes are a popular way to get around the island because they're not affected by traffic restrictions and make it easier to navigate the hills around the island. Many streets around Procida are one way and have traffic restrictions during the summer months, making it challenging at times to get around. To avoid the hassle, consider taking a taxi or microtaxi (small three-wheel vehicles) available at the taxi rank near the ferry terminal on Via Roma. Call Taxi Marina Grande at 081/896-8785 for a taxi in the Marina Grande area.

There are four bus lines operated by **EAV** (www.eavsrl.it; starting at €1.50) that circulate around the island. Line C1 is the bus you'll want to take from the Marina Grande port to reach the Spiaggia del Pozzo Vecchio. Line C2 conveniently connects the port at Marina Grande to Terra Murata, with stops to reach Marina Corricella and the Spiaggia della Chiaia. Buses on both lines run every 30-40 minutes daily 6am-10pm (until 1am or 2am in July and Aug.). Lines L1 and L2 connect the Marina Grande port with Marina Chiaiolella, with buses every 10-40 minutes daily (more frequent service in the summer) from about 6am to 11pm (until about 3am July-Aug.). Buy your tickets in advance at local *tabacchi* (tobacco shops). For one ride, tickets are €1.50, or buy a daily pass for €4.50 for unlimited rides. If you're staying for longer than a day on Procida, there are also three-day tickets for €11 and seven-day tickets for €14.50 available. Be sure to validate your ticket after boarding; the machine is near the driver and you'll only need to do this for the first ride if you're using a daily or multiple-day pass.

Naples

Itinerary Ideas 326
Sights 331
Sports and Recreation..353
Nightlife 354
Entertainment and Events 355
Shopping 358
Food 361
Accommodations 368
Information and Services 373
Getting There 373
Getting Around 375
Around Naples 379

Often described as tumultuous and gritty, Naples is a fascinating city teeming with a vibrant energy and, yes, a touch of chaos. Travelers who get to know this city with its dynamic culture and layers of history often find it captures their heart when they least expect it. From royal palaces to castles, world-class museums, and some of Italy's best street food, Naples is unexpected in the best possible ways.

Naples is a city to be seen from all its many angles. Climb to the top of the **Castel Sant'Elmo** in the Vomero for a bird's-eye view over the city and then stroll along the waterfront to the **Castel dell'Ovo,** guarding over an unusual legend as well as a picturesque fishing village, perfect for seaside dining. Meander through the narrow streets of the *Quartieri Spagnoli* (Spanish Quarter) and *centro storico* (historic center), discovering remarkable small museums and stumbling

Highlights

Look for ★ to find recommended sights, activities, dining, and lodging.

★ **Museo Archeologico Nazionale:** This museum is a must, as it houses one of the finest archaeological collections in the world, including treasures uncovered at the ancient Roman cities of Pompeii and Herculaneum (page 331).

★ **Spaccanapoli:** Walk down this characteristic and vibrant street in the *centro storico*. Its name means "Split Naples" after the way it cuts a straight line through the historic center (page 333).

★ **Complesso Monumentale di Santa Chiara:** This Gothic church was built by the Angevin rulers of Naples. Don't miss the excellent museum, ancient Roman archaeological site, and famous cloister featuring 18th-century majolica tiles (page 333).

★ **Duomo di Napoli:** The Cathedral of Naples includes the earliest baptistery in the western world and the Chapel of San Gennaro, the patron saint of Naples (page 338).

★ **Palazzo Reale:** Get a glimpse of the regal life at the Royal Palace of Naples, where centuries of rulers led the kingdom (page 342).

★ **Galleria Umberto I:** Stroll through a 19th-century shopping center with a soaring iron and glass dome (page 343).

★ **Castel dell'Ovo:** The oldest castle in Naples is set right on the waterfront on an islet near the picturesque little harbor of Borgo Marinari (page 348).

★ **Certosa e Museo di San Martino:** Visit this Carthusian charterhouse and museum to explore the fine art collection and enjoy panoramic views overlooking Naples (page 352).

★ **Museo e Real Bosco di Capodimonte:** Housed in a former royal palace, this museum has an impressive collection of 13th- to 18th-century paintings and decorative arts (page 352).

★ **Reggia di Caserta:** Explore the grandiose 18th-century royal palace and gardens of the Bourbon kings of Naples (page 388).

Greater Naples

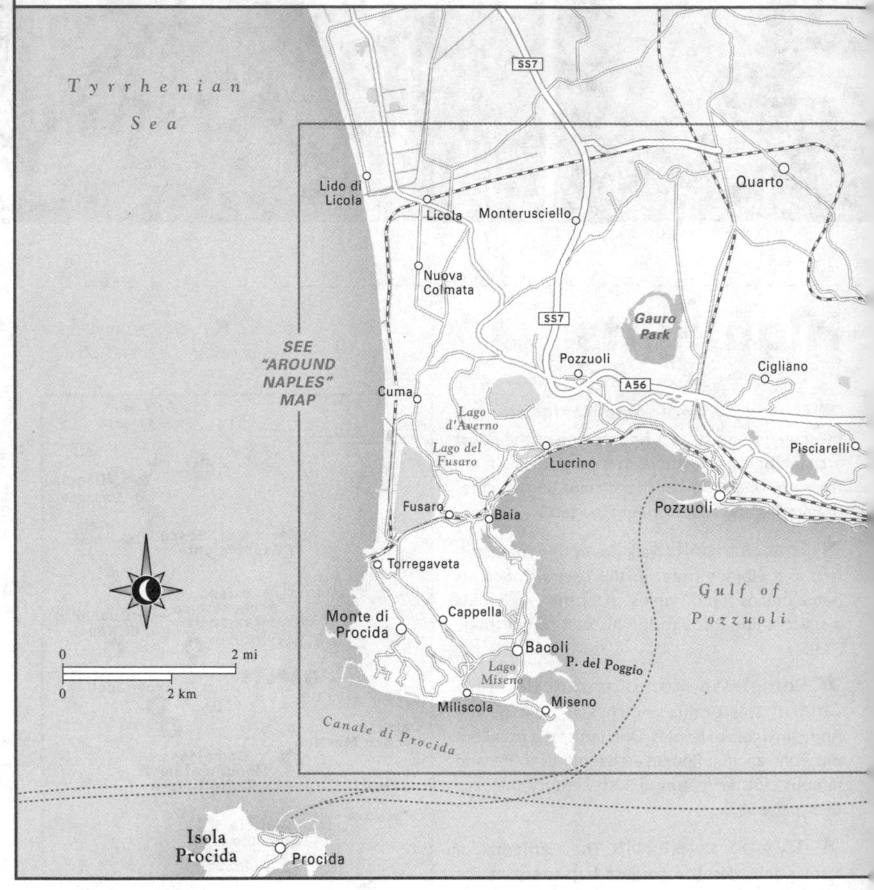

across artistic treasures in the city's hundreds of churches. Travel in time through the history of the city from Greek walls and Roman streets underground to the lavish **Palazzo Reale** (Royal Palace) built for the Bourbon kings, and all the way to the modern Metro stations brought to life with vibrant contemporary art and design.

Naples is a city of too many contrasts to describe. One moment you're gazing up at the impressive glass dome of the **Galleria Umberto I** or admiring Roman statues in the **Museo Archeologico Nazionale,** and the next scooters are zipping past you down impossibly narrow alleyways as you discover artisans continuing centuries-old craft traditions. What's that delicious scent? There's no need to worry about going hungry in Naples, because no matter where you turn, you won't be far from a pizzeria or the sweet scent of *sfogliatelle* (shell-shaped pastry filled with citrus infused ricotta) or strong Neapolitan coffee.

While Naples has enough captivating sights and experiences to fill a vacation, it's also a great jumping-off point to explore the Gulf of Naples as well as Capri, Sorrento, and the

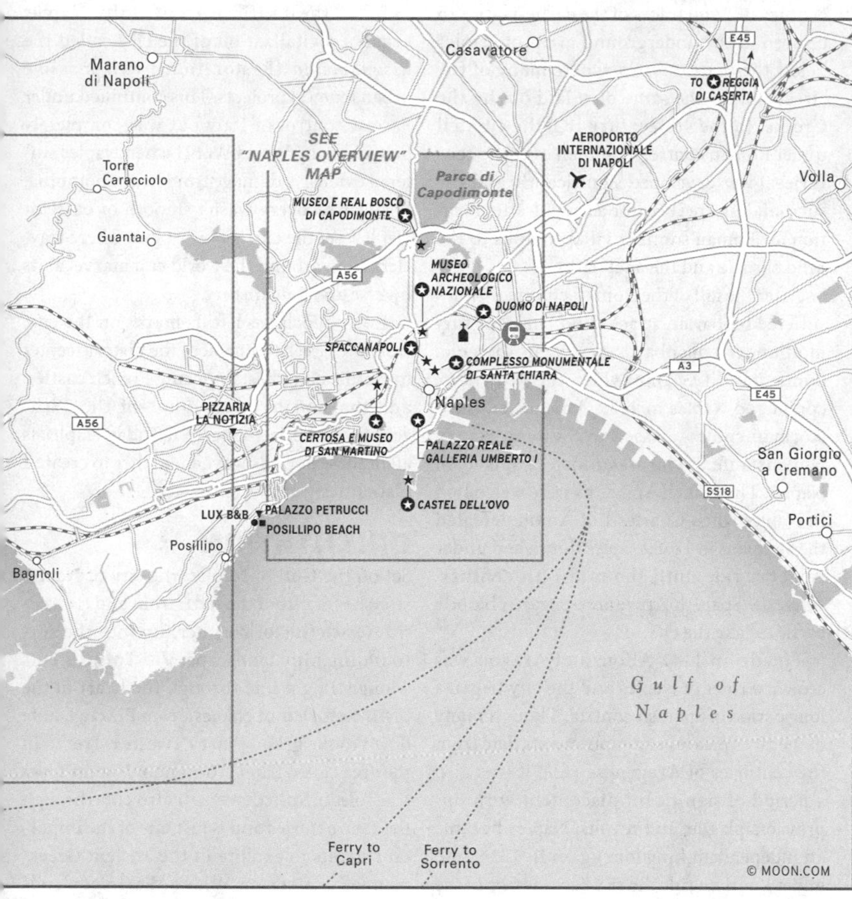

Amalfi Coast. Just west of Naples lies the **Campi Flegrei,** or Phlegraean Fields, a volcanic area rich with archaeological sites and history. After you've explored the royal palaces in Naples, head north to visit the **Reggia di Caserta,** one of the largest palaces in Europe.

HISTORY

Naples, like any big city, has a fascinating story to tell. Delving into the past, you'll find layers of history intertwined, endless plot twists, and plenty of mystery and surprise thrown in for good measure. Its many splendid monuments, fortresses, and museums reflect how Naples has been one of the most important cities in Europe at many points during its rich history.

The first Greek settlers who arrived in the Naples area founded Cumae in 730 BC, and the ruins can still be visited at **Cuma** in the

Previous: view of Mount Vesuvius from Naples waterfront; the Pulcinella sculpture in the historic center of Naples; shopping on Via Chiaia.

Campi Flegrei. Neapolis, the Greek name for Naples, was founded later, likely around 7th century BC, and traces of the earliest city can be seen in the underground areas of Naples below the *centro storico,* where many of the streets follow the same plan laid out by the Greeks. In the 4th century BC, the city fell under Roman control, and then over the centuries it was developed significantly and the surrounding area became a sought-after location for Roman summer villas, thanks to the mild climate and thermal baths.

After the fall of the Roman empire, Naples suffered barbarian attacks and constant turmoil under Longobard and Byzantine rule. Some stability came when the Normans conquered Naples in 1139. This lasted until Norman control passed to Swabian Henry Hohenstaufen, who was much despised in Naples. The French Angevins were welcomed in Naples when Charles I of Anjou defeated the Swabians in 1266. Naples flourished under Angevin rule until the mid-14th century, when the Spanish Aragonese began a bloody battle to take the city.

Finally, in 1442 Alfonso of Aragon was crowned ruler of Naples and the city began a long period of Spanish control. Though many of the city's palaces and monuments date from the centuries of Aragonese rule, it was also a period of significant discontent with oppression, plague, and revolts. Naples became an independent kingdom again in 1734, and under Bourbon rule the city became one of the finest in Europe.

Soon after that, however, the effects of the French Revolution spread across Europe. In 1799, the French defeated Naples and created the Parthenopean Republic, which collapsed after a bloody and tragic time in Naples's history. After a brief return of the Bourbons, the Kingdom of Naples was ruled from 1805 to 1815 by Napoleon's brother Joseph Bonaparte and then later by his brother-in-law Joachim Murat. After Napoleon fell from power, the Bourbons once again returned to control Naples. Yet it was a turbulent time that only set the scene for the arrival of Giuseppe Garibaldi in 1860, and Naples's incorporation into the unified Kingdom of Italy.

After the unification of Italy, Naples began a revitalization of the city called the *Risanamento* (Restoration) with massive urban renewal projects. This continued under Fascist control of Italy but was completely halted during World War II when Naples suffered extensive damage from heavy bombing. Postwar recovery wasn't smooth or easy for Naples, yet the city is now a place where travelers from around the world can marvel at its diverse and long history.

Every epoch has left its marks on the city, from the Greek footprint of the historic center to Gothic churches, imposing French castles, and the soaring glass dome of the 19th-century Galleria Umberto I. Today Naples is all of these periods woven together to create a place utterly unlike any other.

ORIENTATION

Set on the Gulf of Naples, the city of Naples stretches out from the waterfront and flat *centro storico* (historic center) up into the surrounding hilly landscape. **Via Toledo** cuts a long straight line through the heart of the ***centro storico*** of Naples, from Piazza Dante down to the grand Piazza Trieste e Trento in the area called San Ferdinando. Not far from Via Toledo, **Spaccanapoli** also cuts through the *centro storico* and is just one of the important streets to explore in the ancient Greek-planned city center. Where Via Toledo ends (or starts) to the south of the *centro storico* lies the **San Ferdinando** neighborhood, the setting for royal palaces, the grandiose Galleria Umberto I, and the Piazza del Plebiscito.

Along and near the **waterfront,** there are a few neighborhoods to explore. The **Santa Lucia** neighborhood juts out where the Castel dell'Ovo sits on an islet surrounded by the Borgo Marinari, a charming harbor with the atmosphere of a small fishing village. Follow Via Partenope along the waterfront until it becomes Via Caracciolo and runs along the edge of the Villa Comunale gardens. Not far beyond the western edge of the gardens is

Naples and the Amalfi Coast

TRANSPORTATION

If you're looking to explore the Amalfi Coast from Naples, your best option for public transportation is by train as there is no direct ferry service. A stay in the *centro storico* puts you close to the Napoli Centrale train station, where you can catch a train to Salerno and then continue by ferry or bus to the Amalfi Coast. This is the easiest option as the Salerno port is only a few blocks from the train station. The other option is to take the Circumvesuviana commuter train from the Naples train station to Sorrento and continue by bus to the Amalfi Coast. While there is limited ferry service from Sorrento to the Amalfi Coast, if you're traveling by train from Naples, it's a bit of a hike or a bus ride to reach the port in Sorrento from the train station and ferry service is far more limited.

PLANNING TIPS

If you're arriving in, or departing from, Naples and plan to visit the Amalfi Coast, it can be more convenient to schedule your exploration of Naples for the end of your trip prior to departure, especially if you're headed to the United States—flights from Naples to the United States often depart extremely early in the morning. The airport is very near the center of Naples and much more easily reached than the Amalfi Coast if you're using public transportation.

If you're traveling through Naples and have limited time, head straight to the **Castel Nuovo** and enjoy a stroll from there to the **Galleria Umberto I, Piazza del Plebiscito,** and along the waterfront to the Santa Lucia neighborhood to see the **Castel dell'Ovo** and beautiful views along the waterfront of the city with Mount Vesuvius in the distance.

the **Mergellina** harbor, which is one of the most scenic spots to enjoy views of the Gulf of Naples on the waterfront. North of the Villa Comunale is the **Chiaia** neighborhood, a stylish area for shopping, dining, or an evening *aperitivo*. High above Chiaia, the **Vomero** neighborhood offers bird's-eye views from the Castel Sant'Elmo and Certosa di San Martino. Several funicular trains connect the Vomero with Chiaia and the historic center.

In the hills north of the city center, the **Capodimonte** neighborhood is noted especially for its fine Museo di Capodimonte, surrounded by a wooded park. To the west of the historic core of Naples is a fascinating area called the **Campi Flegrei** (Phlegraean Fields), an area of rich history and unique volcanic activity. Enjoy picturesque views along the waterfront of **Posillipo;** continue on to see ancient Roman ruins underwater in **Baia,** and explore the massive Anfiteatro Flavio in Pozzuoli. Farther afield, about 19 miles (30.5 km) north of Naples lies the **Reggia di Caserta,** the impressive royal palace built for the Bourbon kings of Naples in the 18th century.

PLANNING YOUR TIME

With more than 2,700 years of history and culture to explore, Italy's third-largest city deserves at least two to three days for you to cover just the top sights. If you only have a couple of days, read our Itinerary Ideas for the top things to see and do in two days in Naples. Whether you're just visiting for a day or for longer, allow time to explore the *centro storico* to walk along **Spaccanapoli,** visit the churches and layers of history underground, and enjoy the best pizza in Italy. A longer stay means you'll also have time to explore the incredible museums—both the large ones and the smaller artistic gems—and time to take the funicular train up to **Vomero** to see the Castel Sant'Elmo and sweeping views across the city and Gulf of Naples.

In Naples there are plenty of transportation options right at your fingertips, which makes it a convenient base to explore the entire region. You can spend easily up to a week if you plan day trips to popular destinations nearby, such as Pompeii, Herculaneum, Sorrento, or the islands of Capri, Ischia, and Procida. Ferries depart from the port in Naples regularly for the islands and for Sorrento, or you can reach Sorrento on the Circumvesuviana commuter train, which includes stops at the archaeological sites of Pompeii and Herculaneum.

Sightseeing Passes

The **Campania Artecard** (www.campaniartecard.it) is an excellent sightseeing pass for Naples and sights throughout Campania. It covers a large number of art and cultural sights in Naples, including museums, archaeological sites, churches, and more. The pass also includes access to nearly all public transportation systems. A three-day **Naples Card** (€21 adults, €12 youth ages 18-25) covers only sights in the city, whereas a three-day **Campania Card** (€32 adults, €25 youth age 18-25) covers Naples and all of the region; the latter is the better bet if you plan to visit the archaeological cities of Pompeii and Herculaneum. For longer visits, a seven-day **Campania Card** (€34 adults) is also available. All of the cards provide free entry to the first two to five sights, depending on the card selected, and then discounts of up to 50 percent are given for admission to subsequent sights. If you plan to visit many sights in Naples or the surrounding area, the Campania Artecard quickly pays for itself.

Itinerary Ideas

In a city with such an extensive history, seeing all the sights in Naples would require a lifetime. Yet the highlights of the city can be enjoyed in a 48-hour tour that covers the essential sights, panoramic views from the best vantage points, and the gastronomic delights of Naples.

NAPLES ON DAY 1

Day 1 starts with a walking tour through the *centro storico* (historic center), a stop for pizza for lunch, and a visit to the remarkable Museo Archeologico Nazionale. This neighborhood is incredibly rich with historic sights and rewarding museums. So put on some comfortable walking shoes and set off to discover Naples!

1. Start the day with a walk down **Spaccanapoli** through the most characteristic area of Naples.
2. Stop in **Scaturchio** for a shot of strong Neapolitan espresso.
3. Take a left on Via Duomo to visit the **Duomo di Napoli** (Naples Cathedral) with its sumptuous chapel dedicated to the city's patron saint, San Gennaro.
4. Take a detour down **Via San Gregorio Armeno** to see all of the artisan shops selling *presepi* (nativity scenes).
5. Go inside the **Complesso Monumentale di San Lorenzo Maggiore** to see the soaring Gothic nave and explore the archaeological area below the church with Greek and Roman ruins.
6. Stop for a pizza break at **Sorbillo** along Via dei Tribunali.
7. After lunch, stop by the **Museo Cappella Sansevero** to see the *Cristo Velato* (Veiled Christ) statue by Giuseppe Sanmartino.
8. Continue down Via Santa Maria di Costantinopoli to the world-class **Museo Archeologico Nazionale.**
9. Enjoy an *aperitivo* and people watching in **Piazza Bellini,** where nightlife options abound.

NAPLES ON DAY 2

Day 2 begins high in Vomero and continues down to Piazza del Plebiscito, Palazzo Reale, and the waterfront castles of Naples.

1 Make your way to the **Castel Sant'Elmo** in the Vomero neighborhood for panoramic views over Naples.

2 Stop for lunch at **Mostobuono** and enjoy a dish of pasta with traditional *genovese* (meat) sauce.

3 Head to Piazza Fuga to take the **Centrale funicular train** down to the Augusteo stop at the bottom on Via Toledo.

4 Cross Via Toledo and see the **Galleria Umberto I** and stop for a traditional *sfogliatella* pastry at Sfogliatella Mary.

5 Across Piazza Trieste e Trento, visit the **Palazzo Reale,** the stunning royal palace of Naples.

6 Stop for a coffee break at **Gran Caffè Gambrinus** and try their espresso with hazelnut cream.

7 Admire the scale of **Piazza del Plebiscito** and continue along the waterfront to the Borgo Marinari.

8 Climb to the top of **Castel dell'Ovo** for incredible views of the Gulf of Naples with Vesuvius and the island of Capri in the distance.

9 Relax and watch the golden glow of sunset from the **Caruso Roof Garden** at the Grand Hotel Vesuvio with views overlooking the gulf and the charming Borgo Marinari below.

the Borgo Marinari

Itinerary Ideas

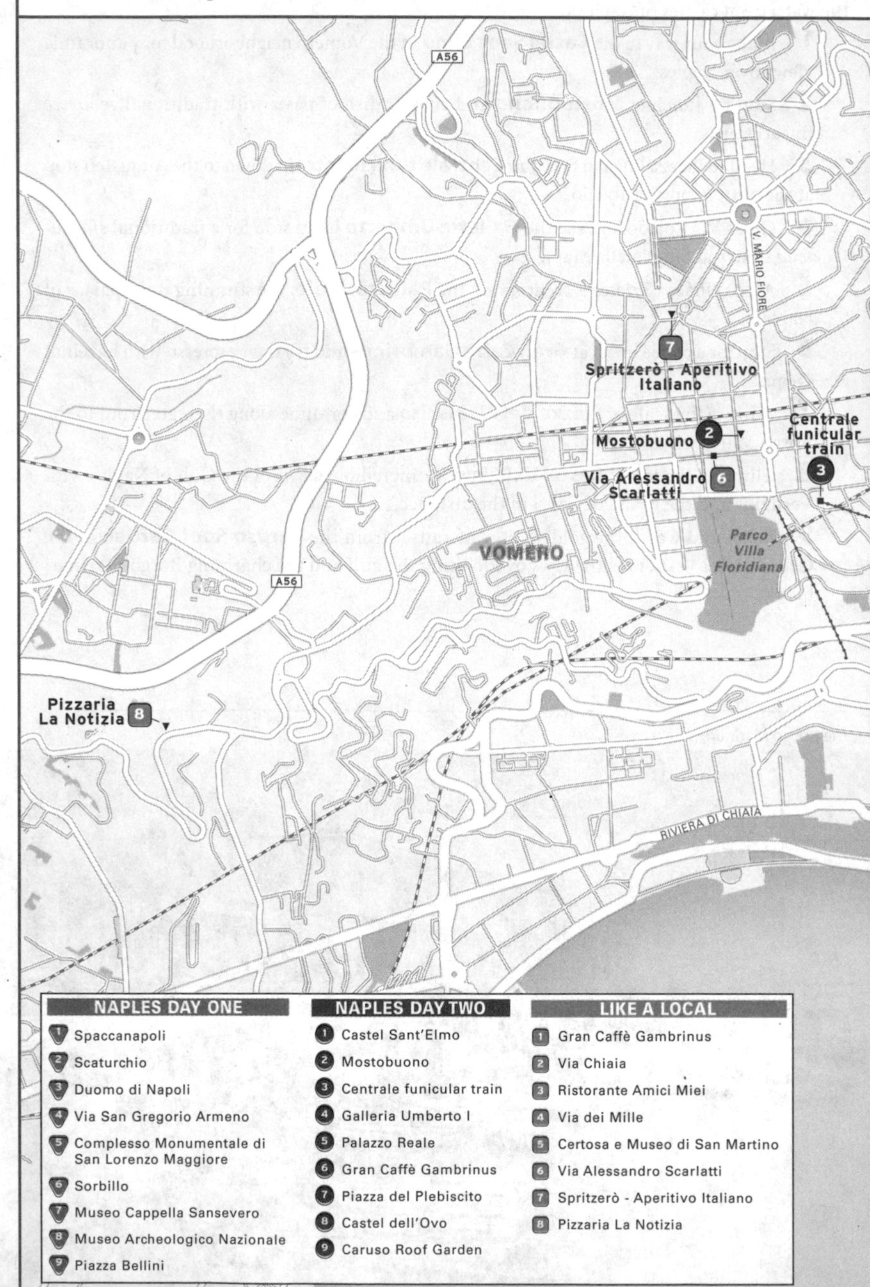
A56
A56
V. MARIO FIORE
7
Spritzerò - Aperitivo Italiano
2
Mostobuono
Centrale funicular train
3
Via Alessandro Scarlatti
6
Parco Villa Floridiana
VOMERO
Pizzaria La Notizia
8
RIVIERA DI CHIAIA
NAPLES DAY ONE
1 Spaccanapoli
2 Scaturchio
3 Duomo di Napoli
4 Via San Gregorio Armeno
5 Complesso Monumentale di San Lorenzo Maggiore
6 Sorbillo
7 Museo Cappella Sansevero
8 Museo Archeologico Nazionale
9 Piazza Bellini
NAPLES DAY TWO
1 Castel Sant'Elmo
2 Mostobuono
3 Centrale funicular train
4 Galleria Umberto I
5 Palazzo Reale
6 Gran Caffè Gambrinus
7 Piazza del Plebiscito
8 Castel dell'Ovo
9 Caruso Roof Garden
LIKE A LOCAL
1 Gran Caffè Gambrinus
2 Via Chiaia
3 Ristorante Amici Miei
4 Via dei Mille
5 Certosa e Museo di San Martino
6 Via Alessandro Scarlatti
7 Spritzerò - Aperitivo Italiano
8 Pizzaria La Notizia

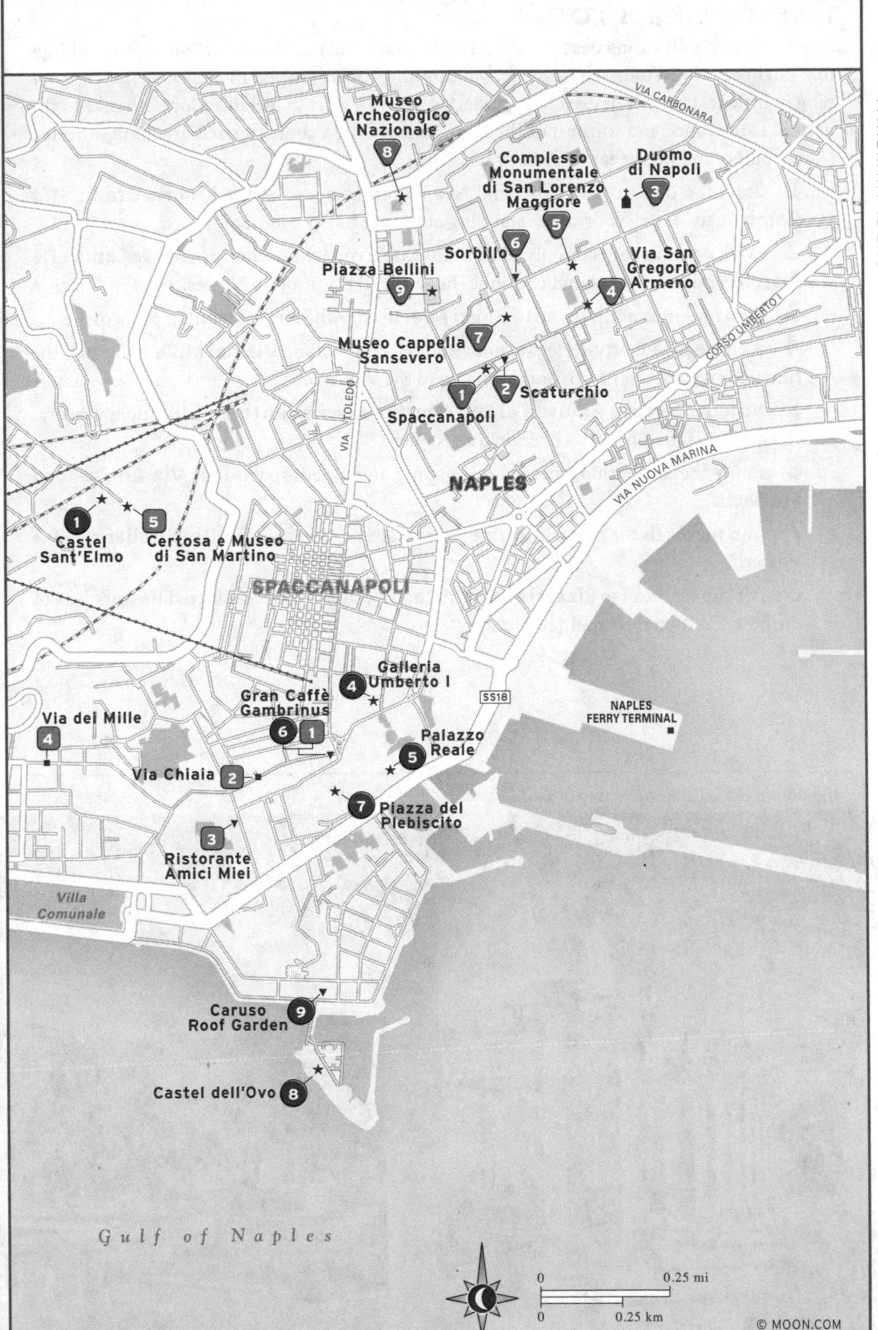
Museo Archeologico Nazionale
8
Complesso Monumentale di San Lorenzo Maggiore
5
Duomo di Napoli
3
VIA CARBONARA
Sorbillo
6
Via San Gregorio Armeno
4
Piazza Bellini
9
Museo Cappella Sansevero
7
CORSO UMBERTO I
Scaturchio
2
1
Spaccanapoli
VIA TOLEDO
VIA NUOVA MARINA
NAPLES
1
Castel Sant'Elmo
5
Certosa e Museo di San Martino
SPACCANAPOLI
Galleria Umberto I
4
Gran Caffè Gambrinus
6
1
SS18
NAPLES FERRY TERMINAL
Via dei Mille
4
Palazzo Reale
5
Via Chiaia
2
7
Piazza del Plebiscito
3
Ristorante Amici Miei
Villa Comunale
Caruso Roof Garden
9
Castel dell'Ovo
8
Gulf of Naples
0
0.25 mi
0
0.25 km
© MOON.COM

NAPLES LIKE A LOCAL

Naples is a city with strong ties to tradition and a somewhat nonchalant attitude toward things that might be termed touristy. However, walking down Spaccanapoli in the *centro storico*, stopping in little restaurants or even busy pizzerias, you can start to feel like a local, thanks to the natural exuberance and warmth of the Neapolitans. Often characterized as a living theater, Naples pulls you into the fabric of daily life.

1 Start the day with a traditional Neapolitan espresso at the historic **Gran Caffè Gambrinus.** Enjoy your coffee standing at the bar like the locals.

2 Walk down pedestrian-only **Via Chiaia** where you'll find iconic shops like **Camiceria Piccolo** and **Rubinacci** that continue the sartorial tradition in Naples.

3 Stop for lunch at **Ristorante Amici Miei** to enjoy hearty Neapolitan pasta dishes.

4 Admire the Liberty-style (art nouveau) buildings along **Via dei Mille** and catch the funicular train from Parco Margherita up to the Vomero.

5 Visit the **Certosa e Museo di San Martino** to see its lovely art collection, peaceful cloister, and fabulous views overlooking Naples.

6 Enjoy the local atmosphere and shopping along pedestrian-only **Via Alessandro Scarlatti.**

7 Join the locals for a classic *spritz aperitivo* at **Spritzerò - Aperitivo Italiano** in the Vomero.

8 For dinner, head to **Pizzaria La Notizia** for what is often considered the very best of the best traditional Neapolitan pizza.

the cloister of the Certosa e Museo di San Martino

Sights

From the waterfront with romantic views across the gulf to the narrow alleys of the historic center and the view from on high in Vomero, Naples is a city to be explored. It's also a city that is best seen on foot to get a feel for all of the city's little quirks and its soul. Most significant sights in Naples are clustered in the historic center and famous Spaccanapoli street, and down Via Toledo to the Piazza del Plebiscito. Plan also to spend some time in the Chiaia area with its chic shopping, take a funicular train up to Vomero to enjoy the views from Castel Sant'Elmo, and explore the fine collection at the Museo di Capodimonte.

CENTRO STORICO

The *centro storico* (historic center) of Naples is incredibly rich with sights, including beautiful Gothic and baroque churches, remarkable small museums, and one of the world's finest archaeological museums. Located over the heart of the ancient Greek and later Roman city, the *centro storico* is basically the city center, from Via Toledo east to the area around the Duomo di Napoli. The center is divided by the *decumani*, three parallel streets dating back to the Greek city, that run roughly east-west and are crossed by a series of streets. Here among this tight grid of narrow streets lie some of Naples's most iconic streets like Spaccanapoli, one of the *decumani*, which cuts a straight line through the center of the city. This is an area for exploring on foot, as it's not very large and, quite literally, around every corner there's something incredible to discover.

TOP EXPERIENCE

★ Museo Archeologico Nazionale

Piazza Museo 19; tel. 848/800-288; www.museoarcheologiconapoli.it; 9am-7:30pm, closed Tues.; €12

For history lovers, a visit to the Museo Archeologico Nazionale, before or after exploring the ancient Roman towns of Pompeii and Herculaneum, is a must. A treasure trove of archaeological finds from the ancient world are on display at this museum, and many of the objects are here thanks to Bourbon kings of Naples, who were fascinated with the discovery and exploration of the ancient sites around Vesuvius. Over the course of the 18th century, Pompeii, Herculaneum, and other sites were excavated, and the finest pieces were gathered together in a collection housed in this museum's current location.

Start on the ground floor in the large galleries dedicated to the Farnese Collection of antiquities, which includes spectacular sculptures. Some of these statues are on a monumental scale like the *Farnese Bull*, a Roman copy of an earlier Greek sculpture that stands over 12 feet (3.7 m) high, or the *Farnese Hercules*, a massive statue dating from the third century. Also part of the Farnese galleries is a collection of carved gems, where the *Farnese Cup*, one of the largest carved cameos in the world, is not to be missed. Spread over the ground floor and the first and second floors, the collection of pieces from Campania's archaeological sites is also on display, including mosaics, frescoes, sculptures, the numismatics collection, and a unique room called the *Gabinetto Segreto* (Secret Cabinet) entirely dedicated to ancient art with an erotic theme. There's also dedicated space with artifacts from prehistoric and protohistoric time, as well as galleries that tell the story of ancient Naples. On the lower level, you'll find a fine Egyptian collection as well.

From exquisitely detailed Roman mosaics to awe-inspiring marble sculptures, the Museo Archeologico Nazionale offers a fascinating exploration of the ancient world and is well worth a visit, even if your time is limited in Naples.

Naples Overview

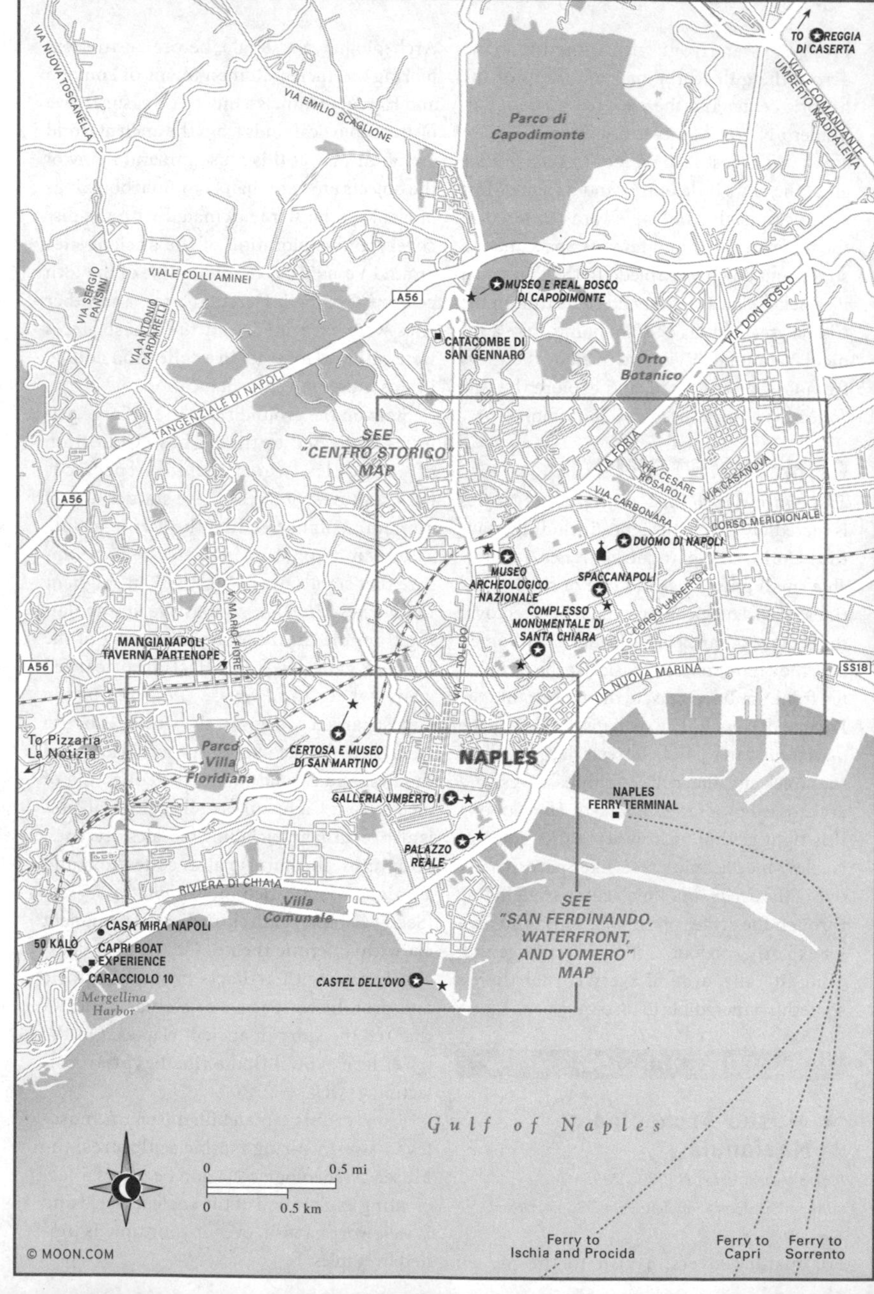

Piazza Dante

Just a short walk south from the Museo Archeologico Nazionale, this large semicircular piazza is named for the statue of the poet Dante Alighieri that stands in the center. Once the setting for a market in the 16th century, the piazza was renovated in 1757 by Neapolitan architect Luigi Vanvitelli for the Bourbon king Charles III. Vanvitelli's elegant colonnade design is the backdrop to a bustling piazza lined with shops and cafés. It marks the starting point for Via Toledo, which runs all the way to Piazza Trieste e Trento. In the northeast corner of the piazza, you'll find the Port'Alba, a large arch that was an entrance gate to the city from the early 17th century. Through the grand arch is an arcade lined with **bookstores** that leads to the nearby Piazza Bellini.

Piazza Bellini

Tucked away behind Piazza Dante, this small square is a lively nightlife spot and is worth a visit to see the ancient Greek walls that are visible below a part of the piazza. Take a look down at the defensive walls that once marked the edge of the Greek city of Neapolis in the 4th century BC. The walls are located well below the modern street level, as the city has been built up in layers over the centuries, literally covering the ancient city.

★ Spaccanapoli

Via Benedetto Croce and Via San Biagio dei Librai, from Piazza Gesù Nuovo to Via Duomo

Running through the heart of Naples's historic center, Spaccanapoli is the popular name for a very straight and long street. Literally meaning "Split Naples," it takes its name from the way it cuts down the middle of the city. Starting in Piazza Gesù Nuovo, the street now is labeled with the modern-day name of Via Benedetto Croce, which then becomes Via San Biagio dei Librai until it crosses Via Duomo. Spaccanapoli is the lower, or southernmost, of the three *decumani*, main streets that date back to the Greek and Roman city. The two parallel streets, Via dei Tribunali and Via Sapienza/Via Anticaglia, form the upper two *decumani*, and all three are crossed by a grid of streets that form the backbone of the ancient city that is still visible today. A stroll down Spaccanapoli is a must, not only to take in the ethos of Naples that is so perfectly captured here but also to see many of the city's most important churches and historic monuments in a very short distance. The streets in the historic center are narrow and can be crowded, especially during the lead up to the Christmas season with so many people heading toward Via San Gregorio Armeno to see the Christmas nativity workshops.

Chiesa di Gesù Nuovo

Piazza del Gesù Nuovo 2; tel. 081/557-8111; www.gesunuovo.it; 7am-1pm and 4pm-8pm

The beautiful Piazza del Gesù Nuovo is one of the city's loveliest with its ornate *Guglia dell'Immacolata* (Spire of the Immaculate, an 18th-century decorative obelisk), elegant palazzos, and the very striking facade of the Chiesa di Gesù Nuovo. Its dark gray stone facade is almost completely covered with carved pyramid-shaped projections, an imposing design that reflects the building's origins as a private *palazzo* in the 15th century. The Jesuits later confiscated the building, completely gutted the inside, and transformed the space into an architectural and artistic treasure. Inside you'll find artworks by some of the most important Neapolitan artists of the 17th century, including Luca Giordano, Francesco Solimena, and Giovanni Lanfranco. The church is free to visit and worth the time to admire the resplendent interior and explore the highly decorated chapels.

★ Complesso Monumentale di Santa Chiara

Via Santa Chiara 49c; tel. 081/551-6673; www.monasterodisantachiara.it; 9:30am-5:30pm Mon.-Sat. and 10am-2:30pm Sun.; €6

At the edge of Piazza del Gesù Nuovo sits the monumental religious complex of the Basilica di Santa Chiara. Built in the early 14th century, the basilica has a stark Gothic facade that stands in striking contrast to the Chiesa

Centro Storico

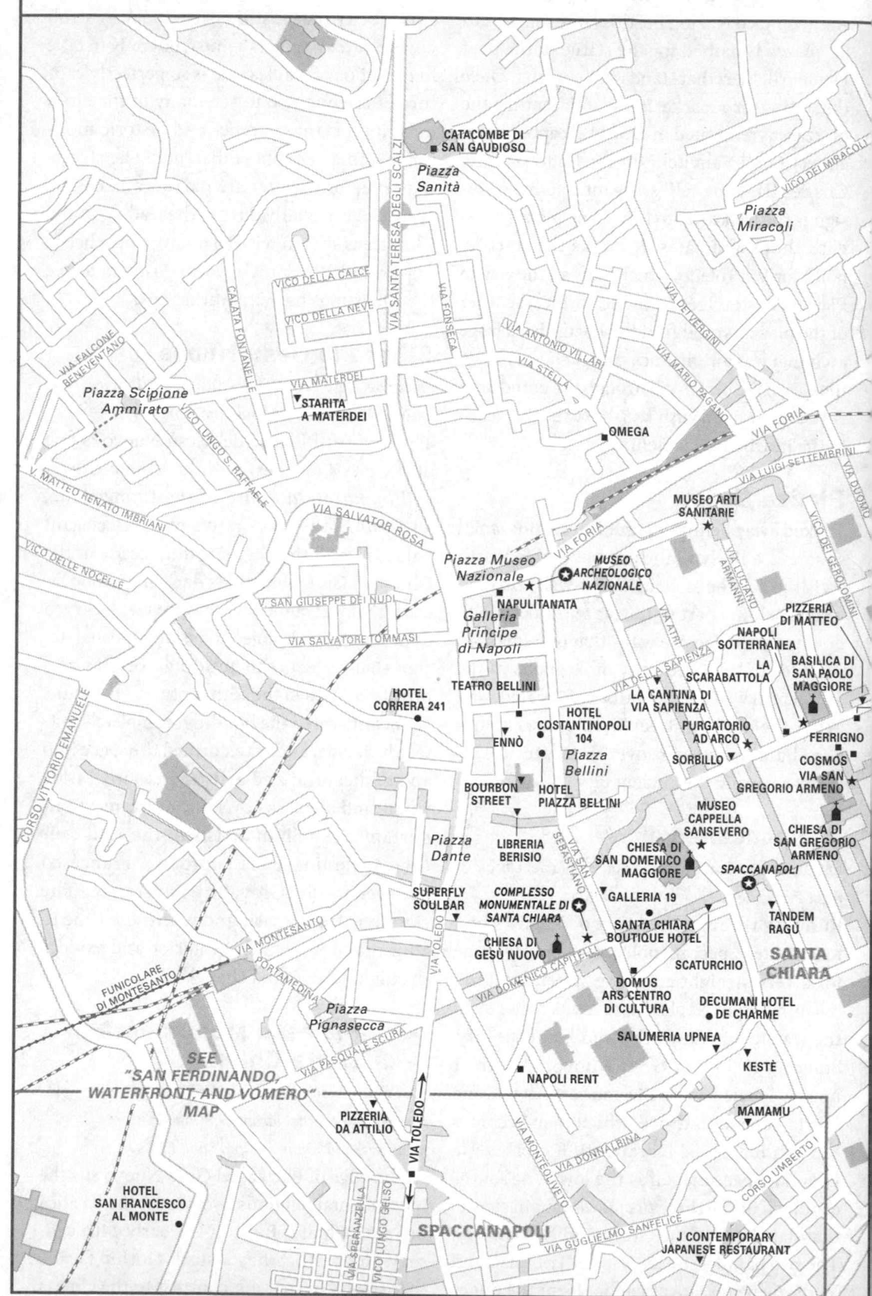
CATACOMBE DI SAN GAUDIOSO
Piazza Sanità
VIA SANTA TERESA DEGLI SCALZI
VICO DEI MIRACOLI
Piazza Miracoli
VICO DELLA CALCE
VICO DELLA NEVE
CALATA FONTANELLE
VIA FONSECA
VIA DEI VERGINI
VIA ANTONIO VILLARI
VIA MARIO PAGANO
VIA STELLA
VIA FALCONE BENEVENTANO
VIA MATERDEI
STARITA A MATERDEI
Piazza Scipione Ammirato
VICO LUNGO S. RAFFAELE
OMEGA
VIA FORIA
VIA LUIGI SETTEMBRINI
VIA DUOMO
V. MATTEO RENATO IMBRIANI
VIA SALVATOR ROSA
MUSEO ARTI SANITARIE
VICO DELLE NOCELLE
VIA LUCIANO ARMANNI
VICO DEI GEROLOMINI
Piazza Museo Nazionale
MUSEO ARCHEOLOGICO NAZIONALE
V. SAN GIUSEPPE DEI NUDI
NAPULITANATA
Galleria Principe di Napoli
VIA ATRI
PIZZERIA DI MATTEO
VIA SALVATORE TOMMASI
NAPOLI SOTTERRANEA
VIA DELLA SAPIENZA
LA SCARABATTOLA
BASILICA DI SAN PAOLO MAGGIORE
TEATRO BELLINI
LA CANTINA DI VIA SAPIENZA
HOTEL CORRERA 241
HOTEL COSTANTINOPOLI 104
PURGATORIO AD ARCO
FERRIGNO
CORSO VITTORIO EMANUELE
ENNÒ
SORBILLO
COSMOS
Piazza Bellini
VIA SAN GREGORIO ARMENO
BOURBON STREET
HOTEL PIAZZA BELLINI
MUSEO CAPPELLA SANSEVERO
CHIESA DI SAN GREGORIO ARMENO
Piazza Dante
LIBRERIA BERISIO
VIA SAN SEBASTIANO
CHIESA DI SAN DOMENICO MAGGIORE
SPACCANAPOLI
SUPERFLY SOULBAR
COMPLESSO MONUMENTALE DI SANTA CHIARA
GALLERIA 19
TANDEM RAGÙ
VIA MONTESANTO
SANTA CHIARA BOUTIQUE HOTEL
CHIESA DI GESÙ NUOVO
SANTA CHIARA
VIA TOLEDO
SCATURCHIO
FUNICOLARE DI MONTESANTO
PORTAMEDINA
VIA DOMENICO CAPITELLI
DOMUS ARS CENTRO DI CULTURA
DECUMANI HOTEL DE CHARME
Piazza Pignasecca
SALUMERIA UPNEA
VIA PASQUALE SCURA
KESTÈ
SEE "SAN FERDINANDO, WATERFRONT, AND VOMERO" MAP
NAPOLI RENT
MAMAMU
PIZZERIA DA ATTILIO
VIA MONTEOLIVETO
VIA DONNALBINA
CORSO UMBERTO I
HOTEL SAN FRANCESCO AL MONTE
VIA SPERANZELLA
VICO LUNGO GELSO
SPACCANAPOLI
VIA GUGLIELMO SANFELICE
J CONTEMPORARY JAPANESE RESTAURANT

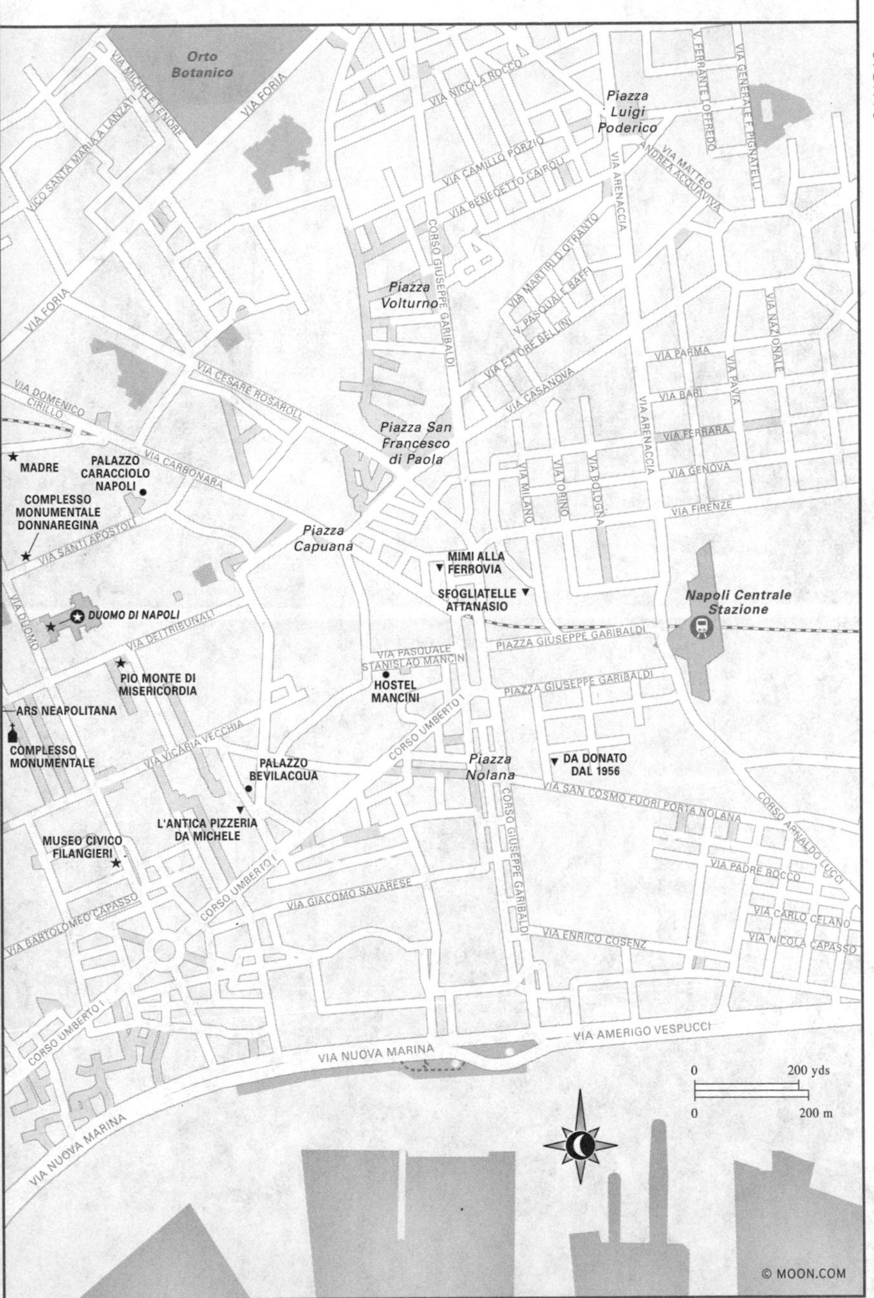
Orto Botanico
Piazza Luigi Poderico
Piazza Volturno
Piazza San Francesco di Paola
Piazza Capuana
Piazza Nolana
Napoli Centrale Stazione
VIA FORIA
VIA MICHELE TENORE
VICO SANTA MARIA A LANZATI
VIA NICOLA ROCCO
VIA CAMILLO PORZIO
VIA BENEDETTO CAIROLI
CORSO GIUSEPPE GARIBALDI
VIA ARENACCIA
V. FERRANTE LOFFREDO
VIA GENERALE F. PIGNATELLI
VIA MATTEO ANDREA ACCUAVIVA
VIA MARTIRI D'OTRANTO
V. PASQUALE BAFFI
VIA ETTORE BELLINI
VIA CASANOVA
VIA NAZIONALE
VIA PARMA
VIA BARI
VIA PAVIA
VIA FERRARA
VIA GENOVA
VIA FIRENZE
VIA MILANO
VIA TORINO
VIA BOLOGNA
VIA DOMENICO CIRILLO
VIA CESARE ROSAROLL
VIA CARBONARA
VIA SANTI APOSTOLI
MADRE
PALAZZO CARACCIOLO NAPOLI
COMPLESSO MONUMENTALE DONNAREGINA
MIMI ALLA FERROVIA
SFOGLIATELLE ATTANASIO
VIA DUOMO
DUOMO DI NAPOLI
VIA DEI TRIBUNALI
PIAZZA GIUSEPPE GARIBALDI
VIA PASQUALE STANISLAO MANCINI
HOSTEL MANCINI
PIO MONTE DI MISERICORDIA
ARS NEAPOLITANA
COMPLESSO MONUMENTALE
VIA VICARIA VECCHIA
CORSO UMBERTO I
PALAZZO BEVILACQUA
DA DONATO DAL 1956
VIA SAN COSMO FUORI PORTA NOLANA
CORSO ARNALDO LUCCI
L'ANTICA PIZZERIA DA MICHELE
MUSEO CIVICO FILANGIERI
VIA PADRE ROCCO
VIA GIACOMO SAVARESE
VIA BARTOLOMEO CAPASSO
VIA CARLO CELANO
VIA NICOLA CAPASSO
VIA ENRICO COSENZ
VIA AMERIGO VESPUCCI
VIA NUOVA MARINA
0
200 yds
0
200 m
© MOON.COM

1

2

di Gesù Nuovo across the piazza. Near the entrance stands a tall bell tower, which also dates from the 14th century yet shows baroque decorations from a later restoration. The church itself was also restored during the baroque period, yet was unfortunately almost completely destroyed by World War II bombardments. After the war, the church was rebuilt in a style to recapture the majestic beauty of the original Gothic design. The chapels along the nave hold tombs of aristocratic Neapolitan families and Angevin sovereigns from the 14th-15th centuries. Behind the main altar is the intricately carved Gothic-style tomb of King Robert of Anjou, created by Florentine sculptors Giovanni and Pacio Bertini in the 14th century.

The monastery was dedicated to the Poor Clares of Santa Chiara and features three cloisters. The most remarkable is the *Chiostro Maiolicato* (Majolica Cloister), which was designed by Domenico Vaccaro from 1739 to 1742 and includes beautiful hand-painted majolica tiles on the 64 octagonal pillars and benches throughout the cloister. Look closely at the benches, which feature a series of scenes from daily life in the 18th century. Off the cloister, look for the room with the large Neapolitan *presepe* (nativity) from the 1700s-1800s.

Beyond the cloister is the **Museo dell'Opera,** which houses a collection of religious artworks saved from the church and archaeological finds from excavations on the site. Part of the museum includes ruins of a Roman bath complex, dating from the 1st century AD, that were discovered during restorations after World War II.

Chiesa di San Domenico Maggiore

Piazza San Domenico Maggiore 8A; tel. 333/863-8997; www.museosandomenicomaggiore.it; 10am-6pm; from €5

Stroll a few minutes down Via Benedetto Croce from Santa Chiara to Piazza San Domenico Maggiore, which you can't miss because it's marked by another distinctive obelisk. Gaze up to see the exterior of the apse of the massive Chiesa di San Domenico Maggiore. This remarkable Gothic church was built in 1283-1324, and together with its museum offers visitors a masterpiece of religious architecture and art in Naples. The soaring basilica is divided into three aisles and is as ornate as Santa Chiara is austere. Here, the Gothic church still retains its resplendent baroque decorations with gilded details and a coffered ceiling. The lavish chapels are the burial place for Aragonese kings and aristocratic families of Naples.

The massive complex, now called **Museo Doma,** can be visited on a guided tour to delve deeper into this rich history. Visits cover the basilica, the sacristy, Aragonese tombs, and highlights of the art collection, which includes 16th-century garments and a painted *Salvator Mundi* attributed to the school of Leonardo da Vinci. Standard visits last about 30 minutes, while the Complete visit lasts 40 minutes and includes additional interesting stops like the room where San Tommaso d'Aquino (St. Thomas Aquinas) lived during his stay at the monastery.

Museo Cappella Sansevero

Via Francesco De Sanctis 19/21; tel. 081/551-8470; www.museosansevero.it; 9am-7pm, closed Tues.; €7

For its intensity and artistic masterpieces, the small Cappella Sansevero is a jewel of Neapolitan baroque design. With pride of place in the center of the chapel is the remarkable *Cristo Velato* (Veiled Christ) statue by Giuseppe Sanmartino. This marble sculpture from 1753 depicts Christ after being taken down from the cross and covered with a sheet. It is so finely carved as to capture the pain and suffering of Christ through the incredible lightness of the sheet. While this fine statue is utterly captivating, the rest of the museum, featuring works by the most prominent 18th-century sculptors and artists, is no less worthy of attention.

1: Museo Archeologico Nazionale **2:** Chiesa di Santa Chiara on the Piazza del Gesù Nuovo

Museo Civico Filangieri

Via Duomo 288; tel. 081/203-175; www.museofilangieri.org; 10am-4pm Mon.-Sat., 10am-2pm Sun; €5

A massive entrance portal and rusticated 15th-century facade greet visitors to the Museo Civico Filangieri, a small museum set in the former home of Prince Gaetano Filangieri (1824-1892). The prince was an avid art collector and historian. In 1888, he transformed the historic palazzo into a home and museum filled with his collection of paintings, sculptures, weapons and armor, decorative arts, and an extensive library with 30,000 volumes. The upper room of the museum features carved wood paneling, an intricate majolica tile floor, and a skylight that fills the room with light. The gallery level of the room has wood cabinets displaying pieces from the museum's porcelain collection.

★ Duomo di Napoli

Via Duomo 147; tel. 081/449-087; www.chiesadinapoli.it; 8:30am-1:30pm and 2:30pm-7:30pm Mon.-Sat., 8:30am-1:30pm and 4:30pm-7:30pm Sun.; free to enter cathedral, €2 to visit baptistery

In a city with no shortage of impressive religious sights, the Duomo (Cathedral of Naples) holds an important place not only as the largest and most important church in the city, but also for its strong connection to Neapolitan traditions and life. Behind the Gothic-revival facade designed by Neapolitan architect Errico Alvino at the end of the 1800s lies a church with layers of history dating back to the 13th century, when the Gothic cathedral was built. Over the centuries the cathedral was rebuilt, expanded, and decorated in a variety of different styles that blend together to tell the story of art in Naples, from the 13th to the 19th century. The central nave soars to about 157 feet (48 m) and combines Gothic elements with later baroque decorations and a coffered and gilded 17th-century ceiling with painted panels. On the upper band of the nave are paintings by celebrated Neapolitan artist Luca Giordano depicting the Apostles and Doctors of the church, and on the lower band are round portraits of important patron saints of Naples.

To the left of the entrance is a large chapel that was once the Basilica of Santa Restituta dating to the 4th century, offering an interesting look at early Christian architecture. Don't miss the **Battistero di San Giovanni in Fonte,** a Byzantine baptistery that is the oldest surviving in the western world. The baptistery is open 8:30am-12:30pm and 2:30pm-6:30pm Monday-Friday, and 8:30am-1pm Sunday. As in much of the *centro storico*, the history below the Duomo dates back to Greek and Roman times. Archaeological excavation has uncovered a Greek street made of tufa with traces of cartwheels carved into the stone, beautiful Roman mosaics, and architectural ruins. Unfortunately, the archaeological area below the Duomo is closed indefinitely for restoration.

The heart and soul of the Duomo is the gleaming **Reale Cappella del Tesoro di San Gennaro,** a sumptuous baroque chapel built in the early 17th century. Dedicated to the city's patron saint and protector San Gennaro, the chapel holds artifacts, reliquaries, and the much-treasured vial of the saint's blood that, faithful say, miraculously liquefies three times a year (first Sun. in May, Sept. 19, and Dec. 16). Besides the chapel, take time to visit the **Museo del Tesoro di San Gennaro** (Via Duomo 149; tel. 081/294-980; www.museosangennaro.it; 9am-4:30pm Mon.-Fri., 9am-5:30pm Sat.; €8) to see the collection of exquisite religious silver objects, textiles, jewels, sculptures, and artwork.

Pio Monte della Misericordia

Via dei Tribunali 253; tel. 081/446-944; www.piomontedellamisericordia.it; 9am-6pm Mon.-Sat., 9am-2:30pm Sun.; €7

Just around the corner from the Duomo, the Pio Monte della Misericordia church is located across from a small piazza with an exquisite obelisk designed by Cosimo Fanzago in 1637. This church was founded in 1602 by seven Neapolitan noblemen to provide charitable works to help the city's poor, offer care for the sick, shelter pilgrims, and help inmates. The institution is still active doing charitable works and is located in the same 17th-century building where it was founded. With more than four centuries of history, Pio Monte della Misericordia has amassed a fine collection of artwork, with the most important and significant being Caravaggio's masterpiece *The Seven Works of Mercy*, created for the main alter in 1607. The cappella is a stunning place to admire this important work by Caravaggio, along with other paintings on display around the chapel. Take time to explore the rest of the church's collection, which includes both historical and contemporary donations by Nepolitan artists Mimmo Jodice and Francesco Clemente.

Napoli Sotterranea (Underground Naples)

Piazza San Gaetano 68; tel. 081/296-944; www.napolisotterranea.org; tours 10am-6pm daily; €10

With two striking churches, Piazza San Gaetano is a natural spot to pause along Via dei Tribunali while exploring the *centro storico* (historic center). This historic piazza is in the exact location of the Greek agora and later Roman forum: the heart of ancient Neapolis. Descend deep down below the busy streets of Naples and you can explore layers upon layers of history. The Napoli Sotterranea tour starts in the caves excavated in the 4th century BC by the Greeks. The caves were later used for cisterns for the city's water supply. The visit includes the remains of a Roman theater and city, World War II air raid shelters, a War Museum, and more. The tour includes steps, but most of the area explored is spacious and well lit, except for one optional part where the space is more narrow and dark, but everyone is given a candle to light the path. Tours last about an hour and are available in English daily every two hours.

Complesso Monumentale di San Lorenzo Maggiore

Piazza San Gaetano 316; tel. 081/211-0860; www.laneapolissotterrata.it; 9:30am-5:30pm daily; €9

To delve deeper into the fascinating tapestry of Naples's history, pay a visit to the Chiesa di San Lorenzo Maggiore, where you'll learn the city's story, from the ancient city to the creation of this important religious complex in Piazza San Gaetano. Beyond the baroque facade designed by Ferdinando Sanfelice in 1742, the interior of the church has largely been restored to its original Gothic design. Dating to the 13th century, the design highlights Gothic forms.

Don't miss the **cloister,** which was located on the spot of the ancient Roman market, with its central stone well carved by Cosimo Fanzago. Travelers should also visit the **Museo dell'Opera** (museum) and the **Sisto V Hall,** the refectory with 17th-century frescoes covering the ceiling. Just off the cloister, a staircase leads down to the **archaeological excavations** below the church, where you can see the Greek and Roman footprint of the city; you'll see a well-preserved Roman street and the ruins of the ancient market shops, including mosaic paving from the 1st to 2nd century BC. It's a unique historical experience to walk down through the medieval layers of the church and to stand in what was the heart of Naples in antiquity.

Basilica di San Paolo Maggiore

Piazza San Gaetano 76

A statue dedicated to San Gaetano stands near the grand double staircase entrance to the Basilica di San Paolo Maggiore. Before visiting, take a moment to look closely at the 17th-century baroque facade of the church and notice the two large Corinthian columns standing about 36 feet (11 m) tall. These are from the Roman Temple of Dioscuri that once stood on this very spot. The church is surprisingly large and bright, which is excellent for admiring the many paintings and frescoes adorning the interior. Significantly damaged during World War II bombings, the church was later restored and repairs can be seen in the transept and roof in this area, which completely collapsed.

Via San Gregorio Armeno

Via San Gregorio Armeno from Via dei Tribunali to Via San Biagio dei Librai

As the hub of Naples's *presepe* (nativity) artisan workshops, this short street is one of the most entertaining in the historic center. Displays with nativity scene figurines and decorations of all sizes spill out onto the street. Take time to look closely at the detailed pieces that are handmade from terra-cotta and require meticulous work. Often in the workshops along the street you can see artisans at work creating new pieces. It's a tradition that has been passed down for generations, and the craftsmanship is spectacular to witness firsthand. The street itself has a heritage of terra-cotta since ancient times, when shops produced votive figurines that were popular offerings to take to the temple dedicated to Ceres, which was located nearby in ancient Neapolis. The holiday season is a particularly busy time to visit the street because the nativity tradition is still an integral part of Christmas celebrations in Italy, but the workshops are open year-round.

Chiesa di San Gregorio Armeno

Via San Gregorio Armeno 1; 9:30am-1pm daily; €4

Take a break from the nativity scenes to visit the Chiesa di San Gregorio Armeno, located about midway down the street. Though it's hard to take in the dark stone baroque facade from the narrow street, go inside to admire the lavish baroque decorations, complete with gold paneling on the walls and ceiling. There are many fine paintings, including more than 50 by Neapolitan artist Luca Giordano. The church and adjacent convent were founded in the 8th century by a group of nuns who fled from persecution in Constantinople with the relics of San Gregorio, a bishop from Armenia. The convent has a peaceful cloister with a marble fountain flanked by two large statues from the early 18th century representing Christ and the Samaritan woman at the well.

Madre

Via Luigi Settembrini 79; tel. 081/197-37254; www.madrenapoli.it; 10am-7:30pm Mon.-Sat., 10am-8pm Sun.; €8

Located in the 19th-century Palazzo Donnaregina, the Madre (Museo d'Arte Contemporanea Donnaregina) museum has a fine collection of contemporary art. The permanent collection, exhibitions, and educational spaces are spread across three floors and 77,500 square feet (7,200 square meters). With a unique juxtaposition of historic and modern architectural styles, the collection includes works by the biggest names in Italian and international art from the past 50 years, including Mimmo Paladino, Richard Serra, Sol Lewitt, Francesco Clemente, Jeff Koons, Anish Kapoor, and many more.

Complesso Monumentale Donnaregina

Largo Donnaregina; tel. 081/557-1365; www.museodiocesanonapoli.com; 9:30am-4:30pm Mon.-Sat. (closed Tues.), 9:30am-2pm Sun.; €6

Covering a large area north of the Duomo, this religious complex dates back to the 8th century with the foundation of the earliest church, Santa Maria Donnaregina Vecchia (*vecchia* means old). The complex today also includes the Santa Maria Donnaregina Nuova (new) church and the Diocesan Museum of Naples, where a wonderful collection of religious art is on display. Visiting the complex, you can see both the Gothic architecture of the Vecchia church and the baroque majesty of the 17th-century Nuova church.

Museo Arti Sanitarie

Via Maria Lorenzo Longo 50; tel. 081/440-647; www.museoartisanitarie.it; 9am-5pm Mon.-Sat., 9am-1pm Sun., closed Tues.; €10

Founded in the early 16th century as a monastery and later transformed into a hospital, the Ospedale degli Incurabili has played an important and fascinating role in medical and scientific history. It was here that doctors

The Nativity Tradition in Naples

the popular Via San Gregorio Aremeno lined with *presepe* shops

Of the many artistic traditions of Naples, one of the most unique is the *presepe*, which is Italian for nativity scene, or Christmas cribs. Dating back to Saint Francis of Assisi in the 13th century, the nativity is still an important part of Christmas celebrations throughout Italy. Starting in the mid-14th century, artists in Naples began creating both small and large-scale *presepi* for churches, private chapels for wealthy families, and eventually for displaying in homes during the Christmas season.

By the 1700s, the Neapolitan *presepe* was a work of art that extended far beyond the traditional manger scene. In addition to figures related to the birth of Jesus, the nativity grew to include an entire landscape that was representative of Neapolitan life in the 1700s. These figures, called *pastori*, include a host of characters, from peasants to farmers, animals, houses, and shops. A traditional Neapolitan nativity scene is a theatrical experience, full of passion and a spark of whimsy.

VIA SAN GREGORIO ARMENO

The heart of the *presepe* tradition is Via San Gregorio Armeno in the historic center, where artisans have been handmaking nativities for centuries. Strolling down the street, you'll find one workshop after the next with elaborate displays of figures and elements for creating *presepi* of all sizes. Traditional figurines are made with terra-cotta or papier-mâché; the finest are delicately painted and feature handmade clothing. Leading up to the Christmas season the street becomes very crowded, but throughout the year you can stop by workshops to see artisans at work.

SHOPS

Located right on Via San Gregorio Armeno, the **Ferrigno** shop is an excellent place to see the traditional Neapolitan nativity scenes created by brothers Giuseppe and Marco Ferrigno. Or just around the corner at Via dei Tribunali 303, stop by **Ars Neapolitana** to see the remarkable figures crafted by hand by the young and talented Neapolitan artist Guglielmo Muoio.

OTHER PLACES TO SEE *PRESEPI*

Some of the finest examples of Neapolitan 18th-century *presepi* can be seen at the **Certosa e Museo di San Martino,** which has a special section dedicated to nativities from the 1700s-1800s in Naples. Just off the *Chiostro Maiolicato* (Majolica Cloister) at the **Complesso Monumentale di Santa Chiara** there's a special room with a large Neapolitan *presepe* from the 18th century. If you visit the **Reggia di Caserta** outside Naples, you'll have the chance to see the Royal Nativity Scene, a massive *presepe* scene re-created based on a design from 1844.

began studying and treating "incurable" diseases of the time. The small yet interesting Museo delle Arti Sanitarie displays historic documents and medical equipment. A real gem is the **Farmacia Degli Incurabili,** a pharmacy dating back to the 18th century where it feels as if time has stopped. Its ornate rococo design includes frescoed ceilings, majolica tiled floor, and carved wooden shelves lined with more than 400 majolica vases. Guided visits last about 1.5 hours and include the Museo delle Arti Sanitarie, the historic pharmacy, medical gardens, and the 16th-century cloister. Information is available in English, and guided visits in English can be arranged in advance.

Purgatorio ad Arco

Via dei Tribunali 39; tel. 081/440-438; www.purgatorioadarco.it; 10am-6pm Mon.-Sat., and 10am-2pm Sun. Apr.-Dec., 10am-2pm Mon.-Fri. and Sun. and 10am-5pm Sat. Jan.-Mar.; €6

Out of all of the churches in Naples, this little one dedicated to Santa Maria delle Anime del Purgatorio is truly one of the city's most unusual. The elegant 17th-century church that you step into on the main level reveals little of what you'll find in the lower church. There lies a burial area housing anonymous remains that are part of a special devotion to the ancient cult of the Purgatory Souls. In the underground church, you'll see tombs, skulls, and wooden boxes used for burial. Though a visit to the church is free, you'll need to buy a ticket and join a guided tour to see the museum and burial site.

SAN FERDINANDO

The area called San Ferdinando is the political and administrative center of Naples—just as it has been for centuries. Yet most travelers head to this part of Naples to stroll through the grand **Piazza del Plebiscito,** shop at the glass domed **Galleria Umberto I,** visit the royal palace, and see the impressive **Castel Nuovo** and other top sights nearby. Here you can go from the depths of the city in **Napoli Sotterranea** (Naples Underground) to the heights of Bourbon dynasty in Naples at the **Palazzo Reale.**

The *Quartieri Spagnoli* (Spanish Quarter) is a tight grid of narrow streets west of Via Toledo sitting at the base of the steep slope up to Vomero. This is where the Spanish Viceroy's soldiers lived in the 16th century, which explains how this intensely Neapolitan neighborhood got its name. This neighborhood's tiny streets, criss-crossed with laundry, make for an interesting stroll.

Castel Nuovo

Piazza Municipio; tel. 081/795-7709; www.comune.napoli.it; 8:30am-6pm Mon.-Sat., closed Sun.; €6

Sitting grandly on the waterfront, the imposing Castel Nuovo, also called the Maschio Angioino, is a castle dating from the late 13th century. Built by the French King Charles I of Anjou, it was later expanded under the Aragonese control of the city. The stunning Triumphal Arch with marble bas-reliefs at the entrance dates from the Aragonese period. Entering through the massive bronze gates, look for the cannonball still embedded in one of the gates, a reminder of the battles this castle has seen over its long history. The view inside the courtyard is an impressive sight. Don't miss the **Cappella Palatina** from the 14th century, **Sala dell'Armeria** (armory), and the **Museo Civico** (Civic Museum), displaying artwork from the medieval period to the late 1800s.

★ Palazzo Reale

Piazza del Plebiscito 1; tel. 081/580-8111; www.palazzorealenapoli.it; 9am-8pm, closed Wed.; €6

Occupying appropriately fine waterfront real estate, the Palazzo Reale is the royal palace of Naples and was built starting at the beginning of the 17th century for Spanish royalty. Designed by noted architect Domenico Fontana, the palace has changed in many ways over the years, including the addition of the grand entrance staircase in 1727. The palace we see now took on its current appearance only in 1858. A visit to the palace includes the throne room and royal apartments, beautifully decorated with historic furniture and artwork from the days of Bourbon rule in Naples. With its frescoes and outstanding sculptural work, the court theater was designed by the architect Ferdinando Fuga to celebrate the marriage of Ferdinand IV to Maria Carolina of Austria in 1768. An audio guide, available in English, is included with the ticket price.

Piazza del Plebiscito

The largest piazza in Naples, and one of the largest in Italy, Piazza del Plebiscito is where much of the city's history has played out over the centuries. Opening from Piazza Trieste e Trento, the large piazza is an impressive sight with the **Palazzo Reale** on the left, a striking colonnade with the **Basilica di San Francesco di Paola** on the right, and a glimpse of the sea in the distance. Two large equestrian statues stand in the piazza, one representing Bourbon king Carlo III and the other his son Ferdinando I. While firmly rooted in the city's royal past, the name Piazza del Plebiscito today refers to the referendum, or plebiscite, in 1860, when the Kingdom of Two Sicilies was annexed to the Kingdom of Italy during the unification. While the Piazza del Plebiscito is occasionally the setting for concerts and events, the rest of the time the large open piazza is a popular spot for kids to run and play, and for locals to enjoy a walk away from the traffic and hustle and bustle of the city.

Basilica di San Francesco da Paola

Piazza del Plebiscito

Built 1817-1846, this impressive church was created at the wish of Ferdinando I as an ex-voto after reclaiming Naples from French control. Situated in the center of a curved colonnade, this fine example of neoclassical Italian architecture was inspired by the Pantheon in Rome. Walk up the small flight of marble steps and past the six Ionic columns that mark the entrance portico. Enter the church to find two side chapels, both with domes, and then the center of the church where the largest dome rises to 174 feet (53 meters). The round nave is surrounded by 34 marble columns and includes a gallery where the royal family would sit during religious services.

Teatro di San Carlo

Via San Carlo 98/F; tel. 081/797-2331; www.teatrosancarlo.it; performances throughout the year

Founded in 1737, the Teatro di San Carlo is the oldest opera house in Europe in continuous use since it first opened. The grand theater was built at the behest of King Carlo III adjacent to the Palazzo Reale. The glittering gold and red theater seats up to 1,379 people with its 184 boxes, including a lavish royal box. It's an extraordinary setting to enjoy an opera, dance, or concert performance. The Teatro San Carlo welcomes visitors outside of performance times with tours available in English daily (€9, hourly 10:30am-12:30pm and 2:30pm-4:30pm), with the option to add a visit to **Memus** (tel. 081/797-2449; www.memus.org; 9am-7pm, closed Wed. and Aug., closes 3pm on Sun.; €6, or €5 with theater tour), the museum and archive of the Teatro San Carlo.

★ Galleria Umberto I

Via San Carlo 15; www.comune.napoli.it; always open

The distinctive soaring glass and metal ribbed dome of the Galleria Umberto I is an arresting sight amid the urban landscape of Naples. Built at the end of the 19th century, the Galleria was a key part of the city's revival and regeneration, called the *Risanamento* (Restoration), which saw massive changes in the historic center. Located across the street from the Teatro San Carlo, the Galleria was envisioned as a public space that would bring together shops, cafés, and living with private apartments on the upper floor. The architectural style is reminiscent of the Galleria Vittorio Emanuele II in Milan. The glass roof is an impressive sight, especially when you stand below the central dome where a large mosaic in the floor depicts the zodiac signs.

San Ferdinando, Waterfront, and Vomero

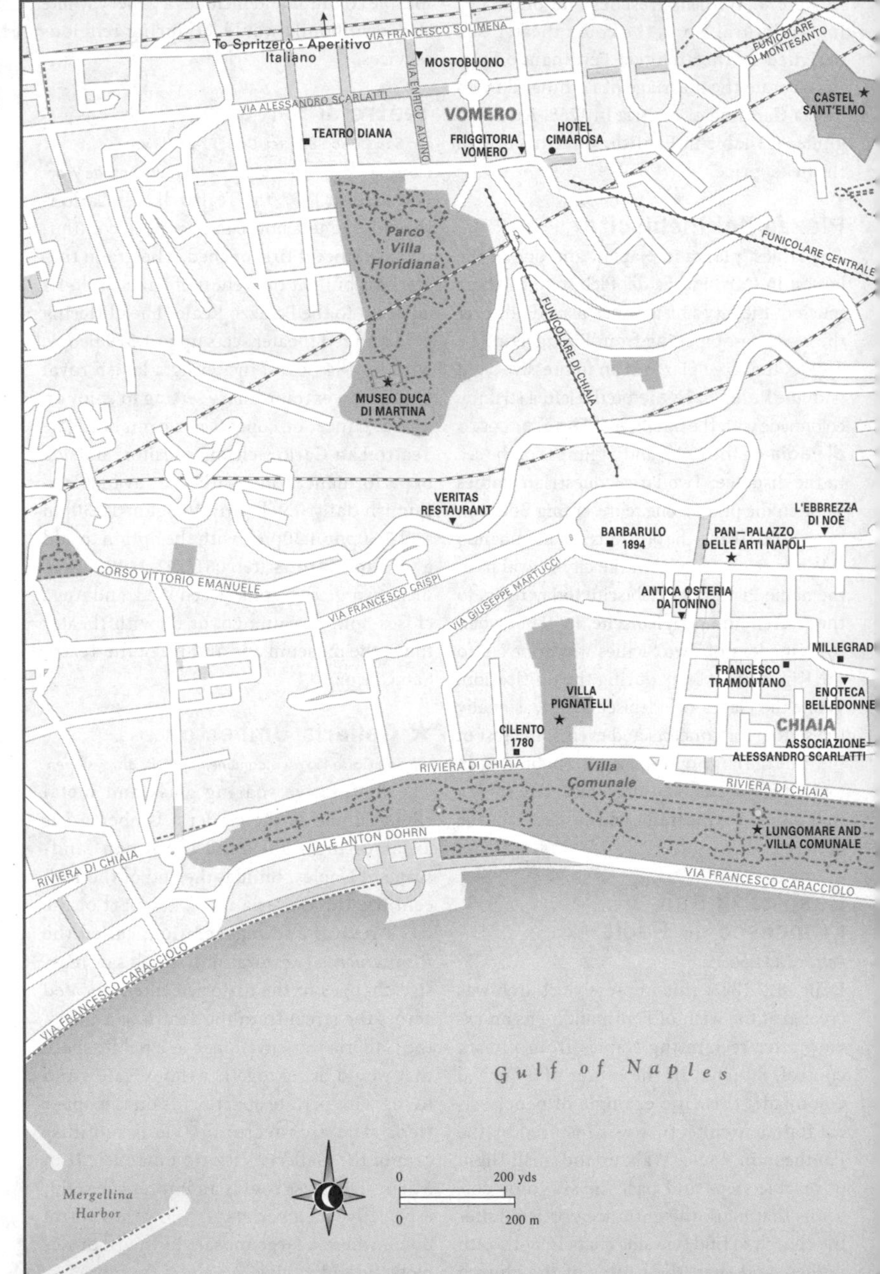
VIA FRANCESCO SOLIMENA
To Spritzerò - Aperitivo Italiano
MOSTOBUONO
FUNICOLARE DI MONTESANTO
VIA ALESSANDRO SCARLATTI
VIA ENRICO ALVINO
CASTEL SANT'ELMO
VOMERO
TEATRO DIANA
FRIGGITORIA VOMERO
HOTEL CIMAROSA
Parco Villa Floridiana
FUNICOLARE CENTRALE
FUNICOLARE DI CHIAIA
MUSEO DUCA DI MARTINA
VERITAS RESTAURANT
L'EBBREZZA DI NOÈ
BARBARULO 1894
PAN—PALAZZO DELLE ARTI NAPOLI
CORSO VITTORIO EMANUELE
VIA FRANCESCO CRISPI
VIA GIUSEPPE MARTUCCI
ANTICA OSTERIA DA TONINO
MILLEGRAD
FRANCESCO TRAMONTANO
ENOTECA BELLEDONNE
VILLA PIGNATELLI
CHIAIA
CILENTO 1780
ASSOCIAZIONE ALESSANDRO SCARLATTI
RIVIERA DI CHIAIA
Villa Comunale
LUNGOMARE AND VILLA COMUNALE
VIALE ANTON DOHRN
VIA FRANCESCO CARACCIOLO
Gulf of Naples
Mergellina Harbor
0
200 yds
200 m

PIZZERIA DA ATTILIO
LA SFOGLIATELLA MARY
VIA TOLEDO
MAMAMU
VIA MONTEOLIVETO
VIA DONNALBINA
CORSO UMBERTO I
HOTEL SAN FRANCESCO AL MONTE
CERTOSA E MUSEO DI SAN MARTINO
SPACCANAPOLI
VIA GUGLIELMO SANFELICE
J CONTEMPORARY JAPANESE RESTAURANT
MARIO TALARICO
SEE "CENTRO STORICO" MAP
CORSO VITTORIO EMANUELE
TOLEDOSTATION BED & BREAKFAST
I BIKE NAPLES
VIA MEDINA
VIA ALCIDE DE GASPERI
RENAISSANCE NAPLES HOTEL MEDITERRANEO
VIA SAN GIACOMO
QUARTIERI SPAGNOLI
HOTEL IL CONVENTO
TOLEDO
ROMEO HOTEL
HOSTEL OF THE SUN
VIA CRISTOFORO COLOMBO
GALLERIE D'ITALIA
TEATRO AUGUSTEO
PINTAURO
LA CILIEGINA LIFESTYLE HOTEL
B&B ATTICO PARTENOPEO
VICO CONTE DI MOLA
VIA SAN MATTIA
CENTRO DI MUSICA ANTICA PIETÀ DE' TURCHINI
LA SFOGLIATELLA MARY
GALLERIA UMBERTO I
CASTEL NUOVO
GAY ODIN
ASCIONE
SAN FERDINANDO
CHIESA DI SAN FERDINANDO
CITY SIGHTSEEING
CORAL MUSEUM ASCIONE
SAN CARLO
IKI SUSHI RESTAURANT
VIA PALAZZO
Parco di Villa Cellamare
NAPOLI SOTTERRANEA
Piazza Trieste e Trento
TEATRO DI SAN CARLO
AZIENDA AUTONOMA DI SOGGIORNO CURA E TURISMO DI NAPOLI
PORTO DI NAPOLI
VIA NARDONES
PIZZERIA BRANDI
OSTERIA LA MATTONELLA
CHIAJA HOTEL DE CHARME
GRAN CAFFÈ GAMBRINUS
Bacino Vittorio Emanuele III
CAMICERIA PICCOLO
VIA CHIAIA
PALAZZO REALE
VIA FERDINANDO ACTON
RUBINACCI
TRAMONTANO
Piazza del Plebiscito
Giardini del Molosiglio
UMBERTO
HOTEL PALAZZO ALABARDIERI
RISTORANTE AMICI MIEI
GALLERIA BORBONICO
BASILICA DI SAN FRANCESCO DA PAOLA
BA-BAR
Piazza dei Martiri
CAPELLA VECCHIA 11
GRAN CAFFÈ LA CAFFETTIERA
E. MARINELLA
VIA VANNELLA GAETANI
LA MASARDONA
VIA CUMA
VIA GIORGIO ARCOLEO
VIA RAFFAELE DE CESARE
Piazza Vittoria
SANTA LUCIA
V. MARINO TURCHI
VIA NAZARIO SAURO
PALAZZO CHIATAMONE
VIA PALEPOLI
HOTEL REX
GRAND HOTEL VESUVIO
CARUSO ROOF GARDEN RESTAURANT
CASTEL DELL'OVO
BORGO MARINARI
© MOON.COM

1

2

3

4

Coral Museum Ascione

Angiporto Galleria Umberto I; tel. 081/421-111; www.ascione.it; 4:30pm-7:30pm Mon., 10:30am-1pm and 4:30pm-7pm Tues.-Sat., closed Sun.; €5

Located inside the Galleria Umberto I, this private museum tells the story of the area's important coral-carving tradition through a display of remarkable coral pieces. Created by Casa Ascione, a historic coral producer from Torre del Greco, the works on display range from 19th-century pieces to contemporary designs. Along with viewing the finished pieces, you can learn more about the history of the art form, local fishing traditions, and the carving process. The museum is open only for guided visits with advance reservation.

Chiesa di San Ferdinando

Piazza Trieste e Trento 5

Overlooking Piazza Trieste e Trento, you might just miss the facade of this church, as it's seemingly absorbed into the surrounding buildings. The church was originally founded by the Jesuits in the early 17th century and dedicated to San Francesco Saverio (St. Francis Xavier), with a design that has been attributed to Cosimo Fanzago (1591-1678), one of the top architects working in Naples during the baroque period. The interior is richly decorated and noted for the stunning baroque frescoes by Paolo De Matteis from the early 1700s. After the Jesuits were expelled from the Kingdom of Naples in 1767, the church was eventually dedicated to San Ferdinando III di Castiglia, a 13th-century Spanish king, who was canonized, and the neighborhood now takes its name from this same saint.

Napoli Sotterranea, L.A.E.S. (Underground Naples)

Vico S. Anna di Palazzo 52; tel. 081/400-256; www.lanapolisotterranea.it; first tour 10am Sat.-Sun., noon Mon.-Fri.; €10

Far below the street level in Naples lies a hidden world, one that dates back to the Greek settlement of the city from 470 BC. The Napoli Sotterranea tour takes you on a journey through the underground city and tells the story of Naples in an intriguing way. You'll see how the city has been built for centuries by excavating the stone from below, and you'll get an up-close look at the cisterns that gathered water for the buildings above. You'll also see the areas that were used for refuge during World War II bombings, including graffiti dating from the war period. Some passageways can be quite narrow, so this tour is not suitable for people who are claustrophobic. Excursions with an English-speaking guide are available Monday-Friday (noon, and 4:30pm in Aug. only), Saturday (10am, noon, 4:30pm, 6pm), and Sunday (10am, noon, 4:30pm). The starting point is in Piazza Trieste e Trento outside the historic Bar Gambrinus. Advance reservation is not necessary. The tour takes about an hour, and comfortable shoes are a good idea.

Gallerie d'Italia

Via Toledo 185; tel. 081/400-256; www.gallerieditalia.com; 10am-7pm Tues.-Fri., 10am-8pm Sat.-Sun., closed Mon.; €5

Along Via Toledo, not far from the Galleria Umberto I, it's hard to miss the imposing and ornate entrance to the beautiful Palazzo Zevallos Stigliano. Built in 1563 as a noble family residence, the palazzo has also served as headquarters for a bank, and in 2014 was transformed into an exquisite gallery space for the collection of the Intesa Sanpaolo bank. The outstanding permanent collection features artwork from the 16th-18th centuries, including important works by Caravaggio, Artemisia Gentileschi, Luca Giordano, and Francesco Solimena. Special exhibitions are hosted throughout the year and are included in the ticket price.

Galleria Borbonico

Vico del Grottone 4; tel. 081/764-5808; www.galleriaborbonica.com; tours Fri.-Sun.; €10-15

Built in the mid-19th century at the request of

1: Piazza del Plebiscito and the Basilica di San Francesco da Paola **2:** Chiesa di San Ferdinando **3:** Castel Nuovo **4:** glass domed shopping center Galleria Umberto I

Coral and Cameos

The art of coral and cameo carving is an ancient one in the Naples area. Since Greek and Roman times there has been a tradition of fine craftsmanship when it comes to creating elegant jewelry from locally sourced coral. In ancient Rome, finely detailed cameos were highly prized and coral was valued because it was thought to protect the wearer from bad luck. From a renewed appreciation of coral carving in the Renaissance to royal patronage in the 1800s to the appeal of the artisan tradition to travelers on the Grand Tour, coral harvesting has long been a part of the local economy, especially in **Torre del Greco,** a seaside town located on the Gulf of Naples between Naples and Pompeii.

Due to significant harvesting and the slow growth of the *corallium rubrum* (red coral) that grows in the Mediterranean, there are many environmental and ethical concerns around the production of coral jewelry. Yet because of the importance of the tradition to the local communities, families have passed down the art form for generations, and some producers and shops in the area, such as Ascione in Naples and Cellini Gallery in Pompeii, claim a commitment to sustainable harvesting and ethically sourced coral. Meanwhile, shoppers should be aware that, though you'll see many stores selling cameos and coral jewelry, much of what's for sale isn't real *corallium rubrum*, and real coral sometimes is imported from other parts of the world that may or may not have a commitment to sustainability.

King Ferdinando II, this massive tunnel was created to connect the Palazzo Reale (Royal Palace) to the military barracks and sea on the other side of Monte Erchie. Opened in 1855 after three years of work that was all done by hand with picks, hammers, and wedges, the tunnel has served many purposes over the years. During World War II, the tunnel and nearby cisterns were used for shelter by 5,000-10,000 Neapolitans during the extensive German and Allied bombings of the city. It's possible to visit the tunnel on four different themed tours, from a standard tour offering a glimpse of the highlights to an adventure tour complete with helmet and flashlight, or a speleological tour for a unique experience deep underground in Naples. Tours are available throughout the day and last 1-1.5 hours. The standard tour doesn't require reservations, but more specialized tours need to be booked in advance. Tickets can be purchased online.

WATERFRONT

The waterfront of Naples, stretching from the Castel dell'Ovo to the harbor at Mergellina, is one of the loveliest spots in in the city. From Piazza del Plebiscito south lies the Santa Lucia neighborhood with elegant buildings overlooking the sea, and the islet with Castel dell'Ovo and the tiny harbor of Borgo Marinari. Heading west leads to the stylish Chiaia neighborhood, which stretches from the Villa Comunale gardens up the slopes until Vomero.

★ Castel dell'Ovo

Borgo Marinari; tel. 081/795-4592; www.comune.napoli.it; 9am-7:30pm Mon.-Sat. (closes 6:30pm in winter), 9am-2pm Sun.; free

One of the most scenic and historic spots in Naples, the Castel dell'Ovo sits on an islet jutting out into the gulf south of Santa Lucia. The earliest Greek settlers landed on this spot and named the island Megaride. Over the centuries it has been a lavish Roman villa, a monastery in the 5th century, and what we see today as the Castel dell'Ovo. Legend says the name, meaning Castle of the Egg, comes from the story that the Roman poet Virgil buried an egg below where the castle stands today. The legend says that, as long as the egg remains unbroken, the castle will stand and Naples will be safe. The castle itself is a fascinating amalgam of styles as it was modified by many rulers of the city since it was first built by the Normans in the 12th century. The castle today largely dates from the Aragonese rulers of Naples in the 15th century. Climb to the top of the castle's terraces for a panoramic view of the Gulf of Naples.

A small causeway leads out to the Castel dell'Ovo and offers an extraordinary up-close view of the castle and the charming **Borgo Marinari,** a small harbor at the base of the castle. An old-world fishing village atmosphere, with boats bobbing in the harbor and seaside restaurants, makes this an especially romantic spot for dinner.

Lungomare and Villa Comunale

Via Francesco Caracciolo and Riviera di Chiaia from Piazza Vittoria to Piazza della Repubblica

Stretching along the waterfront in Chiaia from just west of the Borgo Marinari to Piazza della Repubblica, this large public garden offers green space and a place to stroll by the sea. The sprawling gardens were originally designed by Carlo Vanvitelli from 1778-1780 for the private use of the royal family of King Ferdinand IV. Following the unification of Italy, the gardens were opened to the public and renamed the Villa Comunale in 1869. The gardens are dotted with statues, sculptures, and an ornate art nouveau cast-iron and glass bandstand designed by Errico Alvino in 1887. In the center of the gardens you'll find the **Stazione Zoologica Anton Dohrn** (tel. 081/583-3111; www.szn.it; closed for maintenance), which was founded in 1872 and houses the oldest aquarium in Europe.

Piazza dei Martiri

This elegant piazza is located at the end of Via Chiaia, not far from the *lungomare* (waterfront) and is right in the heart of the elegant shopping district of Chiaia. The triangular-shaped piazza dates to the westward expansion of the city in the 17th century and is lined by elegant palazzos. Find a spot outdoors at one of the cafés to enjoy a moment of people watching and to admire the central column dedicated to all the Neapolitans who have died fighting for freedom in the long history of the city.

Villa Pignatelli

Riviera di Chiaia 200; tel. 081/761-2356; www.polomusealecampania.beniculturali.it; 8:30am-5pm, closed Tues.; €5

Set in a lovely garden, the Villa Pignatelli is a large home that was built in 1826 for Admiral Ferdinando Acton. Its neoclassical design features Ionic pilasters and references to Pompeian designs on its facade. Owned by

view of Castel dell'Ovo on the waterfront of Naples

Carl Mayer von Rothschild (of the German banking family) from Acton's death until after the unification of Italy, the villa now bears a name that refers to Diego Aragona Pignatelli Cortés, who purchased the property in the 19th century, and whose heirs donated the villa and art collection to the Italian state. The historic rooms are richly decorated and offer the chance to explore the collection of furniture, porcelain, and decorative art in situ. An adjacent building houses the **Museo delle Carrozze** with a collection of antique Italian, French, and English carriages from the 1800s-1900s.

Mergellina

Mergellina Harbor

At the base of the hill leading up to Posillipo, this small harbor is a picturesque spot along the waterfront in Naples. Once a small fishing village, it was absorbed into the city as it expanded in the 17th century. As the beach area that once ran along the Villa Comunale was transformed into gardens and eventually paved for Via Francesco Caracciolo, the fishing boats once located along the beach were moved toward the Mergellina marina. Now more of a seaside tourist spot than a place for fishing boats, this area is lovely for a stroll along the harbor to enjoy the excellent view of the Naples waterfront with Mount Vesuvius in the distance. The view is outstanding from the **Fontana del Sebeto,** a large fountain originally designed by Cosimo Fanzago in 1635. At the heart of the statue is an old man representing the Sebeto river, the ancient river that flowed through Naples.

Mergellina's harbor is also a departure point for ferries to Ischia, the Aeolian Islands in Sicily, and the Pontine islands of Ponza and Ventotene.

PAN—Palazzo delle Arti Napoli

Via dei Mille 60; tel. 081/795-8651; www.comune.napoli.it/pan; 9:30am-7:30pm Mon. and Wed.-Sat., 9:30am-2:30pm Sun., closed Tues.; free admission to building, art exhibition prices vary

Set in the Palazzo Roccella, an elegant building dating back to the 17th century, PAN (which stands for Palazzo delle Arti Napoli) has served as a large contemporary art exhibition space since 2005. PAN hosts traveling and specially organized exhibits throughout the year.

VOMERO

Rising steeply above the city center, the Vomero neighborhood is topped by Castel Sant'Elmo and Certosa di San Martino. With its panoramic views and important historical sights, it's a lovely neighborhood to explore and it's easy to reach via the three funicular trains that have connected Vomero with the lower areas of the city since late 19th century.

Castel Sant'Elmo

Via Tito Angelini 22; tel. 081/558-7708; www.polomusealecampania.beniculturali.it; 8:30am-7:30pm daily; €5

Sitting atop the San Martino hill, the Castel Sant'Elmo is perfectly situated to take in views of the city of Naples and the entire Gulf of Naples. Naturally, with such a fine view, it has been the spot for an overlook for centuries. The original construction on this site goes back to the 1200s when the Normans built a fortified residence called Belforte. Expanded and modified many times, the unique hexagonal star-shaped design we see today dates from the 16th century under Spanish rule. From 1860 to 1952, the castle was a military prison and then continued to be used for military purposes until 1976. After an extensive restoration, the castle was transformed into a space for the public to enjoy and visit. It's possible to explore many areas of the castle, which often hosts art exhibitions and events. The **Museo del Novecento** (9am-5pm, closed Tues.) in the castle is dedicated to 20th-century Neapolitan art. Don't miss the views overlooking the Certosa di San Martino and the Gulf of Naples from a variety of different lookout points on the castle walls.

Visiting the Catacombs of Naples

inside the Catacombs of San Gennaro

While in many places the traces of early Christianity have long since been covered with layers upon layers of history, in Naples the catacombs offer a chance to see some of the earliest records of its arrival in the city. The majority of the city's catacombs are located between the historic center and Capodimonte in the Rione Sanità neighborhood, and near the Museo di Capodimonte. Both of the catacombs below are managed by the Catacombe di Napoli organization, and the €9 entrance fee covers both sights. You pay at the first one you visit, and your ticket gives you free access to the other sight. Guided tours are available in English hourly, and written information in English is also available at both catacombs.

CATACOMBE DI SAN GENNARO

Via Capodimonte 13; tel. 081/744-3714; www.catacombedinapoli.it; 10am-5pm Mon.-Sat., 10am-2pm Sun.; €9 includes admission to San Gaudioso

Located below the Basilica della Madre del Buon Consiglio, the Catacombe di San Gennaro is one of the oldest and most important catacomb sites to visit. The paleo-Christian burial area held a strong religious significance when San Gennaro was buried here in the 5th century. Divided into two levels and carved out of tufa rock, the catacombs offer the chance to see the different types of tombs, early chapels, and artwork from pagan designs, from 2nd-century works to Byzantine paintings from the 9th-10th centuries.

CATACOMBE DI SAN GAUDIOSO

Basilica Santa Maria della Sanità, Piazza Sanità 14; tel. 081/744-3714; www.catacombedinapoli.it; 10am-1pm daily; €9 includes admission to San Gennaro

Inside the Basilica Santa Maria della Sanità is the entrance to the fascinating Catacombe di San Gaudioso. Dating from the 4th-5th centuries, these catacombs are the second-largest in Naples, after the Catacombe di San Gennaro. The catacombs contain preserved frescoes and mosaics from the 5th-6th centuries, displaying early Christian symbols, including the lamb, fish, and grapevines. Abandoned during the late Middle Ages, the catacombs were rediscovered and used as a burial site again in the 16th century. To preserve and honor the location, builders constructed the basilica above in the early 17th century with a beautiful baroque design by Fra Nuvolo.

★ Certosa e Museo di San Martino

Largo San Martino 5; tel. 081/229-4502; www.polomusealecampania.beniculturali.it; 8:30am-7:30pm, closed Wed.; €6

Easily spotted atop Vomero hill next to the Castel Sant'Elmo, the Certosa di San Martino is a former Carthusian monastery and now a museum with a remarkable art collection. A visit is highly recommended to explore excellent examples of work by important Neapolitan painters from the 1800s, decorative arts, and historic *presepi* (nativities), and to admire the spectacular view over the Gulf of Naples. Although founded in the 14th century, Certosa has a baroque design that dates to the mid 1600s and is the work of Cosimo Fanzago, the most noted architect working in Naples at the time. Take a stroll around the stunning large cloister surrounded by 60 marble arches and visit the church that is a museum in itself with beautiful paintings and sculptures from the 17th-18th centuries.

Museo Duca di Martina

Villa Floridiana, Via Cimarosa 77; tel. 081/578-8418; www.polomusealecampania.beniculturali.it; 8:30am-5pm, closed Tues.; €4

For decorative arts enthusiasts, a visit to the Museo Duca di Martina is a special experience while in Naples. This small house museum is located in the Villa Floridiana, a stunning neoclassical villa built on the slopes of Vomero for Lucia Migliaccio, the Duchess of Floridia, the second wife of King Ferdinand I. Surrounded by a lush park, the villa is at its most impressive on the south side, where a grand staircase leads down into the gardens with a spectacular view to the sea. Since 1931, the villa has been the home of the Museo Duca di Martina, which houses one of the finest collections of decorative arts in Italy. Created by Placido de Sangro, Duke of Martina, the massive collection of more than 6,000 objects dating from the 12th-19th centuries was donated to the city of Naples in 1911. The museum's collection is spread across three floors of the villa and includes Chinese porcelain and eastern objects on the lowest level; ivories, corals, and majolica from the Middle Ages to the Renaissance and baroque periods on the ground floor; and an incredible collection of 18th-century porcelain on the first floor.

CAPODIMONTE

Once a rural area in hills north of Naples, the Capodimonte area saw many changes during the 18th century, including the construction of the royal palace and development of expansive gardens and woods. Despite the treasures housed in the **Museo di Capodimonte** and the tranquility of the setting, the area was not particularly well connected to the city center until the early 1800s, when a long, straight road and bridge were built over the Sanità neighborhood. Today a visit to Capodimonte is a must for art lovers, but don't miss exploring the area's catacombs as well.

★ Museo e Real Bosco di Capodimonte

Via Miano 2; tel. 081/749-9111; www.museocapodimonte.beniculturali.it; 8:30am-7:30pm closed Wed.; €12

In the hills above Naples, the Museo e Real Bosco di Capodimonte was built in the 18th century by the Bourbon king Carlo III as a royal palace set amidst a lush forest perfect for hunting. It was also intended from the beginning as the setting for the marvelous art collection belonging to Elisabetta Farnese, the mother of Carlo III. Today the Farnese Collection is the heart of the museum, which includes works by Titian, Botticelli, Raphael, and Caravaggio to name only a selection of the highlights. One of the largest art museums in Italy, Capodimonte also houses an excellent collection of paintings and sculptures from the 13th-18th centuries. Decorative art enthusiasts will enjoy the elegant Royal Apartments and extensive porcelain collection, as well as the remarkable *Salottino di Porcellana*, an 18th-century rococo-style salon decorated with delicately painted porcelain. To complete the incredible walk through art history, the museum also includes a gallery dedicated to the 1800s and a contemporary art collection.

Sports and Recreation

Outdoor activities in Naples naturally include boating, kayaking, and other water sports. To go scuba diving, you'll want to head west of Naples to Baia and the Campi Flegrei area for some incredible experiences.

BIKING

I BIKE NAPLES

Via Toledo 317; tel. 081/419-528; www.ibikenaples.it; tours daily; from €30 per person

Though Naples is known for its chaotic traffic, don't let that stop you from exploring the city on two wheels if you enjoy a biking adventure. I Bike Naples offers small group tours for 5-15 people. Tours that travel through the heart of Naples include a 2.5-hour basic tour and a 6-hour excursion with a stop for lunch. Tours are family-friendly, but children must be older than 14. For safety, the tours take place in pedestrian areas and helmets are included. Bike tours in English take place daily throughout the year, but advance booking is required.

BOAT TOURS AND RENTALS

VESUVIA MARE

Borgo Marinari; tel. 348/079-5692; www.vesuviamare.it; starting at €50 per person

Enjoy a private or small group tours of the Naples coastal area as well as Capri, Ischia, Procida, and the Amalfi Coast. Let your English-speaking skipper and hosts Luca and Gabriella share about the history, culture, and traditions of the area while cruising along in comfort. Private tours can be fully customized, or choose from their half-day and full-day cruises or a romantic sunset cruise.

FOOTBALL (SOCCER)

SSC NAPOLI

Piazza Giorgio Ascarelli; tel. 081/509-5344; www.sscnapoli.it; from €25 per person

If there's one thing that is deep at the heart of Neapolitans, it's their love for the local Napoli soccer club. Founded in 1926, the Napoli team has boasted many of the world's best soccer players, including the Argentinian player Diego Maradona from 1984-1991. The Napoli team plays at the highest level (Serie A) of soccer in Italy and is regularly one of the top teams. The soccer season runs from August to May, for a total of 38 games. The Stadio San Paolo is the home stadium for Napoli and is located west of the historic center of Naples.

To enjoy a game at Stadio San Paolo, your best bet is to buy tickets in person in Naples. Advance ticket sales are tricky to come by, given the regulations around sales. You'll find tickets for sale at various points around Naples, including the Box Office (Galleria Umberto I 17; tel. 081/551-9188; 9:30am-8pm Mon.-Fri., 10am-6pm Sat.) or at the stadium in advance of a game. Bring your passport when purchasing tickets because your name will be printed on the ticket. You'll also need your passport as identification to get into the stadium, and the name must match the name on your ticket.

Nightlife

Naples is a vibrant city after dark with a lively and eclectic scene. Although it's a very large city, most of the nightlife spots are small clubs, literary cafés, or wine bars where you're more likely to rub elbows with locals than tourists. The city also has a rich musical heritage, and talented young musicians carry on the Neapolitan traditions. So whether your scene is more a glass of Campania wine, a formal concert, a good jazz club, or dancing until dawn, you'll find plenty of nightlife options, especially in the *centro storico* (historic center) area around Piazza Dante and Piazza Bellini.

CENTRO STORICO

Bars

ENOTECA BELLEDONNE

Vico Belledonne a Chiaia 18; tel. 081/403-162; www.enotecabelledonne.it; 10am-1:30pm and 4pm-2am Tues.-Sat., 4:30pm-1am Mon., 7pm-2am Sun.; drinks from €5

At night, this well-stocked wine store transforms into a popular wine bar, where you can sample a fine selection of wines accompanied by light meals, and cheese and cured meat platters.

ENNÒ

Via Vincenzo Bellini 43; tel. 333/689-8730; www.ennoviabellini.it; 7pm-1am daily; drinks from €5-8

Located in a great nightlife area not far from Piazza Dante and Piazza Bellini, this club offers a large selection of artisan beers, wine, and cocktails along with live music. It's popular with the younger Neapolitan crowd.

LIBRERIA BERISIO

Via Port'Alba 28; tel. 081/549-9090; berisio@libero.it; 9:30am-1:30am Mon.-Thurs., 9:30am-3am Fri., 9:30am-1:30pm and 7pm-3:30am Sat., 6:30pm-1:30am Sun.; drinks from €5

Along Via Port'Alba lined with bookstores, Liberia Bersisio opened its doors in 1956 and is now also a popular local wine and cocktail bar, especially late into the night. Check their schedule for live music events; this place often has a great jazz and blues vibe.

Clubs and Live Music

GALLERIA 19

Via San Sebastiano 18/19; www.galleria19.it; 9pm-3am Thurs., 11:30pm-5am Fri.-Sat., 8pm-1am Sun., closed Mon.-Wed.; admission from €8

From Piazza Bellini, follow Via San Sebastiano south into the musical heart of Naples where this nightclub is tucked away between shops selling musical instruments. This is a popular spot with the university crowd, hosting live DJ sets and performances by local and international artists.

KESTÈ

Largo San Giovanni Maggiore Pignatelli 26/27; tel. 081/781-0034; www.keste.it; 10:30am-2:30am daily; drinks from €2.50

Since 1997, Kestè has been a cornerstone in the music and nightlife scene in Naples. With a live music program throughout the year, as well as art, theater, stand up comedy, and cultural events, it's a popular spot with locals, offering an artistic atmosphere on a little square in the historic center.

BOURBON STREET

Via Vincenzo Bellini 52/53; tel. 338/825-3756; www.bourbonstreetjazzclub.com; 8pm-2am Thurs.-Sun.; drinks from €5

Around the corner from Piazza Dante, Bourbon Street is one of the city's classic nightclubs, completely dedicated to jazz. The setting is intimate, and live music is on the schedule regularly, along with jam sessions.

SUPERFLY SOULBAR

Via Cisterna dell'Olio 12; tel. 081/551-0388; gfiorito6704@yahoo.it; 7pm-1:30am Wed.-Thurs. and Sun.-Mon., 7pm-3am Fri.-Sat., closed Tues.; drinks from €2.50

Superfly Soulbar is an iconic Naples

nightlife spot with a good groove, just south of Piazza Dante in the *centro storico*. The cocktails are expertly mixed, and the setting is perfectly in tune with the jazz and soul music vibe.

MAMAMU

Via Sedile di Porto 46; tel. 320/669-5222; mamamubar@gmail.com; 8pm-2am Thurs.-Sat.; drinks from €2.40

Located near the university, this has been a popular local venue with a great vibe for live music performances since it first opened its doors in 1996. Check their schedule for upcoming live concerts and DJ sets.

WATERFRONT

Bars

ENOTECA BELLEDONNE

Vico Belledonne a Chiaia 18; tel. 081/403-162; www.enotecabelledonne.it; 10am-1:30pm and 4pm-2am Tues.-Sat., 4:30pm-1am Mon., 7pm-2am Sun.; drinks from €5

At night, this well-stocked wine store transforms into a popular wine bar, where you can sample a fine selection of wines accompanied by light meals, and cheese and cured meat platters.

BA-BAR

Via Bisignano 20; tel. 081/764-3525; www.ba-bar.it; 11am-2am Tues.-Thurs. and Sun., 11am-3am Fri.-Sat., 5pm-2am Mon.; drinks from €5-15

A relaxed setting and a comfortable spot for a glass of wine or drinks, Ba-Bar is a blend of bar, bistrot, art gallery, and gathering point in the Chiaia neighborhood. Stop in to enjoy an *aperitivo* or dinner, or catch a soccer game with locals.

SPRITZERÒ–APERITIVO ITALIANO

Largo Antignano 1; tel. 081/1875-2947; appero.spritz@gmail.com; 5:30pm-1:30am Mon.-Fri., 11am-3pm and 5:30pm-1:30am Sat.-Sun.; drinks from €2-6

The classic Aperol *spritz* cocktail has taken the world by storm, and this spot is 100 percent dedicated to celebrating one of Italy's most popular drinks in a casual setting perfect for conversation and fun.

Entertainment and Events

The music and theater scene in Naples has a tremendous history, and for generations it has influenced scores of musicians from Italy and around the world. It's hard to find travelers who aren't familiar with the strains of popular Neapolitan songs like "O Sole Mio." Traditional Neapolitan music is very much alive; it's treasured by the locals and enjoyed by visitors. Naples also offers resplendent opera houses like Teatro San Carlo and Teatro Bellini, and with so many locals dedicated to preserving music traditions, there are plenty of ways for visitors to experience Neapolitan music.

Tradition is also very much at the heart of the biggest religious events throughout the year. Whether it's a festival dedicated to the city's patron saint and protector San Gennaro or a celebration of the city's much-revered pizza, joining the locals in honoring their traditions is a moving experience in a city as full of passion as Naples.

THE ARTS

Centro Storico

NAPULITANATA

Piazza Museo Nazionale 10-11; tel. 348/998-3871; www.napulitanata.com

Set in the arcades of the Galleria Principe near the Museo Archeologico Nazionale, Napulitanata offers a live musical experience dedicated to traditional Neapolitan songs. The relaxed and small concert setting creates a friendly and intimate atmosphere where the heart of Neapolitan music is brought to life through song and dance.

TEATRO BELLINI

Via Conte di Ruvo 14; tel. 081/549-9688; www.teatrobellini.it

Located off of Via Toledo in the *centro storico,* Teatro Bellini is one of the city's important historic theaters. Inagurated in 1878, the theater was restored in the 1980s, bringing back the original splendor of its six tiers of box seats, frescoed ceiling, and 19th-century details. A wide variety of theatrical, musical, and dance performances take place throughout the year.

DOMUS ARS CENTRO DI CULTURA

Via Santa Chiara 10; tel. 081/342-5603; www.domusars.it

Right around the corner from Piazza del Gesù Nuovo, the Chiesa San Francesco delle Monache, originally founded in the 14th century, is the setting for classical concerts organized by the Domus Ars Centro di Cultura.

San Ferdinando

TEATRO DI SAN CARLO

Via San Carlo 98/F; tel. 081/797-2331; www.teatrosancarlo.it

The jewel of Naples's art scene and the oldest opera house in Europe in continuous use, the Teatro San Carlo has been the setting for spectacular opera, dance, and musical performances since its doors opened in 1737. The richly decorated interior is beautiful enough to warrant a visit on its own, but if you can catch a show during your stay in Naples, you'll have a unique chance to experience the celebrated history of this spectacular opera house.

TEATRO AUGUSTEO

Piazzetta Duca D'Aosta 263; tel. 081/414-243; www.teatroaugusteo.it

Set in a lovely little piazza off of Via Toledo, this historic theater was built on the site of an earlier 18th-century theater designed by Luigi Vanvitelli at the same time as the adjacent Funiculare Centrale was constructed in 1929. The theater hosts musicals, plays, and concerts throughout the year.

Waterfront

ASSOCIAZIONE ALESSANDRO SCARLATTI

Piazza dei Martiri 58; tel. 081/411-723; www.associazionescarlatti.it

Founded in 1918, the Associazione Alessandro Scarlatti is dedicated to chamber music, with a rich selection of classical and innovative performances. Concerts are held

Teatro di San Carlo

at various locations around Naples, including the historic Conservatorio di Musica San Pietro a Majella, the Teatro di Corte in the Palazzo Reale, and a variety of churches in the *centro storico*.

CENTRO DI MUSICA ANTICA PIETÀ DE' TURCHINI

Via Santa Caterina da Siena 38; tel. 081/402-395; www.turchini.it

Dedicated to preserving and highlighting the Neapolitan musical and theatrical heritage from the 16th-18th centuries, the Centro di Musica Antica Pietà de' Turchini presents concerts in the Chiesa Monumentale di Santa Catarina da Siena. The beautiful 16th-century baroque church couldn't be a more fitting setting for the classical concerts. Concerts are also held at various churches and the Gallerie d'Italia museum in the historic center.

Vomero

TEATRO DIANA

Via Luca Giordano 64; tel. 081/556-7527; www.teatrodiana.it

This theater in the heart of the Vomero was founded in 1933 and presents a variety of concerts and plays from noted Italian singers and actors. Performances are in Italian, and the theater also hosts classical concerts throughout the year.

Greater Naples

COMPLESSO PALAPARTENOPE

Via Corrado Barbagallo 115; tel. 081/570-0008; www.palapartenope.it

One of the larger music and performance venues in Naples, the Teatro Palapartenope is located west of the historic center in the Fuorigrotta area. The venue has various sized performance areas, and hosts concerts, musicals, dance, and family-friendly performances. This is often the setting for larger concerts by big-name Italian musicians.

FESTIVALS AND EVENTS

WINE & THE CITY

Various locations; tel. 081/681-505; www.wineandthecity.it; May

Launched in 2008 as a creative way to showcase wine in a variety of settings, Wine & The City is an annual festival where wine and gastronomic events take place in various locations across Naples. Events are set in museums, galleries, boutiques, restaurants, artist studios, and more, showcasing more than 100 wineries.

NAPOLI PIZZA VILLAGE

Lungomare Caracciolo; www.pizzavillage.it; June

Every year at the beginning of June along the waterfront, the Napoli Pizza Village celebrates the city's most famous gastronomic contribution. More than 50 pizzerias are present, and there are competitions, events, and live music as well. This is the chance to sample some of the best pizza from Italy's top pizza makers in a festive and fun summer evening in Naples.

FESTA DEL CARMINE

Piazza del Carmine 2; www.santuariocarminemaggiore.it; July 15

One of the most historic religious celebrations in Naples is also one of the most explosive. The Festa del Carmine takes place July 15, the evening before the festival celebrating the Madonna del Carmine (Our Lady of Mount Carmel). After evening Mass in the Santuario del Carmine Maggiore, fireworks are set off from all over the bell tower of the church to create the impression that the bell tower is on fire. Only the arrival of a celebrated portrait of the Madonna del Carmine stops the fire. At 246 feet (75 m) tall, the bell tower is the tallest in Naples. The festival is very popular with Neapolitans, who pack the Piazza del Carmine and surrounding area to watch the event and enjoy the music and stands selling sweets, toys, and food.

FESTA DI SAN GENNARO

Duomo di Napoli; Sat. before first Sun. in May, Sept. 19, Dec. 16

Every day of the year, San Gennaro is the beloved and revered patron saint of Naples, but there are a few very special days when all eyes are on the saint. This is when the reliquary vials holding the blood of the saint are said to miraculously liquefy during a special Mass in the Duomo di Napoli (Naples Cathedral). Tradition says that when the miracle doesn't occur it's a bad omen for the city of Naples, and has in fact coincided with natural disasters and unfortunate events over the centuries. For the festival, the Duomo and surrounding area are crowded with people eager to see the miracle, celebrate the saint with processions, and enjoy the festive atmosphere with stands selling candy, food, and toys.

Shopping

The artisan tradition in Naples dates to ancient times when the Greek and later Roman craftsmen transformed coral into intricately carved treasures. However, it was in the 17th and 18th century that Naples became known for its fine shopping and craftsmanship, thanks to the patronage of the Bourbon kings and aristocracy of the time. Whether you're shopping for handmade nativity figurines, being fitted for a custom shirt or suit, or slipping on a pair of gloves, in Naples you'll find talented artisans preserving family traditions and beautiful artistic traditions.

Many shops in Naples, especially the artisan boutiques and smaller shops, respect the local tradition of closing for a lunch period from 1pm or 1:30pm to about 4pm. If you want to shop during the mid-afternoon, head to Via Toledo where some of the larger chain stores remain open. Many smaller shops will also close on Sunday for the afternoon or entire day, and some take a break for a period in August surrounding the Ferragosto holiday on August 15.

SHOPPING DISTRICTS

VIA TOLEDO

Via Toledo from Piazza Trieste e Trento to Piazza Dante

One of the busiest shopping streets in Naples, Via Toledo starts at Piazza Trieste e Trento at the Galleria Umberto I, the glass domed 19th-century shopping center, and runs to Piazza Dante. The street is largely pedestrian-only and has shops on both sides. Here you'll find Italian and international stores as well as local brands and smaller shops.

VIA CHIAIA

Via Chiaia from Piazza Trieste e Trento to Via Gaetano Filangieri

Via Chiaia is lined with boutiques, the city's historic tailors, and other great shopping finds. The pedestrian-only street is also a pleasant stroll just for window shopping as it connects Piazza Trieste e Trento and Via Toledo with Piazza dei Martiri, another fine shopping area.

VIA DEI MILLE

Via dei Mille Via Gaetano Filangieri to Via Vittoria Colonna

The spot for elegant shopping in Naples, this is where high fashion designer boutiques vie for attention with ornately decorated palazzos, including some in the Liberty style, which is the Italian equivalent of the art nouveau style from the late 1800s and early 1900s.

VIA SAN GREGORIO ARMENO

Via San Gregorio Armeno from Via dei Tribunali to Via San Biagio dei Librai

If you love traditional crafts and Christmas nativities, then a visit to Via San Gregorio Armeno is a must. This narrow street is lined with artisan workshops full to the brim with handmade *presepe* (nativity) figurines and decorations. No matter the size—from tiny figures to grand 18th-century style scenes—you'll find holiday decorations you'll treasure for years to come.

VIA ALESSANDRO SCARLATTI

Via Alessandro Scarlatti from Piazza Vanvitelli to Via Luca Giordano

Vomero's stylish shopping district stretches from Piazza Vanvitelli down the tree-lined and pedestrian-only Via Alessandro Scarlatti to Via Luca Giordano. Be sure to meander down some of the cross streets for more little shops and cafés.

CLOTHING

E. MARINELLA

Via Riviera di Chiaia 287; tel. 081/764-3265; www.emarinella.com; 6:30am-1:30pm and 3pm-8pm daily

If there's one shop to visit to experience Naples's sartorial tradition, it's E. Marinella, a tiny boutique that is known worldwide for its handmade ties. The family-run company was founded in 1914 and all of its ties are hand-sewn in a workshop just a few doors away using handprinted silk. Stepping inside is like being transported back in time with the original woodwork and handcrafted quality, yet the ties have a contemporary style that's fitting for one of the world's finest names in ties.

CAMICERIA PICCOLO

Via Chiaia 41; tel. 081/411-824; www.camiceriapiccolo.com; 10am-1:30pm and 4pm-8pm Mon.-Sat., closed Sun.

Since 1926 when Sabatino Piccolo began creating custom-tailored shirts, the Camiceria Piccolo has been one of the most important names in men's fashion in Naples. Today the business is still family-run, and each shirt is handmade to measure with the highest-quality materials.

RUBINACCI

Via Chiaia 149E; tel. 081/415-793; www.marianorubinacci.net; 10am-1:30pm and 4:30pm-8pm Mon.-Sat., closed Sun.

Distinguished for their bespoke clothing and tailoring since 1930, Rubinacci is an iconic store along Via Chiaia for men's fashion, custom tailoring, and accessories.

CILENTO 1780

Via Riviera di Chiaia 203-204; tel. 081/552-7465; www.cilento1780.it; 9am-1:30pm and 4pm-8pm Mon.-Sat., 9am-1:30pm Sun.

Leaders of Neapolitan fashion since 1780 when the family business was founded, today Ugo Cilento is the eighth generation of the family to guide Cilento 1780. Here you'll find sartorial treasures, accessories, shoes, and shirts made to measure.

JEWELRY

FRANCESCO TRAMONTANO

Via Vittorio Imbriani 44 bis; tel. 081/012-7855; www.tramontanogioielli.com; 10am-1:30pm and 4:30pm-8pm Mon.-Sat., closed Sun. and last two weeks of Aug.

Young goldsmith and designer Francesco Tramontano comes from a long family line of Neapolitan artisans. His jewelry pieces are inspired by Mediterranean elements and are handcrafted in gold, silver, and brass; each one is a unique piece of art.

BARBARULO 1894

Piazza Amedeo 16/i-Passeggiata Colonna; tel. 081/403-512; www.gemellidapolso.it; 10:30am-1:30pm and 4:30pm-8pm Mon.-Sat., closed Sun. and in Aug.

To complement that bespoke suit or custom-made shirt, you need the perfect cuff links. Since 1894, the Barbarulo family have specialized in finely crafted handmade cuff links. Along with traditional pieces, you'll also find a line of women's jewelry and accessories for men.

ASCIONE

Angiporto Galleria Umberto I; tel. 081/421-111; www.ascione.it; 4:30pm-8pm Mon., 10:30am-2pm and 4:30pm-8pm Tues.-Fri., 10:30am-2pm Sat., closed Sun.

Master craftspeople at Ascione have created high-quality coral jewelry for more than 150 years. Here you'll also find cameos, pearls, and fine gems.

LEATHER GOODS

OMEGA

Via Stella 12; tel. 081/299-041; www.omegasrl.com; 9am-6pm Mon.-Fri., by appointment Sat., closed Aug.

Since 1923, the Squillace family have produced the finest-quality leather gloves, and today the fifth generation is hard at work continuing the tradition. Each pair of gloves requires 25 steps to create, and the store is like a living museum where you can see gloves being made.

TRAMONTANO

Via Chiaia 143; tel. 081/414-837; www.tramontano.it; 9:30am-1:30pm and 4:30pm-8pm Mon.-Sat., closed Sun.

Founded in 1865, Tramontano became a top name in leather bags, luggage, and accessories in the 1950s when the second-generation owner Aldo Tramontano focused on highlighting the longstanding leather working tradition in Naples. This brand is now recognized around the world, and their items are all still handmade by top craftsmen.

CHOCOLATE

GAY ODIN

Via Toledo 214; tel. 081/400-063; www.gay-odin.it; 9:30am-8pm Mon.-Sat., 10am-8pm Sunday

At the end of the 1800s, Isidoro Odin created a chocolate shop tucked away between tailors and coffee shops in the stylish Chiaia neighborhood, and set to work making delicious chocolate creations. Neapolitans were enchanted by the unique flavor combinations, and this success led to more shops around the city with the Via Toledo shop opening in 1922. In the 1960s Isidoro Odin and his wife Onorina Gay passed the chocolate-making traditions to the Castaldi-Maglietta family, who still run the business's nine locations around Naples.

CERAMICS

MILLEGRADI

Vico Belledonne 15; tel. 081/764-4959; millegradi@gmail.com; 10am-2pm and 3pm-8pm Mon.-Fri., closed Aug. 10-31

From scenes of Vesuvius on tiles to boldly patterned vases and plenty of Mediterranean blues, this cheerful shop displays beautiful handmade ceramic objects inspired by the colors and traditions of Naples.

COSMOS

Via San Gregorio Armeno 5; tel. 081/193-51165; www.cornocosmos.com; 10:30am-7:30pm Mon.-Sat., 10:30am-2:30pm Sunday

In Naples, small horn-shaped items called *corni* are considered good luck charms and often take the shape of small, red hot peppers that look like the *peperoncino* used in many traditional Neapolitan recipes. Cosmos specializes in the production of handmade *corni* of all types, including customized requests.

NATIVITY

FERRIGNO

Via San Gregorio Armeno 8; tel. 081/552-3148; www.arteferrigno.com; 9am-7:30pm

Along Via San Gregorio Armeno, this very special store is where brothers Giuseppe and Marco Ferrigno continue a family tradition of handmade figures for *presepi*, or nativity scenes. The figurines and nativities are created using the same materials as when the workshop was founded in 1836, including terra-cotta details and silk fabrics, and all created by hand in the workshop on-site.

LA SCARABATTOLA

Via dei Tribunali 50; tel. 081/291-735; www.lascarabattola.it; 10:30am-2pm and 3:30pm-7:30pm Mon.-Fri., 10am-6pm Sat., closed Sun.

Created by three brothers, Salvatore, Emanuele, and Raffaele, this shop is a treasure of hand-carved and remarkably detailed figures for *presepi* as well as contemporary sculptures inspired by Neapolitan masked figure Pulcinella and Neapolitan traditions.

ARS NEAPOLITANA

Via dei Tribunali 303; tel. 081/193-30967; www.arsneapolitana.it; 10am-6:30pm Mon.-Sat., 10am-3pm Sun.

Combining family tradition and original talent, Guglielmo Muoio is a young and highly praised *presepe* artist. He and his wife, Laura Loinam, who adds her expertise at tailoring and embroidery, create inspired nativity pieces in the 18th-century traditional Neapolitan style.

SPECIALTY ITEMS

MARIO TALARICO

Vico Due Porte a Toledo 4b; tel. 081/407-723; www.mariotalarico.it; 9am-8pm Mon.-Sat., closed Sun.

Umbrellas might not be at the top of your holiday shopping list, but that's because you haven't been to Talarico yet. Founded in 1860, this small shop has been producing handmade umbrellas for five generations. Choose from a variety of styles and sizes to brighten up any rainy day with travel memories.

Food

It's not an exaggeration to say that food is a way of life in Naples. While you're in its birthplace, it's a must to try true Neapolitan pizza. Tradition reigns here, whether you're grabbing a quick *pizza fritta* (fried pizza) on the street or enjoying a hearty dish of pasta with a *ragù* sauce that has bubbled away for hours. Neapolitans have strong opinions on the best *ragù* (although it might be their grandma's), the best pizza, and the best place to get a warm *sfogliatella* pastry. With so many options, there are few better pastimes in Naples than trying out different places to find your favorites.

Pizza is an art form in Naples and is taken quite seriously, especially at the historic *pizzerie* where often you'll find pizza, and sometimes only pizza, on the menu. However, at many *pizzerie* you can expect to find delicious fried appetizers, and some restaurants serve full menus in addition to making an excellent pizza. Expect lines at the most popular *pizzerie* because they don't take reservations. As pizza only takes 60-90 seconds to cook in a very hot wood-fire oven, the line usually moves quite quickly. Compared to most restaurant settings in Italy where lingering over a meal is the norm, Naples's *pizzerie* are often bustling places with simple decor and table settings, where it's all about the pizza.

Unlike in the coastal areas and on the islands, many restaurants in Naples close for a period in August. Some may close just for the Ferragosto holiday on August 15, while others will close for a 1-2 week holiday around Ferragosto or even for the entire month.

CENTRO STORICO

Regional Cuisine

SALUMERIA UPNEA

Via San Giovanni Maggiore Pignatelli 34/35; tel. 081/193-64649; www.salumeriaupnea.com; noon-5pm and 7pm-midnight Thurs.-Tues., closed Wed.; €6-10

With an industrial-inspired decor and a great central location, this bistro has an engaging atmosphere and diverse menu where you'll find a series of tempting *panini* (sandwiches) and an extensive menu that includes vegan options, meat and cheese platters, perfectly prepared and seasoned freshly made potato chips, *primi* and *secondi* (first and second courses), and a good drink menu with lots of beer varieties.

MIMI ALLA FERROVIA

Via Alfonso D'Aragona 19/21; tel. 081/553-8525; www.mimiallaferrovia.it; noon-4pm and 7pm-midnight Mon.-Sat., closed Sun.; €7-16

A classic Naples address for beautiful dining, Mimì Alla Ferrovia is a favorite with locals and travelers alike. Start with the *Passeggiata Napoletana,* a series of classic Neapolitan appetizers, and try the delicately flavored ravioli with seabass and lemon. The grilled fish is done superbly. Reservations required for four or more people.

TANDEM RAGÙ

Via Giovanni Paladino 51; tel. 081/190-02468; www.tandem.napoli.it; 12:30pm-3:30pm and 7pm-11:30pm Mon.-Tues., 12:30pm-11:30pm Wed.-Sun.; €8-14

In Naples, *ragù* is essential. This is a tomato sauce simmered for hours upon hours and enriched with various types of meat and quite possibly a touch of magic. Tadem Ragù has a simple menu dedicated to only a handful of *ragù*-based dishes available daily along with a selection of vegetarian options and second courses. As the restaurant is quite small, reservations are a good idea.

LA CANTINA DI VIA SAPIENZA

Via Sapienza 40-41; tel. 081/459-078; www.cantinadiviasapienza.it; 12:30pm-3:30pm Mon.-Sat.; €4-7

A tiny little trattoria not far from the Museo Archeologico Nazionale, La Cantina di Via Sapienza gets its name from the setting in a former cantina, or wine cellar. Stop here for lunch to enjoy Neapolitan homecooked pasta dishes along with plenty of *contorni* (side dishes) of vegetables to choose from. You'll enjoy a delicious, affordable lunch in the *centro storico.*

STARITA A MATERDEI

Via Materdei 27/28; tel. 081/557-3682; www.pizzeriestarita.it; noon-3:30pm and 7pm-midnight, closed Monday; €4-10

A little off the beaten path compared to the *pizzerie* in the *centro storico,* this historic pizzeria is a favorite with locals and attracts a lot of pizza-hunting travelers as well. Don't be surprised if there's a line, but it's worth the wait. Along with a large selection of pizzas, this spot also makes one of the best gluten-free pizzas in Naples. No reservations accepted.

Pizzeria

SORBILLO

Via dei Tribunali 32; tel. 081/446-643;www.sorbillo.it; noon-4pm and 7pm-11pm Mon.-Sat., closed Sun. and Aug. 12-25; €3-9

Coming from a big family of *pizzaioli* (pizza makers), Gino Sorbillo became an expert at a young age and has created one of the most notable pizzerias in Naples, as well as outlets in Milan and Times Square in New York City. The original location on Via dei Tribunali is always packed, but there's also a location Lievito Madre al Mare (Via Partenope 1) as well as the **Antica Pizza Fritta da Zia Esterina Sorbillo** locations (Via dei Tribunali 37, Piazza Trieste e Trento 53, and Via Luca Giordano 35) dedicated to his fabulous *pizze fritte* (fried pizza).

L'ANTICA PIZZERIA DA MICHELE

Via Cesare Sersale 1; tel. 081/553-9204; www.damichele.net; 11am-11pm Mon.-Sat., closed Sun.; €4-5

Easily the most iconic pizzeria in Naples, thanks not only to its divine pizza but also to Elizabeth Gilbert's book *Eat, Pray, Love.* L'Antica Pizzeria da Michele is certainly worthy of all the praise, which is why you can expect to find a good line here most days. Everything here is focused 100 percent on the pizza in its most traditional form. The menu only has two pizzas: the classic pizza Margherita and the marinara, topped with tomatoes, oregano, and garlic. Expect to wait a bit to enjoy this classic Naples experience, as reservations are not accepted.

PIZZERIA DI MATTEO

Via dei Tribunali 94; tel. 081/455-262; www.pizzeriadimatteo.com; 11am-11pm Mon.-Sat., closed Sun.; €4-7

This is one of the most popular pizzerias in

Naples as well as an excellent *friggitoria* (fried food specialist), so throw out the diet when you visit here to try the delicious pizza as well as the traditional *pizze fritte* (fried pizza) and other fried appetizers. It's also a busy a place, and you'll often find a line of eager diners outside.

★ PIZZERIA DA ATTILIO

Via Pignaseca 17; tel. 081/552-0479; www.pizzeriadaattilio.com; noon-4pm and 7pm-midnight Mon.-Sat., closed Sun.; €4.50-10

Just off Via Toledo on the attractive and very typical Neapolitan street Via Pignasecca, this little restaurant is one of the top in Naples. Pizza maker Attilio Bachetti continues a long tradition of excellent pizza started by his grandfather (who was also called Attilio Bachetti) in 1938. From a young age Attilio has been making pizza, and the hard work has paid off as he is a true master of the craft.

Cafés and Bakeries

SCATURCHIO

Piazza San Domenico Maggiore 19; tel. 081/551-7031; www.scaturchio.it; 8am-9pm daily; €2-4

This coffee shop and bakery is a classic stop along Spaccanapoli at Piazza San Domenico Maggiore. Join the locals at the bar inside, which is the traditional way to have coffee in Italy. Listen to the Neapolitan dialect flow as you sip a strong coffee and try something sweet like their delicious rum-soaked *babà* or other tempting pastries.

★ SFOGLIATELLE ATTANASIO

Vico Ferrovia 1-4; tel. 081/285-675; www.sfogliatelleattanasio.it; 6:30am-7pm Tues.-Sun., closed Mon.; €2

Regularly voted the best spot for *sfogliatelle* in Naples, this tiny spot near the train station is easy to find thanks to the crowd as well as the heavenly scent wafting down the street. You'll want to sample both the *sfogiatella riccia* with its flaky crust and the traditional *frolla* variety made with shortcrust pastry.

SAN FERDINANDO

Regional Cuisine

DA DONATO DAL 1956

Via Silvio Spaventa 41; tel. 081/287-828; dadonato1956@gmail.com; 12:30pm-2:30pm and 7:30pm-10:30pm Tues.-Sun., closed Mon.; €7-15

Family-run for four generations, this trattoria and pizzeria is an excellent choice to enjoy a wide variety of homemade Neapolitan-style dishes like the traditional *ragù* or *genovese* pasta sauces that cook for 10-12 hours. The menu changes daily and the staff can guide your choice of a seafood or nonseafood menu, or you can order à la carte. Reservations are a good idea because it's a popular spot.

Pizzeria

PIZZERIA BRANDI

Salita S. Anna di Palazzo 1/2; tel. 081/416-928; www.brandi.it; 12:30pm-4pm and 7:30pm-midnight Tues.-Sun., closed Mon.; €2-22

Every pizzeria in Naples has a good story, but no story is so intimately tied to the origins of Neapolitan pizza as Brandi's. Pizza maker Raffaele Esposito and his wife Maria Giovanna Brandi made pizza in 1889 for King Umberto I and Queen Margherita di Savoia, who were visiting Naples. Of the three types of pizza, the Queen was most pleased by the pizza with mozzarella and tomato, which Esposito then named in her honor. This is how the pizza Margherita, the most classic of all Neapolitan pizzas, was born. In addition to excellent pizza, the restaurant has a full menu.

International

IKI SUSHI RESTAURANT

Via Nardones 103-104; tel.081/186-39120; massimiliano.neri@me.com; 12:30pm-3:30pm and 6:30pm-midnight daily; €10-20

Though Naples might be famous for its pizza, this is a great address when you're ready for something a little different. Created by Massimiliano Neri, the restaurant is a refreshing spot to enjoy sushi and oriental flavors, or simply stop in for a cocktail at the bar. The menu has many tempting creations like the *hikari* roll made with black rice, green peppers, and shrimp tempura.

J CONTEMPORARY JAPANESE RESTAURANT

Via Agostino Depretis 24; tel. 081/580-0543; www.j-japaneserestaurant.com; 8:30pm-midnight Mon.-Sat., closed Sun.; €40-90

Founded in Portici east of Naples and later opened right in the heart of Naples not far from the Castel Nuovo, this restaurant has a hip vibe and specializes in authentic Japanese cuisine and exquisite cocktails.

Cafés and Bakeries

★ GRAN CAFFÈ GAMBRINUS

Via Chiaia 1/2; tel. 081/417-582; www.grancaffegambrinus.com; 7am-1am daily; €2-10

Gambrinus is in a class of its own when it comes to coffee and pastries in Naples. Founded in 1860, the café has beautiful art nouveau rooms; this has been a literary salon and meeting place for generations of Neapolitans. Sitting right between Piazza Trieste e Trento and Piazza del Plebiscito, the café couldn't be better situated for taking a break or just stopping in to try their famous coffee or deserts.

PINTAURO

Via Toledo 275; tel. 081/417-339; www.pintauro.it; 9am-8pm daily; €2

In this small bakery along Via Toledo hangs a sign that honors Pasticceria Pintauro as the birthplace of the famous shell-shaped *sfogliatella* pastry in 1785. The origins of this pastry go back even earlier to a convent on the Amalfi Coast, but it was Pasquale Pintauro who perfected the *sfogliatella* with its flaky crust and citrus-infused ricotta filling that we know today. A stop here is a must on the tour of finding the best *sfogliatella* in Naples.

LA SFOGLIATELLA MARY

Via Toledo 66/Galleria Umberto I; tel. 081/402-218; 11am-8pm Wed.-Sun., closed Mon.-Tues.; €1.80-2.50

Another classic stop for *sfogliatelle* in Naples, this small bakery is located in the Galleria Umberto I just off the entrance from Via Toledo. Yet you'll likely catch the sweet scent before you arrive. Although the specialty is certainly the *sfogliatella*, there are plenty of other traditional Neapolitan desserts like the rum soaked *babà* cake to try as well.

WATERFRONT

Regional Cuisine

CARUSO ROOF GARDEN RESTAURANT

Grand Hotel Vesuvio, Via Partenope 45; www.vesuvio.it; 1pm-3pm and 8:30pm-11pm Tues.-Sun., closed Mon.; €22-30

Atop the Grand Hotel Vesuvio, with unbelievable panoramic views and a romantic setting, the Caruso Roof Garden Restaurant is named after the great tenor Enrico Caruso, who was Neapolitan through and through. Here you can even try a recipe created by Caruso, the *bucatini alla Caruso*, which is hollow spaghetti-shaped pasta served with a sauce made with San Marzano tomatoes, peppers, zucchini, and plenty of basil and oregano. A jacket is suggested for dinner, and reservations are recommended but can only be made a maximum of two weeks in advance.

UMBERTO

Via Alabardieri 30; tel. 081/418-555; www.umberto.it; 12:30pm-3:30pm and 7:15-midnight Tues.-Sun., closed Mon.; €10-20

Founded in 1916, this restaurant has been serving Neapolitan specialties for more than 100 years and doing it exceedingly well. Here you can choose from a rich menu that changes seasonally to highlight locally sourced ingredients and includes both seafood specialties like the *paccheri "d' 'o treddeta* (large tube-shaped pasta served with tomatoes, baby octopus, black olives, and capers) and delicious non-seafood options like the incredible meatballs with *ragù* sauce. The pizza is also an excellent choice.

OSTERIA DELLA MATTONELLA

Via Giovanni Nicotera 13; tel. 081/416-541; www.osteriadellamattonella.com; 12:45pm-3:30pm and

In Search of the Best *Sfogliatella*

sfogliatelle in Naples

Naples has many traditional desserts, but nothing quite tops the shell-shaped *sfogliatella*. This pastry has a citrus-infused ricotta filling and comes in two varieties: The classic *sfogliatella riccia* has a crispy and flaky crust that makes an unavoidable mess as you bite into it, and the *frolla* variety has a soft short-crust pastry shell. The pastry originated on the Amalfi Coast in Conca dei Marini, but was later modified to the sweet treat enjoyed today by Neapolitan pastry maker Pasquale Pintauro at the end of the 1700s. Today it is one of the desserts most commonly associated with Naples, and though it can also be enjoyed throughout the entire region, you've never tasted anything quite like the *sfogliatelle* made right in Naples. Locals hotly debate where to find the best *sfogliatella* in the city, but the tastiest way to find the answer is to throw your diet out the window and try them all. Here's where to start your *sfogliatella* tasting tour in Naples.

- **Pintauro:** This small bakery on Via Toledo is the birthplace of the *sfogliatella* and a fine place to sample both the traditional *sfogliatella riccia* with its flaky crust as well as the *frolla* variety made with short-crust pastry.
- **La Sfogliatella Mary:** Not far away, you'll find this popular bakery right off Via Toledo at the entrance of the Galleria Umberto I.
- **Sfogliatelle Attanasio:** Often considered the top spot for *sfogliatelle* in the city, this tiny bakery is not far from the train station. Stop by to try them still warm from the oven.

7:30pm-11:30pm Mon.-Sat., 1pm-3:30pm Sun.; €22-28

A welcoming, rustic eatery where the walls are lined with bottles of wine, this osteria is a good choice in Chiaia. The menu includes hearty homecooked fare like the *genovese* (meat and onion pasta sance) and the rich yet heavenly pasta with potatoes and *provola* (smoked cheese) that keep the regular customers and locals coming back for more.

RISTORANTE AMICI MIEI

Via Monte di Dio 77/78; www.ristoranteamicimiei.com; noon-3pm and 7:30pm-midnight Tues.-Sat., noon-3pm Sun., closed Mon. and July-Aug.; €7-20

This is a family-run restaurant where the focus is on preserving and sharing Neapolitan culinary traditions, especially recipes closely tied to the land. Try the pasta with mushrooms and truffles, or thick pappardelle noodles served with a tomato sauce enriched with lamb. Second courses include a wonderful selection of steak, grilled meats, and roasts, as well as beautifully prepared seasonal vegetables.

L'EBBREZZA DI NOÈ

Vico Vetriera a Chiaia 8b/9; tel. 081/400-104; www.lebbrezzadinoe.com; 9:30am-1:30pm and 4pm-1am Tues.-Sat., 10:30am-3pm Sun., closed Mon.; €13-20

This excellent wine store is also a cozy dining spot where sommelier and owner Luca shares his passion for all things wine and guides diners to the perfect wine-food pairings. It's a small space, so book ahead to ensure a spot to settle in and sample some lovely local Campania wines and fresh seasonal fare.

VERITAS RESTAURANT

Corso Vittorio Emanuele 141; tel. 081/660-585; www.veritasrestaurant.it; 7:45pm-11pm Tues.-Sat., 1pm-3pm Sun., closed Mon.; €19-30

Located on the slopes of the Vomero hill above Chiaia, this Michelin-starred restaurant offers fine contemporary dining inspired by traditional Neapolitan recipes. While the menu changes seasonally, you'll often find the *Maccaronara al ragù,* where the traditional rich tomato sauce of Naples is served over fresh homemade pasta. Or try the *baccalà* (salted cod) in a variety of exceptional seasonal preparations. Tasting menus are also available. Reservations are recommended.

ANTICA OSTERIA DA TONINO

Via Santa Teresa a Chiaia 47; tel. 081/421-533; osteriadatonino@libero.it; 12:30pm-3:30pm/7:30pm-11:30pm Tuesday-Sunday, 12:30pm-3:30pm Monday; €8-12

A little restaurant with a long history, this osteria is famous for doing all of the traditional Neapolitan dishes especially well. It's hard to choose, but you can't go wrong with the pasta with *genovese* sauce made with meat and onions, or the *braciola al ragù,* an unforgettable tomato sauce over meat rolls stuffed with parmesan cheese, pepper, and garlic. Save room if you can for the *polpette al ragù* (meatballs in tomato sauce).

Pizzeria

50 KALÒ

Piazza Sannazzaro 201/b; tel. 081/192-04667; www.50kalo.it; 12:30pm-4pm and 7pm-12:30am daily; €5-9.50

Not far from the Mergellina harbor and waterfront, this is a spot that pizza enthusiasts from around the world flock to, to taste the creations of master pizza maker Ciro Salvo. Though it's relatively new (opened in 2014), 50 Kalò has quickly become a top choice for pizza in Naples.

★ PIZZARIA LA NOTIZIA

Via Michelangelo da Caravaggio 53; tel. 081/714-2155; www.pizzarialanotizia.com; 7:30pm-midnight Tues.-Sun.; closed Mon.; €7-10

Born and raised in Naples and in the Neapolitan pizza tradition, Enzo Coccia opened his first pizzeria in 1994. With his dedicated attention to the highest-quality ingredients, as well as plenty of passion and hard work, Enzo has created not just one but three of the best pizza places in the city, all on the same street. The original pizzeria at Via Michelangelo da Caravaggio 53 is dedicated to tradition (think the best pizza Margherita of your life), while down the street at number 94 you'll find highly creative and delicious variations with other toppings, and **O Sfizio d''a Notizia** at number 51 is dedicated to the Neapolitan fried pizzas.

LA MASARDONA

Piazza Vittoria 5; tel. 081/281-057; pizzeriamasardona@gmail.com; 7am-4pm Mon.-Sat., closed Sun.; €2-8

In Naples there's pizza, and then there's *pizza fritta* (fried pizza), which is a specialty in itself. Since 1945, La Masardona has specialized in authentic *pizza fritta,* which can be filled with different options like ricotta, *provola,*

TOP EXPERIENCE

True Neapolitan Pizza

traditional Neapolitan pizza Margherita at Sorbillo

In 2017, the art of the Neapolitan *Piazzaiuolo*, or pizza maker, was added to UNESCO's list of Intangible Cultural Heritage of Humanity. It was a moment of great celebration in Naples, where the city's famous gastronomic delight is far more than just pizza. The Neapolitan pizza is truly a work of art and one indelibly connected to Neapolitan identity.

The most classic of Neapolitan pizzas is the pizza Margherita, which dates to 1889 when Raffaele Esposito made pizzas for King Umberto I and Queen Margherita di Savoia during their visit to Naples. The queen enjoyed most the pizza topped with tomatoes, mozzarella, extra virgin olive oil, and basil—to represent the green, white, and red of the Italian flag—and so Raffaele named the pizza in her honor. You'll find pizza Margherita on every pizzeria menu, along with the marinara pizza topped with tomatoes, oregano, garlic, and extra virgin olive oil (no cheese). These two pizzas are considered the most traditional, with some pizzerias only serving those two varieties. However, in most pizzerias you will find a large selection of toppings on the menu. Yet, while in Naples, don't miss the chance to try the classic pizza Margherita and marinara pizzas.

Pizza in Naples Is usually considered individual sized and is served about the size of a large plate. Your pizza will arrive whole and not presliced, so grab your knife and fork and dig in. There are no rules; you can eat it with knife and fork or slice your pizza into quarters and pick up a quarter, fold it in half, and enjoy! Pizza can be a full meal in itself, but sometimes you'll also find a variety of fried appetizers, like the traditional *arancini* (fried rice balls) on the menu. When it comes to fried foods, Naples is also famous for its *pizza fritta* (fried pizza): This is pizza that's topped with a variety of different fillings, like ricotta and salami, and then folded in half and deep fried.

You don't have to go far in Naples to find an excellent pizzeria, and here are some suggestions to get you started.

- **L'Antica Pizzeria da Michele:** Try the classics here—Margherita and marinara are the only two options.
- **Sorbillo:** Among Sorbillo's multiple locations around the city are a restaurant in the *centro storico* and a seaside outpost with a view of the Castel dell'Ovo. Many of their branches specialize in *pizza fritta*.
- **Pizzaria La Notizia:** Located a bit off the beaten path, Pizzzaria La Notizia serves the outstanding pizza created by Enzo Coccia.
- **50 Kalò:** This pizzeria is not far from the Mergellina harbor.
- **Starita a Materdei:** This classic pizzeria also serves gluten-free pizza.

and salami, or topped with arugula, tomatoes, and mozzarella. Above all, these pizzas are best enjoyed Neapolitan-style, by eating with your hands.

Café

GRAN CAFFÈ LA CAFFETTIERA

Piazza dei Martiri 26; tel. 081/764-4243; www.grancaffelacaffettiera.com; 7am-10pm Mon.-Fri., 7am-1am Sat., 7am-midnight Sun.; €3.50-7

This is a lovely spot in Chiaia to stop for coffee, tea, or drinks any time of the day, or late into the night. There's both indoor seating in a salon-style setting and outdoor seating on the elegant Piazza dei Martiri.

VOMERO

Regional Cuisine

★ MOSTOBUONO

Via Enrico Alvino 50; tel. 081/016-8733; www.mostobuono.it; noon-4pm and 6:30pm-1am daily; €10-20

With a great location in Vomero just off the pedestrian-only shopping street Via Alessandro Scarlatti, this restaurant offers a delightful blend of styles. You can enjoy everything from handcut pasta with the traditional *genovese* meat and onion sauce cooked for nine hours to a creative seafood gazpacho and excellent hamburgers. This is also a great spot for wine lovers, as the walls are literally covered with wine bottles and the list is well curated.

FRIGGITORIA VOMERO

Via Domenico Cimarosa 44; tel. 081/578-3130; 8:30am-9pm Mon.-Sat., closed Sun.; €1.50

This small *friggitoria* (fried food shop) is a great spot to try the classic *pizza fritta*, a type of local fried pizza filled with a variety of options like ricotta and salami. Also on the menu are a fried frittata of pasta and fried rice balls. You'll enjoy these tasty and inexpensive snacks while exploring Vomero.

MANGIANAPOLI TAVERNA PARTENOPEA

Via Bernini 85/B; tel. 081/185-80063; www.mangianapoli.eu; 12:30pm-3pm and 7:30pm-11pm Tues.-Sat., , 12:30pm-3:30pm Sun., closed Mon.; €10-15

North of Piazza Vanvitelli in the Vomero, this bright and welcoming restaurant has a simple menu with a good selection of pasta and second courses. Preparations are based on Neapolitan traditions, revisited with an eye to creativity, as well as quality locally sourced and "slow food" ingredients. While the menu changes seasonally throughout the year, you can't go wrong with the delicious pasta with potatoes, *provola* cheese, and pancetta, or the pasta with the traditional Naples *genovese* sauce.

Accommodations

With accommodations ranging from friendly hostels to family-run B&Bs and historic palazzos transformed into modern hotels, Naples has a wide array of accommodations to suit every budget. If you want to be very close to the top sights, look in the San Ferdinando, *Quartieri Spagnoli* (Spanish Quarter), and *centro storico* (historic center) areas. The historic center is an especially good option if you're traveling to the Amalfi Coast via public transportation, because you'll be close to the Napoli Centrale train station. For sea views and a more tranquil atmosphere, look in Santa Lucia, Chiaia, and Mergellina. For the most magnificent views over the city and Gulf of Naples, head for Vomero. Unlike the Amalfi Coast and Capri, Naples offers plenty of accommodations that are open year-round, and breakfast is usually included in the price of the room.

CENTRO STORICO

Under €100

HOSTEL MANCINI

Via Pasquale Stanislao Mancini 33; tel. 081-200-800; www.hostelmancininaples.com; €22 per person for dorm, €35 per person for private room

Located near the Naples train station, this hostel offers comfortable and very cost-effective accommodations in the historic center of the city. Owned by husband-and-wife team Alfredo and Margherita, the hostel welcomes guests to enjoy the large common room and use the fully-equipped kitchen for cooking and dining. Mixed-gender dorms and women-only dorm rooms with private bathrooms are available, in addition to private rooms with shared or en suite bathrooms. This hostel is an excellent choice for a friendly and budget-concious stay in Naples.

★ PALAZZO BEVILACQUA

Via Pietro Colletta 35; tel. 081/015-2412; www.palazzobevilacquanapoli.com; €79 d

A B&B with a lovely family story, the Palazzo Bevilacqua is located in an elegant building built in in 1911 by Pasquale Bevilacqua for his family to live close together. Today the B&B is run by Luigi and Margherita, the fifth generation to live in the palazzo. With a touch of creativity and modern style, they have created an enchanting little B&B with three stylish and comfortable rooms, each with en suite bathroom. With some of the city's best *pizzerie* just steps away, as well as the top sights in the *centro storico*, it's an fine option for an authentic Neapolitan experience.

HOTEL CORRERA 241

Via Correra 241; tel. 081/195-62842; www.correra.it; €90 d

In a city with a dynamic contemporary art scene, this small hotel offers a chance to stay close to the top museums and historic sights. Bright pops of color and modern design prevail here, contrasted with exposed stone walls and the lobby's Greek-Roman cave, which was used as a water cistern until the late 15th century. Double, triple, and two-level family rooms are available, all very distinctive and contemporary.

€100-200

HOTEL PIAZZA BELLINI

Via Santa Maria di Costantinopoli 101; tel. 081/451-732; www.hotelpiazzabellini.com; €135 d

Just a few steps from Piazza Bellini, this small hotel is full of modern style and comfort right in the historic center of Naples. The rooms are bright and modern, and the units with a private terrace are exceptional. Relax in the cozy library or the historic courtyard with a cocktail from the hotel's **Buvette Bar.**

★ PALAZZO CARACCIOLO NAPOLI

Via Carbonara 112; tel. 081/016-0111; www.palazzocaracciolo.com; €150 d

Walk through the imposing entrance and into the courtyard garden of the Palazzo Caracciolo and you'll know you've arrived someplace special. Built in 1584, the palazzo was owned by the Caracciolo family, one of the most important noble families in Naples. The large historic complex has been beautifully remodeled with an air of timeless elegance, and it's now home to 146 finely appointed rooms. Choose from superior rooms, deluxe rooms, or suites, some offering balconies. Dining options include the beautiful **Nel Chiostro** restaurant, set in a cloister from the 16th century.

SANTA CHIARA BOUTIQUE HOTEL

Via Benedetto Croce 23; tel. 081552-7077; http://santachiarahotel.com; €160 d

This boutique hotel harmoniously blends modern style with historic details from the 17th-century palazzo where it is located on Spaccanapoli. Each of the seven suites is beautifully decorated and unique, offering a variety of different layouts from spacious single-level rooms to two-level suites accommodating up to four people.

DECUMANI HOTEL DE CHARME

Via S. Giovanni Maggiore Pignatelli 15; tel. 081/551-8188; www.decumani.com; €174 d

Right in the historic center not far from Santa Chiara, this hotel is set in an 18th-century palazzo that was once the home of Cardinal Sisto Riario Sforza, a bishop from the 19th century. Much of the historic charm has been preserved, including period furniture and the spectacular salon with its 18th-century mirrors and decorative stuccowork covering the walls and ceiling. The 39 rooms range from one single to many double and triple rooms, each one elegantly decorated and featuring large windows.

€200-300

HOTEL COSTANTINOPOLI 104

Via Santa Maria di Costantinopoli 104; tel. 081/557-1035; www.costantinopoli104.it; €225 d

Conveniently located in the historic center not far from Piazza Dante and the Museo Archeologico Nazionale, this small hotel is set in a historic residence with a small garden and swimming pool. The 13 classic rooms are comfortably decorated with warm colors, and the six spacious junior suites are mostly set on two levels, with the garden-facing suites offering private balconies.

SAN FERDINANDO

Under €100

HOSTEL OF THE SUN

Via Guglielmo Melisurgo 15; tel. 081/420-6393; www.hostelnapoli.com; €20 for dorm room, €72 private room

With a cheery atmosphere and a convenient location near the Castel Nuovo and ferry terminal, this hostel offers dorm-style shared rooms as well as private rooms for 2-4 people with private or shared bathroom. Wi-Fi access is fast and available throughout the hostel. The common spaces are welcoming and fun, and breakfast is included. The hostel can help organize excursions, or you can take advantage of the free walking tour of Naples offered by the hostel.

€100-200

TOLEDOSTATION BED & BREAKFAST

Via Toledo 320; tel. 081/283-999; www.toledostation.com; €100 d

One of the top-ranked B&Bs in Naples, ToledoStation is set, as its name suggests, very near the Toledo metro station and is well positioned for guests to walk to the top sights in the San Ferdinando and *Quartieri Spagnoli* neighborhoods, as well as in the *centro storico*. The six rooms, with private bathrooms and balconies, are colorfully decorated in themes inspired by cities around the world.

HOTEL IL CONVENTO

Via Speranzella 137/a; tel. 081/403-977; www.hotelilconvento.it; €110 d

Located in the characteristic and narrow streets of the *Quartieri Spagnoli*, only a block from Via Toledo, this small hotel is set in a palazzo from 1600 that has been fully remodeled yet offers plenty of historic charm. Choose from nicely styled rooms ranging in size from budget single rooms to doubles, triples, and suites.

B&B ATTICO PARTENOPEO

Via Santa Brigida 72; tel. 081/542-4248; www.atticopartenopeo.it; €134 d

This is a welcoming B&B with a fantastic central location right next to Galleria Umberto I. The entire B&B and its eight rooms are decorated with an elegant and artistic touch. Choose a superior room to enjoy a private terrace and views up to Vomero. The rooftop terrace overlooks the glass dome of the Galleria Umberto I and the Chiesa di Santa Brigida next door; hearing the antique bronze bells of the church, which chime on the hour, is a classic Neapolitan experience.

CHIAJA HOTEL DE CHARME

Via Chiaia 216; tel. 081/415-555; www.chiaiahotel.com; €139 d

Full of historic charm and antique decorative touches, this friendly small hotel is set in an 18th-century noble palazzo very near Piazza del Plebiscito. Rooms vary in size, and many are named after stories from the family and building's history. Select rooms have a small balcony overlooking Via Chiaia with its many shops and restaurants below. The breakfast is excellent with only fresh ingredients and locally made pastries.

★ LA CILIEGINA LIFESTYLE HOTEL

Via Paolo Emilio Imbriani 30; tel. 081/197-18800; www.cilieginahotel.it; €180 d

Well situated between Via Toledo and Castel Nuovo, this boutique hotel with 14 jewel-like rooms is an excellent choice for its refreshing Mediterraean style, location, and features. Every aspect of the hotel is beautifully detailed, from luxurious linen sheets to the stylish custom-designed furniture in the rooms to the panoramic rooftop terrace complete with Jacuzzi and sun beds. There's a friendly team dedicated to customer service, and each guest is sent a questionnaire before arrival so the concierge can prepare personalized suggestions and guidance.

RENAISSANCE NAPLES HOTEL MEDITERRANEO

Via Ponte di Tappia 25; tel. 081-797-0001; www.mediterraneonapoli.com; €189 d

Just a short stroll from excellent shopping along Via Toledo, this modern and comfortable hotel offers a wide variety of room choices, from single rooms to deluxe and family rooms. Opt for the High Floor Panoramic rooms for a view of the Castel Nuovo and Vesuvius. There's a solarium with two Jacuzzis, and a sauna as well as a rooftop terrace with good views overlooking the city center and Gulf of Naples

€200-300

ROMEO HOTEL

Via Cristoforo Colombo 45; tel. 081/604-1580; www.romeohotel.it; €285 d

For a five-star modern experience, the Romeo Hotel offers a luxurious stay with elegently designed rooms overlooking the Gulf of Naples. Set just moments from the ferry terminal and the Castel Nuovo along the waterfront, the hotel's 89 rooms include 57 deluxe rooms, 10 junior suites, and 15 truly superb suites. The Studio Corner deluxe rooms are especially nice, with floor-to-ceiling windows and a spacious open-plan layout. This is the only hotel in Naples with a Michelin-starred restaurant, the prestigious **Il Comandante.** Other dining options include the Bar 9850 and the Beluga Lounge Bar & Terrace with sweeping views from Castel Sant'Elmo to Vesuvius in the distance.

WATERFRONT

Under €100

PALAZZO CHIATAMONE

Via Chiatamone 6; tel. 081/248-1179; www.palazzochiatamone.it; €90 d

Located a block from the waterfront between Castel d'Ovo and the Villa Comunale, this lovely little B&B is a convenient spot to reach the top sights in the Chiaia and San Ferdinando areas. A historic palazzo from the 1900s is the setting, and the six rooms are decorated in a shabby chic style, with soft colors and comfortable decor. Each well-lit room includes a private bathroom and small balony.

HOTEL REX

Via Palepoli 12; tel.081/764-9389; www.hotel-rex.it; €95 d

Just moments from the waterfront and set in an art nouveau-style palazzo, this charming three-star hotel offers a very comfortable stay with excellent hospitality in one of the best areas of Santa Lucia. The 34 rooms are spacious and bright, and are decorated in a clean modern style with unique artistic touches like the large paintings depicting Neapolitan scenes. Standard rooms include both doubles and triples, while the executive doubles with lateral sea views are worth the splurge.

€100-200

CAPPELLA VECCHIA 11

Vicolo Santa Maria Cappella Vecchia 11; tel. 081/240-5117; www.cappellavecchia11.it; €100 d

Not far from Piazza dei Martiri in Chiaia, this B&B has six comfortable rooms and a cozy breakfast and sitting area. The rooms are decorated in a streamlined modern style, with bright colors and artwork by local artists inspired by Naples. Parking is available for around €20 per day.

CASA MIRA NAPOLI

Via Giordano Bruno 169; tel. 081/761-1035; www.casamiranapoli.it; €110 d

This small B&B lovingly run by Alessandra, her mother Gina, and family offers a welcoming stay with friendly service and lovely views overlooking the city and Gulf of Naples. Two of the three rooms include a terrace with panoramic views, while the third features a window that frames a view of Vesuvius, the Gulf of Naples, and the Castel dell'Ovo. This property is an easy 5 minute walk from Mergellina harbor and the Villa Comunale gardens nearby.

★ HOTEL PALAZZO ALABARDIERI

Via Alabardieri 38; tel. 081/415-278; www.palazzoalabardieri.it; €145 d

Only a few steps off of Piazza dei Martiri and surrounded by excellent shopping and dining options, this hotel captures the essense of Chiaia's style with its elegant and traditional décor. The classic and superior rooms are all comfortable, but for a splurge consider the junior suite with a view overlooking Piazza dei Martiri.

CARACCIOLO 10

Via Francesco Caracciolo 10; tel. 081/658-4441; www.caracciolo10.it; €120 d

Located along the waterfront by the Mergellina harbor, this B&B offers a cheery stay with its five color-themed and fully modern rooms. Brightly decorated with modern furniture and pieces by contemporary artists, the setting is stylish while making the most of the large spaces of the historic building.

Over €300

GRAND HOTEL VESUVIO

Via Partenope 45; tel. 081/764-0044; www.vesuvio.it; €300

The peak of elegance and refinment in Naples, the Grand Hotel Vesuvio is situated in a prized location along the waterfront overlooking the Borgo Marinari, Castel dell'Ovo, and the Gulf of Naples. Opened in 1882, the hotel maintains a gracious air of old-world charm mixed with modern comforts, including a fitness club with indoor pool, two restaurants with panoramic views, and the top-quality service of a five-star hotel. The 160 rooms and suites are classically decorated and luxurious in every detail. This is a location where the sea view is well worth the splurge.

VOMERO

€100-200

HOTEL CIMAROSA

Via Domenico Cimarosa 29; tel. 081/556-7044; www.hotelcimarosa.it; €129 d

Enjoy a stay in the chic Vomero neighborhood at this boutique hotel situated along the pretty tree-lined streets near Piazza Vanvitelli and Castel Sant'Elmo. Three funicular stations are located nearby, making it easy to explore Naples while also enjoying the atmosphere of Vomero. The rooms offer a calming blend of minimal design with artistic touches, and some feature views over the city and Gulf of Naples all the way to Capri.

€200-300

HOTEL SAN FRANCESCO AL MONTE

Corso Vittorio Emanuele 328; tel. 081/423-9111; www.sanfrancescoalmonte.it; €175 d

One of the most scenic hotels in Naples, the Hotel San Francesco al Monte is set in a 16th-century monastery that is located on the hillside below the Certosa di San Martino and

Castel Sant'Elmo in the Vomero. The property was transformed into a luxury hotel while still preserving and respecting the important religious character of the site. The former monks' cells are now elegant accommodations decorated in soft colors, with breathtaking sea views that bring a sense of calm and reflection. Enjoy the same sweeping views of the Gulf of Naples from the floral roof garden with swimming pool.

Information and Services

VISITOR INFORMATION

AZIENDA AUTONOMA DI SOGGIORNO CURA E TURISMO DI NAPOLI

Via San Carlo 9; tel. 081/402-394; www.inaples.it; info.sancarlo@inaples.it; 9am-5pm Mon.-Sat., 9am-1pm Sun.

The Naples tourist office has several locations, but the largest info point is located at the Galleria Umberto I, just across the street from Teatro San Carlo. There is also an info point in Piazza del Gesù (Piazza del Gesù 7; tel. 081/551-2701; info.piazzagesu@inaples.it; 9am-5pm Mon.-Sat., 9am-1pm Sun.).

MEDICAL AND EMERGENCY SERVICES

For emergency services in Italy, dial 118 for an ambulance and urgent care. The **Antonio Cardarelli hospital** (Via Antonio Cardarelli 9; tel. 081/747-1111) is located northwest of the city center and has a *pronto soccorso* (emergency room) open 24 hours a day. Pharmacies are good resources if you have nonurgent medical issues or questions. Just look for the green cross or signs saying *farmacia*. You'll find several right along Via Toledo in the historic center, including the **Antica Farmacia Augusteo** (Piazzetta Duca D'Aosta 263; tel. 081/416-105; 8am-8:30pm Mon.-Fri., 10am-2pm and 4pm-8pm Sat., closed Sun.) located just across the street from the Galleria Umberto I.

POSTAL SERVICES

For postal services in Naples, head to the main post office (Poste Italiane; Piazza Giacomo Matteotti 2; tel. 081/428-9814; www.poste.it; 8:20am-7:05pm Mon.-Fri., 8:20am-12:35pm Sat., closed Sun.) located not far off of Via Toledo on Piazza Giacomo Matteotti.

Getting There

As Italy's third largest city, Naples is well connected to national and international transportation systems.

BY AIR

AEROPORTO INTERNAZIONALE DI NAPOLI

Viale F. Ruffo di Calabria; tel. 081/789-6259; www.aeroportodinapoli.it

The Aeroporto Internazionale di Napoli, also referred to as Capodichino, is located about 3.7 miles (6 km) northeast of the city center. Though it's not a large airport, it handles more than 8.5 million passengers a year. Direct flights to Naples arrive from destinations across Italy as well as from 80-plus international cities. Direct flights from the United States are occasionally available during the peak travel season from May to October. However, most major European cities offer direct flights to Naples. The airport has received many updates in recent years, including new dining and shopping options. Tourist information, car rentals, currency exchange, and public transportation options are available just outside the baggage claim in the Arrivals hall.

BY TRAIN

NAPOLI CENTRALE STAZIONE

Piazza Giuseppe Garibaldi; www.napolicentrale.it

Located in the heart of Naples at Piazza Garibaldi, the Napoli Centrale Stazione is the city's main train station, where nearly 400 trains pass through the busy station daily. **Trenitalia** (www.trenitalia.com) operates service on the Italian railway lines and runs regional, intercity, and high-speed trains from destinations across Italy. Journey times and prices can vary greatly, depending on the season, time of day, number of transfers, and especially the speed of the train. The fastest and most convenient trains are the **Frecciarossa** high-speed trains that travel from Rome to Naples in only about 70 minutes with prices starting at €16.90. However, the journey from Rome on slower trains like the intercity only takes about 2 hours and prices start at €9.90. From Florence, the Frecciarossa is a great option, as the train is direct and the journey is only 2 hours, 50 minutes, with fares starting at about €29.90. From Venice, the Frecciarossa direct is about 5 hours, 10 minutes with fares starting around €39.90. There are cheaper options, but they take a lot longer and require that you transfer trains. From Milan, the Frecciarosa train takes about 4 hours 20 minutes, and prices start at about €42.90.

The private company **Italotreno** (www.italotreno.it) offers high-speed trains from Torino, Milano, Venice, Bologna, Florence, Rome, and many other smaller cities. The journey from Rome to Naples takes from an hour and 10 minutes to 1 hour 30 minutes, and prices start around €9.90. From Florence to Naples, expect a travel time of about 3 hours and tickets starting at around €19.90. From Venice, the trip is about 5 hours and tickets start at €34.90, while from Milan the journey is about 4 hours 20 minutes with tickets starting at €29.90.

To reach Naples by train from the Amalfi Coast, you will first need to take the bus or ferry from the Amalfi Coast to the closest train stations at Salerno or Sorrento. From Sorrento, you'll catch the **Circumvesuviana** train (www.eavsrl.it; departures approximately every 30 minutes; 1-hour journey; €3.90). The Circumvesuviana train also connects Naples with Pompeii and Herculaneum, with the journey from Pompeii to Naples taking about 40 minutes (€2.80) and from Herculaneum about 20 minutes (€2.20). The Circumvesuviana train platforms are connected to the Napoli Centrale station via an underground walkway.

From Salerno, many Trenitalia trains depart daily every 15-30 minutes for the Napoli Centrale Stazione and the journey ranges from 40 minutes to 1 hour 25 minutes, depending on the type of train, with prices starting at €4.70.

BY BUS

Flixbus (www.flixbus.it) offers bus service to Naples from destinations across Italy for affordable rates. The only station in Naples is located outside the Napoli Centrale station. **Curreri Viaggi** (www.curreriviaggi.it) offers 8-10 daily bus connections from Sorrento and points along the Sorrento peninsula, as well as from Pompeii to the Aeroporto Internazionale di Napoli for €10. The bus ride from Sorrento to the airport takes 1 hour 30 minutes. **SitaSud** (www.sitasudtrasporti.it) has limited bus lines connecting Salerno and the Amalfi Coast to Naples, with a stop at Varco Immacolatella near the ferry terminal. **Pintour** (www.pintourbus.com) operates a shuttle bus service from Amalfi and towns east on the Amalfi Coast (Atrani, Minori, Maiori, Erchie, Cetara, and Vietri sul Mare) to the Aeroporto Internazionale di Napoli for €20 from April to November.

BY BOAT

PORTO DI NAPOLI

Port of Naples; tel. 081/228-3257; www.porto.napoli.it

As one of the largest ports in Italy, the Porto di Napoli (Port of Naples) handles cruise ships, cargo transport, and ferries from the Gulf of

Naples and major ports around the country. Cruise ships usually dock near the **Stazione Marittima,** and the ferry terminal for arrivals from most destinations is nearby at the **Molo Beverello.** Both arrival areas are very near bus and metro options for public transportation at Piazza Municipio, or only a short walk from Castel Nuovo and Piazza Trieste e Trento. Some ferries from Ischia also arrive in the **Mergellina** port to the west of Naples's main port.

BY CAR

Naples is well connected to the *autostrade* (highways) that crisscross Italy. If you're traveling to Naples from points north, take the A1 (Autostrada del Sole) and follow signs indicating Napoli Centro/Porto Marittima/ Stazione Centrale to reach the city center. If you're arriving from Salerno and points south, take the A3 and look for signs for Napoli Centro/Porto Marittima/Stazione Centrale. Driving in Naples can be quite the adventure and is not the recommended means of transportation for exploring the city. Parking in Naples is also challenging. If you're staying in the city center, it's a good idea to contact your hotel in advance for guidance on arriving by car, navigating to the exact location, and parking.

Getting Around

Naples has a busy city center and some of the wildest traffic in Italy. When you consider this, as well as the parking challenges and concentration of sights around the historic center and waterfront, navigating the city on foot and public transportation makes the most sense. When you're out walking, be cautious at all times, even when crossing at crosswalks. Keep an eye out for scooters that zip through traffic and along narrow streets. Although pedestrians do technically have the right of way, it's not something you'll want to test in Naples. Once you're in the city center, public transportation is a great way to get around the city. There are plenty of bus lines, a metro system with modern stations, funicular train lines running up to Vomero, and trains to the surrounding areas.

FROM THE AIRPORT

Alibus (ANM; tel. 800/639-525; www.anm.it; €5) offers a convenient bus line that connects the Aeroporto Internazionale di Napoli at Capodichino with three stops in the Naples city center. The first stop is Piazza Garibaldi for the Napoli Centrale train station or connections to other locations in the city center. The next stops are for the port, with the first at Immacolatella/Porta di Massa and then Molo Angioino/Beverello, which is most convenient for reaching ferries and cruise ships. Tickets are €5 each way and can be purchased onboard. The Alibus stop at the airport is about 100 meters beyond the arrivals exit. Be sure to validate your ticket in the machine onboard and keep it with you for the entire journey. Travel time from the airport to Piazza Garibaldi is about 15 minutes, and it's about 35 minutes to the port. Buses leave the airport about every 20 minutes 6am-11:30pm.

You can also catch a taxi for the short ride from the airport into the center of Naples. The taxi stand is located right outside the arrivals exit at the airport. Fixed rates are available from the airport to the center of Naples, and taxis are required to display the tariff card in the taxi. The rate from the airport to the *centro storico* and Napoli Stazione Centrale train station is about €18, while to the port and the San Ferdinando areas it costs about €21. To Mergellina, Chiaia, and Vomero the fares are about €25. It's essential to let the driver know you would like to have the fixed-rate fare before departing the airport; be sure to agree on the price in advance as well.

PUBLIC TRANSPORTATION

Metro and Railway

Naples has a convenient metro and railway system that travels around the city and the surrounding area. **ANM** (Azienda Napoletana Mobilità; tel. 800/639-525; www.anm.it) operates Line 1 and Line 6 of the metro system. The **Line 1** route is particularly convenient for tourists, as it connects Piazza Garibaldi at the Napoli Centrale train station to the historic center with stops at Municipio for the Piazza Municipio area, Toledo along the busy shopping street Via Toledo, Dante at Piazza Dante, Museo for the Museo Archeologico Nazionale, and Vanvitelli for the Vomero. **Line 6** runs from Mergellina to the western suburbs of Naples. **Line 2** is a metro train line that's actually operated by **Trenitalia** (www.trenitalia.com; departures every 10 minutes; €1.30) and runs from Piazza Garibaldi as well, with stops at Cavour, Museo (to transfer to Line 1), Montesanto, Amedeo, Mergellina, and points west to Pozzuoli.

To reach the archaeological sites of Pompeii and Herculaneum as well as points along the Sorrentine Peninsula to Sorrento, the Circumvesuviana train line operated by **EAV** (www.eavsrl.it; departures about every 30 minutes; 60-minute journey from Naples to Sorrento; €2.80 to Pompei, €2.20 to Herculaneum, €3.90 to Sorrento) departs from Piazza Garibaldi at the Napoli Centrale station. To reach the Campi Flegrei area, the **Cumana** train line also operated by EAV (www.eavsrl.it; departures about every 20 minutes; 25-minute journey; €1.30) departs from Naples at Montesanto.

Bus and Tram

ANM (Azienda Napoletana Mobilità; tel. 800/639-525; www.anm.it) operates a large bus transit network that covers the city center day and night. From the Napoli Centrale train station, Line **R2** runs from Piazza Garibaldi to Piazza Trieste e Trento to reach the Galleria Umberto I, Piazza del Plebiscito, and Via Toledo area. Bus Line **151** connects Piazza Garibaldi with Piazza Vittoria in Chiaia, with stops for the port near Molo Beverello and Castel Nuovo. For the *centro storico*, bus Line **E1** runs a loop around the historic center starting in Piazza del Gesù Nuovo and following Corso Umberto I to Via Duomo, past Piazza Cavour and the Museo Archeologico Nazionale down Via Toledo and back to Piazza del Gesù Nuovo. To explore the Vomero area, Line **V1** covers much of the area, including a convenient connection from near Piazza Vanvitelli and the Cimarosa and Morghen funicular train stations to reach the Castel Sant'Elmo and Certosa di San Martino. To reach the Museo di Capodimonte, catch the **178** bus at the Piazza Museo outside the Museo Archeologico Nazionale and get off at the Tondo di Capodimonte piazza to visit the Catacombe di Napoli, or stay on a little longer for the Museo di Capodimonte stop to walk through the park to reach the museum.

A single ride ticket costs €1.10, or you can choose a 90-minute ticket for €1.60 that allows for transfers. Daily tickets for the ANM transit network (buses, funicular trains, trams, and metro lines 1 and 6) are €3.50, or weekly passes are available for €12.50. Buy your tickets at most *tabacchi* (tobacco shops), some newsstands, or at the ticket machines available at some metro or train stations. Single-use or timed tickets must be validated at the machine when you board the bus or before boarding at the metro or train station. If you have a daily or weekly ticket, validate it the first time you use it and be sure to fill out the name and date information on the ticket. Be prepared to show ID if the ticket inspector asks. It is worth making sure you validate your tickets properly, or you may be fined.

Funicular

Naples has three funicular train lines, called *funicolari*, also operated by **ANM** (Azienda Napoletana Mobilità; tel. 800/639-525; www.anm.it) that connect the *centro storico* and Chiaia area with the Vomero. These train lines run vertically up the mountainside and provide quite a convenient and unique way to get around in the city. The **Funicolare Centrale** line starts in the Augusteo station just off Via Toledo opposite the Galleria Umberto 1 and arrives at the Fuga station in Piazza Ferdinando Fuga in the Vomero. The **Funicolare di Chiaia** starts at the Amedeo station in Piazza Amedeo and ends at the Cimarosa station just south of Piazza Vanvitelli in the Vomero. The **Funiculare di Montesanto** starts in the Quartieri Spagnoli and runs to the Morghen station not far from the Castel Sant'Elmo in Vomero. The funicular trains are primarily used by locals to move between the higher and lower parts of the city. Each line makes several stops along the way, mostly connecting residential areas of Naples. It's not a problem to transport luggage on the trains.

Funicular trains run in both directions on all the lines, about every 10 minutes, 7am-10pm. Ticketing is the same as for buses, and a single ride costs €1.10. Daily and weekly ANM tickets also include rides on the funicular lines.

Taxi

Taxis in Naples offer both metered and fixed-rate tariffs that you can choose from for each ride. Fixed-rate fares are available to and from the main transporation hubs like the airport, train station, and port. You must opt for a fixe-rate tariff at the beginning of a journey and tell the driver. Metered fares start at €3.50 Monday-Saturday and €6.50 on Sundays and holidays; the fare increases €.05 every 157 feet (48 m) and every 8 seconds stopped. There are extra fees for bags, more than four passengers, airport pickups or drop-offs, and more. All taxis must display the tariff card (in Italian and English) that is regulated by the city of Naples. Though you can flag a taxi down, getting a taxi is much easier if you go to the nearest taxi stand. They are located throughout the city at the transportation hubs and at major landmarks and piazzas. It is also possible to call a taxi by phoning **Radio Taxi** (tel. 081/8888; www.radiotaxinapoli.it), **Consortaxi** (tel. 081/2222; www.consortaxi.it), or **Radio Taxi La Partenope** (tel. 081/0101; www.radiotaxilapartenope.it).

Ferry

The large **Porto di Napoli** (www.porto.napoli.it) offers frequent ferry connections that make it easy to get around the Gulf of Naples to see Sorrento and the islands of Capri, Ischia, and Procida. Ferry service is available year-round from Naples, but the number

Funicular trains connect Chiaia and the historic center to the Vomero neighborhood.

of ferries daily is reduced during the winter months. Ferry service direct from Naples to the Amalfi Coast is not available, but you can take a ferry to Sorrento and Capri and connect from those destinations to ferry services to the Amalfi Coast (available seasonally, usually May-Oct.).

DOCKING AREAS

The Naples Port is divided into many different docking areas. Just across from the Castel Nuovo, you'll find the **Molo Beverello,** where the majority of the passenger ferries depart and arrive. Just to the left of the Molo Beverello (looking toward the sea), a very large pier juts out into the harbor with the **Stazione Marittima** (Piazzale Stazione Marittima; tel. 081/551-4448; www.terminalnapoli.it), which is where cruise ships usually dock. Continuing along the port to the left beyond Piazzale Immacolatella is the **Calata Porta di Massa,** where larger passenger and vehicle ferries depart for Ischia, Procida, and Capri. From Molo Beverello to the Calata Porta di Massa it's a 15-minute walk, or there is often a free shuttle bus that circulates between the two that you can take.

BOAT SERVICES

Many different companies run boat service from Naples's port, offering a variety of options, from high-speed jets to *aliscafo* (hydrofoil) and slower *traghetti* (ferries) that transport passengers and vehicles. Most ferry companies offer advance ticket purchase online, which is a good idea during the busy summer months. You can also purchase tickets from the ticket booths before boarding; just arrive with time to spare, in case there are lines at the ticket booths.

- **NLG** (tel. 081/552-0763; www.navlib.it; starting at €13.10 per person) operates jet routes to Capri and Sorrento.
- **Gescab** (tel. 081/428-5259; www.gescab.it; starting at €19) has jet routes from Naples to Capri and Sorrento as well.
- **SNAV** (tel. 081/428-5555; www.snav.it; starting at €15.50) operates lines to Ischia, Procida, and Capri.
- **Caremar** (tel. 081/189-66690; www.caremar.it; starting at €12.30 for passengers and €28.50 for vehicles) offers ferry service also, to transport vehicles to Sorrento, Capri, Ischia, and Procida.
- **Medmar** (tel. 081/333-4411; www.medmargroup.it; starting at €12.40 for passengers) also offers vehicle transport and ferry service from the **Calata Porta di Massa** in the Naples port to Ischia and Procida.
- **Alilauro** (tel. 081/551-3236; www.alilaurogruson.it; starting at €21.10 per person) runs ferry departures from the **Mergellina** port to Sorrento and Ischia.

CAR AND SCOOTER RENTAL

Navigating Naples's famously chaotic traffic and maze of streets in the historic center is not a recommended way to get around. Outside Naples, however, having a car gives you more freedom to move around.

NAPOLI RENT

Calata Trinità Maggiore 28; tel. 081/1925-9711; www.napolirent.it; scooters from €26 per day and cars from €31.50 per day

If you're willing to brave the streets or are looking to head out of Naples, Napoli Rent offers car and scooter rental options with different locations to pick up your rental in Naples, including the airport, Piazza Garibaldi at the Napoli Centrale train station, or near the Molo Beverello at the port.

BUS TOURS

CITY SIGHTSEEING

Info point at Largo Castello Piazza Municipio; tel. 335/780-3812; www.city-sightseeing.it/it/napoli; from €23

For a worry-free way to get around Naples, City Sightseeing offers a city tour on easy-to-spot, bright red, double-decker buses with open seating on the top. With the company's convenient hop-on hop-off policy, you can explore the city for an entire day, getting on and off as many times as you wish. Line 1 makes a loop through the **historic center** and includes stops at all the top sights, including the **Museo Archeologico Nazionale** and **Museo di Capodimonte.** Line 2 runs along the waterfront to **Mergellina** and along Posillipo to **Capo Posillipo.** Tickets are €23 per person for adults and €11.50 for children ages 5-15; children 4 and under ride for free.

Around Naples

Just west of Naples lies a stretch of coastline that is well off the beaten path yet is enormously rich in archaeological treasures and history. Head southwest from Mergellina to explore the rugged coastline and scenic views of **Posillipo.** Beyond lie the fabled **Campi Flegrei** (burning fields) or Phlegraean Fields, named for the volcanic activity in the area surrounding the Gulf of Pozzuoli. From ancient Greek times to the Bourbon dynasty, this area has been noted for its natural beauty, thermal spas, and air of mystery.

While Naples holds incredible artistic and architectural treasures from the Bourbon era, the finest royal residence is the **Reggia di Caserta** about an hour north of the city. This 18th-century palace is one of the largest in Europe and is well worth a day trip from Naples.

POSILLIPO

Following the coastline from Mergellina southwest leads to a hilly residential area of Naples called Posillipo. Along the promontory that ends at Capo Posillipo, a well-developed residential area covers the slopes of the hillside and reaches down to villas at sea level. That beautiful coastline and the splendid views across the Gulf of Naples with Vesuvius in the distance have always made this an appealing place to live. Ancient Greek settlers, the first to live on the promontory, called this area *Pausilypon*, which means "respite from pain." Later the Romans built lavish villas here, the ruins of which can be seen today at the **Parco Archeologico del Pausilypon** and below the sea in what is now a protected marine area. A coastline rich with history and beautiful little beaches, Posillipo still offers a respite to travelers who are curious to venture outside the historic center of Naples.

Sights

AREA MARINA PROTETTA PARCO SOMMERSO DI GAIOLA

Discesa Gaiola; tel. 081/240-3235; www.areamarinaprotettagaiola.it; info@areamarinaprotettagaiola.it; 10am-4pm Apr.-Sept., 10am-2pm Oct.-Mar., closed Mon.; tours from €6 per person

The extensive archaeological ruins in the Posillipo area are managed by the Area Marina Protetta Parco Sommerso di Gaiola, which offers guided tours of the Parco Archeologico del Pausilypon and the underwater **Roman ruins** around the Gaiola islands. In an incredible natural setting surrounded by lush greenery and steep cliffs to the sea is the **villa of Publius Vedius Pollio,** who was a wealthy Roman and friend of Emperor Augustus. While much of his estate has been lost to time, there are still remnants, including parts of an amphitheater that once seated 2,000 people, a smaller theater, and other parts of what was once an incredibly lavish seaside villa. The ruins are accessed through a 2,297-foot (770m) long tunnel called the **Grotta di Seiano** that also dates back to Roman times. Guided tours last about 1.5 hours and are available in English with advance booking via phone or email.

Many more Roman ruins lie submerged below the sea level, and the Area Marina Protetta Parco Sommerso di Gaiola offers a variety of different options to explore underwater. A glass-bottomed boat ride is a

Around Naples

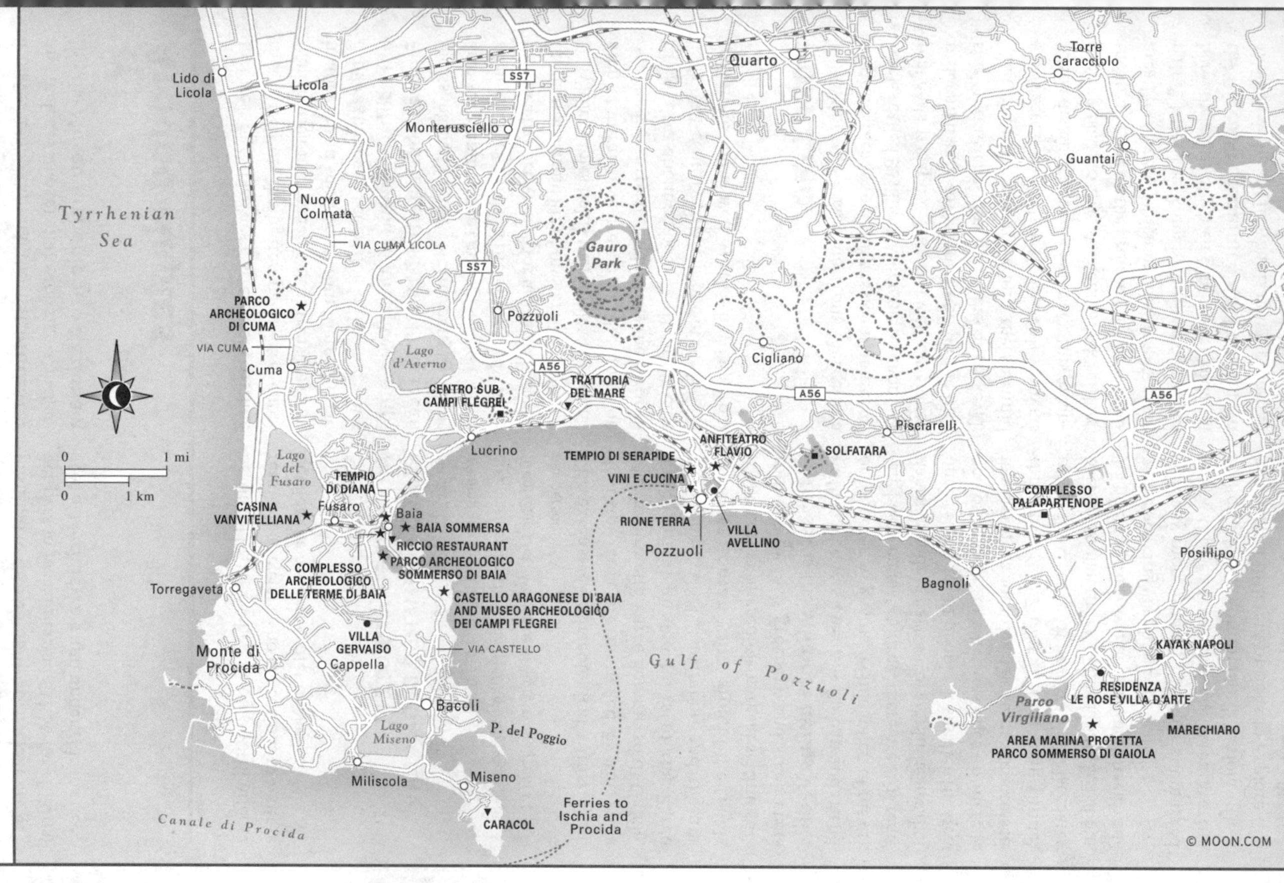

comfortable option to get a glimpse of the ruins, or for an even closer look there are also snorkeling and scuba diving experiences available. Located just off the very tip of the Posillipo promontory are two small islands called Gaiola that are connected to one another by a small bridge. Tours are available in English with advance booking and last about 1.5 hours (€12 per person). Snorkeling and scuba diving excursions are also available and start at €20 per person. Contact in advance for help booking your tour or excursion.

PARCO VIRGILIANO

Viale Virgilio; 7am-8:30pm

Near the tip of the Posillipo promontory and about 492 feet (150 m) above sea level, this large park offers unbeatable panoramic views of the Gulf of Naples from Vesuvius down the Sorrento coast to the islands of Capri and Ischia in the distance and the nearby islands of Gaiola and Nisida. To the west is an excellent view of the Gulf of Pozzuoli to Capo Miseno and the island of Procida beyond.

Beaches

POSILLIPO BEACH

Via Posillipo just west of Mergellina

Posillipo's main beach, which is the closest beach to Naples, affords beautiful views of the gulf and the evocative **Palazzo Donn'Anna** that sits right at the edge of the sea at the western side of the beach. This grand 17th-century villa was once the home of Anna Carafa, the wife of Ramiro Núñez de Guzmán, the Spanish Viceroy of Naples. She commissioned prominent architect Cosimo Fanzago to create this luxurious palazzo on the sea. Construction began in 1642 yet was never completed. Though it's private property, the villa creates an evocative backdrop for a swim at this sandy little beach, and it's a popular place for kayak tours to paddle by on the sea. **Bagno Ideal** (Via Posillipo 18; tel. 081/248-3087; Apr.-Oct.) offers sun bed rentals and beach services like showers and changing rooms.

MARECHIARO

Via Marechiaro

Located near Capo Posillipo, this tiny seaside village dates back to the 13th century, when it was home to fishermen. Today the sea is as clear as the name suggests (*marechiaro* means "clear sea") yet the beach is a rocky one. A series of beach clubs (*stabilimenti balneari*) line the cove and offer sunbathing platforms built out into the sea and on rocky outcroppings nearby. This area is perfect for swimmers who like to explore rocky beaches and coves. Nearby at the edge of the sea is the **Palazzo degli Spiriti,** Roman ruins dating back to the 1st century BC that were once a part of the lavish Pausilypon villa in the hills nearby.

Sports and Recreation

KAYAK NAPOLI

Via Posillipo 68 and Via Posillipo 357; tel. 331/987-4271; www.kayaknapoli.com; tours from €25 per person

The best way to explore the Posillipo coastline with its caves and beautiful seaside villas is from the sea. Kayak Napoli offers both kayak and stand-up paddleboard rentals, as well as guided kayak tours along the coast. A variety of themed tours and sunset tours are available from two different starting points. From Bagno Sirena (Via Posillipo 357), the **Naples and its Villas** tour offers a close-up look at some of the historic villas of the area, including Palazzo Donn'Anna. Farther west down the coastline, starting at the Baia delle Rocce Verdi (Via Posillipo 68), the **Wild Posillipo** tour highlights the natural landscape, archaeological ruins, and marine-protected area of Gaiola. Tours are offered with an English-speaking guide and take place throughout the year, weather permitting. To reach both beach areas for the kayak tours, you can take the 140 bus from Naples that runs along Via Posillipo.

Food

Along with seaside restaurants and beach clubs offering snacks, you'll find a variety of dining options, including restaurants, *pizzerie*, and cafés around Piazza San Luigi, located along Via Posillipo.

PALAZZO PETRUCCI

Via Posillipo 16c; tel. 081/575-7538; www.palazzopetrucciristorante.it; 7pm-10:30pm Mon., noon-2:30pm and 7pm-10:30pm Tues.-Sat., noon-2:30pm Sun.; €28-40

Founded in the heart of Naples in 2007 and receiving the first Michelin star in Naples in 2008, this iconic restaurant moved to its beautiful beachside setting overlooking Palazzo Donn'Anna in 2016. With panoramic views and an exquiste menu crafted by master chef Lino Scarallo, the dishes here blend tradition and innovation with equal attention to seafood and non-seafood recipes inspired by classic Neapolitan flavors. Tasting menus are available. Reservations are highly recommended.

Accommodations

LUX B&B

Via Posillipo 382; tel 338/138-3154; www.lux-beb.com; €100 d

Not far from Posillipo's beach and the Palazzo Donn'Anna, this small B&B offers a welcoming stay and unforgettable panoramic views from its three rooms. The standard rooms have a large window while the superior room has a balcony. This B&B is in an excellent location near the beach, and parking is available with advance notice for an extra charge.

RESIDENZA LE ROSE VILLA D'ARTE

Discesa Gaiola 73; tel. 081/575-3851; www.residenzalerose.it; €75 d

Located on Posillipo hill not far from the Parco Virgiliano, this unique B&B has a quiet setting and artistic touches in all of its six rooms and common spaces. The rooms function like little art galleries in themselves with contemporary art displays. The villa overlooks a lush garden and is an ideal setting for a tranquil holiday escape.

Getting There and Around

Located about 3.7 miles (6 km) west of the Naples city center, Posillipo is accessible via bus lines that run from Naples along the coastline, connecting all the main sights. Via Posillipo begins just west of Mergellina and follows the coastline, beginning close to the sea and gradually climbing higher on the hill. **Via Petrarca** is the main road running down the promontory in the upper part of Posillipo hill. To get around via public transportation, the **ANM** (Azienda Napoletana Mobilità; tel. 800/639-525; www.anm.it; buses every 15-20 minutes; from €1.10) 140 bus line runs on Via Posillipo. It departs from the center of Naples at Santa Lucia south of the Piazza del Plebiscito and passes by Piazza Vittoria, the Riveria di Chiaia, and Mergellina before running along Via Posillipo all the way to Capo Posillipo. The **City Sightseeing** (Piazza Municipio Largo Castello; www.city-sightseeing.it/it/napoli; starting at €23) bus company offers a hop-on hop-off route (Linea B) from Piazza Municipio with stops at Capo Posillipo, the road leading down to Marechiaro, and the Parco Virgiliano with other scenic stops along the route. The entire journey takes 70 minutes if you stay onboard.

POZZUOLI

Pozzuoli sits at the heart of the Campi Flegrei and Gulf of Pozzuoli, an area that has been admired for its natural beauty since ancient times. An ancient Greek myth says that the Lago d'Averno near Pozzuoli was an entryway to hell, but the Romans built lavish seaside villas here nevertheless. This area also held fascination for travelers on the Grand Tour, like the author Johann Wolfgang von Goethe, who was captivated by the ruins and fascinating history. Set in the Campi Flegrei, Pozzuoli stretches from the port up into a hilly area that includes several volcanic craters, such as Atroni, Monte Nuovo, the crater that is now Lago d'Averno, and the steaming Solfatara. To the west, the terrain of Pozzuoli levels as it reaches the sea, and the ruins of ancient Cuma, the earliest Greek settlement in the Naples area, spreads out by the sea. Once one of the most important ports for the entire Roman Empire, modern day Pozzuoli is still an active port where ancient ruins have been absorbed into the fabric of daily life. Exploring Pozzuoli reveals incredible historic treasures, intriguing legends, and the chance to enjoy those alluring natural landscapes.

Sights

RIONE TERRA

Rione Terra; tel. 081/199-36286; prenotazioni@comune.pozzuoli.na.it; 9am-noon and 1:30pm-4:30pm Sat.-Sun. only; €5

Sitting above the port of Pozzuoli, this raised part of town is the earliest settlement in the area and dates back to the Roman colony founded at the end of the 1st century BC. This historic neighborhood has been compared to the pages of a book, with each layer of history placed on top of another. Over the centuries much of the area's history had quite literally been covered. It was well populated until 1970 when, due to concerns over the stability of the area, it was completely evacuated. Rione Terra remained a ghost town until the 1990s when work began to reclaim the area. It was during this work that the remarkable ruins of the Roman city, complete with soaring marble columns of a temple dedicated to Augustus, were discovered. Today the Rione Terra is again open on the weekends, and a self-guided itinerary leads through the archaeological area and the highlights of this historic neighborhood. Visitors are admitted hourly during opening hours. Advance reservation is required.

ANFITEATRO FLAVIO

Corso Nicola Terracciano 75; tel. 081/526-6007; www.parcoarcheologicocampiflegrei.beniculturali.it; 9am-sunset, closed Tues.; €4

Right in the center of modern day Pozzuoli, the Anfiteatro Flavio is a remarkable reminder of just how important a place Pozzuoli held in the Roman Empire. This massive amphitheater seated up to 40,000 spectators and was the third-largest in the empire after the Colosseum in Rome and the amphitheater in Capua north of Naples. Likely built by the same architects as the Colosseum, the Anfiteatro Flavio's construction was completed in the second half of the 1st century. Excavations in the 19th century revealed a remarkably intact series of underground passageways that can be explored today.

TEMPIO DI SERAPIDE

Via Serapide 13

Although referred to as a temple dedicated to the god Serapide, this archaeological area along the waterfront in Pozzuoli was once the center of the busy market, or *macellum*, of the ancient Roman town. Dating back to the 1st century, the ruins now sit well below street level. The sight is one of great archaeological and geological interest due to the way the water surrounding the three large columns and much of the ruins changes levels. It's one of the clearest examples of bradyseism, a slow movement of the earth due to underground magma chambers or hydrothermal activity, which impacts the entire Campi Flegrei area. Scientists have discovered that at one time the columns were submerged in water by at least 23 feet (7 m). Bradyseism is also the reason that many archaeological sites now lie underwater, like those in nearby Baia and the Area Marina Protetta Parco Sommerso di Gaiola in Posillipo. While the ruins cannot be visited, it's possible to walk around most of the site and get a good view.

LAGO D'AVERNO

Via Lago d'Averno

West of Pozzuoli's historic center a large round lake sits in the crater of a now extinct volcano. The name Averno comes from the Greek word meaning "without birds" and reflects how both the Greeks and later Romans thought birds flying over the lake were killed by the gases released by the volcano. Even more ominously, it was considered the opening to Hades. The Roman poet Virgil wrote about Lago d'Averno in the *Aeneid* as the place where Aeneas goes with Sibyl to enter the underworld. A footpath encircles the lake, where you can spot different types of waterfowl that apparently aren't aware of the lake's dark story. At the eastern end of the lake are the ruins of the **Tempio di Apollo,** once a grand temple that is thought to have been part of a bathing complex that is now mostly underground.

PARCO ARCHEOLOGICO DI CUMA

Via Monte di Cuma 3; tel. 081/804-0430; www.parcoarcheologicocampiflegrei.beniculturali.it; 9am-sunset daily; €4

On the western edge of the Campi Flegrei and bordered by the Tyrrhenian Sea, Cuma is now a part of larger Pozzuoli nearby, yet it has a fascinating heritage. It was here that ancient Greeks settlers founded Cumae in 730 BC, the first colony on the Italian mainland after that of Pithecusae on the island of Ischia. The ruins of the ancient town of Cumae are now part of the **Parco Archeologico di Cuma,** where it's possible to explore part of the excavations in the 136-acre (55-hectare) site. Highlights include the ruins of the Temple of Apollo, Acropolis with the Temple of Jupiter, and the most intriguing of all, the Antro della Sibilla. This trapezoidal shaft is the legendary location of the Cumean Sibyl, a prophetess whom the Roman Poet Virgil wrote about in the *Aeneid*, though it was more likely part of a military defense system. Guided tours are not available.

Food

VINI E CUCINA

Via Caldaia 17; tel. 081/341-7997; viniecucinapozzuoli@gmail.com; 7pm-11pm Mon.-Tues. and Thurs.-Fri., 12:30pm-3pm Sun., closed Wed. and first three weeks of Sept.; €7.50-11

Set in a pedestrian-only area just steps from the port of Pozzuoli, this small restaurant has a trattoria vibe and good homecooked-style meals. The menu changes seasonally, but you can't go wrong with the pasta with mussels and *tarallo* (a typical savory biscuit made in Naples) or pasta with mussels and beans if they're on the menu.

TRATTORIA DEL MARE

Via Campi Flegrei 58; tel. 081/341-6055; www.trattoriadelmarepozzuoli.it; 6pm-midnight Tues.-Thurs., noon-midnight Fri.-Sat., noon-8pm Sun., closed Mon.; €7-14

Seafood is the specialty of this friendly trattoria located in the western part of Pozzuoli. Local flavors are combined in new ways in unexpected combinations, like the traditional

Tempio di Serapide

Steaming Solfatara

Just outside Pozzuoli lies one of the most intriguing and storied areas of the Campi Flegrei. The Solfatara is a volcanic crater that, despite being classified as a dormant volcano, has active fumaroles that spew sulfurous fumes and pools of bubbling hot mud. The name (and quite distinctive smell) comes from the Latin *sulpha terra*, meaning "land of sulfur" or "sulfur earth." Created about 4,000 years ago, this has been a place of fascination since at least ancient Roman times, when it was thought to be the home of Vulcan, the god of fire; with its steaming fumaroles and hot earth, one can easily imagine why. The Romans were the first to recognize and use the vapors and mud for their healing properties.

In AD 305, this otherworldly place was the location where San Gennaro, the patron saint of Naples, was martyred, along with six other Christians. The nearby **Santuario di San Gennaro** (Via San Gennaro Agnano 7, Pozzuoli; tel. 081/526-1114; www.santuariosangennaro.it) preserves the rock where the saint is believed to have been beheaded.

During the 18th-19th centuries, the Solfatara was a must for travelers on the Grand Tour who were captivated by the otherworldly landscape and took advantage of the medicinal qualities of the mud and steams. First opened to the public in the early 1900s, the area has been popular spot for tours, thanks to its rare volcanic activity and fascinating setting. However, the area was closed in October 2017 after the tragic deaths of a family of three visiting the site. There is no date scheduled to reopen the site, but you can visit **Vulcano Solfatara** online (www.solfatara.it) to find out more.

spaghetti with clams infused with a zucchini cream, or shrimp covered with almonds and honey.

Accommodations

VILLA AVELLINO

Via Carlo Maria Rosini 21-29; tel. 081/303-6812; www.villaavellino.it; open year round; €116 d

Set right in the center of Pozzuoli near all the top sights, Villa Avellino is a historic residence dating back to the 16th century. Beautifully restored and set next to a large park, this property offers 18 apartments, from studios to family suites, all with fully equipped kitchens. Some of the apartments are located on two levels and include sea views, balconies, or terraces. Breakfast is included.

Getting There and Around

Pozzuoli is located west of Naples and is connected to the center of the city by train lines. The Metro Line 2 is a regional line operated by **Trenitalia** (www.trenitalia.com; departures every 10 minutes; 40-minute journey; €2.20) that connects Piazza Garibaldi (stops at Piazza Cavour, Piazza Amedeo, Montesante, and Mergellina) in Naples with the Pozzuoli Solfatara station very near the Anfiteatro Flavio, which is only a 10-minute walk from the Tempio di Serapide and the waterfront, and 15 minutes from Rione Terra. The Cumana train line operated by **EAV** (www.eavsrl.it; departures every 20 minutes; 25-minute journey; €1.30) connects Naples at Montesanto to the Pozzuoli station located near the port. For the archaeological sites of Cuma and Lago d'Averno, it is easiest to explore by car.

BAIA AND BACOLI

Set along the western side of the Gulf of Pozzuoli, Baia has a small harbor surrounded by scenic hills and has been a popular holiday spot since ancient Roman times, when luxury villas were constructed here. In Baia, more than any other location on the Campi Flegrei, the ancient past seems to be ever present. Just above the harbor lie extensive ruins of Roman thermal baths while not far offshore, at the underwater archaeological area, the rest of the city lies covered with water as a result of bradyseism: the slow movement of the earth's surface that is prominent in the Campi Flegrei. Near the harbor, you'll also spot the **Tempio di Diana** (Via Bellavista 35) and the **Tempio di Venere** (Via Lucullo), two Roman structures that were once thought to be temples but are now believed to be ancient thermal baths or spas.

Continuing down the coastline leads to Bacoli and the tip of Capo Miseno, the western defining point of the Gulf of Pozzuoli and also the much larger Gulf of Naples. Much like Baia, the area has been a holiday spot and is dotted with Roman ruins. Capo Miseno is named after Misenus, a companion to Aeneus in Virgil's *Aeneid*, who supposedly died here. A place of ancient lore and historical importance as the base for the Roman naval fleet, Bacoli and the narrow stretch of land leading to Capo Miseno are popular today for their beautiful natural setting and views across to the island of Procida.

Sights

COMPLESSO ARCHEOLOGICO DELLE TERME DI BAIA

Piazza Alcide de Gasperi, Baia; tel. 081/804-0430; www.parcoarcheologicocampiflegrei.beniculturali.it; 9am to an hour before sunset, closed Mon.; €4

Set on the hills right above the harbor, the ruins of ancient Baia are an evocative sight to see, surrounded by the modern-day city. The extensive Roman thermal baths spread across multiple terraces and are only a part of the Roman city. The remainder of the city now lies underwater and can be visited thanks to the Parco Archeologico Sommerso di Baia. The ruins on land are often referred to as the Terme di Baia (Thermal Baths of Baia), because much of what has been uncovered is part of an extensive series of thermal baths and summer villas that were built over the span of four centuries. Everyone from emperors to the most noted writers of the period—such as Virgil, Cicero, Ovid, and Horace—spent time here. The quiet archaeological site is an evocative place to look out over the bay and imagine the hustle and bustle of summer in ancient Roman times.

PARCO ARCHEOLOGICO SOMMERSO DI BAIA

Dicesa Baia; tel. 081/240-3235; www.gaiola.org; 10am-4pm Tues.-Sun. Apr.-Sept., 10am-2pm Tues.-Sun. Oct, 10am-2pm Tues., Thurs., and Sat. Nov.-Mar.

The ruins of the ancient city of Baia lie submerged off the coastline as a result of bradyseism, the slow movement of the earth's surface. The natural setting is spectacular, with fish swimming among the ruins, elaborate mosaics just below a dusting of sand, sculptures, Roman roads, and a tranquility that is haunting. There are various ways to see the underwater park. Scuba diving and snorkeling are offered by **Centro Sub Campi Flegrei** for a close-up look, or enjoy a more relaxed glimpse of the ruins aboard a glass-bottom boat tour from **Baia Sommersa.** (Both providers are detailed below under Sports and Recreation.)

CASTELLO ARAGONESE DI BAIA AND MUSEO ARCHEOLOGICO DEI CAMPI FLEGREI

Via Castello 39, Baia; tel. 081/523-3797; www.parcoarcheologicocampiflegrei.beniculturali.it; 9am-1:30pm, closed Mon.; €4

Sitting on a promontory south of Baia's harbor, the Castello Aragonese is a grand fortress that was built from 1490-93 on top of a Roman villa that is commonly thought to have been a summer residence of Julius Caesar or Emperor Nero. Today it houses the Museo Archeologico dei Campi Flegrei, dedicated to the rich archaeological history of the area. The museum includes finds uncovered at Baia, Pozzuoli, Cuma, Miseno, and surrounding areas. Among the archaeological treasures, the museum displays models and didactic information (also in English) to help re-create the original setting where the artifacts were uncovered.

CASINA VANVITELLIANA

Piazza Gioacchino Rossini 1, Bacoli; tel. 348/428-8342; www.parcovanvitelliano.it; 10am-8pm Sat.-Sun. Apr.-Oct. and 10am-6pm Nov.-Mar.; €3

Similar to nearby Lago d'Averno, the Lago

Fusaro is located over an extinct volcanic crater. During the Bourbon rule of Naples, the lake and surrounding area were popular hunting and fishing ground for the kings. In 1782, Carlo Vanvitelli, son of the celebrated architect Luigi Vanvitelli, completed a royal fishing lodge located in the lake that was only accessible by boat. Now connected by a bridge from the shore, the two-level baroque building is quite unique in its elegant octagonal shape and can be visited for a small fee.

Sports and Recreation

CENTRO SUB CAMPI FLEGREI

Via Miliscola 165 at Lido Montenuovo beach, Pozzuoli; tel. 081/853-1563; www.centrosubcampiflegrei.it; summer dive times: 9am, 11:30am, or 2:30pm Mon.-Fri. and 8:30am, 11:30am, or 2:30pm Sat.-Sun Apr.-Oct., winter dive times: 8:30am, 11:30am, or 2:30pm Sat.-Sun Nov.-Mar.; €20-35

Situated between Pozzuoli and Baia's harbor, this well-equipped diving center is set very near the Parco Archeologico Sommerso di Baia. Guided scuba diving and snorkeling excursions are available to see all of the most interesting archaeological spots, as well as diving areas farther afield near the islands of Ischia, Procida, and Nisida. The center includes showers, changing room, and lockers. Book in advance for guided excursions in English. Snorkeling trips begin at €20 per person, while single dives for certified scuba divers start at €35 per person. Trial dives are available for non-certified divers and start at €50 per person. There is an additional required fee of €3-5 per person for diving in the Parco Archeologico Sommerso di Baia that goes to maintaining the underwater site.

BAIA SOMMERSA

Via Molo di Baia, Baia; tel. 349/497-4183; www.parcosommersobaia.it; baiasommersa@gmail.com; mid-Mar.-early Nov.; tours in English with advance reservation; €10 per person

Climb aboard a glass-bottom boat that seats up to 48 passengers for a tour of the Parco Archeologico Sommerso di Baia. You can gaze down on the submerged ancient city below as a guide shares historical information on the sights. Information is only available in Italian unless you prebook a tour with an English-speaking guide. English tours must be booked at least 48 hours in advance via email or phone.

Food

CARACOL

Via Faro 44, Bacoli; tel. 081/523-3052; www.caracolgourmet.it; 8pm-11:30pm Mon.-Sat., closed Sun. May-Sept., 8pm-11:30pm Wed., 1pm-3:30pm and 8pm-11:30pm Thurs.-Sat., 1pm-3:30pm Sun. Oct.-Dec., closed Jan.-Apr.; €22-26

With equally beautiful indoor and outdoor seating areas, Caracol offers an unforgettable setting with a view of Procida, Ischia, and Capri across the Gulf of Naples. The gourmet menu here is carefully crafted by chef Angelo Carannante, who is originally from the Campi Flegrei area but trained in Michelin-starred kitchens throughout Italy. Tasting menus are available and reservations are recommended.

RICCIO RESTAURANT

Via Molo di Baia 47, Baia; tel. 081/868-8617; robertadimeo@live.it; 1pm-3pm and 8pm-11pm Mon.-Tues. and Thurs.-Sat., 1pm-3pm Sun., closed Wed.; €13-18

Set along the harbor in Baia, this is a great spot to stop for a break from exploring archaeological sites to sample some of the seafood specialties of the region. If you've never tried it, this is the place to experience *riccio* (sea urchin), which is prepared beautifully in *spaghetti al riccio.*

Accommodations

VILLA GERVASIO

Via Bellavista 176; tel. 081/868-7892; www.villagervasio.it; €100 d

With a sweeping view of the Gulf of Pozzuoli and the Castello Aragonese, this small boutique hotel offers a stylish stay and a friendly atmosphere. The six rooms are elegantly designed with an artistic touch and modern style blended with comfort. Choose from standard rooms or the superior rooms with balcony to savor the fine views. The on-site restaurant boasts an especially romantic view over the Gulf of Pozzuoli.

Getting There and Around

Located along the western side of the Gulf of Pozzuoli, both Baia and Bacoli are more isolated and challenging to reach on public transportation. The closest train station to Baia is Fusaro on the Cumana regional train line operated by **EAV** (www.eavsrl.it; departures every 20 minutes; 35-minute journey; €1.30); from there it's a 20-minute walk (.6 miles or 1 km) to reach the port. Driving from Naples, the best route to Baia is via the **A56** highway, also called the **Tangenziale di Napoli,** that passes northwest of the center of Naples. Exit at Pozzuoli and continue south on Via Miliscola, which becomes Via Montegrillo before reaching Baia. The drive from Naples to Baia takes 30-40 minutes.

★ REGGIA DI CASERTA

Of all of the architectural treasures created by the Bourbon kings of Naples, the largest and most impressive lies about an hour outside of the city in Caserta. This was the secluded location chosen by King Charles VII in the 18th century to build the Reggia di Caserta, a royal palace and gardens that rival Versailles for their size and splendor.

Sights

REGGIA DI CASERTA

Viale Douhet 2/a; tel. 082/344-8084; www.reggiadicaserta.beniculturali.it; 8:30am-7:30pm Wed.-Mon., closed Tues.; €12

The first sight of the Reggia di Caserta is awe inspiring, no matter the approach. The palace is an 18th-century architectural treasure that was created for Charles VII of Bourbon by Luigi Vanvitelli (1700-1773). The scale of the Reggia is truly immense. The building has a rectangular plan divided into four sections, each one with a large inner courtyard, and covers a surface area of about 505,904 square feet (47,000 square meters). When multiplied by the building's five floors, that brings the space to a whopping 2,529,520 square feet (235,000 square meters). With its 1,200 rooms and 1,700 windows, the space is almost too large to conceptualize. Unfortunately, Charles never lived in the palace he started, as he left in 1759 to be crowned king of Spain. Building continued under King Ferdinand IV of Bourbon and was finally finished in 1845 for King Ferdinand II of the Two Sicilies by Vanvitelli's son Carlo Vanvitelli. A century later, the end of World War II was marked on May 7, 1945, with the signing of the unconditional surrender of German forces, which took place in the royal apartments of the Reggia.

A visit to the Reggia offers the chance to step inside the palatial surroundings and see the opulence of the Bourbon court. Begin by climbing the imposing staircase guarded by two large marble lion statues and topped by an elliptical vault. See the splendid **Palatine Chapel** with its design inspired by Versailles, blending neoclassical, Renaissance, and baroque elements. The **Royal Apartments** span the 18th-19th centuries and include a series of richly decorated antechambers leading to the gilded **Throne Room,** the most resplendent of all the palace's many rooms.

Also fascinating is the glimpse of more relaxed moments of royal life inside the **Murat Apartment,** set up for Gioacchino Murat at the beginning of the 19th century. This part of the palace also includes the apartments where Ferdinand IV and Queen Maria Carolina lived at the end of the 18th century, including the enchanting, thematic **Rooms of the Seasons,** the **King's Apartment,** the **Queen's Apartment,** the **Palatine Library,** and the impressive **Royal Nativity Scene** set up similar to the nativity created at the palace in 1844.

The grandeur of the Reggia di Caserta continues outside in the **Royal Park,** which was also designed by Luigi Vanvitelli and finished by his son Carlo. The massive park covers 297

1: Casina Vanvitellina **2:** entry of the Aragonese Castle of Baia **3:** Complesso Archeologico delle Terme di Baia **4:** gardens of Reggia di Caserta

1
2
3
4

acres (120 hectares) and includes an English-style garden and a long alley called the Via d'Acqua that stretches more than 1.8 miles (3 km) and features a series of fountains inspired by classical mythology. At the very top of the alley is the impressive **Fountain of Diana and Actaeon** set at the base of a waterfall that was carefully man-made to appear natural. The view looking back toward the Reggia di Caserta from the end of the alley is a sight fit for royalty.

REAL BORGO DI SAN LEUCIO

Belvedere di San Leucio; tel. 082/327-3151; www.sanleucio.it; 9:30am-6pm, closed Tues.; reservations required; €6

A little over 2 miles (3.5 km) from the Reggia di Caserta lies a small town created by the Bourbon kings in the 18th century. The Real Borgo di San Leucio was established in 1778, and an entire town was created that was dedicated the production of silk fabrics. The colony not only housed the specially trained artisans, but also provided education and other benefits for all members of their families. A splendid royal residence was also built here. Today the **Complesso Monumentale del Belvedere di San Leucio** allows visitors to see the royal apartments, English-style gardens, the historic factory, and a museum dedicated to the artistic silk traditions. Reservations are required to visit the site and guided tours are available in English.

CASERTAVECCHIA

Located in the mountains northeast of the Reggia di Caserta, Casertavecchia (old Caserta) is a well preserved medieval village with a distinctive 12th-century cathedral, Norman castle, and lots of historic charm to enjoy while strolling along its cobblestoned, winding streets. The cathedral, now called the Duomo di Casertavecchia, is dedicated to San Michele Archangelo and was built by the Normans. It is an excellent example of Norman-Arab architecture with its interlacing arches and includes elements from an earlier paleochristian church and a Roman temple.

Food

LE COLONNE MARZIALE

Viale Giulio Douchet 7; tel. 082/346-7494; www.lecolonnemarziale.it; 8am-10:30pm Fri.-Sat., 8am-6pm Sun., 8am-7:30pm Mon. and Wed.-Thurs., closed Tues.; €20-26 or tasting menus from €70 per person

Just a 10-minute walk west of the Reggia di Caserta, this elegant restaurant is a popular destination for fine dining in Campania. After growing up in her family's restaurant, Rosanna Marziale is now the chef, and along with her family has created a very special place where Michelin-starred dining is combined with a warm atmosphere and local traditions. The variety of tasting menus are an excellent choice. Here *mozzarella di bufala* is a dream, both in terms of quality and the creative way it's used, or try the buffalo steak filet topped with ricotta. Reservations are recommended by calling or emailing info@lecolonnemarziale.it.

OSTERIA LA MEDIOEVALE

Via Federico II di Svevia; tel. 082/337-1410; www.osterialamedioevale.it; noon-3pm and 6:30pm-11:30pm, closed Thursday; €8-13

Set in the charming historic center of Casertavecchia, this family-run restaurant is an inviting spot to enjoy hearty local fare and try out the restaurant's signature dish, *pasta alla medioevale* (medieval style pasta), thick handmade pasta served with a tomato sauce enriched with *guanciale* (cured pork).

Accommodations

HOTEL DEI CAVALIERI PALACE OF CASERTA

Piazza Luigi Vanvitelli 12; tel. 082/335-5859; www.deicavaliericollection.com; €99 d

Overlooking a garden square in Piazza Luigi Vanvitelli, this modern hotel is just a short walk from the Reggia di Caserta and Via Giuseppe Mazzini, lined with restaurants and shops. The hotel's 86 rooms are decorated in warm tones with wood accents and include classic, superior, and junior suite options. Many superior rooms overlook the garden square, while the junior suites offer a balcony with view of the Reggia di Caserta.

Getting There

The Reggia di Caserta is located about 19 miles (30.6 km) north of Naples and makes an excellent day trip. Trains run regularly (www.trenitalia.com, every 20-30 minutes, starting at €3.40 for regional trains) from the Napoli Centrale train station, and the journey is 40-50 minutes depending on the type of train. The train station is located across Piazza Carlo III from the entrance to the Reggia di Caserta. **City Sightseeing** (www.city-sightseeing.it; closed Tues.; €15) offers a shuttle bus from Naples to Caserta. There's one morning departure from Naples at Piazza Municipio at 9:30am and Piazza Garibaldi at 9:45, and there's one daily return from Caserta at 2:15pm to Naples. Tickets are purchased onboard.

To explore the Caserta area, including the **Real Borgo di San Leucio** and **Casertavecchia,** you'll need a car. From Naples, it's about a 35-minute drive to Caserta. Take the A1 highway north from Naples and exit at *Caserta nord* to continue east on SS7/Via Nazionale Appia to reach the Reggia di Caserta. To visit the Real Borgo di San Leucio from Caserta, follow SS7 west and then take a right to head north on Via Passionisti. Continue along as it changes to Via Sant'Anastasio, Via San Leucio, and Via Papa Gennaro. Go left at Via del Giardini Reale to reach San Leucio. For Casertavecchia, instead stay on Via Papa Gennaro, which becomes Via della Pineta, a narrow and scenic road through the mountains leading to the small town. The drive from the Reggia di Caserta to San Leucio takes about 15 minutes, while to Casertavecchia it takes about 30 minutes.

Pompeii, Herculaneum, and Vesuvius

Itinerary Ideas 396
Pompeii 397
Herculaneum 408
Vesuvius...............413

Whether you're relaxing by the sea in Sorrento or strolling along the waterfront in Naples, the distinctive humpbacked slopes of Mount Vesuvius dominate the Gulf of Naples. Although its lush green appearance may make it seem innocuous, this volcano is considered one of the most dangerous in the world because of the densely populated areas surrounding the base. In among the urban sprawl are the ruins of the ancient cities of Pompeii and Herculaneum: two of the world's most important archaeological sites.

These two Roman towns were frozen in time by the explosive eruption of Mount Vesuvius in AD 79. Though this massive eruption destroyed many luxurious Roman villas in the area as well, the sites of Pompeii and Herculaneum offer a rare look at life in ancient

Highlights

Look for ★ to find recommended sights, activities, dining, and lodging.

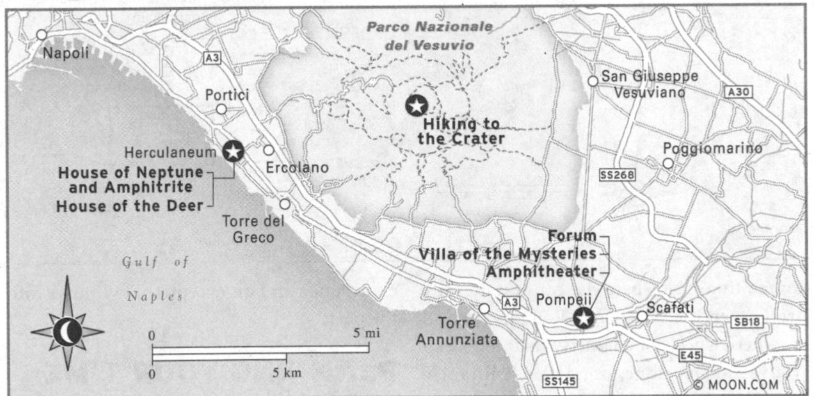

★ **Forum, Pompeii:** Stand in the middle of what was Pompeii's city center and imagine what everyday life was like for the people who lived here (page 401).

★ **Villa of the Mysteries, Pompeii:** A prime example of a Roman agricultural estate, its name comes from a series of stunning, but mysterious, frescoes (page 404).

★ **Amphitheater, Pompeii:** Visit this arena on the outskirts of the city for a glimpse into Roman sporting life (page 406).

★ **House of Neptune and Amphitrite, Herculaneum:** One of the loveliest houses in Herculaneum, this site is known for its intricate and colorful wall mosaics (page 412).

★ **House of the Deer, Herculaneum:** A series of statues, including some of deer being attacked by dogs, were uncovered in the garden of this sophisticated seaside villa (page 412).

★ **Hiking to the Crater, Vesuvius:** Hike to the summit of Vesuvius to take in panoramic views of the Naples area and the Sorrentine Peninsula (page 414).

Pompeii, Herculaneum, and Vesuvius

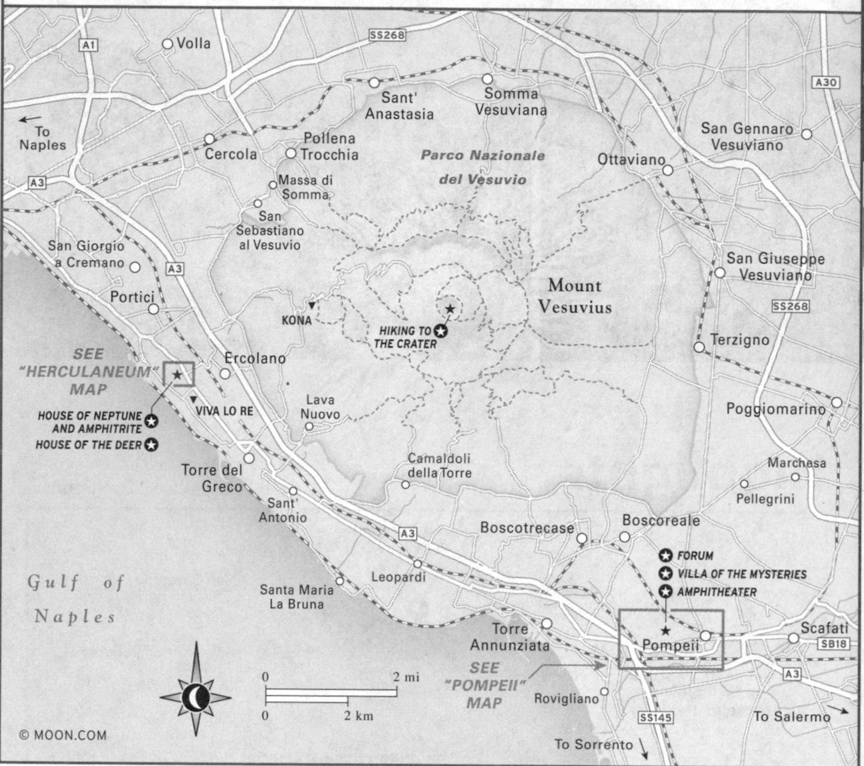

Roman times. Nowhere else can you literally stroll down the streets of a Roman city and see where wheels of countless carts left deep grooves in the stone, or admire brilliantly colored frescoes and minutely detailed mosaics preserved by volcanic ash. A full picture of daily life comes into focus as you discover everything from the advanced heating and plumbing systems of the ancient cities to street food businesses, and see close-up how Romans of all social levels lived, worked, ate, and spent their free time.

A visit to Pompeii and Herculaneum, as well as the volcano that destroyed them so many centuries ago, is an eye-opening experience and an exceptional glimpse into the past.

PLANNING YOUR TIME

Mount Vesuvius and the ancient cities of Pompeii and Herculaneum are located southeast of Naples and north of the Sorrentine Peninsula, making them ideal day trip destinations from both areas. Though both archaeological sites can be visited in one day, it requires a good deal of walking on uneven surfaces and there's a lot of ground to cover, especially if you're getting around on public transportation. It's a good idea to break it up into two days of sightseeing if your travel

Previous: ruins of Pompeii; a mosaic from the House of Neptune and Amphitrite at Herculaneum; the crater of Mount Vesuvius.

schedule allows, or elect to visit only one of the sites. Pompeii is the popular choice if time only permits one site, because its larger size offers a more complete look at an ancient Roman city. However, Herculaneum has many historical gems and is usually the less crowded of the two. A visit to either archaeological site can be combined with a visit to Mount Vesuvius. A guided tour is highly recommended for Pompeii and Herculaneum, and a group or private tour that includes transportation to the sites, or combines one or both of the cities with Vesuvius, can save you time and hassle.

Tours

RIMONTI TOURS

Via Monte di Dio 9, Naples; tel. 081/764-4934; www.rimontitours.com; 10am-6pm Mon.-Fri.; group tours from €65 per person, private tours €330

If you're based in Naples, Rimonti Tours offers private and small-group excursions to Pompeii, Herculaneum, and Vesuvius. This provider can help you plan the excursion that's right for you, whether that's a fully private customized tour with a guide and transportation, or a small-group tour from Naples to Vesuvius, Herculaneum, and Pompeii. There's a wide variety of options that can include a tour guide, entrance fees, and transportation from Naples. Group tours are often scheduled for set days of the week and require a minimum of 8 people to run, so check in advance to see what is being offered during your visit. Bookings for daily excursions must be made in advance and can be done easily via the website.

ACAMPORA TRAVEL

Via del Mare 22; tel. 081/532-9711; www.acamporatravel.it; Apr.-Oct.; group tours from €36 per person

For daily group excursions to Pompeii, Herculaneum, and Vesuvius from Sorrento, Acampora Travel organizes a variety of half-day tours to the individual locations, and full-day combo tours that visit more than one site. Group tours include accommodation pickup and a guide, but not entrance fees. Different tours are scheduled for different set days of the week, so contact the company in advance to book.

SUNLAND

Corso Reginna 82, Maiori; tel. 089/877-455; www.sunland.it; Apr.-Oct.; group tours from €42 per person

From the Amalfi Coast, the Sunland travel agency offers many tour options, including private and group excursions to Pompeii and Vesuvius, Pompeii and Herculaneum, or to only Pompeii on a half-day excursion in the morning or afternoon. Tours include a guide and bus pickup in towns along the Amalfi Coast. Tours of the archaeological sites take place on set days during the week and vary per tour, so it's worth checking the schedule ahead of time. Advance bookings are required and can be made online.

Itinerary Ideas

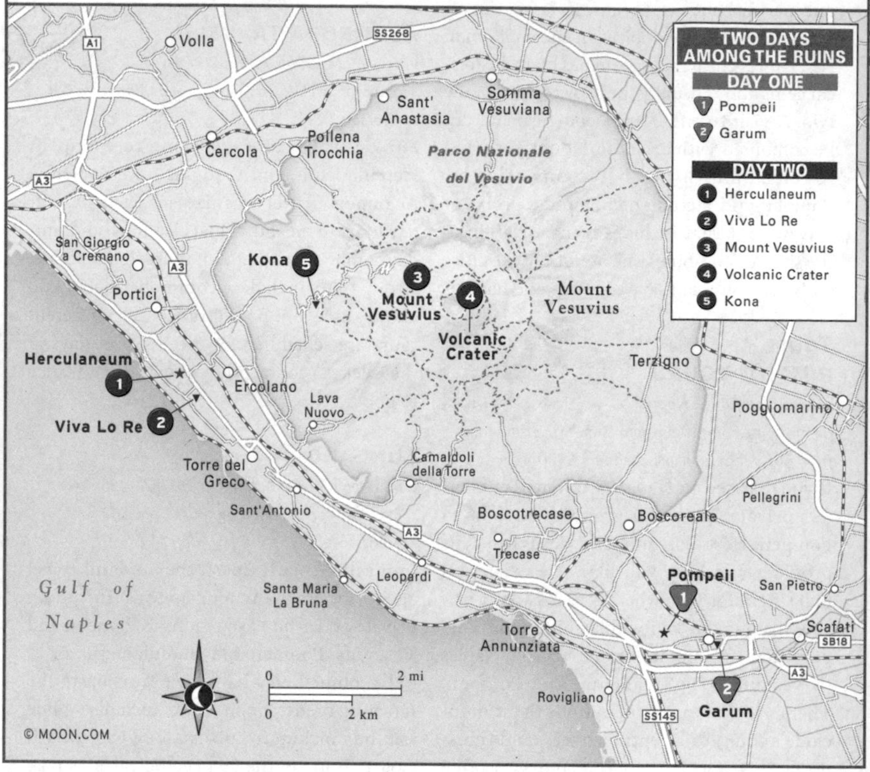

TWO DAYS AMONG THE RUINS

DAY ONE
1 Pompeii
2 Garum

DAY TWO
1 Herculaneum
2 Viva Lo Re
3 Mount Vesuvius
4 Volcanic Crater
5 Kona

Itinerary Ideas

Day 1

Start your two-day exploration with a visit to Pompeii followed by an optional afternoon visit to the Museo Archeologico Nazionale (National Archaeological Museum) in Naples, to see the treasures uncovered at Pompeii and archaeological sites in the Gulf of Naples area.

1 Arrive in **Pompeii** by car or by public transportation. Begin your visit at the **Porta Marina** entrance, and follow the Walking Tour of Pompeii Highlights (page 402).

2 After a long day of walking, enjoy a hearty dinner at **Garum.**

Day 2

The second day focuses on the ancient city of Herculaneum and a visit to Mount Vesuvius. This is a good combination because Herculaneum is a more manageable size than Pompeii and is a bit nearer the volcano.

1 Start your day by traveling to **Herculaneum** by car, and spend two or three hours exploring the archaeological ruins.

2 Stop for lunch at **Viva Lo Re** near the archaeological site to enjoy dishes inspired by traditional recipes and seasonal ingredients.

3 Continue to **Mount Vesuvius** by car.

4 From the parking area closest to the summit, continue on foot up to the *Gran Cono* (Big Cone) to **hike** around the edge of the **volcanic crater.** Enjoy panoramic views over the entire Gulf of Naples from the Sorrentine Peninsula to the islands of Capri and Ischia and over to Naples.

5 After your hike, pop into **Kona** for an early dinner.

Pompeii

TOP EXPERIENCE

With more than 3.4 million visitors annually, Pompeii is one of the most popular sights in all of Italy. Its massive appeal is due to the one-of-a-kind experience the archaeological ruins offer to visitors, to virtually step back in time. Before Mount Vesuvius erupted in AD 79, freezing Pompeii in time, it was a large Roman city in Campania. The origins of the city date back to the sixth century BC, when the city was founded by the Oscans from central Italy. Over centuries, it passed from Etruscans to Greeks to Samnites, and eventually into Roman control. In the 1st century AD, Pompeii sat much closer to the seaside than it does today, and the city was prized for its location near the sea and the Sarno river, which made it an important trading city.

Pompeii is situated not far from the base of Mount Vesuvius, which the ancient Romans didn't know to be a dangerous volcano, as it had been dormant for more than 800 years. In AD 62, a violent earthquake caused significant damage to Pompeii, but that was only a prelude to what was coming. The hustle and bustle of daily life came to a dramatic end for the people of Pompeii on that fateful day in AD 79, when the explosive eruption of Mount Vesuvius covered the city with ash and pumice from the violent pyroclastic flows. Every part of life stopped in time and was preserved for centuries by the ash that covered the city. After the eruption, the city was abandoned and forgotten until it was accidentally rediscovered, first in 1599 and later in 1748 when official excavations began to uncover the city. Early archaeological treasures, including statues, mosaics, and frescoes were uncovered and removed from the site, and many are now on display in the **Museo Archeologico Nazionale** in **Naples.**

There's a solemnity about Pompeii that lingers in the air. We can walk the same streets that the ancient Romans walked only because of the dramatic way in which the city and its residents were lost to time. Today, the massive amphitheater may be empty, but once thousands upon thousands of Romans crowded its seats to watch spectacles like gladiator fights. Where the scent of bread once filled the air, the ovens are now empty. Walking through homes, you can see how families lived, worshipped, and conducted their daily business. Every detail of life, from how the city was run to daily pleasures and entertainment, can be discovered while exploring Pompeii.

Pompeii

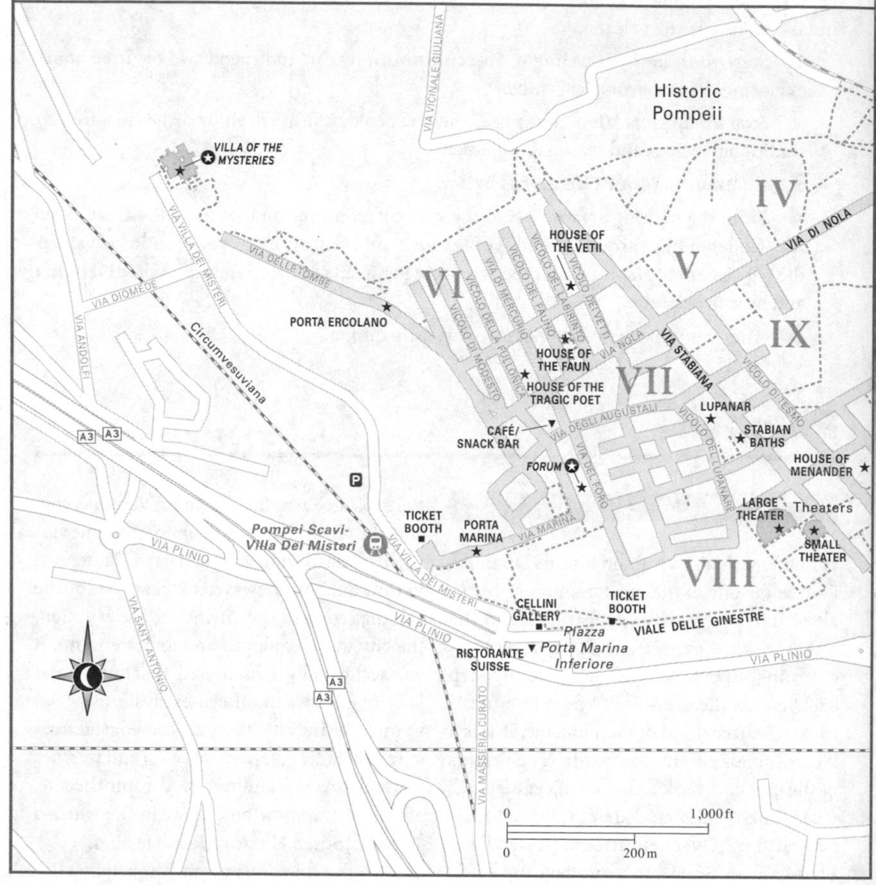

ORIENTATION

The massive archaeological site of Pompeii covers roughly 163 acres (66 hectares) enclosed by about 2 miles (3 km) of city walls. Seven entrance gates to the city have been uncovered as well as the main streets that crisscrossed the city. **The Forum,** located in the southwest area of Pompeii, was the heart of the city. Two main streets, the **Via dell'Abbondanza** and **Via di Nola,** run southwest to northeast through the city and are crossed by the main street **Via Stabiana.** The **Via dell'Abbondanza** leads to the large amphitheater at the easternmost edge of Pompeii.

A Roman from AD 79 wouldn't be able to get around with the street names we use today because they are modern conventions, often based on important buildings and finds. Archaeologists have divided the site into nine areas (called *regio*), each subdivided into blocks with numbers for each building. The map and booklet you'll receive at the ticket booth is divided into these areas with the main sites numbered.

Entrance to the archaeological site

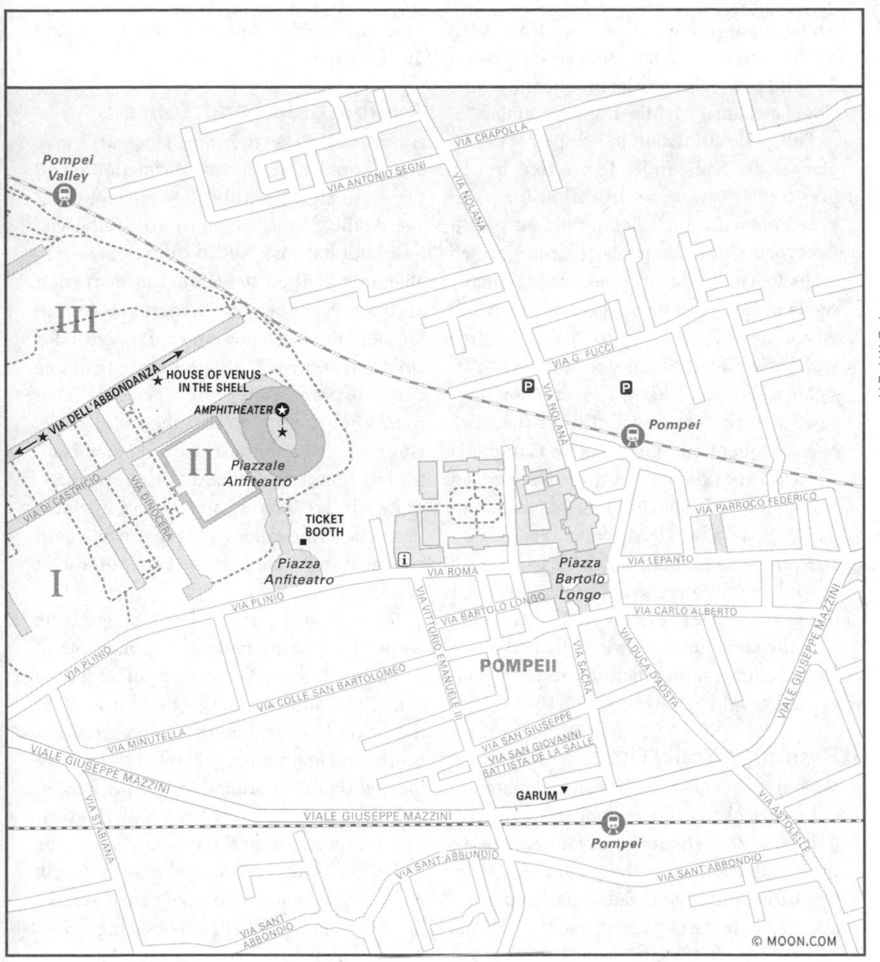

is through the ancient entrance gate to Pompeii at **Porta Marina** in the southwesternmost point of Pompeii or at **Piazza Anfiteatro** on the easternmost side. You can exit Pompeii from either gate and from the **Porta Ercolano** on the northwestern side of Pompeii. However, note that you cannot enter Pompeii via the Porta Ercolano. The most convenient entrance for most travelers is the main entrance at Porta Marina, which leads to Via Marina and the Forum. Another convenient entrance is southeast of Porta Marina at **Piazza Porta Marina Inferiore** (Piazza Esedra), where after the ticket booth you can follow the **Viale delle Ginestre** and enter the site on the southern side near the Teatro Grande. The entrance at **Piazza Anfiteatro** on the southeastern side of Pompeii is largely used for school groups and it's on the opposite side of Pompeii from public transportation.

VISITING POMPEII

Entrance to the **Parco Archeologico di Pompei** (tel. 081/857-5111; www.pompeiisites.org) includes access to the entire archaeological park and all the sights. It is open

9am-7:30pm (last entrance 6pm) from April to October, and 8:30am-5pm (last entrance 3:30pm) November to March. The site is only closed on January 1, May 1, and December 25.

Full-price admission to Pompeii is €15.00 per person. Kids under 18 are free, but be prepared to show identification for older kids. Pompeii is included in the **Campania Artecard** (www.campaniartecard.it), which offers free and discounted entrance to many sights in Naples as well as both Pompeii and Herculaneum. Entrance to Pompeii is free with the Artecard if it is one of the first two sights where you present the card; you'll receive a 50 percent discount if it's the third or subsequent site visited. The Campania Artecard is available in a three-day version (€32 adults, €25 youth age 18-25) and a seven-day Campania card (€34 adults) version.

Keep in mind that your ticket to Pompeii is valid for only one entrance. Once you enter you won't be able to exit the park and re-enter with the same ticket. However, there is a café for refreshments and there are restrooms located throughout the excavation site.

Planning Your Time

With such a large footprint and so many archaeological treasures, Pompeii's ruins require at least 3-4 hours for anyone even to see the highlights, such as the Forum area, thermal baths, the city's theaters and amphitheater, homes in the city center, and the Villa dei Misteri outside the city walls. A longer visit will allow you to stop to see more homes and explore more areas of the city, but do prepare for a good deal of walking.

Given Pompeii's popularity, there's not necessarily a good time of day to avoid crowds. Early afternoon is often a good time to visit, but you will still have to navigate crowds and groups. Inclement weather can turn Pompeii muddy, so it's best to adjust your schedule if possible and avoid the site if it's raining hard.

Much of Pompeii requires walking on uneven stone roads and there's limited shade on sunny days. Bring water, sunscreen, and a hat on hot days. Comfortable closed walking shoes are the best option for the rough and dusty setting.

Audio Guides and Tours

An entrance ticket to Pompeii includes a map and a booklet with brief information on all the main sights within the archaeological site. Audio guides and tours are available at an additional cost. **Audio guides** are available only at the **Porta Marina entrance** and cost €8 per person for adults, €6.50 each for more than one person, €5 per person for children, and €4.50 each for more than one child. Be prepared to leave a personal ID of some kind in order to rent the audio guide. However, given the vast size of Pompeii and the fact that it can be hard to navigate many of its similar looking streets and intersections, the audio guide and map can be a hard combination to manage and can lead to a lot of wandering.

Hiring a **private guide** or joining a **tour** is one of the best ways to get the most out of a visit to Pompeii. Authorized guides for the region of Campania can be hired near all of the ticket booths. You can join a group of people and enjoy a roughly two-hour tour of the highlights for around €10-15 per person. Groups usually include 12-15 people. You can also opt for a two- or three-hour private tour with a guide that will cost roughly €100-120. As Pompeii includes areas of active excavation as well as restoration to existing sights, it's not uncommon for some areas to be closed. Guides are up to date on the openings, and can save you a lot of time by showing you only the houses that are currently open. After seeing the highlights and learning about the history on a guided tour, you can always choose to stay in the archaeological site and continue exploring on your own.

SIGHTS

The sights included here are the top highlights of Pompeii, but this only scratches the surface of all that Pompeii offers with its multitude of houses, civic and religious buildings, public baths, and buildings to explore at the site.

★ Forum

Via Villa dei Misteri at Via Marina/Via dell'Abbondanza

Located in the oldest part of the city, the Forum was the bustling city center and the heart of the political, religious, and commercial life of Pompeii. The large rectangular area is surrounded by temples dedicated to Jupiter, Apollo, Vespasian, and Venus. On the south side, what is called the Basilica today was home to the law and commerce courts. The city's largest meat and fish market, called the Macellum, is located on the northeastern side of the Forum. Along the western side, stop to peer into the Forum Granary, which was once a large fruit and vegetable market, where you'll now see row after row of tall shelves lined with archaeological finds, including amphorae (large vases used for storage), pots and pans for cooking, statues, architectural details, and, most poignant, plaster casts of the bodies of victims of Pompeii that were created by archaeologists during the excavation process. The terrifying final moments of life in Pompeii are captured in the different positions of the plaster cast bodies. Seeing them is a somber experience that can be unsettling to some visitors, especially young travelers. However, moments like this offer the chance to reflect on both the broad historical significance of Pompeii and the tragic loss of individual lives.

Standing in the middle of the Forum today, you can imagine Pompeiians of all types passing through here going about their business, shopping, or visiting a temple. Looking toward the Temple of Jupiter on the northern side of the Forum you'll also find a perfectly framed view of Mount Vesuvius in the distance.

Stabian Baths

Via dell'Abbondanza 15

Located east of the Forum, the Stabian baths are the oldest public baths in Pompeii dating back as early as the third century BC. The pristine state of the baths allows a rare glimpse into the splendid plumbing and heating systems that were used; the clever heating system is still quite intact. Public baths were a regular part of life in ancient Rome, and as was the custom the Stabian baths are divided into separate areas for men and women. You can walk through the changing rooms to another series of rooms, each one with a different water temperature. While the men's rooms are larger and more lavishly decorated with paintings, both the men's and women's areas offer a look at the multistep bathing process as well as the heating system with double floors and terra-cotta pipes in the walls where hot air was circulated throughout the structure from a furnace. There are two other interesting public baths in Pompeii, including the **Forum Baths** just north of the Forum and the **Central Baths** north of the Stabian Baths along Via Stabiana.

Theaters

Near intersection of Via Stabiana and Via del Tempio d'Iside

South of the Stabian Baths, Via Stabiana leads to a beautiful part of Pompeii where the city's theaters are located. Here the **Large Theater** (Teatro Grande) is built into the hillside with steep seating and excellent acoustics. The theater was built around the 2nd century BC and seated up to 5,000 people. Today it is still occasionally used as a particularly evocative setting for cultural and musical events. Next to the Large Theater, the Odeon or **Small Theater** (Teatro Piccolo), was originally a covered theater used for more intimate musical performances. Just south of the Large Theater, a large square—surrounded by 74 gray Doric columns—that was previously connected to the theater was transformed into a barracks for gladiators after the earthquake in AD 62.

Lupanar

Vicolo del Lupanare at Vicolo del Balcone Pensile

Among the variety of entertainments available in Pompeii, many brothels have been brought to light during archaeological excavations. The largest is located along Vicolo del Lupanare, and the name of both the structure and the street come from the Latin word *lupa*, meaning prostitute. This two-level building has five

Walking Tour of Pompeii's Highlights

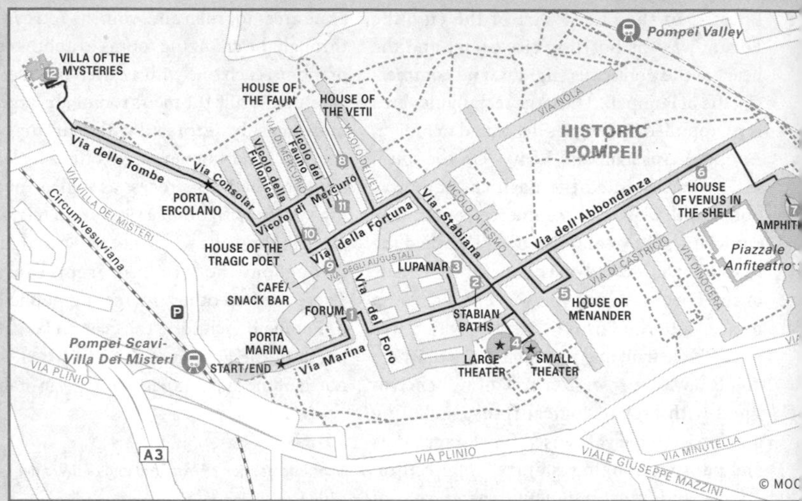

To see many of the highlights of Pompeii, pull on a comfortable pair of walking shoes and follow this itinerary to hit all the top spots in the archaeological site. To cover the sights included here, allow 3-4 hours for the visit, and longer if you want to explore more of the buildings, temples, and sights you'll pass along the way.

1. Enter Pompeii through the Porta Marina gate and follow Via Marina until you reach the **Forum,** the heart of the ancient city. See the temples, commercial buildings, and courts, and enjoy a perfectly framed view of Mount Vesuvius.
2. From the Forum, follow Via dell'Abbondanza a few blocks east to see the **Stabian Baths,** the oldest public baths in Pompeii.

rooms on the lower level, each one fitted with a built-in bed and that could be closed off with curtains. Along the main corridor are erotic-themed paintings that are thought to have encouraged clients or perhaps been used to communicate with clients speaking different languages. Let's just say they set the scene.

A visit to the Lupanar is included in most guided visits to Pompeii, but it can be skipped if it's not to a visitor's taste. However, it is interesting to note that erotic themes weren't particularly taboo in Roman culture. A large amount of art with erotic themes has been uncovered in Pompeii over the centuries, and much of it can be seen at the *Gabinetto Segreto* (Secret Cabinet) room at the **Museo Archeologico Nazionale** in Naples. It's also not uncommon to find erotic symbolism in the streets and houses of Pompeii, some of which are thought to have been a sort of *porta fortuna* (good luck symbol) for Romans.

Via dell'Abbondanza

One of the main roads of Pompeii, the Via dell'Abbondanza runs from the Forum northeast all the way to the Porta Sarno on the eastern side of the city. This area is one of the most intriguing and characteristic in Pompeii, with a mix of large and richly decorated private homes interspersed with shops, bakeries,

3. Walk north a couple of blocks on Vicolo del Lupanare to visit the **Lupanar,** one of the brothels of the ancient city.
4. Return down Vicolo del Lupanare, cross Via dell'Abbondanza, and continue to the two well-preserved **theaters** where plays, music, and events were held.
5. Go back the way you came, take a right on Via dell'Abbondanza, and continue along it as it heads northeast into a residential area of the city where you can walk through many fine Roman homes like the **House of Menander.**
6. The **House of Venus in the Shell** is also worth a look for its fresco of Venus reclining in a large shell. As you walk along Via dell'Abbondanza, don't miss the fine examples of the ancient equivalent of fast food restaurants, where food was served from large terra-cotta vases sunk into the counters.
7. At the end of Via dell'Abbondanza head south to visit the impressive **Amphitheater** built around 70 BC for gladiator fights.
8. Turn back toward the center of Pompeii along Via dell'Abbondanza and take a right on Via Stabiana and a left on Via della Fortuna. Stop to see the **House of the Vetii,** the most finely decorated house excavated at Pompeii.
9. Back on Via della Fortuna, take a left on Via del Foro to stop at the **café and snack bar** for a break.
10. From Via del Foro, take a left and then an immediate right on Vicolo della Fullonica to see the **House of the Tragic Poet,** which is famous for its entry mosaic depicting a large dog with the words *Cave Canem,* meaning "Beware of the Dog."
11. Continue straight and take a right on Vicolo di Mercurio to see the **House of the Faun,** which is well worth the mini-detour to explore one of the largest houses in the ancient city.
12. Return back along Vicolo di Mercurio to Via Consolare and take a right. Keep walking as it passes through the ancient gate of Porta Ercolano and becomes Via delle Tombe, leading to the **Villa of the Mysteries.** This large country estate is fascinating to explore and is famous for its captivating frescoes.

You can exit the archaeological site near the Villa of the Mysteries or return along Via delle Tombe, Via Consolare, back through the Forum, and to Via Marina and the **Porta Marina gate.**

and inns. Walking down the once busy street, where the wheels of countless carts left deep grooves in the stone paving, visitors can envision moments of daily life in ancient Pompeii. Archaeologists have discovered many of the original shop functions as well as incredible details that reveal the names of the original shopkeepers in some cases.

While walking down Via dell'Abbondanza, stop to see some well preserved examples of *thermopolia*, which were somewhat like modern-day takeout or fast food restaurants. You'll recognize them when you see their countertops with terra-cotta jars set into them, where ready-to-serve food was stored in the small restaurants, or dried goods were kept in the shops. Just beyond the crossroad of Vicolo dell'Efebo, stop to see the house and *thermopolium* (tavern) of Vetutius Placidus. Drinks and hot food were served at the front of the building, and the owner's house located at the rear. During excavation, about 6.6 pounds (3 kg) of coins were found in one of the terra-cotta pots set into the counter, a testament to the popularity of this particular tavern.

Pompeii's Houses

Pompeii has an embarrassment of riches when it comes to residential architecture to explore, with more houses and villas than you could possibly visit in one day. One thing to keep in mind is that, unlike the larger buildings, many of Pompeii's houses may be closed at any given time for restoration work. It is hard to tell in advance if, or how long, a house will be closed. Yet, while some houses may have been closed for years, ongoing restoration and excavation means that houses are also continually reopening. The Pompeii website (www.pompeiisites.org) does include a list of buildings open to the public, but the surest way to avoid wasting time is to hire a guide or join a guided tour, as the local authorized guides are up to date on the latest openings and closures. Below are some fine houses that you'll want to see if they're open during your visit.

Any direction you walk from the Forum leads to archaeological treasures. Heading north from the Forum leads toward the northwestern section of the city where some of the largest homes were located. You won't have to go far to reach the **House of the Tragic Poet** (Via della Fullonica between Via delle Terme and Vicolo di Mercurio). This somewhat small house has one of Pompeii's most famous mosaics right at the entrance. You'll go in through a side entrance where glass covers the mosaic of a large and rather intimidating black dog with the words *Cave Canem* (Beware of the Dog) below.

Continuing down Vicolo di Mercurio leads to the **House of the Faun** (Vicolo di Mercurio between Vicolo del Fauno and Vicolo del Labrinto), among the largest houses in Pompeii. The name comes from a bronze statue of a faun in one of the atriums. A replica stands in place of the original, which is now at the Museo Archeologico Nazionale along with the original of the remarkable mosaic scene depicting the Battle of Alexander, which has also been replaced by a replica. Just beyond is the **House of the Vetii** (Vicolo dei Vetti at Vicolo di Mercurio), one of the richest and most finely decorated of all the houses excavated at Pompeii. The house belonged to rich merchants who spared no expense in filling it with paintings and friezes inspired by mythological themes. There's also a large garden with a central fountain that featured jets of water.

Following Via dell'Abbondanza from the Forum into the southeastern area of the city, you'll come to another particularly rich area with homes to explore. Take a detour south of Via dell'Abbondanza to reach the **House of Menander** (Vicolo del Menandro between Vicolo del Citarista and Vicolo di Pasquius Proculus), where you can explore one of Pompeii's most beautiful homes. Walking through the atrium you can see frescoes depicting scenes from Homer's *Iliad* and *Odyssey*, and the artistic theme continues in the frescoes around the large and elegant peristyle garden with a portrait of the Greek playwright Menander.

Not far north of the Amphitheater, the **House of Venus in the Shell** (Via dell'Abbondanza between Vicolo della Venere and Vicolo di Giulia Felice) is a very appealing house with a garden atrium surrounded by rooms with detailed frescoes. The house is named after the impressive fresco of Venus reclining in a large shell.

★ Villa of the Mysteries

Via Villa dei Misteri 2

As you work your way toward the periphery of Pompeii, you'll notice the houses tend to get larger as more space was available for gardens and private estates. The Villa dei Misteri (Villa of the Mysteries) is located outside the city walls northwest of Pompeii; this large villa is a fine example of a wealthy Roman agricultural estate. Built around large peristyle courtyard, the sprawling villa has many rooms you can explore on various levels. Because the villa received less damage during the eruption of Vesuvius than much of the rest of Pompeii suffered, you can get an excellent sense of the original spaces with many ceilings and frescoes remarkably well intact. Its name comes from one series of captivating

1: remains of walls and columns of the House of the Faun **2:** one of the bathrooms in the Stabian Baths **3:** the Forum at Pompeii **4:** fresco in the Villa of Mysteries.

1
2
3
4

yet cryptic frescoes that have puzzled art historians. This highly debated fresco frieze is beautifully detailed with a striking red background. It runs around three walls of a room and is one of the largest and finest examples of painting from antiquity. The frieze depicts scenes of women performing various rituals along with a host of mythological figures, and the prevailing thought is that they depict scenes from rites dedicated to Dionysus who appears in the center of the frieze.

★ Amphitheater

Piazzale Anfiteatro

Set in the far southeastern part of the city, Pompeii's large Amphitheater offers a fascinating glimpse into an important element of Roman culture that is often of interest to modern-day travelers: gladiators. While smaller than more impressive amphitheaters like the Colosseum in Rome, Pompeii's oval Amphitheater is notable as the earliest known example of a large theater built primarily for gladiator combat. Built around 70 BC, it seated up to 20,000 people, who crowded in to watch the popular fights between gladiators and animals. With so many people coming and going, the Amphitheater was built on the outskirts to lessen the noise and crowding impact on daily life in Pompeii. Though there's no roar of the crowd today, the Anfiteatro is an impressive place to stand right in the center, gaze around, and imagine the scene in all its glory.

SHOPPING

CELLINI GALLERY

Piazza Porta Marina Inferiore 1, Pompei; tel. 081/862-4200; www.cellinigallery.com; 8:15am-5:30pm daily Apr.-Oct., 8:15am-4pm Nov.-Mar.

Near the main entrance to Pompeii, you'll find this shop specializing in beautiful cameos and coral. Founded in 1960, the shop upholds the antique tradition of coral and cameo carving, which dates back to Greek and Roman times. You'll also souvenirs of your visit to Pompeii.

FOOD

Inside the archaeological site of Pompeii, a **café** located near the Forum offers a variety of snacks, sandwiches, and light meals as well as drinks. The restaurants below are located outside of the archaeological site.

RISTORANTE SUISSE

Piazza Porta Marina Inferiore 10/13, Pompei; tel. 081/862-2536; www.suissepompei.com; 8am-7pm daily Apr.-Oct., 8am-5pm daily Nov.-Mar.; €15-30

This popular restaurant is located in the piazza between the Porta Marina entrance and

Large Theater of Pompeii

the entrance nearby off of Piazza Porta Marina Inferiore. With a full restaurant, self-service bar for a quick meal, and pizzeria, there are plenty of options to choose from for the whole family. Stop for a coffee and something sweet in the morning before starting your tour, or have a snack or meal after a visit to the ruins.

GARUM

Viale Giuseppe Mazzini 63, Pompei; tel. 081/850-1178; www.ristorantegarumpompei.it; noon-4pm and 7pm-11:30pm Mon.-Sat., noon-4pm Sun., closed Wed.; €8-17

Not far from the archaeological site near the modern-day city of Pompei, this restaurant specializes in traditional dishes and Campania wines. Special attention is given to ingredients like the antique garum fish sauce used in ancient Rome, which is featured in a variety of dishes, including a lovely spaghetti with tomatoes, pine nuts, raisins, and local anchovies.

GETTING THERE

BY TRAIN

Pompeii is easily reached by train from Naples and Sorrento with the **Circumvesuviana** train operated by **EAV** (www.eavsrl.it; departures every 30 minutes). The journey is 40 minutes from Naples (€2.80) and 30 minutes from Sorrento (€2.40). Exit at the Pompeii Scavi-Villa dei Misteri stop, and across the street from the station you'll find the Porta Marina entrance to Pompeii. Keep in mind that the Circumvesuviana is a commuter train for the area and can be quite crowded. However, it does provide an inexpensive way to reach Pompeii without the hassle of driving.

BY BUS

Multiple bus lines connect Pompeii with surrounding cities. From Naples and Sorrento, the journey is much faster and more convenient by train. However, **City Sightseeing** (www.city-sightseeing.it) offers a comfortable bus service from Naples to Pompeii. The easy-to-spot red buses depart from Molo Beverello port in Naples and from Piazza Garibaldi near the train station. The price is €15 round-trip (€8 for children 3-17 and free for children 2 and younger), including audio commentary in English. From May to October there are four departures in the morning and four returns in the afternoon, while from November to April there are two in the mornings and two returns in the afternoon.

From Salerno, **Busitalia Campania** (www.fsbusitaliacampania.it; €4) has two lines that connect the historic center of Salerno with Pompeii, stopping near Piazza Porta Marina Inferiore. Line 4 passes by the Salerno train station and takes about 1 hour and 40 minutes to reach Pompeii. Line 50 also departs from Salerno's train station and takes about 1 hour and 10 minutes to Pompeii.

To reach Pompeii from the Amalfi Coast, the easiest option is to first take the ferry or bus to Salerno and continue by bus, or first head to Sorrento and continue to Pompeii on the Circumvesuviana train.

BY CAR

Pompeii is located just off the **A3** autostrada (highway) connecting Naples and Salerno. The drive from Naples to Pompeii takes about 30 minutes, while from Salerno it is 35-40 minutes. To reach Pompeii from Sorrento, follow the SS145 east along the Sorrentine Peninsula to where it meets the A3 autostrada and shortly after joining the A3 you'll exit for Pompeii. Whether you're coming from Naples, Salerno, or Sorrento, exit at Pompei Scavi and in moments you'll arrive at the Porta Marina entrance. There's a variety of paid parking areas around the archaeological site, including one conveniently located near the Porta Marina entrance operated by Camping Zeus (tel. 081/861-5320; www.campingzeus.it; from €2.50 per hour).

GETTING AROUND

Once you're at the Pompeii archaeological site, the only way to get around and explore the ruins is on foot. Expect to navigate some hills, steps, and uneven stone walkways while visiting the site.

Herculaneum

The same devastating volcanic eruption that brought the ruin of Pompeii also destroyed the nearby city of Herculaneum. Much smaller than Pompeii, the town wasn't a commercial center like its larger neighbor but was instead a popular seaside resort town that was home to luxurious homes and villas. While Pompeii was covered with ash, Herculaneum's proximity to Vesuvius meant that it was buried below a very deep layer of mud combined with ash and volcanic materials. Though this was a horrendous end for the town's population, the volcanic mud preserved Herculaneum's buildings. That's why today we can still see wooden structures like ceiling beams, upper floors of buildings, furniture, and doors in more detail than what remains in Pompeii.

In the **Villa dei Papiri** (Villa of the Papyri), one of the most sumptuous private houses in Herculaneum, more than 1,800 papyrus scrolls were discovered: a truly rare and precious find. They are now housed in the **Biblioteca Nazionale di Napoli** (National Library of Naples), where they are still undergoing intense study. The villa is unfortunately closed to the public, but its famous sculptures are located in the Museo Archeologico Nazionale in Naples and the architectural design of the lavish villa was the inspiration for the J. Paul Getty Museum in Los Angeles, California.

The ruins of Herculaneum, located in modern-day Ercolano, were discovered in 1709 before those of Pompeii. Yet the excavation of Herculaneum has always been a challenge compared to Pompeii because the 52 feet (16 meters) of volcanic mud covering the town turned into solid rock. And unlike Pompeii, much of the ancient city of Herculaneum lies below the city of Ercolano. However, what has been uncovered so far of ancient Herculaneum has revealed true archaeological gems, and the site is certainly worth a visit.

ORIENTATION

The excavation site of Herculaneum is located well below the street level and is accessed via a long, inclined walkway that offers a great view over the ruins before you even arrive. However, much of the ancient city remains covered; only about 11 acres (4.5 hectares) of the estimated 49 acres (20 hectares) has been excavated. Based on the areas that have been brought to light, it's possible to get an idea of the city's original urban plan. As was traditional in Roman cities, Herculaneum is laid out in a grid, divided by at least three *decumani*, the main streets, of which only two have been uncovered. These are the roughly southwest-northeast running **Decumano Inferiore** and the **Decumano Massimo.** These two roads were crossed perpendicularly by five roads, called Cardo III, Cardo IV, and Cardo V on today's maps of Ercolano. The remaining two of the five cross roads lie in an unexcavated area northwest of the archaeological site. Since the Decumano Massimo is a noticeably larger street, researchers think it may mark where the Forum or center of the city started.

Before the eruption of AD 79, Herculaneum sat right at the edge of the sea. The volcanic material from the eruption moved the city much farther out to where we see it today. After you pass the ticket booth, look down to the right as you pass by the barrel-vaulted buildings below; these were originally boathouses opening to the beach. Herculaneum's most noted sight, the Villa of the Papyri, remains only partially excavated and is not open to the public. The ancient theater, which was the first sight at Herculaneum discovered in the early 18th century, is completely underground north of the archaeological area below modern-day Ercolano, and it is only rarely open to the public.

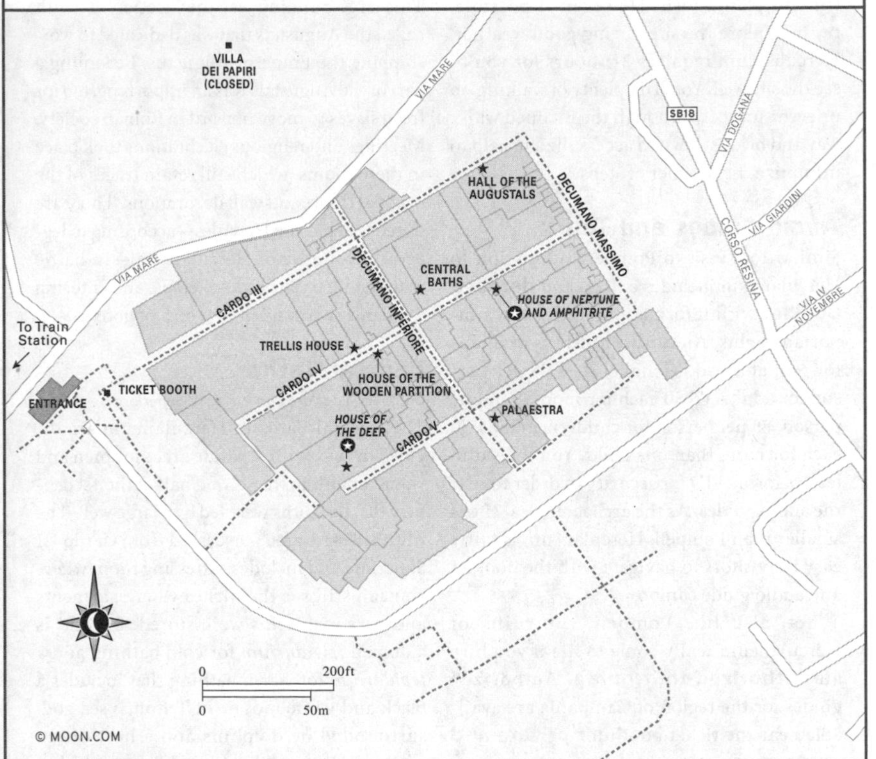

VISITING HERCULANEUM

The Herculaneum archaeological site is managed by the **Parco Archeologico di Ercolano** (Corso Resina, Ercolano; tel. 081/777-7008; www.ercolano.beniculturali.it) and is open 8:30am-7:30pm (last entrance 6pm) from April through October, and 8:30am-5pm (last entrance 3:30pm) from November through March. The site is open daily and is only closed on January 1 and December 25.

Full-price admission to Herculaneum is €13.00 per person. Kids under 18 get free admission, but bring identification, especially for older kids. If you purchase the **Campania Artecard** (www.campaniartecard.it), it includes many sights in Naples as well as free admission to both Herculaneum and Pompeii if the sites are the first two where you present the card; the card gives you a 50 percent discount if it's the third or subsequent site you visit. The Campania Artecard is available in a three-day version (€32 adults, €25 youth age 18-25) and a seven-day version called the Campania Card (€34 adults).

Planning Your Time

Herculaneum doesn't receive the massive number of visitors that Pompeii gets, but still do expect to find groups. The flow of visitors depends on the season and the number of cruise ships docked in nearby Naples and Sorrento, which means there's no one best time to plan a visit. However, if possible, try to explore the site during good weather. Herculaneum requires 2-3 hours for you to see the site well. You'll do plenty of walking on uneven surfaces, although the inclined walkway and bridge down to access the site help to minimize the number of steps.

Audio Guides and Tours

Similar to a visit to Pompeii, admission to Herculaneum includes a **map** and **detailed booklet** with information on the most important sights. An **audio guide** is available for rent at an additional cost of €8 per person for adults, €6.50 each for more than one person, €5 per person for children, and €4.50 each for more than one child. You'll need to leave a form of ID for security in order to rent the audio guides. As the archaeological site is smaller than Pompeii, Herculaneum is fairly easy for visitors to navigate with the booklet and audio guide combo.

Yet, also like Pompeii, the ruins of Herculaneum really come to life if you hire an **authorized tour guide.** Authorized guides for the region of Campania are available near the ticket booth for **private and group tours.**

SIGHTS

At Herculaneum, you'll find examples of many of the same types of buildings as at Pompeii, including public baths, shops and eating establishments, and you'll enjoy the experience of walking down the streets of an ancient Roman town. Herculaneum has fine examples of houses, many with details that are even better preserved than at Pompeii. Each site has something different to offer, so history buffs in particular will enjoy exploring both. The sights mentioned here are a selection of the top highlights, but there are many more to explore during a visit to Herculaneum.

Hall of the Augustals

Cardo III Superiore near Decumano Massimo

This large building was the location of a cult called the Augustals that was dedicated to worshipping the Emperor Augustus. Becoming a part of the Augustals was an important step for freed slaves to move upward in Roman society. Meetings and religious celebrations took place in these rooms, which still retain traces of the original floors and wall decorations. There are frescoes depicting Hercules—according to legend the founder of Herculaneum—in battle with the Etruscan god Achelous, and entering Olympus surrounded by a host of gods.

Central Baths

Cardo III Superiore and Cardo IV Superiore

The Central Baths in Herculaneum are divided in two, with separate areas for men and women. Built in the second half of the 1st century BC, the baths were fed by a large well. The **Men's Baths** area is accessed from Cardo III Superiore and includes a dressing room where you can still see the niches where garments and personal items were stored. Beyond is a domed *frigidarium* for cold bathing and a *tepidarium* for warm bathing that includes a black and white mosaic of Triton, a sea god, surrounded by dolphins and a host of sea creatures. Beyond that is a *caldarium*, the hot room of the baths.

The **Women's Baths** are entered from Cardo IV Superiore and follow a similar progression of rooms, from the barrel-vaulted changing room to the *tepidarium* where shelves were located for personal items. This is followed by the *caldarium* with a large vaulted ceiling and two unusually fancy seats: one made of marble and the other a dark red stone. Behind the *caldarium* is the furnace used to heat the rooms and water, in addition to the well for the baths that drew water from a depth of about 27 feet (8.25 meters). Adjacent to the baths is a large courtyard, surrounded by porticos, that was used as a palaestra, or gymnasium.

1: garden statue in the House of the Deer **2:** mosaic in the Central Baths **3:** the ruins of Herculaneum

1
2
3

★ House of Neptune and Amphitrite

Cardo IV Superiore

One of Herculaneum's loveliest houses, this building is noted for its remarkable wall mosaics, which are often considered the most beautiful uncovered in Herculaneum. Although not a particularly large house, it has a highly detailed décor indicating its owner was wealthy. The most impressive mosaic depicts the god Neptune and his wife Amphitrite surrounded by decorative floral patterns and columns, and topped with a fan-shaped design, all in brilliantly preserved shades of deep red, blue, yellow, and green. Nearby, there's also a *nymphaeum*, or water garden, covered with floral and animal-themed mosaics and topped with marble theatrical masks. Admiring the brightly colored mosaics with all of the captivating intricacies of their designs, it's fascinating to image just how lavish the fully decorated room would have looked before the eruption of Vesuvius.

Trellis House

Cardo IV Inferiore

Easy to spot from the street with its wooden balcony supported by brick columns, this was originally a two-level boarding house with space for several families on the upper level; there's a separate entrance from the apartment on the lower level. Not only was the wooden balcony structure discovered remarkably intact, but archaeologists also found carbonized wooden remains of furniture.

House of the Wooden Partition

Cardo IV Inferiore

Just across the street from the Trellis House, this house is named after a very particular detail that was remarkably preserved. Beyond the atrium entry that's standard in most Roman homes, the family here added a wooden partition, an ancient version of a sliding door, that could be closed for more privacy between the atrium and the tablinum, the room located between the atrium and the peristyle garden. The wooden partition survived and is the only known example of this type of design from Greek or Roman antiquity.

★ House of the Deer

Cardo V Inferiore

This elegant villa covers about 11,840 square feet (1,100 square meters) and includes many rooms centered around a central garden. This is where archaeologists uncovered statues of deer being attacked by dogs, as well as statues of a Satyr and one of drunken Hercules, and round marble tables with ornately carved legs. Replicas of these statues and tables are located in the center of the garden. Surrounding the garden is a *cryptoporticus*, a covered passageway with windows, that has frescoes along the walls and a white mosaic floor. On the north side you'll find a large portal entrance to a sitting room with traces of highly detailed mosaics depicting cherubs riding sea animals and the head of the sea god Oceanus. With the villa's position near the walls of the city by the sea, there would have once been a fine sea view from the terrace located off of the garden. Since the ancient city sits well below street level today and the sea is no longer in sight, it takes some imagination today to picture the enviable seaside setting villas like this one once boasted.

Palaestra

Cardo V Superiore at Decumano Inferiore

The entrance to this building, between two large columns, leads into what was once a very large complex used for sporting activities. In the center there was originally a grand open space with a cross-shaped pool in the center, surrounded on three sides by arcades with columns and a corridor on the north side. The gymnasium complex included a variety of rooms, including a vast hall that was likely used for religious or cult ceremonies. Only a small area of the central garden and pool has been uncovered, but one of the finds includes a bronze fountain sculpture of the Lernaean Hydra, which was a frightening mythical monster with many snake heads.

FOOD

VIVA LO RE

Corso Resina 261, Ercolano; tel. 081/739-0207; www.vivalore.it; noon-4pm and 7pm-11pm Tues.-Sat., noon-4pm Sun., closed Mon.; €12-18

South of the archaeological park in Ercolano, this *osteria* and *enoteca* (wine bar) is a good spot to stop for a meal before or after visiting Herculaneum. Locally sourced ingredients are key, and are used beautifully to create traditional dishes with a twist, such as the lovely *zuppa d'orzo con frutti di mare* (barley soup with mixed seafood). The excellent wine list offers more than 1,500 labels.

GETTING THERE

BY TRAIN

The **Circumvesuviana** train run by EAV (www.eavsrl.it; departures every 30 minutes; journey about 20 minutes from Naples and costs €2.20 and about 40 minutes from Sorrento and costs €2.90) is the most comfortable public transportation option to reach Herculaneum. Exit at the Ercolano Scavi stop and head straight down Via Vittorio Veneto toward the sea and across the traffic circle to continue along Via IV Novembre for about 10 minutes. This will take you right to the entrance gate of the ruins.

BY CAR

Herculaneum is located off the **A3** autostrada (highway) that connects Naples and Salerno. It's about a 30-minute drive from Naples and at least 45 minutes from Salerno. Exit at either the Ercolano or Portici/Ercolano exit and follow the signs indicating Scavi di Ercolano for a short distance to the archaeological site. There are paid parking lots southeast of the site with rates usually starting at €2 per hour.

GETTING AROUND

Once you're at the Herculaneum archaeological site, the only way to navigate the ruins is on foot. The area is significantly smaller than Pompeii, so is a good choice between the two sites if extensive walking is an issue. However, you should still be prepared for uneven surfaces; and sturdy, comfortable shoes are recommended.

Vesuvius

In ancient Roman times, the massive volcano Mount Vesuvius, called Vesuvio in Italian, was known as Monte Somma. The fertile land surrounding the mountain southeast of Naples was valued by the Romans, who were largely unaware that the lush green slopes of Vesuvius concealed a deadly, explosive volcano. Until the massive eruption in AD 79, only a few Roman scholars suspected the true nature of Monte Somma. Pliny the Elder had been studying the mountain, and the geographer Strabo had written about stones on the mountain that looked as if they had been burned by fire. Yet the devastation of the eruption left no doubt of the fierce natural power below Vesuvius. Letters written by Pliny the Younger describe the events of that fateful day that killed his uncle Pliny the Elder as he tried to escape.

Though there hasn't been an eruption of the same level of devastation as the AD 79 eruption, Vesuvius has erupted regularly over the centuries. It is classified as a stratovolcano, a type of volcano made up of many layers of hardened lava, pumice, ash, and other materials. This type of volcano is known for periodic and violent eruptions, similar to Mount St. Helens in the United States. Vesuvius is considered one of the most dangerous volcanos in the world due to its unpredictable nature and the nearly three million people who live in the area surrounding the volcano. The last major eruption was in 1944 during World War II and was captured on film and video by the United States Air Force stationed near Naples at the time.

Today you can only occasionally catch a glimpse of wisps of steam coming out of the crater, but Vesuvius remains as much a threat as ever. It will come as no surprise that it's a heavily studied and constantly monitored volcano. Nevertheless, its gently curved slopes are an undeniable symbol of Naples. A climb to the top of the crater is a moving experience, both for the spectacular views and for the chance to be so close to such an incredible force of nature.

PARCO NAZIONALE DEL VESUVIO

Strada Provinciale Ercolano-Vesuvio; tel. 081/575-2524; www.parconazionaledelvesuvio.it; hours to visit crater 9am-3pm Jan.-Feb. and Nov.-Dec., 9am-4pm Mar. and Oct., 9am-5pm Apr.-June and Sept., 9am-6pm July-Aug.; €10

The Parco Nazionale del Vesuvio (Mount Vesuvius National Park) was created in 1995 to protect the entire area surrounding the volcano, along with its natural landscape, animal and plant species, and unique geological elements. The vast park covers 20,959 acres (8,482 hectares), from the base of the volcano to the upper part around the cone. The fertile soil of the volcano has created a rich forest of pine and holm oak trees, along with maple, alder, chestnut, and oak trees. The park is especially rich in Mediterranean vegetation, with up to 23 types of orchids and several varieties of broom. Following the meandering road up the slopes of Vesuvius to the top leads through the natural landscape from the forested base up to the rugged, rocky area around the *Gran Cono*, the main cone of the volcano.

Even though the volcano is surrounded by a dense urban environment, the park is home to many different species of mammals, birds, and reptiles. Foxes, rabbits, and beech martens all call the slopes of the volcano home, along with more than 100 different species of birds, including migratory, wintering, and breeding birds. It's a beautiful sight to catch a glimpse of a peregrine falcon gliding through the air along the slopes of the volcano.

★ Hiking to the Crater

Piazzale di quota 1,000 (parking area nearest the crater)

By far the biggest draw at Vesuvius is the experience hiking around the crater, or *Gran Cono*, the highest point around the crater of the volcano. To hike to the crater, start with a drive or bus ride to the parking lot located at

path on Mount Vesuvius

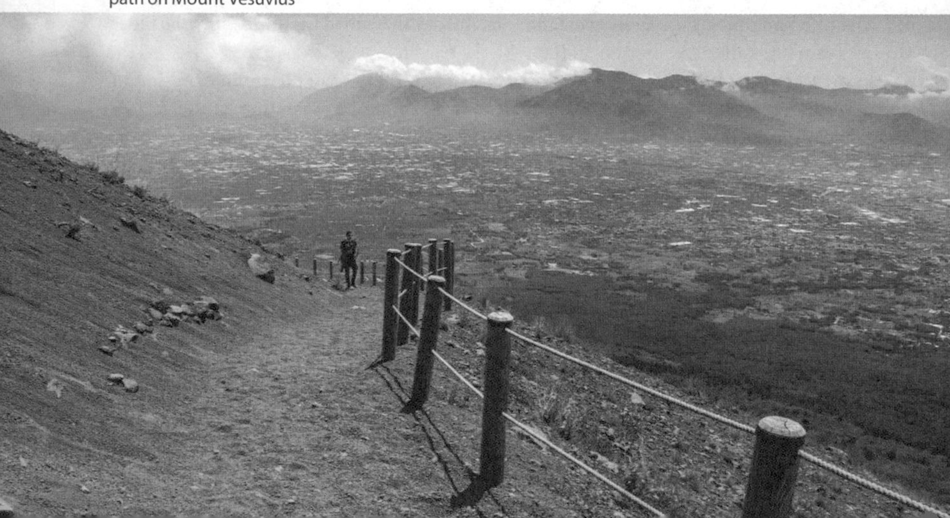

about 3,280 feet (1,000 m). First you'll need to purchase a ticket (€10 per person) at the ticket stand before the parking lot in order to access the pathway up to the crater. After buying your ticket, the steep and rocky pathway zigzags up to the edge of the crater. The path up to the crater is not shaded at all and rugged in parts, but there are plenty of spots to stop off and rest. Along the way, look over to the other peak on the other side of the volcano; it rises to 4,203 feet (1,281 m), and down to the valley of lava flow from the 1944 eruption.

Once you're at the top, the pathway levels out and opens to great views down into the crater and panoramic views over the entire Naples area south to the Sorrentine Peninsula, and on a clear day to the islands of Capri, Ischia, and Procida in the Gulf of Naples. Along the crater you'll find an information and services booth where you can get more details on the volcano (available in English). Enjoy exploring the crater area and walking along the rocky pathway leading around a long section of the crater. The pathway has wooden fences along either side and is a good vantage point to look down into the steep slopes of the crater. The hike up takes 20-30 minutes, depending on the number of photo stops or breaks you take. Plan to spend at least that long visiting the crater as well before doubling back on the same pathway for the 20-30 minute walk down. Mornings are the best time to visit the crater, as the view over the Gulf of Naples tends to be clearer and in the summer you can avoid the midday heat. To avoid having to rush, be sure to park in the lot area 1.5-2 hours before the park closes.

Keep in mind that the temperature at the summit can be quite cool, so it's a good idea to bring layers, even in the summer. Services are quite limited, though, so be sure to bring water and sunscreen. Comfortable footwear is highly recommended for the climb, but hiking boots are certainly not required. Note that the summit of Mount Vesuvius can be closed due to adverse weather conditions. To find out in advance if the crater is open, call the Parco Nazionale del Vesuvio for information (tel. 081/575-2524).

FOOD

KONA

Contrada Osservatorio, Ercolano; tel. 081/777-3968; ristorantekona@email.it; 11:30am-6pm daily and 7pm-11pm Fri.-Sun.; €8-15

Located along the road leading from the town of Ercolano up the slopes of Vesuvius, this restaurant is convenient to stop for a pizza or hearty lunch while you're driving to the crater of Vesuvius. There's a large dining area with indoor and outdoor seating and great views. The service is friendly and welcoming, and you can't go wrong with either the pizza or menu with traditional first and second course options. Set menus feature plenty of seafood and non-seafood choices.

GETTING THERE

Vesuvius is located about 6 miles (9.7 km) from Naples, 5 miles (8 km) from Pompeii, and 4.3 miles (7 km) from Herculaneum. The volcano is a popular day trip often combined with a visit to Pompeii or Herculaneum.

BY TRAIN

The **Circumvesuviana** train (www.eavsrl.it) stops at both the Pompeii and Herculaneum archaeological sites, where you can then connect to buses to reach the nearest point of the summit of Vesuvius before continuing on foot.

BY BUS

From Pompeii, the public bus company **EAV** (www.eavsrl.it; departures every 50 minutes; approximately an hour journey; Apr.-Sept.; €2.70) operates a bus line during the tourist season connecting Pompeii with the *Gran Cono* of Vesuvius. Buses depart from the Piazza Anfiteatro with a stop at the Pompeii Scavi-Villa dei Misteri Circumvesuviana train station near the Porta Marina entrance. Tickets can be purchased onboard and cost €2.70 each ride. Buses run 8am-3:30pm from Pompeii and return from Vesuvius to Pompeii 9am-5:40pm. Buses can be very crowded at times and may be standing-room-only during peak periods. Be prepared for a bit of an adventure and do plan to be patient with crowds and schedules if you choose this inexpensive way to reach Vesuvius from Pompeii.

There are also bus companies that specialize in bus transfers from Pompeii and Herculaneum to Vesuvius. **Busvia del Vesuvio** (www.busviadelvesuvio.com; Apr.-Oct.; €10 for return trip) runs a line from Pompeii to Vesuvius, departing from the Pompeii-Villa dei Misteri Circumvesuviana train station near the Porta Marina entrance to Pompeii. Keep in mind that entrance to Vesuvius is not included in the price; it's an additional €10 per person. Buses can be crowded and schedules might not be on the mark during peak season.

From Ercolano, **Vesuvio Express** (tel. 081/739-3666; www.vesuvioexpress.info; operates all year; €10 for return trip or €20 including entrance to Vesuvius) operates a bus route departing from the Ercolano Circumvesuviana train station. Both Busvia del Vesuvio and Vesuvio Express services include the round-trip transfer and free time to hike to the crater of Vesuvius.

BY CAR

From the A3 autostrada connecting Naples and Salerno, exit at Ercolano and follow signs for Parco Nazionale del Vesuvio. The road begins to climb up Via Vesuvio. The setting, landscape, and views improve as you continue to drive up. The road winds its way to a small parking area at an altitude of about 3,280 feet (1,000 meters). You must park in the paid lot there before continuing on foot to the ticket booth. Expect to pay around €5 to park.

Background

The Landscape

The Landscape.........417
Plants and Animals.....419
History..................421
Government and Economy............431
People and Culture 434

Whether you're gazing out the airplane window and seeing the distinctive humpbacked slopes of Vesuvius, looking up at the rugged mountains of the Amalfi Coast from the ferry, or zipping through the lush countryside on a high-speed train, your first glimpse of the Campania landscape will be captivating. The coastline, mountains, and fertile fields have shaped the history of this region for centuries.

The landscape explains a lot about the rich history of this area. It explains how culture can change within such short distances, why words are pronounced differently from one area to the next, and how culinary

traditions have developed. Nature has been instrumental in the development of Italy. The vineyards, olive groves, hilltop villages, and mountain ranges that define the region's geography have evolved over centuries while people have adapted to and transformed the natural setting. From the slopes of Vesuvius to the islands in the Gulf of Naples and the soaring mountain peaks along the Sorrentine Peninsula, it's a land that has fostered genius and civilization, and a landscape that is as memorable as the food, art, and people you'll meet.

GEOGRAPHY

Italy is roughly the size of Colorado but has enough geologic diversity to fill a continent. The long, boot-shaped peninsula was formed millions of years ago in the Cenozoic Era, when tectonic plates underneath Europe and Africa slowly collided and transformed the earth's surface. Over the past million years, alternating warm and glacial periods shaped the terrain and formed mountain ranges, valleys, lakes, and rivers. A journey down the length of the country reveals Alpine peaks, active volcanoes, hot springs, and desert-like settings.

The region of Campania is the third most populous of Italy and covers an area of 5,247 square miles (13,590 square km), with a coastline of about 217 miles (350 km) on the Mediterranean Sea. It is bordered by the regions of Lazio to the northwest where Rome is located, Molise directly to the north, Puglia to the northeast, and Basilicata to the east and south. Its coastline and two large gulfs are divided by the Sorrentine Peninsula, with the Gulf of Naples to the north and the Gulf of Salerno to the south. The Gulf of Naples is home to the islands of Capri, Ischia, and Procida.

Volcanic Activity

Perhaps the most defining geographic feature of Campania is **Mount Vesuvius,** the massive volcano that soars 4,203 feet (1,281 m) above the city of Naples and surrounding areas. The volcano is only a part of the Campania volcanic region, which formed some 34,000 years ago and stretches along the coastline west of Naples to the Campi Flegrei and to the islands of Ischia and Procida. This volcanic area comprises active, dormant, and extinct volcanoes. You'll observe hydrothermal activity, steaming craters at the Solfatara in the Campi Flegrei, fumaroles and thermal hot springs on Ischia, and fascinating Bradyseism in Pozzuoli, where the level of the earth's surface has moved up and down significantly over the centuries.

Because of centuries of volcanic activity, the Campania area has always been prized for its rich soil and productive farming. During Roman times the area was called *Campania felix*, meaning "fertile countryside" or "happy countryside." Agriculture is still an important part of the economy, both on a large scale in the plains around Vesuvius and on a smaller scale with the lemon production on the Amalfi Coast and small vineyards that produce high-quality wines throughout much of the region.

CLIMATE

The weather in Campania ranges from a warm Mediterranean climate along the coastline and islands to a cooler climate as you head inland toward the mountains. Yet in the Amalfi Coast and Naples area, the Mediterranean climate with warm summers and mild winters makes Campania an appealing travel destination for much of the year.

The classic sight of laundry drying on balconies and clotheslines is a good indication of what the weather is like much of the year. Summers are hot and dry with abundant sunshine, while the spring and autumn shoulder seasons are excellent times to travel, to enjoy pleasant weather and avoid the heat. In early spring, from March through April, the

Previous: lemon tree growing on the Amalfi Coast

weather begins warming up, with occasional rain and temperatures ranging from lows of 43-46°F (6-8°C) to highs of 59-64°F (15-18°C). May and June temperatures are among the most pleasant, with lows from 54-61°F (12-16°C) and highs from 72-79°F (22-26°C). The hottest period is from July to August, with temperatures ranging from an average low of 64°F (18°C) to an average high of 86°F (30°C). September is very much a continuation of the warm summer weather, with only a slightly cooler average low of 59°F (15°C) and a high of 79°F (26°C).

Temperatures begin cooling off in late autumn, from October and November, when there will be some rainy days as well as gorgeous sunny days. Expect average lows to range from 45-52°F (7-11°C) and highs from 63-72°F (17-22°C). Although winters are relatively mild in the Amalfi Coast area, temperatures drop to their lowest from December to February, with average lows from 37-41°F (3-5°C) and average highs from 54-55°F (12-13°C). Yet, it's not uncommon during this period for temperatures to drop enough for a dusting of snow to arrive occasionally on the top of Mount Vesuvius or along the mountains of the Sorrentine Peninsula. November to January is when the most rainfall occurs on the Amalfi Coast.

If you're planning a seaside holiday, the beach season usually begins around April or May and continues through October in most coastal areas. The sea temperatures are the warmest during July and August, with an average of about 78.8°F (26°C). The water can be a bit chilly in the spring and autumn months, yet on a sunny day that can be quite refreshing. June and September are also excellent times for swimming, as the water is on average about 75°F (24°C). Though there are some brave locals who swim year round, the winter sea temperatures drop to an average of about 57-59°F (14-15°C) from January to April.

ENVIRONMENTAL ISSUES

Italy's environmental concerns range from poor building practices in earthquake-prone areas to air and water pollution. Over the past decade, seasons have begun to stray from their clockwork patterns and people have started to recognize the greater variability. Summers aren't just hot, they can be excruciating, and local TV broadcasts advise viewers throughout July and August on how to avoid sunstroke and heat exhaustion.

Italy also suffers from environmental criminals who think dumping toxic waste into rivers and fields is the business of the future. Unfortunately, the practice is very profitable and difficult to stop. Many acres of productive agricultural land have been tarnished in southern Italy, and it's not uncommon for Italians living in affected areas to wonder if local food is safe to eat.

Plants and Animals

From rugged mountains to Mediterranean islands, the natural landscape of the Amalfi Coast area supports rich and diverse wildlife and plantlife.

TREES

The slopes of the mountains along the Sorrentine Peninsula as well as the surrounding areas are home to thick forests with many different types of trees, including pine, oak, beech, and chestnut. The towns of Scala and Tramonti on the Amalfi Coast are particularly noted for their large forests of chestnut trees. Occasionally, you'll also see palm trees and the iconic umbrella pine trees, which were introduced to the area during Roman times. The *noci di Sorrento* is a variety of walnut typically found on the Sorrento coastline, but it's cultivated in many areas of Campania.

Limone Costa d'Amalfi and Limone di Sorrento

Though citrus trees like mandarin and orange are common in the area, the lemons of the Amalfi Coast and Sorrentine Peninsula are world famous. Two types of lemons are grown in these areas, the *limone Costa d'Amalfi* and the *limone di Sorrento*, and these two varieties have garnered the IGP (*Indicazione Geografica Protetta*) status, which indicates a protected product unique to a geographic area. The *limone Costa d'Amalfi* is the *Sfusato Amalfitano* variety, which is noted for its tapered shape, very bright and medium-thick peel, and intense aroma. It is rich in essential oils and the pulp is juicy with a moderate acidic level, making it popular for use in creating the classic *limoncello* liqueur as well as in traditional cooking. These lemons are exclusively grown in terraced groves along the Amalfi Coast, with large groves in the Amalfi, Minori, and Maiori areas.

Along the Sorrento coastline you'll find the *limone di Sorrento*, a slightly smaller and more oval-shaped lemon compared to the *Sfusato Amalfitano*. The juice has a higher acidity level and is rich in vitamin C. The peels are also extremely fragrant and are used to create excellent *limoncello* and lemon sweets.

Olives

Olive trees are typical at lower elevations along the Sorrentine Peninsula and Amalfi Coast, where groves climb nearly vertically up and down terraces on the mountain slopes. Their silvery green leaves are a common sight throughout the year. During autumn harvest you can spot the black and green nets placed below the trees to catch the olives.

PLANTS AND FLOWERS

The mild Mediterranean climate is ideal for plants and flowers, which grow in abundance in the Campania area. Wildflowers fill the mountainsides with color and their sweet scent starting in the spring. You'll see many varieties of orchids, as well as cyclamen, crocuses, freesias, lilies, poppies, valerian, lavender, honeysuckle, buttercups, geraniums, and even wild garlic. Bright bursts of bougainvillea in various shades of purple and pink dot the area along with delicate wisteria in the spring. Jasmine grows particularly well here and fills the early summer air with a divine scent. Along rugged slopes you'll see the characteristic wisps of green and yellow of the many broom plants. Herbs grow wild here, including rosemary, thyme, oregano, and sage.

Along the stone footpaths of the Amalfi Coast it's common to see wild cyclamen popping out of tiny crevices in stone walls or to find large caper plants growing in the most unexpected spots. Deep in the Valle delle Ferriere, the mountain valley above Amalfi, there are rare examples of the *Woodwardia radicans*, a giant fern dating back to prehistoric times. Far easier to spot is the prickly pear, a type of cactus with fruit that is edible.

Grapevines and vineyards are common in the area, but they can be found in the most unlikely places. Along the Amalfi Coast, for instance, a vineyard may spread vertically along terraces with the vines trained to grow on trellises. Keen to maximize every inch of space available, growers often plant small vegetable gardens below the trellises.

MAMMALS AND REPTILES

Deep in the mountains of the Sorrentine Peninsula and inland in Campania, it's possible to find wild boar, foxes, and hare. However, the types of animals you're more likely to encounter while out hiking and walking along the old stone footpaths of the Amalfi Coast are the mules and donkeys that traditionally help to move material in the area. Outfitted with metal baskets to carry their loads—which in the summer may be tourists' suitcases—these beasts of burden are often seen clattering up and down the steps in long rows. Sheep and goats are also traditional in the area, and you'll hear the tinkling of their bells before you see them making their way along the mountainside. On Capri, you will occasionally spot wild goats that pick their way carefully along the rocky, steep cliffs of the island.

While you're out hiking, you're sure to happen across lizards and geckos sunning themselves or darting across your path. There are snakes in the rural areas, but most are relatively harmless except for vipers. The most common snakes are long and dark and are nonpoisonous. You will want to keep an eye out for vipers, which have a triangular head, lighter color, and smaller size. They'll stay away from you and are only defensive when startled.

SEALIFE

The Mediterranean is home to a variety of sealife, much of which is a rare treat to see in person. Occasionally, dolphins can be spotted jumping alongside boats, especially in the early morning. The Gulf of Salerno and Gulf of Naples are home to many different types of fish, from the tiny *alici* (anchovies), to large tuna in the deeper waters off the coast, as well as squid, octopus, and sea urchin. While swimming, you might run into a jellyfish (*medusa*), which can be an unpleasant experience but is not dangerous. Locals are keen to spot jellyfish and will likely alert you if they have been seen in the area. If you are stung, you can find creams or lotions that offer relief at any local *farmacia* (pharmacy).

BIRDS

The cry of seagulls is a familiar sound in the coastal regions, where you'll see colonies perched on rocks along the shore or high atop rugged cliffs on the islands. It's also not unusual to see falcons and other birds of prey gently gliding through the air. At night, you may hear the calls of owls, especially in the mountaintop villages of the Amalfi Coast.

Many types of migratory birds pass over the area in the spring and autumn while traveling between breeding grounds in northern Europe and winter nesting areas in Africa. Capri has long been a resting place during migration periods. The varieties of birds passing over the island and their flight patterns captured the interest of Swedish doctor Axel Munthe. In 1904, he bought the entire mountain above his Villa San Michele in Anacapri to protect native and migratory birds from being hunted and to study the birds as they stopped to rest on the island. Today the Capri Bird Observatory at Villa San Michele still welcomes ornithologists who continue to study and track migratory patterns on the island.

History

GREEKS, ETRUSCANS, AND ITALIC TRIBES

(8th-5th Centuries BC)

Inhabited since Paleolithic times, the region of Campania was home to many ancient Italic tribes and was colonized by the Greeks and Etruscans. **Greek** colonists founded some of the earliest settlements along the coastal areas of Campania. The first Greek colony in the area was Pithecusa on the island of Ischia, which was founded by Greeks from Euboea around 775 BC near the modern-day town of Lacco Ameno. From there, the Greeks moved to the mainland and founded Cumae around 730 BC. The ruins of the ancient city can be visited at Cuma in the Campi Flegrei west of Naples. Cumae developed into one of the finest colonies of Magna Graecia and was a strong foothold for the Greek expansion and foundation of nearby cities, including Neapolis (what is now modern-day Naples) around the 7th century BC.

Farther south, Greek colonists from Sybaris founded Poseidonia (today called Paestum) around 600 BC, and Elea (Velia) was founded by settlers from Phocaea in 541-535 BC. Poseidonia became a thriving Greek city and during the period from 560 to 450 BC, the three Doric temples that are still visible today were built. These temples are nearly as impressive as anything built in Athens and have remained in much better shape.

Meanwhile, the **Etruscans,** the first major civilization to settle in modern-day Italy, began to spread throughout the center of the peninsula in the 9th century BC and continued south to Campania, founding colonies in the inland areas like Capua around 600 BC.

It wasn't long before Greeks and Etruscans battled over the coastal areas, along with the Osci, a local Italic tribe that had founded towns such as Pompeii along the coastline. The Etruscans lost two major battles to the Greeks in Cumae in 524 and 474 BC. Much weakened, the Etruscans were unable to resist the Samnites, an Italic tribe of Oscan-speaking people, who expanded their territory from the mountainous internal regions of Italy toward the coast in the 5th century BC. Around the same time, the Lucanians, another Oscan-speaking Italic tribe, moved into Campania from the south and conquered Poseidonia in 400 BC. Not long after, the Samnites took Cumae in 421 BC.

ROMANS

(4th Century BC-4th Century AD)

The Romans began their expansion south in the 4th century BC, meeting great resistance from local Italic tribes and especially from the Samnites. During the period from 343 BC to 290 BC, Rome fought three wars with the Samnites until the Romans finally took control of the area, including Neapolis. It took even longer, however, for the Romans to dominate the Samnites, who continued to rebel. By 273 BC, Romans had arrived in Poseidonia, which they called Paestum, and they later refounded Pozzuoli in 194 BC and established a naval base in the Campi Flegrei at Misenum, near Capo Miseno on the Gulf of Pozzuoli.

Over the following centuries, Campania became fully Romanized. Roman ruins are still visible in Salerno, Sorrento, and Capri, as well as on the Amalfi Coast, throughout the Campi Flegrei, and especially in Naples where Roman streets and ruins lie just below the modern-day streets. Take a Napoli Sotterranea (Naples Underground) tour and you can literally walk along the streets of ancient Neapolis and see the ruins of markets, theaters, and more.

Lavish Villas

For the Romans, Capri had a particular appeal. Emperor Augustus (63 BC-AD 14) was so enamored of the island's beauty that he gave the island of Ischia to Neapolis in exchange for Capri. He started many large-scale building projects but was never able to call the island home. The island remained the property of the imperial family and was a favorite spot for Tiberius, the successor of Augustus, who completed many fine villas and ruled the Roman Empire from the island for the last 10 years of his life, from AD 27 to 37. During this time, the historian Tacitus reports there were 12 imperial villas across the island. Today, only the ruins of a few remain. Villa Jovis, the largest villa, sits atop Monte Tiberio while the ruins of Villa Damecuta in Anacapri reveal a grand terrace where the emperor could take in fine views of the Gulf of Naples.

The Sorrentine Peninsula and Amalfi Coast attracted wealthy Romans who built lavish villas along the coastline. Brilliantly colored frescoes have been found below the Chiesa di Santa Maria Assunta in Positano, while the Villa Romana in Minori offers the chance to walk through an ancient Roman villa.

Roman Decline

The Roman cities of Pompeii and Herculaneum around the base of Mount Vesuvius thrived until the violent eruption of the volcano in AD 79 completely destroyed the cities. As the Roman Empire started to decline, much of the once-thriving agricultural plains in Campania were abandoned. **Constantine** (AD 272-337) moved the capital to Constantinople (modern-day Istanbul) in AD 312, which led to the split of the Roman Empire. Though the eastern half survived for another 1,000 years in the guise of the **Byzantine Empire,** the west could not stop the Vandals, Franks, and Visigoths from pouring over the Alps in the north. The western Roman Empire officially came to an end in AD 476, with some sources indicating that the last emperor, Romulus Augustulus, died at the Roman villa that once stood where the Castel dell'Ovo stands in Naples today.

Despite persecution, **Christianity** grew and eventually became an officially recognized religion. The first Christian temples that were built later formed the foundations (literally) on which the Duomo di Napoli and many other churches in the area were built.

MIDDLE AGES

(5th-13th Centuries AD)

After the fall of the Western Empire, foreign invasion became the norm in Italy. **Lombards** arrived and founded their capital in Pavia, only to be replaced by the **Franks** and **Charlemagne** (742-814), who was crowned Holy Roman Emperor. The Lombards then moved south and vied for control of much of Campania. From the south, **Saracen** pirates landed in Sicily and Campania, followed by **Normans** who went on to build some of their most impressive fortifications in southern Italy. The **Byzantine Empire** continued to fight for control of the area after taking Naples in the 6th century.

Many battles for Naples, Salerno, and the Amalfi Coast areas were waged between the **Goths** invading from the north and the Byzantines before the Goths were finally driven out by the Byzantine Empire. Later, the Lombards arrived and took much of Campania, with the Byzantines only managing to keep hold of Naples, Sorrento, and the Amalfi Coast. Salerno fell to the Lombards in 646 and was absorbed into the Duchy of Benevento. Naples would continue on as an independent duchy under Byzantine influence until the 12th century.

Independent Republics

In the fray of the early Middle Ages many cities managed to form independent republics. Along with Venice, Genoa, and Pisa, Amalfi became one of the most powerful maritime republics of Italy. The peak of the **Duchy of Amalfi** stretches from the 10th to the 11th century, when the republic included much of the Amalfi Coast. As its trading ships crisscrossed the Mediterranean, traveling as far as Africa, Constantinople, and Jerusalem, this was the peak of wealth and culture on the Amalfi Coast. Many of the richly decorated churches and sprawling estates, like the Villa Rufolo in Ravello, date from this period. The Duchy of Amalfi was sacked by the Republic of Pisa in 1137, which was the beginning of the area's decline as powers shifted to the cities of Salerno and Naples. After a series of attacks, plagues, and misfortunes, the Amalfi Coast settled into a simple, rural existence as the centuries passed.

Salerno grew in prominence during the late Middle Ages under Lombard rule. After the seat of the Duchy of Benevento was moved to Salerno in 774, the city thrived and was known as a center of culture and art, and for founding the Schola Medica Salernitana, among the earliest medical schools in the world. In 954, the relics of San Matteo (St. Matthew) were brought to Salerno and the city's grand cathedral was built.

The relative stability of the area was turned on its head with the arrival of the Normans. From their first settlement at Aversa, not far from Naples, they would go on to conquer all of southern Italy over the next century. Amalfi fell to the Normans in 1073, and in 1076 they took Salerno, which became an important center for Normans in the area. Naples was the final territory in the area to fall to the Normans in 1139. Under the Normans, Naples was fortified with the construction of walls and the Castel dell'Ovo.

In 1194, power shifted in Naples and the south, from the Normans to the Swabians, the Hohenstaufen dynasty of kings from Germany. The period was not an easy transition for the population of Naples, who were highly resistant to their new leaders. Nevertheless, Naples began to grow under

King Frederick II Hohenstaufen, who founded the University of Naples—the first state-run, secular university in the west—in 1224. Yet after the king's death in 1250, the city revolted once again under Swabian rule.

ANJOU AND ARAGONESE RULE

(13th-15th Centuries)

The Swabian rule of Naples came to an end when Charles I of Anjou arrived in the city in 1266. As the ruler of the French Angevin kingdom, which covered all of southern Italy and Sicily, Charles set about developing Naples as an intellectual and artistic capital in Europe, and these efforts were continued by his grandson, Robert of Anjou (1275-1343). Defending Naples was also key, and it was Charles I who built the Castel Nuovo along the waterfront in Naples; later Angevin rulers built the Castel Sant'Elmo in the hills above the city.

Religious Monuments

Yet, grand building plans during this period weren't limited to castles. During Angevin rule, the Gothic Complesso Monumentale di Santa Chiara religious complex was built and became the final resting place for the sovereigns. Inside are a number of chapels and tombs, including that of King Robert of Anjou. Other Gothic masterpieces in Naples include the Duomo di Napoli cathedral, the Complesso Monumentale di San Lorenzo Maggiore and the Chiesa di Santa Maria Donnaregina Vecchia with its marvelous frescoes inspired by Giotto.

Power Shifts and Cultural Growth

As the Angevin dynasty began to crumble from internal family struggles in the early 15th century, the Aragonese took the chance to attack Naples. After a bloody battle, Alfonso of Aragon conquered Naples in 1442 and arrived in triumphal fashion in early 1443. The period of Aragonese rule only lasted a little over half a century, though, and it was marked by near constant turmoil. The Aragonese rulers were widely disliked, but it was a vibrant period for the arts and learning, attracting notable Renaissance poets and painters to the city. In addition to enlarging the Castel dell'Ovo in Naples, the Aragonese expanded existing fortifications on Ischia at the Castello Aragonese and connected the castle to the island with a stone bridge. In the Gulf of Pozzuoli, they also built the Castello Aragonese in Baia, a fortress constructed on top of a Roman villa that was once the summer residence ancient Roman emperors.

Though the Aragonese controlled much of the Campania area, Salerno and its territory came under the rule of the Princes of Sanseverino, feudal lords who controlled the area starting in the 14th century. The wealthy lords were pulled into the battle between the Angevin and Aragonese rulers, taking sides between the two back and forth, depending on what was most beneficial for Salerno.

SPANISH RULE

(16th-17th Centuries)

By the end of the 15th century, both France and Spain were vying for the Kingdom of Naples. The French first took control in 1501 but power passed to the Spanish King Ferdinand III by 1504. This began about 200 years of Spanish rule, largely under the Hapsburg dynasty in Spain, with Naples governed by a series of viceroys. One of the most notable was Pedro Álvarez de Toledo, who was viceroy from 1532 to 1552. Though he was known for urban planning initiatives like expanding the city walls, constructing Via Toledo, and building the tightly packed residential area to house the Spanish troops (still called the Quartieri Spagnoli or Spanish Quarters), he was also known for his harsh rule of the city.

Growth of Naples

Nevertheless, under Spanish rule Naples very quickly grew to be one of the largest cities in Europe. Overcrowding and poverty became significant issues. However, the 17th century was one of the peak moments of art and architecture for Naples. Many fine churches and monasteries were built in the lavish Neapolitan baroque style, and Cosimo Fanzago (1591-1678) was one of the most notable architects of the day. The first truly Neapolitan school of painting began in the early 17th century, largely inspired by the work of Caravaggio (1571-1610), who spent a short time in the city and gifted it with masterpieces like *The Seven Works of Mercy* at the Pio Monte della Misericordia. Neapolitan artists, such as Battistello Caracciolo (1578-1635), Luca Giordano (1634-1705), and Francesco Solimena (1657-1747), to mention only a few, were hard at work decorating all of the new churches being built during the period.

The period of Spanish rule was also punctuated by a series of revolts to oppressive taxes, including an uprising in 1647 led by Tommaso Aniello, called Masaniello (1620-1647). The young fisherman led a riot on July 7 that turned into a citywide uprising that lasted until Masaniello was assassinated on July 16, 1647. Capitalizing on the disorder, the French attempted to take back Naples, but by 1648 order was restored under a new Spanish viceroy.

By the second half of the 17th century, the situation in the Kingdom of Naples was falling apart. In 1656, the plague hit Naples and Campania in full force, killing more than half of the population in Naples alone. A strong earthquake in 1688 caused significant destruction in the historic center of Naples, setting the city's recovery back even further. Outside of Naples, Salerno finally passed from the last descendants of the Sanseverino family to the Kingdom of Naples.

THE BOURBONS

(18th Century)

After the tumultuous Spanish period, the 1700s brought great changes to Naples. During the War of the Spanish Succession (1701-1714), as the Austrian Habsburg and Bourbon families fought over the Spanish Empire, Naples was ceded to Austria in 1707. The Austrian viceroyalty rule lasted only until 1734 when the Bourbon king Charles VII (future Charles III, King of Spain) conquered Naples and set about transforming it into a European capital. Grand urban plans and a focus on public works marked the Bourbon era in Naples and the surrounding areas.

Under Charles VII, and later his son Ferdinand IV, Naples became one of the finest cities in Europe. The arts flourished as well as new industries like silk production at the Real Borgo di San Leucio and the prized porcelain of the Real Fabbrica di Capodimonte (Royal Factory of Capodimonte). During this period, the Teatro San Carlo opened in 1734 and became one of the most celebrated opera houses in Europe. In the hills above the city center, the grand museum known as the Museo e Real Bosco di Capodimonte was developed as a palace and home to the royal art collection. The finest Bourbon addition to Naples is the grand Reggia di Caserta, the massive royal palace built to rival Versailles in France.

Rediscovering Pompeii and Herculandum

It was during Bourbon rule that Herculaneum was accidentally rediscovered during construction of yet another royal residence. The first real exploration of the archaeological site began in 1738, and in 1748 Pompeii was rediscovered through intentional excavations in search of the ancient city. The treasures uncovered were highly valued by the kings of Naples and were extremely influential during the neoclassical movement in Naples.

As Naples garnered attention from across Europe, the first tourists began to arrive. This took the form of the Grand Tour, the popular tour across Europe that was an integral part of an aristocratic education in the 18th century. After visiting Florence, Venice, and Rome, many travelers continued south to appreciate the fine music, art, and cultural experiences of Naples, as well as to marvel at the ancient temples in Paestum and walk among the ruins of Pompeii and Herculaneum. Many travelers would continue on to Sorrento during this period, drawn by the romantic views across the

Gulf of Naples and artisan traditions like intarsia (inlaid woodwork). A few travelers also braved the boat ride or mountainous journey to visit villages on the Amalfi Coast, which were still extremely isolated. By the early 1800s, especially after the rediscovery of the Grotta Azzurra in 1826, Capri's allure as an international travel destination had begun.

PARTHENOPEAN REPUBLIC AND UNIFICATION

(19th Century)

At the end of the 18th century, the wave of revolutionary ideas of the French Revolution arrived in Naples. When Marie Antoinette—who was the sister of King Ferdinand IV's wife Maria Carolina—was beheaded in 1793, the revolution became very personal to the Bourbon rulers of Naples. After battling with the French, the king and queen escaped to Palermo and left Naples to the French, who established the Parthenopean Republic in 1799. This was a short-lived moment of confusion, which ended after only six months when a counter revolution lead by the Bourbons ousted the republic and brutally executed republican sympathizers.

Despite the return of the Bourbon monarchy, the beginning of the 19th century in Naples was a period of turmoil. The French returned in 1805, this time more successfully. In 1806, Napoleon made his brother Joseph Bonaparte King of Naples, a role that was passed to Napoleon's brother-in-law Joachim Murat in 1808. The French were never fully embraced by the Neapolitans, and when the French lost power in 1815 the Neapolitans welcomed Ferdinand IV back to rule as Ferdinand King of the Two Sicilies.

Resurgence and Restoration

The Bourbon family continued to rule Naples for the rest of the first half of the 19th century, which was a period of great unrest in Naples. The birth of a nationalist movement determined to unite a fragmented peninsula and free it from foreign domination began to spread across Italy. The ***Risorgimento*** (Resurgence) was a challenging endeavor. One of the great leaders of the period was the charismatic **Giuseppe Garibaldi** (1807-1882). He was a George Washington-like figure whose dedication and perseverance never waned. There's a statue, square, or street dedicated to him in practically every village, town, and city in Italy.

One of the major hurdles in the unification of Italy was the south: namely, the **Kingdom of the Two Sicilies,** overseen by Bourbon monarchs who ruled over southern Italy from their capital in Naples. In 1860, Garibaldi set off from Genoa with 1,000 volunteers equipped with hand-me-down weapons and red shirts for uniforms. What they lacked in training and equipment, however, they made up for in spirit. After landing in Marsala, they captured Palermo and the rest of Sicily with little bloodshed. The going was tougher in Campania, but the Bourbons eventually surrendered Naples and the entire Kingdom of the Two Sicilies was incorporated into the Kingdom of Italy.

The period post-unification in Naples saw widespread poverty in the densely populated city center. A terrible cholera epidemic in 1884 led to a massive urban renewal plan, called the ***Risanamento*** (Restoration). Streets where widened and entire neighborhoods were demolished and rebuilt in an attempt to revitalize the city. Large-scale building projects like the Galleria Umberto I date from this period, as well as the city's first funicular train to the Vomero neighborhood of Naples.

WORLD WAR I

(1914-1919)

Italy entered the 20th century united under a single king but still in search of itself. The country was not threatened, yet politicians and intellectuals alike succumbed to the fervor of war as the events rocking other European capitals spread to Rome. Which side Italy actually joined wasn't settled until the last days, when the Allies made a better offer and promised to expand Italy's borders and regain lands from Austrian control. It wasn't until the end of **World War I,** when Austria ceded Trentino and Trieste, that Italy reached its current territorial state.

The country entered the war with little preparation and forethought for what everyone predicted to be a short conflict. The army eagerly set off, badly equipped and ill commanded, toward the Alps. Reality set in after the **Battle of Caporetto** in 1917, when Italian forces suffered a major defeat and nearly buckled under a combined German and Austro-Hungarian offensive. A long, hard-fought campaign ensued that saw very little progress. By 1919 more than 650,000 Italians had died and a million had been wounded in fighting of little strategic significance.

FASCISM

(1920-1945)

Postwar Italy was greatly deprived, and it was during this period that many peasants packed their bags and headed for the United States, Argentina, and Australia. Naples was one of the primary ports of embarkation, and both the city and the surrounding areas saw massive emigration during the Italian diaspora, which started after the unification and continued into the early 20th century. Many of those who remained survived on a meager diet, and the feeling of disappointment was rife throughout society. The promises of war had not been fulfilled, and territorial gains seemed like small compensation for people's constant suffering. The economy was weak and a revolution in Russia gave workers something to contemplate. Extreme factions began to form, and both sides were convinced that the government's liberal policies were outdated.

One proponent of change was **Benito Mussolini** (1883-1945). Before the war, Mussolini had been an editor of the Socialist Party newspaper and had displayed a talent for increasing circulation. His idea of **Fascism** evolved slowly and remained heavy on propaganda and light on philosophy. Economic hardship made recruiting easy, and a private security force known as the **Blackshirts** was established to protect landowners, fight communists, and beat Slavs. In October 1922 Mussolini announced he would march on Rome. King Emmanuel III refused to sign a decree of martial law that might have stopped the Fascists, and instead he promoted Mussolini to prime minister.

Order was quickly restored, trains started arriving on time, and opponents of the party could still show their faces. Things changed after the elections of 1924 and the assassination of Giacomo Matteotti, a socialist politician who spoke out against corruption and dictatorship. Over the next few years Fascists used parliamentary means to convert Italy into a virtual dictatorship and inspired other European dictators to do the same. Mussolini used large-scale public works projects to keep workers employed, and manipulated the new media of cinema and radio to glorify his achievements and reinforce his hold on Italy. In Naples, the Palazzo delle Poste, which still serves as the main post office, was built from 1928 to 1936 in the sleek rationalist style typical of Fascist architecture. The Stazione Marittima in the port also dates from this period and was part of the Fascist regime's plan to increase the productivity and importance of the port of Naples in Mediterranean trade.

WORLD WAR II

(1939-1945)

One of Mussolini's favorite slogans was, "Whoever stops is lost." He didn't stop and Italians lacked the democratic means to stop him. He invaded Ethiopia and joined the Spanish Civil War on the side of Franco in 1936. This endeavor forged an alliance with Hitler that would eventually be fatal. Once again Italy was led unprepared into a world conflict, except this time they chose to fight on the wrong side. The military and civilian casualties were greater than during World War I, and even the magic of propaganda could not sugarcoat defeats in North Africa and the Balkans.

Historical Timeline

8th century BC	Greek settlers arrive on Ischia and later Cuma.
7th century BC	Greek city of Neapolis (modern day Naples) is founded.
474 BC	First castle is built on the Castello Aragonese in Ischia.
560-450 BC	Three large Greek temples are built in Paestum.
3rd century BC	Romans arrive in Campania and establish settlements.
27-37 AD	Emperor Tiberius rules Roman Empire from his lavish Villa Jovis on Capri.
1st century AD	Anfiteatro Flavio is built in Pozzuoli and is the third largest amphitheater in the Roman Empire.
79 AD	Violent eruption of Mount Vesuvius destroys Roman cities of Pompeii and Herculaneum.
305	San Gennaro (St. Januarius) martyred in Pozzuoli.
5th century	Campania area is ruled by Byzantines, Goths, and Lombards.
9th century	The Schola Medica Salernitana, the first medical school of its kind, is founded in Salerno.
954	Relics of San Matteo (St. Matthew) arrive in Salerno and construction of cathedral already underway is ramped up.
10th-11th centuries	The Republic of Amalfi reaches its peak.
1057	Bronze doors of the Duomo di Amalfi are cast in Constantinople.
1139	Naples becomes part of the Norman kingdom that already includes Amalfi and Salerno.
1208	Relics of Sant'Andrea (St. Andrew) arrive in Amalfi.
1266	Angevin dynasty gains control of Naples.
1343	Massive tsunami hits Amalfi and destroys much of the town.
1442	Alfonso of Aragon conquers Naples and begins the Aragonese dynasty in Naples.
1504	Naples becomes a colony of Spain and two centuries of Spanish rule begin.
1558	Sorrento is sacked by Barbary pirates.

U.S. and British troops commanded by Generals Patton and Montgomery reached Sicilian shores in July 1943, by which time it was clear the tide had turned against Mussolini and his Axis allies. An **armistice** was hastily drafted and signed in Brindisi, but that didn't end the conflict. German divisions were sent to defend Italy and made the Allies pay a heavy price for every mile they advanced up the peninsula after the **Landing of Salerno** on September 9, 1943. After a four-day popular uprising in Naples against German forces, the allied troops arrived on October 1 for the **Liberation of Naples.**

The **Battle of Monte Cassino,** northwest of Naples, in 1944 was one of the bloodiest five-month periods of the war and a throwback to the futility of trench warfare. Throughout the Italian campaign a network

1647	Masaniello leads revolution in Naples against Spanish rule.
1734	Bourbon dynasty begins in the Kingdom of Naples.
1737	Teatro San Carlo opens in Naples.
1738	Herculaneum is rediscovered, and 10 years later Pompeii is found again.
1752	Construction begins on the massive Reggia di Caserta royal palace.
1799	Parthenopean Republic established after bloody revolution in Naples.
1815	Bourbons take back control of Naples.
1832	Construction begins on the Amalfi Coast Road.
1861	Italian city-states and regions unify into a single nation governed by a constitutional monarchy.
1883	Earthquake on Ischia causes severe destruction in town of Casamicciola Terme.
1886	A school dedicated to teaching the inlaid woodwork tradition opens in Sorrento.
1943	Operation Avalanche, also known as the Landing of Salerno, during World War II takes place on September 9.
1943	Naples is liberated from German occupation September 27-30.
1945	The Surrender of Caserta is signed at the Reggia di Caserta on April 29, ending the Italian campaign of World War II.
1946	Italians choose to become a democratic republic in national referendum.
1953	John Steinbeck writes influential essay on Positano for *Harper's Bazaar.*
1962	First Lady Jacqueline Kennedy spends a summer vacation on the Amalfi Coast and visits Capri.
1987	Napoli soccer team wins the *scudetto* (Coppa Campioni d'Italia) and the Coppa Italia with Diego Maradona on the team.
1988	Russian dancer Rudolf Nureyev buys the Li Galli islands off of Positano.
1997	The Amalfi Coast, Pompeii, Herculaneum, and the Reggia di Caserta are listed as UNESCO World Heritage Sites.
2010	The Auditorium Oscar Niemeyer is inaugurated in Ravello.

of Italian resistance fighters, organized behind the enemy lines, aided the Allies. The **Partisans** hampered German movement and managed to liberate many parts of northern Italy before Allied tanks rolled into the region toward the end of the war. Mussolini was caught trying to escape to Switzerland in April 1945. He and his mistress were shot, and their tortured bodies were publicly displayed in Milan. He remains popular with a small segment of the population, and his granddaughter was elected to parliament several times.

The Most Bombed City in Italy

Naples suffered a significant amount of damage from allied bombing during World War II. There were more than 200 air strikes from 1940 to '44, and the city holds the unfortunate record as the most-bombed Italian city during the war. The approximate toll of civilian casualties ranges from 20,000 to 25,000 people. During bombing raids, the city's residents fled to the underground areas of the city, which can now be visited on Napoli Sotterranea (Naples Underground) tours. To cap off this period, Mount Vesuvius erupted in 1944 (its last major eruption), which destroyed a number of towns around the base of the volcano as well as planes from the United States Army Air Forces (USAAF) 340th Bombardment Group, which was based near Naples at the time.

The end of World War II in Italy is connected to the Reggia di Caserta (Royal Palace of Caserta), where the **Surrender of Caserta** was signed on April 29, 1945. This was the written agreement that ended the Italian campaign of World War II and formalized the surrender of German forces in Italy.

POSTWAR AND CONTEMPORARY TIMES

(1946-Present)

A **referendum** was held in 1946 to choose between monarchy and democracy. The majority of Italians voted for the latter, although Naples as a city voted for the monarchy. A new constitution was adopted and the **Italian Republic** was born. There were still many years of rationing and hunger ahead, as the country recovered from the war, and Naples had a significant uphill battle to rebuild from the extensive damage. However, by the late 1950s and 1960s Naples, along with much of Italy, began a period of growth that transformed cities and saw new neighborhoods and infrastructure emerge from the ashes. In many parts of Naples, especially the Posillipo area, indiscriminate, unchecked building was a widespread problem. Recovery postwar was also hindered by the Camorra, the mafia of Naples and Campania. Industrialization was slower in Naples than in other areas, as well, which led to high unemployment and mass emigration, this time largely to the north of Italy and throughout Europe.

Largely untouched during World War II, the Amalfi Coast and island of Capri quickly became popular tourist destinations postwar, starting in the 1950s and '60s. Capri offered the epitome of the *La Dolce Vita* (The Sweet Life) style, attracting the jet set crowd of movie stars, royalty, and other rich celebrities.

Starting in the 1990s, political leaders in Naples began a war on corruption and criminality as well as a focus on preserving and enhancing the historic treasures of Naples and Campania. The region has seen a remarkable transformation and is now one of the top tourist destinations in Italy. Its public transportation network continues to be improved, and large pedestrian-only areas in the historic center have given the city an open-air museum atmosphere where travelers can marvel at the city's many cultural treasures and fascinating layers of history.

Government and Economy

Italian government can appear enigmatic to outsiders. Even Italians have trouble understanding their election laws, which are often changed and appear designed to ensure no party gains a significant majority. More than 60 governments have been formed since the end of World War II, and it's rare for politicians to finish their mandate. Elections often end in stalemate, and the 2018 vote exemplifies the problem. The two winning parties have spent months negotiating the political future of the country with very little progress, and recently they set the record for the longest period of time Italy has operated without a government in place. New elections may be held to resolve the turmoil of the last ones, which explains why many Italians have lost confidence in politicians and voter turnout is declining.

Fortunately, a country doesn't need politicians to run. Below the politicians are the bureaucrats and government agencies that keep the country in business; it's a big organization that has had a difficult time adapting to new realities. Italians pay more for their government than citizens of other western democracies, and most wouldn't say they are getting their money's worth. The system does supply TV talk shows with plenty of content and allows new parties to periodically emerge with promises of reform. Yet change remains elusive, and passing meaningful legislation can be an excruciatingly long process.

ORGANIZATION

The Italian parliament consists of a **Chamber of Deputies** and a **Senate.** According to the Constitution of 1948, both have the same rights and powers. They are independent of each other and joint sessions are rare. The main business is the enactment of laws. For a bill to become law it must receive a majority in both houses. The bill is discussed in one house, and is then amended and approved or rejected. If approved, it is passed to the other house, which can amend, approve, or reject. If everything runs smoothly, the text is proclaimed law by the President of the Republic and enacted.

The **president,** however, is more of a figurehead than a leader. That job is reserved for the **prime minister,** who nominates key ministers and is susceptible to losing power if the majority is lost. It's also not uncommon for members of parliament to switch parties. A vote of confidence can be called at any time, and should a government fail to pass such a test it must resign and make way for new elections. That means fixed terms aren't guaranteed, and stability can be difficult to attain.

The Italian **justice system** has its own problems and is regularly in conflict with politicians who seek to reduce its power and openly criticize its judgments. The **Constitutional Court** is Italy's version of a Supreme Court. It's composed of 15 judges. One-third are appointed by the president, one-third elected by parliament, and the remainder are elected by lesser courts. They have their work cut out for them, and there is a tremendous backlog of cases throughout the system. Both civil and criminal judgments can take years to obtain and lack the efficiency required to make the wheels of justice run smoothly.

POLITICAL PARTIES

Italy is as far as you can get from a two-party system. There are dozens of officially organized groups that run the gamut from hardcore communist to right-wing separatist. In between are small- and medium-sized groups, none of whom are large enough to govern on their own. The political landscape is divided into right, left, center, and radical. Obtaining a majority can be hard, which explains why the country has experienced so many governments since the end of World War II. In

Italy governments don't last for a designated amount of time; they can be toppled whenever the ruling party loses its majority in parliament. The result is instability and gridlock that hampers the country's legislative needs.

The rise of Silvio Berlusconi and his *Forza Italia* (Italian Power) party in the early 1990s led to political consolidation. Since the turn of the 21st century there has been a trend toward three or four large political forces vying for power. These include the centrist *Partito Democratico (Democratic Party)*, which lost significant parts of its electorate in the last election (2018), and the right-leaning Lega (League), which currently has significant influence over policy making and is the second-most popular party in the country.

One of the newest political players is the Movimento *5 Stelle* (5 Star Movement) that was founded in 2009 and has capitalized on discontent with politicians. Their founder, Beppe Grillo, is a comedian with a sharp tongue and popular blog who helped nurture a new generation of politicians. They have gradually gained seats at local and national levels, including the mayoral seats of Rome and Turin. This is currently the most popular party, which is why they're often labeled as populist and feared by old-school politicians. Things can change quickly in Italian politics, however, and often do.

ELECTIONS

The **Chamber of Deputies** is located in Palazzo Montecitorio in Rome and has 630 members elected by Italian citizens over the age of 18. Deputies are elected for five-year terms unless the president dissolves parliament. Reforms in 2005 significantly complicated matters. The electoral system combines proportional representation with priority for the coalition securing the largest number of votes, so a ruling government can achieve a majority. That hasn't been the case in recent elections and there's now talk of further electoral reform.

The **Senate** is located in Palazzo Madama and has 315 members, elected for five-year terms by Italian citizens over the age of 25. Members are elected by proportional representation based on party lists from each of Italy's 20 regions. Six Senators represent Italians living abroad, and seven are granted senatorship for life.

Italians don't elect leaders directly. They vote for parties and those parties determine who represents the people. It's like buying a car without specifying the model, and guarantees the same old faces. Turnout is generally high and hovers around 80 percent for national elections. Participation has declined as of late as electors lose faith in the system, which has led to political mayhem and resulted in compromised leaders. The electoral system is subject to intense debate and is regularly modified. Meanwhile, the politicians seem uniquely unqualified to fix the problem and are more interested in avoiding term limits and guaranteeing perennial power than they are in resolving matters.

ECONOMY

Italy is the eighth-largest economy in the world with a GDP of $2.1 trillion and an average income per capita of over $35,000. The introduction of the **euro**, however, has taken its toll on disposable income and salaries have not increased as fast as prices. Growth is beneath the European average and has suffered from stagnation since the recession of 2008. In addition, there's a striking economic divide between regions in the north and those in the south. The country's main trading partners are Germany, France, Switzerland, and the United States. Unemployment hovers around 10 percent and is particularly high among young adults.

Many advanced industries operate in Italy; however, a decline in research-and-development investment has led thousands of recent graduates and researchers to search for opportunities abroad. Turning this around is one of the political challenges of the future.

Fiscal pressures are high in Italy and tax evasion is common. The Italian tax agency estimates billions of euros go unpaid every year, and their collection would have a significant impact on GDP. For this reason, the government has passed legislation encouraging a transition toward a cashless society, and you can pay for nearly everything using a debit or credit card.

Industry

Italy has a long history of innovation. Today, agriculture, aerospace, automobiles, light industry, textiles, tourism, and creative services make up the main economic activities. From 1951 to 1963, the economy grew by more than 6 percent per year. **Fiat** led the economic postwar recovery, and its cars still make up the largest slice of the domestic market. Other goods include precision machinery, pharmaceuticals, home appliances, luxury goods, textiles, clothing, and ceramics. Agriculture is still an important industry in Campania, with a large production of fruit and vegetables as well as notable wines. Naples is a major port for cargo transport and is one of the Mediterranean's busiest port cities.

The country lacks deposits of iron, coal, or oil. Most raw materials and much of the country's energy sources must be imported. One of Italy's strengths is small and medium-size businesses. More than 90 percent of all companies employ fewer than 10 people. These firms take pride in their work and manage to maintain high levels of craftsmanship.

The Minister of Finance has one of the toughest jobs in Italy. The country must balance a rising trade deficit, high labor costs, and substantial national debt. "Reform" is a dirty word, and taxes couldn't be any higher. Italian companies are at a disadvantage compared to their European rivals and competition from Asia has driven many manufacturers out of business. Nevertheless, the words "Made in Italy" still matter to consumers around the world, and there are plenty of success stories.

Tourism

Italy is the fifth most visited country in the world and attracted more than 52 million visitors in 2016. Germans (10.8 million), Americans (4.5 million), and French (4.3 million) are the tourists you're most likely to meet, although the country is also a favorite with Chinese and British travelers. The Naples and Amalfi Coast areas are among the most popular destinations in Italy, with a notable increase in visitors every year. Cruise ships dock in the large ports of Naples and Salerno, while at Amalfi, Sorrento, and Capri, cruise ships drop anchor and tender travelers to shore. Because this region is such a popular travel destination, tourism is well organized and nearly every large town and city has a tourist center.

The impact of tourism in Italy has been making the news, with some cities taking a deeper look at how to handle the mass influx of tourists. In 2011, the town of Amalfi opened a large parking area that was tunneled out of the mountain. Meanwhile, the island of Capri is revisiting ferry schedules and investigating other ways to help visitors get around the island more easily. Cultural initiatives like **Slow Tourism** are designed to address the impact of overtourism, encouraging travelers to spend longer and get a deeper understanding of the places they visit.

People and Culture

DEMOGRAPHY

Italy is one of the most densely populated countries in Europe, with more than 60 million inhabitants. Rome is the largest city, with a population of 4.3 million, followed by Milan (3.2 million) and Naples (3.1 million). The average life expectancy is 85 years for females and 80 for males. There are also plenty of people pushing 100, and the country has a median age of 45.5. (It's 38.1 in the United States, 40.5 in the United Kingdom, and 38.7 in Australia.) That's the fifth-highest in the world, due to low birth rates and the high life expectancy. Immigration, however, prevents the population from declining.

IMMIGRATION

Immigration is a relatively new phenomenon in Italy. Up until 1989 more people left the country than arrived. Today, the official number of foreign-born residents is around five million and represents 8.3 percent of the total population.

The largest immigrant communities are from Romania, Albania, Poland, Morocco, and China. Most are men who moved to Rome or cities in northern Italy, where the chances of finding a job are better than in the south. Many work as day laborers, builders, cleaners, dishwashers, and caretakers. The second generation of this immigration wave is now emerging in Italian society, and it's not uncommon to see Italo-Bangladeshi chefs preparing pizza, Italo-Nigerian children on their way to school, or Italo-Chinese contestants on TV quiz shows.

Ongoing conflict in Syria and sub-Saharan Africa has greatly increased immigration to Europe overall. The issue has reached crisis proportions in the past few years, with some nations unable or unwilling to deal with the influx. Several Eastern European countries have built fences, but that only diverts refugees to other destinations. Italy is not a primary haven for Middle Eastern migrants, who usually travel through Turkey and into Greece on their way to Germany and Nordic countries. Most immigrants and refugees to Italy cross the Mediterranean from Africa, and smugglers regularly pack boats with people desperate to start a new life abroad. You'll see some selling bags and other items to tourists in the center of Naples and other large cities.

Italians generally favor legal immigration and recognize their own emigrant past, but immigration is one of the hot political topics, with several parties making it a pillar of their platform.

RELIGION

The vast majority of Italians are **Catholic,** although the number of those who regularly attend church is on the decline. The Lateran Agreement of 1929 officially formalized the relationship between the Italian state and the Vatican, which continues to benefit from substantial tax breaks. Although church and state are divided in the constitution it's not uncommon to see crucifixes in police stations, hospitals, and schools. Every town has a patron saint that is still celebrated with feasts and festivals.

Islam, Buddhism, and Orthodox Christianity are the fastest-growing religions in Italy. Many Muslims face Mecca inside improvised mosques, as some Italian cities have been reluctant to provide building permits for new mosques. Jews have been present in Italy since the reign of Julius Caesar, and the **oldest synagogue in Europe** can be found in Ostia, outside of Rome. In Naples, the Jewish community dates to the 1st century under Roman control of the city. The 15th-16th centuries brought much persecution, with all Jews being forced to leave in 1541. In the 19th century, the community grew thanks to the thriving branch of the Rothschild family bank in Naples. Today the

Breaking the Language Barrier

Learning a new language takes time, dedication, and practice. If you want to experience a fundamental aspect of Italian culture, you must start before your trip. Set aside 20 minutes per day for undistracted study at least two weeks before arrival. Download an Italian learning app (**Duolingo** or **Babbel**), invest in a book, or enroll in a course. Listen to Italian music on your way to work, and browse the headlines of Italian newspapers online. Discover Italian singers (Jovanotti, Giorgia, Ligabue, Subsonica, etc.) you like and add them to your playlist, watch short films or cartoons, and, if you have the benefit of a friend or traveling partner, try out new grammar and vocabulary as often as possible.

Imagine situations you're likely to encounter (restaurant, ticket office, bar, etc.), and role-play interactions until you're comfortable ordering a cappuccino and asking for a bottle of house wine. It's impossible to master a new language in a month, but you can absorb enough grammar and vocabulary to adapt to the linguistic surroundings and break through the language barrier. Stimulating your eyes and ears with as many sources of Italian as possible will make it easier to understand and use Italian once you arrive. The more effort you put in at home, the more gratifying your journey will be.

Jewish community of Naples is only around 200 people and there is one synagogue (Comunità ebraica di Napoli; Vico Santa Maria a Cappella Vecchia 31; tel. 081/764-3480; www.napoliebraica.it).

LANGUAGE

Modern Italian derives from Latin and owes a great debt to **Dante Alighieri** (1265-1321), who was the first to codify and utilize the dialects spoken on the Renaissance streets of Florence in his tales of heaven and hell. Not all Italian sounds the same, however. There is a big difference between the accent you'll hear in the north and the one you'll hear in Rome and central Italy, or farther south around Naples and the Amalfi Coast. There are also minority languages spoken, such as Sardo, used by more than a million people in Sardinia; and Friulano, widely used in Friuli. Ladino is confined to an alpine valley in Alto Adige, and Catalan is spoken on the northwestern coast of Sardinia; both are remnants of foreign occupation, and their gradual mixture with Italian has led to colorful words and expressions that aren't found in dictionaries.

Neapolitan

In Naples and much of southern Italy, your ear will pick up a highly expressive and unique dialect called Neapolitan. Though it's not officially a language and isn't taught in school, the dialect sounds distinctly different from Italian even though it shares a great deal of vocabulary. The pronunciation of Neapolitan is what largely sets it apart from Italian, although there are significant grammatical differences as well. The dialect can even be almost incomprehensible to Italian speakers. Yet one thing Neapolitans excel at is the use of highly demonstrative gestures, which is a seemingly integral part of communication in the area. Stay long enough and you'll likely find yourself gesturing to communicate as well. The Neapolitan dialect is indelibly linked with the cultural history of Naples, thanks to an especially rich musical, theatrical, and literary heritage that is still appreciated around the world today.

LITERATURE AND PHILOSOPHY

Naples and the surrounding areas have been important cultural centers since ancient Greek and Roman times. South of Paestum, the town Elea (Velia) was home to the Greek philosopher Parmenides, founder of Eleaticism, an important pre-Socratic school of philosophy that also counted philosopher and mathematician Zeno of Elea as a member.

Naples was later a center of Epicureanism, a school of philosophy arguing that pleasure or happiness is the chief good in life. Writings by noted Epicurean philosopher Philodemus of Gadara have been uncovered among the charred papyrus scrolls at the Villa dei Papiri in Herculaneum.

Letters from Mount Vesuvius

Roman writer and natural philosopher Pliny the Elder was among the many victims of the eruption of Mount Vesuvius in AD 79 that destroyed Pompeii and Herculaneum. His nephew, **Pliny the Younger,** wrote two letters to the great historian Tacitus describing the eruption of Vesuvius and death of his uncle; the letters serve as remarkable pieces of historical evidence of the tragic events.

The Roman poet **Virgil** (70-19 BC), author of the epic poem *The Aeneid*, is also associated with Naples, from the legend of the egg he placed below the Castel dell'Ovo to the mysterious allure of his supposed tomb west of Naples (in fact, it is not his tomb at all). Naples was a place of pilgrimage for other writers, as well, including Dante Alighieri (1265-1321), Francesco Petrarca (1304-1374), and Giovanni Boccaccio (1313-1375). Boccaccio lived for years in Naples and used the city as the setting for *The Decameron* and later works.

Influential philosopher and theologian **San Tommaso d'Aquino** (St. Thomas Aquinas) lived and worked in Naples at the Chiesa di San Domenico Maggiore in the 13th century. The city was also home to philosophers Giordano Bruno (1548-1600), Giambattista Vico (1668-1744), and Benedetto Croce (1866-1952), who adopted Naples as his hometown.

Today's Neapolitan Writers

The allure of Naples has continued to tempt many writers over the centuries. More recent examples include Neapolitan writer **Roberto Saviano,** who gained fame for his stories of the Camorra crime syndicate; and bestselling author **Elena Ferrante,** whose Neapolitan novels have captivated readers around the world.

VISUAL ARTS

Architecture

With its remarkable churches, royal palaces, and castles, Naples has an incredibly rich architectural heritage. It's a city that has, at many moments in its history, been a center of culture and arts in Europe. Below the city lie the ruins of the ancient Greek and Roman city, where you can walk down Roman streets, and see ruins of markets as well as a theater where performances were once held. It is fascinating to explore on a Napoli Sotteranea (Naples Underground) tour. Above the ancient city, layer upon layer of history has created modern-day Naples, which is an intriguing blend of soaring Gothic churches and lavishly decorated baroque ones: all masterpieces of architecture, full of artistic treasures around every corner.

GREEK AND ROMAN RUINS

Beyond Naples, the greater region of Campania is home to many remarkable ancient architectural treasures. Just south of Salerno at Paestum you can see some of the best preserved ancient **Greek temples,** and explore the Greek and Roman ruins of the ancient city. The archaeological sites of Pompeii and Herculaneum offer the rare chance to walk through Roman towns and envision moments of daily life. The ruins of the Villa Romana in Minori and a Roman villa below the Chiesa di Santa Maria Assunta in Positano offer a glimpse into Roman seaside villas, and the Villa Jovis on Capri is the once lavish villa where Emperor Tiberius ruled the Roman Empire.

FORTIFIED CITIES

Centuries of turmoil gave the entire coastal region a great deal of defensive architecture. The Amalfi Coast is dotted with **watchtowers,** and in the town of Cetara you can visit the 14th-century Torre di Cetara. **Castles** are abundant in the area, from the Castello Aragonese in Ischia, which was founded in 474 BC, to the 8th-century Castello di Arechi, high above Salerno. In Naples, three of the city's castles are easy to spot: Along the waterfront, the Castel dell'Ovo sits on a small islet where some of the earliest settlers of the city landed. The grand Castel Nuovo, dating from the 13th century, sits right on the waterfront of the city and its dark crenellated towers are an impressive site. High above the city, the Castel Sant'Elmo dates to the 1200s but has a unique hexagonal star-shaped design from the 16th century.

GOTHIC AND BAROQUE CHURCHES

The first of many extraordinary churches in Naples dates to the Angevin rule in the 13th century. The Complesso Monumentale di San Lorenzo Maggiore is a fine example of **Gothic architecture** that has maintained much of its original style. Many churches in Naples were remodeled during the baroque period, a time when creativity flourished and the city became one of the great centers of architecture in Italy. The work of Cosimo Fanzago (1591-1678) exemplifies the Neapolitan baroque style, including his work at the Certosa di San Martino, the Chiesa di San Ferdinando, and various sculptures in Naples, along with the Palazzo Donn'Anna in Posillipo.

Naples is full of **baroque gems,** and inside the Museo Cappella Sansevero, itself a jewel of baroque architectural design, you'll find the superb *Cristo Velato* (Veiled Christ) statue created by Giuseppe Sanmartino (1720-1793). From the end of the 1600s to the beginning of the 1700s, Neapolitan painter, sculptor, and architect Domenico Antonio Vaccaro (1678-1745) worked on many churches in Naples, including the splendid Chiostro Maiolicato (Majolica Cloister) in the Complesso Monumentale di Santa Chiara.

The baroque style was used to remodel churches throughout the area, including the Duomo di Amalfi and the Cattedrale di Salerno, to mention two fine examples in the Amalfi Coast area. Yet it's often the smaller churches that reveal architectural treasures, like the exquisite 18th-century hand-painted ceramic tile floor of the Chiesa Monumentale di San Michele in Anacapri, depicting the Garden of Eden, or the Chiesa del Soccorso atop a picturesque promontory in Forio on the island of Ischia, where you'll find votive offerings of sailing ships incorporated into the architecture.

ROYAL PALACES

As the capital of the Kingdom of Naples, the city is home to many splendid **royal palaces.** In the 17th century, Domenico Fontana (1543-1607) designed the grand Palazzo Reale on the waterfront in Naples, and later Ferdinando Fuga (1699-1782) added the lavish court theater inside. Next came a royal palace in Capodimonte, now the Museo e Real Bosco di Capodimonte, which was built in 1738 in the hills above Naples by the Bourbon king Charles VII as a royal palace for hunting. However, from the beginning it was also used to store the royal art collection and today it is one of the finest art museums in Italy. Yet, the jewel in the crown of royal palaces is the Reggia di Caserta, a masterpiece of 18th-century architecture designed by prominent architect Luigi Vanvitelli (1700-1773). It is one of the largest palaces in Europe, with 1,200 rooms and truly immense monumental gardens.

The shift toward **neoclassicism** in Naples was greatly influenced by the rediscovery of the ruins of Herculaneum in 1738 and Pompeii in 1748, and the re-evaluation of the ancient city of Paestum. Naples was at the forefront of this shift in styles, and classical influences, symmetry, and simplicity reigned in architecture and design. In Piazza del Plebiscito, the grand curved colonnade and the Basilica di San Francesco da Paola, inspired by the Pantheon in Rome, are the most striking examples of neoclassicism in the city. The Villa Pignatelli in Naples is a fine example of neoclassical residential architecture, including references to designs from Pompeii in its elegant facade.

URBAN RENEWAL

The urban footprint of Naples was dramatically changed in the 19th century, during a period called the *Risanamento (Restoration)*, a revival and regeneration of the city similar to large-scale urban renewal projects that took place in other cities across Europe. Streets were widened, and old buildings were cleared and replaced with some of the impressive architectural sights of Naples today, such as the soaring glass dome of the Galleria Umberto I, which was built at the end of the 19th century.

A few interesting examples of **modern and contemporary architecture** can be found while exploring the Campania area, including the unusual Villa Malaparte on Capri, a striking red villa created by Italian writer Curzio Malaparte. In more contemporary times, the Auditorium Oscar Niemeyer in Ravello was opened in 2012 and is named after its Brazilian architect. The venue makes a bold and rare contemporary addition to the UNESCO World Heritage-protected Amalfi Coast. Not far down the coastline, the Stazione Marittima in Salerno, with its sleek roofline and smooth lines, was designed by Zaha Hadid and opened in 2016.

Painting

For a glimpse of incredible frescoes and pictorial decorations from the ancient world, a stroll through the ruins of Pompeii and Herculaneum is a one-of-a-kind experience. Many fine examples of frescoes uncovered at the archaeological sites are on display at Museo Archeologico Nazionale in Naples. You can go back even further in time at the Museo Archeologico Nazionale in **Paestum,** as you admire the Tomb of the Diver, a rare example of an ancient Greek burial tomb with painted figures.

The **Neapolitan School** of painting only began in the 17th century. In 1606, Caravaggio (1571-1610) arrived in Naples, and though he only spent about eight months in the city, his stay created a lasting impression on many artists of the day, including Battistello Caracciolo (1578-1635). In Naples, you'll find impressive works by Caravaggio, including *The Seven Works of Mercy* at the Pio Monte della Misericordia, what is likely his final painting, *Martirio di Sant'Orsola* (*The Martyrdom of Saint Ursula*) at the Gallerie d'Italia, and other works at the Museo di Capodimonte. In addition, you'll find many paintings in churches and museums in Naples by local artists who were inspired by Caravaggio's dramatic use of *chiaroscuro*, defined by its strong contrast between light and dark.

Also very active in the 17th century, the noted Italian painter Luca Giordano (1634-1705) was born in Naples and contributed his lively and particularly colorful style to many churches. Exploring the city's churches, you'll also find masterpieces by local artist Francesco Solimena (1657-1747), who was the most important painter in the 1700s in Naples. In addition to the churches in Naples, head to the Museo di Capodimonte to explore an extensive collection of paintings from the 13th-18th centuries.

By the 19th century, painting styles had become decidedly more naturalistic and romantic, and the **Posillipo School** of painters were drawn to the natural beauty of the Gulf of Naples. Domenico Morelli (1823-1901), a leading artist of the 19th century, was known for his fine historical and religious paintings. He was also an influential professor at the Accademia di Belle Arti di Napoli (Naples Academy of Fine Arts) and later its president. Morelli was the designer of the mosaics depicting the Triumph of Christ and the Twelve Apostles on the facade of the Duomo di Amalfi.

In the 1970s, the **Transavanguardia movement,** an Italian version of neo-expressionism, was developed by a group of artists in Naples, including Francesco Clemente and Mimmo Paladino. Visit the Madre (Museo d'Arte Contemporanea Donnaregina) museum in Naples to see fine examples of their work as well as pieces by other top Italian and international artists from the past 50 years.

Decorative Arts and Crafts

The creative talents of generations of artisans have always brought an artistic touch to daily life in Campania. A strong artisan tradition dating back centuries is still thriving in many locations, from the dramatic baroque-influenced ***presepe*** (nativity), still hand crafted in Naples, to the intricate **intarsia** (inlaid woodwork) in Sorrento. You can still walk down the Via San Gregorio Armeno in the historic center of Naples and see artisans at work creating nativity figures. In Sorrento, the labor-intensive tradition of inlaid woodwork is passed down through generations; many examples of the craft are on display at the excellent Museobottega della Tarsialignea museum dedicated to intarsia.

A strong decorative arts and craft tradition has long flourished on the Amalfi Coast. **Ceramic production** is traditional in the entire area, but is especially strong in the town of Vietri sul Mare on the Amalfi Coast. There you'll find streets lined with ceramic workshops as well as the Museo della Ceramica, a small museum dedicated to the history of ceramic production in Vietri sul Mare. Since ancient times, coral and cameo carving has been a tradition in the Gulf of Naples, especially in Torre del Greco, located between Naples and Pompeii.

Famous for producing European porcelain, Capodimonte flourished under Bourbon control of Naples. The Real Fabbrica di Capodimonte (Royal Factory of Capodimonte) produced remarkable porcelain pieces from 1743-1759, and many fine examples can be seen at the Museo di Capodimonte in Naples. After the Real Fabbrica di Capodimonte was transferred to Madrid, **porcelain production** continued to be a popular local craft throughout the 18th century. Some small factories still produce pieces in the Capodimonte style today.

MUSIC, THEATER, AND DANCE

Music

Nothing captures the spirit of Naples quite like traditional Neapolitan songs, and the city's contributions to musical history began in the 16th century, when many important conservatories were founded. During the baroque period, Alessandro Scarlatti was the founder of the Neapolitan school of opera and was noted for his operas and chamber cantatas. Known as the "conservatory of Europe," Naples was noted not only for its many important composers, such as Domenico Cimarosa, but also for attracting other famous composers like the young Mozart, who was smitten with the city, as well as Gioachino Rossini. Opened in 1737, the Teatro San Carlo is the oldest continuously active opera house in the world.

Starting in the 1800s, traditional Neapolitan popular songs, called *canzone napoletana*, took center stage. Songs like ***"O Sole Mio," "Torna a Surriento,"*** and ***"Funiculì Funiculà"*** became internationally known and are just as popular today. Neapolitan tenor Enrico Caruso had great success in America and was an important ambassador of opera and Neapolitan song around the world. Later, the recordings of Renato Carosone had an international success with songs like "Tu Vuò fà l'Americano," which was later performed by Sophia Loren in the movie *It Started in Naples* with Clark Gable. In Naples, you can enjoy a live performance of iconic Neapolitan songs at Napulitanata (www.napulitanata.com).

Neapolitan music is popular throughout the region of Campania. On the Amalfi Coast, the town of Ravello is known as the City of Music and has a long tradition of opera and other musical performances. In 1880, German composer Richard Wagner visited Ravello and found inspiration for this opera *Parsifal* among the terraced gardens of the Villa Rufolo. This was the origin of a Wagnerian music festival in 1930s that eventually transformed into the **Ravello Festival,** a music and performing arts festival that takes place every summer.

Theater

There's one masked figure that you'll encounter often in Naples. This is **Pulcinella.** With a long nose and distinctive black mask, a baggy white costume, and often a pointy white hat,

Pulcinella is a much loved and often mischievous character from the 17th-century *commedia dell'arte* (art comedy) theater tradition in Italy. The character of Pulcinella inspired many different iterations across Europe, most notably Mr. Punch, of Punch and Judy, in London in the 17th century.

With its vibrant music and literary scene, Naples has been a rich setting for theater. Eduardo Scarpetta (1853-1925) was one of the most notable theatrical actors and writers working in the Neapolitan dialect from the end of the 1800s to the beginning of the 1900s. He created an artistic dynasty that was continued by his son Eduardo de Filippo (1900-1984) and siblings, Peppino and Tatiana de Filippo. Eduardo de Filippo was extremely active as an actor, playwright, screenwriter, and author, and he is considered one of the most important Italian artists of the 20th century.

Naples wouldn't be Naples without **Totò** (1898-1967), one of the most characteristic and entertaining actors, often considered the most popular Italian comedian of all time. Neapolitan through and through, Totò first gained success as a stage actor before appearing in many films from the 1940s-'60s, many of which are still regularly aired on TV. One of the classics is *Totò, Peppino e la Malafemmina,* featuring Totò and Peppino de Filippo and including the beautiful song "*Malafemmena,*" written by Totò.

Dance

Popular throughout southern Italy, the Tarantella is a folk dance, and the **Tarantella Napoletana** is the traditional variation that is connected to Naples. Dating back to the 1700s, it's a lively and flirtatious dance typically performed by couples or groups of couples, and accompanied by tambourines and castanets. You can see performances of the dance in Sorrento at the Sorrento Musical or the Tarantella Show (www.cinemateatroarmida.it).

On Ischia in the small mountain town of Buonopane, the traditional dance **'Ndrezzata** is a fascinating folk dance that features 18 men dressed in traditional fishermen's costumes from the 17th century. The dance, accompanied by a song and rhythmic beating of wooden sticks and swords, is a tradition passed down from one generation to the next. You can see it during the festival of San Giovanni Battista on June 24 and on the Monday following Easter.

Essentials

Transportation

Transportation 441
Visas and Officialdom ..447
Recreation 448
Food 449
Shopping 453
Accommodations 454
Health and Safety 456
Conduct and Customs ..457
Practical Details 460
Traveler Advice 465

GETTING THERE

By Air

The **Aeroporto Internazionale di Napoli** (NAP; Viale F. Ruffo di Calabria; tel. 081/789-6259; www.aeroportodinapoli.it), also referred to as the Capodichino airport, is the Naples International Airport, located about 3.7 miles (6 km) northeast of the city center of Naples. Although it's not a large airport, it handles more than 8.5 million passengers a year and is the main airport for Naples and the region of

Campania, including travelers visiting the Amalfi Coast, Sorrentine Peninsula, and the islands of Capri, Ischia, and Procida.

FROM NORTH AMERICA

Direct flights from the United States to Naples are very limited, but **United** (www.united.com) does offer one daily direct flight from Newark to Naples during the peak travel season, from the end of May through the beginning of October. However, there are more than 50 daily nonstop flights from the United States to Italy, with most landing in Rome or Milan. There are many connecting flights daily from Rome and Milan to Naples. **Alitalia** (www.alitalia.com), **Delta** (www.delta.com), **American** (www.aa.com), **United** (www.united.com), and **Air Canada** (www.aircanada.com), along with their European partners, operate most of the flights from major North American cities to destinations in Italy, with connecting service to Naples.

FROM EUROPE

Alitalia (www.alitalia.com) operates most domestic flights within Italy to Naples. Direct flights to Naples are available from most major cities across Italy as well as from more than 80 European and international cities. There are many direct flights from London, Paris, Frankfurt, and Amsterdam via **Air France** (www.airfrance.com), **BA** (www.britishairways.com), or **Lufthansa** (www.lufthansa.com). Low-cost airlines like **EasyJet** (www.easyjet.com), **Vueling** (www.vueling.com), and **Ryanair** (www.ryanair.com) also fly to Naples from many European capitals and major cities. **Aer Lingus** (www.aerlingus.com) operates flights from Dublin airport, which is equipped with a U.S. immigration office. Passengers are screened in Ireland and bypass customs when returning to the United States.

FROM AUSTRALIA AND NEW ZEALAND

Getting to Italy from down under is a long journey, and there are no direct flights to Naples or even to larger cities like Rome. **Quantas** (www.qantas.com), **Emirates** (www.emirates.com), and **Etihad** (www.etihad.com) operate daily departures to Italy from Sydney, Melbourne, and Perth. Most flights require a transfer in Dubai or Abu Dhabi, and total travel time is around 24 hours. **China Southern** (www.csair.com) is often the cheapest option but requires one or two stops in China and can take up to 40 hours. Travelers from Auckland can transfer in Australia with the above airlines or fly **Qatar** (www.qatarairways.com), **Korean Air** (www.koreanair.com), and **Emirates** on single-stop flights with transfers in Hamad, Seoul, or Dubai. You will then need to catch a connecting flight to reach Naples. Recently **flydubai** (www.flydubai.com), a low cost airline based in Dubai, announced it will be starting direct flights from Dubai to Naples in the summer of 2019.

FROM SOUTH AFRICA

While there are no direct flights from South Africa to Naples, travelers from Durban, Cape Town, and Johannesburg can reach Rome with **Ethiopian Airlines, Qatar, Emirates,** and **Turkish Airlines,** each of which requires a transfer in its respective hub. **Alitalia** offers direct flights (about 10 hours) between Johannesburg and Rome. From Rome, you will need to catch a connecting flight to Naples.

By Train

European train networks are well integrated, but getting between countries by rail can still take a long time. There are daily departures from Paris to Naples onboard the **Thello** (www.thello.com) service that leaves the

Previous: Amalfi Coast ferry

French capital in the early evening and arrives the following morning. If you want to avoid a neck ache, it's worth purchasing a berth in one of the sleeping cabins (*couchettes*). There are also many trains from northern European cities to Naples, often with a transfer in Milan or Rome. Single tickets can be purchased through www.trenitalia.it; if you are on a European vacation and visiting many countries, purchase a rail pass from **Eurail** (www.eurail.com) or **Rail Europe** (www.raileurope.com).

Over the last decade successive Italian governments have invested billions in an expanding network of high-speed tracks that have drastically reduced journey times between Italian cities. Today, traveling to Naples or Salerno from major cities like Milan, Rome, Florence, and Venice is fast, easy, and convenient. There are two operators. The state-owned **Trenitalia** (www.trenitalia.com) and private **Italo** (www.italo.it) both provide frequent daily departures to the Napoli Centrale station in Naples and to Salerno. The Trenitalia **Frecciarossa** (red arrow) service is slightly more expensive and operates more trains, making it popular with business travelers; tourists generally prefer Italo. Both companies use the same track and leave from the same stations. Journey times vary significantly, depending on the type of train and number of stops or transfers, but the high-speed direct journey time to Naples is about 1 hour and 15 minutes from Rome, about 3 hours from Florence, about 5 hours from Venice, and about 4 hours and 30 minutes from Milan. Salerno's train station is also served by both Trenitalia and Italo trains, with the travel time taking 35-40 minutes more than to Naples.

Italian high-speed trains are modern and clean, and are equipped with Wi-Fi, electrical outlets, leather upholstery, snack machines, and bar cars. Tickets can be purchased online or at train stations from automated machines or service booths. The Italo website is easier to navigate and if you sign up for the newsletter you'll receive special offers every month. There are several levels of comfort onboard but even standard seating is adequate.

Trenitalia also operates local and intercity trains throughout Italy. These are slower and make more stops. Tickets are inexpensive, and train interiors have a romantic wear and tear about them. However, it is a very affordable way to reach Naples and Salerno from destinations across Italy.

By Bus

Buses are an inexpensive alternative to trains. **Flixbus** (www.flixbus.com) is the main company offering bus service to Naples and Salerno from many points throughout Italy, and more limited service to Sorrento. Buses seat around 40 passengers with one-way tickets starting as low as €4.99 and rarely exceeding €20. Buses arrive and depart from near the Napoli Centrale train station in Naples, from Piazza della Concordia in Salerno, and from Corso Italia right outside the train station in Sorrento. All are equipped with free Wi-Fi, electrical outlets, restrooms, and baggage storage. There are stops along the way, and travel is two or three times longer than train service.

By Boat

Naples is one of the busiest ports in Italy, handling a large number of ferries, cruise ships, and commercial vessels daily. Many of the cruise ship companies offering Mediterranean cruises stop in Naples. Cruise ships usually dock at the Stazione Marittima. Naples is well connected by ferries from destinations across Italy, including Sicily and Sardinia, as well as destinations around the Mediterranean. Ferries from destinations in the Gulf of Naples, such as Sorrento, Capri, Ischia, and Procida, arrive at either the Molo Beverello near the Stazione Marittima or the Calata Porta di Massa, where larger passenger and vehicle ferries from Ischia, Procida, and Capri arrive. Ferries from Ischia, the Aeolian Islands, and Ponza also arrive at the Mergellina port in Naples.

Farther south, Salerno continues to grow

as a popular cruise ship destination. Ferry service also connects many ports around the Mediterranean to Salerno. Ferry service to the Amalfi Coast and Capri is also available seasonally from April to October.

By Car

The **Schengen Agreement** removed border controls between members of the European Union and made travel hassle-free. Ongoing immigration issues, however, have led some governments to reinstate checks. Entering Italy from France, Switzerland, Austria, or Slovenia isn't a problem, but leaving Italy can be trickier as border officials check incoming vehicles.

As many highways in northern Italy are at high altitudes, snow and fog in winter can lead to delays. Millions of northern Europeans head south during the summer and traffic near crossing points, such as the Brenner Pass and Ventimiglia, is heavy throughout July and August. The 2018 Genova bridge collapse along the A7 highway will disrupt traffic to and from France until it is rebuilt. Smaller roads that cross the Alps are best driven during the day at low speeds.

Italy's **highways** *(autostrade)* are generally very good. Drivers collect tickets at booths as they enter the network and pay tolls in cash or credit, based on distance traveled, upon exiting highways. **Autostrade** (www.autostrade.it) manages highways and provides real-time traffic information in English. Signage should be familiar to drivers from around the world; however, there's a much greater use of **yield,** and **roundabouts** are frequent in urban areas. To review the rules of the Italian road, visit the **Italian Office of Tourism** (www.italia.com).

GETTING AROUND

By Train

Trenitalia (www.trenitalia.com) operates frequent train service between Naples and Salerno daily with travel times ranging from 40 minutes to 1 hour 25 minutes, depending on the type of train. Salerno is the closest major train station to the Amalfi Coast. From the station you can catch buses to the Amalfi Coast or walk a short distance to the port nearby, where ferries depart for the Amalfi Coast towns and to Capri seasonally from April to October.

The **Circumvesuviana train** line operated by EAV (www.eavsrl.it) connects Naples with the archaeological sites of Pompeii and Herculaneum as well as Sorrento. The full journey from Naples to Sorrento takes about 60 minutes. This regional commuter train runs frequently throughout the day and is an inexpensive way to travel between Naples and Sorrento. To reach the Amalfi Coast from Sorrento, you can catch a bus right outside the Sorrento train station.

For the Campi Flegrei area, the **Cumana and Circumflegrea train lines** also operated by EAV depart from Naples at Montesanto station. From the Napoli Centrale station, you can take the Trenitalia metro Linea 2 to Montesanto to connect to the Cumana and Circumflegrea lines.

By Car and Scooter

Cars can be rented from **Avis** (www.avisautonoleggio.it), **Budget** (www.budgetautonoleggio.it), **Europcar** (www.europcar.com), **Sixt** (www.sixt.com), **Maggiore** (www.maggiore.com), **Hertz** (www.hertz.com), and other companies upon arrival at the Aeroporto Internazionale di Napoli, from rental offices located near the train stations in Naples and Salerno, or with smaller local companies along the Amalfi Coast. **Skyscanner** (www.skyscanner) and **Kayak** (www.kayak.com) can help find the best rental prices.

Naples is famous for its chaotic traffic, and driving in the city is not for the timid. Given the extensive public transportation system, challenging parking, and the **limited traffic zone** (ZTL) in the historic center of Naples, getting around by car in Naples is not recommended. It's best to park at a supervised lot and continue to explore the city via public transportation.

The Amalfi Coast Road is famous for

its beautiful views and twists and turns. However, the road is not the easiest to negotiate and parking is limited, so getting around the area by car can be more of a hassle than it's worth. Scooters are a popular choice because they're easier to maneuver along the winding road and are usually easier to park as well. With extremely narrow and busy roads, it's also not recommended to get around the islands of Capri, Ischia, and Procida by car. The small size of Capri and Procida make public transportation a good choice. Ischia is larger, and renting a scooter can be helpful for getting around the island. You'll find scooter rental agencies in many of the towns along the Amalfi Coast, as well as Sorrento, Capri, Ischia, and Procida.

RULES AND DOCUMENTATION

You'll need a **passport** and a **driver's license** if you plan to rent a scooter or car. (Specify automatic transmission for cars if you're unfamiliar with manual drive.) For U.S. citizens, an **international driver's permit** is not required but can help you avoid confusion if you're pulled over. It's available from **AAA** (www.aaa.com) for $20. The **minimum driving age** in Italy is 18. Police and *Carabinieri* frequently set up control posts along roads and randomly stop cars. The **blood alcohol limit** in Italy is 0.5 which is lower than in the United States and UK (both 0.8) but is on par with most European nations.

DRIVING WARNING AND RECOMMENDATIONS

Whether you rent a car or scooter, always get the maximum insurance. Anything can happen on Italian roads, especially the ones around Naples and the Amalfi Coast. If you observe cars carefully, you'll notice a high percentage of dents on many vehicles. Most cars are manual transmission, so be sure to request or reserve automatic if you're not comfortable tackling the mountains and tight curves of the Amalfi Coast with a stick shift.

In contrast to the relaxing atmosphere in a lot of the coastal areas, drivers in the area are usually in a hurry. Passing is a very common practice, especially on the Amalfi Coast. If traffic seems to want to move faster than you're comfortable, find a straight section to slow down or pull over to let traffic pass. Naturally, if you're the one passing, pay extra careful attention to the curves, taking advantage of the mirrors placed on the side of the road in especially tight curves for guidance. Scooters, motorcycles, and cyclists can appear very suddenly around curves, so it's best for drivers who are unfamiliar with the road to go with the flow of traffic.

By Bus

On the **Amalfi Coast**, buses are operated by **SITA SUD** (www.sitasudtrasporti.it), with Amalfi as the central hub. The main lines run from Amalfi to Sorrento and from Amalfi to Salerno, with stops in all of the towns along the way. Buses for Ravello and Scala depart from Amalfi. In Positano, an internal bus line operated by **Mobility Amalfi Coast** (info@mobilityamalficoast.com) circles through the town's internal road and extends to the hamlets located in the mountains above.

For the **Sorrentine Peninsula**, buses are operated by both **SITA SUD** (www.sitasudtrasporti.it) and **EAV** (www.eavsrl.it). Within Sorrento, EAV runs four lines that circulate around the city, connecting main spots like Marina Piccola, Piazza Tasso, and the train station. To explore the Sorrentine Peninsula, EAV has bus lines connecting Sorrento to Massa Lubrense, while **SITA SUD** buses run from the train station in Sorrento to Massa Lubrense, Nerano, Marina del Cantone, and Sant'Agata sui Due Golfi.

On **Capri,** the island's small public buses are operated by **A.T.C.** (tel. 081/837-0420) and connect all the main points on Capri, including Marina Grande, Capri town, Anacapri, Marina Piccola, Punta Carena, and the Grotta Azzurra. **Ischia** and **Procida** are well connected via many bus lines that go to all the towns on the islands. All buses are operated by **EAV** (www.eavsrl.it) and offer an inexpensive option for exploring the island.

While you're in Naples, you can get around on public buses operated by **ANM** (www.anm.it). The large bus transit network covers the city center day and night. The **City Sightseeing** (www.city-sightseeing.it) hop-on hop-off buses in Naples are often more convenient for reaching top sights in the historic center. They also offer a line from the historic center to the Museo di Capodimonte, another line along the coastline in Posillipo, and a shuttle to the Reggia di Caserta. From Sorrento, City Sightseeing runs a hop-on hop-off route around the Sorrentine Peninsula, as well as a route from Sorrento to Positano and Amalfi. On the Amalfi Coast, you can catch their easy-to-spot red open-top buses that run between Amalfi, Ravello, Minori, and Maiori. For City Sightseeing buses, you can purchase tickets directly onboard and they come with an audio guide.

Tickets in all cities must be **validated** upon boarding the bus; this is done with a small machine located near the driver. Controllers do occasionally check passengers and will fine anyone without a ticket. Daily and multiday travel cards are available in most areas and can be more convenient and affordable than single tickets.

By Boat

Ferries are the most comfortable and scenic modes of transportation between destinations in the Gulf of Naples and Gulf of Salerno. **Travelmar** (www.travelmar.it) and **Alicost** (www.alicost.it) are the main ferry companies connecting Salerno, the Amalfi Coast, Capri, and Sorrento. On the Amalfi Coast, ferry service runs between Positano, Amalfi, Minori, Maiori, Cetara, and Salerno. Amalfi and Positano serve as the main ferry terminals on the Amalfi Coast with the most departures daily. In Positano, **Positano Jet** (www.lucibello.it) also offers ferry service connecting Positano, Amalfi, and Capri. Ferry service is highly seasonal on the Amalfi Coast, running from April through the beginning of November.

The Naples port (www.porto.napoli.it) is very large and offers frequent ferry connections to destinations around the Gulf of Naples, including Sorrento and the islands of Capri, Ischia, and Procida. Many different companies operate ferry service from Naples, ranging from high-speed jets to *aliscafo* (hydrofoil) and slower *traghetti* (ferries) that transport passengers and vehicles. **NLG** (www.navlib.it) operates jet routes to Capri and Sorrento, while **Gescab** (www.gescab.it) has jet routes from Naples to Capri and Sorrento as well. **SNAV** (www.snav.it) operates lines to Ischia, Procida, and Capri. **Alilauro** (www.alilaurogruson.it) has routes connecting Naples to Sorrento and Ischia. To transfer vehicles, you'll need to book through **Caremar** (www.caremar.it) for ferry service to Sorrento, Capri, Ischia, and Procida, or **Medmar** (www.medmargroup.it) for service to Ischia and Procida. Ferry departures are also available from the Mergellina port in Naples to Ischia with **Alilauro** (www.alilaurogruson.it). Though ferry service is available year-round from Naples, the number of ferries daily is reduced during the winter months. Ferry service direct from Naples to the Amalfi Coast is not available, but you can take a ferry to Sorrento and Capri and connect to ferry services to the Amalfi Coast; these are available seasonally (usually May-Oct.).

All ferries to Capri arrive in the island's Marina Grande port. Service is seasonal from Salerno, the Amalfi Coast, and the islands of Ischia and Procida, while it is available year round from Sorrento and Naples. On Ischia, the island's main port is in Ischia town, with more limited ferry service to the towns of Casamicciola Terme and Forio. Procida is connected by frequent ferry service from Ischia and Naples, and all ferries arrive in the port of Marina Grande. Ferries to Ischia and Procida run throughout the year from Naples, while they operate seasonally during the summer from Capri, Sorrento, and the Amalfi Coast.

You can purchase tickets in advance online from most ferry companies, which is a good idea during the busy summer months. Tickets are also available to purchase before boarding from ticket booths in the ports.

By Taxi

In Naples, cabs are stationed at taxi stands near large squares, at the train station, and near the port, day and night. Vehicles are privately owned and range in size. They are usually white and topped with signage that indicates whether cars are free or in service. Spontaneously hailing taxis is possible but rarely done by locals. It's easier to get a taxi at a taxi stand or to reserve one by phone. Response time is fast and travelers rarely wait more than ten minutes. Call the local companies Radio Taxi (tel. 081/8888; www.radiotaxinapoli.it), Consortaxi (tel. 081/2222; www.consortaxi.it), or Radio Taxi La Partenope (tel. 081/0101; www.radiotaxilapartenope.it). Taxis operate 24 hours, and vehicles for special-needs passengers are available.

Taxi fares in Naples are relatively high and are calculated according to time and distance. Weekend and night rates are higher. Drivers don't expect tips but fares can be rounded up to the nearest euro. Fixed tariffs for popular journeys are set by the city of Naples and rates must be posted inside the taxi. However, it is essential to notify the driver before departure that you want the fixed-rate fare. The same goes for Capri, Ischia, and Procida, where you'll want to inquire about fares in advance in order to avoid a higher rate than expected upon arrival.

Taxis on the Amalfi Coast can be found in the center of most towns. It's important to note that taxis in this area function more like private transfers than a taxi, with costs much higher than a city taxi. Many cities have fixed tariffs determined by the city for journeys between towns on the Amalfi Coast, but some do not. If there are not fixed-rate fares, try to negotiate a rate with the driver in advance.

Visas and Officialdom

PASSPORTS AND VISAS

United States and Canada

Travelers from the United States and Canada do not need a visa to enter Italy for visits of 90 days or less. All that's required is a passport valid at least three months after your intended departure from the European Union.

EU/Schengen

Citizens from all 28 countries belonging to the European Union can travel visa-free within the European Union. The United Kingdom will remain a full member of the European Union until its exit is made official.

Australia and New Zealand

Visas are not required for Australian or New Zealand citizens who visit Italy for 90 days or less within any 180-day period in the Schengen Area (European Union). New Zealanders between the ages of 18 and 30 can apply for a special working holiday visa at the Italian Embassy in Wellington.

South Africa

Visas are required to visit Italy from South Africa and can be obtained through **Capago** (tel. 087/231-0313, www.capago.eu). The application process begins online and requires stopping into one of the visa application centers located in Cape Town, Durban, Sandton, and Pretoria. Getting a visa takes two weeks and there is a fee.

Electronic Registration

In 2021, a pre-travel electronic registration system (European Travel Information and Authorisation System or ETIAS) is planned for travelers from Schengen visa-waiver countries. If traveling in or after 2021, be sure to check with the state department or foreign affairs ministry in your home country for more information.

CONSULATES

The majority of foreign embassies and consulates in Italy are located in Rome. However, the **U.S. Consulate General in Naples** (Piazza della Repubblica, Naples; tel. 081/583-8111; https://it.usembassy.gov/embassy-consulates/naples) offers passport and emergency services for U.S. citizens. For emergencies, call the consulate at 081/583-8111, which is a 24-hour hotline. For help with **lost or stolen passports,** you can apply in person for same-day emergency passports at the consulate in Naples. The consulate is closed during Italian and U.S. holidays. For bureaucratic questions before arriving to Italy call the **U.S. Department of State** (tel. 1-888/407-4747 from the United States, 1-202/501-4444 from other countries; 8am-8pm EST Mon.-Fri.).

CUSTOMS

Travelers entering Italy are expected to declare any cash over €10,000 and are prohibited from importing animal-based food products into the country. Duty-free imports for passengers from outside the European Union are limited to one liter of hard alcohol, two liters of wine, 200 cigarettes, 50 cigars, and 250 grams of smoking tobacco.

Bags are likely to be heavier upon leaving Italy than they were when you packed. U.S. citizens are limited to $800 worth of goods deemed for personal use. Anything over that amount must be declared and will be taxed. Fresh fruit and vegetables, cheese, and animal-based products are not allowed into the United States. Further details regarding what can and cannot be imported into the country are available from the **U.S. Department of State** (www.state.gov).

Canadian regulations are fairly lenient and allow cheese, herbs, condiments, dried fruits, baked goods, and candies; for a complete list, visit the **Canadian Border Services Agency** (www.cbsa-asfc.gc.ca). Australian regulations are particularly stringent and customs officers go to great lengths to avoid contamination. All fruit, vegetables, and meat products are forbidden. Fake designer goods will also be confiscated and may lead to a fine. If you're in doubt, consult the **Australian Department of Immigration and Border Protection** (www.border.gov.au).

Recreation

HIKING

Outdoor enthusiasts will find plenty of fine hiking opportunities on the Amalfi Coast, Sorrentine Peninsula, and the islands of Capri and Ischia. Most walks are along stone steps and pathways, but you can certainly go deeper into the woods of the Monte Lattari, the mountains that run down the Sorrentine Peninsula. Hiking boots are not essential for most hikes in the area, unless you're doing serious hiking up into the mountains or are more comfortable with the support. For the walks and hikes included in this book, regular sneakers or athletic shoes with support will be fine. Most hikes include a significant change in altitude, so do be prepared for a lot of steps and steep walking up or down. However, the fine views are a wonderful compensation for the effort.

BEACHES

The beaches are among the biggest draws to the Amalfi Coast and islands in the Gulf of Naples. Similar to the rugged and mountainous landscape, the beaches here are rocky and tucked away in scenic spots along the coastline. Expect anything from small pebbles to larger rocks on the beaches instead of fine sand. A handful of beaches do have finer dark sand, but it's a good idea to pack water shoes or flip-flops to make walking on the beaches and wading into the sea more comfortable.

Going to the beach in Italy might be a different experience from what you're used to at home. Beaches are divided into two areas, one that is free and the other where you must pay to gain access. The free areas are called *spiaggia libera*, literally meaning free beach, where you can simply throw down a towel and enjoy swimming. However, if you see rows of sun beds and umbrellas neatly lined up, that is a *stabilimente balneare*, or a private beach club. To access those beach areas, you will need to rent a sun bed and umbrella for the day. The rental also includes beach services that vary depending on the size of the *stabilimente balneare*, but usually you'll have access to changing rooms and showers. Most *stabilimenti balneari* will also offer snack bar and drink options, or even complete seaside restaurants. Given the rocky nature of the beaches, renting a sun bed and having beach services is certainly the most comfortable way to enjoy a relaxing day at the beach.

WATER SPORTS

Water sports are not as popular in the Amalfi Coast area as might be expected. Yet there are some great experiences to be had, and many are highlighted in individual chapters about areas offering water sports options. Kayaking is one of the best ways to experience the coastlines of the Amalfi Coast and Sorrentine Peninsula up close. Glide along the sea to discover little coves and beaches only accessible from the sea and swim in secluded spots. To explore the undersea beauty of the region, there are scuba diving centers on the Amalfi Coast, Sorrentine Peninsula, Capri, and Ischia. For a one of a kind experience, go diving or snorkeling through ancient Roman ruins underwater in the Parco Archeologico Sommerso di Baia in the Gulf of Pozzuoli.

Food

ITALIAN EATERIES

Restaurants

The most common sit-down eateries are **trattorias, *osterie,*** and ***ristoranti.*** The first two have humble origins and are cheaper than a *ristorante.* The typical trattoria serves local dishes within a rustic atmosphere. The best have been in business for generations and have a devoted local following. Service can be ad hoc, and waiters are not overly concerned with formality. An *osteria* is similar, but has fewer items on the menu and rarely strays from tradition. A *ristorante* is more expensive and elegant, with uniformed waiters, an extensive wine cellar along with a sommelier, and fine table settings. Menus often diverge from tradition and combine flavors in novel ways. All three types of eateries are open lunch and dinner, but continuous service throughout the day is not the norm. During the summer months on the Amalfi Coast and Capri, you can usually find a handful of restaurants in the main piazzas that are open continuously from lunch through dinner.

Pizzerias

With the strong Neapolitan pizza tradition, you don't have to go far to find an excellent pizzeria. In Naples, there are pizzerias dedicated just to making the classic wood-fire oven pizza. There the menus will focus only on pizza and sometimes a few appetizer options. However, on the Amalfi Coast, islands, and remaining areas in Campania, most pizzerias also offer trattoria or *ristorante* menu options.

Street Food

The most popular street food in Naples is pizza. Both ***pizza al taglio*** (pizza by the slice) style and ***pizza fritta*** (fried pizza) are available in small food shops from midmorning

Dine Like a Local

Italians have their own way of doing things, especially when it comes to food. Here's how to blend in with locals:

- **Embrace a light breakfast.** Forget about eggs and bacon. Sidle up to locals at the nearest bar and order a cappuccino and a pastry. While the *cornetti* (croissants) are a top choice, try other local specialties like the *sfogliatella*, a crunchy and flaky pastry shell filled with citrus-infused ricotta.
- **Know the coffee culture.** Italians drink coffee at specific times. Cappuccinos are rarely ordered after noon or in restaurants, and should never accompany or immediately precede a meal. Instead, espressos are ordered at the end of lunch and/or dinner, and during midday or midafternoon breaks.
- **Skip the salt and olive oil.** Salt, pepper, olive oil, and *parmigiano* (Parmesan) aren't a given on restaurant tables, so don't expect to find them wherever you go. *Parmigiano* is not served with every type of pasta and will often only appear when it is considered appropriate for a dish. Note that *parmigiano* is not served with fish-based pasta dishes.
- **Forget about eating on the go.** Italians eat standing at bars and sitting at restaurants, but you'll rarely see them eating while they walk. The only exception is gelato, which makes strolling through historic streets even better.
- **Accept the slowness.** Service may be slower than you're used to. It might be hard to get the waiter's attention, or the second bottle of wine may never arrive. Just remember the sun is probably shining and you are in Italy. A little patience along with good-natured persistence will ensure a pleasant time. Frustration won't. Remember that your bill will not be brought to your table until you request it.

onward. These standing-room-only shops with little or no seating offer varieties of pizza waiting to be cut, and customers line up to order. In Naples you can also find excellent *friggitoria* (fried food shop) options, which offer *pizza fritta*, fried pizza filled with a variety of options like ricotta and salami, as well as other typical fried snacks like frittata of pasta or fried rice balls: They make a tasty and inexpensive snack while sightseeing.

By midmorning, coffee bars will begin serving ***panini*** (sandwiches) stacked behind glass counters. These cost €2-4 and can be eaten at the counter or table, or taken away. *Tavola calda* (cafeterias) offer home cooked-style selections of first- and second-course dishes. They offer complete meals with water and coffee for about €15.

Bakeries and *Pasticceria*

Fornaio (bakeries) open before dawn and remain busy until midafternoon. There's one in every neighborhood in bigger towns and cities and they supply locals with all types of bread, buns, and sweets. You'll also find cakes, cookies, tarts, pastries, and unique treats served during holidays. Most items are priced by the kilo and purchased for takeaway.

Pasticceria shops are entirely dedicated to sweets; they open early in the morning and remain busy until midafternoon. If combined with a coffee bar, they may be open all day long and late into the night. They prepare cookies, tarts, and cakes along with an array of smaller finger-sized pastries that Italians serve as midafternoon snacks (*merenda*) or offer to visiting friends. Some *pasticceria* serve coffee and prepare one or two signature items for which they are famous. The Neapolitan tradition of pastries is strong in the entire area, and there are unique varieties of cakes and sweets to be found from Naples to the Amalfi Coast and islands. On the Amalfi

Coast, try the lemon-infused sweets like the *delizia al limone*, a cake with lemon filling and topped with a lemon cream. Procida is famous for its *lingue di bue* (ox tongues), a name that refers to the pastry's long, oval shape. This puff pastry dessert filled with lemon cream can only be found on the island. In Capri, you'll often find *torta Caprese*: a rich flourless almond and chocolate cake.

Coffee Bars

Coffee bars and cafés open nearly as early as bakeries and provide different services throughout the day. In the morning, they supply locals with espressos or cappuccinos and **cornetti** (croissants), which are either plain or filled with cream, jelly, or chocolate. *Cornetti* rarely exceed €1 and provide a cheap and tasty way to start the day. Most bars are supplied by bakeries, but some have their own ovens.

Bars usually operate on a "consume now, pay later" policy, with a dedicated cashier off to one side who calculates checks. Counter service is cheaper and faster, and that's where most locals do their eating and drinking. Sitting at table to linger over your coffee and pastries will cost more than standing inside, but the experience may be worth it. If you're sitting at a **café** in Capri's Piazzetta or the Piazza Duomo in Amalfi, you can expect prices to be higher than what you'd pay at a small bar tucked away on a small street. In other words, you'll pay for the view and atmosphere, and the tables outside are usually filled with tourists.

Gelaterie

Gelaterie (ice cream shops) are nearly as common as bars in Italy and stay open late during the summer. They specialize in gelato and sorbet, which come in countless flavors. The best gelato is made on the spot with seasonal ingredients, while less passionate owners cut corners by using preservatives and compressed air to give gelato bright colors and gravity-defying forms. Gelato is priced by the scoop and served in a cone or cup.

MENUS

Italian menus are divided into courses with an established order. ***Antipasti*** (starters) are first, and can be as simple as *bruschette* (toasted bread topped with tomatoes) or *fiori di zucchini* (fried zucchini flowers stuffed with cheese). The point of *antipasti* is to relieve hunger and prepare stomachs for the meal to come. House starters *(antipasto della casa)* are a safe bet, and plates of local cold cuts and cheeses are meant to be shared.

The ***primo*** (first course) can be pasta, risotto, or soup. There are hundreds of traditional pasta shapes, all of which are combined with particular sauces that include vegetables, meat, or fish. Pasta with seafood is featured at many restaurants, especially on the coast and islands. Risotto is often served with a simple yet beautiful lemon infusion, or with fish or crustaceans.

While it's fine to order just one course, try to leave room for the ***secondo*** (second course). It consists of meat or fish and is the gastronomic main event. Let waiters know if you want meat rare *(al sangue)*, medium rare *(cotta)*, or well done *(ben cotta)*. Unless you order a ***contorno*** (side), your fish or steak will be lonely. These generally consist of grilled vegetables or roasted potatoes and are listed at the end of the menu along with desserts and drinks.

Restaurants often have a separate wine menu and daily specials, which waiters will translate when possible. Food is relatively inexpensive in Italy, and a satisfying three-course lunch or dinner with dessert and coffee runs around €25-40 per person.

DRINKS

Italy has hundreds of natural springs, and Italians drink more **mineral water** per capita than any other people in the world. The first question waiters often ask is the type of ***acqua*** (water) you want. You can choose between ***frizzante*** (sparkling) or ***naturale*** (still). A liter costs around €3, and sometimes there's a choice of brands. That's not to say ***acqua del rubinetto*** (tap water) is bad. It's regularly tested by authorities and safe to drink.

It's difficult to find a restaurant that doesn't have a decent **wine** list. Many eateries have a separate wine menu that includes local, regional, and international bottles. House wine is also available and generally very good. It can be ordered by the glass or in different-sized carafes.

Most Italians end lunch with an **espresso** and usually conclude dinner with a ***digestivo*** (digestif). The latter is some kind of high-grade alcoholic spirit infused with a variety of fruits or herbs and reputed to help digestion. The most famous of these in the area is *limoncello*, a very strong lemon-infused liqueur. It is served ice-cold in small glasses and is sipped. Each area has its typical *digestivo* options to try, including other citrus fruits, wild fennel, or licorice liqueurs on the Amalfi Coast, and the *rucola* liqueur infused with arugula (rocket) made on Ischia. **Soft drinks** are widely available but are not often seen on Italian restaurant tables.

REGIONAL AND SEASONAL SPECIALTIES

The Mediterranean coastal setting of the Amalfi Coast and surrounding areas means **seafood** is the top regional specialty that you'll find on nearly every menu. Yet that doesn't mean you won't find anything you'll like if you don't care for seafood or are vegetarian or vegan. The regional cuisine is divided into *mare* (sea) and *terra* (land), reflecting the sea and the mountainous setting as well as the strong agricultural tradition of Campania. The majority of dining spots, even ones specializing in seafood, will have *primi* and *secondi* options highlighting seasonal vegetables and meat as well.

If you do enjoy seafood, you are in for some excellent gastronomic experiences, as it is fresh and prepared in an unfussy way that highlights the natural flavors. You'll often find spaghetti or linguine with *vongole* (clams) or *cozze* (mussels). Pasta with freshly caught fish is another classic, as is grilled or baked fish for a second course. Cetara, a small fishing village on the Amalfi Coast, is noted for *alici* (anchovies), which are prepared in a variety of ways. Squid and octopus are also popular, and are served fried as an appetizer, prepared with pasta or potatoes, and grilled or stuffed for *secondi*. Even if you've not tried squid or even *ricci* (sea urchins), it's well worth stepping out of your comfort zone to try the regional seafood specialties.

Though Campania isn't particularly noted for its steak like some other regions of Italy, you will still find nicely prepared beef on many menus. The local tradition, especially on the Amalfi Coast, leans more toward **pork.** The sausage is excellent, especially in the autumn when it's served grilled with the seasonal broccoli. Rabbit is traditional on the islands of Ischia and Procida, especially on the slopes of Monte Epomeo on Ischia.

Vegetables and legumes are important parts of the traditional Campania diet, especially when it comes to home cooking. Pasta with zucchini is a classic dish to try in Nerano, a seaside town near the tip of the Sorrentine Peninsula, and in many other towns on the Amalfi Coast. Pasta is also served with chickpeas, beans, and lentils. Some areas are known to combine *mare* and *terra* with dishes like a thick soup of *cozze e fagioli* (mussels and beans). Grilled locally grown vegetables are a popular antipasto, as is the famous *parmigiana di melanzane* (eggplant parmesan). Vegetables appear on menus very seasonally, from artichokes and asparagus in the spring to zucchini, eggplant, and peppers in the summer, and pumpkin and broccoli in the autumn. Other notable seasonal specialties include Amalfi Coast chestnuts, which are celebrated in the town of Scala with a food festival every October.

Nothing compares to **pizza in Naples,** where it is truly a gastronomic art form. Be sure to try the classic pizza Margherita topped with tomatoes, mozzarella, basil, and olive oil. Or go even more traditional by enjoying the pizza marinara with tomatoes, oregano, garlic, extra virgin olive oil, and no cheese. Of course, you'll find plenty of options for toppings at most pizzerias. In Naples, you won't want to miss the *pizza fritta* (fried pizza). This is a pizza filled with a variety of different fillings, like ricotta and salami, which is then folded in half and fried. Forget the diet for the day—you're in Naples!

No visit to the Amalfi Coast region is complete without trying the local lemons. It's an easy task since the famous lemons cultivated in the area are incorporated into many of the regional specialties. Squeeze lemons over your fresh fish or salad, enjoy traditional lemon desserts, like *delizia al limone*, and finish off your meal with a chilled glass of *limoncello*, a lemon-infused liqueur.

HOURS

Restaurants are typically open 12:30pm-2:30pm for lunch and 7:30pm-10:30pm for dinner. Most close one day a week, except for during the peak of summer, and many take an extended break from January to March in the coastal areas and islands. Reservations aren't usually necessary, but to guarantee a seat at especially popular eateries it's wise to book ahead or to arrive early or late. Bakeries open before sunrise and close in the midafternoon, while coffee bars remain open all day long and pizzerias and *gelaterie* stay open late. Italians tend to eat later in summer when they wait for the sun to set and temperatures to fall.

TIPPING

Tipping is neither required nor expected in Italy. Most restaurants include a €1-3 surcharge *(coperto)* for bread, utensils, and service per customer. Waiters earn a decent living, but rounding your bill up or leaving €3-5 behind after a good meal is one way to show appreciation. The other way to express gastronomic gratitude is with words. Italians are proud of their cuisine and compliments are always welcome. Customers at coffee bars often leave a low-denomination coin on the counter.

Shopping

The majority of family-owned shops are dedicated to one thing and one thing only. This can be a single product like shoes, hats, books, clothing, or furniture, or materials like leather, ceramics, paper, or glass. These shops are true treasures in Campania, where you can often see artisans at work painting ceramics on the Amalfi Coast, carving wood in Sorrento, or creating the traditional *presepe* (nativity) figures in Naples.

Most businesses are small and have few employees. Department and flagship stores exist in the center of Naples and Salerno but attract as many tourists as locals, who often shop more at malls and outlets on the outskirts of cities. If you're looking for luxury boutiques, you'll find them concentrated around Via Dei Mille in Naples and even more in the shopping haven that is Capri. From the Piazzetta down Via Vittorio Emanuele and along Via Camerelle, you'll find just about every name in high-end Italian and international fashion design.

SHOPPING ETIQUETTE

Italians entering a shop (or bar) nearly always greet shopkeepers with *buongiorno* or *buonasera* (good morning/good evening). Most shop owners and employees are not overbearing and welcome browsing. They're happy to leave shoppers alone; however, they are professional and helpful once you demonstrate interest in an item and will happily find your size or explain how something is made. When leaving a store, it's traditional to say *grazie* (thank you) or *arrivederci* (goodbye), regardless of whether you've made a purchase.

SHIPPING ITEMS HOME

Don't worry if something that's larger than your suitcase catches your eye. Stores, especially ones selling ceramics, are accustomed to tourists and can arrange for shipment directly to your door. Expect to pay up to 10 percent of the purchase price for home delivery.

SALES

January to February and July to August are the best times to shop in Campania. All stores begin the official sale season in unison during these months and windows are plastered with discounts. Every price tag should contain the original and sale price. Check items carefully before buying and don't hesitate to try clothes on, as Italian sizes generally run smaller and fit slightly differently. The sale season lasts for more than a month, but most of the good stuff and sought-after sizes disappear after the first couple of weeks.

HOURS

Italy has its own unique rhythm, and nowhere is that more evident than in shops. Family-owned stores and smaller businesses nearly always close between 1pm and 3pm. Many also close on Sundays and Monday mornings. However, larger stores and those located in heavily trafficked areas have continuous hours. If you're shopping in Naples, Salerno, and on Ischia, do plan on shops closing mid-afternoon for a break. However, if you're in Amalfi, Positano, Sorrento, or Capri, you'll find shops open daily and with continuous hours. If you're traveling off season, many shops on the Amalfi Coast and Capri close for a period after Christmas through early spring, but the length of time varies from a couple of weeks to a month or longer. Just keep in mind that from early January through March many shops will be closed in those areas. This is not the case in larger cities like Salerno and Naples.

Accommodations

MAKING RESERVATIONS

The Amalfi Coast and Capri are among the most popular travel destinations in Italy, so accommodations can fill up very quickly. Despite the large number of accommodation options on the Amalfi Coast, many hotels in the area can be fully booked well in advance. If you have your eye on a particular hotel for its features or views, it's wise to book ahead of time, especially if you're going to be traveling from July to August. Yet even during the shoulder seasons certain hotels can be booked up many months ahead of time. Lower priced hotels in Positano, Amalfi, and Capri fill up especially fast. Keep in mind that many hotels or B&Bs might only have a handful of rooms and are relatively small compared to large chain hotels in other parts of the world.

Accommodations in Naples and Salerno are open throughout the year, but most hotels on the Amalfi Coast, Sorrentine Peninsula, and islands of Capri, Ischia, and Procida close for a period in the winter. This may be the entire winter season from November to March or for a shorter period from January to March. Some smaller B&Bs will operate year round or you will find vacation apartment rentals available throughout the winter season in these areas.

HOTELS

Italian hotels are graded on a system of stars that ranges from one to five. How many stars an establishment receives depends on infrastructure and services. Criteria varies from region to region, but most three-star hotels are quite comfortable. The Amalfi Coast is a very popular tourist destination, and the quality of accommodations on the coast and other areas covered in this book is very high. Breakfast is included, and all hotel rooms include en suite bathrooms. Reservations can be made online and most hotels have multilingual websites. A **passport** or ID card is required when checking in and early arrivals can usually leave luggage at the front desk. Many smaller hotels operate a "leave the key" policy in which keys must be left and retrieved whenever entering or leaving the accommodation.

Valuables are best carried or deposited in a hotel safe if one is available. In addition to the room rate, expect to be charged a city **hotel tax** of €1.50-5 per guest/per day depending on the number of stars and accommodation type. (Kids younger than 10 are exempt.) Some towns only collect the city hotel tax seasonally from April to November while others charge you year-round. The city tax is usually required to be paid in cash when you leave. It's a small price to pay for waking up in beautiful spots like Amalfi, Positano, or Capri.

HOSTELS

Hostels (*ostelli*) aren't just for young travelers; there's no maximum age limit to stay in one. They provide clean, affordable accommodation and many are less sparse than you might expect. Most include single, double, and quad options in addition to classic dormitory-style rooms. A bed starts around €20 per person and may include breakfast. Expect higher than usual hostel rates in locations like Positano. The best thing about hostels, however, is the feeling of community. They're filled with travelers from all over at various stages of round-the-world adventures. Bathrooms are often shared, although many also have private rooms with en suite baths. Italian hostels are overseen by the **Associazione Italiana Alberghi per la Gioventù** (tel. 06/487-1152; www.aighostels.it).

BED AND BREAKFASTS AND APARTMENTS

Italy has experienced a **B&B** boom over the last decade and the country now offers thousands of options. It allows you not only to stay with local residents and gain an insider's perspective but also to enjoy a truly local stay.

To feel truly at home while on holiday, rent an **apartment** or **villa** to get an instant native feel. Short-term rental is especially convenient for families and groups of traveling friends. Not only are prices lower than many hotels, but also staying in an apartment allows you to call the mealtime shots and relax in a home away from home. **Airbnb** (www.airbnb.com) and **VRBO** (www.vrbo.com) offer a wide variety of options on the Amalfi Coast and surrounding areas. A word to the wise if you're considering a short-term vacation rental on the Amalfi Coast: Be sure to check for the number of stairs to access the property. Though most hotels have easy access or elevators available, many private residences or villas may require climbing a significant number of steps to reach the property. If number of steps or access information is not indicated on the website where you're searching, it's a good idea to ask in advance before booking if there are steps and how many. It is far better than arriving to your vacation rental and finding a daunting flight of stairs to navigate daily.

LOCATION RECOMMENDATIONS

Choosing a holiday destination can be a challenging task with so many fine options on the **Amalfi Coast**. If you're planning a visit of only a few days, Amalfi is the most convenient choice because it offers easy ferry and bus connections to the entire area. If you're staying longer, Positano and Ravello are also fine choices. For an experience a bit more off the beaten path, consider Minori or Cetara, two smaller towns that also offer convenient ferry and public transportation connections.

If you're booking a short-term rental on the Amalfi Coast, keep in mind that many towns are quite spread out and include *frazioni*, or hamlets, that can be quite a distance from the town center. In some towns, like Positano or Amalfi, you will find rentals available in *frazioni* that are located very high in the mountains above the center of town. In this case, you will need to use local buses to reach the town first for beaches, shopping, and dining options. These more remote lodging options offer a quieter experience, but if you're not prepared, it can be quite a surprise and you may use up some valuable vacation time waiting for buses that can be very crowded in the summer months. Don't assume that a town name in an address guarantees that a short-term rental will be conveniently located. Map the precise location before booking so you know exactly what you're getting.

Health and Safety

EMERGENCY NUMBERS

In case of a **medical emergency,** dial **118.** Operators are multilingual and will provide immediate assistance and ambulance service. The **U.S. Consulate General in Naples** (tel. 081/583-8111) offers U.S. citizens phone access any time for matters regarding illness or victimization of any sort. ***Carabinieri*** (112), **police** (113), and the **fire department** (115) also operate around-the-clock emergency numbers.

POLICE

The law enforcement in Italy is divided into different agencies. The two main agencies are the *polizia* and the *Carabinieri*, who are responsible essentially for the same duties. The *Carabinieri* are a military corps that perform both military and civilian police duties, whereas the *polizia* is the more customary civilian police force. Either one can help in an emergency situation because they both handle law enforcement duties, investigations, and traffic incidents. The *polizia* tend to be more involved in patrolling the *Autostrade* (highways), yet both forces also perform periodic and random traffic stops. If you are driving and see the *polizia* or *Carabinieri* on the side of the road flag you to stop, be prepared to show your documents and vehicle registration or rental information. The *Carabinieri* uniforms are black with a red stripe on the pants while the vehicles are dark blue, also with red stripe details. *Polizia* uniforms are gray and blue, and their vehicles light blue and white.

Although you're less likely to encounter them while sightseeing, the *Guardia di Finanza* are another military police force who are responsible for policing financial and drug crimes. They are usually outfitted in gray uniforms and the vehicles are also gray. On a city level, the *vigili urbani*, which are part of the *polizia municipale* (municipal police), are usually on hand in every town to help with traffic, parking violations, and local law enforcement.

MEDICAL SERVICES

Italian medical and emergency services are relatively modern and are ranked second in the world by the World Health Organization. First aid can be performed by all public hospitals, and urgent treatment is entirely free of charge. A symbolic copayment is often required for non-life-threatening treatment but does not exceed €30. The emergency medical service number is **118.** If you can't wait, go directly to the *pronto soccorso* (emergency room) located in most hospitals.

Vaccines are not required for entering Italy, but a flu shot can prevent unnecessary time in bed if you're visiting in winter.

PHARMACIES

A pharmacy is called a *farmacia* in Italian, and they are recognizable by their green neon signs. They are very common in cities and even smaller town centers. If a pharmacy is closed, you can always find a list of the closest open ones posted in the window. Pharmacists can be very helpful in Italy and provide advice and nonprescription medicine for treating minor ailments. You'll also find practical items such as toothbrushes, sunscreen, baby food, and dietary foods like gluten-free products along with automated prophylactic vending machines out front.

CRIME

Italian cities are safe and muggings and violent crime are rare. The Amalfi Coast area, along with Sorrentine Peninsula, the islands of Capri, Ischia, and Procida are very safe. Of course, you'll want to keep an eye on your personal items, but even petty crimes are rare.

Though Naples has a reputation regarding organized crime, violent crimes are usually restricted to the *Camorra* (local mafia) and generally do not affect tourists. Petty crime is the main issue, as in any large city in the world. Being street savvy is your best defense against thieves. Most petty criminals work in teams and can be quite young. Crowded train stations and subways are ideal places for thieves. Leave the eye-catching jewelry and expensive accessories at home and opt for a cross-body bag, carried in front, that closes well. It's best to keep wallets and other valuables in a front pocket or locked in a hotel safe. Distribute what you carry with you in different front pockets, or even better, use a money belt and leave out just the cash that you need to be easily accessible for the day. Keep smart phones and cameras out of sight as much as possible, and always keep a close eye on your bags.

If you're driving in Naples, it's best to park your car in an attended parking garage rather than on the street. Be sure to lock the vehicle and leave no valuables in the car.

Before traveling, make a photocopy of your passport and other vital documents and call your credit card company immediately if your wallet is stolen. If you are the victim of a pickpocket, have a bag snatched, or have issues with car theft, report it within 24 hours to the nearest police station. You'll need a copy of the police report (*denuncia*) in order to make an insurance claim.

Conduct and Customs

LOCAL HABITS

Italians are attached to their habits, especially those related to food. Mealtimes are fairly strict, and most eating is done sitting down at precise hours. Locals generally have a light breakfast and save themselves for lunch and dinner, which are served at 1pm and 8pm. You won't see many Italians snacking on the subway or bus, or walking while they eat. When eating out, Italians usually divide the bill between friends, but no one will take offense if you offer to pay. Rounds of drinks are not offered as they are in the United States; each person buys his or her own drink. Drinking in general is done over a meal rather than with any intention of getting drunk, and displays of public drunkenness are rare.

Most behavior that is considered rude in North America is also considered rude in Italy. One exception is cutting in line, which is a frequent occurrence. Italian lines are undisciplined, and if you don't defend your place by saying *scusi* or coughing loudly, you may be waiting all day for a cappuccino or slice of pizza. Fortunately, number dispensers are used in larger post offices and deli counters, but don't expect an orderly line while waiting to get on the bus or other forms of transportation. Personal space in general is smaller than in some other countries, and Italians tend to use their hands as well as words to emphasize ideas.

GREETINGS

Italians are exceptionally sociable and have developed highly ritualized forms of interaction. Daily exchanges with friends and acquaintances often involve physical contact, and kisses on both cheeks are common. Bars and squares are the urban settings for unhurried conversation, which is a normal part of everyday Italian life. The proliferation of the cell phone has fueled the passion to communicate, and in some cases has led to an overreliance that can be witnessed

Italian Survival Phrases

- ***Ciao*** [ch-OW] This world-famous word is an informal greeting that means both hello and good-bye. It's used between friends or once you have gotten acquainted with someone.
- ***Buongiorno*** [bwon-JUR-no] and ***Buonasera*** [bwo-na-SEH-ra] The first means hello (or literally, good day) and the latter good evening. These are formal variations of *ciao* and the first words to say when entering a restaurant or shop.
- ***Scusi*** [SKU-zee] is an invaluable word that sounds very much like its English counterpart: excuse me. It can be used whenever you want to get someone's attention, ask for something, or need to excuse yourself.
- ***Per favore*** [PEAR fa-VOR-eh] and ***Grazie*** [GRA-zee-eh] are pillars of Italian politeness. *Per favore* is useful when ordering at a bar or restaurant and can go at the beginning or end of a sentence (*un caffé per favore* or *per favore un caffè*). Once you've been served something, it's always polite to say *grazie* (thank you).
- ***Dov'è...?*** [doe-VAY...?] The Italian phrase for *where* can save you from getting lost. Just add the location to the end and do your best to comprehend the answer.
- ***Parli inglese?*** [par-LEE in-GLAY-zay?] should only be used as a last resort, but if you must it's more polite than launching directly into English.

on public transportation and sidewalks of Italian cities.

Kissing is how Italians demonstrate respect, friendship, and love. The practice is as Italian as pizza. The most common form is the double-cheek kiss. It can be uncomfortable for the uninitiated but no one will impose it on you, and a handshake is equally acceptable. If you observe carefully you'll see women kissing women, women kissing men, men kissing women, men kissing men, and everyone kissing children.

Kisses are exchanged at the beginning and end of most social encounters. An Italian man introduced to an Italian woman (or vice versa) will exchange kisses. Men will shake hands with each other, and women may kiss or shake hands. Non-Italians can greet however they please. While citizens of other countries tend to exchange good-byes quickly, Italians love to linger. The time between verbal indication of departure and actual physical departure can be surprisingly long and is generally spent discussing the next day and making preliminary plans for a future meeting.

ALCOHOL AND SMOKING

Legislation regarding alcohol consumption is more relaxed than in North America. Alcohol can be consumed in public and purchased in supermarkets, grocery stores, and specialty shops all week long by anyone over 18. Most locals are not prone to excessive drinking, and public drunkenness is rare.

Smoking has been banned in bars, restaurants, and public spaces since 2005, and if you want to take a puff you'll need to step outside or request an outdoor table. Although there is a high percentage of smokers in Italy that number is falling, and laws regarding non-smoking areas are respected. Cigarettes are sold at specialized *tabacchi* (tobacco shops) for around €5 a pack.

DRUGS

Italy's position in the center of the Mediterranean, coupled with the country's 4,971-mile (8,000-kilometer) coastline, makes drug smuggling difficult to eradicate. There are major markets for heroin, cocaine, hashish, and synthetic drugs imported by sea from

South America, North Africa, the Balkans, and Afghanistan. That said, it's very rare to be offered drugs in Italy during the day, and the hardest drug you're likely to be offered at night is hashish (a substance derived from cannabis and mixed with tobacco). Most dealers aren't threatening and will take no for an answer. Discos and nightclubs are more likely to be the scene of cocaine or amphetamines, which kill their share of Italian teenagers every year. Marijuana and hashish are classified as light drugs and are illegal but have been decriminalized since 1990. Personal use of marijuana in public will not lead to arrest but may bring about a fine or warning. It's not worth the risk, and there's enough perfectly legal wine to go around. Harder drugs such as cocaine, heroin, ecstasy, LSD, and so on are all illegal.

DRESS

Italians like to look good. Even if the standards of formality have fallen in recent years, locals of all ages remain well groomed and careful about appearance. It's not just the clothes that are different but the way Italians wear clothes and the overall homogeneity that exists on city streets. Women are elegant, men well fitted, and even retirees look like they're wearing their Sunday best. It's easy to differentiate locals from tourists, who are blissfully unaware of the fashion faux pas they are committing. Tourists can usually be spotted a kilometer away: They're the ones wearing the baseball caps, white socks with sandals, and khaki shorts. If you're concerned about fitting in style-wise, you might need to take your normal style up a notch and may even need to do some shopping to acquire Italian style.

That being said, the coastal areas of the Amalfi Coast and the islands are more relaxed in style than many Italian cities. On the coast, you'll see more of a resort-chic style, including a lot of linen for both men and women, flowing summer dresses to keep cool, and handmade sandals or leather loafers. And while the skimpy Speedo-style swimsuits for men and the proliferation of bikinis on the beach might give the idea of a relaxed beach vibe everywhere, Italians cover up when leaving the beach. It's not appropriate, or even allowed in many towns, to walk around in only swimwear except on the beach. A beach cover-up and flip-flops are fine for getting from your accommodation to the beach, but you won't see Italians dining anywhere except a beachside restaurant in a beach cover-up.

At Places of Worship

It is assumed travelers will dress more conservatively when visiting churches in Italy. Most churches have a dress code, which may be posted outside. Though modest dress codes are not as strictly enforced in this region as in other parts of Italy, if you are revealing too much skin you might be denied entry. Even if a sign isn't posted, it's polite to avoid going into churches while wearing miniskirts, above-the-knee shorts, bare-midriff tops, or bare shoulders. For women, it can be handy to carry a scarf to cover your shoulders while visiting religious sites during the summer months.

Entry may be restricted during Mass and a certain amount of decorum (maintaining silence, refraining from eating and drinking, and acting in a respectful manner) should be observed at all times. Photography is usually allowed but rules vary. Flash photography is not permitted inside some churches and museums where light can damage delicate works of art.

Practical Details

WHAT TO PACK

What to pack depends on the season and length of stay, but always beware of overpacking; traveling to an area famous for its many steps can quickly make you regret packing those extra five pairs of shoes. It's probably best to leave expensive watches and jewelry at home, especially if you'll be spending time in Naples. Finally, it's a good idea to email yourself a copy of your passport and any important credit card codes or customer service numbers as backup in case you lose your wallet or bag.

Luggage: A wheeled suitcase makes getting around airports and hotels easier. It can be bumpy going on Italy's cobblestone streets, but it's often still worth it to avoid carrying heavy bags. Backpacks or handbags are good for daily excursions and should have zippers to dissuade pickpockets. A money belt can be useful for storing cash and valuables.

Paperwork: You'll need your passport and a driver's license if you plan on renting a moped or car. An international permit is not required but can prevent confusion if you're pulled over.

Clothing, shoes, and accessories: Select comfortable clothes that can be mixed and matched. Layers are important in spring and fall when mornings are chilly and temperatures vary throughout the day. Formal clothes may be necessary if you plan on any fine dining or clubbing. Remember that knees and shoulders should be covered when entering religious buildings. Flip-flops are essential for the rocky beaches. If you have very sensitive feet, consider packing a pair of water shoes. You might not win style awards, but being comfortable on your beach holiday is more important. Pack some beach cover-ups for seaside dining and getting to and from the beach. Sunglasses are essential during the summer, especially if you'll be doing any driving, and hats are useful for the beach and hiking. You'll do a lot of walking, often on uneven stone streets and steps, so bring at least two comfortable pairs of shoes. For hiking and walking, a good pair of supportive athletic shoes will be fine and you can save space leaving your hiking boots at home.

Toiletries and medication: A high-SPF sunscreen is vital during summer. It's handy to pack some as it can be quite costly in seaside locations. If you take medication, make sure to bring enough and have a copy of your prescription in case you need a refill. If you forget something, pharmacies in Italy are useful for replacing lost toiletries or picking up aspirin. Most hotels and B&Bs provide hair dryers, but if you're staying in a hostel you may want to pack one. It should be adaptable to Italy's 220 voltage. **Hand sanitizer** can be useful to remove bacteria while on the go. Tuck several **travel tissue** packs into your bag as it's not uncommon to find bathrooms without toilet paper.

Electronics: Voltage is 220 in Italy and plugs have two round prongs. Electronic devices that need recharging require an adapter. Simple U.S.-to-European **travel adapters** are available for under $10 at electronic stores (and double that at airports). Adapters are harder to find once you're in Italy, but many hotels supply them to guests free of charge. Digital photographers will definitely want to bring extra memory cards, and a portable battery charger can prevent phones and other devices from going dark.

MONEY

Currency

The euro has been Italy's currency since 2000. Banknotes come in denominations of €5, €10, €20, €50, €200, and €500 (which is currently being phased out). Denominations are different colors and sizes to facilitate recognition. Coins come in €0.01, €0.02, €0.05, €0.10, €0.20, €0.50, €1, and €2 denominations; these also vary in color, shape, and size. The euro is used in 19 nations across Europe, and each country decorates and mints its own coins. Take time to familiarize yourself with the different values, and count your change after each purchase for practice.

Currency Exchange

Fluctuation between the dollar and euro can have a major impact on expenditures. Over the past decade exchange rates haven't favored U.S. travelers, but since 2014 the dollar has strengthened considerably, and one dollar is now worth roughly €0.85.

There are several options for obtaining euros. You can exchange at your local bank before departure, use **private exchange** agencies located in airports and near major monuments, or simply use **ATM machines** in Italy. Banks generally offer better rates but charge commission, while agencies charge low commission but offer poor rates. Certainly the easiest and best option is to withdraw the cash you need from ATMs as you go.

ATMs and Banks

ATMs are easy to find and are located inside or outside all Italian banks. They accept foreign debit and credit cards, and exchange rates are set daily. Before withdrawing cash in Italy, ask your bank or credit card company what fees they charge. Most charge an international processing fee that can be a fixed amount or a percentage of the total withdrawal. **Charles Schwab** is one of the few financial institutions that does not charge either. Italian banks also charge a small fee for cardholders of other banks using their ATMs.

The maximum daily withdrawal at most banks is €500. ATMs provide instructions in multiple languages. Be aware of your surroundings when withdrawing cash late at night or on deserted streets. If the card doesn't work, try another bank before contacting your bank back home. Italian banks are generally open weekdays 8:30am-1:30pm and more limited hours in the afternoons, from about 2:30pm-4:30pm.

Debit and Credit Cards

Before your departure, inform your bank and/or credit card company of your travel plans, as many will block cards after unexpected foreign activity.

Debit cards are a ubiquitous form of payment in Italy, and recent legislation meant to encourage cashless transactions has removed monetary limits. Yet it's still best not to assume you can use a credit or debit card absolutely everywhere. Do plan on always having some cash on hand for transactions like bus tickets or small purchases, as not all small businesses are equipped to process cards. However, you can use credit cards at most museums, restaurants, and shops. Newsstands are about the only places that don't accept plastic, and cash-only restaurants are rare. Most Italian smart cards use a chip-and-PIN system. If your card requires old-fashioned swiping, you may need to alert cashiers.

Credit cards are also widely accepted. **Visa** (tel. 800/877-232) and **MasterCard** (tel. 800/870-866) are the most common. **American Express** (tel. 06/4211-5561) comes a distant third, and Discover is unknown. Cards provide the most advantageous exchange rates, and a low 1-3 percent commission fee is usually charged on every transaction.

Sales Tax

The Italian government imposes a value-added tax (IVA) of 22 percent on most goods. Visitors who reside outside the European Union are entitled to **tax refunds** (www.taxrefund.it) on all purchases over €154.94 on the same day within stores that participate in the tax-back program. Just look for the **Euro Tax Free** or **Tax Free Italy** logo, have your passport ready, and fill out the yellow refund form. You'll still have to pay tax at the time of purchase but you are entitled to reimbursement at airports and refund offices. Forms must be stamped by customs officials before check-in and brought to the refund desk, where you can choose to receive cash or have funds wired to your credit card.

Lines move slowly and it's usually faster to be refunded at private **currency exchange agencies** such as **Forexchange** (www.forexchange.it) in Naples. They facilitate the refund process for a small percentage of your refund. All claims must be made within three months of purchase.

COMMUNICATIONS

Telephones

To call Italy from outside the country, dial the **exit code** (011 for the United States and Canada), followed by **39** (Italy country code), and the number. All large Italian cities have a 2- or 3-digit **area code** (081 for the city of Naples and surrounding areas and 089 for the province of Salerno), and numbers are 6-11 digits long. Landline numbers nearly always start with a zero, which must be dialed when making calls in Italy or calling Italy from abroad. Cell phone numbers have a 3-digit prefix (347, 390, 340, etc.) that varies according to the mobile operator, and cell phone numbers are 10 digits long total.

To call the United States or Canada from Italy, dial the 001 country code followed by area code and number. For collect calls to the United States, first dial 172-1011 (AT&T), 172-1022 (MCI), or 172-1877 (Sprint).

Numbers that start with 800 in Italy are toll-free, 170 gets you an English-speaking operator, and 176 is **international directory assistance.** Local calls cost €0.10 per minute and public phone booths are slowly disappearing. Fees for calling cell phones are higher.

CELL PHONES

Your smart phone will work in Italy if it uses the GSM system, which is the mobile standard in Europe. All iPhones, Samsung Galaxy, and Google Nexus devices function, although rates vary widely between operators. Voice calls to the United States can vary from as much as $1.79 (Verizon) to $0.20 (T-Mobile) per minute, depending on your plan. Most companies offer international bundles that include a certain amount of text messaging, data transfer, and voice traffic. If you don't want any unexpected bills, compare offers and choose one that meets your expected needs.

You can also purchase a SIM card in Italy at any mobile shop and use it in your phone. **Wind** (www.wind.it), **Tim** (www.tim.it), and **Vodafone** (www.vodafone.it) are the most common operators, with stores in Naples and throughout the region. This option will require a passport or photo ID and may take a little longer, but it can be the cheapest and will be useful if you plan to make a lot of domestic and international calls.

If your phone doesn't use GSM you can buy one in Italy. New phones are inexpensive and available from the European telecom operators mentioned above. A basic flip phone can cost as little as €29 and can be purchased with prepaid minutes. ID is required, and some operators offer special deals for foreign travelers.

You can save on telephone charges altogether if you have access to Wi-Fi. Many hotels and bars have hot spots, and using Facetime, Skype, or other VOIP operators is free.

PAY PHONES

The advent of cell phones has led to a steady decline of public pay phones. Those still standing operate with coins or phone cards that can be purchased at *tabacchi* or newsstands. Ask for a *scheda telefonica* (phone card), which can be inserted into a slot in the telephone.

Wi-Fi

Getting online in Italy is easy. Many towns have free Wi-Fi networks that make it simple to stay connected throughout a journey. Access is free; however, registration is required and there are time and traffic limits. Both Trenitalia and Italo train operators provide onboard Wi-Fi, as do most Italian airports and hotels.

Postal Services

Francobolli (stamps) for standard-size postcards and letters can be purchased at *tabacchi* (tobacco shops). Larger parcels will require a trip to the post office. **Poste Italiane** (tel.

800/160-000; www.poste.it) offices are yellow; larger branches are usually open weekdays 8:30am-7pm, while smaller branches will only be open from about 8:30am-1:30pm. Grab a numbered ticket at the entrance and prepare for a short wait. A postcard to the United States costs €0.85 as long as it doesn't exceed 20 grams and remains within standard dimensions. The cost of sending letters and other goods varies according to weight; such items can be sent *posta prioritaria* (express) for a couple euros extra. Mailboxes are red and have slots for international and local mail. Travel time varies and it can take weeks for a postcard to reach its destination.

OPENING HOURS

Opening hours can vary based on the season and location throughout the region of Campania. In larger cities like Naples and Salerno, you can expect to find many shops, especially smaller ones, closed in the afternoons from around 1:30pm to 4:30pm. In Salerno, shops often close on Monday morning as well, especially during the winter, while in more popular tourist spots like Amalfi, Positano, Ravello, Sorrento, and Capri, shops will be open daily and offer continuous hours. On Ischia and Procida, many shops will close for the afternoon from around 1:30pm to 4:30pm even in the peak of summer.

Shop hours also vary significantly by season. In the top tourist spots, shops will likely be open daily and continuous hours during the summer months, with extended evening hours from July to August. Hours will be shorter over the winter months and some shops may close entirely on the Amalfi Coast and islands for a period after Christmas or for the entire winter period.

Restaurants will often close one day a week, but the day varies between Monday, Tuesday, or Wednesday. In the coastal areas and islands, restaurants will usually be open daily in August or for the entire summer period, but will close for much or all of the winter season.

Nothing is worse than arriving at a museum you are eager to visit and finding it closed. Most of the major museums in Naples, including the Museo Archeologico Nazionale, MADRE museum, the Museo Cappella Sansevero, and many smaller museums, are closed Tuesday. The Reggia di Caserta is also closed on Tuesday while the Museo di Capodimonte and Certosa e Museo di San Martino are closed Wednesday. In Sorrento, the Museo Correale di Terranova is closed Monday, while the Museobottega della Tarsialignea is open daily. As for museums in Salerno, the Museo Archeologico Provinciale and Pinacoteca Provinciale are closed Monday while the Museo Diocesano is closed Wednesday. On the Amalfi Coast, the Museo della Carta in Amalfi is closed Monday from November to January and is closed for the entire month of February, while the Museo della Ceramica is closed Monday throughout the year.

PUBLIC HOLIDAYS

Public holidays in Italy usually mean that banks and offices will be closed. It also means that grocery stores will be closed, or open for reduced hours. In addition to public holidays, each town has one or more days dedicated to celebrating its local patron saint. Though this usually doesn't impact the hours of banks or public offices, you may sometimes find that shops keep more limited hours. However, along the Amalfi Coast, on the islands and other peak tourist spots, you will find all restaurants and shops open during the summer months and for public holidays, like the *Festa della Repubblica* and *Ferragosto*.

- **January 1:** Capodanno (New Year's Day)
- **January 6:** Epifania (Epiphany)
- **Pasqua** (Easter Sunday)
- **Pasquetta** (Easter Monday)
- **April 25:** Festa della Liberazione (Liberation Day)
- **May 1:** Festa del Lavoro (International Worker's Day)
- **June 2:** Festa della Repubblica (Republic Day)

- **August 15:** Ferragosto (Assumption Day)
- **November 1:** Tutti i Santi (All Saints' Day)
- **December 8:** Immacolata (Immaculate Conception)
- **December 25:** Natale (Christmas)
- **December 26:** Santo Stefano (St. Stephen's Day)

WEIGHTS AND MEASURES

Italy uses the **metric system.** A few helpful conversions: 5 centimeters is about 3 inches, 1 kilogram is a little more than 2 pounds, and 5 kilometers is around 3 miles. **Celsius** is used to measure temperature, and 20°C (68°F) is a good air-conditioning setting inside hotels and cars. Summers often break the 35°C (95°F) barrier, and when that happens it's best to head to the beach early in the day and spend the hottest midday hours indoors as many Italians do.

Italy is on **Central European Time,** six hours ahead of the U.S. East Coast and nine ahead of the West Coast. Military/24-hour time is frequently used. Just subtract 12 from any number after midday so that 13:00 becomes 1pm and 20:15 is 8:15pm.

Italians use commas where Americans use decimal points, and vice versa. That means €10,50 is 10 euros and 50 cents, while €1.000 is a thousand euros. Italians order dates by day, month, and year, which is important to remember when booking hotels and tours.

TOURIST INFORMATION

Tourist Offices

You'll find tourist offices in major destinations: on the Amalfi Coast and the islands, and in Sorrento and Naples, where city travel cards, maps, and event information can be obtained. Hours vary but most are open nonstop from 9:30am until around 6pm during the tourist season, with more limited hours during the winter months. Staff are multilingual and can help put you in touch with local guides, order tickets, or get directions. Tourist offices are located in the city center and are usually well indicated with signs.

Sightseeing Passes

The Campania Artecard (www.campaniartecard.it) is the main sightseeing pass for Naples and sights throughout Campania. It covers many art and cultural sights in Naples, including museums, archaeological sites, churches, and more. The pass also includes access to nearly all public transportation systems. Available passes include a 3-day Naples card (€21 adults, €12 youth ages 18-25) that covers only Naples and a 3- or 7-day Campania card (3-day: €32 adults, €25 youth age 18-25, and 7-day: €34 adults, no youth card available) that covers Naples and the region. As the Campania card includes the archaeological cities of Pompeii and Herculaneum, it is often the better choice. The cards provide free entry to the first 2-5 sights, depending on the card selected, and reductions of up to 50 percent for subsequent sights visited. If you plan to visit many sights in Naples or the surrounding area, the Campania Artecard quickly pays for itself and saves you money on sightseeing and travel.

Maps

Maps are available at most tourist offices and at newsstands and bookstores in Naples. Keep in mind that the towns of the Amalfi Coast and the islands are all quite small and easy to navigate. Usually there are only one or two main streets or piazzas, and a maze of little passageways weaving through the town. Often a quick glance at a map is enough to orient yourself and memorize major landmarks and sights. Studying maps and getting an idea of the layout of each city beforehand will make getting around easier once you arrive.

Finding the name of a street you're standing on is simple, but finding that same street on a map can be tricky. Often, it's quicker to locate a piazza or a nearby cathedral, museum, or monument. Also, asking for directions is the best way to start a conversation with a stranger and learn something new.

One of the most enjoyable experiences on the Amalfi Coast or the islands is putting away the map and simply meandering through town. You'll happen across moments of daily life and experience the joy of discovering quiet spots.

For hiking on the Amalfi Coast, Sorrentine Peninsula, and Capri, Cart&Guide (www.carteguide.com) produces the most in-depth maps of the hiking and walking paths. These maps are available online and in bookstores in the area. The Amalfi Coast is divided into four separate maps that cover the entire coastline from Vietri sul Mare to Punta Campanella, and a there's a separate Capri map that details 14 walks on the island.

Traveler Advice

OPPORTUNITIES FOR STUDY AND EMPLOYMENT

With unemployment rates quite high in Italy, finding job opportunities in the area is challenging at best. An easier option is to consider studying abroad in order to experience a more extended time in Italy, learn about the history and culture of the area, and to learn and practice Italian. Language study programs are among the best options in the area, with the **Accademia Italiana Salerno** (www.accademia-italiana.it), the **Istituto Italia 150** (www.istitutoitalia150.it/italian), and the **Sant'Anna Institute** in Sorrento (www.sorrentolingue.com) offering a variety of courses throughout the year.

ACCESS FOR TRAVELERS WITH DISABILITIES

For a country with predominantly historic buildings that were not designed to be wheelchair-accessible, Italy has been making great strides to improve accessibility in airports, train stations, hotels, and sights. However, not all historic churches and sights, or even restaurants, are wheelchair-accessible, so it's always a good idea to call in advance before visiting to confirm. Calling ahead is also a good idea because some sights offer wheelchair access, but it must be reserved.

The Amalfi Coast presents many barriers for travelers with disabilities or mobility issues simply due to the mountainous setting and many steps involved in navigating the towns along the coastline. Positano is one of the most challenging places to visit for anyone in a wheelchair because the town center is located near the beach and is only accessible on foot along a steep pathway that includes many steps. Of all the towns along the Amalfi Coast, Amalfi is one of the most wheelchair-friendly. The waterfront and historic center—including Piazza Duomo and the main street through town, lined with shops and restaurants—are relatively flat. Large cobblestones in the historic center make it a bit bumpy, but along the waterfront the sidewalks are smoother and there are ramps. The Marina Grande beach is accessible via a ramp on the western side of the beach nearest Piazza Flavio Gioia. The towns of Minori and Maiori are also relatively flat and wheelchair-friendly, with Maiori offering a long waterfront area and main street with smoother sidewalks and ramps.

The historic center of Naples has many pedestrian-only areas, but the cobblestone streets and chaotic atmosphere can present challenges for special-needs travelers. Sorrento is somewhat easier to navigate in that it is not as chaotic, but those classic Italian cobblestones are ubiquitous. Yet cultural sightseeing in Naples and Sorrento is well ahead of the curve in Italy. It's safe to say that nearly all of the museums are accessible and offer special services. The Museo Archeologico Nazionale in Naples (www.museoarcheologiconapoli.it) is entirely wheelchair-accessible and offers both wheelchairs and tablets with **video guides in Italian Sign Language** at the Infopoint. **Tactile itineraries and workshops** are available for blind and partially sighted travelers, but must be reserved in advance.

Though the uneven terrain and large stone streets of the archaeological sites of Pompeii and Herculaneum present challenges, there are new initiatives to make them both more accessible. **Pompeii** has a special route called *Pompeii per tutti* (Pompei for everyone) that leads through a specially designed 2.2-mile (3.5km) tour through the ruins, with ramps to make it more manageable for mobility-impaired visitors. While it's a fantastic endeavor, you'll still want to keep in mind that you're entering an archaeological site; there are ramps or slopes of more than 8 percent at times, as well as stretches of ancient and uneven pavement and certain points that may present challenges for wheelchair users to move independently. **Herculaneum** is a much smaller site than Pompeii and offers wheelchair-accessible ramps and walkways to enter the ancient city. Movement within is, again, somewhat challenging given the uneven terrain and steps required to enter some of the houses. **Paestum** has some barrier-free paths through its archaeological park as well as wheelchair access to all areas of the museum.

Turismo Accessibile (www.turismoaccessibile.org) provides detailed information on accessibility in Naples, yet much of the information is only available in Italian. **Sage Traveling** (www.sagetraveling.com) is a travel company specializing in disabled travel. In the Naples area, the company offers a number of day tours that are wheelchair-friendly, including tours to Pompeii, Herculaneum, Sorrento, Capri, and the Amalfi Coast.

TRAVELING WITH CHILDREN

Italians go crazy for kids, and if you're traveling with a baby or toddler expect people to sneak peaks inside the stroller or ask for the name, age, and vital statistics of your child. Restaurants and hotels generally welcome young travelers, and some high-end accommodations offer babysitting services for parents who want to sightsee on their own. Not all restaurants offer booster seats or high chairs, but many will create half-size portions (*mezza porzione*) for small appetites. Tickets to museums and public transportation are usually discounted for children under 12, and are free for kids under 6.

Strollers

Keep in mind that steps, and often a lot of them, are hard to avoid on the Amalfi Coast, which can make getting around with a stroller challenging. You're going to want a lightweight and easy-to-fold stroller in order to navigate steps. For infants and young children, baby wraps, carriers, or a hip seat can be helpful to make handling the steps a little easier. Be sure to check the number of steps required to reach your accommodation. The vertical setting of Positano is particularly challenging for strollers and tiring for little legs. However, if Positano is your dream family destination, just look for an accommodation close to the beach to make it easier to get around once you've arrived.

The archaeological sites like Pompeii, Herculaneum, and Paestum can also be challenging to navigate with a stroller. Herculaneum is a much smaller site to cover, yet offers all of the intriguing aspects of ancient Roman life to capture the interest of young visitors. A tour guide can also help bring the history to life for children in fun and engaging ways.

Beaches

Most of the beaches in this area have pebbles or are rocky, so a pair of beach shoes will keep little feet safe and can help make the beach experience more enjoyable for the whole family. (Adults will want water shoes or flip-flops for the beach as well.) Hiring a boat or booking a boat excursion is a family-friendly way to explore the coastline and islands, allowing you to stop and swim in beautiful coves, older kids to explore the rugged coastline and little grottoes.

Managing the Heat

During the hot days of summer, do like the Italians do and head to the beach in the morning. Then return to your accommodation for a midafternoon break during the hottest part of the day to rest up for evening adventures. You'll find that most Italian children have later bedtimes, especially during the summer, and it's normal for families to be out to dinner late, even with young children. With some advance planning, it's hard for kids not to love Italy. Involving them as much as possible in the journey will help leave an impression they'll never forget.

WOMEN TRAVELING ALONE

Women attract the curiosity of Italian men whether traveling alone or in groups. Italians in general are less shy about staring than many female travelers may be accustomed to at home. This may make women feel uncomfortable, but for the most part, men in southern Italy are respectful. The stereotype of Italians and their wandering hands is uncommon here and would be looked upon as shameful by the locals. Advances are usually good-natured and can simply be ignored. If you do feel threatened, enter a shop, bar, or other public space. Should harassment persist, call the **police** (113) and remain in a crowded area. In Naples women should be more aware of their surroundings at all times. It's best to avoid unlit streets and train stations at night. If you must pass through these areas, walk quickly and keep your guard up. Having a cell phone handy is a wise precaution, and periodically keeping in touch with family back home never hurts. Hotels often go out of their way to assist single travelers and will be happy to order a taxi or make reservations whenever necessary.

SENIOR TRAVELERS

Italy has a high life expectancy (83) and median age (46), which makes gray hair a common sight and visiting seniors feel young again. There's also a general respect for older people, who are an integral part of economic and social life. You'll see that the steps of the Amalfi Coast don't stop local seniors from getting around. They just take the slow and steady approach and stop to chat along the way. Take a cue from them and enjoy sightseeing at a relaxed pace. If mobility and steps are problematic, be sure to check on the number of steps at your accommodation and confirm there is an elevator. Nearly all hotels have elevators, but smaller accommodations and B&Bs may not.

Special Discounts

Seniority has benefits. Anyone over age 65 is entitled to discounts at museums, theaters, and sporting events, as well as on public transportation and for many other services. A passport or valid ID is enough to prove age, even if these are rarely checked. **Carta Argento** (Silver Card) is available from **Trenitalia** for over-60s traveling by train and provides a 15 percent discount on first- and second-class seating. The card costs €30 but is free for those over 75. It's valid for one year and can be purchased at any train station. **Italo** offers anyone over 60 a 40 percent discount on all first-class train tickets.

Health While Traveling

Italy gets very hot in the summer so it's important to remain hydrated and avoid peak temperature times. You'll also walk a lot, so take frequent breaks and join bus or ferry tours whenever you need a rest. If you take medication, bring as much as you need, as prescriptions can be hard to fill.

LGBTQ TRAVELERS

Italians in general are accepting and take a live-and-let-live approach. It's not uncommon to see same-sex couples holding hands today, and the sexual preferences of emperors and Renaissance artists are all well known. Violence against LGBTQ people is rare, although cases of physical and verbal harassment in Naples do occasionally make headlines. Capri has long been known for its open community and appeal for gay travelers. For an LGBTQ nightlife scene, your best bet is Naples, though the scene is more modest than in other large cities in Italy, such as Rome or Milan. The **Mediterranean Pride of Naples** (www.napolipride.org) parade and festival take place in July in the streets of Naples.

Italian homosexual couples have benefited from the same civil union status as heterosexuals since 2016. Italy was one of the last European countries to enact such legislation, doing so more than 20 years after Denmark. Still, it was a big step, and a sign Italian society (or Italian politicians) is open to change.

TRAVELERS OF COLOR

The face of Italy has been changing since the 1980s, and the country has become increasingly diverse, with communities of Eastern Europeans, Asians, South Americans, and Africans contributing to the cultural mix. Ethnic minorities no longer turn heads, and if any Italians are surprised to find you in their bar, hotel, or restaurant they certainly won't show it. Blatant discrimination is rare, but if you think you've been refused service based on race, report the incident to local police or *Carabinieri*, who treat all acts of racism seriously.

Resources

Glossary

A

aeroporto: airport
albergo: hotel
alcolici: alcohol
alimentari: grocery store
aliscafo: hydrofoil (high-speed ferry)
ambasciata: embassy
analcolico: nonalcoholic
aperitivo: appetizer
aperto: open
arrivo: arrival
autista: driver
autobus: bus
autostrada: highway

B

bagaglio: suitcase
bagno: bathroom
banca: bank
bibita: soft drink
biglietteria: ticket office
biglietto: ticket
buono: good

C

calcio: soccer
caldo: hot
cambio: exchange
camera: room
cameriere: waiter
carta di credito: credit card
cartolina: postcard
cassa: cashier
cattedrale: cathedral
centro storico: historic center
chiesa: church
chiuso: closed
città: city
climatizzato: air-conditioned
coincidenza: connection (transport)
consolate: consulate
contante: cash
conto: bill

D E

destinazione: destination
discoteca: disco
dogana: customs
duomo: cathedral
edicola: newsstand
enoteca: wine bar
entrata: entrance
escursione: excursion

F G

farmacia: pharmacy
fermata: bus/subway stop
ferrovia: railway
fontana: fountain
forno: bakery
francobollo: stamp
gratuito: free
grazie: thanks

L

letto: bed
libreria: bookshop
lontano: far
limone: lemon
lungomare: waterfront

M N O

macchina: car
mare: sea
mercato: market
metropolitana: subway
moneta: coin
monumento: monument
mostra: exhibition
museo: museum
negozio: shop
orario: timetable
ospedale: hospital
ostello: hostel

P Q R

palazzo: building
panino: sandwich
parcheggio: parking lot
parco: park
partenza: departure
passeggiata: walk
pasticceria: pastry shop
pasto: meal
periferia: outskirts
piazza: square
polizia: police
ponte: bridge
prenotazione: reservation
prezzo: price
quartiere: neighborhood
ristorante: restaurant

S T

sconto: discount
soccorso: assistance
spiaggia: beach
spuntino: snack
stabilimento balneare: seaside beach club
stazione: station
strada: road
tabaccherie: tobacco shop
teatro: theater
traghetto: ferry
trattoria: restaurant (casual)
torre: tower
treno: train

U V

uscita: exit
via: street
viale: avenue

Italian Phrasebook

Many Italians in the Amalfi Coast area have some knowledge of English, ranging from managing basic communication to being fully fluent. Of course, whatever vocabulary they lack is compensated for with gesticulation. It is, however, more rewarding to attempt to communicate in Italian, even a little bit, and your efforts will often be greeted with encouragement from locals.

Fortunately, Italian pronunciation is straightforward. There are 7 vowel sounds (one for *a*, *i*, and *u*, and two each for *e* and *o*) compared to 15 in English, and letters are nearly always pronounced the same way. Consonants will be familiar, although the Italian alphabet has fewer letters (no j, k, w, x, or y). If you have any experience with French, Spanish, Portuguese, or Latin you have an advantage, but even if you don't, learning a few phrases is simple and will prepare you for a linguistic dive into Italian culture. Inquiring how much something costs or asking for directions in Italian can be a little daunting, but it's also exciting and much more gratifying than relying on English.

PRONUNCIATION

Vowels

a like *a* in *father*
e short like *e* in *set*
é long like *a* in *way*
i like *ee* in *feet*
o short like *o* in *often*, or long like *o* in *rope*
u like *oo* in *foot*, or *w* in *well*

Consonants

b like *b* in *boy,* but softer
c before e or i like *ch* in *chin*
ch like *c* in *cat*
d like *d* in *dog*
f like *f* in *fish*
g before e or i like *g* in *gymnastics* or like *g* in *go*
gh like *g* in *go*
gl like *ll* in *million*
gn like *ni* in *onion*
gu like *gu* in *anguish*
h always silent
l like *l* in *lime*
m like *m* in *me*
n like *n* in *nice*
p like *p* in *pit*
qu like *qu* in *quick*
r rolled/trilled similar to *r* in Spanish or Scottish
s between vowels like *s* in *nose* or *s* in *sit*
sc before e or i like *sh* in *shut* or *sk* in *skip*
t like *t* in *tape*
v like *v* in *vase*
z either like *ts* in *spits* or *ds* in *pads*

Accents

Accents are used to indicate which vowel should be stressed and to differentiate between words with different meanings that are spelled the same.

ESSENTIAL PHRASES

Hi Ciao
Hello Salve
Good morning Buongiorno
Good evening Buonasera
Good night Buonanotte
Good-bye Arrivederci
Nice to meet you Piacere
Thank you Grazie
You're welcome Prego
Please Per favore
Do you speak English? Parla inglese?
I don't understand Non capisco
Have a nice day Buona giornata
Where is the restroom? Dov'è il bagno?
Yes Si
No No

TRANSPORTATION

Where is...? Dov'è...?
How far is...? Quanto è distante...?
Is there a bus to...? C'è un autobus per...?
Does this bus go to...? Quest'autobus va a...?
Where do I get off? Dove devo scendere?
What time does the bus/train leave/arrive? A che ora parte/arriva l'autobus/treno?
Where is the nearest subway station? Dov'è la stazione metro più vicina?
Where can I buy a ticket? Dove posso comprare un biglietto?
A round-trip ticket/a single ticket to... Un biglietto di andata e ritorno/andata per...

FOOD

A table for two/three/four... Un tavolo per due/tre/quattro...
Do you have a menu in English? Avete un menu in inglese?
What is the dish of the day? Qual è il piatto del giorno?
We're ready to order. Siamo pronti per ordinare.
I'm a vegetarian. Sono vegetariano (male) / Sono vegetariana (female)
May I have... Posso avere...
The check please? Il conto per favore?
beer birra
bread pane
breakfast colazione
cash contante
check conto
coffee caffè
dinner cena
glass bicchiere
hors d'oeuvre antipasto
ice ghiaccio
ice cream gelato
lunch pranzo
restaurant ristorante
sandwich(es) panino(i)
snack spuntino
waiter cameriere

water acqua
wine vino

SHOPPING

money soldi
shop negozio
What time do the shops close? A che ora chiudono i negozi?
How much is it? Quanto costa?
I'm just looking. Sto guardando solamente.
What is the local specialty? Quali sono le specialità locali?

HEALTH

drugstore farmacia
pain dolore
fever febbre
headache mal di testa
stomachache mal di stomaco
toothache mal di denti
burn bruciatura
cramp crampo
nausea nausea
vomiting vomitare
medicine medicina
antibiotic antibiotico
pill/tablet pillola/pasticca
aspirin aspirina
I need to see a doctor. Ho bisogno di un medico.
I need to go to the hospital. Devo andare in ospedale.
I have a pain here... Ho un dolore qui...
She/he has been stung/bitten. È stata punta/morsa.
I am diabetic/pregnant. Sono diabetico/incinta.
I am allergic to penicillin/cortisone. Sono allergico alla penicillina/cortisone.
My blood group is...positive/negative. Il mio gruppo sanguigno è... positivo/negative.

NUMBERS

0 zero
1 uno
2 due
3 tre
4 quattro
5 cinque
6 sei
7 sette
8 otto
9 nove
10 dieci
11 undici
12 dodici
13 tredici
14 quattordici
15 quindici
16 sedici
17 diciassette
18 diciotto
19 diciannove
20 venti
21 ventuno
30 trenta
40 quaranta
50 cinquanta
60 sessanta
70 settanta
80 ottanta
90 novanta
100 cento
101 centouno
200 duecento
500 cinquecento
1,000 mille
10,000 diecimila
100,000 centomila
1,000,000 un milione

TIME

What time is it? Che ora è?
It's one/three o'clock. E l'una/sono le tre.
midday mezzogiorno
midnight mezzanotte
morning mattino
afternoon pomeriggio
evening sera
night notte
yesterday ieri
today oggi
tomorrow domani

DAYS AND MONTHS

week settimana
month mese
Monday Lunedì
Tuesday Martedì
Wednesday Mercoledì
Thursday Giovedì
Friday Venerdì
Saturday Sabato
Sunday Domenica
January Gennaio
February Febbraio
March Marzo
April Aprile
May Maggio
June Giugno
July Luglio
August Agosto
September Settembre
October Ottobre
November Novembre
December Dicembre

VERBS

to have avere
to be essere
to go andare
to come venire
to want volere
to eat mangiare
to drink bere
to buy comprare
to need necessitare
to read leggere
to write scrivere
to stop fermare
to get off scendere
to arrive arrivare
to return ritornare
to stay restare
to leave partire
to look at guardare
to look for cercare
to give dare
to take prendere

Suggested Reading

HISTORY AND CULTURE

Banks Amendola, Barbara. *The Mystery of the Duchesss of Malfi*. In-depth research and fine storytelling bring to life the enigmatic Giovanna d'Aragona, the Duchess of Amalfi, and detail the historical context of her life, her secret marriage, and her death, which has since been shrouded in mystery.

Beard, Mary. *The Fires of Vesuvius: Pompeii Lost and Found*. This is an excellent look at life in Pompeii, written in a compelling narrative style that brings the history of the ancient city to life.

Hazzard, Shirley. *The Ancient Shore: Dispatches from Naples*. Celebrated Australian writer Shirley Hazzard first visited Naples in the 1950s, beginning a lifelong love affair with the city. This volume brings together her many writings on Naples.

Kelly, Chantal. *The Amalfi Coast Up Close & Personal*. In a beautiful homage to the Amalfi Coast, author and photographer Chantal Kelly shares a personal look at the history, culture, and charms of the area through her stories and many photos. This is a follow-up to her entertaining travel narrative *Gelato Sisterhood on the Amalfi Shore*.

La Capria, Raffaele. *Capri and No Longer Capri*. This intriguing portrait of Capri by an Italian novelist and screenwriter blends the island's history with personal tales and beautiful descriptions of Capri.

Lancaster, Jordan. *In the Shadows of Vesuvius: A Cultural History of Naples*. Lancaster delves into the history of Naples with a special focus on ancient Naples to the Medieval, Spanish, and Bourbon eras of the city.

Lewis, Norman. *Naples '44: A World War II Diary of Occupied Italy.* This is a classic look at Naples during World War II by noted British writer Norman Lewis, famous for his travel writing, who was stationed in Naples in 1944 as an Intelligence Officer.

Lima, Chiara. *Mamma Agata: Traditional Italian Recipes of a Family That Cooks with Love and Passion in a Simple and Genuine Way.* Both a cookbook and the story of a family dedicated to traditional cooking on the Amafi Coast, this book will enchant you with its photos and help you re-create the delicious flavors of the coastline in your own home.

Munthe, Axel. *The Story of San Michele.* The memoir of Swedish-born doctor Axel Munthe was a bestseller when it was first published in 1929 and continues to offer a captivating glimpse into his life and time spent in his beloved Villa San Michele on the island of Capri.

Saviano, Roberto. *Gomorrah.* Saviano provides a frightening and unforgettable insider's account of the inner workings of the Camorra, the organized crime network in the Naples area.

LITERATURE

Adler, Elizabeth. *The House in Amalfi* and *Sailing to Capri.* International bestselling author Elizabeth Adler has brought a charming combination of romance, intrigue, and love of travel to her two novels set on the Amalfi Coast and Capri. This is fun and light travel reading for a beach holiday.

Ferrante, Elena. *Neapolitan Novels: My Brilliant Friend, The Story of a New Name, Those Who Leave and Those Who Stay, The Story of the Lost Child.* This four-part novel follows a captivating friendship between two young girls and how it carries through their lives. Set in the Naples area—with episodes in the first book, *My Brilliant Friend,* taking place on Ischia—the books have become an international success.

Hazzard, Shirley. *The Bay of Noon.* This novel, set in Naples following World War II, was written by Australian writer and Naples enthusiast Shirley Hazzard. This book is not generally considered one of her finest works, but the city of Naples is depicted beautifully.

de Lamartine, Alphonse. *Graziella.* Published in 1852 and based on firsthand experiences of French writer Alphonse de Lamartine in Procida, the novel is the story of an ill-fated relationship between a young French man and poor young woman named Graziella, the granddaughter of a fisherman.

Mazzoni, Jan. *Stones of the Madonna.* Taking place on the Amalfi Coast in 1939, this novel of lust and betrayal is set against the beautiful backdrop of Positano.

Morante, Elsa. *Arturo's Island.* Set on the island of Procida, this celebrated novel written by Italian author Elsa Morante in 1957 follows Arturo and his family life on the island.

Sontag, Susan. *The Volcano Lover.* This is a compelling historical novel about Sir William Hamilton, British Ambassador to the Kingdom of Naples from 1764-1800, his wife Emma Hamilton, and her scandalous affair with Lord Nelson.

HIKING GUIDES AND MAPS

Cart&Guide Maps. For the most in-depth maps of the hiking and walking paths of the Amalfi Coast and Capri, you'll want to get your hands on the series of maps by Cart&Guide (www.carteguide.com). The Amalfi Coast is divided into four separate maps, stretching from Vietri sul Mare to Punta Campanella. A Capri map with 14 walks is also available.

Cavaliere, Gabriele. *Strolling Through Amalfi*. Divided into seven walks themed around art, history, and tradition, this book is packed with detailed trail maps, information, and photos.

Cavaliere, Gabriele. *Ravello*. Full of color photos, maps, and information about Ravello, this book includes six walks in Ravello and the surrounding area, including Minori, Atrani, and Scala, as well as the Valle delle Ferriere.

Price, Gillian. *Walking on the Amalfi Coast: Ischia, Capri, Sorrento, Positano and Amalfi*. This is a helpful Cicerone guide by experienced Italian hiker Gillian Price.

Tippett, Julian. *Sorrento, Amalfi and Capri: 7 Car Tours, 72 Walk Segments*. Tippett's pocket-sized book includes drives on the Sorrentine Peninsula, as well as detailed walking and hiking directions on the Amalfi Coast and Capri. Walks in Ischia, Capri, Sorrento, and the Amalfi Coast are also included.

Suggested Films

Beat the Devil (1953) John Huston. An entertaining and, at times, comic parody of a film noir, this movie was filmed in Ravello and various spots on the Amalfi Coast, and stars Humphrey Bogart, Jennifer Jones, and Gina Lollobrigida. Bogart's character teams up with a band of crooks to buy a uranium-rich piece of land in Africa. While they are waiting in Italy to depart for Africa, a series of encounters sets off a chain of unexpected events.

L'Oro di Napoli (1954) Vittorio De Sica. Meaning "The Gold of Naples," this film is a tribute to the city by Italian director and actor Vittorio De Sica. Composed of six episodes, the film features some of the most iconic names in Italian film, including Totò, Eduardo De Filippo, and Sophia Loren.

It Started in Naples (1960) Melville Shavelson. This fun love story features the great duo of Clark Gable and Sophia Loren. Despite the title, the movie was filmed mostly on Capri and really shows off the island beautifully as it was in the '60s.

Avanti! (1972) Billy Wilder. Set on Ischia, this comedy features Jack Lemmon, who arrives on the island after his father is killed in a car accident only to discover that nothing is quite as it seemed. The movie was filmed on Ischia, in Sorrento, and various other locations on the Amalfi Coast and Capri.

Il Postino (1994) Massimo Troisi, Michael Radford. This now iconic film featuring Massimo Troisi was nominated for five academy awards in 1995, winning the Academy Award for Best Music for an Original Dramatic Score. Filmed on Procida, it's a story of an unlikely friendship between the poet Pablo Neruda and his postman.

Only You (1994) Norman Jewison. This romantic comedy with Robert Downey Jr. and Marisa Tomei follows a grand tour from Venice to Rome and Positano. The movie's poolside scenes in Positano were filmed at the Le Sirenuse hotel.

The Talented Mr. Ripley (1999) Anthony Minghella. A movie adaptation of Patricia Highsmith's 1955 novel, this thriller has the powerhouse cast of Matt Damon, Jude Law, and Gwyneth Paltrow. For the film, Procida was used for the novel's fictional seaside town of Mongibello, with scenes also shot in Positano.

Under the Tuscan Sun (2003) Audrey Wells. This much-loved film, based on the book of the same name by Frances Mayes, has a Positano interlude featuring Italian actor Raoul Bova.

A Good Woman (2004) Mike Barker. Based on *Lady Windermere's Fan* by Oscar Wilde, this captivating film is set in the 1930s and features Helen Hunt and Scarlett Johansson. It was filmed on the Amalfi Coast, with especially beautiful scenes in Atrani.

Love Is All You Need (2012) Susanne Bier. This romantic comedy with Pierce Brosnan tells the story of Brosnan's character falling in love alongside the character played by Danish actress Trine Dyrholm. Sorrento shines as the setting, and you'll easily fall in love with the place as well as the characters.

Si Accettano Miracoli (2015) Alessandro Siani. Neapolitan actor and director Alessandro Siani shot this film on the Amalfi Coast, with much of the filming taking place in the peaceful town of Scala near Ravello.

Internet and Digital Resources

TRAVEL AND TOURIST TIPS

www.incampania.com

The official tourist website for Campania is a great place to start looking for inspiration, with information on the landmarks, museums, culture, gastronomy, and natural landscape of the region.

www.viator.com

This site offers an extensive selection of private and group tours for the Amalfi Coast area, including Sorrento, Naples, Capri, and more.

TRANSPORTATION

www.skyscanner.com, www.kayak.com, www.hipmunk.com, www.momondo.com

These flight aggregators help find the cheapest fares. Momondo often pulls in the lowest fares, while Hipmunk has a clean interface and practical features like timelines and maps that simplify planning. They all also offer hotel and car-rental services.

www.rome2rio.com

Here you'll find door-to-door transportation details with distances, departures times, and prices for planes, trains, buses, and ferries. There's also a carbon emissions estimate for the ecologically inclined.

www.seatguru.com

Learn your legroom options and read unbiased advice on where to sit on a flight. The database includes all major airlines, along with diagrams, photos, and descriptions of Airbus and Boeing interiors.

www.jetlagrooster.com

Avoid jet lag by creating a personalized sleep plan for a smooth transition between time zones. Just log on 3-4 days before departure and follow their recommended bedtimes.

www.italo.com, www.trenitalia.com

These are the sites of Italy's high-speed rail operators. Tickets can be printed at home or saved on mobile devices. If your trip is still months away, sign up for the Italo newsletter and receive monthly travel offers.

www.aeroportodinapoli.it

The Aeroporto Internazionale di Napoli website offers travel information in English for arrivals, departures, traveling to and from the airport, and amenities available while you're in transit.

www.autostrade.it

Drivers can calculate mileage (in kilometers) and toll costs for planned routes. Rest areas are listed, as are the cheapest gas stations. It's also useful for traffic alerts and brushing up on the rules of the Italian road.

ACCOMMODATIONS

www.airbnb.com, www.booking.com, www.slh.com

Search for B&Bs, apartments, or boutique hotels. Sites include realistic visuals, plus advice and reviews from people who have traveled before you.

www.tripadvisor.com

Get feedback and user ratings on sights, services, and hotels. Comments are detailed and often highlight inconveniences like a bad view or small bathroom.

www.xe.com

Calculate what a buck is worth and know exactly how much you're spending. The site's sister app is ideal for the financially conscious and allows travelers to track expenditures on the go.

APPS

Alitalia

Italy's main airline has an app with flight status, boarding information, and baggage claim info.

Trenitalia, Italo

Italy's two train companies offer English-language apps with timetables, the latest train status information, and the ability to purchase tickets via the apps.

Costa Eventi

Find out about local events, concerts, and the latest happenings on the Amalfi Coast.

Procida Island

The island of Procida offers a detailed app with ferry, bus, and transportation schedules, as well as information on local sights and things to see and do.

Moovit

This excellent app covers transportation for the entire area, including trains, metro, buses, funicular trains, and ferries. Offline maps of Naples's train and Metro lines are available to download.

Travelmar

Find schedules and purchase tickets in advance for ferries along the Amalfi Coast to Salerno, Cetara, Minori, Maiori, Amalfi, and Positano.

Google Translate

This helpful dictionary and translation app helps travelers decipher and pronounce Italian.

The Weather Channel

Here you'll find the latest reliable weather information and forecasts for the Amalfi Coast area.

Index

A

Abbazia di Crapolla: 212, 214
Abbazia di San Michele Arcangelo: 313, 315
Abbazia di Santa Maria de Olearia: 150
abbeys: 150, 163, 214, 313
accessibility: 465–466
accommodations: 454–456; Capri 255–258; Naples 368–373; *see also specific place*
adapters (electronic): 29, 460
Aeneid (Virgil): 383–384, 386, 436
Aeroporto Internazionale di Napoli (Capodichino Airport): 26–27, 209, 373, 375, 441
A. Gargiulo & Jannuzzi (woodworking): 198, 202
Agricola Fore Porta: 102
air travel: 26–27, 373–374, 375, 441–442
alcohol: 458
Amalfi (town): 28, 30, 51, 56, 57, 93–116; map 94–95
Amalfi Coast: 7–21
Amalfi Coast Road (SS163): 40, 43, 46–47; *see also specific place*
Amalfi Coast towns: 22, 28, 30–32, 34, 38, 39–40, 41–181, 455–456; Amalfi 93–116; maps 44–45, 46–47, 52–53, 58, 94–95, 122, 169, 180; Ravello 120–137; transportation 43, 46–50; *see also specific town*
Amalfi Lemon Experience tour: 33, 103
Amphitheater (Pompeii): 393, 406
Anacapri: 227, 228; accommodations 256–257; festivals 247; food 253–254; nightlife 247; shopping 250–251; sights 235–240; walking/hiking 243
anchovies *(alici)*: 33, 42, 57, 156, 158–159
anchovy oil *(colatura di alici)*: 33, 57, 157–159
Anfiteatro Flavio amphitheater: 383
Angevin/Anjou rule (Naples): 324, 337, 424, 437
Antica Pizzeria da Michele: 33, 362, 367
Antica Trattoria: 205
Antiquarium Silio Italico: 212
apartment rentals: 455
Aragonese rule (Naples): 272, 324, 424
Arcate, Le: 118
archaeological museums: 170–171, 179, 181, 198, 212, 290, 331, 386
archaeological sites: 59, 144–145, 179–181, 379, 381, 383, 384; *see also* Herculaneum; Pompeii
architecture: 436–438
Arco Naturale (Natural Arch): 232, 237, 242
Arco Naturale to Belvedere di Tragara Walk: 225, 238, 242–243
Area Marina Protetta di Punta Campanella (Protected Marina Area of Punta Campanella): 218
Area Marina Protetta Parco Sommerso di Gaiola: 379, 381
Arienzo Beach: 35, 59, 64
Arsenale: 98
Ars Neapolitana: 341, 361
Art Hotel Villa Fiorella: 190, 218–219
art museums: 57; Naples 337, 338, 340, 347, 350, 352–353; Salerno 170, 171; Sorrento 198–199
Associazione Alessandro Scarlatti: 356–357
ATMs: 461
Atrani: 116–120
Atrani Beach (Marina di Atrani): 34, 117
Auditorium Oscar Niemeyer: 128

B

Badia Della Santissima Trinita: 163
Bagni della Regina Giovanna: 190, 200
Baia/Bacoli: 385–388
Baia di San Montano: 35, 276, 292–293
Baia di Sorgeto: 276, 287, 305
bakeries: 92, 110, 176, 308, 317, 363, 364, 450–451
banks: 461
Barano d'Ischia: 36, 276, 303, 304–310
Bar dal Cavaliere: 317
baroque architecture: 437
bars: *see also* nightlife
Basilica (Temple of Hera): 179
Basilica di San Francesco da Paola: 343
Basilica di San Paolo Maggiore: 339
Basilica di Sant'Antonino: 196
Basilica di Santa Trofimena: 144
Basilica di Sant'Eustachio: 138, 140
Basilica of the Crucifix: 98
baths, public (Roman): 401, 410
Battistero di San Giovanni in Fonte: 338
B&B (bed and breakfasts): 455; *see also* accommodations
beach clubs (stabilimente balneari): 48, 449; *see also specific beach; specific place*
beaches: 34–36, 48, 56, 276, 448–449, 466; Capri 35, 240–242; Ischia/Procida 35–36, 274–277, 284, 292, 300, 305, 313–314; *see also specific beach; specific place*
Beckett, Ernest William (Grimthorpe, 2nd Baron of): 126
Belvedere della Migliera Walk: 238–239, 243
biking: 292, 319, 353

birds: 414, 421
Blu Bar: 138
Blue Flag beaches: 62, 64, 216, 219, 221
Blue Grotto (Grotta Azzurra): 235–237, 245
boat travel: *see* ferry service
boat trips/rentals: Amalfi Coast towns 38, 66, 88–89, 89–91, 102, 152, 200; Capri 200, 235–236, 239, 245; Ischia 277, 300, 306; Naples area 353, 378, 387; Sorrento area 200
bookshops: 278, 315, 333
bradyseism: 383
Buco, Il: 205
bus tours: *see* City Sightseeing bus lines
bus travel: 27, 443, 445–446; Amalfi Coast towns 47–49, 177–178, 445; Capri 259–260, 445; Naples 178, 374, 376, 446; *see also specific place*
Byzantine New Year: 106

C

cable cars (funicular trains): 212, 260, 376–377
Caffe Calce: 128
cameo carving: 348
Camiceria Piccolo: 359
Campania Artecard: 326, 400, 409, 464
Campanian Mineralogical Museum (Museo Mineralogico Campano): 211–212
Campania region: 418
Campanile dell'Annunziata: 145
Campi Flegrei (Phlegraean Fields): 325, 376, 379, 382, 418
Cantine Giuseppe Apicella: 33, 85, 142
Cantine Marisa Cuomo: 33, 85, 87
Cap' e' Fierr: 274, 278
Capodanno (New Year's Eve): 28, 103
Capodichino Airport (Aeroporto Internazionale di Napoli): 26–27, 209, 373, 375, 441
Capo di Conca promontory: 89
Capodimonte (Naples): 325, 352–353, 439
Capo Sottile: 77
Cappella dei Crociati (Chapel of the Crusaders): 170
Cappella della Madonna delle Neve: 89
Capri (island): 23, 32, 36, 224–260; maps 226–227, 230
Capri Rooftop: 239, 246
Capri Town: 227, 228; accommodations 255–256; festivals 247; food 252–253; map 230; nightlife 246–247; shopping 248–250; sights 229–235, 238–239
Caravaggio: 339, 347, 352, 425, 438
Cartaromana beach: 276, 277
car travel: 27, 187–189, 444–445; Amalfi Coast towns 43, 46; Capri 259; Naples 378; *see also specific place*
Caruso, Enrico: 190, 208, 364, 439
Caruso Roof Garden Restaurant: 364
Casa d'Ambra: 33, 300
Casa di Graziella, La: 313
Casa e Bottega: 71
Casamicciola Terme: 283–285, 286, 287, 288–289
Casa Rossa: 239
Casertavecchia: 390
Casina Vanvitelliana: 386–387
Castel dell'Ovo: 321, 348–349
Castello Aragonese (Ischia): 19, 38, 262, 272–274
Castello Aragonese di Baia: 386
Castello di Arechi: 171
Castel Nuovo (Maschio Angioino): 342
Castel Sant'Elmo: 38, 350
Castiglione Beach: 117–118
castles: 436–437; Ischia 272–274; Naples 38, 342, 348–349, 350, 436–437; Salerno 171
Catacombe di San Gaudioso: 351
Catacombe di San Gennaro: 351
catacombs (Naples): 351
cathedrals: Amalfi 96–98; former designation 144, 211, 216; Ischia 274; Naples and area 338, 358, 390; Salerno 170; Sorrento 183, 194–195, 198; *see also* churches
Cattedrale di Salerno (Cathedral of San Matteo): 170
Cattedrale di Sorrento: 183, 194–195, 198
Cattedrale Santa Maria dell'Assunta: 274
Cavallo Morto beach: 151
caves/grottoes: 88–89, 235–237
cell phone services: 462
Central Baths (Herculaneum): 410
Centro Caprense Ignazio Cerio: 231
Centro di Musica Antica Pietà de' Turchini: 357
centro storico (Naples): 324, 325, 326; accommodations 369–370; arts 355–356; food 361–363; map 334–335; nightlife 354–355; sights 331–342
centro storico (Salerno): 42, 168, 170, 174–175, 179
centro storico (Sorrento): 183, 195
Ceramica Artistica Solimene factory: 164
Ceramica Pinto factory: 164–165
ceramics: history 162; museums 162, 198–199; shops/factories 68, 107–108, 164–165, 284, 360; tile floor 238–239, 437; Vietri sul Mare 57, 161, 162, 164–165, 438
Certosa di San Giacomo: 231–232
Certosa e Museo di San Martino: 321, 341, 352
Cetara: 25, 28, 33, 42, 55, 57, 154–161
Cetara Beach (Marina di Cetara): 35, 156
Cetarii shop: 159
Chapel of the Crusaders (Cappella dei Crociati): 170
Chasing Syrens kayaks: 38, 220
Chestnut Festival (Festa della Castagna): 140
Chiaia neighborhood (Naples): 325, 348, 358
Chiaro Di Luna: 317

Chiesa dei Marinai (Church of the Fishermen): 283
Chiesa dell'Annunziata (Minori): 145
Chiesa dell'Annunziata (Scala): 138
Chiesa della Santissima Annunziata: 190, 211
Chiesa dell'Immacolata: 273
Chiesa del Soccorso: 262, 297–298
Chiesa di Buon Consiglio: 283
Chiesa di Gesù Nuovo: 333
Chiesa di San Domenico Maggiore: 337
Chiesa di San Ferdinando: 347
Chiesa di San Francesco (Ravello): 124
Chiesa di San Francesco and Cloister (Sorrento): 196
Chiesa di San Francesco d'Assisi (Cetara): 155
Chiesa di San Francesco d'Assisi (Ischia): 298
Chiesa di San Gaetano: 298
Chiesa di San Gennaro: 77–78
Chiesa di San Giovanni Battista (Scala): 138
Chiesa di San Giovanni Battista (Vietri sul Mare): 161
Chiesa di San Giovanni del Toro: 124
Chiesa di San Gregorio Armeno: 340
Chiesa di San Lorenzo Maggiore: 339
Chiesa di San Luca Evangelista: 78
Chiesa di San Michele Arcangelo: 127
Chiesa di San Pancrazio: 89
Chiesa di San Pietro Apostolo: 155
Chiesa di San Salvatore de Birecto: 117
Chiesa di Sant'Agostino: 124
Chiesa di Santa Maria a Gradillo: 124
Chiesa di Santa Maria Assunta: 57, 59
Chiesa di Santa Maria delle Grazie: 211, 216
Chiesa di Santa Maria di Costantinopoli: 155–156
Chiesa di Santa Maria Visitapoveri: 298
Chiesa di Santa Restituta: 290
Chiesa di Santo Stefano: 229, 230–231
Chiesa Monumentale di San Michele: 225, 238–239
children, tips for travelers with: 466–467
children's activities: 34, 38, 286
chocolate: 108, 360
Christianity: 351, 423, 434
churches: 437; Capri 230–231, 238–239; Ischia/Procidia 283, 290, 297–298, 313, 315; Naples 333, 337, 338–340, 342, 343, 347; *see also* cathedrals; *specific place*
Cioccolato Andrea Pansa: 108
City of Music (Ravello): 28, 42, 121, 128, 439
City Sightseeing bus lines: 446; Amalfi Coast towns 48–49, 76, 115, 137, 148, 154; Naples and area 378–379, 382, 391, 407; Sorrento 209, 211
cliff jumping: 87
climate: 24, 418–419
Clock Palace (Palazzo dell'Orologio): 274
Clock Tower (Torre dell'Orologio): 229–230
Cloister of Paradise: 12, 97–98
clothing shops: Amalfi 107; Capri 250; Ischia 278; Naples 359; Positano 68; Ravello 130
clothing tips: 27, 29, 134, 459, 460
coffee bars: 450, 451
colatura di alici (anchovy oil): 33, 57, 157–159
Collegiata di Santa Maria a Mare: 149–150
Collegiata di Santa Maria Maddalena: 117
communications: 462–463
Complesso Archeologico delle Terme di Baia: 386
Complesso Monumentale di San Lorenzo Maggiore: 339
Complesso Monumentale di Santa Chiara: 321, 333, 337, 341
Complesso Monumentale di Sant'Andrea: 98
Complesso Monumentale Donnaregina: 340
Complesso Museale di Villa Arbusto: 290
Complesso Palapartenope: 357
Conca dei Marini: 25, 56, 88–93
concerts: 81, 128–130, 201, 202, 355–357
consulates: 448
cooking classes: 127–128, 245–246
coral carving: 123–124, 347, 348
Coral Museum Ascione: 347
Corso Italia: 191, 194
Corso Reginna: 149, 152, 154
Corso Sant'Agata: 211, 221
Corso Umberto I: 161, 164–165
Corso Vittoria Colonna: 272, 282
Corso Vittorio Emanuele: 168, 174
Costa d'Amalfi DOC (Denomination of Controlled Origin) wines: 25, 33, 85
crafts: 438–439
credit cards: 461
Crestarella, La (beach): 163
crime: 457
Cristo Velato (Sanmartino): 337, 437
crowds, avoiding: 24–26, 50, 54–55, 77, 116, 330
cultural customs: 453, 457–459
Cuma, Parco Archeologico di: 384
currency/currency exchange: 460–462, 464
customs regulations: 448
cycling: *see* biking

D

Da Ferdinando: 62, 70
dancing: 67, 440
D'Anton Design & Bistrot: 206
Da Paolino: 251–252
Da Teresa: 100
dates/time: 464, 472–473
debit cards: 461
decorative arts: 352, 438–439
decumani streets: 331, 333, 408
demographics: 434
desserts: 92, 147, 317, 363, 364, 365, 450–451
Deus Neptunus: 308

De Vivo: 294
digestivo (digestif): 452
disabilities, tips for travelers with: 465–466
discounts for seniors: 467
diving, scuba/snorkeling: 80, 200, 218, 277, 306, 387
diving competitions: 87
Domus Ars Centro di Cultura: 356
Don Alfonso 1890: 222
dress codes/standards: 27, 29, 459
drinks: 33, 450–451, 457
driving tour: 187–189
drugs: 458–459
Duchy of Amalfi: 106, 423
Due Fratelli, I (rock formation): 163
Duoglio beach: 34, 100
Duomo (Cattedrale di Salerno): 170
Duomo (Ravello): 121, 123
Duomo di Amalfi: 12, 42, 96–98
Duomo di Casertavecchia: 390
Duomo di Napoli (Naples Cathedral): 321, 338, 358
Duomo di San Lorenzo: 138

E

Easter and Holy Week: 28, 103–104, 201, 315
economy: 432–433
elections: 431, 432
electronics: 29, 460
embassies: 448
Emerald Grotto (Grotta dello Smeraldo): 88–89
emergency numbers: 456
emergency services: *see* medical services
entertainment/events: Capri 246–247; Naples 355–358; *see also specific place*
environmental issues: 419
Erchie: 151, 154
Ercolano: 408
Esposito, Raffaele: 363, 367
espresso: 450, 451, 452
Etruscans: 422

F

family activities/tips: 34, 38, 276, 466–467
Fanzago, Cosimo: 347, 352, 425, 437
Faraglioni, I (rocks): 232, 237, 238, 240
Faraglioni beach: 239, 240
farmacia (pharmacies): 208, 373, 456
Farnese collections: 331, 352
fascism: 427
Fauno Bar: 205
Ferragosto (Feast of the Assumption of Mary): 28, 67
Ferrigno: 341, 360
ferry service: 27, 443–444, 446–447; Amalfi Coast towns 49–50; Capri 258–259; Naples 377–378; *see also specific place*
Festa a Mare Agli Scogli di Sant'Anna: 28, 277–278
Festa del Carmine: 357
Festa della Castagna (Chestnut Festival): 140
Festa della Colatura di Alici: 158–159
Festa del Pesce (Fish Festival): 28, 67
Festa di San Costanzo: 247
Festa di San Gennaro: 28, 358
Festa di San Giovan Giuseppe della Croce: 278
Festa di San Michele Arcangelo (Procida): 315
Festa di Sant'Antonio (Anacapri): 247
Festa di Santa Restituta: 292
Festa di San Vito: 300–301
Festa San Michele Arcangelo (Ischia): 306
Festival of La Maddalena: 118
Festival of San Giovanni Battista: 164, 308, 440
Festival of San Lorenzo: 140
Festival of San Matteo: 173–174
Festival of San Pantaleone: 130
Festival of San Pietro: 156
Festival of Santa Maria a Mare: 152
Festival of Sant'Andrea: 28, 104
Festival of Sant'Antonio (Amalfi): 104
Festival of Sant'Antonio (Sorrento): 201
Festival of Santa Trofimena: 145–147
Festival of Santi Anna e Gioacchino: 201–202
festivals: 28; Capri 247; Naples 357–358; *see also specific festival; specific place*
50 Kalò pizzeria: 33, 366, 367
film festival: 277
Fiordo di Furore: 42, 85–87
fishing: 66, 80, 154, 156, 158; *see also* seafood
flowers: 420
Fontana del Sebeto: 350
Fontana di Sant'Andrea: 96
Fontana Moresca: 144
Fonte delle Ninfe Nitrodi spa: 287, 304
food festivals: 28, 67, 140, 147, 156, 158–159, 357
food/restaurants: 25, 33, 56–57, 92, 449–453, 471–472; Capri 25, 251–254; Naples 361–368; *see also specific food; specific place*
football (soccer): 353
forests: 419–420
Forio: 263, 276, 296–303; map 291
Fornillo: 59, 62, 64
fortified cities: 311, 436–437
Forum (Pompeii): 393, 401
Foundation for Environment Education: 62, 216
Franco's Bar: 67
frazioni (villages): 59, 137, 161, 185, 216, 303, 455
fried pizza *(pizza fritta)*: 366–368, 449, 450, 453
funicular trains (cable cars): 212, 260, 376–377
Furore: 25, 84–88

G

Gabinetto Segreto (Secret Cabinet): 331, 402
Galleria Borbonico tunnel: 347–348
Galleria Umberto I: 321, 343
Gallerie d'Italia: 347
gardens: Capri 231; Ischia 296–297, 298; Naples 349, 388–390; Ravello 123, 124–126; Salerno 171; Sorrento 190, 196, 199; Tramonti 142
Garibaldi, Giuseppe: 283, 324, 426
garum fish oil (anchovies): 33, 57, 158
Garum restaurant: 407
Gavitella, La (beach): 77, 78, 80
gay and lesbian travelers, tips for: 467–468
gelaterie (ice cream shops): 206, 214, 253, 308, 317, 451
geography: 418
geology: 211–212, 383
Geranio, Il: 239, 252
Giardini di Augusto (Gardens of Augustus): 225, 231, 238
Giardini La Mortella (Mortella, La): 262, 296–297
Giardini Poseidon Terme: 286, 298–300
Giardini Ravino: 298
Giardino della Minerva: 171
Giardino Segreto dell'Anima: 142
Giordano, Luca: 340, 425, 438
glossary: 469–470
Gothic architecture: 437
government: 431
Gran Caffè (Amalfi): 110
Gran Caffè Gambrinus (Naples): 364
Grand Hotel Excelsior Vittoria: 190, 208
Grand Tour of Europe: 191, 385, 425–426
gratuities: 453
Greek myths: 60
Greeks, ancient: 421–422, 436; Capri 229; Ischia/Lacco Amena 289–290; Naples 323–324, 331, 333, 338, 339, 347, 348; Naples area 379, 382, 384, 436; Sorrento 191, 195, 200; temples (Paestum) 25, 42, 179–181, 436
Green Grotto (Grotta Verde): 236, 237
Green Island *(Isola Verde)*: 261
greetings: 457–458, 471
Grimthorpe, 2nd Baron of (Ernest William Beckett): 126
Grotta Azzurra (Blue Grotto): 225, 235–237, 245
Grotta Bianca (White Grotto): 236, 237
Grotta dello Smeraldo (Emerald Grotto): 88–89
Grotta di Matermania: 242
Grotta Meravigliosa (Marvelous Grotto): 236
Grotta Rossa (Red Grotto): 236, 237
Grotta Verde (Green Grotto): 236, 237
Gulf of Naples: 418, 421, 446
Gulf of Salerno: 418, 421, 446
Gusta Minori (A Taste of Minori): 147

H

Hall of the Augustals: 410
health: 456, 467, 472; *see also* medical services; spas (Ischia)
Herculaneum: 24, 25, 38, 392–397, 408–413, 425; maps 394, 396, 409
hiking: 57, 134–135, 448; Amalfi 100, 102; Amalfi Coast overview 25, 42, 57, 134–135; Capri 243–245; guides 65, 245; Ischia 305–306; maps 126, 134, 465; Positano 57, 64–65; Ravello 57, 126–127; Scala 57, 140, 145; Vesuvius 414–415; *see also* walking
Hiking to the Crater (Vesuvius): 393, 414–415
history: 323–324, 421–430; *see also* Greeks, ancient; medieval heritage; Romans, ancient
holidays, public: 463–464
hospitals: *see* medical services
hostels *(ostelli)*: 455
hotels: 454–455; *see also* accommodations
hours, opening: 453, 454, 463
House of Neptune and Amphitrite: 393, 412
House of the Deer: 393, 412
House of the Wooden Partition: 412
Houses of Pompeii: 403–404

IJK

immigration: 434
industries: 433
information/services: 464–465; Capri 258; Ischia/Procida 281, 295, 318; Naples 373; *see also specific place*
insurance, automobile: 445
intarsia (inlaid wood): 194–195, 195–196, 198, 202, 439
Ischia: 23, 35–36, 36–37, 261–310; Barano d'Ischia 36, 276, 303, 304–310; Casamicciola Terme 283–285, 286, 287, 288–289; Forio 263, 276, 291, 296–303; Ischia Town 28, 272–283; Lacco Ameno 35, 263, 276, 289–296; maps 264–265, 270–271, 273, 291; Sant'Angelo 262, 266, 276, 303, 304–310; Serrara Fontana 303, 309–310
Ischia Film Festival: 277
Ischia Ponte: 263, 272
Ischia Porto: 263, 272
Ischia Town: 28, 272–283; map 273
Isola di Vivara Riserva Naturale Statale: 314–315
Isola Verde (Green Island): 261
Italian language: 435, 458, 466, 470–473
Italic tribes: 422
itineraries, suggested: Amalfi (town) 30, 51; Amalfi Coast towns 30–32, 39–40, 51–56; Capri 32, 36, 228–229; Ischia/Procida 36–37, 268–271; Naples 32, 326–330; Pompeii/Herculaneum/Vesuvius 32, 396–397, 402–403; Positano 30–31, 51, 54; Procida 37, 269, 271;

Ravello 31, 54; Sorrentine Peninsula 187–189; Sorrento 31–32, 36, 186–187
jazz festivals: 202
jewelry: 359–360
Jewish community: 434–435
kayaking: Amalfi Coast towns 66, 80, 102, 145; Ischia/Procida 306, 314; Posillipo 381; Sorrento area 17, 38, 200, 220
Kingdom of Italy: 324, 426
Kingdom of Two Sicilies: 343, 426
kissing: 458
Kona restaurant: 415

L

Lacco Ameno: 35, 263, 276, 289–296; map 291
Lago d'Averno: 383–384
Lampara, La: 279
language: 435, 458, 466, 470–473
L'Antica Pizzeria da Michele: 33, 362, 367
L'Antica Trattoria: 205
Lattari Mountains (Monti Lattari): 184, 212
Laurito Beach: 34, 59, 64
leather goods: 360
Lemonjazz Festival: 202
lemons/lemon products: 33, 103, 108, 145, 204, 420
Lemon Twist cooking class: 33, 246
Letters from Mt. Vesuvius: 436
LGBTQ travelers, tips for: 467–468
Lido Azzurro: 108
Li Galli Islands: 60
limoncello liqueur: 33, 204, 420, 452
limone Costa d'Amalfi: 420
limone di Sorrento: 420
literature: 435–436
locals, habits of: 54–55, 330, 450, 457
Lombards: 423
luggage tips: 460
Luminaria di San Domenico festival: 81
lungomari (waterfront promenades): Maiori 149, 154; Naples 349; Salerno 168, 173
Lupaner (Pompeii): 401–402

M

MacKowen, John Clay: 239
Madonna of the Sea (Santa Maria A Mare) statue: 149–150
Madre (Museo d'Arte Contemporanea Donnaregina): 340
Maiori: 54, 149–154
Maiori Beach: 34, 150
Malanga, Patrizia: 162–163
Maliblu Sunset: 239, 247
Mamma Agata: 127–128
mammals: 414, 420–421
maps, tourist: 126, 134, 464–465
Marechiaro: 381
Margherita pizza: 363, 367
Marina Corricella: 21, 262, 310, 316
Marina del Cantone beach: 35, 183, 190, 219–220
Marina di Atrani (Atrani Beach): 34, 117
Marina di Cetara (Cetara Beach): 35, 156
Marina di Conca: 56, 89
Marina di Erchie: 151
Marina di Praia: 34, 42, 77, 80
Marina di Puolo: 216, 218
Marina di Vico: 214
Marina di Vietri: 163
Marina Grande beach (Amalfi): 99
Marina Grande harbor (Procida): 310, 315
Marina Grande harbor (Sorrento): 14, 35, 183, 191, 199–200
Marina Grande port (Capri): 227, 240, 251–252, 257–258
Marina Piccola (Capri): 13, 35, 225, 239, 241–242
Marina Piccola (Sorrento): 191, 199, 209
Marinella, La (beach): 99
Mario D'Ischia Sandali: 294
Maritime Station (Stazione Marittima di Salerno): 168, 178
Marmeeting Mediterranean Cup: 85, 87
marquetry: *see* intarsia (inlaid wood)
Marvelous Grotto (Grotta Meravigliosa): 236
Masaniello Art Café: 103
Maschio Angioino (Castel Nuovo): 342
Massa Lubrense: 184, 185, 190, 211, 216–219
Massine, Léonide: 60, 67
meals/mealtimes: 450, 457
measurements (metric): 464
medical museum: 340, 342
medical services: 456, 472; Amalfi 114; Capri 258; Ischia 295; Naples 373; Ravello 136; Salerno 177; Sorrento 208
medieval heritage (Middle Ages): 98, 106, 121, 150, 423–424; *see also* castles; cathedrals; churches; Republic of Amalfi
Medieval Museum (Museo Medievale): 171
menu courses: 450
Mergellina: 350
Meta: 185
metro system (Naples): 376
Minori: 34, 54, 56, 144–148
Minuta: 137
Miramare e Castello: 281
mobile phone services: 462
Moda Positano, La (Positano Fashion): 69
Molo Foraneo pier: 93
Molo Manfredi: 168, 178
Monastero di San Paolo al Deserto: 190, 211, 221–222
Monastero Santa Rosa: 92

money: 460–462, 464
Monte Epomeo: 261, 262, 263, 303, 305–306, 306–307
Monte Faito: 190, 212
Monte Gambera: 60
Montepertuso: 59, 60
Monte Solaro: 14, 38, 225, 237–238, 243–245
Monte Tiberio: 227, 232, 234
Monte Vico: 289
Monti Lattari (Lattari Mountains): 184, 212
Morelli, Domenico: 438
Moresca, La: 131, 158
Mortella, La (Giardini La Mortella): 262, 296–297
Mostobuono: 368
motorcycle travel: *see* scooter travel
Mount Vesuvius: 20, 24, 38, 392–397, 413–416, 418, 430, 436; maps 394, 396; *see also* Herculaneum; Pompeii
Mt. Vesuvius National Park (Parco Nazionale del Vesuvio): 414
Munthe, Axel: 236–237
Museo Angelo Rizzoli: 290
Museo Archeological Romano Santa Maria Assunta: 59
Museo Archeologico dei Campi Flegrei: 386
Museo Archeologico di Pithecusae: 290
Museo Archeologico Nazionale (National Archaeological Museum, Naples): 18, 321, 331
Museo Archeologico Nazionale (Paestum): 181
Museo Archeologico Provinciale: 170–171
Museo Arti Sanitarie: 340, 342
Museobottega della Tarsialignea: 16, 38, 183, 195–196, 198
Museo Cappella Sansevero: 337
Museo Civico del Torrione: 298
Museo Civico Filangieri: 338
Museo Correale di Terranova: 183, 198–199
Museo d'Arte Contemporanea Donnaregina (Madre): 340
Museo del Corallo: 123–124
Museo della Bussola e del Ducato Marinaro di Amalfi (Museum of the Compass and Duchy of Amalfi): 98
Museo della Carta (papermaking): 38, 98
Museo della Ceramica (Provincial Museum of Ceramics): 162
Museo delle Carrozze (carriages): 350
Museo dell'Opera (Naples): 337
Museo dell'Opera del Duomo (Ravello): 123
Museo del Mare (Museum of the Sea): 274
Museo del Tesoro di San Gennaro: 338
Museo di Capodimonte (Museo e Real Bosco di Capodimonte): 321, 352–353, 379
Museo Diocesano (Amalfi): 98
Museo Diocesano (Salerno): 170
Museo Doma: 337
Museo Duca di Martina: 352
Museo e Real Bosco di Capodimonte (Museo di Capodimonte): 321, 352–353, 379, 437
Museo Medievale (Medieval Museum): 171
Museo Mineralogico Campano (Campanian Mineralogical Museum): 211–212
Museum of Rural Life Arts and Crafts: 103
Museum of the Compass and Duchy of Amalfi (Museo della Bussola e del Ducato Marinaro di Amalfi): 98
Museum of the Sea (Museo del Mare): 274
music events/venues: 81, 128–130, 201, 202, 355–357, 439
music overview: 439
Mussolini, Benito: 427, 429

N

Naples: 8, 24, 25, 32, 38, 320–391, 437–438; accommodations 369–370; arts/culture 355–357, 425, 435–437, 438–440; festivals/events 28, 357–358; food 33, 361–363; history 323–324, 423–426, 429–430; information/services 373; maps 322–323, 328–329, 332, 334–335, 344–345, 380; nearby 379–391; neighborhoods 324–325; nightlife 354–355; shopping 358–361; sights 331–342; sports/recreation 353–354; transportation 373–379
Naples Cathedral (Duomo di Napoli): 321, 338, 358
Napoli Centrale Stazione: 374
Napoli Pizza Village festival: 28, 357
Napoli Sotterranea (Underground Naples): 38, 339
Napoli Sotterranea, L.A.E.S. (Underground Naples): 38, 347
Napulitanata: 355
National Archaeological Museum (Museo Archeologico Nazionale, Naples): 18, 321, 331
nativities *(presepi)*: 204, 340, 341, 360–361
Natural Arch (Arco Naturale): 232, 237, 242
nature reserve: 314–315
naval/nautical history: 98, 274
'Ndrezzata folk dance: 306, 308, 440
Neapolitan music (traditional): 201, 355, 357, 439
Neapolitan opera: 343, 355, 356–357, 439
Neapolitan pizza: 19, 33, 367, 449
Negombo spa: 286, 287, 290, 292
Nerano: 17, 25, 35, 190, 219–221
New Year's Eve (Capodanno): 28, 103
Niemeyer, Oscar: 128
nightlife: Amalfi 103; Capri 246–247; Naples 354–355; Positano 67; Praiano 80–81; Ravello 128; Salerno 173; Sorrento 202
Nocelle: 57, 59, 60, 62, 65
Normans: 423

Notte delle Lampare (Night of the Fishing Lights): 28, 156, 158
Notte di Masaniello, La: 118

OPQ

Odyssey, The (Homer): 60
olives: 420
opera: 343, 355, 356, 357, 439
osteria eateries: 449
outdoor recreation: 25, 39–40
packing tips: 27, 29, 460
Paese Che Non C'è, Il (The Town that Doesn't Exist): 84
Paese Dipinto, Il (The Painted City): 84
Paestum: 25, 42, 43, 179–181; map 180
Painted City, The *(Il Paese Dipinto)*: 84
painting: 438
palaces (Naples): 342–343, 352–353, 388–391, 437
Palaestra (Roman sports): 412
Palazzo Avino: 135–136
Palazzo Cerio (Palazzo Arcucci): 231
Palazzo dell'Oroglogio (Clock Palace): 274
Palazzo Donn'Anna: 381
Palazzo Mezzacapo: 150
Palazzo Reale (Royal Palace): 321, 342–343, 437
PAN - Palazzo delle Arti Napoli: 350
paper, shopping for: 107
papermaking (Museo della Carta): 38, 98
parades: 106, 152, 468
Parco Archeologico del Pausilypon: 379
Parco Archeologico di Cuma: 384
Parco Archeologico di Ercolano: 409
Parco Archeologico di Paestum: 179
Parco Archeologico di Pompei: 399–400
Parco Archeologico Sommerso di Baia: 386
Parco Castiglione Resort & Spa: 284, 286
Parco Nazionale del Vesuvio (Mt. Vesuvius National Park): 414
Parco Virgiliano: 381
parking: *see* car travel
parks: 314–315, 381; *see also specific parco*
Parsifal (Wagner): 123, 130, 133, 439
Parthenopean Republic (Naples): 426
passports: 26, 447
Pasticceria Pansa: 92, 110
pasticceria shops: 450; *see also* bakeries; desserts
Pathway of the Forts (Sentiero dei Fortini): 243
Pathway of the Gods (Sentiero degli Dei) trail: 25, 57, 64–65, 81, 135
Pathway of the Lemons (Sentiero dei Limoni): 33, 135, 145
pathways: *see* walking
pay phones: 462
performing arts: 173, 355–357, 439–440
perfume: 69, 248, 316
Pescatore, Il: 316
pharmacies *(farmacia)*: 208, 373, 456
philosophy: 435–436
phrases/phrasebook: 458, 470–473
Piano di Sorrento: 185
Piazza Bellini: 333
Piazza Dante: 333
Piazza dei Dogi: 96
Piazza dei Martiri: 349
Piazza dei Mulini: 57, 68
Piazza del Gesù Nuovo: 333
Piazza del Plebiscito: 342, 343
Piazza Duomo (Amalfi): 93, 96, 104
Piazza Duomo (Ravello): 121
Piazza Fontana Moresca: 124
Piazza Marina: 283
Piazza Martiri Ungheresi: 155
Piazza Municipio (Amalfi): 96
Piazza Municipio (Scala): 137–138
Piazza San Francesco: 154–155
Piazza Sant'Antonino: 201
Piazza Tasso: 191, 194
Piazza Umberto I (Atrani): 117
Piazza Umberto I (Capri town): 229–230
Piazza Umberto I (Vico Equense): 211
Piazzetta, La (Capri town): 229–230
Pinacoteca Provinciale di Salerno: 171
Pintauro, Pasquale: 92, 364, 365
Pintauro bakery: 364, 365
Pio Monte della Misericordia: 338–339
pizza: 33, 367, 449–450; festival 357; Naples 25, 33, 361, 363, 452–453; Neapolitan 19, 33, 367, 449; Tramonti 142–143; Vico Equense 214
Pizza a Metro da Gigino: 33, 214
pizza fritta (fried pizza): 366–368, 449, 450, 453
Pizzaria Criscemunno: 33, 175
Pizzaria La Notizia: 33, 366, 367
Pizzeria Donna Stella: 110
planning tips: 22–29, 465–468; Amalfi Coast towns 22, 50, 56–57, 325; Capri 23, 228; Ischia/Procida 23, 267; Naples 24, 325–326; Pompeii/Herculaneum/Vesuvius 24, 394–395, 400, 409–410; Sorrento/Sorrentine Peninsula 22–23, 186
plants: 420
Pliny the Younger: 436
police agencies: 456
political parties: 431–432
Pompeii: 20, 24, 25, 32, 331, 392–396, 397–407, 425; maps 394, 396, 398–399, 402
Pontone: 137, 138–140
porcelain production: 439
Porta Marina (Sorrento restaurant): 33, 204
Porta Marina entrance (Pompeii): 399, 400, 402, 407
Porto di Cetara: 156
Porto di Napoli (Port of Naples): 27, 374–375, 377

Porto Turistico (Salerno): 178
Posillipo: 379–382
Posillipo Beach: 381
Positano: 28, 30–31, 34, 35, 39–40, 51, 54, 56–77; map 58
Positano Fashion *(La Moda Positano)*: 69
Positano Premia La Danza Léonide Massine: 67
postal services (Poste Italiane): 462–463; Amalfi 114; Naples 373; Positano 74; Ravello 136; Salerno 177
Postino, Il (movie): 263, 276, 314, 475
Pozzuoli: 382–385
Praiano: 77–84
Praiano NaturArte: 78
presepi (nativities): 204, 340, 341, 360–361
Principe e la Civetta, Il: 158, 165
Procida: 23, 36, 37, 262, 267, 269, 276, 310–319; maps 265, 271, 311
Profumi di Positano: 69
pronunciation guide: 470–471
Protected Marina Area of Punta Campanella (Area Marina Protetta di Punta Campanella): 218
Provincial Museum of Ceramics (Museo della Ceramica): 162
public holidays: 463–464
public transportation: 376
Punta Campanella: 185, 218
Punta Carena: 35, 237, 242
Purgatorio ad Arco: 342
Quartieri Spagnoli (Spanish Quarter): 342, 368, 424

R

racially diverse travelers, tips for: 468
railway travel: *see* train travel
Raito: 161, 162–163, 167
Ravello: 25, 28, 31, 40, 54, 57, 120–137, 439; map 122
Ravello Festival: 28, 42, 128–130, 439
Ravello to Atrani hike: 127, 135
Ravello to Minori hike: 127, 135
Real Borgo di San Leucio: 390
Reale Cappella del Tesoro di San Gennaro: 338
recreation: 39–40, 448; *see also specific activity; specific place*
Red Grotto (Grotta Rossa): 236, 237
Regata dei Tre Golfi: 247
Regatta of the Ancient Maritime Republics (Regata delle Antiche Repubbliche Marinare): 106
Reggia di Caserta: 27, 321, 341, 388–391, 437
Regina Isabella Terme & Spa: 286, 287, 292
relics of San Matteo (St. Matthew): 170
religion: 434–435
rental cars/scooters: 444–445
reptiles: 421
Republic of Amalfi: 57, 106, 120, 137, 138, 142, 149
reservations: 454–456; *see also* accommodations
restaurants: 449–453; *see also* food/restaurants
Riccio, Il: 239, 253
Rione Terra: 383
Risanamento (Restoration): 324, 343, 426, 438
Riso, Salvatore de: 147
Ristorante Amici Miei: 365–366
Ristorante Don Alfonso 1890: 222
ristorante eateries: 449
Ristorante Garden: 131
Ristorante Il Cantuccio: 211, 218
Ristorante Il Geranio: 239, 252
Ristorante Lo Scoglio: 220
Ristorante Marina Grande: 109
Ristorante Michel'angelo: 245–246, 252
Ristorante Pizzeria Al Convento: 159
Ristorante Pizzeria Nettuno: 152
Ristorante San Giovanni: 141
Ristorante San Pietro: 33, 159
Rizzoli, Angelo: 290, 295
rock climbing: 65–66
Rolex Capri Sailing Week: 247
Romans, ancient: 422–423, 436; Amalfi Coast towns 59, 144–145, 168, 170; Capri 232–234, 239–240, 422; Ischia 304; Naples and nearby 331, 338, 339, 379, 383, 385–386; Sorrento 191, 195; *see also* Herculaneum; Mount Vesuvius; Pompeii
Rome: 177
Rossellinis: 131
Royal Palace (Palazzo Reale): 321, 342–343, 437
Rubinacci: 359
ruins, ancient: 436; *see also* Greeks, ancient; Romans, ancient

S

safety: 456–457
Sagra del Pesce Spada: 292, 294
sailing (regattas): 106, 247
Sal de Riso: 147
Salerno: 43, 57, 168–179, 423; map 169
Salerno day trip: 179–181
sales tax: 461–462
Salicerchie beach: 150–151
San Ferdinando (Naples): 324; accommodations 370–371; arts 356; food 363–364; sights 342–343, 347–350
San Matteo (St. Matthew), relics of: 170
Santa Croce beach: 35, 56, 100
Sant'Agata sui Due Golfi: 190, 211, 221–222
Sant'Agnello: 185
Santa Maria A Mare (Madonna of the Sea) statue: 149–150
Sant'Angelo: 262, 266, 276, 303, 304–310
Santa Rosa, Sfogliatella: 92, 365
Santuario della Madonna del Carmine: 194

Scala: 55, 57, 137–141; map 122
Scala to Amalfi hike: 135, 140
Scaturchio: 363
Schola Medica Salernitana: 168, 171, 423
scooter travel: 444–445; Amalfi Coast towns 43, 46–47; Capri 260; Naples 378; *see also specific place*
Scuderia del Duca, La: 107
seafood: 25, 33, 67, 156, 158–159, 452; *see also specific place*
sealife: 421
seaside destinations: *see* beaches
seasons: 24, 26, 48, 50, 65, 418–419, 467
Secret Cabinet (Gabinetto Segreto): 331, 402
Sedil Dominova: 195
Seggiovia Monte Solaro chairlift: 238
senior travelers, tips for: 467
Sentiero degli Dei (Pathway of the Gods) trail: 25, 57, 64–65, 81, 135
Sentiero dei Fortini (Pathway of the Forts): 243
Sentiero dei Limoni (Pathway of the Lemons): 33, 135, 145
Serrara Fontana: 303, 309–310
Serrara Fontana Belvedere: 303
Settembrata Anacaprese festival: 247
Settimana Santa (Easter week): 28, 315
Seven Works of Mercy, The (Caravaggio): 339, 438
Sfogliatella Attanasio: 363, 365
Sfogliatella dessert: 92, 363, 364, 365
Sfogliatella Mary, La: 364, 365
shipping: 454
shoes, packing tips for: 29, 77, 134, 448–449, 460
shoe/sandal shops: 68, 204, 248–250, 294
shopping: 453–454, 472; Capri 248–251; Naples 358–361; *see also specific place*
sightseeing passes: 326, 400, 409, 464
Sirene beach, Le: 100
smoking: 458
Solfatara (volcanic crater): 385
Solimena, Francesco: 171, 333, 425, 438
solo travelers, tips for: 467
Sorbillo pizzeria: 33, 362, 367
Sorrento Musical and Tarantella Show: 201
Sorrento/Sorrentine Peninsula: 182–223; maps 184–185, 187, 188–189, 192–193; Sorrentine Peninsula 23, 35, 38, 182–190, 210–223; Sorrento 22–23, 28, 31–32, 35, 36, 38, 182–190, 191–210
Sounds of the Gods, The (I Suoni Degli Dei): 81
spa/beauty products: 278
Spaccanapoli: 321, 324, 333
Spanish Quarter *(Quartieri Spagnoli)*: 342, 368, 424
Spanish rule (Naples): 424–425
spas (Ischia): 20, 25, 262, 263, 284, 286–287, 290–292, 298–300, 304–305
Spiaggia Citara: 276, 300
Spiaggia degli Inglesi: 277
Spiaggia dei Maronti beach: 36, 266, 276, 305
Spiaggia dei Pescatori: 274, 276, 277
Spiaggia della Chiaia beach: 36, 276, 313–314
Spiaggia della Chiaiolella: 314
Spiaggia della Marina: 284
Spiaggia del Lannio: 156
Spiaggia delle Fumarole: 305
Spiaggia del Porto: 99
Spiaggia del Postino: 276, 314
Spiaggia del Pozzo Vecchio: 276, 314
Spiaggia di Chiaia: 300
Spiaggia di Fornillo beach: 34, 38, 59, 62, 64
Spiaggia di San Francesco: 276, 300
Spiaggia di San Montano: 292
Spiaggia di San Pietro: 274
Spiaggia di Sant'Angelo: 276, 305
Spiaggia Grande beach (Minori): 145
Spiaggia Grande beach (Positano): 11, 30–31, 34, 42, 62
sports: 449; *see also specific place; specific sport*
Spritzerò-Aperitivo Italiano: 355
SSC Napoli: 353
Stabian Baths: 401
stabilimente balneari: *see* beach clubs
Stadio San Paolo: 353
Starita a Materdei pizzeria: 362, 367
Stazione di Salerno: 177
Stazione Marittima di Salerno (Maritime Station): 168, 178
steps/stairs, warnings about: 77, 127, 134, 448, 455, 460, 465–466
Stinga Tarsia: 198, 204
store hours: 358, 454
Story of San Michele, The (Munthe): 236
street food: 449–450
studying, opportunities for: 465
Suoni Degli Dei, I (The Sounds of the Gods): 81
Surrender of Caserta: 430
Surrentum (Roman town): 195
sweets: *see pasticceria* shops
swimming: *see* beaches

T

Tagliata, La: 70
Taste of Minori, A (Gusta Minori): 147
taxis: 50, 447; Amalfi 116; Capri 260; Ischia 267, 282–283; Naples 377; Positano 76–77; *see also specific place*
tax refunds: 461–462
Teatro Augusteo: 356
Teatro Bellini: 356
Teatro Diana: 357
Teatro di San Carlo: 343, 356
Teatro Giuseppe Verdi: 173
Teatro Palapartenope: 357

telephones: 462
temperatures: 419
Tempio di Serapide: 383
Temple of Athena: 181
Temple of Hera (Basilica): 179
Temple of Neptune: 179, 181
temples, Greek (Paestum): 25, 42, 179–181, 436
Tenuta San Francesco Vineyard: 33, 85, 142
Terme di Cavascura spa: 287, 304–305
Terme Manzi Hotel & Spa: 284
Terra Madre: 294
Terra Murata: 262, 311–313
theater: 439–440
theaters (Pompeii): 401
thermal spas: *see* spas (Ischia)
Tiberius (Roman Emperor): 232–234
time/dates: 464, 472–473
timeline, historical: 428–429
tipping: 453
toiletries, packing tips for: 460
Toledo, Pedro Álvarez de: 424
Torre a Mare watchtower: 80
Torre Cerniola watchtower: 151
Torre dell'Orologio (Clock Tower): 229–230
Torre dello Ziro watchtower hike: 135, 140
Torre di Cetara watchtower: 155
Torre di Clavel watchtower: 62
Torre di Sant'Angelo: 304
Torre Museo: 123
Torre Normanna watchtower: 152–153
Torre Saracena beach: 241
Torre Trasita watchtower: 59
tourism: 430, 433
tourist offices: 464; Capri 258; Naples 373; *see also specific place*
tours/tour guides: Amalfi Coast towns 66, 103; nature reserve 314–315; Pompeii/Herculaneum/Vesuvius 395, 400, 404, 410; *see also* boat trips/rentals
Town that Doesn't Exist, The *(Il Paese Che Non C'è)*: 84
train travel: 27, 442–443, 444; Capri 260; Naples 43, 177, 374, 376–377; *see also specific place*
Tramonti: 25, 85, 142–143
transportation: 26–27, 441–447, 471; Amalfi Coast towns 43, 47–50, 325; Capri 258–260; Naples 325, 373–379; *see also specific place*
Trattoria da Cumpà Cosima: 131
Trattoria Da Lorenzo: 33, 141
Trattoria Da Maria: 108–109, 158
trattoria eateries: 449
travelers, tips for: *see* planning tips
trees: 419–420
Trellis House: 412

UV

Ufficio Informazioni Turistiche di Praiano: 83
Underground Naples: 38, 339, 347
UNESCO Intangible Cultural Heritage of Humanity list: 367
UNESCO World Heritage sites: 22, 41, 438
urban renewal (Naples): 437–438
Valle dei Mulini, La: 33, 108
Valle delle Ferriere trail (Valle delle Mulini trail): 12, 25, 39, 100, 102, 135, 140
Vallone dei Mulini: 194
Vertical City (Positano): 41, 56
Vesuvius: *see* Mount Vesuvius
Vettica Maggiore: 77
Via Alessandro Scarlatti: 359
Via Camerelle: 248
Via Chiaia: 358
Via dei Mille: 358
Via dell'Abbondanza: 402–403
Viale Enrico Caruso: 194
Viale Pasitea: 57, 68
Via Magna Grecia: 179, 181
Via Mercanti: 168, 174–175
Via Positanesi d'America: 59
Via Roma: 310, 318
Via San Gregorio Armeno: 340, 341, 358–359
Via Toledo: 324, 358
Via Vittorio Emanuele: 248
Vico Equense: 185, 190, 210–216
Vietri sul Mare: 57, 85, 158, 161–167, 439
viewpoints: Capri 238–239; Ischia/Procida 276; Sorrentine Peninsula 183, 190
Vigne di Raito, Le: 33, 85, 162–163
Villa Cimbrone: 16, 42, 121, 124–126
Villa Comunale gardens (Naples): 349
Villa Comunale gardens (Salerno): 171
Villa Comunale gardens (Sorrento): 190, 196
Villa dei Misteri (Villa of the Mysteries): 393, 404–406
Villa dei Papiri (Villa of the Papyri): 408
Villa di Damecuta: 239–240, 422
Villa Fiorentino: 201, 202
Villa Jovis: 225, 232–234, 238, 422
Villa Lysis: 234–235, 237
Villa Malaparte: 237, 243
Villa Pignatelli: 349–350
Villa Romana: 144–145, 422
Villa Rufolo: 121, 123
villas, history of: 422
Villa San Michele: 225, 236–237, 238
vineyards: 33, 420; Amalfi Coast towns 25, 33, 85, 87, 142, 162–163; Ischia 33, 300; Vico Equense 212, 214
Virgil: 383–384, 386, 436

visas: 26, 447–448
visitor information: *see* tourist offices
Vittoria Colonna: 272
Viva Lo Re: 413
volcanic activity: 385, 397, 408, 413–414, 418
Vomero (Naples): 325; accommodations 372–373; arts 357; food 368; shopping 359; sights 350, 352

W

Wagner, Richard: 123, 128, 130, 439
walking: 59, 77, 78, 80, 93, 173, 242–243; *see also* hiking; *lungomari* (waterfront promenades); steps/stairs, warnings about
Walking Tour of Pompeii Highlights: 402–403
Walton, Sir William and Susan: 296–297
watchtowers: 59, 62, 80, 135, 140, 151, 152–153, 155, 436
water, drinking: 451–452
waterfront neighborhood (Naples): 324–325; accommodations 371–372; arts 356–357; food 364–368; nightlife 355; sights 348–350
waterfront promenades: *see lungomari* (waterfront promenades)
water sports: 449; Amalfi Coast towns 34, 66, 80, 102; Ischia/Procidia 276, 277, 306, 314; Sorrento/Sorrentine Peninsula 200, 218
weather: 24, 418–419
wheelchair accessibility: 465–466
whistles, ceramic: 284
White Grotto (Grotta Bianca): 236, 237
Wi-Fi networks: 462
wildflowers: 420
windsurfing: 80, 102
Wine and the City festival: 357
wines/wine tours: 66, 87, 142, 300, 357, 452; *see also* vineyards
women travelers, tips for: 467
woodwork, inlaid (intarsia): 194–196, 195–196, 198, 202, 439
World War I: 426–427
World War II: 149, 348, 388, 427–430

List of Maps

Front Map

Amalfi Coast: 4–5

Discover Amalfi Coast

chapter divisions map: 23

Amalfi Coast

Amalfi Coast and Paestum: 44–45
Amalfi Coast: 46–47
Itinerary Ideas: 52–53
Positano: 58
Amalfi: 94–95
Ravello and Scala: 122
Salerno: 169
Paestum: 180

Sorrento and the Sorrentine Peninsula

Sorrento and the Sorrentine Peninsula: 184–185
One Day in Sorrento: 187
Driving Tour of the Sorrentine Peninsula: 188–189
Sorrento: 192–193

Capri

Capri: 226–227
Itinerary Idea: 229
Capri Town: 230

Ischia and Procida

Ischia and Procida: 264–265
Itinerary Ideas: 270–271
Ischia Town: 273
Lacco Ameno and Forio: 291
Procida: 311

Naples

Greater Naples: 322–323
Itinerary Ideas: 328–329
Naples Overview: 332
Centro Storico: 334–335
San Ferdinando, Waterfront, and Vomero: 344–345
Around Naples: 380

Pompeii, Herculaneum, and Vesuvius

Pompeii, Herculaneum, and Vesuvius: 394
Itinerary Ideas: 396
Pompeii: 398–399
Herculaneum: 409

Photo Credits

All photos © Laura Thayer except: title page photo © Francesco Riccardo Iacomino/123rf.com; page 2 © Massimobuonaiuto | Dreamstime.com; page 6 © (top left) Tannjuska | Dreamstime.com; (top right) Mikolaj64 | Dreamstime.com; (bottom) Aleh Varanishcha | Dreamstime.com; page 7 © (top) Freesurf69 | Dreamstime.com; (bottom left) Tat'jana Michaljova /123rf.com; (bottom right) Anton Ivanov /123rf.com; page 8 © (top) Francesca Sciarra | Dreamstime.com; page 9 © (top) Janos Gaspar | Dreamstime.com; (bottom left) Zdeněk Matyáš | Dreamstime.com; (bottom right) Selinairina77 | Dreamstime.com; page 10 © Lorenzobovi | Dreamstime.com; page 13 © darios/123rf.com; page 15 © (top) Ig0rzh | Dreamstime.com; (bottom) Felis | Dreamstime.com; page 16 © (top) Sergiomonti - Dreamstime.com; (bottom) Museobottega della Tarsialignea; page 17 © Marco Cesarano | Dreamstime.com; page 18 © Kanokrat Tawokhat | Dreamstime.com; page 19 © (top) Floriano Rescigno | Dreamstime.com; (bottom) PFMphotostock/ Shutterstock; page 20 © (top) Sorin Colac | Dreamstime.com; (bottom) shutterstock; page 21 © Mikolaj64 | Dreamstime.com; page 22 © (bottom) Erdalakan | Dreamstime.com; page 29 © (top) Selinairina77 | Dreamstime.com; page 34 © (bottom) Josef Skacel /123rf.com; page 41 © Natursports | Dreamstime.com; page 65 © Massimobuonaiuto | Dreamstime.com; page 79 © (top) Gastonebaldo | Dreamstime.com; page 86 © (bottom) Giacomo Scandroglio | Dreamstime.com; page 92 © Maurice Naragon / Monastero Santa Rosa; page 97 © (top) Laszlo Konya | Dreamstime.com; page 105 © (bottom right) Rinofelino | Dreamstime.com; page 125 © (top) Wieslaw Jarek | Dreamstime.com; (left middle) Leklek73 | Dreamstime.com; (bottom) Pino Izzo / Ravello Festival; page 129 © (bottom) Pino Izzo / Ravello Festival; page 133 © Tyson Sadlo / Belmond Hotel Caruso; page 157 © (bottom) Pfeifferv | Dreamstime.com; page 217 © (top) Cristiano Nunziata; page 220 © Adeliepenguin | Dreamstime.com; page 223 © (top) Giuseppemasci | Dreamstime.com; page 233 © (bottom) Ig0rzh | Dreamstime.com; page 235 © Casadphoto | Dreamstime.com; page 241 © Mikolaj64 | Dreamstime.com; page 244 © (top right) Wipark Kulnirandorn | Dreamstime.com; (bottom) Felis | Dreamstime.com; page 261 © Beriliu | Dreamstime.com; page 269 © Monticelllo | Dreamstime.com; page 275 © (top) Ig0rzh | Dreamstime.com; (right middle) Esherez | Dreamstime.com; (bottom) Jacob Moore | Dreamstime.com; page 276 © Beach with umbrellas,Italy San angelo, on Ischia, island in bay of Naples, italy; page 287 © Morozova Oxana/Shutterstock.com; page 293 © (bottom) Eugenesergeev | Dreamstime.com; page 297 © Maddalena Di Gregorio | Dreamstime.com; page 299 © (top left) Mariyasiyanko | Dreamstime.com; (bottom left) Danilo Mongiello | Dreamstime.com; (bottom right) Anastasiia Pliekhova | Dreamstime.com; page 307 © (top left) Massimo Buonaiuto | Dreamstime.com; page 327 © Enzodebe | Dreamstime.com; page 330 © Rcgcristi | Dreamstime.com; page 336 © (top) Enrico Della Pietra | Dreamstime.com; page 346 © (top) Laraslk | Dreamstime.com; (bottom) Christophefaugere | Dreamstime.com; page 351 © Enrico Della Pietra | Dreamstime.com; page 356 © Photogolfer | Dreamstime.com; page 365 © Stefano Carnevali | Dreamstime.com; page 384 © Raffaele1 | Dreamstime.com; page 389 © (top) Enzodebe | Dreamstime.com; (left middle)Lucamato | Dreamstime.com; (right middle)Tiziano Casalta | Dreamstime.com; (bottom) Perseomedusa | Dreamstime.com; page 392 © Martin Molcan | Dreamstime.com; page 405 © (top) Pablo Boris Debat | Dreamstime.com; (left middle) Maxim Sergeenkov | Dreamstime.com; (right middle) Alexandre Fagundes De Fagundes | Dreamstime.com; (bottom) Floriano Rescigno | Dreamstime.com; page 406 © Yi Liao | Dreamstime.com; page 411 © (top left) Merlin1812 | Dreamstime.com; (top right) Porojnicu | Dreamstime.com; (bottom) Nicolas De Corte | Dreamstime.com; page 414 © Rcgcristi | Dreamstime.com; page 417 © Pfeifferv | Dreamstime.com; page 441 © Jamie Frattarelli | Dreamstime.com.

Acknowledgments

A place as beautiful as the Amalfi Coast is a dream for inspiration, especially with the rich artistic and cultural heritage and warmth of the locals in Campania. Many thanks to everyone I encountered who helped me with details, history, and stories while I was writing.

This book is a labor of love that never would have happened without the inspiration of my mother, Sandra Thayer, who first brought me to the Amalfi Coast in 2007 on a mother-daughter holiday. Thank you for being my biggest cheerleader always and for supporting my journey every step of the way.

A huge thank you to all of my family and to my friends who stuck with me through this project, especially the ones who checked in every once in a while to make sure I was still here. A heartfelt thanks to Michelle Kaminsky who kept me laughing every day—no matter what.

Many thanks to the team at Moon who helped bring the book to life. Special appreciation to Grace Fujimoto who really was the saving grace of the book from start to finish.

A special thank you to my husband, Lello Brandi, for sharing this beautiful place in the world and our life together.

MAP SYMBOLS

Roads and routes	Places	Services	Features
Expressway	City/Town	Information Center	Park
Primary Road	State Capital	Parking Area	Golf Course
Secondary Road	National Capital	Church	Unique Feature
Unpaved Road	Highlight	Winery	Waterfall
Trail	Point of Interest	Trailhead	Camping
Ferry	Accommodation	Train Station	Mountain
Railroad	Restaurant/Bar	Airport	Ski Area
Pedestrian Walkway	Other Location	Airfield	Glacier
Stairs			

CONVERSION TABLES

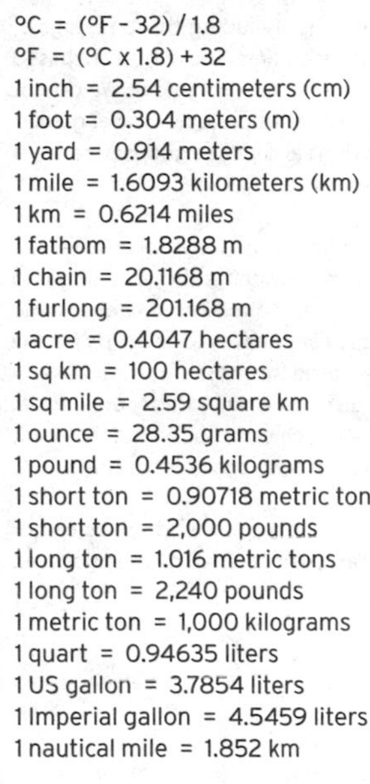

°C = (°F - 32) / 1.8
°F = (°C x 1.8) + 32
1 inch = 2.54 centimeters (cm)
1 foot = 0.304 meters (m)
1 yard = 0.914 meters
1 mile = 1.6093 kilometers (km)
1 km = 0.6214 miles
1 fathom = 1.8288 m
1 chain = 20.1168 m
1 furlong = 201.168 m
1 acre = 0.4047 hectares
1 sq km = 100 hectares
1 sq mile = 2.59 square km
1 ounce = 28.35 grams
1 pound = 0.4536 kilograms
1 short ton = 0.90718 metric ton
1 short ton = 2,000 pounds
1 long ton = 1.016 metric tons
1 long ton = 2,240 pounds
1 metric ton = 1,000 kilograms
1 quart = 0.94635 liters
1 US gallon = 3.7854 liters
1 Imperial gallon = 4.5459 liters
1 nautical mile = 1.852 km

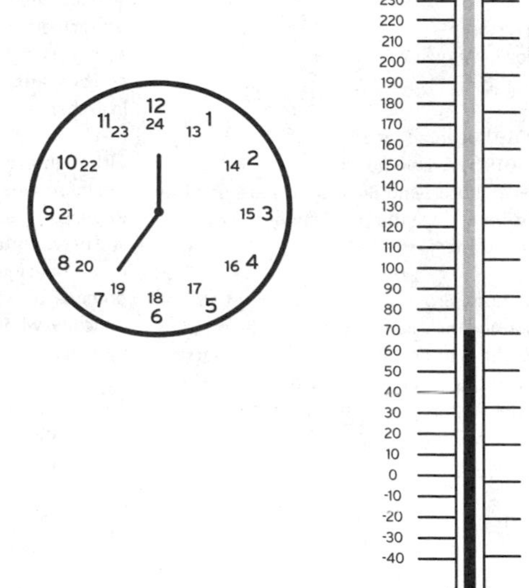

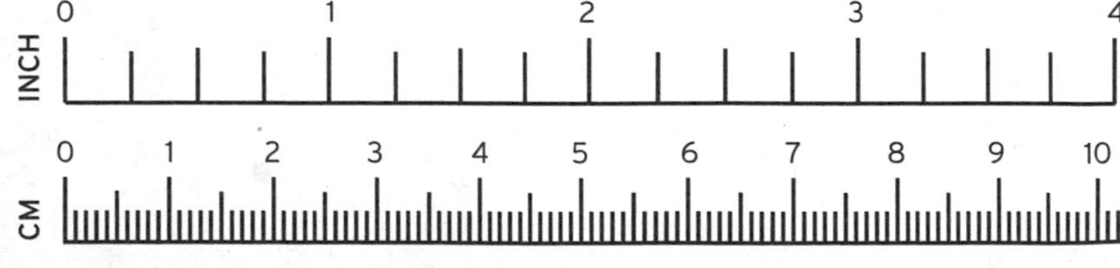

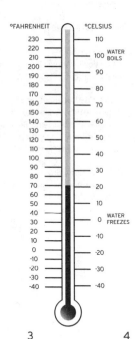

MOON AMALFI COAST
Avalon Travel
Hachette Book Group
1700 Fourth Street
Berkeley, CA 94710, USA
www.moon.com

Editor: Ada Fung
Series Manager: Kathryn Ettinger
Copy Editor: Barbara Schultz
Production and Graphics Coordinator: Rue Flaherty
Cover Design: Faceout Studios, Charles Brock
Interior Design: Domini Dragoone
Moon Logo: Tim McGrath
Map Editor: Kat Bennett
Cartographers: Moon Street Cartography (Durango CO), Kat Bennett
Proofreader: Jessica Gould
Indexer: Sam Arnold-Boyd

ISBN-13: 978-1-64049-035-2

Printing History
1st Edition — August 2019
5 4 3 2 1

Front cover photo: Atrani and Amalfi coast road © Jorg Greuel/Getty Images

Back cover photo: Cauco beach and Cerniola castle near Erchie © Felis | Dreamstime.com

Printed in Canada by Friesens